Business Environments:
Law Regulation and Ethics
Prepared for
Willis W. Hagen and Paul D. Frederickson

Eleventh Edition

Mann/Roberts/Bagley/Savage/Bohlman/Dundas

THOMSON

SOUTH-WESTERN

Australia · Canada · Mexico · Singapore · Spain · United Kingdom · United States

THOMSON

SOUTH-WESTERN

Business Environments: Law Regulation and Ethics
Mann/Roberts/Bagley/Savage/Bohlman/Dundas

Executive Editors:
Michele Baird, Maureen Staudt &
Michael Stranz

Project Development Manager:
Linda de Stefano

Marketing Coordinators:
Lindsay Annett and Sara Mercurio

Production/Manufacturing Supervisor:
Donna M. Brown

Pre-Media Services Supervisor:
Dan Plofchan

Kalina Hintz and Bahman Naraghi

Cover Image
Getty Images*

Rights and Permissions Specialists:

For permission to use material from this text or product, contact us by:
Tel (800) 730-2214
Fax (800) 730 2215
www.thomsonrights.com

The Adaptable Courseware Program consists of products and additions to existing Thomson products that are produced from camera-ready copy. Peer review, class testing, and accuracy are primarily the responsibility of the author(s).

Business Environments: Law Regulation and Ethics /
Mann/Roberts/Bagley/Savage/Bohlman /Dundas – Eleventh Edition
p. 874
ISBN 0-324-53507-4

International Divisions List

Asia (Including India):
Thomson Learning
(a division of Thomson Asia Pte Ltd)
5 Shenton Way #01-01
UIC Building
Singapore 068808
Tel: (65) 6410-1200
Fax: (65) 6410-1208

Australia/New Zealand:
Thomson Learning Australia
102 Dodds Street
Southbank, Victoria 3006
Australia

Latin America:
Thomson Learning
Seneca 53
Colonia Polano
11560 Mexico, D.F., Mexico
Tel (525) 281-2906
Fax (525) 281-2656

Canada:
Thomson Nelson
1120 Birchmount Road
Toronto, Ontario
Canada M1K 5G4
Tel (416) 752-9100
Fax (416) 752-8102

UK/Europe/Middle East/Africa:
Thomson Learning
High Holborn House
50-51 Bedford Row
London, WC1R 4L$
United Kingdom
Tel 44 (020) 7067-2500
Fax 44 (020) 7067-2600

Spain (Includes Portugal):
Thomson Paraninfo
Calle Magallanes 25
28015 Madrid
España
Tel 34 (0)91 446-3350
Fax 34 (0)91 445-6218

Custom Contents

from Smith & Roberson's Business Law

Business Ethics and the
Social Responsibility of Business

CHAPTER

2

Business ethics is a subset of ethics: there is no special set of ethical principles that applies only to the world of business. Immoral acts are immoral, whether or not a businessperson has committed them. But before a behavior, in business or elsewhere, is judged immoral, special attention must be accorded the circumstances surrounding it. For example, suppose a company discovers a new cost-effective technology that enables it to outperform its competitors. Few would condemn the company for using the technology even if it put one or more competitors out of business. After all, the economic benefits derived from the new technology would seem to so outweigh the social costs of unemployment that it would be difficult to conclude that the business acted immorally.

On the other hand, unethical business practices date from the very beginning of business and continue today. As one court stated in connection with a securities fraud,

> Since the time to which the memory of man runneth not to the contrary, the human animal has been full of cunning and guile. Many of the schemes and artifices have been so sophisticated as almost to defy belief. But the ordinary run of those willing and able to take unfair advantage of others are mere apprentices in the art when compared with the manipulations thought up by those connected in one way or another with transactions in securities.

In the last decade, the almost daily reporting of business wrongs has included, among countless others, insider trading, the Beech-Nut adulterated apple juice scandal, the Bhopal disaster, the Dalkon Shield tragedy, and the savings and loan industry depredations.

Ethics can be broadly defined as the study of what is right or good for human beings. It pursues the questions of what people ought to do, what goals they should pursue. In *Business Ethics*, 5th ed., Richard T. DeGeorge provides the following explanation of ethics:

> In its most general sense *ethics is a systematic attempt to make sense of our individual and social moral experience, in such a way as to determine the rules that ought to govern human conduct, the values worth pursuing, and the character traits deserving development in life.* The attempt is systematic and therefore goes beyond what reflective persons tend to do in daily life in making sense of their moral experience, organizing it, and attempting to make it coherent and unified. . . . Ethics concerns itself with human conduct, taken here to mean human activity that is done knowingly and, to a large extent, willingly. It does not concern itself with automatic responses, or with, for example, actions done in one's sleep or under hypnosis.

Business ethics, as a branch of applied ethics, is the study and determination of what is right and good in business settings. Business ethics seeks to understand the moral issues that arise from business practices, institutions, and decision making and their relationship to generalized human values. Unlike the law, analyses of ethics have no central authority, such as courts or legislatures, upon which to rely; nor do they have clear-cut, universal standards. Despite these inherent limitations, making meaningful ethical judgments is still possible. To improve ethical decision making, it is important to understand how others have approached the task.

14

Some examples of the many ethics questions confronting business may help to clarify the definition of business ethics. In the employment relationship, countless ethical issues arise regarding the safety and compensation of workers, their civil rights (such as equal treatment, privacy, and freedom from sexual harassment), and the legitimacy of whistle-blowing. In the relationship between business and its customers, ethical issues permeate marketing techniques, product safety, and consumer protection. The relationship between business and its owners bristles with ethical questions involving corporate governance, shareholder voting, and management's duties to the shareholders. The relationship among competing businesses involves numerous ethical matters, including efforts to promote fair competition over the temptation of collusive conduct. The interaction between business and society at large has additional ethical dimensions: pollution of the physical environment, commitment to the community's economic and social infrastructure, and the depletion of natural resources. At the international level, these issues not only recur but couple themselves to additional ones, such as bribery of foreign officials, exploitation of less-developed countries, and conflicts among differing cultures and value systems.

In resolving the ethical issues raised by business conduct, it is helpful to use a seeing-knowing-doing model. First, the decision maker should *see* (identify) the ethical issues involved in the proposed conduct, including the ethical implications of the various available options. Second, the decision maker should *know* (resolve) what to do by choosing the best option. Finally, the decision maker should *do* (implement) the chosen option by developing implementing strategies.

This chapter first surveys the most prominent ethical theories, then examines ethical standards in business, and concludes by exploring the ethical responsibilities of business.

> **http:**   Ethics Resource Center: http://www.ethics.org
> Council for Ethics in Economics: http://www.businessethics.org/
> Business for Social Responsibility: http://www.bsr.org
> International Business Ethics Institute: http://www.business-ethics.org/
> Center for Applied Ethics: http://www.ethics.ubc.ca/resources/business/

LAW VERSUS ETHICS

As discussed in Chapter 1, the law is strongly affected by moral concepts, but law and morality are not the same. Although it is tempting to say that "if it's legal, it's moral," such a proposition is inaccurate and generally too simplistic. For example, it would seem gravely immoral to stand by silently while a blind man walks off a cliff if one could prevent the fall by shouting a warning, even though one is under no legal obligation to do so.

Similarly, moral questions arise concerning "legal" business practices, such as failing to fulfill a promise that is not legally binding; exporting products banned in the United States to third world countries, where they are not prohibited; manufacturing and selling tobacco or alcohol products; or slaughtering baby seals for fur coats. The mere fact that these practices may be legal does not prevent them from being challenged on moral grounds.

Just as it is possible for legal acts to be immoral, it is equally possible for illegal acts to seem morally preferable to following the law. It is, for example, the moral conviction of the great majority of people that those who sheltered Jews in violation of Nazi edicts during World War II and those who committed acts of civil disobedience in the 1950s and 1960s to challenge racist segregation laws in the United States were acting properly and that the laws themselves were immoral.

ETHICAL THEORIES

Philosophers have sought for centuries to develop dependable universal methods for making ethical judgments. In earlier times, some thinkers analogized the discovery of ethical principles with the derivation of mathematical proofs. They asserted that people could discover fundamental ethical rules by applying careful reasoning *a priori*. (*A priori* reasoning is based on theory rather than experimentation and deductively draws conclusions from cause to effect and from generalizations to particular instances.) In more recent times, many philosophers have concluded that although careful reasoning and deep thought assist substantially in moral reasoning, experience reveals that the complexities of the world defeat most attempts to fashion precise, *a priori* guidelines. Nevertheless, reviewing the most significant ethical theories can help to analyze issues of business ethics.

Ethical Fundamentalism

Under **ethical fundamentalism**, or absolutism, individuals look to a central authority or set of rules to guide them in ethical decision making. Some look to the Bible; others look to the Koran or the writings of Karl Marx or to any number of living or deceased prophets. The essential characteristic of this approach is a reliance upon a central repository of wisdom. In some cases, such reliance is total. In others, it occurs to a lesser degree: followers of a religion or a spiritual leader may believe that all members of the group have an obligation to assess moral dilemmas independently, according to each person's understanding of the dictates of certain fundamental principles.

Ethical Relativism

Ethical relativism is a doctrine asserting that individuals must judge actions by what they feel is right or wrong for themselves. It holds that both parties to a disagreement regarding a moral question are correct, because morality is relative. While ethical relativism promotes open-mindedness and tolerance, it has limitations. If each person's actions are always correct for that person, then his behavior is, by definition, moral, and no one can truly criticize it. If a child abuser truly felt it right to molest children, a relativist would accept the proposition that the child abuser was acting properly. As almost no one would accept the proposition that child abuse could ever be ethical, few can truly claim to be relativists. Once a person concludes that criticizing or punishing behavior is, in some cases, appropriate, he abandons ethical relativism and faces the task of developing a broader ethical methodology.

Although bearing a surface resemblance to ethical relativism, situational ethics actually differs substantially. **Situational ethics** holds that developing precise guidelines for navigating ethical dilemmas is difficult because real-life decision making is so complex. To judge the morality of someone's behavior, the person judging must actually put herself in the other person's shoes to understand what motivated the other to choose a particular course of action. In this respect, situational ethics shares with ethical relativism the notion that we must judge actions from the perspective of the person who actually made the judgment. From that point on, however, the two approaches differ dramatically. Ethical relativism passes no judgment on what a person did other than to determine that he truly believed the decision was right for him. Much more judgmental, situational ethics insists that once a decision has been viewed from the actor's perspective, a judgment can be made as to whether or not her action was ethical. Situational ethics does not cede the ultimate judgment of propriety to the actor; rather, it insists that another evaluate the actor's decision or act from the perspective of a person in the actor's shoes.

Utilitarianism

Utilitarianism is a doctrine that assesses good and evil in terms of the consequences of actions. Those actions that produce the greatest net pleasure compared with the net pain are better in a moral sense than those that produce less net pleasure. As Jeremy Bentham, one of the most influential proponents of utilitarianism, proclaimed, a good or moral act is one that results in "the greatest happiness for the greatest number."

The two major forms of utilitarianism are act utilitarianism and rule utilitarianism. **Act utilitarianism** assesses each separate act according to whether it maximizes pleasure over pain. For example, if telling a lie in a particular situation produces more overall pleasure than pain, then an act utilitarian would support lying as the moral thing to do. Rule utilitarians, disturbed by the unpredictability of act utilitarianism and by its potential for abuse, follow a different approach by holding that general rules must be established and followed even though, in some instances, following rules may produce less overall pleasure than not following them. In applying utilitarian principles

to developing rules, **rule utilitarianism** thus supports rules that on balance produce the greatest satisfaction. Determining whether telling a lie in a given instance would produce greater pleasure than telling the truth is less important to the rule utilitarian than deciding if a general practice of lying would maximize society's pleasure. If lying would not maximize pleasure generally, then one should follow a rule of not lying, even though telling a lie occasionally would produce greater pleasure than would telling the truth.

Utilitarian notions underlie cost-benefit analysis, an analytical tool used by many business and government managers today. **Cost-benefit analysis** first quantifies in monetary terms and then compares the direct and indirect costs and benefits of program alternatives for meeting a specified objective. Cost-benefit analysis seeks the greatest economic efficiency, given the underlying notion that acts achieving the greatest output at the least cost promote the greatest marginal happiness over less efficient acts, other things being equal.

The primary purpose of cost-benefit analysis is to choose from alternative courses of action the program that maximizes society's wealth. For example, based on cost-benefit analysis, an auto designer might choose to devote more effort to perfecting a highly expensive air bag that would save hundreds of lives and prevent thousands of disabling injuries than to developing an improved car hood latching mechanism that would produce a less favorable cost-benefit ratio.

The chief criticism of utilitarianism is that in some important instances it ignores justice. A number of situations would maximize the pleasure of the majority at great social cost to a minority. Under a strict utilitarian approach, it would, for example, be ethical to compel a few citizens to undergo painful, even fatal medical tests to develop cures for the rest of the world. For most people, however, such action would be unacceptable. Another major criticism of utilitarianism is that measuring pleasure and pain in the fashion its supporters advocate is extremely difficult, if not impossible.

Deontology

Deontological theories (from the Greek word *deon*, meaning "duty" or "obligation") address the practical problems of utilitarianism by holding that certain underlying principles are right or wrong regardless of calculations regarding pleasure or pain. Deontologists believe that actions cannot be measured simply by their results but must be judged by means and motives as well.

Our criminal laws apply deontological reasoning. Knowing that John shot and killed Marvin is not enough to tell us how to judge John's act. We must know whether John shot Marvin in anger, self-defense, or by mistake. Although under any of these motives Marvin is just as dead, we judge John quite differently depending on the mental process that we believe led him to commit the act. Similarly, deontologists judge the morality of acts not so much by their consequences but by the motives that lead to them. To act morally, a person not only must achieve just results but also must employ the proper means.

The best-known deontological theory was proffered by the eighteenth-century philosopher Immanuel Kant. Kant asserted what he called the **categorical imperative**, which has been summarized as follows:

1. Act only according to that maxim by which you can, at the same time, will that it should become a universal law.
2. Act as never to treat another human being merely as a means to an end.

Thus, for an action to be moral, it (1) must possess the potential to be made a consistently applied universal law and (2) must respect the autonomy and rationality of all human beings and avoid treating them as an expedient. That is, one should avoid doing anything that he or she would not have everyone do in a similar situation. For example, you should not lie to colleagues unless you support the right of all colleagues to lie to one another. Similarly, you should not cheat others unless you advocate everyone's right to cheat. We apply Kantian reasoning when we challenge someone's behavior by asking, What if everybody acted that way?

Under Kant's approach, it would be improper to assert a principle to which one claimed personal exception, such as insisting that it was acceptable for you to cheat but not for anyone else to do so. Because everyone would then insist on similar rules by which to except themselves, this principle could not be universalized.

Kant's philosophy also rejects notions of the end justifying the means. To Kant, every person is an end in himself or herself and deserves respect simply because of his or her humanity. Thus, any sacrifice of a person for the greater good of society would be unacceptable to Kant.

In many respects, Kant's categorical imperative is a variation of the Golden Rule. Like the Golden Rule, the categorical imperative reflects the idea that people are, to a certain extent, self-centered. As one writer on business ethics notes, this is what makes the Golden Rule so effective:

> It is precisely this self-centeredness of the Golden Rule that makes it so valuable, and so widely acknowledged, as a guide. To inquire of yourself, "How would I feel in the other fellow's place?" is an elegantly simple and reliable method of focusing in on the "right" thing to do. The Golden Rule works not in spite of selfishness, but because of it. Tuleja, *Beyond the Bottom Line.*

As does every theory, Kantian ethics has its critics. Just as deontologists criticize utilitarians for excessive pragmatism and flexible moral guidelines, utilitarians and others criticize deontologists for rigidity and excessive formalism. For example, if one inflexibly adopts as a rule to tell the truth, one ignores situations in which lying might well be justified. A person hiding a terrified wife from her angry, abusive husband would seem to

be acting morally by falsely denying that the wife is at the person's house. Yet, a deontologist, feeling bound to tell the truth, might ignore the consequences of truthfulness, tell the husband where his wife is, and create the possibility of a terrible tragedy. Less dramatically, one wonders whether the world would effect a higher ethical code by regarding as immoral "white lies" concerning friends' appearance, clothing, or choice of spouse.

Social Ethics Theories

Social ethics theories assert that special obligations arise from the social nature of human beings. Such theories focus not only on each person's obligations to other members of society, but also on the individual's rights and obligations within society. For example, **social egalitarians** believe that society should provide all persons with equal amounts of goods and services regardless of the contribution each makes to increase society's wealth.

Two other ethics theories have received widespread attention in recent years. One is the theory of **distributive justice** proposed by Harvard philosopher John Rawls, which seeks to analyze the type of society that people in a "natural state" would establish if they could not determine in advance whether they would be talented, rich, healthy, or ambitious, relative to other members of society. According to Rawls, the society contemplated through this "veil of ignorance" should be given precedence in terms of development because it considers the needs and rights of all its members. Rawls did not argue, however, that such a society would be strictly egalitarian. That would unfairly penalize those who turned out to be the most talented and ambitious. Instead, Rawls suggested that such a society would stress equality of opportunity, not of results. On the other hand, Rawls stressed that society would pay heed to the least advantaged to ensure that they did not suffer unduly and that they enjoyed society's benefits. To Rawls, society must be premised on justice. Everyone is entitled to her fair share in society, a fairness all must work to guarantee.

In contrast to Rawls, another Harvard philosopher, Robert Nozick, stressed liberty, not justice, as the most important obligation that society owes its members. **Libertarians** stress market outcomes as the basis for distributing society's rewards. Only to the extent that one meets the demands of the market does one deserve society's benefits. Libertarians oppose interference by society in their lives as long as they do not violate the rules of the marketplace; that is, as long as they do not cheat others and as long as they honestly disclose the nature of their transactions with others. The fact that some end up with fortunes while others accumulate little simply proves that some can play in the market effectively while others cannot. To libertarians, this is not unjust. What is unjust to them is any attempt by society to take wealth earned by citizens and then distribute it to those who did not earn it.

These theories and others (e.g., Marxism) judge society in moral terms by its organization and by its method of distributing goods and services. They demonstrate the difficulty of ethical decision making in the context of a social organization: behavior that is consistently ethical from individual to individual may not necessarily produce a just society.

Other Theories

The preceding theories do not exhaust the possible approaches to evaluating ethical behavior, but represent the most commonly cited theories advanced over the years. Several other theories also deserve mention. **Intuitionism** holds that a rational person possesses inherent powers to assess the correctness of actions. Though an individual may refine and strengthen these powers, they are just as basic to humanity as our instincts for survival and self-defense. Just as some people are better artists or musicians, some people have more insight into ethical behavior than others. Consistent with intuitionism is the **good persons** philosophy, which declares that individuals who wish to act morally should seek out and emulate those who always seem to know the right choice in any given situation and who always seem to do the right thing. One variation of these ethical approaches is the **"Television Test,"** which directs us to imagine that every ethical decision we make is being broadcast on nationwide television. Adherents of this approach believe an appropriate decision is one we would be comfortable broadcasting on television for all to witness.

ETHICAL STANDARDS IN BUSINESS

This section will explore the application of the theories of ethical behavior to the world of business.

Choosing an Ethical System

In their efforts to resolve the moral dilemmas facing humanity, philosophers and other thinkers have struggled for years to refine the various systems discussed previously. No one ethical system is completely precise, however, and each tends occasionally to produce unacceptable prescriptions for action. But to say that a system has limits is not to say it is useless. On the contrary, many such systems provide insight into ethical decision making and help us formulate issues and resolve moral dilemmas. Furthermore, concluding that moral standards are difficult to articulate and that the boundaries are imprecise is not the same as concluding that moral standards are unnecessary or nonexistent.

Research by noted psychologist Lawrence Kohlberg provides insight into ethical decision making and lends credibility to the notion that moral growth, like physical growth, is part of the human condition. Kohlberg observed that people progress through stages of moral development according to two major variables: age and education. During the first level—the **preconventional level**—a child's conduct is a reaction to the fear of punishment and, later, to the pleasure of reward. Although people who operate at this level may behave in a moral manner, they do so without understanding why their behavior is moral. The rules are imposed upon them. During adolescence—Kohlberg's **conventional level**—people conform their behavior to meet the expectations of groups, such as family, peers, and eventually society. The motivation for conformity is loyalty, affection, and trust. Most adults operate at this level. According to Kohlberg, some people reach the third level—the **postconventional level**—where they accept and conform to moral principles because they understand *why* the principles are right and binding. At this level, moral principles are voluntarily internalized, not externally imposed. Moreover, individuals at this stage develop their own universal ethical principles, and even question the laws and values that society and others have adopted.

Kohlberg believed that these stages are sequential and that not all people reach the third, or even the second, stage. He therefore argued that exploring ways of enabling people to develop to the advanced stage of postconventional thought was essential to the study of ethics. Other psychologists assert that individuals do not pass from stage to stage but rather function in all three stages simultaneously.

Whatever the source of our ethical approach, we cannot avoid facing moral dilemmas that challenge us to recognize and to do the right thing. Moreover, for those who plan business careers, such dilemmas will necessarily have implications for many others: employees, shareholders, suppliers, customers, and society at large.

◆ **SEE FIGURE 2-1**   **Kohlberg's Stages of Moral Development**

Corporations as Moral Agents

Because corporations are not persons but artificial entities created by the State, it is not obvious whether they can or should be held morally accountable. As Lord Chancellor Thurlow lamented two hundred years ago, "A company has no body to kick and no soul to damn, and by God, it ought to have both." Clearly, individuals within corporations can be held morally responsible, but the corporate entity presents unique problems.

Commentators are divided on the issue. Some, like philosopher Manuel Velasquez, insist that only people can engage in behavior that can be judged in moral terms. Opponents of this view, like philosophers Kenneth Goodpaster and John Matthews, Jr., concede that corporations are not persons in any literal sense but insist that the attributes of responsibility inherent in corporations are sufficient in number to permit judging corporate behavior from a moral perspective.

◆**Figure 2-1**   **Kohlberg's Stages of Moral Development**

Levels	Perspective	Justification
Preconventional (Childhood)	Self	Punishment/Reward
Conventional (Adolescent)	Group	Group Norms
Postconventional (Adult)	Universal	Moral Principles

ETHICAL RESPONSIBILITIES OF BUSINESS

Many people assert that the only responsibility of business is to maximize profit and that this obligation overrides any other ethical or social responsibility. Although our economic system of modified capitalism is based on the pursuit of self-interest, it contains components to check this motivation of greed. Our system has always recognized the need for some form of regulation, whether it be the "invisible hand" of competition, the self-regulation of business, or government regulation.

Regulation of Business

As explained and justified by Adam Smith in *The Wealth of Nations* (1776), the capitalistic system is composed of six "institutions": economic motivation, private productive property, free enterprise, free markets, competition, and limited government. Economic motivation assumes that a person who receives an economic return for his effort will work harder; therefore, the economic system should provide greater economic rewards for those who work harder. Private productive property, the means by which economic motivation is exercised, permits individuals to innovate and produce while securing to them the fruits of their efforts. Jack Behrman, a professor of business ethics, has described how the four other institutions combine with these two to bring about industrialized capitalism:

Free enterprise permits the combination of properties so people can do things together that they can't do alone. Free enterprise means a capitalistic combination of factors of production under decisions of free individuals. Free enterprise is the group expression of the use of private property, and it permits greater efficiency in an industrial setting through variation in the levels and kinds of production.

. . . The free market operates to equate supply and demand—supply reflecting the ability and willingness to offer certain goods or services, and demand reflecting the consumer's ability and willingness to pay. Price is adjusted to include the maximum number of *both* bids and offers. The market, therefore, is *the* decision-making mechanism outside of the firm. It is the *means* by which basic decisions are made about the use of resources, and all factors are supposed to respond to it, however they wish.

. . . Just in case it doesn't work out that way, there is one more institution—the *Government*—which is supposed to set rules and provide protection for the society and its members. That's all, said Smith, that it should do: it should set the rules, enforce them, and stand aside. J. Behrman, *Discourses on Ethics and Business*, 25–29.

As long as all these constituent institutions continue to exist and operate in a balanced manner, the factors of production—land, capital, and labor—combine to produce an efficient allocation of resources for individual consumers and for the economy as a whole. To achieve this outcome, however, Smith's model requires the satisfaction of several conditions: "standardized products, numerous firms in markets, each firm with a small share and unable by its actions alone to exert significant influence over price, no barriers to entry, and output carried to the point where each seller's marginal cost equals the going market price." E. Singer, *Antitrust Economics and Legal Analysis*, 2.

History has demonstrated that the actual operation of the economy has satisfied almost none of these assumptions. More specifically, the actual competitive process falls considerably short of the classic economic model of perfect competition:

Competitive industries are never perfectly competitive in this sense. Many of the resources they employ cannot be shifted to other employments without substantial cost and delay. The allocation of those resources, as between industries or as to relative proportions within a single industry, is unlikely to have been made in a way that affords the best possible expenditure of economic effort. Information is incomplete, motivation confused, and decision therefore ill informed and often unwise. Variations in efficiency are not directly reflected in variations of profit. Success is derived in large part from competitive selling efforts, which in the aggregate may be wasteful, and from differentiation of products, which may be undertaken partly by methods designed to impair the opportunity of the buyer to compare quality and price. C. Edwards, *Maintaining Competition*.

In addition to capitalism's failure to allocate resources efficiently, it cannot be relied on to achieve all of the social and public policy objectives a pluralistic democracy requires. For example, the free enterprise model simply does not comprehend or address equitable distribution of wealth, national defense, conservation of natural resources, full employment, stability in economic cycles, protection against economic dislocations, health and safety, social security, and other important social and economic goals. Because the "invisible hand" and self-regulation by business have failed not only to preserve the competitive process in our economic system but also to achieve social goals extrinsic to the efficient allocation of resources, governmental intervention in business has become increasingly common. Such intervention attempts to (1) regulate both "legal" monopolies, such as those conferred by law through copyrights, patents, and trade symbols, and "natural" monopolies, such as utilities, transportation, and communications; (2) preserve competition by correcting imperfections in the market system; (3) protect specific groups, especially labor and agriculture, from failures of the marketplace; and (4) promote other social goals. Successful government regulation involves a delicate balance between regulations that attempt to preserve competition and those that attempt to advance other social objectives. The latter should not undermine the basic competitive processes that provide an efficient allocation of economic resources.

Corporate Governance

In addition to the broad demands of maintaining a competitive and fair marketplace, another factor demanding the ethical and social responsibility of business is the sheer size and power of individual corporations. The five thousand largest U.S. firms currently produce more than half of the nation's gross national product. Statutorily, their economic power should be delegated by the shareholders to the board of directors, who in turn appoint the officers of the corporation.

> In reality, this legal image is virtually a myth. In nearly every large American business corporation, there exists a management autocracy. One man—variously titled the President, or the Chairman of the Board, or the Chief Executive Officer—or a small coterie of men rule the corporation. Far from being chosen by the directors to run the corporation, this chief executive or executive clique chooses the board of directors and, with the acquiescence of the board, controls the corporation. R. Nader, M. Green, and J. Seligman, *Taming the Giant Corporation.*

In a classic study published in 1932, Adolf Berle and Gardner Means concluded that significant amounts of economic power had been concentrated in a relatively few large corporations, that the ownership of these corporations had become widely dispersed, and that the shareholders had become far removed from active participation in management. Since their original study, these trends have steadily continued. The large publicly held corporations—numbering 500 to 1,000—own the great bulk of the industrial wealth of the United States. Moreover, these corporations are controlled by a small group of corporate officers.

Historically, the boards of many publicly held corporations consisted mainly or entirely of inside directors (corporate officers who also serve on the board of directors). During the past two decades, however, as a result of regulations by the U.S. Securities and Exchange Commission and the stock exchanges, the number and influence of outside directors have increased substantially. Now the boards of the great majority of publicly held corporations consist primarily of outside directors, and these corporations have audit committees consisting entirely of outside directors. Nevertheless, a number of instances of corporate misconduct have been revealed in the first years of this century. In response to these business scandals—involving companies such as Enron, WorldCom, Global Crossing, and Arthur Andersen—in 2002 Congress passed the Sarbanes-Oxley Act. This legislation seeks to prevent these types of scandals by increasing corporate responsibility through imposing additional corporate governance requirements on publicly held corporations.

These developments raise social, policy, and ethical issues about the governance of large, publicly owned corporations. Many observers insist that companies playing such an important role in economic life should have a responsibility to undertake projects that benefit society in ways that go beyond mere financial efficiency in producing goods and services. In some instances, the idea of corporate obligation comes from industrialists themselves. Andrew Carnegie, for example, advocated philanthropy throughout his life and contributed much of his fortune to educational and social causes.

> `http:` **Corporate Governance OECD:** http://www.oecd.org/ daf/corporate-affairs
> **Corporate Governance Network:** http://www. corpgov.net

Arguments against Social Responsibility

Among the arguments opposing business involvement in socially responsible activities are profitability, unfairness, accountability, and expertise.

Profitability   As economist Milton Friedman and others have argued, businesses are artificial entities established to permit people to engage in profit-making, not social, activities. Without profits, they assert, there is little reason for a corporation to exist and no real way to measure the effectiveness of corporate activities. Businesses are not organized to engage in social activities; they are structured to produce goods and services for which they receive money. Their social obligation is to return as much of this money to their direct stakeholders as possible. In a free market with significant competition, the selfish pursuits of corporations will lead to maximizing output, minimizing costs, and establishing fair prices. All other concerns distract companies and interfere with achieving these goals.

Unfairness Whenever companies stray from their designated role of profit-maker, they take unfair advantage of company employees and shareholders. For example, a company may support the arts or education or spend excess funds on health and safety; however, these funds rightfully belong to the shareholders or employees. The company's decision to disburse these funds to others who may well be less deserving than the shareholders and employees is unfair. Furthermore, consumers can express their desires through the marketplace, and shareholders and employees can decide independently if they wish to make charitable contributions. In most cases, senior management consults the board of directors about supporting social concerns but does not seek the approval of the company's major stakeholders. Thus, these shareholders are effectively disenfranchised from actions that reduce their benefits from the corporation.

Accountability Corporations, as previously noted, are private institutions that are subject to a lower standard of accountability than are public bodies. Accordingly, a company may decide to support a wide range of social causes and yet submit to little public scrutiny. But a substantial potential for abuse exists in such cases. For one thing, a company could provide funding for causes its employees or shareholders do not support. It could also provide money "with strings attached," thereby controlling the recipients' agendas for less than socially beneficial purposes. For example, a drug company that contributes to a consumer group might implicitly or explicitly condition its assistance on the group's agreement never to criticize the company or the drug industry.

This lack of accountability warrants particular concern because of the enormous power corporations wield in modern society. Many large companies, like General Motors or IBM, generate and spend more money in a year than all but a handful of the world's countries. If these companies suddenly began to vigorously pursue their own social agendas, their influence might well rival, and perhaps undermine, that of their own governments. In a country like the United States, founded on the principles of limited government and the balance of powers, too much corporate involvement in social affairs might well present substantial problems. Without clear guidelines and accountability, the corporate pursuit of socially responsible behavior might well distort the entire process of governance.

There is a clear alternative to corporations engaging in socially responsible action. If society wishes to increase the resources devoted to needy causes, it has the power to do so. Let corporations seek profits without the burden of a social agenda, let the consumers vote in the marketplace for the products and services they desire, and let the government tax a portion of corporate profits for socially beneficial causes.

Expertise Even though a corporation has an expertise in producing and selling its product, it may not possess a talent for recognizing or managing socially useful activities.

Corporations become successful in the market because they can identify and meet customers' needs. Nothing suggests that this talent spills over into nonbusiness arenas. In fact, critics of corporate engagement in social activities worry that corporations will prove unable to distinguish the true needs of society from their own narrow self-interest.

Arguments in Favor of Social Responsibility

First, it should be recognized that even business critics acknowledge that the prime responsibility of business is to make a reasonable return on its investment by producing a quality product at a reasonable price. They do not suggest that business entities be charitable institutions. They do assert, however, that business has certain obligations beyond making a profit or not harming society. Critics contend that business must help to resolve societal problems, and they offer a number of arguments in support of their position.

The Social Contract Society creates corporations and accords them a special social status, including the grant of limited liability, which insulates the owners from liability for debts the organization incurs. Supporters of social roles for corporations assert that limited liability and other rights granted to companies carry a responsibility: corporations, just like other members of society, must contribute to its betterment. Therefore, companies owe a moral debt to society to contribute to its overall well-being. Society needs a host of improvements, such as pollution control, safe products, a free marketplace, quality education, cures for illness, and freedom from crime. Corporations can help in each of these areas. Granted, deciding which social needs deserve corporate attention is difficult; however, this challenge does not lessen a company's obligation to choose a cause. Corporate America cannot ignore the multitude of pressing needs that still remain, despite the efforts of government and private charities.

A derivative of the social contract theory is the stakeholder model for the societal role of the business corporation. Under the **stakeholder model**, a corporation has fiduciary responsibilities to all of its stakeholders, not just its stockholders. Historically, the stockholder model for the role of business has been the norm. Under this theory, a corporation is viewed as private property owned by and for the benefit of its owners—the stockholders of the corporation. (For a full discussion of this legal model, see Chapter 36.) The stakeholder model, on the other hand, holds that a corporation is responsible to society at large and more directly, to all those constituencies on which it depends for its survival. Thus, it is argued that a corporation should be managed for the benefit of all of its stakeholders—stockholders, employees, customers, suppliers, and managers, as well as the local communities in which it operates. Compare Figure 2-2 with Figure 36-1.

◆ **See Figure 2-2** The Stakeholder Model

◆**Figure 2-2**   **The Stakeholder Model**

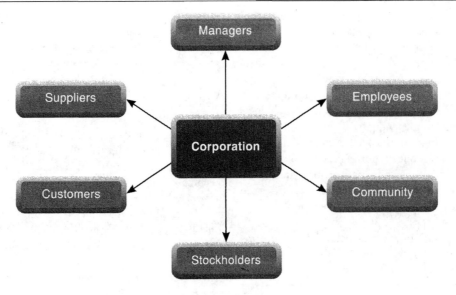

Less Government Regulation According to another argument in favor of corporate social responsibility, the more responsibly companies act, the less regulation the government must provide. This idea, if accurate, would likely appeal to those corporations that typically view regulation with distaste, perceiving it as a crude and expensive way of achieving social goals. To them, regulation often imposes inappropriate, overly broad rules that hamper productivity and require extensive record-keeping procedures to document compliance. If companies can use more flexible, voluntary methods of meeting a social norm such as pollution control, then government will be less tempted to legislate norms.

The argument can be taken further. Not only does anticipatory corporate action lessen the likelihood of government regulation, but social involvement by companies creates a climate of trust and respect that reduces the overall inclination of government to interfere in company business. For example,

a government agency is much more likely to show some leniency toward a socially responsible company than toward one that ignores social plights.

Long-Run Profits Perhaps the most persuasive argument in favor of corporate involvement in social causes is that such involvement actually makes good business sense. Consumers often support good corporate images and avoid bad ones. For example, consumers generally prefer to patronize stores with "easy return" policies. Even though such policies are not required by law, companies institute them because they create goodwill—an intangible though indispensable asset for ensuring repeat customers. In the long run, enhanced goodwill often leads to stronger profits. Moreover, corporate actions to improve the well-being of their communities make these communities more attractive to citizens and more profitable for business.

——— **C H A P T E R   S U M M A R Y** ———

Definitions	**Ethics** study of what is right or good for human beings **Business Ethics** study of what is right and good in a business setting
Ethical Theories	**Ethical Fundamentalism** individuals look to a central authority or set of rules to guide them in ethical decision making **Ethical Relativism** actions must be judged by what individuals subjectively feel is right or wrong for themselves **Situational Ethics** one must judge a person's actions by first putting oneself in the actor's situation

Utilitarianism moral actions are those that produce the greatest net pleasure compared with net pain
- *Act Utilitarianism* assesses each separate act according to whether it maximizes pleasure over pain
- *Rule Utilitarianism* supports rules that on balance produce the greatest pleasure for society
- *Cost-Benefit Analysis* quantifies the benefits and costs of alternatives

Deontology actions must be judged by their motives and means as well as their results

Social Ethics Theories focus is on a person's obligations to other members in society and also on the individual's rights and obligations within society
- *Social Egalitarians* believe that society should provide all its members with equal amounts of goods and services regardless of their relative contributions
- *Distributive Justice* stresses equality of opportunity rather than results
- *Libertarians* stress market outcomes as the basis for distributing society's rewards

Other Theories
- *Intuitionism* a rational person possesses inherent power to assess the correctness of actions
- *Good Person* individuals should seek out and emulate good role models

Ethical Standards in Business	**Choosing an Ethical System** Kohlberg's stages of moral development is a widely accepted model (see Figure 2-1) **Corporations as Moral Agents** because a corporation is a statutorily created entity, it is not clear whether it should be held morally responsible
Ethical Responsibilities of Business	**Regulation of Business** governmental regulation has been necessary because all the conditions for perfect competition have not been satisfied and free competition cannot by itself achieve other societal objectives **Corporate Governance** vast amounts of wealth and power have become concentrated in a small number of corporations, which are in turn controlled by a small group of corporate officers **Arguments against Social Responsibility** • *Profitability* because corporations are artificial entities established for profit-making activities, their only social obligation should be to return as much money as possible to shareholders • *Unfairness* whenever corporations engage in social activities such as supporting the arts or education, they divert funds rightfully belonging to shareholders and/or employees to unrelated third parties • *Accountability* a corporation is subject to less public accountability than public bodies are • *Expertise* although a corporation may have a high level of expertise in selling its goods and services, there is absolutely no guarantee that any promotion of social activities will be carried on with the same degree of competence **Arguments in Favor of Social Responsibility** • *The Social Contract* because society allows for the creation of corporations and gives them special rights, including a grant of limited liability, corporations owe a responsibility to our society • *Less Government Regulation* by taking a more proactive role in addressing society's problems, corporations create a climate of trust and respect that has the effect of reducing government regulation • *Long-Run Profits* corporate involvement in social causes creates goodwill, which simply makes good business sense

Civil Dispute Resolution

As discussed in Chapter 1, substantive law establishes the rights and duties of individuals and other legal entities while procedural law determines the means by which these rights are asserted. Procedural law attempts to accomplish two competing objectives: (1) to be fair and impartial and (2) to operate efficiently. The judicial process in the United States represents a balance between these two objectives as well as a commitment to the adversary system.

The first part of this chapter describes the structure and function of the Federal and State court systems. The second part deals with jurisdiction; the third part discusses civil dispute resolution, including the procedure in civil lawsuits.

The Court System

Courts are impartial tribunals (seats of judgment) established by governmental bodies to settle disputes. A court may render a binding decision only when it has jurisdiction over the dispute and the parties to that dispute; that is, when it has a right to hear and make a judgment in a case. The United States has a dual court system: The Federal government has its own independent system, as does each of the fifty States plus the District of Columbia.

THE FEDERAL COURTS

Article III of the U.S. Constitution states that the judicial power of the United States shall be vested in one Supreme Court and such lower courts as Congress may establish. Congress has established a lower Federal court system consisting of a number of special courts, district courts, and courts of appeals. The Federal court system is staffed by judges who receive lifetime appointments from the President, subject to confirmation by the Senate.

♦ SEE FIGURE 3-1 Federal Judicial System

http: Information about Federal courts: http://www.uscourts.gov/about.html

District Courts

The district courts are the general trial courts in the Federal system. Most cases begin in a district court, and it is here that issues of fact are decided. The district court is generally presided over by *one* judge, although in certain cases three judges preside. In a few cases, an appeal from a judgment or decree of a district court is taken directly to the Supreme

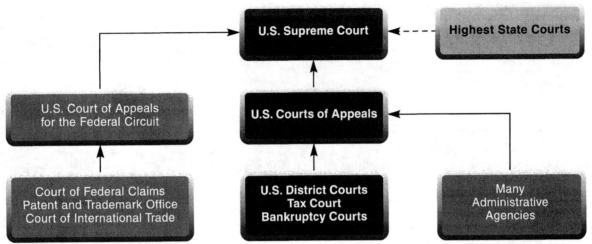

Court. In most cases, however, appeals go to the Circuit Court of Appeals of the appropriate circuit, the decision of which is, in most cases, final.

Congress has established 94 judicial districts, each of which is located entirely in a particular State. All States have at least one district, while certain States contain more than one. For instance, New York has four districts, Illinois has three, and Wisconsin has two, while a number of less populated States comprise a single district.

 Information about and cases decided by the U.S. district courts: http://www.law.emory.edu/FEDCTS/
http://www.law.cornell.edu/federal/districts.html#circuit

Courts of Appeals

Congress has established twelve judicial circuits (eleven numbered circuits plus the D.C. Circuit), each having a court known as the Court of Appeals, which primarily hears appeals from the district courts located within its circuit. In addition, these courts review decisions of many administrative agencies, the Tax Court, and the Bankruptcy Court. Congress has also established the U.S. Court of Appeals for the Federal Circuit, which is discussed in the section on "Special Courts." The United States Courts of Appeals generally hear cases in panels of *three* judges, although in some instances all of the judges of the circuit will sit *en banc* to decide a case.

The function of appellate courts is to examine the record of a case on appeal and to determine if the trial court committed prejudicial error. If so, the appellate court will **reverse** or **modify** the judgment and if necessary **remand** it (send it back) to the lower court for further proceeding. If no prejudicial error exists, the appellate court will **affirm** the decision of the lower court.

 Cases decided by the U.S. Courts of Appeals: http://www.law.emory.edu/FEDCTS/

◆ **SEE FIGURE 3-2** Circuit Courts of the United States

The Supreme Court

The nation's highest tribunal is the United States Supreme Court, which consists of nine justices (a Chief Justice and eight Associate Justices) who sit as a group in Washington, D.C. A quorum consists of any six justices. In certain types of cases, the U.S. Supreme Court has original jurisdiction (the right to hear a case first). The Court's principal function, nonetheless, is to review decisions of the Federal Courts of Appeals and, in some instances, decisions involving Federal law made by the highest State courts. Cases reach the Supreme Court under its appellate jurisdiction by one of two routes. Very few come by way of **appeal by right**—cases the Court must hear should a party request the review. In 1988, Congress enacted legislation that almost completely eliminated the right to appeal to the U.S. Supreme Court.

The second way in which the Supreme Court may review a decision of a lower court is by the discretionary **writ of certiorari**, which requires a lower court to produce the records of a case it has tried. Now almost all cases reaching the Supreme Court come to it by means of writs of *certiorari*. The Court uses the writ as a device to choose the cases it wishes to hear. The Court grants writs for cases involving a Federal question of substantial importance or a conflict in the decisions of the U.S. Circuit Courts of Appeals. Only a small percentage of the petitions to the Supreme Court for review by *certiorari* are granted, however. The vote of four justices is required to grant a writ.

 Information about the U.S. Supreme Court: http://www.supremecourtus.gov/about/about.html

◆ FIGURE 3-2   **Circuit Courts of the United States**

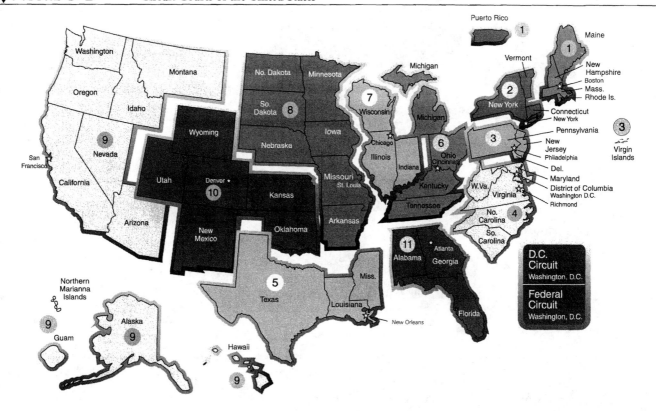

Source: Administrative Office of The United States Courts, January 1983

Special Courts

The special courts in the Federal judicial system include the U.S. Court of Federal Claims, the U.S. Tax Court, the U.S. Bankruptcy Courts, and the U.S. Court of Appeals for the Federal Circuit. These courts have jurisdiction over particular subject matter. The U.S. Court of Federal Claims has national jurisdiction to hear claims against the United States. The U.S. Tax Court has national jurisdiction over certain cases involving Federal taxes. The U.S. Bankruptcy Courts have jurisdiction to hear and decide certain matters under the Federal Bankruptcy Act, subject to review by the U.S. District Court. The U.S. Court of Appeals for the Federal Circuit has nationwide jurisdiction and reviews decisions of the Court of Federal Claims, the Patent and Trademark Office, patent cases decided by the U.S. District Court, the United States Court of International Trade, the Merit Systems Protection Board, and the U.S. Court of Veterans Appeals.

> **http:** Information about and cases decided by the U.S. Court of Federal Claims: http://www.uscfc.uscourts.gov/
> Information about and cases decided by the U.S. Bankruptcy Courts: http://www.law.cornell.edu/federal/districts.html#circuit

STATE COURTS

Each of the fifty States and the District of Columbia has its own court system. In most States the voters elect judges for a stated term.

◆ **SEE FIGURE 3-3** State Court System

Inferior Trial Courts

At the bottom of the State court system are the inferior trial courts, which decide the least serious criminal and civil matters. Usually, inferior trial courts do not keep a complete written record of trial proceedings. Such courts, which are referred to as municipal courts, justice of the peace courts, or traffic courts, hear minor criminal cases such as traffic offenses. They also conduct preliminary hearings in more serious criminal cases.

Small claims courts are inferior trial courts which hear civil cases involving a limited amount of money. Usually there is no jury, the procedure is informal, and neither side employs an attorney. An appeal from small claims court is taken to the trial court of general jurisdiction, where a new trial (called a trial *de novo*), in which the small claims court's decision is given no weight, is begun.

◆ **FIGURE 3-3**   **State Court System**

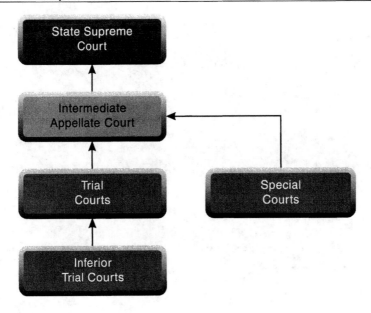

Trial Courts

Each State has trial courts of general jurisdiction, which may be called county, district, superior, circuit, or common pleas courts. (In New York the trial court is called the Supreme Court.) These courts do not have a dollar limitation on their jurisdiction in civil cases and hear all criminal cases other than minor offenses. Unlike the inferior trial courts, these trial courts of general jurisdiction maintain formal records of their proceedings as procedural safeguards.

Special Courts

Many States have special courts that have jurisdiction over particular areas. For example, many States have probate courts with jurisdiction over the administration of wills and estates. Many States also have family courts, which have jurisdiction over divorce and child custody cases. Appeals from these special courts go to the general State appellate courts.

Appellate Courts

At the summit of the State court system is the State's court of last resort, a reviewing court generally called the Supreme Court of the State. Except for those cases in which review by the U.S. Supreme Court is available, the decision of the highest State tribunal is final. Most States also have created intermediate appellate courts to handle the large volume of cases seeking review. Review by such a court is usually by right. Further review is in most cases at the highest court's discretion.

 Information about and cases decided by State courts: http://www.ncsc.dni.us/COURT/SITES/Courts.htm
State court decisions: http://www.ncsconline.org/

Jurisdiction

Jurisdiction means the power or authority of a court to hear and decide a given case. To resolve a lawsuit, a court must have two kinds of jurisdiction. The first is subject matter jurisdiction. Where a court lacks jurisdiction over the subject matter of a case, no action it takes in the case will have legal effect.

The second kind of jurisdiction is over the parties to a lawsuit. This jurisdiction is required for the court to render an enforceable judgment that affects the rights and duties of the parties to the lawsuit. A court usually may obtain jurisdiction over the defendant if she lives and is present in the court's territory or the transaction giving rise to the case has a substantial connection to the court's territory. The court obtains jurisdiction over the plaintiff when he voluntarily submits to the court's power by filing a complaint with the court.

SUBJECT MATTER JURISDICTION

Subject matter jurisdiction refers to the authority of a particular court to adjudicate a controversy of a particular kind. Federal courts have *limited* subject matter jurisdiction, as set forth in the U.S. Constitution, Article III, Section 2. State courts have jurisdiction over *all* matters that the Constitution or Congress has not given exclusively to the Federal courts or expressly denied the State courts.

Federal Jurisdiction

The Federal courts have, to the exclusion of the State courts, subject matter jurisdiction over some areas. Such jurisdiction is called **exclusive Federal jurisdiction**. Federal jurisdiction is exclusive only if Congress so provides, either explicitly or implicitly. If Congress does not so provide and the area is one over which Federal courts have subject matter jurisdiction, they share this jurisdiction with the State courts. Such jurisdiction is known as **concurrent Federal jurisdiction**.

Exclusive Federal Jurisdiction   The Federal courts have exclusive jurisdiction over Federal criminal prosecutions; admiralty, bankruptcy, antitrust, patent, trademark, and copyright cases; suits against the United States; and cases arising under certain Federal statutes that expressly provide for exclusive Federal jurisdiction.

Concurrent Federal Jurisdiction   There are two types of concurrent Federal jurisdiction: Federal question jurisdiction and diversity jurisdiction. The first arises whenever there is a Federal question over which the Federal courts do not have exclusive jurisdiction. A **Federal question** is any case arising under the Constitution, statutes, or treaties of the United States. For a case to be treated as "arising under" Federal law, either Federal law must create the plaintiff's cause of action or the plaintiff's right to relief must depend upon the resolution of a substantial question of Federal law in dispute between the parties. There is no minimum dollar requirement in Federal question cases. When a State court hears a concurrent Federal question case, it applies Federal substantive law but its own procedural rules.

Diversity jurisdiction arises where there is "diversity of citizenship" and the amount in controversy exceeds $75,000. Then private litigants may bring an action in a Federal district court or a State court. **Diversity of citizenship** exists (1) when the plaintiffs are all citizens of a State or States different from the State or States of which the defendants are citizens; (2) when a foreign country brings an action against citizens of the United States; or (3) when the controversy is between citizens of a State and citizens of a foreign country. The citizenship of an individual litigant is the State in which the litigant resides or is domiciled, whereas that of a corporate litigant is both the State of incorporation and the State in which its principal place of business is located. For example, if the amount in controversy exceeds $75,000, then diversity of citizenship jurisdiction would be satisfied if Ada, a citizen of California, sues Bob, a citizen of Idaho. If, however, Carol, a

citizen of Virginia, and Dianne, a citizen of North Carolina, sue Evan, a citizen of Georgia, and Farley, a citizen of North Carolina, diversity of citizenship would not exist because both Dianne, a plaintiff, and Farley, a defendant, are citizens of North Carolina.

The $75,000 jurisdictional requirement is satisfied if the plaintiff makes a good faith claim to the amount in the complaint, unless it is clear to a legal certainty that the claim does not exceed the required amount.

◆ **SEE CASE 3-1**

When a Federal district court hears a case solely under diversity of citizenship jurisdiction, no Federal question is involved, and, accordingly, the Federal court must apply substantive State law. The conflict of laws rules of the State in which the district court is located determine which State's substantive law the court will use. (Conflict of laws is discussed later.) Federal courts apply Federal procedural rules in diversity cases.

In any case involving concurrent jurisdiction, the plaintiff has the choice of bringing the action in either an appropriate Federal court or State court. If the plaintiff brings the case in a State court, however, the defendant usually may have it **removed** (shifted) to a Federal court for the district in which the State court is located.

State Jurisdiction

Exclusive State Jurisdiction   The State courts have exclusive jurisdiction over *all other matters* not granted to the Federal courts in the Constitution or by Congress. Accordingly, exclusive State jurisdiction would include cases involving diversity of citizenship where the amount in controversy is $75,000 or less. In addition, the State courts have exclusive jurisdiction over all cases to which Federal judicial power does not reach. These matters include, but are by no means limited to, property, torts, contract, agency, commercial transactions, and most crimes.

◆ **SEE FIGURE 3-4** Federal and State Jurisdiction

◆ **SEE FIGURE 3-5** Subject Matter Jurisdiction

Choice of Law in State Courts   A court in one State may be a proper forum for a case even though some or all of the relevant events occurred in another State. For example, a California plaintiff may sue a Washington defendant in Washington over a car accident that occurred in Oregon. Because of Oregon's connections to the accident, Washington may choose, under its **conflict of laws rules**, to apply the substantive law of Oregon. Conflict of laws rules vary from State to State.

◆ **SEE CASE 3-1**

◆ **Figure 3-4**   Federal and State Jurisdiction

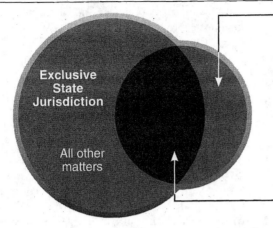

Exclusive Federal Jurisdiction
1. Federal crimes
2. Bankruptcy
3. Patents
4. Copyright and trademarks
5. Admiralty
6. Antitrust
7. Suits against the United States
8. Specified Federal statutes

Concurrent Jurisdiction
1. Federal questions
2. Diversity of citizenship

Stare Decisis in the Dual Court System

The doctrine of *stare decisis* presents certain problems when there are two parallel court systems. Consequently, in the United States, *stare decisis* functions approximately as follows:

1. The United States Supreme Court has never held itself to be bound rigidly by its own decisions, and lower Federal courts and State courts have followed that course with respect to their own decisions.
2. A decision of the U.S. Supreme Court on a Federal question is binding on all other courts, Federal or State.
3. On a Federal question, although a decision of a Federal court other than the Supreme Court may be persuasive in a State court, the decision is not binding.
4. A decision of a State court may be persuasive in the Federal courts, but it is not binding except where Federal jurisdiction is based on diversity of citizenship. In such a case the Federal courts must apply State law as determined by the highest State tribunal.
5. Decisions of the Federal courts (other than the U.S. Supreme Court) are not binding upon other Federal courts of equal or inferior rank, unless the latter owe obedience to the deciding court. For example, a decision of

the Fifth Circuit Court of Appeals binds district courts in the Fifth Circuit but binds no other Federal court.
6. A decision of a State court is binding upon all courts inferior to it in its jurisdiction. Thus, the decision of the supreme court in a State binds all other courts in that State.
7. A decision of a State court is not binding on courts in other States except where the latter courts are required, under their conflict of laws rules, to apply the law of the former State as determined by the highest court in that State. For example, if a North Carolina court is required to apply Virginia law, it must follow decisions of the Virginia Supreme Court.

◆ **See Figure 3-6** *Stare Decisis* in the Dual Court System

JURISDICTION OVER THE PARTIES

The second essential type of jurisdiction a court must have is the power to bind the parties involved in the dispute. The court obtains jurisdiction over the *plaintiff* when she voluntarily submits to the court's power by filing a complaint with the court. With respect to the *defendant*, a court may meet the

◆ **Figure 3-5**   Subject Matter Jurisdiction

Types of Jurisdiction	Court	Substantive Law Applied	Procedural Law Applied
Exclusive Federal	Federal	Federal	Federal
Concurrent: Federal Question	Federal State	Federal Federal	Federal State
Concurrent: Diversity	Federal State	State State	Federal State
Exclusive State	State	State	State

◆ **FIGURE 3-6**   *Stare Decisis* in the Dual Court System

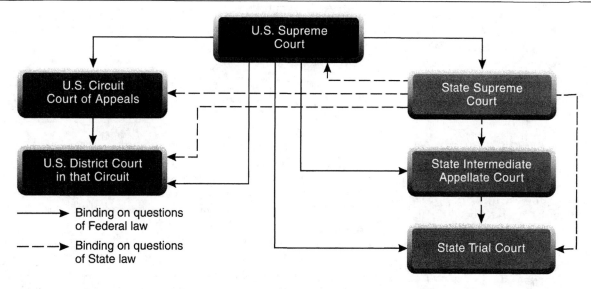

requirements for this type of jurisdiction, called **jurisdiction over the parties**, in any of three ways: (1) *in personam* jurisdiction, (2) *in rem* jurisdiction, or (3) attachment jurisdiction. In addition, the exercise of jurisdiction must satisfy the constitutionally imposed requirements of due process: reasonable notification and a reasonable opportunity to be heard. Moreover, the court's exercise of jurisdiction is valid under the Due Process Clause of the U.S. Constitution only if the defendant has minimum contacts with the State sufficient to prevent the court's assertion of jurisdiction from offending "traditional notions of fair play and substantial justice." For a court constitutionally to assert jurisdiction over a defendant, the defendant must have engaged in either purposeful acts in the State or acts outside the State that are of such a nature that the defendant could reasonably foresee being sued in that State. This overriding limitation on jurisdictional power is imposed upon the Federal and State courts through the U.S. Constitution, as discussed more fully in Chapter 4.

What notice is due depends on several factors but generally must be "notice reasonably calculated, under the circumstances, to apprise interested parties of the pendency of the action and afford them the opportunity to present their objections."

◆ **SEE CASE 3-2**

In Personam Jurisdiction

In personam jurisdiction, or **personal jurisdiction**, is jurisdiction of a court over the parties to a lawsuit, in contrast to jurisdiction over their property. A court obtains *in personam* jurisdiction over a defendant either (1) by serving process on the party within the State in which the court is located or (2)

by reasonable notification to a party outside the State in those instances where a "long-arm statute" applies. To *serve process* means to deliver a summons, which is an order to respond to a complaint lodged against a party. (The terms *summons* and *complaint* are explained more fully later in this chapter.)

Personal jurisdiction may be obtained by personally serving a person within a State if that person is domiciled in that State. The U.S. Supreme Court has held that a State may exercise personal jurisdiction over a nonresident defendant who is temporarily present if the defendant is personally served in that State. Personal jurisdiction may also arise from a party's consent. For example, parties to a contract may agree that any dispute concerning that contract will be subject to the jurisdiction of a specific court.

Most States have adopted **long-arm statutes** to expand their jurisdictional reach beyond those persons who may be personally served within the State. These statutes allow courts to obtain jurisdiction over nonresident defendants whose contacts with the State in which the court is located are such that the exercise of jurisdiction does not offend traditional notions of fair play and substantial justice. The typical long-arm statute permits a court to exercise jurisdiction over a defendant, even though process is served beyond its borders, if the defendant (1) has committed a tort (civil wrong) within the State, (2) owns property within the State and that property is the subject matter of the lawsuit, (3) has entered into a contract within the State, or (4) has transacted business within the State and that business is the subject matter of the lawsuit.

In Rem Jurisdiction

Courts in a State have the jurisdiction to adjudicate claims to property situated within the State if the plaintiff gives those persons who have an interest in the property reasonable notice and an opportunity to be heard. Such jurisdiction over property is called **in rem** jurisdiction, from the Latin word *res*, which means "thing." For example, if Carpenter and Miller are involved in a lawsuit over property located in Kansas, then an appropriate court in Kansas would have *in rem* jurisdiction to adjudicate claims with respect to this property so long as both parties are given notice of the lawsuit and a reasonable opportunity to contest the claim.

Attachment Jurisdiction

Attachment jurisdiction, or **quasi** *in rem* jurisdiction, is jurisdiction over property rather than over a person. Attachment jurisdiction is invoked by seizing the defendant's property located within the State to obtain payment of a claim against the defendant that is *unrelated* to the property seized. For example, Allen, a resident of Ohio, has obtained a valid judgment in the amount of $20,000 against Bradley, a citizen of Kentucky. Allen can attach Bradley's automobile, which is located in Ohio, to satisfy his court judgment against Bradley.

◆ **SEE FIGURE 3-7** Jurisdiction

Venue

Venue, which often is confused with jurisdiction, concerns the geographical area in which a lawsuit *should* be brought. The purpose of venue is to regulate the distribution of cases within a specific court system and to identify a convenient forum. In the Federal court system, venue determines the district or districts in a given State in which a suit may be brought. State rules of venue typically require that a suit be initiated in a county where one of the defendants resides. In matters involving real estate, most venue rules require that a suit be initiated in the county where the property is situated. A defendant may, however, object to the venue for various reasons.

Civil Dispute Resolution

As mentioned in Chapter 1, one of the primary functions of law is to provide for the peaceful resolution of disputes. Accordingly, our legal system has established an elaborate set of governmental mechanisms to settle disputes. The most prominent of these is judicial dispute resolution, called *litigation*. The rules of civil procedure, discussed in the first part of this section, govern judicial resolution of civil disputes. Judicial resolution of criminal cases is governed by the rules of criminal procedure, which are covered in Chapter 6. Dispute resolution by administrative agencies, which is also very common, is discussed in Chapter 5.

As an alternative to governmental dispute resolution, several nongovernmental methods of dispute resolution, such as arbitration, have developed. These are discussed in the second part of this section.

CIVIL PROCEDURE

Civil disputes that enter the judicial system must follow the rules of civil procedure. These rules are designed to resolve the dispute justly, promptly, and inexpensively.

◆ **FIGURE 3-7**   **Jurisdiction**

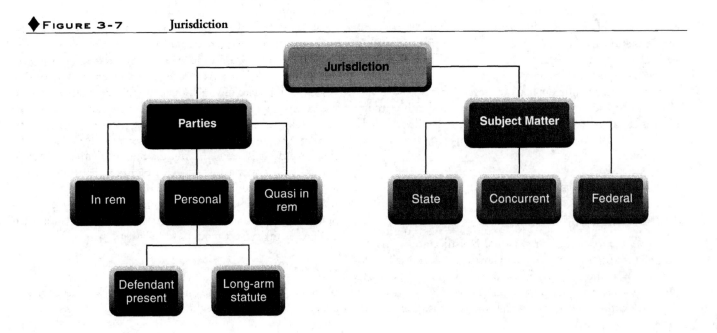

To acquaint the student with civil procedure, it will be helpful to carry a hypothetical action through the trial court to the highest court of review in the State. Although there are technical differences in trial and appellate procedure among State and Federal courts, the following illustration will provide a general understanding of the trial and appeal of cases. Assume that Pam Pederson, a pedestrian, while crossing a street in Chicago, is struck by an automobile driven by David Dryden. Pederson suffers serious personal injuries, incurs heavy medical and hospital expenses, and is unable to work for several months. Pederson desires that Dryden pay her for the loss and damages she sustained. After attempts at settlement fail, Pederson brings an action at law against Dryden. Pederson is the plaintiff, and Dryden the defendant. Each is represented by a lawyer. Let us follow the progress of the case.

http: State civil procedure laws: http://www.law.cornell.edu/topics/civil_procedure.html

The Pleadings

The **pleadings** are a series of responsive, formal, written statements in which each side to a lawsuit states its claims and defenses. The purpose of pleadings is to give notice and to establish the issues of fact and law that the parties dispute. An "issue of fact" is a dispute between the parties regarding the events that gave rise to the lawsuit. In contrast, an "issue of law" is a dispute between the parties as to what legal rules apply to these facts. Issues of fact are decided by the jury, or by the judge when there is no jury, whereas issues of law are decided by the judge.

Complaint and Summons   A lawsuit commences when Pederson, the plaintiff, files with the clerk of the trial court a **complaint** against Dryden which contains (1) a statement of the claim and supporting facts showing that she is entitled to relief and (2) a demand for that relief. Pederson's complaint alleges that while exercising due and reasonable care for her own safety, she was struck by Dryden's automobile, which was negligently being driven by Dryden, causing her personal injuries and damages of $50,000, for which Pederson requests judgment.

Once the plaintiff has filed a complaint, the clerk issues a **summons** to be served upon the defendant to notify him that a suit has been brought against him. If the defendant has contacts with the State sufficient to show that the State's assertion of jurisdiction over him is constitutional, proper service of the summons establishes the court's jurisdiction over the person of the defendant. The sheriff of the county or a deputy sheriff serves a summons and a copy of the complaint upon Dryden, the defendant, commanding him to file his appearance and answer with the clerk of the court within a specific time, usually thirty days from the date the summons

was served. A number of States permit the server to leave a copy of the summons at the defendant's home with a person of "suitable age and discretion." Most long-arm statutes allow service of the summons to be sent to out-of-state defendants by registered mail. If the defendant is a corporation, the statutes typically authorize actual service to the company's general or managing agent. When direct methods of notifying the defendant are unavailable, service by publication may be allowed.

Responses to Complaint   At this point Dryden has several options. If he fails to respond at all, a **default judgment** will be entered against him for the relief the court determines in a hearing. He may make **pretrial motions** contesting the court's jurisdiction over him or asserting that the action is barred by the statute of limitations, which requires suits to be brought within a specified time. Dryden also may move that the complaint be made more definite and certain, or that the complaint be dismissed for failure to state a claim upon which the court may grant relief. Such a motion, sometimes called a **demurrer**, essentially asserts that even if all of Pederson's allegations were true, she still would not be entitled to the relief she seeks, and that, therefore, there is no need for a trial of the facts. The court rules on this motion as a matter of law. If it rules in favor of the defendant, the plaintiff may appeal the ruling.

If he does not make any pretrial motions, or if they are denied, Dryden will respond to the complaint by filing an **answer**, which may contain admissions, denials, affirmative defenses, and counterclaims. Thus, Dryden might answer the complaint by denying its allegations of negligence and stating, on the other hand, that he, Dryden, was driving his car at a low speed and with reasonable care (a **denial**) when his car struck Pederson (an **admission**), who had dashed across the street in front of Dryden's car without looking in any direction to see whether cars or other vehicles were approaching; that, accordingly, Pederson's injuries were caused by her own negligence (an **affirmative defense**) and that, therefore, she should not be permitted to recover any damages. Dryden might further state that Pederson caused damages to his car and request a judgment for $2,000 (a **counterclaim**). These pleadings create an issue of fact regarding whether Pederson or Dryden, or both, failed to exercise due and reasonable care under the circumstances and were thus negligent and liable for their carelessness.

If the defendant counterclaims, the plaintiff must respond by a **reply,** which may also contain admissions, denials, and affirmative defenses.

Pretrial Procedure

Judgment on Pleadings   After the pleadings, either party may move for **judgment on the pleadings**, which requests the judge to rule as a matter of law whether the facts as alleged in the pleadings, which for the purpose of the motion are taken to be as the nonmoving party alleges them, form a sufficient basis to warrant granting the requested relief.

Discovery   In preparation for trial and even before completion of the pleadings stage, each party has the right to obtain relevant evidence, or information that may lead to evidence, from the other party. This procedure is known as **discovery**. It includes (1) pretrial **depositions** consisting of sworn testimony, taken out of court, of the opposing party or other witnesses; (2) sworn answers by the opposing party to **written interrogatories**; (3) **production** of documents and physical objects in the possession of the opposing party or, by a court-ordered subpoena, in the possession of nonparties; (4) a relevant court-ordered physical and/or mental **examination**, by a physician, of the opposing party; and (5) admissions of facts obtained by a **request for admissions** submitted to the opposing party. By properly using discovery, each party may become fully informed of relevant evidence and avoid surprise at trial. Another purpose of this procedure is to encourage and facilitate settlements by providing both parties with as much relevant information as possible.

Pretrial Conference   Also furthering these objectives is the pretrial conference between the judge and the attorneys representing the parties. The basic purposes of the **pretrial conference** are (1) to simplify the issues in dispute by amending the pleadings, admitting or stipulating facts, and identifying witnesses and documents to be presented at trial; and (2) to encourage settlement of the dispute without trial. (More than 90 percent of all cases are settled before going to trial.) If no settlement occurs, the judge will enter a pretrial order containing all of the amendments, stipulations, admissions, and other matters agreed to during the pretrial conference. The order supersedes the pleadings and controls the remainder of the trial.

Summary Judgment   The evidence disclosed by discovery may be so clear that a trial to determine the facts becomes unnecessary. Thus, after discovery, either party may move for a summary judgment, which requests the judge to rule that, because there are no issues of fact to be determined by trial, the party thus moving should prevail as a matter of law. A **summary judgment** is a final binding determination on the merits made by the judge before a trial.

◆ See Case 3-3

Trial

In all Federal civil cases at common law involving more than $20, the U.S. Constitution guarantees the right to a jury trial. In addition, nearly every State constitution provides a similar right. In addition, Federal and State statutes may authorize jury trials in cases not within the constitutional guarantees. Under Federal law and in almost all States, jury trials are *not* available in equity cases. Even in cases where a jury trial is available, the parties may waive (choose not to have) a trial by jury. When a trial is conducted without a jury, the judge serves as the fact finder and will make separate findings of fact and conclusions of law. When a trial is conducted with a jury, the judge determines issues of law and the jury determines questions of fact.

Jury Selection   Assuming a timely demand for a jury has been made, the trial begins with the selection of a jury. The jury selection process involves a *voir dire*, an examination by the parties' attorneys (or, in some courts, by the judge) of the potential jurors. Each party may make an unlimited number of **challenges for cause**, which prevent a prospective juror from serving if the juror is biased or cannot be fair and impartial. In addition, each party has a limited number of **peremptory challenges**, which allow the party to disqualify a prospective juror without showing cause. The Supreme Court has held that the U.S. Constitution prohibits discrimination in jury selection on the basis of race or gender.

Conduct of Trial   After the jury has been selected, both attorneys make an **opening statement** concerning the facts that they expect to prove in the trial. The plaintiff and her witnesses then testify upon **direct examination** by the plaintiff's attorney. Each is then subject to **cross-examination** by the defendant's attorney. Thus, in our hypothetical case, the plaintiff and her witnesses testify that the traffic light at the street intersection where Pederson was struck was green for traffic in the direction in which Pederson was crossing but changed to yellow when she was about one-third of the way across the street.

During the trial the judge rules on the admission and exclusion of evidence on the basis of its relevance and reliability. If the judge does not allow certain evidence to be introduced or certain testimony to be given, the attorney may preserve the question of admissibility for review on appeal by making an **offer of proof**. The law does not regard the offer of proof as evidence, and the offer, which consists of oral statements of counsel or witnesses showing for the record the substance of the evidence which the judge has ruled inadmissible, is not heard by the jury.

After cross-examination, followed by redirect examination of each of her witnesses, Pederson rests her case. At this point, Dryden may move for a directed verdict in his favor. A **directed verdict** is a final binding determination on the merits made by the judge after a trial but before the jury renders a verdict. If the judge concludes that the evidence introduced by the plaintiff, which is assumed for the purposes of the motion to be true, would not be sufficient for the jury to find in favor of the plaintiff, then the judge will grant the directed verdict in favor of the defendant. In some States, the judge will deny the motion for a directed verdict if there is *any* evidence on which the jury might possibly render a verdict for the plaintiff. If a directed verdict is reversed on appeal, a new trial is necessary.

If the judge denies the motion for a directed verdict, the defendant then has the opportunity to present evidence. The defendant and his witnesses testify that Dryden was driving his car at a low speed when it struck Pederson and that Dryden at the time had the green light at the intersection.

After the defendant has presented his evidence, the plaintiff and the defendant may be permitted to introduce rebuttal evidence. Once both parties have rested (concluded), either party may move for a directed verdict. By this motion the party contends that the evidence is so clear that reasonable persons could not differ as to the outcome of the case. If the judge grants the motion for a directed verdict, he takes the case away from the jury and enters a judgment for the party making the motion.

If the judge denies the motion, the plaintiff's attorney makes a **closing argument** to the jury, reviewing the evidence and urging a verdict in favor of Pederson. Dryden's attorney then makes a closing argument, summarizing the evidence and urging a verdict in favor of Dryden. Pederson's attorney is permitted to make a short argument in rebuttal.

Jury Instructions The attorneys previously have tendered possible written **jury instructions** on the applicable law to the trial judge, who gives to the jury those instructions he approves and denies those he considers incorrect. The judge also may give the jury instructions of his own. These instructions (called "charges" in some States) advise the jury of the particular rules of law that apply to the facts the jury determines from the evidence.

Verdict The jury then retires to the jury room to deliberate and to reach a **general verdict** in favor of one party or the other. If it finds the issues in favor of the defendant, its verdict is that the defendant is not liable. If, however, it finds the issues for the plaintiff and against the defendant, its verdict will hold the defendant liable and will specify the amount of the plaintiff's damages. In this case, the jury found that Pederson's damages were $35,000. Upon returning to the jury box, the foreman either announces the verdict or hands it in written form to the clerk to give to the judge, who reads the general verdict in open court. In some jurisdictions, the jury must reach a **special verdict** by making specific written findings on each factual issue. The judge then applies the law to these findings and renders a judgment.

Motions Challenging the Verdict The unsuccessful party may then file a written motion for a new trial or for judgment notwithstanding the verdict. The judge may grant a **motion for a new trial** if (1) the judge committed prejudicial error during the trial, (2) the verdict is against the weight of the evidence, (3) the damages are excessive, or (4) the trial was not fair. The judge has the discretion to grant a motion for a new trial (on grounds 1, 3, or 4 above) even if substantial evidence supports the verdict. On the other hand, he must deny the motion for judgment notwithstanding the verdict (also called a judgment n.o.v.) if any substantial evidence supports the verdict. This motion is similar to a motion for a directed verdict, only it is made *after* the jury's verdict. To grant the **motion for judgment notwithstanding the verdict**, the judge must decide that the evidence is so clear that reasonable people could not differ as to the outcome of the case. If a judgment n.o.v. is reversed on appeal, a new trial is *not* necessary, and the jury's verdict is entered. If the judge denies the motions for a new trial and for a judgment notwithstanding the verdict, he enters **judgment on the verdict** for $35,000 in favor of Pederson.

Appeal

The purpose of an appeal is to determine whether the trial court committed prejudicial error. Most jurisdictions permit an appeal only from a final judgment. As a general rule, an appellate court reviews only errors of law. Errors of law include the judge's decisions to admit or exclude evidence; the judge's instructions to the jury; and the judge's actions in denying or granting a motion for a demurrer, a summary judgment, a directed verdict, or a judgment notwithstanding the verdict. Appellate courts review errors of law *de novo*. An appellate court will reverse errors of fact only if they are so clearly erroneous that the court considers them to constitute an error of law.

Assume that Dryden directs his attorney to appeal. The attorney files a notice of appeal with the clerk of the trial court within the prescribed time. Later, Dryden, as appellant, files in the reviewing court the record on appeal, which contains the pleadings, transcript of the testimony, rulings by the judge on motions made by the parties, arguments of counsel, jury instructions, the verdict, posttrial motions, and the judgment from which the appeal is taken. In States having an intermediate court of appeals, such court will usually be the reviewing court. In States having no intermediate courts of appeal, a party may appeal directly from the trial court to the State supreme court.

Dryden, as appellant, is required to prepare a condensation of the record, known as an abstract, or pertinent excerpts from the record, which he files with the reviewing court together with a brief and argument. His **brief** contains a statement of the facts, the issues, the rulings by the trial court which Dryden contends are erroneous and prejudicial, grounds for reversal of the judgment, a statement of the applicable law, and arguments on his behalf. Pederson, the appellee, files an answering brief and argument. Dryden may, but is not required to, file a reply brief. The case is now ready for consideration by the reviewing court.

The appellate court does not hear any evidence; rather, it decides the case upon the record, abstracts, and briefs. After **oral argument** by the attorneys, if the court elects to hear one, the court then takes the case under advisement and makes a decision based upon majority rule, after which the court prepares a written opinion containing the reasons for its decision, the applicable rules of law, and its judgment. The judgment may **affirm** the judgment of the trial court, or, if the appellate court finds that reversible error was committed, the judgment may be **reversed**, or the case may be **reversed and remanded** for a new trial. In some instances the appellate court will affirm the lower court's decision in part and reverse it in part. The losing party may file a petition for rehearing, which is usually denied.

If the reviewing court is an intermediate appellate court, the party losing in that court may decide to seek a reversal of its judgment by filing within a prescribed time a notice of appeal, if the appeal is by right, or a petition for leave to appeal to the State supreme court, if the appeal is by discretion. This petition corresponds to a petition for a writ of *certiorari* in the U.S. Supreme Court. The party winning in the appellate court may file an answer to the petition for leave to appeal. If the petition is granted or if the appeal is by right, the record is certified to the supreme court, where each party files a new brief and argument. Oral argument may be held, and the case is taken under advisement. If the Supreme Court concludes that the judgment of the appellate court is correct, it affirms. If it decides otherwise, it reverses the judgment of the appellate court and enters a reversal or an order of remand. The unsuccessful party may again file a petition for a rehearing, which is likely to be denied. Barring the remote possibility of an application for still further review by the U.S. Supreme Court, the case either has reached its termination or, upon remand, is about to start its second journey through the courts, beginning, as it did originally, in the trial court.

Enforcement

If Dryden does not appeal or if the reviewing court affirms the judgment if he does appeal and Dryden does not pay the judgment, the task of enforcement remains. Pederson must request the clerk to issue a **writ of execution**, demanding payment of the judgment, which is served by the sheriff upon the defendant. If the writ is returned "unsatisfied," Pederson may post bond or other security and order a levy on and sale of specific nonexempt property belonging to Dryden, which is then seized by the sheriff, advertised for sale, and sold at public sale under the writ of execution. If the proceeds of the sale do not produce sufficient funds to pay the judgment, plaintiff Pederson's attorney may institute a supplementary proceeding in an attempt to locate money or other property belonging to Dryden. In an attempt to collect the judgment, Pederson's attorney also may proceed by **garnishment** against Dryden's employer to collect from Dryden's wages or against a bank in which Dryden has an account.

If Pederson cannot satisfy the judgment with Dryden's property located within Illinois (the State where the judgment was obtained), Pederson will have to bring an action on the original judgment in other States where Dryden owns property. Because the U.S. Constitution requires each State to accord judgments of other States **full faith and credit**, Pederson will be able to obtain a local judgment that may be enforced by the methods described above.

◆ **See Figure 3-8** Stages in Civil Procedure

ALTERNATIVE DISPUTE RESOLUTION

Litigation is complex, time-consuming, and expensive. Furthermore, court adjudications involve long delays, lack special expertise in substantive areas, and provide only a limited range of remedies. In addition, the litigation process offers little opportunity for compromise and often causes or exacerbates animosity between the disputants. Consequently, in an attempt to overcome some of the disadvantages of litigation, several nonjudicial methods of dealing with disputes have developed. The most important of these alternatives to litigation is arbitration. Others include conciliation, mediation, "mini-trials," and summary jury trials.

The various techniques differ in a number of ways, including (1) whether the process is voluntary, (2) whether the process is binding, (3) whether the disputants represent themselves or are represented by attorneys, (4) whether the decision is made by the disputants or by a third party, (5) whether the procedure used is formal or informal, and (6) whether the basis for the decision is law or some other criterion.

Which method of civil dispute resolution—litigation or one of the nongovernmental methods—is better for a particular dispute depends on several factors, including the financial circumstances of the disputants, the nature of their relationship (commercial or personal, ongoing or limited), and the urgency of their need for a quick resolution. Alternative dispute resolution methods are especially suitable where privacy, speed, preservation of continuing relations, and control over the process—including the flexibility to compromise—are important to the parties. Nevertheless, the disadvantages of using alternative dispute mechanisms may make court adjudication more appropriate. For example, except for arbitration, only courts can compel participation and provide a binding resolution. In addition, only courts can establish precedents and create public duties. Furthermore, the courts provide greater due process protections and uniformity of outcome. Finally, the courts are independent of the disputants and are publicly funded.

◆**FIGURE 3-8**   **Stages in Civil Procedure**

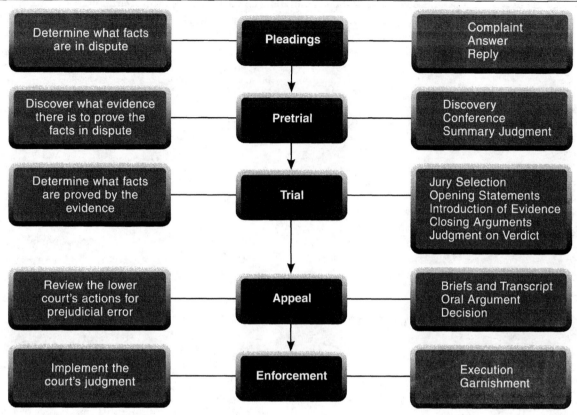

◆**SEE FIGURE 3-9** **Comparison of Adjudication, Arbitration, and Mediation/Conciliation**

http: **Information about alternate dispute resolution:** http://www.abanet.org/dispute and http://www.adr.org

Arbitration

In **arbitration,** the parties select a neutral third person or persons (the arbitrator[s]) who render(s) a binding decision after hearing arguments and reviewing evidence. Because the presentation of the case is less formal and the rules of evidence are more relaxed, arbitration usually takes less time and costs less than litigation. Moreover, in many arbitration cases the parties are able to select an arbitrator with special expertise concerning the subject of the dispute. Thus, the quality of the arbitrator's decision may be higher than that available through the court system. In addition, arbitration normally is conducted in private, which enables the parties to avoid unwanted publicity. Arbitration is commonly used in commercial and labor management disputes.

Types of Arbitration   Arbitration is of two basic types—consensual, which is by far the most common, and compulsory.

Consensual arbitration occurs whenever the parties to a dispute agree to submit the controversy to arbitration. They may do this in advance by agreeing in their contract that disputes arising out of the contract will be resolved by arbitration. Or, after a dispute arises, they may agree to submit the dispute to arbitration. In either instance, such agreements are enforceable under the Federal Arbitration Act (FAA) and statutes in more than forty States. The great majority of these States have adopted the Uniform Arbitration Act (UAA); the others have adopted substantially similar legislation. (In 2000, the National Conference of Commissioners on Uniform State Laws promulgated the Revised Uniform Arbitration Act to provide State legislatures with a more up-to-date statute to resolve disputes through arbitration. To date, only a few States have adopted the Revised UAA.) In **compulsory arbitration**, which is relatively infrequent, a Federal or State statute requires arbitration for specific types of disputes, such as those involving public employees like police officers, teachers, and firefighters.

http: **Federal Arbitration Act:** http://caselaw.lp.findlaw.com/casecode/uscodes/9/toc.html

Revised Uniform Arbitration Act: http://www.law.upenn.edu/bll/ulc/uarba/arbitrat1213.htm

◆ **FIGURE 3-9**   **Comparison of Adjudication, Arbitration, and Mediation/Conciliation**

	Court Adjudication	Arbitration	Mediation/Conciliation
Advantages	Binding	Binding	Preserves relations
	Public norms	Parties control process	Parties control process
	Precedents	Privacy	Privacy
	Uniformity	Special expertise	Flexible
	Publicly funded	Speedy resolution	
	Compels participation		
Disadvantages	Expensive	No public norms	Not binding
	Time-consuming	No precedent	Lacks finality
	Long delays	No uniformity	No compelled participation
	Limited remedies		No precedent
	Lacks special expertise		No uniformity
	No compromise		
	Disrupts relationships		
	Publicity		

Source: Adapted from Table 4 of *Report of the Ad Hoc Panel on Dispute Resolution and Public Policy,* prepared by the National Institute for Dispute Resolution.

Procedure   Usually the parties' agreement to arbitrate specifies how the arbitrator or arbitrators will be chosen. If it does not, the Federal Arbitration Act and State statutes provide methods for selecting arbitrators. Although the requirements for arbitration hearings vary from State to State, they generally consist of opening statements, case presentation, and closing statements. Case presentations may include witnesses, documentation, and site inspections. The parties may cross-examine witnesses and the parties may be represented by attorneys.

The decision of the arbitrator, called an **award**, is binding on the parties. Nevertheless, it is subject to very limited judicial review. Under the Federal Arbitration Act and the Revised UAA grounds for review include (1) the award was procured by corruption, fraud, or other undue means; (2) the arbitrators were partial or corrupt; (3) the arbitrators were guilty of misconduct prejudicing the rights of a party to the arbitration proceeding; and (4) the arbitrators exceeded their powers. Historically, the courts were unfriendly to arbitration; now, however, they favor the procedure.

International Arbitration   Arbitration is a commonly used means for resolving international disputes. The United Nations Committee on International Trade Law (UNCITRAL) and the International Chamber of Commerce have promulgated arbitration rules which have won broad international adherence. The Federal Arbitration Act has provisions implementing the United Nations Convention on the Recognition and Enforcement of Foreign Arbitral Awards. A number of States have enacted laws specifically governing international arbitration; some of the statutes have been based on the Model Law on International Arbitration drafted by UNCITRAL.

Court-Annexed Arbitration   A growing number of Federal and State courts have adopted court-annexed arbitration in civil cases where the parties seek limited amounts of damages. The arbitrators are usually attorneys. Appeal from this type of *nonbinding* arbitration is by trial *de novo*.

Many States have enacted statutes requiring the arbitration of medical malpractice disputes. Some States provide for mandatory nonbinding arbitration before bringing a case to court. Other States provide for voluntary but binding arbitration agreements which patients sign before receiving medical treatment.

◊ **SEE CASE 3-4**

Conciliation

Conciliation is a nonbinding, informal process in which the disputing parties select a neutral third party (the conciliator) who attempts to help them reach a mutually acceptable agreement. The duties of the conciliator include improving communications, explaining issues, scheduling meetings, discussing differences of opinion, and serving as an intermediary between the parties when they are unwilling to meet.

Mediation

Mediation is a process in which a neutral third party (the mediator) selected by the disputants helps them to resolve their disagreement. In addition to employing conciliation techniques to improve communications, the mediator, unlike the conciliator, proposes possible solutions for the parties to consider. Like the conciliator, the mediator lacks the power to render a binding decision. Mediation is commonly used by the judicial system in such tribunals as small claims courts, housing courts, family courts, and neighborhood justice centers. In 2001 the National Conference of Commissioners on Uniform State Laws promulgated the Uniform Mediation Act, which was amended in 2003. The Act establishes a privilege of confidentiality for mediators and participants. To date two States have adopted it.

 Uniform Mediation Act: http://www.law.upenn.edu/bll/ulc/mediat/2003finaldraft.htm

Sometimes the techniques of arbitration and mediation are combined in a procedure called "med-arb." In med-arb, the neutral third party serves first as a mediator. If all issues are not resolved through such mediation, she then serves as an arbitrator authorized to render a binding decision on the remaining issues.

Mini-Trial

A mini-trial is a structured settlement process that combines elements of negotiation, mediation, and trials. Mini-trials are most commonly used when both disputants are corporations. In a mini-trial, attorneys for the two corporations conduct limited discovery and then present evidence to a panel consisting of managers from each company, as well as a neutral third party, who may be a retired judge or other attorney. After the lawyers complete their presentations, the managers try to negotiate a settlement without the attorneys. The managers may consult the third party on how a court might resolve the issues in dispute.

Summary Jury Trial

A summary jury trial is a mock trial in which the parties present their case to an advisory jury. Though not binding, the jury's verdict does influence the negotiations in which the parties must participate following the mock trial. If the parties do not reach a settlement, they may have a full trial *de novo*.

Negotiation

Negotiation is a consensual bargaining process in which the parties attempt to reach an agreement resolving their dispute. Negotiation differs from other methods of alternate dispute resolution in that there are no third parties involved.

———— CHAPTER SUMMARY ————

The Court System

Federal Courts

District Courts trial courts of general jurisdiction that can hear and decide most legal controversies in the Federal system

Courts of Appeals hear appeals from the district courts and review orders of certain administrative agencies

The Supreme Court nation's highest court, whose principal function is to review decisions of the Federal Courts of Appeals and the highest State courts

Special Courts have jurisdiction over cases in a particular area of Federal law and include the U.S. Court of Federal Claims, the U.S. Tax Court, the U.S. Bankruptcy Courts, and the U.S. Court of Appeals for the Federal Circuit

State Courts

Inferior Trial Courts hear minor criminal cases, such as traffic offenses, and civil cases involving small amounts of money; conduct preliminary hearings in more serious criminal cases

Trial Courts have general jurisdiction over civil and criminal cases

Special Courts trial courts, such as probate courts and family courts, having jurisdiction over a particular area of State law

Appellate Courts include one or two levels; the highest court's decisions are final except in those cases reviewed by the U.S. Supreme Court

Jurisdiction

Subject Matter Jurisdiction

Definition authority of a court to decide a particular kind of case
Federal Jurisdiction
- *Exclusive Federal Jurisdiction* Federal courts have sole jurisdiction over Federal crimes, bankruptcy, antitrust, patent, trademark, copyright, and other specified cases
- *Concurrent Federal Jurisdiction* authority of more than one court to hear the same case; State and Federal courts have concurrent jurisdiction over (1) Federal question cases (cases arising under the Constitution, statutes, or treaties of the United States) that do not involve exclusive Federal jurisdiction and (2) diversity of citizenship cases involving more than $75,000

State Jurisdiction State courts have exclusive jurisdiction over all matters to which the Federal judicial power does not reach

Jurisdiction over the Parties

Definition the power of a court to bind the parties to a suit
In Personam **Jurisdiction** jurisdiction based upon claims against a person, in contrast to jurisdiction over the person's property
In Rem **Jurisdiction** jurisdiction based on claims against property
Attachment Jurisdiction jurisdiction over a defendant's property to obtain payment of a claim not related to the property
Venue geographical area in which a lawsuit should be brought

Civil Dispute Resolution

Civil Procedure

The Pleadings a series of statements that give notice and establish the issues of fact and law presented and disputed
- *Complaint* initial pleading by the plaintiff stating his case
- *Summons* notice given to inform a person of a lawsuit against her
- *Answer* defendant's pleading in response to the plaintiff's complaint
- *Reply* plaintiff's pleading in response to the defendant's answer

Pretrial Procedure process requiring the parties to disclose what evidence is available to prove the disputed facts; designed to encourage settlement of cases or to make the trial more efficient
- *Judgment on Pleadings* a final ruling in favor of one party by the judge based on the pleadings
- *Discovery* right of each party to obtain evidence from the other party
- *Pretrial Conference* a conference between the judge and the attorneys to simplify the issues in dispute and to attempt to settle the dispute without trial
- *Summary Judgment* final ruling by the judge in favor of one party based on the evidence disclosed by discovery

Trial determines the facts and the outcome of the case
- *Jury Selection* each party has an unlimited number of challenges for cause and a limited number of peremptory challenges
- *Conduct of Trial* consists of opening statements by attorneys, direct and cross-examination of witnesses, and closing arguments
- *Directed Verdict* final ruling by the judge in favor of one party based on the evidence introduced at trial
- *Jury Instructions* judge gives the jury the particular rules of law that apply to the case proves

- **Verdict** the jury's decision based on those facts the jury determines the evidence proves
- **Motions Challenging the Verdict** include motions for a new trial and a motion for judgment notwithstanding the verdict

Appeal determines whether the trial court committed prejudicial error

Enforcement plaintiff with an unpaid judgment may resort to a writ of execution to have the sheriff seize property of the defendants and to garnishment to collect money owed to the defendant by a third party

Alternative Dispute Resolution	**Arbitration** a nonjudicial proceeding in which a neutral party selected by the disputants renders a binding decision (award) **Conciliation** a nonbinding process in which a third party acts as an intermediary between the disputing parties **Mediation** a nonbinding process in which a third party acts as an intermediary between the disputing parties and proposes solutions for them to consider **Mini-Trial** a nonbinding process in which attorneys for the disputing parties (typically corporations) present evidence to managers of the disputing parties and a neutral third party, after which the managers attempt to negotiate a settlement in consultation with the third party **Summary Jury Trial** mock trial followed by negotiations **Negotiation** consensual bargaining process in which the parties attempt to reach an agreement resolving their dispute without the involvement of third parties

CASES

**CASE
3-1**

Concurrent Federal Jurisdiction/Choice of Law
RAM PRODUCTS CO., INC. v. CHAUNCEY
United States District Court, N.D. Indiana, South Bend Division, 1997
967 F.Supp. 1071

Sharp, C. J.

[Defendant, Warren C. Chauncey (Chauncey), is an Indiana resident, who briefly held the position of Vice President of Sales and Marketing while employed at RAM Products. He is fifty-nine years old and has been in the plastics industry for twenty-five years. Defendant, Replex Plastics (Replex), is an Ohio Corporation now employing Chauncey in a management position. Plaintiff, RAM Products (RAM), a Michigan corporation, and Replex are both in the plastics industry. The employment contract in controversy was entered into between Chauncey and RAM in St Joseph County, Michigan on November 18, 1991 and contained a clause prohibiting former employees from competing against RAM for a period of one year after termination of employment with RAM. On December 3, 1996, Chauncey was released from his employment at RAM and soon after began employment with Replex.

The plaintiff contends that this was a breach of its former employment contract's covenant not to compete, that Chauncey has converted and continues to convert RAM's property and trade secrets, and that he has made derogatory

remarks regarding RAM to its customers and the general public. The plaintiff argues that Chauncey's breach of contract causes irreparable harm to it through the disclosure of confidential information, the loss of client confidence, loss of goodwill, and loss of business reputation. The plaintiff seeks a preliminary injunction requiring Chauncey to cease his employment with Replex until the one year time period required by the contract has expired, an injunction restraining Chauncey from working for any other competitor during the one year period, and damages originally in the amount of $50,000. The defendant Chauncey asserts that he is not violating his former employment contract, that the contract is void due to RAM's failure to perform certain provisions of the contract, that the non-competition clause is overly-broad and unenforceable, and that he has not disclosed any trade secrets or confidential information.]

The court heard oral argument regarding the issues on February 5, 1997, at which time the court directed the parties to brief the issues. Subsequently, the parties entered into settlement negotiations with the Magistrate and requested several

Criminal Law

As discussed in Chapter 1, the civil law defines duties the violation of which constitutes a wrong against the injured party. The criminal law, on the other hand, establishes duties the violation of which is a societal wrong against the whole community. Civil law is a part of private law, whereas criminal law is a part of public law. In a civil action, the injured party sues to recover compensation for the damage and injury that he has sustained as a result of the defendant's wrongful conduct. The party bringing a civil action (the plaintiff) has the burden of proof, which he must sustain by a preponderance (greater weight) of the evidence. The purpose of the civil law is to compensate the injured party.

Criminal law, by comparison, is designed to prevent harm to society by defining criminal conduct and establishing punishment for such conduct. In a criminal case, the defendant is prosecuted by the government, which must prove the defendant's guilt beyond a reasonable doubt, a burden of proof significantly higher than that required in a civil action. Moreover, under our legal system, guilt is never presumed. Indeed, the law presumes the innocence of the accused, and the defendant's failure to testify in her own defense does not affect this presumption. The government still has the burden of affirmatively proving the guilt of the accused beyond a reasonable doubt.

Of course, the same conduct may, and often does, constitute both a crime and a tort, which is a civil wrong. (Torts are discussed in Chapters 7 and 8.) But an act may be criminal without being tortious; by the same token, an act may be a tort but not a crime.

Because of the increasing use of criminal sanctions to enforce governmental regulation of business, criminal law is an essential part of business law. Moreover, businesses sustain considerable loss as victims of criminal actions. Accordingly, this chapter covers the general principles of criminal law and criminal procedure as well as specific crimes relevant to business.

 U.S. Department of Justice, Bureau of Justice Statistics: http://www.ojp.usdoj.gov/bjs/
**U.S. Department of Justice, Bureau of Justice Statistics Crime & Justice Electronic
Data Abstracts:** http://www.ojp.usdoj.gov/bjs/dtdata.htm
FBI, Uniform Crime Reports: http://www.fbi.gov/ucr/ucrquest.htm

NATURE OF CRIMES

A **crime** is any act or omission forbidden by public law in the interest of protecting society and made punishable by the government in a judicial proceeding brought by it. Punishment for criminal conduct includes fines, imprisonment, probation, and death. In addition, some States and the Federal government have enacted victim indemnification statutes which establish funds, financed by criminal fines, to provide indemnification in limited amounts to victims of criminal activity. Crimes are prohibited and punished on grounds of public policy, which may include the protection and safeguarding of government (as in treason), human life (as in murder), or private property (as in larceny). Additional purposes of the criminal law include deterrence, rehabilitation, and retribution.

Historically, criminal law was primarily common law. Today, however, criminal law is almost exclusively statutory. All States have enacted comprehensive criminal law statutes (or codes) covering most, if not all, common law crimes. Moreover, these statutes have made the number of crimes defined in criminal law far greater than the number of crimes defined under common law. Some codes expressly limit crimes to those included in the codes, thus abolishing common law crimes. Nonetheless, some States do not statutorily define all of their crimes; their courts, therefore, must rely on the common law definitions. Because there are no Federal common law crimes, all Federal crimes are statutory.

Within recent times the scope of criminal law has increased greatly. The scope of traditional criminal conduct has been expanded by numerous regulations and laws which contain criminal penalties pertaining to nearly every phase of modern living. Typical examples in the field of business law are those laws concerning the licensing and conduct of a business, antitrust laws, and the laws governing the sales of securities.

Essential Elements

In general, a crime consists of two elements: (1) the wrongful or overt act (*actus reus*) and (2) the criminal intent (*mens rea*). For example, to support a larceny conviction it is not enough to show that the defendant stole another's goods; it must also be established that he intended to steal the goods. Conversely, criminal intent without an overt act is not a crime. For instance, Ann decides to rob the neighborhood grocery store and then really "live it up." Without more, Ann has committed no crime.

Actus reus refers to all the nonmental elements of a crime, including the physical act that must be performed, the consequences of that act, and the circumstances under which it must be performed. The *actus reus* required for specific crimes will be discussed later in this chapter.

Mens rea, or mental fault, refers to the mental element of a crime. Most common law and some statutory crimes require subjective fault, other crimes require objective fault, while some statutory crimes require no fault at all. The American Law Institute's Model Penal Code and most modern criminal statutes recognize three possible types of **subjective fault:** purposeful, knowing, and reckless. A person acts *purposely* or *intentionally* if his conscious object is to engage in the prohibited conduct or to cause the prohibited result. Thus, if Arthur, with the desire to kill Donna, shoots his rifle at Donna, who is seemingly out of gunshot range, and in fact does kill her, Arthur had the purpose or intent to kill Donna. If Benjamin,

desiring to poison Paula, places a toxic chemical in the water cooler in Paula's office and unwittingly poisons Gail and Victor, Benjamin will be found to have purposefully killed Gail and Victor because Benjamin's intent to kill Paula is transferred to Gail and Victor, regardless of Benjamin's feelings toward Gail and Victor.

A person acts *knowingly* if he is aware that his conduct is of a prohibited type or that a prohibited consequence is practically certain to result. A person acts *recklessly* if he consciously disregards a substantial and unjustifiable risk (1) that his conduct is prohibited or (2) that it will cause a prohibited result.

Objective fault involves a gross deviation from the standard of care that a reasonable person would observe under the circumstances. Criminal statutes refer to objective fault by such terms as *carelessness* or *negligence*. Such conduct occurs when a person *should* be aware of a substantial and unjustifiable risk that his conduct is prohibited or will cause a prohibited result. Examples of crimes requiring objective fault are involuntary manslaughter (negligently causing the death of another), carelessly driving an automobile, and, in some States, issuing a bad check.

Many regulatory statutes have totally dispensed with the mental element of a crime by imposing criminal liability without fault. Without regard to the care that a person exercises, criminal liability without fault makes it a crime for a person to commit a specified act or to bring about a certain result. Statutory crimes imposing **liability without fault** include the sale of adulterated food and the sale of alcoholic beverages to a minor. Most of these crimes involve regulatory statutes dealing with health and safety and impose only fines for violations.

◆ **See Figure 6-1**   Degrees of Mental Fault

Classification

Historically, crimes were classified *mala in se* (wrongs in themselves or morally wrong, such as murder) or *mala prohibita* (not morally wrong but declared wrongful by law, such as the prohibition against making a U-turn). From the standpoint of the seriousness of the offense, a crime is also classified as a **felony** (any crime punishable by death or imprisonment in the penitentiary) or as a **misdemeanor** (any crime punishable by a fine or imprisonment in a local jail).

Vicarious Liability

Vicarious liability is liability imposed upon one person for the acts of another. Employers are vicariously liable for any authorized criminal act of their employees if the employer directed, participated in, or approved of the act. For example, if an employer directs an employee to fix prices with the employer's competitors, and the employee does so, both the employer and employee have criminally violated the Sherman Antitrust Act. On the other hand, employers are ordinarily not liable for the

◆ **FIGURE 6-1** **Degrees of Mental Fault**

Type	Fault Required	Examples
Subjective Fault	Purposeful Knowing Reckless	Larceny Embezzlement
Objective Fault	Negligent Careless	Careless driving Issuing bad checks (some States)
Liability Without Fault	None	Sale of alcohol to minor Sale of adulterated food

unauthorized criminal acts of their employees. As previously discussed, most crimes require mental fault; this element is absent, so far as criminal responsibility of the employer is concerned, where the employee's criminal act was not authorized.

Employers nonetheless may be subject to a criminal penalty for the unauthorized act of a manager acting in the scope of employment. Moreover, employers may be criminally liable under liability without fault statutes for certain unauthorized acts of their employees, whether those employees are managerial or not. For example, many States have statutes that punish "every person who by himself or his employee or agent sells anything at short weight," or "whoever sells liquor to a minor and any sale by an employee shall be deemed the act of the employer as well."

Liability of the Corporation

Historically, corporations were not held criminally liable because, under the traditional view, a corporation could not possess the requisite criminal intent and, therefore, was incapable of committing a crime. The dramatic growth in size and importance of corporations changed this view. Under the modern approach, a corporation may be liable for violation of statutes imposing liability without fault. In addition, a corporation may be liable where the offense is perpetrated by a high corporate officer or the board of directors. The Model Penal Code provides that a corporation may be convicted of a criminal offense for the conduct of its employees if:

1. the legislative purpose of the statute defining the offense is to impose liability on corporations and the conduct is within the scope of the [employee's] office or employment;
2. the offense consists of an omission to discharge a specific, affirmative duty imposed upon corporations by law; or
3. the offense was authorized, requested, commanded, per-

Punishment of a corporation for crimes is necessarily by fine, not imprisonment. Nonetheless, individuals bearing responsibility for the criminal act face fines, imprisonment, or both. The Model Penal Code provides that the corporate agent having primary responsibility for the discharge of the duty imposed by law on the corporation is as accountable for a reckless omission to perform the required act as though the duty were imposed by law directly upon him.

On November 1, 1991, the Federal Organizational Corporate Sentencing Guidelines took effect. The overall purpose of the guidelines is to impose sanctions that will provide just punishment and adequate deterrence. To that end, the guidelines mandate corporations to formulate and implement compliance programs reasonably designed to prevent potential legal violations by the corporation and its employees.

The guidelines provide for a base fine for each criminal offense, calculated by one of the following: (a) the amount listed in the guidelines' offense-level fine table (fines range from $5,000 to $72.5 million), (b) the pecuniary gain to the organization, or (c) the pecuniary loss as a result of the offense, to the extent that the loss was intentionally, knowingly, or recklessly caused. In addition, restitution is available to victims whenever possible. In the most extreme case, a corporation's charter can be revoked. If a corporation successfully adopts and implements an adequate compliance program, the corporate fine can be reduced to as little as 5 percent of the scheduled fine. On the other hand, if a company does not have a proper program in place, the fine can be multiplied by up to four times.

An adequate compliance program should include the following:

1. a written code of conduct,
2. assignment of a senior corporate official to be responsible for the overall compliance program,

4. ongoing monitoring of the program,
5. proper delegation of program-related authority within the organization,
6. disciplinary measures appropriate to enforce the program, and
7. periodic reviews of the program.

| http: | **United States Sentencing Commission:** http://www.ussc.gov/ |

WHITE-COLLAR CRIME

White-collar crime has been defined in various ways. The Justice Department defines it as nonviolent crime involving deceit, corruption, or breach of trust. It also has been defined to include crimes committed by individuals—such as embezzlement and forgery—as well as crimes committed on behalf of a corporation—such as commercial bribery, product safety and health crimes, false advertising, and antitrust violations. A less precise definition is crime "committed by a person of respectability and high social status in the course of his occupation," while a more narrow definition identifies white-collar crime as fraud or deceit practiced through misrepresentation to gain an unfair advantage. Regardless of its definition, such crime costs society billions of dollars; estimates range from $40 billion to more than $200 billion per year. Historically, prosecution of white-collar crime was de-emphasized because such crime was not considered violent. Now, however, many contend that white-collar crime often inflicts violence but does so impersonally. For example, unsafe products cause injury and death to consumers while unsafe working conditions cause injury and death to employees. Indeed, many contend that white-collar criminals should receive stiff prison sentences due to the magnitude of their crimes.

| http: | **Department of Justice:** http://www.usdoj.gov/ |

In response to the business scandals involving companies such as Enron, WorldCom, Global Crossing, and Arthur Andersen, in 2002 Congress passed the Sarbanes-Oxley Act, which is more fully discussed in Chapter 44, Securities Regulation. The Act, according to President George W. Bush, constitutes "the most far-reaching reforms of American business practices since the time of Franklin Delano Roosevelt [President from 1932 until 1945]." The legislation seeks to prevent such scandals by increasing corporate responsibility; adding new financial disclosure requirements; creating new criminal offenses and increasing the penalties of existing Federal crimes; and creating a powerful new five-person Accounting Oversight Board with authority to review and discipline auditors.

The Act establishes new criminal penalties including: (1) making it a crime to defraud any person or to obtain any money or property fraudulently in connection with any security of a public company, with penalties of a fine and/or up to 25 years imprisonment, and (2) imposing fines and/or imprisonment of up to 20 years for knowingly altering, destroying, mutilating, or falsifying any document with the intent of impeding a Federal investigation. In addition, the Act substantially increases the penalties for existing crimes including: (1) mail and wire fraud (five-year maximum increased to twenty-five year maximum) and (2) violation of the Securities and Exchange Act (ten-year maximum increased to twenty-year maximum).

❖ **SEE CASE 6-1**

Computer Crime

One special type of white-collar crime is computer crime, which involves the use of a computer to steal money or services, to remove personal or business information, and to tamper with information. Computer crimes can be broken down into five general categories: (1) theft of computer hardware, software, or secrets; (2) unauthorized use of computer services; (3) theft of money by computer; (4) vandalism of computer hardware or software; and (5) theft of computer data. For a more complete discussion of computer crime, see Chapter 48, CyberLaw.

Detecting crimes involving computers is extremely difficult. In addition, many businesses, loath to imply that their security is lax, often do not report computer crimes. Nonetheless, losses due to computer crimes are estimated to be in the tens of billions of dollars. Moreover, given society's ever-increasing dependence upon computers, this type of crime will in all likelihood continue to increase.

Computer crimes already have become commonplace. Examples abound. Software piracy (the unauthorized copying of copyrighted software) is now so widespread that an estimated two out of every three copies of software are illegally obtained. A computer consultant hired by Security Pacific Bank wrongfully transferred $10 million from the bank to his own Swiss bank account. Six employees stole TRW's credit-rating data and offered to repair poor credit ratings for a fee. Disgruntled or discharged employees have used computer programs to destroy company software.

As a consequence, enterprises are spending large sums of money to increase computer security. In addition, nearly all fifty States have enacted computer crime laws, though the Federal government, despite numerous attempts, has yet to pass comprehensive legislation prohibiting computer crime. The absence of such legislation has been defended on three grounds: (1) computer crime is not unique and can be addressed under existing criminal law statutes, (2) State legislation can deal with the problem, and (3) writing effective legislation is difficult. Congress has, however, enacted specific legislation (the Counterfeit Access Device and Computer Fraud and Abuse Act) making it a Federal crime to (1) gain unauthorized access to a computer used by the government, by a financial institution, or in interstate or foreign commerce or communication; (2) cause damage, without authorization, to a computer; (3) traffic in the interstate distribution of computer passwords with the intent to defraud; or (4) extort money or other items of value by means of threats to cause damage to a computer.

http: **Department of Justice Computer Crime:** http://www.usdoj.gov/criminal/cybercrime/ **Counterfeit Access Device and Computer Fraud and Abuse Act:** http://www4.law.cornell.edu/uscode/18/ 1001.html

Racketeer Influenced and Corrupt Organizations Act (RICO)

The Racketeer Influenced and Corrupt Organizations Act (RICO) was enacted in 1970 with the stated purpose of terminating the infiltration of organized crime into legitimate business. The act subjects to severe civil and criminal penalties enterprises that engage in a pattern of racketeering, defined as the commission of two or more predicate acts within a period of ten years. A "predicate act" is any of several criminal offenses listed in RICO. Included are nine major categories of State crimes and and more than thirty Federal crimes, such as murder, kidnapping, arson, extortion, drug dealing, securities fraud, mail fraud, and bribery. The most controversial issue concerning RICO is its application to businesses that are not engaged in organized crime but that do meet the "pattern of racketeering" test under the Act. Criminal conviction under the law may result in a prison term of up to 20 years plus a fine of up to $25,000 per violation. In addition, businesses will forfeit any property obtained due to a RICO violation, and individuals harmed by RICO violations may invoke the statute's civil remedies, which include treble damages and attorneys' fees.

Other areas of Federal law that impose both civil and criminal penalties include bankruptcy (Chapter 39), antitrust (Chapter 41), securities regulation (Chapter 44), and environmental regulation (Chapter 46).

http: **RICO:** http://www4.law.cornell.edu/uscode/18/1961.html

CRIMES AGAINST BUSINESS

Criminal offenses against property greatly affect businesses, amounting to losses in the hundreds of billions of dollars each year. This section covers the following crimes against property: (1) larceny, (2) embezzlement, (3) false pretenses, (4) robbery, (5) burglary, (6) extortion and bribery, (7) forgery, and (8) bad checks.

Larceny

The crime of larceny is the (1) trespassory (2) taking and (3) carrying away of (4) personal property (5) of another (6) with the intent to deprive the victim permanently of the goods. All six elements must be present for the crime to exist. Thus, if Barbara pays Larry $5,000 for an automobile that Larry agrees to deliver the following week, and Larry does not do so, Larry is *not* guilty of larceny because he has not trespassed on Barbara's property. Larry has not taken anything from Barbara; he has simply refused to turn the automobile over to her. Larceny applies only when a person takes personal property from another without the other's consent. Here, Barbara voluntarily paid the money to Larry, who has not committed larceny but who may have obtained the $5,000 by false pretenses (which is discussed later). Likewise, if Carol takes Dan's 1968 automobile without Dan's permission, intending to use it for a joyride and to then return it to Dan, Carol has not committed larceny because she did not intend to deprive Dan permanently of the automobile. (Nevertheless, Carol has committed the crime of unauthorized use of an automobile.) On the other hand, if Carol left Dan's 1968 car in a junkyard after the joyride, she most likely would be held to have committed a larceny because of the high risk that her action would permanently deprive Dan of the car.

Embezzlement

Embezzlement is the fraudulent conversion of another's property by one who was in lawful possession of it. A **conversion** is any act that seriously interferes with the owner's rights in the property, such as exhausting the resources of the property, selling it, giving it away, or refusing to return it to its rightful owner. This statutory crime was first enacted in response to a 1799 English case in which a bank employee was found not guilty of larceny for taking money given to him for deposit in the bank because the money had been voluntarily handed to him. Thus, embezzlement is a crime intended to prevent individuals who are lawfully in possession of another's property from taking such property for their own use.

The key distinction between larceny and embezzlement, therefore, is whether the thief is in lawful possession of the property. While both crimes involve the misuse of another's property, in larceny the thief unlawfully possesses the property, whereas in embezzlement the thief possesses it lawfully. A second distinction between larceny and embezzlement is that, unlike larceny, embezzlement does not require the intent to deprive the owner permanently of his property. Nonetheless, to constitute an embezzlement, an act must interfere significantly with the owner's rights to the property.

False Pretenses

Obtaining property by **false pretenses**, like embezzlement, is a crime addressed by statutes enacted to close a loophole in the requirements for larceny. False pretenses is the crime of obtaining title to property of another by making materially false representations of an existing fact, with knowledge of their falsity and with the intent to defraud. Larceny does not cover this situation because here the victim voluntarily transfers the property to the thief. For example, a con artist who goes door to door and collects money by saying he is selling stereo equipment, when he is not, is committing the crime of false pretenses. The test of deception is *subjective*: if the victim is actually deceived, the test is satisfied even though a reasonable person would not have been deceived by the defendant's lies. Therefore, the victim's gullibility or lack of due care is no defense.

Many courts hold that a false statement of intention, such as a promise, does not constitute false pretenses. In addition, a false expression of opinion regarding value is usually not considered a misrepresentation of fact and thus will not suffice for false pretenses.

Other specialized crimes that are similar to false pretenses include mail, wire, and bank fraud as well as securities fraud. **Mail fraud**, unlike the crime of false pretenses, does not require the victim to be actually defrauded; it simply requires the defendant to use the mails (or private carrier) to carry out a scheme that attempts to defraud others. Due to its breadth and ease of use, mail fraud has been employed extensively by Federal prosecutors. The **wire fraud** statute prohibits the transmittal by wire, radio, or television in interstate or foreign commerce of any information with the intent to defraud. The Federal statute prohibiting **bank fraud** makes it a crime knowingly to execute or attempt to execute a scheme to defraud a financial institution or to obtain by false pretenses funds under the control or custody of a financial institution. Securities fraud is discussed in Chapter 44.

Robbery

Under the common law as well as most statutes, robbery is a larceny with the additional elements that (1) the property is taken directly from the victim or in the immediate presence of the victim and (2) the act is accomplished through either force or the threat of force which need not be against the person from whom the property is taken. For example, a robber threatens Sam, saying that unless Sam opens his employer's safe, the robber will shoot Maria. Moreover, the victim's presence may be actual or constructive. *Constructive presence* means that the defendant's actual or threatened force prevents the victim from being present. For example, if the robber knocks the victim unconscious or ties her up, the victim is considered constructively present.

Many laws distinguish between simple robbery and aggravated robbery. Robbery can be aggravated by any of several factors, including (1) the use of a deadly weapon; (2) the robber's intent to kill or to kill if faced with resistance; (3) serious bodily injury to the victim; *or* (4) commission of the crime by two or more persons.

Burglary

At common law, **burglary** was defined as breaking and entering the dwelling of another at night with the intent to commit a felony. Many modern statutes differ from the common law definition by requiring merely that there be (1) an entry (2) into a building (3) with the intent to commit a felony in the building. Thus, these statutory definitions omit three elements of the common law crime: the building need not be a dwelling house, the entry need not be at night, and the entry need not be a technical breaking. Nonetheless, so greatly do the modern statutes vary (except for the idea that each contains some, but not all, of the common law elements) that generalization is nearly impossible.

Extortion and Bribery

Although frequently confused, extortion and bribery are two distinct crimes. **Extortion**, or blackmail as it is sometimes called, is generally held to be the making of threats for the purpose of obtaining money or property. For example, Lindsey tells Jason that unless he pays her $10,000, she will tell Jason's customers that he was once arrested for disturbing the peace. Lindsey has committed the crime of extortion. In a few jurisdictions, however, the crime of extortion occurs only if the defendant actually causes the victim to give up money or property.

Bribery, on the other hand, is the act of offering money or property to a public official to influence the official's decision. The crime of bribery is committed when the illegal offer is made, whether accepted or not. Thus, if Andrea offered Edward, the mayor of New Town, a 20-percent interest in Andrea's planned real estate development if Edward would use his influence to have the development proposal approved, Andrea would be guilty of criminal bribery. In contrast, if Edward had threatened Andrea that unless he received a 20-percent interest in Andrea's development he would use his influence to prevent the approval of the development, Edward would be guilty of criminal extortion. Bribery of foreign officials is covered by the Foreign Corrupt Practices Act, discussed in Chapter 44.

Some jurisdictions have gone beyond traditional bribery law by adopting statutes that make commercial bribery illegal. **Commercial bribery** is the use of bribery to acquire new business, obtain secret information or processes, or receive kickbacks.

Forgery

Forgery is the intentional falsification or false making of a document with the intent to defraud. Accordingly, if William prepares a false certificate of title to a stolen automobile, he is guilty of forgery. Likewise, if an individual alters some receipts to increase her income tax deductions, she has committed the crime of forgery. The most common type of forgery is the signing of another's name to a financial document.

Bad Checks

A statutory crime that has some relation to both forgery and false pretenses is the passing of **bad checks**—that is, writing a check on an account containing funds insufficient to cover the check. All jurisdictions have now enacted laws making it a crime to issue bad checks; however, these statutes vary greatly from jurisdiction to jurisdiction. Most jurisdictions simply require that the check be issued; they do not require that the issuer receive anything in return for the check. Also, although most jurisdictions require that the defendant issue a check with knowledge that she does not have enough money to cover the check, the Model Penal Code and a number of States provide that knowledge is presumed if the issuer had no account at the bank or if the check was not paid for lack of funds and the issuer failed to pay the check within ten days.

❖ **See Case 6-2**

DEFENSES TO CRIMES

Even though a defendant is found to have committed a criminal act, he will not be convicted if he has a valid defense. The defenses most relevant to white-collar crimes and crimes against business include defense of property, duress, mistake of fact, and entrapment. In some instances, a defense proves the absence of a required element of the crime; other defenses provide a justification or excuse that bars criminal liability.

Defense of Person or Property

Individuals may use reasonable force to protect their property. This defense enables a person to commit, without any criminal liability, what the law would otherwise consider the crime of assault, battery, manslaughter, or murder. Under the majority rule, deadly force is *never* reasonable to safeguard property, because life is deemed more important than the protection of property. For this reason, individuals cannot use a deadly mechanical device, such as a spring gun, to protect their property. If, however, the defender's use of reasonable force in protecting his property is met with an attack upon his person, then he may use deadly force if the attack threatens him with death or serious bodily harm.

Duress

A person who is threatened with immediate, serious bodily harm to himself or another unless he engages in criminal activity has the valid defense of **duress** (sometimes referred to as compulsion or coercion) to criminal conduct other than murder. For example, Ann threatens to kill Ben if he does not assist her in committing larceny. Ben complies. Because of duress, he would not be guilty of the larceny.

Mistake of Fact

If a person reasonably believes the facts surrounding his conduct to be such that his conduct would not constitute a crime, then the law will treat the facts as he reasonably believes them to be. Accordingly, an honest and reasonable **mistake of fact** will justify the defendant's conduct. For example, if Ann gets into a car that she reasonably believes to be hers—the car is the same color, model, and year as hers, is parked in the same parking lot, and is started by her key—she will be relieved of criminal responsibility for taking Ben's automobile.

Entrapment

The defense of **entrapment** arises when a law enforcement official induces a person to commit a crime when that person would not have done so without the persuasion of the police official. The rationale behind the rule which applies only to government officials and agents, not to private individuals, is to prevent law enforcement officials from provoking crime and from engaging in reprehensible conduct.

CRIMINAL PROCEDURE

Each of the States and the Federal government have procedures for initiating and coordinating criminal prosecutions. In addition, the first ten amendments to the U.S. Constitution, called the Bill of Rights, guarantee many defenses and rights of an accused. The Fourth Amendment prohibits unreasonable searches and seizures to obtain incriminating evidence. The Fifth Amendment requires indictment for capital crimes by a grand jury, prevents double jeopardy and self-incrimination, and prohibits deprivation of life or liberty without due process of law. The Sixth Amendment requires that an accused receive a speedy and public trial by an impartial jury and that he be informed of the nature of the accusation, be confronted with the witnesses who testify against him, be given the power to obtain witnesses in his favor, and have the right to competent counsel for his defense. The Eighth Amendment prohibits excessive bail, excessive fines, and cruel or unusual punishment.

Most State constitutions have similar provisions to protect the rights of accused persons. In addition, the Fourteenth Amendment prohibits State governments from depriving any person of life, liberty, or property without due process of law. Moreover, the U.S. Supreme Court has held that most of the Constitutional protections just discussed apply to the States through the operation of the Fourteenth Amendment.

Although the details of criminal process differ in various jurisdictions, the process retains several common objectives. In every jurisdiction, the primary purpose of the process is to enforce the criminal law, but this purpose must be accomplished within the limitations imposed by other goals. These goals include advancing an adversary system of adjudication, requiring the government to bear the burden of proof, minimizing erroneous convictions, minimizing the burdens of defense, respecting individual dignity, maintaining the appearance of fairness, and achieving equality in the administration of the process.

We will first discuss the steps in a criminal prosecution; we will then focus on the major Constitutional protections for the accused in our system of criminal justice.

◆ **SEE FIGURE 6-2** **Constitutional Protection for the Criminal Defendant**

Steps in Criminal Prosecution

Although the particulars of criminal procedure vary from State to State, the following provides a basic overview. After arrest, the accused is booked and appears (first appearance) before a magistrate, commissioner, or justice of the peace, where formal notice of the charges is given, the accused is advised of his rights, and bail is set. Next, a **preliminary**

hearing is held to determine whether there is probable cause to believe the defendant is the one who committed the crime. The defendant is entitled to be represented by counsel.

If the magistrate concludes that probable cause exists, she will bind the case over to the next stage, which is either an indictment or information, depending upon the jurisdiction. The Federal system and some States require indictments for all felony prosecutions (unless waived by the defendant), while the other States permit but do not mandate indictments. A grand jury, which is not bound by the magistrate's decision at the preliminary hearing, issues an **indictment**, or true bill, if it finds sufficient evidence to justify a trial on the charge brought. Unlike the preliminary hearing, the grand jury does not hear evidence from the defendant, nor does the defendant appear before the grand jury. A grand jury traditionally consisted of not less than sixteen and not more than twenty-three people. Today, many States use a smaller grand jury, not infrequently composed of twelve members. An **information**, by comparison, is a formal accusation of a crime brought by a prosecuting officer, not a grand jury. Such a procedure is used in misdemeanor cases and in some felony cases in those States that do not require indictments. The indictment or information at times precedes the actual arrest.

At the **arraignment**, the defendant is brought before the trial court, where he is informed of the charge against him and where he enters his plea. The arraignment must be held promptly after the indictment or information has been filed. If his plea is "not guilty," the defendant must stand trial. He is entitled to a jury trial for all felonies and for misdemeanors

◆ **FIGURE 6-2**   **Constitutional Protection for the Criminal Defendant**

Amendment	Protection Conferred
Fourth	Freedom from unreasonable search and seizure
Fifth	Due process Right to indictment by grand jury for capital crimes* Freedom from double jeopardy Freedom from self-incrimination
Sixth	Right to speedy, public trial by jury Right to be informed of accusations Right to confront witnesses Right to present witnesses Right to competent counsel
Eighth	Freedom from excessive bail

punishable by more than six months imprisonment. Most States also permit a defendant to request a jury trial for lesser misdemeanors. If the defendant chooses, however, he may have his guilt or innocence determined by the court sitting without a jury, which is called a "bench trial."

A criminal trial is somewhat similar to a civil trial, but with some significant differences: (1) the defendant is presumed innocent, (2) the burden of proof on the prosecution is to prove criminal guilt beyond a reasonable doubt, and (3) the defendant is not required to testify. The trial begins with the selection of the jury and the opening statements by the prosecutor and the attorney for the defense. The prosecution presents evidence first; then the defendant presents his. At the conclusion of the testimony, closing statements are made, and the jury, instructed as to the applicable law, retires to arrive at a verdict. If the verdict is "not guilty," the case is over. The State has no right to appeal from an acquittal; and the accused, having been placed in "jeopardy," cannot be tried a second time for the same offense. If the verdict is "guilty," the judge will enter a judgment of conviction and set the case for sentencing. The defendant may make a motion for a new trial, asserting that prejudicial error occurred at his original trial, necessitating a retrial of the case. He may also appeal to a reviewing court, alleging error by the trial court and asking for either his discharge or a remandment of the case for a new trial.

Fourth Amendment

The Fourth Amendment, which protects all individuals against unreasonable searches and seizures, is designed to safeguard the privacy and security of individuals against arbitrary invasions by government officials. Although the Fourth Amendment by its terms applies only to acts of the Federal government, the Fourteenth Amendment makes it applicable to State government action as well.

When evidence has been obtained in violation of the Fourth Amendment, the general rule prohibits the introduction of the illegally seized evidence at trial. The purpose of this **exclusionary rule** is to discourage illegal police conduct and to protect individual liberty, not to hinder the search for the truth. In *Weeks v. United States*, 232 U.S. 383 (1914), the United States Supreme Court ruled,

> If letters and private documents can thus be seized and held and used in evidence against a citizen accused of an offense, the protection of the Fourth Amendment declaring his right to be secure against such searches and seizures is of no value, and, so far as those thus placed and concerned, might as well be stricken from the Constitution. The efforts of the courts and their officials to bring the guilty to punishment, praiseworthy as they are, are not to be aided by the sacrifice of those great principles established by years of endeavor and suffering which have resulted in their embodiment in the fundamental law of the land.

Nonetheless, in recent years the U.S. Supreme Court has limited the exclusionary rule.

To obtain a warrant to search a particular person, place, or thing, a law enforcement official must demonstrate to a magistrate that he has probable cause to believe that the search will reveal evidence of criminal activity. **Probable cause** means "[t]he task of the issuing magistrate is simply to make a practical, common-sense decision whether, given all the circumstances set forth . . . before him, . . . , there is a fair probability that contraband or evidence of a crime will be found in a particular place." *Illinois v. Gates*, 462 U.S. 213 (1983).

Even though the Fourth Amendment requires that a search and seizure generally be made after a valid search warrant has been obtained, in some instances a search warrant is not necessary. For example, it has been held that a warrant is not necessary where (1) there is hot pursuit of a fugitive, (2) the subject voluntarily consents to the search, (3) an emergency requires such action, (4) there has been a lawful arrest, (5) evidence of a crime is in plain view of the law enforcement officer, or (6) delay would significantly obstruct the investigation.

http: **U.S. Constitution:** http://www.law.cornell.edu/ constitution/constitution.table.html

Fifth Amendment

The Fifth Amendment protects persons against self-incrimination, double jeopardy, and being charged with a capital or infamous crime except by grand jury indictment.

The prohibitions against self-incrimination and double jeopardy also apply to the States through the Due Process Clause of the Fourteenth Amendment; the Grand Jury Clause, however, does not.

The privilege against self-incrimination extends only to testimonial evidence, not to physical evidence. The Fifth Amendment "privilege protects an accused only from being compelled to testify against himself, or otherwise provide the State with evidence of a testimonial or communicative nature." *Schmerber v. California*, 384 U.S. 757 (1966). Therefore, a person can be forced to stand in a lineup for identification purposes, provide a handwriting sample, or take a blood test. Most significantly, the Fifth Amendment does not protect the records of a business entity such as a corporation or partnership; it applies only to papers of individuals. Moreover, the Fifth Amendment does not prohibit examination of an individual's business records as long as the individual is not compelled to testify against himself.

The Fifth Amendment and the Fourteenth Amendment also guarantee due process of law, which is basically the requirement of a fair trial. Every person is entitled to have the charges or complaints against him made publicly and in writing, whether in civil or criminal proceedings, and to receive the opportunity to defend himself against those charges. In criminal prosecutions, due process includes the right to counsel; to confront and cross-examine adverse witnesses; to testify in one's own behalf, if desired; to produce witnesses and offer other evidence; and to be free from any and all prejudicial conduct and statements.

Sixth Amendment

The Sixth Amendment specifies that the Federal government shall provide the accused with a speedy and public trial by an impartial jury, inform her of the nature and cause of the accusation, confront her with the witnesses against her, have compulsory process for obtaining witnesses in her favor, and allow her to obtain the assistance of counsel for her defense. The Fourteenth Amendment extends these guarantees to the States.

The Supreme Court has explained the purpose of guaranteeing the right to a trial by jury as follows: "[T]he purpose of trial by jury is to prevent oppression by the Government by providing a safeguard against the corrupt or overzealous prosecutor and against the compliant, biased, or eccentric judge. . . . [T]he essential factors of a jury trial obviously lie in the interposition between the accused and his accuser of the common sense judgment of a group of laymen." *Apodaca v. Oregon*, 406 U.S. 404 (1972). Nevertheless, a defendant may forgo her right to a jury trial.

Historically, juries consisted of twelve jurors, but the Federal courts and the courts of certain States have since reduced the number to six. Noting no observable difference between the results reached by a jury of twelve and those reached by a jury of six, nor any evidence to suggest that a jury of twelve is more advantageous to a defendant, the Supreme Court has held that the use of a six-member jury in a criminal case does not violate a defendant's right to a jury trial under the Sixth Amendment. The jury need only be large enough "to promote group deliberation, free from outside attempts at intimidation, and to provide a fair possibility for obtaining a representative cross section of the community." Moreover, State court jury verdicts need not be unanimous, provided the vote is sufficient to ensure adequate deliberations. Thus, the Supreme Court has upheld jury votes of 11–1, 10–2, and 9–3 but rejected as insufficient a 5–1 vote.

CHAPTER SUMMARY

Nature of Crimes

Definition any act or omission forbidden by public law
Essential Elements
- *Actus Reus* wrongful or overt act
- *Mens Rea* criminal intent or mental fault

Classification
- *Felony* a serious crime
- *Misdemeanor* a less serious crime

Vicarious Liability liability imposed for acts of employees if the employer directed, participated in, or approved of the acts
Liability of a Corporation under certain circumstances a corporation may be convicted of crimes and punished by fines

---

White-Collar Crime

Definition nonviolent crime involving deceit, corruption, or breach of trust
Computer Crime use of a computer to commit a crime
Racketeer Influenced and Corrupt Organizations Act (RICO) Federal law intended to stop organized crime from infiltrating legitimate businesses

---

Crimes Against Business

Larceny trespassory taking and carrying away of personal property of another with the intent to deprive the victim permanently of the property
Embezzlement taking of another's property by a person who was in lawful possession of the property
False Pretenses obtaining title to property of another by means of representation one knows to be materially false; made with intent to defraud

Robbery committing larceny with the use or threat of force

Burglary under most modern statutes, an entry into a building with the intent to commit a felony

Extortion making threats to obtain money or property

Bribery offering money or property to a public official to influence the official's decision

Forgery intentional falsification of a document to defraud

Bad Checks knowingly issuing a check without funds sufficient to cover the check

---

Defenses to Crimes

Defense of Person or Property individuals may use reasonable force to protect themselves, other individuals, and their property

Duress coercion by threat of serious bodily harm; a defense to criminal conduct other than murder

Mistake of Fact honest and reasonable belief that conduct is not criminal

Entrapment inducement by a law enforcement official to commit a crime

---

Criminal Procedure

Steps in Criminal Prosecution generally include arrest, booking, formal notice of charges, preliminary hearing to determine probable cause, indictment or information, arraignment, and trial

Fourth Amendment protects individuals against unreasonable searches and seizures

Fifth Amendment protects persons against self-incrimination, double jeopardy, and being charged with a capital crime except by grand jury indictment

Sixth Amendment provides the accused with the right to a speedy and public trial, the opportunity to confront witnesses, a process for obtaining witnesses, and the right to counsel

---

CASES

CASE

6-1

White Collar Crime
PEOPLE v. FARELL
Supreme Court of California, 2002
28 Cal.4th 381, 121 Cal.Rptr.2d 603
http://caselaw.lp.findlaw.com/data2/californiastatecases/s092183.doc

George, C. J.

In this case we determine whether Penal Code section 1203.044, which requires the imposition of a minimum county jail sentence as a condition of probation upon conviction of certain theft offenses, applies to the theft of property other than money, including trade secrets. We conclude that it does.

I

On April 18, 1997, [a] * * * complaint was filed charging defendant with the theft of a trade secret * * * . It was further alleged as a sentence enhancement that the loss exceeded $2.5 million * * * , and as a restriction on the granting of probation that the theft was of an amount exceeding $100,000 within the meaning of sections 1203.044 * * * . Defendant pleaded no

contest to the theft charge, * * *. He objected, however, to the potential application of section 1203.044 to his sentence. * * *

A hearing was held in the superior court on the limited question of whether section 1203.044 applies to the theft of property other than money, including trade secrets. The court concluded that the provision applies to the theft of all property of a certain value, including trade secrets. * * * In accordance with the requirements of section 1203.044, the court suspended imposition of sentence and placed defendant on probation for a period of three years on condition that he serve three months in county jail, with credit for time served of seven days. The court granted a stay of the jail term pending appeal.

The Court of Appeal reversed, concluding that section 1203.044 applies only to the theft of what it termed "monetary

Relationship of Principal and Agent

By using agents, one person (the principal) may enter into any number of business transactions as though he had personally carried them out, thus multiplying and expanding his business activities. The law of agency, like the law of contracts, is basic to almost every other branch of business law. Practically every type of contract or business transaction can be created or conducted through an agent. Therefore, the place and importance of agency in the practical conduct and operation of business cannot be overemphasized.

This is particularly true in the case of partnerships, corporations, and other business associations. Partnership is founded on the agency of the partners. Each partner is an agent of the partnership and, as such, has the authority to represent and bind the partnership in all usual transactions of the partnership. A corporation, being an artificial legal entity, must act through the agency of its officers and employees. Limited liability companies act through the actions of their members, managers, or both. Thus, practically and legally, agency is an essential part of partnerships, corporations, and other business associations. In addition, sole proprietors also may employ agents in the operations of their business. Business, therefore, is largely conducted not by owners themselves but by their agents or representatives.

The law of agency divides broadly into two main and somewhat overlapping parts: the internal and the external. An agent functions as an agent by dealing with third persons, thereby establishing legal relationships between the principal and those third persons. These relationships, which constitute the external part of agency law, are discussed in the next chapter. This chapter will cover the internal relationship between principal and agent, including the nature of agency, the creation of an agency, the duties of agent to principal, the duties of principal to agent, and the termination of agency.

Agency is primarily governed by State common law. An orderly presentation of this law is found in the Restatement (Second) of the Law of Agency published by the American Law Institute (ALI). Regarded as a valuable authoritative reference work, the Restatement is extensively cited and quoted in reported judicial opinions and by legal scholars. The ALI is in the process of preparing a third Restatement of Agency.

NATURE OF AGENCY

Agency is a consensual relationship between two persons, known as principal and agent, through which the agent is authorized to act for and on behalf of the principal. Restatement, Section 1. An agent, therefore, is one who represents another, the principal, in business dealings with a third person; the operation of agency therefore involves three persons: the principal, the agent, and a third person. In dealing with a third person, the agent acts for and in the name and place of the principal, who, along with the third person, is, if properly entered into, a party to the transaction, which is usually contractual. When the agent is dealing with the third person, the principal, in legal effect, is present in the person of the agent; and the result of the agent's functioning is exactly the same as if the principal had dealt directly with the third person. If, moreover, the existence and identity of the principal are disclosed, the agent acts not as a party but simply as an intermediary.

Within the scope of the authority granted to her by her principal, the agent may negotiate the terms of contracts with others and bind her principal to such contracts. In addition, the negligence of an agent who is an employee in conducting the business of her principal exposes the principal to tort liability for injury and loss suffered by third persons. The old maxim "*Qui facit per alium, facit per se*" (Who acts through another, acts himself) accurately describes the relationship between principal and agent. The rights and liabilities of the parties where an agent enters into a contract with a third party or commits a tort against a third party are discussed in the next chapter.

Scope of Agency Purposes

As a general rule, a person may do through an agent whatever business activity he may accomplish personally. Conversely, whatever he cannot legally do himself, he cannot authorize another to do for him. Thus, a person may not validly authorize another to commit an illegal act or crime. Any such agreement is illegal and therefore unenforceable. Restatement, Section 19. Also, a person may not appoint an agent to perform acts that are so personal that their performance may not be delegated to another, as in the case of a contract for personal services. Restatement, Section 17. For example, Howard, a painter, contracts to paint a portrait of Doris. But Howard has one of his students execute the painting and tenders it to Doris. This is not a valid tender because the duty to paint Doris's portrait is not delegable.

Other Legal Relationships

Two other legal relationships overlap with agency: employer-employee and principal-independent contractor. In the **employment relationship** (historically referred to as the master-servant relationship), the employer has the right to *control* the physical conduct of the employee. Restatement, Section 2. In contrast, a person who engages an **independent contractor** to do a specific job does not have the right to control the conduct and activities of the independent contractor in the performance of his contract. Restatement, Section 2(3). The latter simply contracts to do a job and is free to choose the method and manner in which to perform it. For example, a full-time chauffeur is an employee, whereas a taxicab driver hired to carry a person to the airport is an independent contractor engaged by the passenger.

In determining whether a person acting for another is an employee or an independent contractor, the courts consider several factors listed in Section 220 of the Restatement:

(a) the extent of control which, by the agreement, the master may exercise over the details of the work;

(b) whether or not the one employed is engaged in a distinct occupation or business;

(c) the kind of occupation, with reference to whether, in the locality, the work is usually done under the direction of the employer or by a specialist without supervision;

(d) the skill required in the particular occupation;

(e) whether the employer or the workman supplies the instrumentalities, tools, and the place of work for the person doing the work;

(f) the length of time for which the person is employed;

(g) the method of payment, whether by the time or by the job;

(h) whether or not the work is a part of the regular business of the employer;

(i) whether or not the parties believe they are creating the relation of master and servant; and

(j) whether the principal is or is not in business.

All employees are agents, even those employees not authorized to contract on behalf of the employer or otherwise to conduct business with third parties. Thus, an assembly-line worker in a factory is an agent of the company employing her.

Although all employees are agents, not all agents are employees. Agents who are not employees are independent contractors. For instance, an attorney retained to handle a particular transaction would be an independent contractor-agent regarding that particular transaction. Other examples are auctioneers, brokers, and factors. Finally, not all independent contractors are agents. For example, the taxicab driver in the example above is not an agent. Likewise, if Pam hires Bill to build a stone wall around her property, Bill is an independent contractor who is not an agent.

The distinction between employee and independent contractor has several important legal consequences. For example, as discussed in the next chapter, a principal is liable for the torts committed by an employee within the scope of his employment but ordinarily is not liable for torts committed by an independent contractor. In addition, the obligations of a principal under numerous Federal and State statutes apply only to agents who are employees. These statutes cover such matters as labor relations, employment discrimination, disability, employee safety, workers' compensation, social security, minimum wage, and unemployment compensation. These and other statutory enactments affecting the employment relationship are discussed in Chapter 43.

❦ **SEE CASE 19-1**

CREATION OF AGENCY

Agency is a consensual relationship that the principal and agent may form by contract *or* agreement. The Restatement defines an agency relationship as "the fiduciary relation which results from the manifestation of consent by one person [the principal] to another [the agent] that the other shall act on his behalf and subject to his control, and consent by the other so to act." Section 1. The Restatement further provides that "[a]n agency relation exists only if there has been a manifestation by the principal to the agent that the agent may act on his account, and consent by the agent so to act." Section 15. Thus, whether an agency relationship has been created is determined by an *objective* test. If the principal requests another to act for him with respect to a matter and indicates that the other is to act without further communication, and the other consents to act, the relation of principal and agent exists. For example, Paula writes to Austin, a factor whose business is purchasing goods for others, telling him to select described goods and ship them at once to Paula. Before answering Paula's letter, Austin does as directed, charging the goods to Paula. He is authorized to do this because an agency relationship exists between Paula and Austin.

The principal has the right to control the conduct of the agent with respect to the matters entrusted to the agent. Restatement, Section 14. The principal's right to control continues throughout the duration of the agency relationship.

The relationship of principal and agent is consensual and not necessarily contractual; therefore, it may exist without consideration. Restatement, Section 16. An agency created without consideration is a **gratuitous agency**. For example, Patti asks her friend Andrew to return for credit goods recently purchased from a store. If Andrew consents, a gratuitous agency has been created. The power of a gratuitous agent to affect the principal's relationships with third persons is the same as that of a paid agent, and his liabilities to and rights against third persons also are the same. Nonetheless, agency by contract, the most usual method of creating the relationship, must satisfy all the requirements of a contract.

In some circumstances a person is held liable as a principal, even though no actual agency has been created. Called **agency by estoppel**, apparent agency, or ostensible agency, this liability arises when (1) a person (P) intentionally or negligently causes a belief that another person (A) has authority to act on P's behalf, (2) a third person (T) reasonably and in good faith relies on the appearances created by P, and (3) T changes her position in reliance on A's apparent authority. Restatement, Section 8B. When these requirements are met, P is liable to T for the loss T suffered by changing her position.

◊ See Case 19-2

Formalities

As a general rule, a contract of agency requires no particular formality. Usually the contract is express or inferred from the conduct of the principal. In some cases, however, the contract must be in writing. For example, the appointment of an agent for a period of more than a year comes within the one-year clause of the statute of frauds and thus must be in writing to

be enforceable. In some States, the authority of an agent to sell land must be stated in a writing signed by the principal. Some States have "equal dignity" statutes providing that a principal must grant his agent in a written instrument the authority to enter into any contract required to be in writing. See Chapter 48 for a discussion of State and Federal legislation giving electronic records and signatures the legal effect of traditional writings and signatures.

A **power of attorney** is a written instrument that evidences the formal appointment of an agent, who is known as an attorney in fact. Under a power of attorney, a principal may, for example, appoint an agent not only to execute a contract for the sale of the principal's real estate, but also to execute the deed conveying title to the real estate to the third party. A number of States have created an optional statutory short form power of attorney based on the Uniform Statutory Form Power of Attorney Act.

> **http:** Uniform Statutory Form Power of Attorney Act:
> http://www.law.upenn.edu/bll/ulc/ulc_frame.htm

Capacity

The capacity to be a principal, and thus to act through an agent, depends upon the capacity of the principal to do the act herself. For example, contracts entered into by a minor or an incompetent not under a guardianship are voidable. Consequently, the appointment of an agent by a minor or an incompetent not under a guardianship—and any resulting contracts—are voidable, regardless of the agent's contractual capacity. The capacity of a business association to be a principal is determined by the law governing that business association.

Almost all of the States have adopted the Uniform Durable Power of Attorney Statute providing for a durable power of attorney under which an agent's power survives or is triggered by the principal's loss of mental competence. A **durable power of attorney** is a written instrument that expresses the principal's intention that the agent's authority will not be affected by the principal's subsequent incapacity or that the agent's authority will be come effective upon the principal's subsequent incapacity.

Any person, including individuals, corporations, partnerships, and other associations, has the capacity to act as an agent. Restatement, Section 21. Because the act of the agent is considered the act of the principal, the incapacity of an agent to bind himself by contract does not disqualify him from making a contract that is binding on his principal. The agent's liability, however, depends upon the agent's capacity to contract. Thus, although the contract of agency may be voidable, an authorized contract between the principal and the third person who dealt with the agent is valid. An "electronic agent" is a computer program or other automated means used independently to initiate an action or respond to electronic records or performances in whole or in part without review or action by an individual. Electronic agents are not persons and, therefore, are not considered agents. See Chapter 48 for a discussion of the legal effect given to electronic agents.

DUTIES OF AGENT TO PRINCIPAL

As the principal-agent relationship ordinarily is created by contract, the duties of the agent to the principal are determined primarily by the provisions of the contract. In addition to these contractual duties, the agent is subject to various other duties imposed by law, unless the parties agree otherwise. Restatement, Section 376. Normally, a principal bases the selection of an agent on the agent's ability, skill, and integrity. Moreover, the principal not only authorizes and empowers the agent to bind him on contracts with third persons, but also frequently places the agent in possession of his money and other property. As a result, the agent is in a position, either through negligence or dishonesty, to injure the principal. Accordingly, an agent as a **fiduciary** (a person in a position of trust and confidence) owes his principal the duties of obedience, diligence, and loyalty; the duty to inform; and the duty to provide an accounting. Moreover, the agent "is subject to liability for loss caused to the principal by any breach of duty." Restatement, Section 401.

A gratuitous agent is subject to the same duty of loyalty that is imposed upon a paid agent and is liable to the principal for the harm he causes by his careless performance. Although the lack of consideration usually places a gratuitous agent under no duty to perform for the principal, such an agent may be liable to the principal for failing to perform a promise on which the principal has relied.

Duty of Obedience

The duty of obedience requires the agent to act in the principal's affairs only as authorized by the principal and to obey all reasonable instructions and directions of the principal. Restatement, Sections 383 and 385. Except where the instructions are ambiguous, an agent is liable to the principal for unauthorized acts that are the result of the agent's misinterpretation of the principal's directions. An agent is not, however, under a duty to follow orders to perform illegal or unethical acts, such as misrepresenting the quality of his principal's goods or those of a competitor. Still, he may be subject to liability to his principal for breach of the duty of obedience (1) because he entered into an unauthorized contract for which his principal is liable, (2) because he has improperly delegated his authority, or (3) because he has committed a tort for which the principal is liable. Thus, an agent who sells on credit in violation of his principal's explicit instructions has breached the duty of obedience and is liable to the principal for any amounts the purchaser does not pay. Moreover, an agent who breaches his duty of obedience loses his right to compensation. Restatement, Section 469.

Duty of Diligence

A paid agent must act with reasonable care and skill in performing the work for which she is employed. She must also exercise any special skill that she may have. Restatement, Section 379. By failing to exercise the required care and skill, she is liable to the principal for any resulting loss. For example, Peg appoints Alvin as her agent to sell goods in markets where the highest price can be obtained. Although by carefully obtaining information he could have obtained a higher price in a nearby market, Alvin sells goods in a glutted market, receiving only a low price. Consequently, he is liable to Peg for breach of the duty of diligence.

Duty to Inform

An agent must use reasonable efforts to provide the principal with information relevant to the affairs entrusted to her and that, as the agent knows or should know, the principal would desire to have. Restatement, Section 381. The rule of agency providing that notice to an agent is notice to his principal makes this duty imperative. Examples of information that an agent is under a duty to communicate to his principal include the following: that a customer of the principal has become insolvent; that a debtor of the principal has become insolvent; that a partner of a firm with which the principal has previously dealt, and with which the principal or agent is about to deal, has withdrawn from the firm; or that property which the principal has authorized the agent to sell at a specified price can be sold at a higher price.

Duty to Account

The agent is under a duty to maintain and provide the principal with a true and complete account of money or other property that the agent has received or expended on the principal's behalf. Restatement, Section 382. An agent also must keep the principal's property separate from his own.

Fiduciary Duty

A fiduciary duty arises out of a relationship of trust and confidence. A duty imposed by law, an agent owes it to his principal and an employee to his employer. The **fiduciary duty** is one of utmost loyalty and good faith. Although it occurs under many circumstances involving principals and their agents, the fiduciary duty arises most frequently in the following situations.

Conflicts of Interest An agent must act solely in the interest of his principal, not in his own interest or in the interest of another. In addition, an agent may not represent his principal in any transaction in which the agent has a personal interest. Nor may he act on behalf of adverse parties to a transaction without both principals' approval to the dual agency. An agent may take a position that conflicts with the interest of his principal only if the principal, with full knowledge of all of the facts, consents. For example, A, an agent of P who desires to purchase land, agrees with C, who represents B, a seller of land, that A and C will endeavor to effect a transaction between their principals and will pool their commissions. A and C have committed a breach of fiduciary duty to P and B.

Self-dealing   The courts closely scrutinize transactions between an agent and her principal. Because the agent may not deal at arm's length with her principal, she thus owes her principal a duty of full disclosure of all relevant facts that affect the transaction. Moreover, the transaction must be fair. Thus, an agent who is employed to buy may not buy from himself without the principal's consent. Restatement, Section 389. For example, Penny employs Albert to purchase for her a site suitable for a shopping center. Albert owns such a site and sells it to Penny at the fair market value, but does not disclose to Penny that he had owned the land. Penny may rescind the transaction. An agent who is employed to sell may not become the purchaser nor may he act as agent for the purchaser without the consent of the principal. The agent's loyalty must be undivided, and he must devote his actions exclusively to represent and promote the interests of his principal.

◆ **See Case 19-3**

Duty Not to Compete   An agent cannot compete with his principal or act on behalf of a competitor. After the agency terminates without breach by the agent, however, unless otherwise agreed, the agent may compete with his former principal. The courts will enforce by injunction a contractual agreement by the agent not to compete after the agency terminates if the restriction is reasonable as to time and place and is necessary to protect the principal's legitimate interest. Contractual agreements not to compete are discussed in Chapter 13. Moreover, as discussed in Chapter 48, contracts not to compete may be subject to different standards for Internet companies and their employees.

◆ **See Case 13-1**

Confidential Information   An agent may not use or disclose confidential information obtained in the course of the agency for his own benefit or contrary to the interest of his principal. Confidential information is information that, if disclosed, would harm the principal's business or that has a value because it is not generally known. Such information includes unique business methods, trade secrets, business plans, and customer lists. An agent may, however, reveal confidential information that the principal is committing, or is about to commit, a crime.

   Once the agency terminates, unless otherwise agreed, the agent may not use or disclose to third persons confidential information. The agent may, however, utilize the skills, knowledge, and general information she acquired during the agency relationship. Restatement, Section 396.

Duty to Account for Financial Benefits   Unless otherwise agreed, an agent is accountable to the principal for any financial benefit she has received as a direct result of transactions conducted on behalf of the principal. Such benefits would include bribes, kickbacks, and gifts. Moreover, an agent may not profit secretly from any transaction subject to the agency. All profits belong to the principal, to whom the agent must account. Thus, if an agent, authorized to sell certain property of his principal for $1,000, sells it for $1,500, he may not secretly pocket the additional $500. Further, suppose Peabody employs real estate broker Anderson to sell his land for a commission of 6 percent of the sale price. Anderson, knowing that Peabody is willing to sell for $20,000, agrees secretly with a prospective buyer who is willing to pay $22,000 for the land that he will endeavor to obtain Peabody's consent to sell for $20,000, in which event the buyer will pay Anderson $1,000, or one-half of the amount that the buyer believes she is saving on the price. The broker has violated his fiduciary duty and must pay to Peabody the secret profit of $1,000. Furthermore, Anderson loses the right to any commission on the transaction.

Principal's Remedies   An agent who violates his fiduciary duty is liable to his principal for breach of contract, in tort for losses caused, and in restitution for profits he made or property he received in breach of the fiduciary duty. Moreover, he loses the right to compensation. Restatement, Section 469. The principal may avoid a transaction in which the agent breached his fiduciary duty, even though the principal suffered no loss. A breach of fiduciary duty may also constitute just cause for discharge of the agent.

DUTIES OF PRINCIPAL TO AGENT

Although both principal and agent have rights and duties arising out of the agency relationship, more emphasis is placed on the duties of the agent. This is necessarily so because of the nature of the agency relationship. First, the acts and services to be performed, both under the agency contract and as may be required by law, are to be performed mostly by the agent. Second, the agent is a fiduciary and as such is subject to the duties discussed earlier. Nonetheless, an agent has certain rights against the principal, both under the contract and by the operation of law. Correlative to these rights are certain duties, based in contract and tort law, which the principal owes to the agent.

◆ **See Figure 19-1**   **Duties of Principal and Agent**

Contractual Duties

The contractual duties owed by a principal to an agent are the duties of compensation, reimbursement, and indemnification; each may be excluded or modified by agreement between the principal and agent. Although a gratuitous agent

◆ FIGURE 19-1   Duties of Principal and Agent

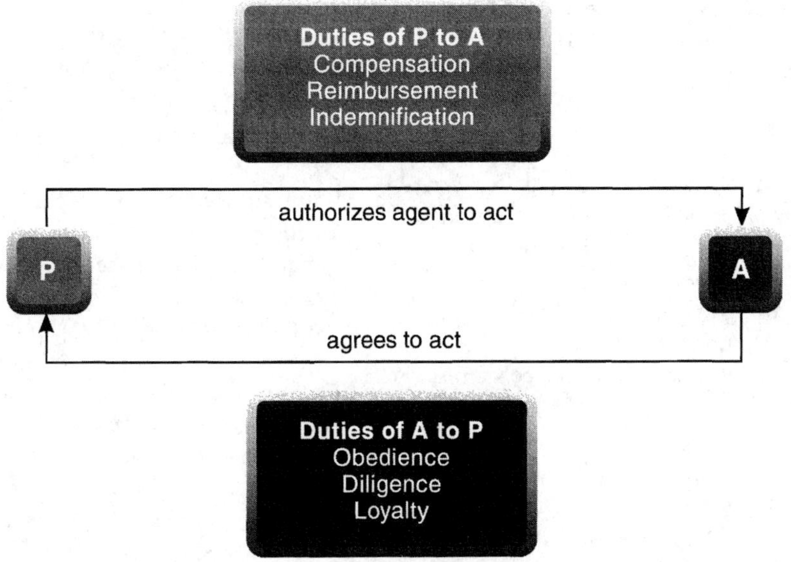

Duties of P to A
Compensation
Reimbursement
Indemnification

authorizes agent to act

P   **A**

agrees to act

Duties of A to P
Obedience
Diligence
Loyalty

is not owed a duty of compensation, she is entitled to reimbursement and indemnification.

As with any party to a contract, a principal is under a duty to perform his part of the contract according to its terms. The most important duty of the principal, from the standpoint of the agent, is to compensate the agent as specified in the contract. It is also the duty of the principal not to terminate the agency wrongfully. Whether the principal must furnish the agent with the means of employment or the opportunity for work will depend upon the particular case. For example, a principal who employs an agent to sell his goods must supply the agent with conforming goods, whereas in other cases, the agent must create his own opportunity for work, as in the case of a broker employed to procure a buyer for his principal's house. How far, if at all, the principal must assist or cooperate with the agent will depend on the particular agency. Usually, cooperation on the part of the principal is more necessary where the agent's compensation is contingent upon the success of his efforts than where the agent is paid a fixed salary regularly over a period of permanent employment.

Compensation A principal has a duty to compensate her agent unless the agent has agreed to serve gratuitously. If the agreement does not specify a definite compensation, a principal is under a duty to pay the reasonable value of the authorized services her agent has performed. Restatement, Section 443. An agent loses the right to compensation by (1) breaching the duty of obedience, (2) breaching the duty of loyalty, or (3) willfully and deliberately breaching the agency contract. Furthermore, an agent whose compensation depends upon her accomplishing a specific result is entitled to the agreed compensation only if

she achieves the result within the time specified or within a reasonable time, if no time is stated. A common example is a listing agreement between a seller and a real estate broker providing for a commission to the broker if he finds a buyer ready, willing, and able to buy the property on the terms specified in the agreement. A principal also has a duty to maintain and provide to the agent a true and complete account of the money or property due to her.

❖ SEE CASE 19-4

Reimbursement A principal is under a duty to reimburse his agent for authorized payments the agent makes on the principal's behalf and for authorized expenses the agent incurs. Restatement, Section 438. For example, an agent who reasonably and properly pays a fire insurance premium for the protection of her principal's property is entitled to reimbursement for the payment. "The authority to pay money to third persons on account of the principal or to incur liabilities in the course of the principal's business may be created by specific directions or may be the result of the course of business between the principal and the agent, or of the customs of the business in which the agent is engaged for the principal." Section 439, Comment c.

Indemnification The principal is under a duty to indemnify the agent for losses the agent incurred or suffered while acting as directed by the principal in a transaction that is neither illegal nor known by the agent to be wrongful. Restatement, Sections 438 and 439. To **indemnify** is to make good or pay a loss. Suppose that Perry, the principal, has in his possession goods belonging to Margot. Perry directs Alma, his agent, to sell these goods. Alma, believing Perry to be the owner, sells the goods to Turner. Margot then sues Alma for the conversion of her goods and recovers a judgment, which Alma pays to Margot. Alma is entitled to payment from Perry for her loss, including the amount she reasonably expended in defense of the action brought by Margot.

Tort Duties

A principal owes to any agent the same duties under tort law that the principal owes to all parties. Restatement, Section 470. Moreover, a principal is under a duty to disclose to an agent risks of which the principal knows or should know, if the principal should realize that the agent is unaware of such risks in the agency. For instance, in directing his agent to collect rent from a tenant who is known to have assaulted rent collectors, the principal has a duty to warn the agent of the risk involved.

Where the agent is an employee, the principal owes the agent additional duties. Among these is the duty to provide reasonably safe conditions of employment and to warn the employee of any unreasonable risk involved in the employment. A negligent employer is also liable to her employees for injury caused by the negligence of other employees and of other agents doing work for her. The tort duties an employer owes to an employee are discussed more fully in Chapter 43.

TERMINATION OF AGENCY

Because the authority of an agent is based upon the consent of the principal, the agency is terminated when such consent is withdrawn or otherwise ceases to exist. Upon termination of the agency, the agent's actual authority ends; and he is not entitled to compensation for services subsequently rendered, although his fiduciary duties may continue. As discussed in the next chapter, in some situations apparent authority also terminates, whereas in others apparent authority continues until a third party has knowledge or notice of the termination of agency. Termination may take place by the acts of the parties or by operation of law.

Acts of the Parties

Termination by the acts of the parties may occur by the provisions of the original agreement, by the subsequent acts of both principal and agent, or by the subsequent act of either one of them.

Lapse of Time Authority conferred upon an agent for a specified time terminates when that period expires. If no time is specified, authority terminates at the end of a reasonable period. Restatement, Section 105. For example, Palmer authorizes Avery to sell a tract of land for him. After ten years pass without communication between Palmer and Avery, though Avery purports to have sold the tract, his authorization has terminated due to lapse of time.

Fulfillment of Purpose The authority of an agent to perform a specific act or to accomplish a particular result terminates when the agent performs the act or accomplishes the result. Restatement, Section 106. Thus, if Porter authorizes Alford to sell or lease Porter's land, Alford's authority terminates when he leases the land to Taft; he may not thereafter sell or lease the land without receiving new authorization.

Mutual Agreement of the Parties The agency relationship is created by agreement and may be terminated at any time by mutual agreement of the principal and the agent.

Revocation of Authority A principal may revoke an agent's authority at any time by giving notice to the agent. Restatement, Section 119. If, however, such revocation constitutes a breach of contract, the agent may recover damages from the principal. For example, Patrick, in consideration of Alice's agreement to advertise and give her best energies to the sale of Patrick's property, Blackacre, grants to Alice "a power of attorney, irrevocable for one year." Alice advertises and spends time trying to sell Blackacre. At the end of three months, Patrick informs Alice that he is revoking the power of attorney. Although her authority is terminated, Alice may recover damages from Patrick. Restatement, Section 118, Illustration 1. Nonetheless, where the agent has seriously breached the agency contract, willfully disobeyed, or violated the fiduciary duty, the principal is not liable for revocation. In addition, a principal ordinarily may revoke a gratuitous agency without liability to the agent.

Renunciation by the Agent The agent also has the power to end the agency by notice to the principal that she renounces the authority given her. If the parties have contracted for the agency to continue for a specified time, an unjustified renunciation prior to the expiration of that time is a breach of contract. If the agency is gratuitous, however, the agent ordinarily may renounce it without liability to the principal.

Operation of Law

The occurrence of certain events will automatically terminate an agency relationship by the operation of law. These events either make it impossible for the agent to perform or unlikely that the principal would want the agent to act. As a matter of law, the occurrence of any of the following events ordinarily terminates agency.

Bankruptcy Bankruptcy is a Federal court proceeding that affords relief to financially troubled debtors. (See Chapter 39.) The filing of a petition in bankruptcy, which initiates the proceedings, usually terminates all the debtor's existing agency relationships. The trustee in bankruptcy, however, may assume an executory contract of agency unless under State law the contract is not assignable. If the credit standing of the agent is important to the agency relationship, the relationship will terminate upon the bankruptcy of the agent. Restatement, Section 113. Thus, Arnold is appointed by Pacific Securities, Inc., an investment house, to act as its agent in advising Pacific's local clients as to investments. When Arnold becomes bankrupt, he is no longer authorized to act for Pacific.

Death Because the authority given to an agent by a principal is strictly personal, the agent's death terminates the agent's actual authority. The death of the principal also terminates the authority of the agent. For example, Polk employs Allison to sell Polk's line of goods under a contract specifying Allison's commission and the one-year period for which the employment is to continue. When, without Allison's knowledge, Polk dies, Allison no longer has authority to sell Polk's goods, even though the contract specified that she would be employed for one year. The death of Polk, the principal, terminated the authority of the agent and voided the contract. The Uniform Durable Power of Attorney Act allows the holder of *any* power of attorney, durable or otherwise, to exercise it on the death of the principal, if its exercise is in good faith and without knowledge of the principal's death.

Incapacity Incapacity of the principal that occurs after the formation of the agency terminates the agent's authority. To illustrate, Powell authorizes Anna to sell in the next ten months an apartment complex for not less than $2 million. Without Anna's knowledge, Powell is adjudicated incompetent two months later. Anna's authority to sell the apartment complex is terminated. Likewise, the subsequent incapacity of an agent to perform the acts authorized by the principal terminates the agent's authority.

If an agent is appointed under a durable power of attorney, the authority of an agent survives, or is triggered by, the incapacity of the principal. Moreover, the Uniform Durable Power of Attorney Act allows the holder of a power that is *not* durable to exercise it on the incapacity of the principal, if its exercise is in good faith and without knowledge of the principal's incapacity.

Change in Business Conditions Notice or knowledge of a change in the value of the subject matter, or of a change in business conditions from which the agent should reasonably infer that the principal would not wish the agent to exercise the authority given him, terminates an agent's authority. Restatement, Section 109. Thus, Patricia authorizes Aaron to sell her eighty acres of farmland for $800 per acre. Subsequently, oil is discovered on nearby land, which causes Patricia's land to increase greatly in value. Because Aaron knows of this, but Patricia does not, Aaron's authority to sell the land is terminated.

Loss or Destruction of Subject Matter Where the authority of the agent relates to a specific subject matter that becomes lost or is destroyed, her authority is thereby terminated.

Depending on the agreement between the principal and the agent, authority terminates either immediately or only when the agent has notice of the loss or destruction. For example, Paul authorizes Allan to make a contract for the sale of Paul's residence. The next week, as Allan is aware, the residence burns completely. Allan's authority is terminated.

Disloyalty of Agent If an agent, without the knowledge of her principal, acquires interests adverse to those of the principal or otherwise breaches her duty of loyalty to the principal, her authority to act on behalf of the principal is terminated. Restatement, Section 112. Thus, Parker employs Agnes, a realtor, to sell Parker's land. Unknown to Parker, Agnes has been authorized by Trent to purchase this land from Parker. Consequently, Agnes is not authorized to sell the land to Trent.

Change in Law A change in the law that takes place after the employment of the agent and that makes the performance of the authorized act illegal or criminal terminates the authority of the agent. Restatement, Section 116. Thus, Pablo directs his agent, Arp, to ship young elm trees from State X to State Y. To control elm disease, State X establishes a quarantine upon the shipment of elm trees into any other State, making any such shipment punishable by fine. Arp's authority to ship the elm trees is terminated.

Outbreak of War Where the outbreak of war places the principal and agent in the position of alien enemies, the authority of the agent is terminated because its exercise is illegal. Otherwise, the outbreak of war of which the agent has notice terminates his authority if conditions are so changed that the agent should infer that the principal would not consent to further exercise of the authority. Restatement, Section 115.

Irrevocable Agencies

In the foregoing discussion of the various ways in which the authority of an agent may be terminated, the agency relationship was assumed to be the ordinary one in which the agent has no security interest in the power conferred upon him by the principal. Where the agency is coupled with an interest of the agent in the subject matter, as, for example, where the agent has advanced funds on behalf of the principal and his power to act is given as security for the loan, the principal may *not* revoke the authority of the agent. (This relationship is also referred to as a "power given as security.") In addition, neither the incapacity nor bankruptcy of the principal terminates the authority or the power of the agent. Nor will the death of the principal terminate the agency, unless the duty for which the security was given terminates with the death of the principal. Restatement, Section 139. An agency coupled with an interest is terminated by an event that discharges the obligation secured by it. Thus, in the example above, when the principal repays the loan, the agency coupled with an interest is terminated.

CHAPTER SUMMARY

Nature of Agency

Definition of Agency relationship authorizing one party (the agent) to act for and on behalf of the other party (the principal)

Scope of Agency Purposes generally, whatever business activity a person may accomplish personally he may do through an agent

Other Legal Relationships

- *Employment Relationship* one in which the employer has the right to control the physical conduct of the employee
- *Independent Contractor* a person who contracts with another to do a particular job and who is not subject to the control of the other

Creation of Agency

Formalities though agency is a consensual relationship that may be formed by contract or agreement between the principal and agent, agency may exist without consideration

- *Requirements* no particular formality usually is required in a contract of agency, although appointments of agents for a period of more than one year must be in writing
- *Power of Attorney* written, formal appointment of an agent

Capacity

- *Principal* if the principal is a minor or an incompetent not under a guardianship, his appointment of another to act as an agent is voidable
- *Agent* any person may act as an agent, as the act of the agent is considered the act of the principal

Duties of Agent to Principal

Duty of Obedience an agent must act in the principal's affairs only as authorized by the principal and must obey all reasonable instructions and directions

Duty of Diligence an agent must act with reasonable care and skill in performing the work for which he is employed

Duty to Inform an agent must use reasonable efforts to give the principal information relevant to the affairs entrusted to her

Duty to Account an agent must maintain and provide the principal with a true and complete account of money or other property that the agent has received or expended on behalf of the principal

Fiduciary Duty an agent owes a duty of utmost loyalty and good faith to the principal

- *Conflicts of Interest*
- *Self-dealing*
- *Duty Not to Compete*
- *Confidential Information*
- *Duty to Account for Financial Benefits*

Duties of Principal to Agent

Contractual Duties

- *Compensation* a principal must compensate the agent as specified in the contract, or for the reasonable value of the services provided, if no amount is specified
- *Reimbursement* the principal must pay back to the agent authorized payments the agent has made on the principal's behalf
- *Indemnification* the principal must pay the agent for losses the agent incurred while acting as directed by the principal

Tort Duties include the duty to provide an employee with reasonably safe conditions of employment and to warn the employee of any unreasonable risk involved in the employment

---

Termination of Agency

Acts of the Parties
- *Lapse of Time*
- *Fulfillment of Purpose*
- *Mutual Agreement of the Parties*
- *Revocation of Authority*
- *Renunciation by the Agent*

Operation of Law
- *Bankruptcy* the bankruptcy of the principal usually terminates all of the principal's agency relationships; if the credit of the agent is important to the agency relationship, the relationship will be terminated by the bankruptcy of the agent
- *Death* of either the principal or the agent
- *Incapacity* of either the principal or the agent
- *Change in Circumstances*
- *Loss or Destruction of the Subject Matter*
- *Disloyalty of Agent*
- *Change in Law*
- *Outbreak of War*

Irrevocable Agencies an agency coupled with an interest is irrevocable and occurs where the agent has a security interest in the subject matter of the agency

---

CASES

CASE
19-1

Other Legal Relationships: Employment
versus Independent Contractors
JAEGER v. WESTERN RIVERS FLY FISHER
United States District Court, District of Utah, 1994
855 F.Supp. 1217

Sam, J.

A review of the record reveals the following summary of undisputed, material facts. Western, operating under license of the U.S. Forest Service, is an "outfitter," a corporation in the business of arranging fishing expeditions on the Green River. Defendant Michael D. Petragallo is licensed by the Forest Service as a guide to conduct fishing expeditions but cannot do so by himself as the Forest Service only licenses outfitters to float patrons down the Green River. Western and several other licensed outfitters contact Petragallo to guide clients on fishing trips. Because the Forest Service licenses only outfitters to sponsor fishing expeditions, every guide must display on the boat and vehicle he uses the insignia of the outfitter sponsoring the particular trip. Western has classified the river into different sections for purposes of such fishing trips and, based upon Forest Service regulations, may suggest to clients areas in which to fish. Petragallo may agree

or refuse to take individuals Western refers to him, and Western does not restrict him from guiding expeditions for other outfitters. Western pays Petragallo a certain sum per fishing trip, does not make any deductions from his compensation, supplies him with a 1099 independent contractor tax form, and the Internal Revenue Service has determined that Western is properly treating him and other river guides it hires as independent contractors, for tax purposes. Petragallo's responsibilities include: transporting patrons to the Green River, using his own boat for fishing trips, providing food and overnight needs for patrons, assisting patrons in fly fishing, and transporting them from the river to their vehicles.

Prior to May 1992, Robert McMaster contacted Western and arranged for a fishing trip for himself and two others. Plaintiff was a member of McMaster's fishing party. McMaster paid Western, which set the price for the trip, and Western planned the itinerary for the McMaster party, rented fishing

Relationship with Third Parties

The purpose of an agency relationship is to allow the principal to extend his business activities by authorizing agents to enter into contracts with third persons on the principal's behalf. Accordingly, it is important that the law balance the competing interests of principals and third persons. The principal wants to be liable *only* for those contracts he actually authorizes the agent to make for him. The third party, on the other hand, wishes the principal bound on *all* contracts that the agent negotiates on the principal's behalf. As this chapter discusses, the law has adopted an intermediate outcome: the principal and the third party are bound to those contracts the principal *actually* authorizes *plus* those the principal has *apparently* authorized.

While pursuing her principal's business, an agent may tortiously injure third parties, who then may seek to hold the principal personally liable. Under what circumstances should the principal be held liable? Similar questions arise concerning a principal's criminal liability for an agent's violation of the criminal law. The law of agency has established rules to determine when the principal is liable for the torts and crimes his agents commit. These rules are discussed in this chapter.

Finally, what liability to the third party should the agent incur, and what rights should she acquire against the third party? Usually, the agent has no liability for, or rights under, the contracts she makes on behalf of her principal. As discussed in this chapter, however, in some situations the agent has contractually created obligations or rights or both.

Relationship of Principal and Third Persons

This section will first consider the contract liability of the principal; then it will examine the principal's potential tort liability.

CONTRACT LIABILITY OF THE PRINCIPAL

The power of an agent is his ability to change the legal status of his principal. An agent having either actual or apparent authority has the power to bind his principal. Thus, whenever an agent, acting within his authority, makes a contract for his principal, he creates new rights or liabilities for his principal, thereby changing his principal's legal status. This power of an agent to act for his principal in business transactions is the basis of agency.

A principal's contract liability also depends upon whether the principal is disclosed, partially disclosed, or undisclosed. The principal is a **disclosed principal** if at the time of a transaction an agent conducts, the other party has notice that the agent is acting for a principal and also has notice of the principal's identity. The principal is a **partially disclosed principal** if at the time of the transaction, the other party has notice that the agent is or may be acting for a principal but has no notice of the principal's identity. (Some courts refer to the partially disclosed principal as an "unidentified principal.") An example is an auctioneer who sells on behalf of a seller who is not identified: the seller is a partially disclosed principal since it is understood that the auctioneer acts as an agent. The principal is an **undisclosed principal** if the other party has no notice that the agent is acting for a principal. Restatement, Section 4.

Types of Authority

Authority is of two basic types: actual and apparent. **Actual authority** depends upon consent that the principal manifests to the agent. It may be either express or implied. In either case, such authority is binding and confers upon the agent both the power and the right to create or affect the principal's legal relations with third persons. Where the principal is undisclosed, an agent acting with actual authority in making the contract will contractually bind the principal and the third party unless the terms of the contract exclude the principal from being a party or unless the agent fraudulently conceals the principal's existence from the third party.

Apparent authority is based upon acts or conduct of the principal that lead a third person to believe that the agent, or supposed agent, has actual authority, upon which belief the third person *justifiably* relies. This manifestation, which confers upon the agent the power to create a legal relationship between the principal and a third party, may consist of words or actions of the principal as well as other facts and circumstances that induce the third person reasonably to rely upon the existence of an agency relationship.

Actual Express Authority   The express authority of an agent, found in the spoken or written words the principal communicates to the agent, is actual authority stated in language directing or instructing the agent to do something specific. Thus, if Perkins, orally or in writing, requests his agent Abbott to sell Perkins's automobile for $6,500, Abbott's authority to sell the car for this sum is actual and express. Actual express authority does not depend on the third party having knowledge of the manifestations or statements made by the principal to the agent.

Actual Implied Authority   Implied authority is not found in express or explicit words of the principal but is inferred from words or conduct that the principal manifests to the agent, who has implied authority to do that which she reasonably infers the principal desires her to do, in light of the principal's manifestations to her and all other facts she knows or should know. Restatement, Section 33. Implied authority may arise from customs and usages of the principal's business. In addition, the authority granted to an agent to accomplish a particular purpose necessarily includes the authority to employ the means reasonably required to accomplish it. Restatement, Section 35. For example, Pearson authorizes Arlington to manage her eighty-two-unit apartment complex but says nothing about expenses. In order to manage the building, Arlington must employ a janitor, purchase fuel for heating, and arrange for ordinary maintenance. Even though Pearson has not expressly granted him the authority to incur such expenses, Arlington may, because such expenses are necessary to proper apartment management, infer the authority to incur them from the express authority to manage the building.

Unless otherwise agreed, the authority to make a contract is inferred from the authority to conduct a transaction, if the making of such a contract is incidental to the transaction, usually accompanies such a transaction, or is reasonably necessary to accomplish it. Restatement, Section 50. Thus, Paragon, Inc., appoints Astor as the general manager of Paragon's manufacturing business. Astor's authority is interpreted as including authority to make contracts for the employment of necessary employees. On the other hand, suppose Paige employs Arthur, a real estate broker, to find a purchaser for her residence at a stated price. Arthur has no authority to contract for its sale.

General authority to manage or operate a business for a principal confers implied authority upon the agent to buy and sell property for the principal to the extent usual and customary in such operation; to make contracts which are incidental to the business, are usually made in it, or are reasonably necessary in conducting it; to employ, supervise, or discharge employees; to receive payment due the principal and to pay debts due from the principal arising out of the business enterprise; and to direct the ordinary operations of the business. Restatement, Section 73.

◆ **SEE FIGURE 20-1**   **Contract Liability of Disclosed Principal**

Apparent Authority   Apparent authority is power arising from words or conduct of a disclosed or partially disclosed principal that, when manifested to third persons, reasonably induce them to rely upon the assumption that actual authority exists. Restatement, Sections 27 and 159. Apparent authority confers upon the agent, or supposed agent, the power to bind the disclosed or partially disclosed principal in contracts with third persons and precludes the principal from denying the existence of actual authority. Thus, when authority is apparent but not actual, the disclosed or partially disclosed principal is nonetheless bound by the act of the agent. By exceeding his actual authority, however, the agent violates his duty of obedience and is liable to the principal for any loss the principal suffers as a result of the agent's acting beyond his actual authority.

Common ways in which apparent authority may arise include the following:

◆ F ɪ ɢ ᴜ ʀ ᴇ 20-1   **Contract Liability of Disclosed Principal**

Agent Has Actual Authority

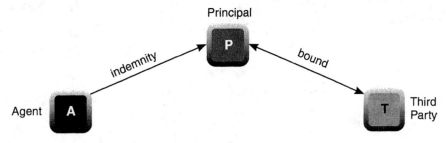

Agent Has Apparent Authority But Not Actual Authority

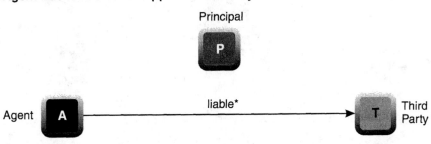

Agent Has No Actual or Apparent Authority

*Agent is liable for breach of implied warranty of authority or misrepresentation, as discussed later in this chapter.

1. When a principal appoints an agent to a position in an organization, third parties may reasonably believe that the agent has the authority to do those acts customary of an agent in such a position. (Apparent authority for agents of various business associations is discussed in Parts 6 and 7 of this text.)

2. If a principal has given an agent general authority to engage in a transaction, subsequently imposed limitations or restrictions will not affect the agent's apparent authority to engage in that transaction until third parties are notified of the restrictions.

3. The principal's acquiescence in prior similar transactions between the agent and a third party may create a basis for the third party reasonably to believe that the agent has apparent authority.

4. The agent shows the third party a document, such as a power of attorney, from the principal authorizing the agent to enter into such a transaction.

5. As discussed further below, after many terminations of authority an agent has lingering apparent authority until the third party has actual knowledge or receives notice of the termination.

For example, Peter writes a letter to Alice authorizing her to sell his automobile and sends a copy of the letter to Thomas, a prospective purchaser. On the following day, Peter writes a letter to Alice revoking the authority to sell the car but does not send a copy of the second letter to Thomas, who is not otherwise informed of the revocation. Although Alice has no actual authority to sell the car, she continues to have apparent authority with respect to Thomas. Or suppose that Arlene, in the presence of Polly, tells Thad that Arlene is Polly's agent to buy lumber. Although this statement is not true, Polly does not deny it, as she easily could. Thad, in reliance upon the statement, ships lumber to Polly on Arlene's order. Polly is obligated to pay for the lumber because Arlene had apparent authority to act on Polly's behalf. This apparent authority of Arlene exists only with respect to Thad. If Arlene were to give David an order for a shipment of lumber to Polly, David would be unable to hold Polly liable. Arlene would have had neither actual authority nor, as to David, apparent authority.

Because apparent authority is the power resulting from acts that appear to the third party to be authorized by the principal, apparent authority cannot exist where the principal is undisclosed. Nor can apparent authority exist where the third party knows that the agent has no actual authority.

◆ **SEE FIGURE 20-2** **Contract Liability of Partially Disclosed Principal**

◆ **SEE FIGURE 20-3** **Contract Liability of Undisclosed Principal**

◈ **SEE CASE 20-1**

Delegation of Authority

Because the appointment of an agent reflects the principal's confidence in and reliance upon the agent's personal skill, integrity, and other qualifications, the agent ordinarily has no power to delegate her authority to a subagent. Restatement, Section 18.

Nonetheless, in certain situations it is clear that the principal intended to permit the agent to delegate the authority granted to her. Such an intention may be gathered from the express authorization of the principal, the character of the business, the

◆ **FIGURE 20-2**   **Contract Liability of Partially Disclosed Principal**

Agent Has Actual Authority

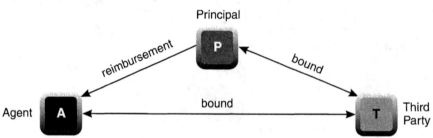

Agent Has Apparent Authority But Not Actual Authority

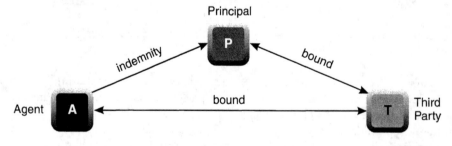

Agent Has No Actual or Apparent Authority

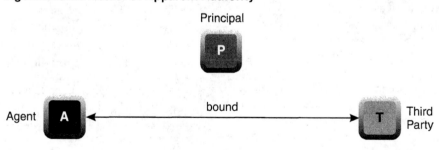

◆ FIGURE 20-3   **Contract Liability of Undisclosed Principal**

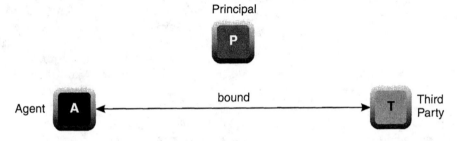

Agent Has Actual Authority

Agent Has No Actual Authority

usages of trade, or the prior conduct of the parties. Restatement, Sections 78–81. For example, if a check is deposited in a bank for collection at a distant place, the bank is impliedly authorized to employ another bank at the place of payment. Similarly, sub-agency is necessarily involved whenever a corporation is the agent since corporations may act only through their agents.

If an agent is authorized to appoint or select other persons, called **subagents**, to perform or assist in the performance of the agent's duties, the acts of the subagent are as binding on the principal as those performed by the agent. As an agent of both the principal and the agent, the subagent owes a fiduci-ary duty to both. For example, P contracts with A, a real estate broker (agent), to sell P's house. P knows that A employs sales-persons to show houses to prospective purchasers and to make representations about the property. The salespersons are A's employees and P's subagents.

If an agent having no authority to delegate her authority does so nevertheless, the acts of the subagent do not impose upon the principal any obligations or liability to third persons. Likewise, the principal acquires no rights against such third persons.

Effect of Termination of Agency on Authority

When an agency terminates, the agent's *actual authority* ceases. When the termination is by the death or incapacity of the prin-cipal or agent, the agent's *apparent authority* also expires, as notice of such termination to third persons is not required. Thus, in a case where Thomas, a tenant of the principal, Plato, paid rent to Plato's agent, Augustus, in ignorance of Plato's

death, and Augustus failed to account for the payment, Thomas is liable to Plato's estate for payment of the amount of the rent. The same holds where the performance of an authorized trans-action is rendered impossible, such as where the subject matter of the transaction is destroyed or the transaction is made illegal. Restatement, Section 124. The bankruptcy of the principal ter-minates without notice the power of an agent to affect the prin-cipal's property that has passed to the bankruptcy trustee.

In other cases, apparent authority continues until the third party has actual knowledge or receives actual notice, if that third party is one (1) with whom the agent had previously dealt on credit, (2) to whom the agent has been specially accredited, or (3) with whom the agent has begun to deal, as the principal should know. Restatement, Section 136(2). **Actual notice** requires a communication to the third party, either oral or writ-ten. If notice is given by mail, it is effective as actual notice upon delivery, not upon dispatch. All other third parties as to whom there was apparent authority must have actual knowledge or be given **constructive notice** through, for example, publication in a newspaper of general circulation in the area where the agency is regularly carried on. Restatement, Section 136(3).

To illustrate: Alfred is the general agent of Pace, who carries on business in Chicago. Carol knows of the agency but has never dealt with Alfred. Daphne sells goods on credit to Alfred, as the agent of Pace. Pace revokes Alfred's authority and pub-lishes a statement to that effect in a newspaper of general cir-culation published in Chicago. Carol does not see the statement and deals with Alfred in accordance with and in reliance upon the former agency. Daphne, who also does not see the statement and has no knowledge of the revocation, sells more goods to Alfred, as the agent of Pace. Because Pace has given sufficient notice of revocation as to Carol, Alfred's apparent authority has terminated with respect to Carol. On the other hand, Pace has not given sufficient notice of revocation as to Daphne; consequently, Pace is bound to Daphne by the contract of sale that Alfred made on Pace's behalf.

◆ **SEE FIGURE 20-4**   Termination of Apparent
                                  Authority

Ratification

Ratification is the confirmation or affirmance by one person of a prior unauthorized act performed by another who is, or who purports to be, his agent. The ratification of such act or contract binds the principal and the third party as if the agent or purported agent had been acting initially with actual authority. Restatement, Section 82. Once made, a valid ratification is irrevocable.

Requirements of Ratification   Ratification may relate to acts that have exceeded the authority granted to an agent, as well as to acts that a person without any authority performs on behalf of an alleged principal. Nonetheless, for the act to be ratified, the actor must have indicated to the third person that he was acting on a principal's behalf. There can be no ratification by an undisclosed principal. Thus Archie, without any authority, contracts to sell to Tina an automobile belonging to Pierce. Archie states that the auto is his. Tina promises to pay $5,500 for the automobile. Pierce subsequently learns of the agreement and affirms. Pierce's affirmation of Archie's action would not be a ratification because Archie did not purport to act on Pierce's behalf.

To effect a ratification, the principal must manifest an intent to do so with knowledge of all material facts concerning the transaction, Restatement, Section 91. The principal does not need to communicate this intent, which may be manifested by express language or implied from her conduct, such as accepting or retaining the benefits of a transaction. Thus, if Amanda, without authority, contracts in Penelope's name for the purchase of goods from Tate on credit, and Penelope, having learned of Amanda's unauthorized act, accepts the goods from Tate, she thereby impliedly ratifies the contract and is bound on it. If formalities are required for the authorization of an act, the same formalities apply to a ratification of that act. Restatement, Section 93. In any event, the principal must ratify the entire act or contract. Restatement, Section 96.

To be effective, ratification must occur before the third person gives notice of his withdrawal to the principal or agent. Restatement, Section 88. If the affirmance of a transaction occurs when the situation has so materially changed that it would be inequitable to subject the third party to liability, the third party may elect to avoid liability. For example, Alex has no authority, but, purporting to act for Penny, contracts to sell Penny's house to Taylor. The next day, the house burns down. Penny then affirms. Taylor is not bound. Moreover, the power to ratify is terminated by the death or loss of capacity of the third party and by the lapse of a reasonable time.

For ratification to be effective, the purported principal must have been in existence when the act was done. For example, a promoter of a corporation not yet in existence may enter into contracts on behalf of the corporation. In the vast majority of States, however, the corporation cannot ratify these acts because it did not exist when the contracts were made. Instead, the corporation may **adopt** the contract. Adoption differs from ratification because it is not retroactive and does not release the promoter from liability. See Chapter 34.

◆ **FIGURE 20-4**   **Termination of Apparent Authority**

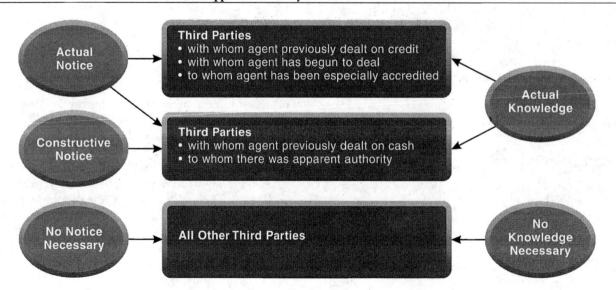

If a principal's lack of capacity entitles her to avoid transactions, the principal may also avoid any ratification made when under the incapacity. The principal may, however, ratify a contract that is voidable because of her incapacity when the incapacity no longer exists. Thus, after she reaches majority, a principal may ratify an unauthorized contract made on her behalf during her minority. She may also avoid any ratification made prior to attaining majority.

Effect of Ratification   Ratification is equivalent to prior authority, which means that the effect of ratification is substantially the same as if the agent or purported agent had been actually authorized when she performed the act. The respective rights, duties, and remedies of the principal and the third party are the same as if the agent had originally possessed actual authority. Both the principal and the agent are in the same position as they would have been if the principal had actually authorized the act originally. The agent is entitled to her due compensation and, moreover, is freed from liability to the principal for acting as his agent without authority or for exceeding her authority, as the case may be. Between the agent and the third party, the agent is released from any liability she may have to the third party by reason of her having induced the third party to enter into the contract without the principal's authority.

Fundamental Rules of Contractual Liability

The following rules summarize the contractual relations between the principal and the third party:

1. A disclosed principal and the third party are contractually bound if the agent acts within her actual or apparent authority in making the contract (see Figure 20-1).
2. A partially disclosed principal and the third party are contractually bound if the agent acts within her actual or apparent authority in making the contract (see Figure 20-2).
3. An undisclosed principal and the third party are contractually bound if the agent acts within her actual authority in making the contract unless (a) the terms of the contract exclude the principal or (b) his existence is fraudulently concealed (see Figure 20-3).
4. No principal is contractually bound to a third party if the agent acts without any authority, unless the principal is disclosed or partially disclosed and he ratifies the contract.

TORT LIABILITY OF THE PRINCIPAL

In addition to being contractually liable to third persons, a principal may be liable in tort to third persons because of the acts of her agent. Tort liability may arise directly or indirectly (vicariously) from authorized or unauthorized acts of an agent. Also, a principal is liable for the unauthorized torts an agent commits in connection with a transaction that the purported principal, with full knowledge of the tort, subsequently ratifies. Restatement, Section 218. Cases involving unauthorized but ratified torts are extremely rare. Of course, in all of these situations the wrongdoing agent is personally liable to the injured persons because he committed the tort.

◆ **SEE FIGURE 20-5**   Tort Liability

Direct Liability of Principal

A principal is liable for his own tortious conduct involving the use of agents. Such liability primarily arises in one of two ways. First, a principal is directly liable in damages for harm resulting from his directing an agent to commit a tort. Second, the principal is directly liable if he fails to exercise care in employing competent agents.

Authorized Acts of Agent   A principal who authorizes his agent to commit a tortious act with respect to the property or person of another is liable for the injury or loss that person sustains. Restatement, Section 212. The authorized act is that of the principal. Thus, if Phillip directs his agent, Anthony, to enter upon Clark's land and cut timber, which neither Phillip nor Anthony has any right to do, the cutting of the timber is a trespass, and Phillip is liable to Clark. Or, suppose Phillip instructs his agent, Anthony, to make certain representations as to Phillip's property, which Anthony is authorized to sell. Phillip knows these representations are false, but Anthony does not. Such representations by Anthony to Dryden, who buys the property in reliance on them, constitute a deceit for which Phillip is liable to Dryden.

Unauthorized Acts of Agent   A principal who negligently or recklessly conducts activities through an employee or other agent is liable for harm resulting from such conduct. Specifically, a principal is liable if he negligently or recklessly (1) gives improper or ambiguous instructions, (2) fails to make proper regulations, (3) employs improper persons as agents, (4) provides improper instruments, tools, or materials to agents, (5) supervises the activities of agents, or (6) fails to prevent tortious acts by persons on his premises or with instrumentalities under his control. Restatement, Section 213.

The liability of a principal under this provision—called **negligent hiring**—arises when the principal does not exercise proper care in selecting an agent for the job to be done. For example, if Patricia lends to her employee, Art, a company car with which to run a business errand knowing that Art is incapable of driving the vehicle, Patricia would be liable for her own negligence to anyone injured through Art's unsafe driving. The negligent hiring doctrine has also been used to impose liability on a principal for intentional torts committed by an agent against customers of the principal or members of the public, where the principal either knew or should have known that the agent was violent or aggressive.

◆ **FIGURE 20-5**   **Tort Liability**

Agent's Tort Authorized

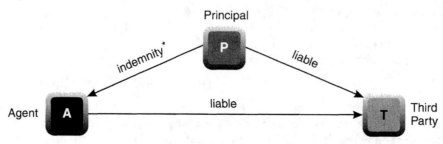

Employee's Tort Unauthorized But Within Scope of Employment

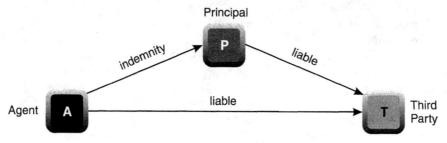

Employee's Tort Outside Authority and Scope of Employment or Independent Contractor's Tort Unauthorized

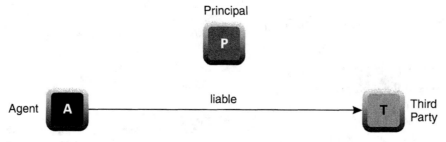

*If not illegal or known by A to be wrongful.

◊ **SEE CASE 20-2**

Vicarious Liability of Principal for Unauthorized Acts of Agent

The liability of a principal for the unauthorized torts of an agent depends primarily on whether the agent is an employee or not. An employee is an agent whose physical conduct in the performance of services for the principal–employer is controlled by the principal or is subject to the principal's right to control. By comparison, an agent whose physical conduct is not controlled by, or subject to the control of, the principal is an independent contractor, not an employee. The general rule is that a principal is not liable for physical harm caused by the tortious conduct of an agent who is an independent contractor if the principal did not intend or authorize the result or the manner of performance. Restatement, Section 250. Conversely, a principal is liable for an unauthorized tort

committed by an employee in the course of his employment. Restatement, Sections 216 and 219.

On the other hand, the liability of a principal whose agent makes an unauthorized yet tortious **misrepresentation** does not depend upon whether the agent is an employee. Rather, the principal is liable for loss caused to another who relies upon a tortious representation made by an agent (whether an employee or an independent contractor) if the representation is apparently authorized. Restatement, Section 257. For example, Pillsbury engages Adams as an agent to sell some land. While negotiating with Trent, Adams states that a stream running through the property has not overflowed its banks during the past ten years. Adams knows that this is false. In reliance upon this false statement, Trent purchases the land. Pillsbury is liable to Trent for fraudulent misrepresentation.

Respondeat Superior An employer may be liable for an unauthorized tort committed by his employee, even one that is in flagrant disobedience of his instructions, if the employee committed the tort in the course of his employment. This form of employer liability without fault is based upon the doctrine of *respondeat superior* (let the superior respond). It does not matter how carefully the employer selected the employee, if in fact the latter tortiously injures a third person while engaged in the employer's business. Moreover, an *undisclosed* principal–employer is liable for the torts committed by her employee within the scope of employment. Restatement, Section 222.

The doctrine of *respondeat superior* is fundamental to the operation of tort law in the United States. The rationale of this doctrine is that a person who conducts his business activities through the use of employees should be liable for the employees' tortious conduct in carrying out those activities. The employer is more likely to insure against liability and is more likely to have the assets to satisfy a tort judgment than the employee. Moreover, *respondeat superior* creates an economic incentive for employers to exercise care in choosing, training, and supervising employees.

The liability of the principal under *respondeat superior* is vicarious or derivative and depends upon proof of wrongdoing by the employee *in the course of his employment*. Restatement, Section 219. Frequently both principal and employee are joined as defendants in the same suit. Because the liability of the employer is based upon the employee's tortious conduct, if the employee is not held liable, the principal is not liable either. A principal who is held liable for her employee's tort has a right of **indemnification** against the employee, or the right to be reimbursed for the amount that she was required to pay as a result of the employee's wrongful act. Frequently, however, an employee is unable to reimburse his employer, who then must bear the brunt of the liability.

The wrongful act of the employee must be connected with his employment and within its scope if the principal is to be held liable for injuries or damage resulting to third persons. Section 228 of the Restatement provides a general rule for determining whether the conduct of an employee ("servant") is within the scope of employment:

(1) Conduct of a servant is within the scope of employment if, but only if:
  (a) it is of the kind he is employed to perform;
  (b) it occurs substantially within the authorized time and space limits;
  (c) it is actuated, at least in part, by a purpose to serve the master [employer]; and
  (d) if force is intentionally used by the servant against another, the use of force is not unexpectable by the master.
(2) Conduct of a servant is not within the scope of employment if it is different in kind from that authorized, far beyond the authorized time or space limits, or too little actuated by a purpose to serve the master.

For example, Eugene, while delivering gasoline for Packer Oil Co., lights his pipe and negligently throws the blazing match into a pool of gasoline that has dripped onto the ground during the delivery. The gasoline ignites, burning Ray's filling station. Packer is subject to liability for the resulting harm because the negligence of the employee who delivered the gasoline relates directly to the manner in which he handled the goods in his custody. But if a chauffeur, while driving his employer's car on an errand for his employer, suddenly decides to shoot his pistol at pedestrians for target practice, the employer would not be liable to the pedestrians. This willful and intentional misconduct is not related to the performance of the services for which the chauffeur was employed, nor is it expectable by the employer.

To further illustrate, if Page employs Earl to deliver merchandise to Page's customers in a given city, and while driving a delivery truck to or from a place of delivery Earl negligently causes the truck to hit and injure Fred, Page is liable to Fred for the injuries he sustains. But if, after making the scheduled deliveries, Earl drives the truck to a neighboring city to visit a friend and while so doing negligently causes the truck to hit and injure Dottie, Page is not liable. In the latter case, Earl is said to be on a "frolic of his own." By using the truck to accomplish his own purposes, not those of his employer, he has deviated from the purpose of his employment.

A principal may be held liable for the intentional torts of his employee if the commission of the tort is so reasonably connected with the employment as to be within its scope. For example, a principal would be liable if his employee were to make fraudulent statements about the products she is selling, defame a competitor, or disparage the competitor's product.

◆ **SEE CASE 20-3**

Torts of Independent Contractor As previously indicated, an independent contractor is not the employee of the person for whom he is performing work or rendering services. Hence, the doctrine of *respondeat superior* generally does not apply to torts committed by an independent contractor. For example, Parnell authorizes Bob, his broker, to sell land for him. Parnell, Teresa, and Bob meet in Teresa's office, where Bob arranges the sale to Teresa. While Bob is preparing the deed for Parnell to sign, he negligently knocks over an inkstand and ruins a valuable rug belonging to Teresa. Bob, but not Parnell, is liable to Teresa. Similarly, Patty employs Igor, a roofer, as an independent contractor to repair her roof. Igor drops a hammer upon Wanda, a pedestrian walking by on the public sidewalk. Igor, but not Patty, is liable to Wanda.

Nonetheless, the principal may be *directly* liable if she fails to exercise reasonable care in selecting an independent contractor. For example, Melanie employs Gordon, whom she knows to be an alcoholic, as an independent contractor to repair her roof. Gordon attempts the repairs while heavily intoxicated and negligently drops a fifty-pound bundle of shingles upon Eric, a pedestrian walking on the sidewalk. Both Gordon and Melanie are liable to Eric.

Moreover, under some circumstances a principal will be *vicariously* liable for torts committed by a carefully selected independent contractor. Certain duties imposed by law are nondelegable, and a person may not escape the consequences of their nonperformance by having entrusted them to an independent contractor. For example, a landowner who permits an independent contractor to maintain a dangerous condition on his premises, such as an excavation, neither surrounded by a guardrail nor lit at night, adjoining a public sidewalk is liable to a member of the public who is injured by falling into the excavation.

A principal is also vicariously liable for an independent contractor's negligent conduct in carrying on an ultrahazardous activity, such as using fire or high explosives. Finally, a principal is vicariously liable if an independent contractor negligently conducts an inherently dangerous activity, such as excavating a public road, demolishing a building, or spraying crops.

CRIMINAL LIABILITY OF THE PRINCIPAL

A principal is liable for the authorized criminal acts of his agents only if the principal directed, participated in, or approved of the acts. For example, if an agent, at his principal's direction or with his principal's knowledge, fixes prices with the principal's competitors, both the agent and the principal have criminally violated the antitrust laws. Otherwise, a principal ordinarily is not liable for the unauthorized criminal acts of his agents. One of the elements of a crime is mental fault, and this element is absent, so far as the criminal responsibility of the principal is concerned, where the principal did not authorize the agent's act.

An employer may, nevertheless, be subject to a criminal penalty for the act of an advisory or managerial person acting in the scope of employment. Restatement, Section 217D, Comment d. Moreover, an employer may be criminally liable under liability without fault statutes for certain unauthorized acts of an employee, whether the employee is managerial or not. These statutes, which usually are regulatory, do not require mental fault. For example, many States have statutes that punish "every person who by himself or his employee or agent sells anything at short weight," or "whoever sells liquor to a minor and any sale by an employee shall be deemed the act of the employer as well." Another example is a statute prohibiting the sale of unwholesome or adulterated food. See Chapter 6 for a more detailed discussion of this topic.

Relationship of Agent and Third Persons

The function of an agent is to assist in the conduct of the principal's business by carrying out his orders. Generally, the agent acquires no rights against third parties and likewise incurs no liabilities to them. There are, however, several exceptions to this general proposition. In certain instances, an agent may become personally liable to the third party for contracts she made on behalf of her principal. In some of these situations, the agent also may acquire rights against the third party. In addition, an agent who commits a tort is personally liable to the injured third party. These circumstances involving the personal liability of an agent, as well as those in which an agent may acquire rights against third persons, will be covered in this section.

CONTRACT LIABILITY OF AGENT

The agent normally is not a party to the contract he makes with a third person on behalf of a disclosed principal. An agent who exceeds his actual and apparent authority, however, may be personally liable to the third party. In addition, an agent acting for a disclosed principal may become liable if he expressly assumes liability on the contract. When an agent enters into a contract on behalf of a partially disclosed principal or an undisclosed principal, the agent becomes personally liable to the third party on the contract. Furthermore, an agent who knowingly enters into a contract on behalf of a nonexistent or incompetent principal is personally liable to the third party on that contract.

Disclosed Principal

As explained earlier, an agent acts for a disclosed principal when, at the time of the transaction, the other party has notice both of the fact that the agent is acting for a principal and of the principal's identity. The agent is not normally a party to the contract she makes with a third person on behalf of a disclosed principal. The third person is on notice that he is transacting business with an agent who is acting for an identified principal and that the agent is not personally undertaking to perform the contract but is simply negotiating on behalf of her principal. The resulting contract, if within the agent's actual authority, is between the third person and the principal, and the agent ordinarily incurs no liability on the contract to either party. Restatement, Section 320. Thus, Angela, who has actual authority to sell circuit boards manufactured by Pinter, writes to Toni, "On behalf of Pinter, I offer to sell you 5,000 circuit boards for $15,000." Toni accepts; consequently, a contract exists between Toni and Pinter. Angela is not a party to that contract and has no liability to Pinter or Toni. This is also true of unauthorized contracts that are subsequently ratified by the principal. If, however, the agent has apparent authority but no actual authority, he has no liability to the third party but is liable to the principal for any loss he causes by exceeding his actual authority.

◆ **See Figure 20-1**   **Contractual Liability of Disclosed Principal**

Unauthorized Contracts   If an agent exceeds his actual *and* apparent authority, the principal is not bound. The fact that the principal is not bound does not, however, make the agent a party to the contract. The agent's liability, if any, arises from express or implied representations about his authority that he makes to the third party. For example, an agent may **expressly warrant** that he has authority by stating that he has authority and that he will be personally liable to the third party if he does not in fact have the authority to bind his principal.

Moreover, a person who undertakes to make a contract on behalf of another gives an **implied warranty** that he is in fact authorized to make the contract on behalf of the party whom he purports to represent. If the agent does not have authority to bind the principal, the agent is liable to the third party for damages unless the principal ratifies the contract or the third party knew that the agent was unauthorized. No implied warranty exists, however, if the contract expressly provides that the agent shall not be responsible for any lack of authority or if the agent, acting in good faith, discloses to the third person all of the facts upon which his authority rests. For example, agent Larson has received an ambiguous letter of instruction from his principal, Dan. Larson shows it to Carol, stating that it represents all of the authority that he has to act, and both Larson and Carol rely upon its sufficiency. Larson has made no implied or express warranty of his authority to Carol.

If a purported agent **misrepresents** to a third person that he has authority to make a contract on behalf of a principal whom he has no power to bind, he is liable in a tort action to the third person for the loss she sustained in reliance upon the misrepresentation. If the third party knows, however, that the representation is false, then the agent is not liable.

Agent Assumes Liability   An agent may agree to become liable on a contract between the principal and the third party (1) by making the contract in her own name, (2) by co-making the contract with the principal, or (3) by guaranteeing that the principal will perform the contract between the third party and the principal. In each situation, the agent's liability is separate unless the parties agree otherwise. Therefore, the third party may sue the agent separately without joining the principal and may obtain a judgment against either the principal or the agent or both. If the principal satisfies the judgment, the agent is discharged. If the agent pays the judgment, he usually will have a

right of reimbursement from the principal. This right is based upon the principles of suretyship, discussed in Chapter 38.

Partially Disclosed Principal

An agent, as previously discussed, acts for a partially disclosed principal (or unidentified principal) if the third party has notice that the agent is acting for a principal but has no notice of the principal's identity. The use of a partially disclosed principal may be helpful where, for example, the third party might inflate the price of property he was selling if he knew the principal's identity. Partial disclosure also may occur inadvertently, when the agent fails through neglect to inform the third party of the principal's identity.

Unless otherwise agreed, an agent making a contract for a partially disclosed principal is a party to the contract. Restatement, Section 321. For example, Ashley writes to Terrence offering to sell a rare painting on behalf of its owner, who wishes to remain unknown. Terrence accepts. Ashley is a party to the contract.

Whether the particular transaction is authorized or not, an agent for a partially disclosed principal is liable on the contract to the third party. If the agent is actually authorized to make the contract, then both the agent and the partially disclosed principal are liable. In any event, the agent is separately liable, and the third party may sue her individually without joining the principal and may obtain a judgment against either the principal or the agent or both. If the principal satisfies the judgment, the agent is discharged. If the agent pays the judgment, he has the right to be reimbursed by the principal.

◆ **See Figure 20-2**   **Contract Liability of Partially Disclosed Principal**

Undisclosed Principal

An agent acts for an undisclosed principal when she appears to be acting in her own behalf and the third person with whom she is dealing has no knowledge that she is acting as an agent. The principal has instructed the agent to conceal not only the principal's identity but also the agency relationship. Such concealment can also occur if the agent simply neglects to disclose the existence and identity of her principal. Thus, the third person is dealing with the agent as though she were a principal.

The agent is personally liable upon a contract she enters into with a third person on behalf of an undisclosed principal, unless the third person, after discovering the existence and identity of the principal, elects to hold the principal to the contract. The agent is liable because the third person has relied upon the agent individually and has accepted the agent's personal undertaking to perform the contract. Obviously, where the principal is undisclosed, the third person does not know of the interest of anyone in the contract other than that of himself and the agent.

After the third person has learned of the identity of the undisclosed principal, he may hold either the principal or the agent to performance of the contract, but not both; and his choice, once made, binds him irrevocably. Nevertheless, to avoid the possibility that evidence at trial will fail to establish the agency relationship, the third person may bring suit against both the principal and agent. In most States, this act of bringing suit and proceeding to trial against both is not an election, but before the entry of any judgment, the third person is compelled to make an election because he is not entitled to a judgment against both. A judgment against the agent by a third party who knows the identity of the previously undisclosed principal discharges the liability of the principal. Restatement, Section 210. In this case, the agent would have the right to be reimbursed by the principal. If, however, the third party obtains a judgment against the agent before learning the principal's identity, the principal is not discharged. Finally, the agent is discharged from liability if the third party gets a judgment against the principal. Restatement, Section 337. (Some States have recently rejected the election rule, holding that a third party's rights against the principal are *additional* and not alternative to the third party's rights against the agent.)

◆ **See Figure 20-3** Contract Liability of Undisclosed Principal

◊ **See Case 20-4**

A person who purports to act as agent for a principal, whom both the agent and the third party know to be nonexistent or wholly incompetent, is personally liable on a contract entered into with a third person on behalf of such a principal. Restatement, Section 326. For example, a promoter of a corporation who enters into contracts with third persons in the name of a corporation yet to be organized is personally liable on such contracts. Not yet in existence, and therefore unable to authorize the contracts, the corporation is not liable. If, after coming into existence, the corporation affirmatively adopts a preincorporation contract made on its behalf, it, in addition to the promoter, becomes bound. If the corporation enters into a new contract with such a third person, however, the prior contract between the promoter and the third person is discharged, and the liability of the promoter is terminated. This is a novation.

◆ **See Figure 34-1** Promoter's Preincorporation Contracts Made in Corporation's Name

Incompetent Principal

An agent who makes a contract for a disclosed principal whose contracts are voidable for lack of contractual capacity is *not* liable to the third party. Restatement, Section 332. There are two exceptions to this rule: (1) if the agent warrants or represents that the principal has capacity or (2) if the agent has reason to know both of the principal's lack of capacity and of the third party's ignorance of that incapacity.

TORT OF LIABILITY OF AGENT

An agent is personally liable for his tortious acts that injure third persons, whether the principal authorizes such acts or not and whether or not the principal may also be liable. Restatement, Section 343. For example, an agent is personally liable if he converts the goods of a third person to his principal's use. An agent is also liable for making representations that he knows to be fraudulent to a third person who in reliance sustains a loss.

RIGHTS OF AGENT AGAINST THIRD PERSON

An agent who makes a contract with a third person on behalf of a disclosed principal usually has no right of action against the third person for breach of contract. Restatement, Section 363. The agent is not a party to the contract. An agent for a disclosed principal may sue on the contract, however, if it provides that the agent is a party to the contract. Furthermore, an agent for an undisclosed principal or a partially disclosed principal may maintain in her own name an action against the third person for breach of contract. Restatement, Section 364.

CHAPTER SUMMARY

Principal and Third Persons

Contract Liability of Principal	**Types of Principals** • *Disclosed Principal* principal whose existence and identity are known • *Partially Disclosed Principal* principal whose existence is known but whose identity is not known • *Undisclosed Principal* principal whose existence and identity are not known

Authority power of an agent to change the legal status of the principal
- *Actual Authority* power conferred upon the agent by actual consent given by the principal
- *Actual Express Authority* actual authority derived from written or spoken words of the principal
- *Actual Implied Authority* actual authority inferred from words or conduct manifested to the agent by the principal
- *Apparent Authority* power conferred upon the agent by acts or conduct of the principal that reasonably lead a third party to believe that the agent has such power

Delegation of Authority is usually not permitted unless expressly or impliedly authorized by the principal; if the agent is authorized to appoint other subagents, the acts of these subagents are as binding on the principal as those of the agent

Effect of Termination of Agency on Authority ends actual authority
- *Termination by Operation of Law* apparent authority also ends without notice to third parties
- *Termination by Act of Parties* apparent authority ends when third parties have actual knowledge or when appropriate notice is given to third parties: actual notice must be given to third parties with whom the agent has previously dealt on credit, has been specially accredited, or has begun to deal; all other third parties as to whom there was apparent authority need be given only constructive notice

Ratification affirmation by one person of a prior unauthorized act that another has done as her agent or as her purported agent

Fundamental Rules of Contractual Liability
- *Disclosed Principal* is contractually bound with the third party if the agent acts within her actual or apparent authority in making the contract
- *Partially Disclosed Principal* is contractually bound with the third party if the agent acts within her actual or apparent authority in making the contract
- *Undisclosed Principal* is contractually bound with the third party if the agent acts within her actual authority in making the contract

---

Tort Liability of Principal

Direct Liability of Principal a principal is liable for his own tortious conduct involving the use of agents
- *Authorized Acts of Agent* a principal is liable for torts she authorizes another to commit
- *Unauthorized Acts of Agent* a principal is liable for failing to exercise care in employing agents whose unauthorized acts cause harm

Vicarious Liability of Principal for Unauthorized Acts of Agent
- *Respondeat Superior* an employer is liable for unauthorized torts committed by an employee in the course of his employment
- *Independent Contractor* a principal is usually not liable for the unauthorized torts of an independent contractor

---

Criminal Liability of Principal

Authorized Acts the principal is liable if he directed, participated in, or approved the criminal acts of his agents

Unauthorized Acts the principal may be liable either for a criminal act of a managerial person or under liability without fault statutes

Agent and Third Persons

Contract Liability of Agent

Disclosed Principals the agent is not normally a party to the contract she makes with a third person if she is authorized or if the principal ratifies an unauthorized contract

- *Unauthorized Contracts* if an agent exceeds her actual and apparent authority, the principal is not bound but the agent may be liable for breach of warranty or for misrepresentation
- *Agent Assumes Liability* an agent may agree to become liable on a contract between the principal and the third party

Partially Disclosed Principal an agent who acts for a partially disclosed principal is a party to the contract with the third party unless otherwise agreed

Undisclosed Principal an agent who acts for an undisclosed principal is personally liable on the contract to the third party

Nonexistent or Incompetent Principal a person who purports to act as an agent for a principal whom both the agent and the third party know to be nonexistent or wholly incompetent is personally liable on a contract entered into with a third person on behalf of such a principal

---

Tort Liability of Agent

Authorized Acts the agent is liable to the third party for his own torts

Unauthorized Acts the agent is liable to the third party for his own torts

---

Rights of Agent

Disclosed Principal the agent usually has no rights against the third party

Partially Disclosed Principal the agent may enforce the contract against the third party

Undisclosed Principal the agent may enforce the contract against the third party

---

CASES

CASE

20-1

Types of Authority

SCHOENBERGER v. CHICAGO TRANSIT AUTHORITY

Appellate Court of Illinois, First District, First Division, 1980
84 Ill.App.3d 1132, 39 Ill.Dec. 941, 405 N.E.2d 1076

Campbell, J.

The plaintiff, James Schoenberger, brought a small claims action * * * in the * * * circuit court of Cook County against the defendant, Chicago Transit Authority (hereinafter C.T.A.) to recover contract damages. The trial court ruled in favor of the defendant and against the plaintiff. The plaintiff appeals from this judgment. At issue is whether the C.T.A. may be held liable under agency principles of a promise allegedly made by an employee of the C.T.A. to the plaintiff at the time that he was hired to the effect that he would receive a $500 increase in salary within a specified period of time. We affirm.

Schoenberger was employed by the C.T.A. from August 16, 1976, to October, 1976, at a salary of $19,300. The facts surrounding his employment with the C.T.A. are controverted. The plaintiff's position at the trial was that he took the job with the C.T.A. at a salary of $19,300 upon the condition that he would receive a $500 salary increase, above and beyond any merit raises, within a year. Schoenberger testified at trial that, after filling out a job application and undergoing an initial interview with a C.T.A. Placement Department interviewer, he

met several times with Frank ZuChristian, who was in charge of recruiting for the Data Center. At one of the meetings with ZuChristian, the Director of Data Center Operations, John Bonner, was present. At the third meeting held between ZuChristian and the plaintiff, ZuChristian informed the plaintiff that he desired to employ him at $19,800 and that he was making a recommendation to this effect. Schoenberger told ZuChristian that he would accept the offer. ZuChristian informed him that a formal offer would come from the Placement Department within a few days. However, when the offer was made, the salary was stated at $19,300. Schoenberger did not accept the offer immediately. Rather, he called ZuChristian for an explanation of the salary difference. After making inquiries, ZuChristian informed Schoenberger that a clerical error had been made and that it would take a number of weeks to have the necessary paperwork reapproved because several people were on vacation. To expedite matters, ZuChristian suggested Schoenberger take the job at the $19,300 figure and that he would see that the $500 would be made up to him at the April, 1976, October, 1976, or at the

Products Liability: Warranties and Strict Liability in Tort

This chapter considers the liability of manufacturers and sellers of goods to buyers, users, consumers, and bystanders for damages caused by defective products. The rapidly expanding development of case law has established products liability as a distinct field of law that combines and enforces rules and principles of contracts, sales, negligence, strict liability in tort, and statutory law.

One reason for the expansion of this liability is the modern method of distributing goods. Today, retailers serve principally as conduits of prepackaged goods that are widely advertised by the manufacturer or distributor. This has brought about the extension of product liability coverage to include manufacturers and other parties along the chain of distribution. The extension of product liability to manufacturers, however, has not lessened the liability of the retailer to his immediate purchaser. Rather, it has broadened the base of liability through the development and application of new principles of law.

Currently, the entire area of products liability has attracted a great deal of public attention. According to the U.S. Consumer Product Safety Commission, thirty-six million Americans are injured each year in consumer product-related accidents. Of those injured, twenty-eight thousand die while many others are permanently disabled. The resultant cost of maintaining product liability insurance has skyrocketed, causing great concern in the business community. In response to the clamor over this insurance crisis, more than forty States have revised their tort laws to make successful product liability lawsuits more difficult to bring. Nevertheless, repeated efforts to pass Federal product liability legislation have been unsuccessful.

The liability of manufacturers and other sellers of goods for a defective product, or for its failure to perform adequately, may be based upon one or more of the following: (1) negligence, (2) misrepresentation, (3) violation of statutory duty, (4) warranty, and (5) strict liability in tort. The first three causes of actions have been covered in Chapters 8 and 11. This chapter will explore the last two.

Warranties

A **warranty** creates a duty on the part of the seller that the goods she sells will conform to certain qualities, characteristics, or conditions. A seller, however, is not required to warrant the goods; and, in general, she may, by appropriate words, disclaim, exclude, negate, or modify a particular warranty or even all warranties.

In bringing a warranty action, the buyer must prove that (1) a warranty existed, (2) the warranty has been breached, (3) the breach of the warranty proximately caused the loss suffered, and (4) notice of the breach was given to the seller. The seller has the burden of proving defenses based on the buyer's conduct. If the seller breaches his warranty, the buyer may reject or revoke acceptance of the goods. Moreover, whether he has accepted or rejected the goods, the buyer may recover a judgment against the seller for damages. Harm for which damages are recoverable include personal injury, damage to property, and economic loss. Economic loss most commonly involves damages for loss of bargain and consequential damages for lost profits. (Damages for breach of warranty are discussed in the next chapter.) This section will examine the various types of warranties as well as the obstacles to a cause of action for breach of warranty.

TYPES OF WARRANTIES

A warranty may arise out of the mere existence of a sale (a warranty of title), any affirmation of fact or promise made by the seller to the buyer (an express warranty), or the circumstances under which the sale is made (an implied warranty). In a contract for the sale of goods, it is possible to have all three types of warranties. All warranties are construed as consistent with each other and cumulative, unless such a construction is unreasonable.

Article 2A carries over the warranty provisions of Article 2 with relatively minor revision to reflect differences in style, leasing terminology, or leasing practices. The creation of express warranties and, except for finance leases, the imposition of the implied warranties of merchantability and fitness for a particular purpose are virtually identical to their Article 2 analogues. Article 2 and Article 2A diverge somewhat in their treatment of the warranties of title and infringement as well as in their provisions for the exclusion and modification of warranties.

Warranty of Title

Under the Code's warranty of title, the seller implicitly warrants (1) that the title conveyed is good and its transfer rightful and (2) that the goods have no security interest or other lien (a claim on property by another for payment of debt) of which the buyer was not aware at the time of purchase. Section 2–312(1). In a lease, title does not transfer to the lessee. Accordingly, Article 2A's analogous provision protects the lessee's right to possession and use of the goods from the claims of other parties arising from an act or omission of the lessor. Section 2A–211(1).

For example, Iris acquires goods from Sherman in a transaction that is void and then sells the goods to Brenda. Sherman brings an action against Brenda and recovers the goods. Iris has breached the warranty of title: because she did not have good title to the goods, her transfer of the goods to Brenda was not rightful. Accordingly, Iris is liable to Brenda for damages.

The Code does *not* label the warranty of title as an implied warranty, even though it arises from the sale and not from any particular words or conduct. Consequently, the Code's general disclaimer provision for implied warranties does not apply to a warranty of title, which instead is subject to its own disclaimer provision. Nevertheless, a seller of goods does implicitly warrant title to those goods.

A seller who is a merchant makes an additional warranty in sales of goods of the kind in which he regularly deals: that such goods shall be delivered free of the rightful claim of any third person that the goods infringe (use without authorization) upon any existing patent. Section 2–312(3); Section 2A–211(2).

Express Warranties

An express warranty is an explicit undertaking by the seller with respect to the quality, description, condition, or performability of the goods. The undertaking may consist of an affirmation of fact or a promise that relates to the goods, a description of the goods, or a sample or model of the goods. In each of these instances, the undertaking must become or be made part of the basis of the bargain in order for an express warranty to be created. The seller need not, however, have a specific intention to make a warranty or use formal words such as "warrant" or "guarantee." Moreover, to be liable for a breach of express warranty a seller need not know that she has made a false statement; the seller may be acting in good faith. For example, if John mistakenly asserts to Sam that a rope will easily support 300 pounds and Sam is injured when the rope breaks while supporting only 200 pounds, John is liable for breach of an express warranty.

Creation The seller can create an express warranty either orally or in writing. One of the ways in which an express warranty can be created is through an **affirmation of fact** or a **promise** relating to the goods that becomes part of the basis of the bargain. Section 2–313(1)(a); Section 2A–210(1)(a). The statement can be in regard to the quality, condition, capacity, performability, or safety of the goods. For example, a statement made by a seller that an automobile will get 42 miles to the gallon of gasoline or that a camera has automatic focus is an express warranty.

The Code further provides that a statement affirming the **value** of the goods or purporting merely to be the seller's **opinion** or recommendation of the goods does not create a warranty. Section 2–313(2); Section 2A–210(2). Such statements are not factual and do not deceive the ordinary buyer, who accepts them merely as opinions or as puffery (sales talk). For example, a statement by a salesperson that "this is one terrific deal" would likely be considered puffery. On the other hand, a statement that "this car gets 30 miles to the gallon" would be considered an express warranty, given its specificity. A statement of value may be an express warranty, however, where the seller states the price at which the goods were purchased from a former owner, or where she gives market figures relating to sales of similar goods. As statements of events, not mere opinions, these are statements of facts; and the seller is liable for breach of warranty if they are untrue. Moreover, although a statement of opinion by the seller is not ordinarily a warranty, if the seller is an expert and gives her opinion as such, she may be liable for breach of warranty. Thus, if an art expert states that a certain painting is a genuine Rembrandt, and this becomes part of the basis of the bargain, then the expert warrants the accuracy of her professional opinion.

An express warranty also can be created by the use of a **description** of the goods that becomes part of the basis of the bargain. Section 2–313(1)(b); Section 2A–210(1)(b). Under such a warranty, the seller expressly warrants that the goods shall conform to the description. Examples include statements regarding a particular brand or type of goods, technical specifications, and blueprints.

The use of a **sample** or model is another means of creating an express warranty. Section 2–313(1)(c); Section 2A–210 (1)(c). If a sample or model is part of the basis of the bargain, the seller expressly warrants that the entire lot of goods sold shall conform to the sample or model. A sample is a good drawn from the bulk of goods comprising the subject matter of the sale. A model, by comparison, is offered for inspection when the subject matter is not at hand; it is not drawn from the bulk. Section 2–313, Comment 6.

━━━━━ C I S G ━━━━━

The seller must deliver goods which conform to quality and description required by the contract. In addition, the goods must possess the qualities of any sample or model used by the seller.

Basis of Bargain The Code does not require that the buyer rely on the affirmations, promises, descriptions, samples, or models the seller makes or uses but only that they constitute a part of the basis of the bargain. If they are part of the buyer's assumption underlying the sale, then reliance by the buyer is presumed. Some courts merely require that the buyer know of the affirmation or promise for it to be presumed to be part of the basis of the bargain. Relaxing the reliance requirement more often forces sellers to live up to their express warranties than does a rule requiring reliance.

Because they may constitute part of the basis of the bargain just as much as statements in advertisements or catalogs would, statements or promises the seller makes to the buyer prior to the sale may be express warranties. Furthermore, under the Code, statements or promises made by the seller subsequent to the contract of sale may become express warranties even though no new consideration is given. Sections

2–209(1) and 2A–208(1) provide that an agreement modifying a sale or lease needs no consideration to be binding. Thus, a statement, promise, or assurance with respect to the goods that the seller makes to the buyer at the time of delivery may be considered a binding modification of the prior contract of sale and held to be an express warranty basic to the bargain.

❧ **SEE CASES 24–1 AND 24–2**

Implied Warranties

An implied warranty, unlike an express warranty, is not found in the language of the sales contract or in a specific affirmation or promise by the seller. Instead, an **implied warranty** is an obligation imposed by operation of law upon the transfer of property or contract rights. This warranty, which arises out of the circumstances under which the parties enter into their contract, depends on factors such as the type of contract or sale entered into, the seller's merchant or non-merchant status, the conduct of the parties, and the applicability of other statutes. The law has developed implied warranties not as something to which the parties must agree but as a departure from the early rule of *caveat emptor*.

Merchantability At early common law, a seller was not held to any implied warranty as to the quality of goods. Under the Code, however, a **merchant seller** impliedly warrants the merchantability of goods that are of the kind in which she deals. The implied warranty of **merchantability** provides that the goods are reasonably fit for the ordinary purposes for which they are used, pass without objection in the trade under the contract description, and are of fair, average quality. Section 2–314; Section 2A–212. Because the warranty arises as a matter of law, the buyer does not need to prove that she relied on the warranty or that the warranty formed a basis of the bargain. The warranty applies automatically unless disclaimed by the seller. The official Comments to the Code further provide that a contract for the sale of secondhand goods "involves only such obligation as is appropriate to such goods for that is their description."

The Code in Sections 2–314(3) and 2A–212(3) expressly provides that implied warranties may arise from course of dealing or usage of trade. Thus, where the seller of a new automobile failed to lubricate it before delivery to the buyer, and the evidence established that it was the regular custom and usage of new car dealers to do so, the seller was held liable to the buyer for the resulting damages to the automobile in an action for breach of implied warranty.

The Code further provides that the serving for value of food or drink to be consumed on the premises or elsewhere is a sale. Section 2–314(1). Where a nonedible substance in food causes an injury, however, an implied warranty may not exist if the substance is natural to the food. A minority of jurisdictions distinguish between natural objects in food, such as fish bones in fish, and foreign objects such as a pebble, a piece of wire, or glass. The modern and majority test is the reasonable expectation of the consumer. That a substance is natural to a product in one stage of preparation does not necessarily imply that the consumer will reasonably anticipate or expect it to be in the final product.

◆ SEE CASE 24-2

―――――――――― C I S G ――――――――――

The seller must deliver goods, unless otherwise agreed, which are fit for any particular purpose expressly or impliedly made known to the seller by the buyer, except, where the buyer did not rely on the seller's skill and judgment where it was unreasonable for the buyer to rely on the seller.

Fitness for Particular Purpose Unlike the warranty of merchantability, the implied warranty of fitness for a particular purpose applies to *any* seller, whether he is a merchant or not. The **implied warranty of fitness for a particular purpose** arises if at the time of sale the seller had reason to know the buyer's particular purpose and that the buyer was relying upon the seller's skill and judgment to select suitable goods. Section 2–315; Section 2A–213.

The implied warranty of fitness for a particular purpose does not require any specific statement by the seller. Rather, the warranty requires only that the seller know that the buyer is relying on the seller's expertise in selecting a product for the buyer's specific purpose. The buyer need not specifically inform the seller of her particular purpose; it is sufficient if the seller has reason to know it. On the other hand, the implied warranty of fitness for a particular purpose would not arise if the buyer were to insist on a particular product and the seller simply conveyed it to her.

In contrast to the implied warranty of merchantability, the implied warranty of fitness for a particular purpose pertains to the *specific* purpose of the goods. The courts disagree whether an ordinary purpose of goods can be a particular purpose. Goods that are fit for ordinary purposes, and therefore are merchantable, may nonetheless be unfit for a particular purpose. A particular purpose may be a specific use or relate to a special situation in which the buyer intends to use the goods. Thus, if Miller has reason to know that Levine is purchasing a pair of shoes for mountain climbing and that Levine is relying upon Miller's judgment to furnish shoes suitable for this purpose, an implied warranty of fitness for a particular purpose would arise in this sale. If Miller sold Levine shoes suitable only for ordinary walking purposes, Miller would breach this implied warranty. Likewise, a buyer indicates to a seller that she needs a stamping machine to stamp 10,000 packages in an

eight-hour period and that she relies on the seller to select an appropriate machine. By selecting the machine, the seller impliedly warrants that the machine selected will stamp 10,000 packages in an eight-hour period.

Reliance is therefore required for this warranty, unlike an express warranty, which requires only that the affirmation meet the broad "basis of the bargain" test, or the implied warranty of merchantability, which requires no proof of reliance. In order to prevail in a case involving an implied warranty of fitness for a particular purpose, the buyer must be able to demonstrate specifically that she relied on the seller's skill or judgment in selecting or furnishing suitable goods.

◆ SEE CASE 24-2

―――――――――― C I S G ――――――――――

The seller must deliver goods, unless otherwise agreed, which are fit for the purposes for which goods of the same description would ordinarily be used.

OBSTACLES TO WARRANTY ACTIONS

In certain respects, warranty claims offer injured persons many advantages. Generally, a plaintiff need only establish the existence and breach of a warranty, an injury resulting from the breach, and the giving of notice in order to recover in a warranty action. This makes warranty claims easier to bring than negligence cases, which require the plaintiff to show that the defendant failed to act with due care—often a difficult task. Nonetheless, a number of technical obstacles limit the effectiveness of warranty as a basis for recovery. These include disclaimers of warranties, limitations or modifications of warranties, privity, notice of breach, and the conduct of the plaintiff. These obstacles vary considerably from jurisdiction to jurisdiction.

Disclaimer of Warranties

The Code calls for a reasonable construction of words or conduct to **disclaim** (negate) or limit warranties. Section 2–316; Section 2A–214. The Code makes clear that the seller should not rely on a time-honored formula of words and expect to obtain a disclaimer that may go unnoticed by the buyer. To be effective, disclaimers must be positive, explicit, unequivocal, and conspicuous.

Express Exclusions A **warranty of title** may be excluded only by specific language or by certain circumstances, including judicial sales or sales by sheriffs, executors, or foreclosing lienors. Section 2–312(2); Section 2A–214(4). In the latter cases the seller is manifestly offering to sell only such right or title as he or a third person might have in the goods, as it is apparent that the goods are not the property of the person selling them.

In general, a seller cannot provide an **express warranty** and then disclaim it. A seller can avoid making an express warranty, however, by carefully refraining from making any promise or affirmation of fact relating to the goods, refraining from making a description of the goods, or refraining from using a sample or model. Section 2–313; Section 2A–210. A seller also may be able to negate an express warranty by *clear, specific, unambiguous* language. The Code, however, provides that words or conduct relevant to the creation of an express warranty and words or conduct negating a warranty shall be construed wherever reasonable as consistent with each other and that a negation or limitation is inoperative to the extent that such construction is unreasonable. Section 2–316; Section 2A–214. For example, a seller and a buyer enter into a written contract for the sale of a camera in which the seller warrants that the camera being sold is free of defects. This express warranty renders inoperative another provision in the contract that attempts to disclaim liability for any repairs necessitated by defects in the camera. The inconsistency between the two contractual provisions makes the disclaimer ineffective. Moreover, if the seller's disclaimer attempts to negate "all express warranties," this general disclaimer would be ineffective against the specific express warranty providing that the camera is free of defects. Finally, oral warranties made prior to the execution of a written agreement that contains an express disclaimer are subject to the parol evidence rule. Thus, as discussed in Chapter 15, if the parties intend the written contract to be the final and complete statement of the agreement between them, oral evidence of warranties that contradict the terms of the written contract is inadmissible.

To exclude an **implied warranty of merchantability,** the language of disclaimer must mention merchantability and, in the case of a writing, must be *conspicuous.* Section 2–316(2). Article 2A requires that a disclaimer of an implied warranty of merchantability mention merchantability, be in writing, and be conspicuous. Section 2A–214(2). For example, Bart wishes to buy a used refrigerator from Ben's Used Appliances Store for $100. Given the low purchase price, Ben is unwilling to guarantee the refrigerator's performance. Bart agrees to buy it with no warranty protection. To exclude the warranty, Ben writes conspicuously on the contract, "This refrigerator carries no warranties, including no warranty of MERCHANTABILITY." Ben has effectively disclaimed the implied warranty of merchantability. Some courts, however, do not require the disclaimer to be conspicuous where a *commercial* buyer has actual knowledge of the disclaimer. The Code's test for whether a provision is *conspicuous* is whether a

reasonable person against whom the disclaimer is to operate ought to have noticed it. Section 1–201(10).

To exclude or to modify an **implied warranty of fitness** for the particular purpose of the buyer, the disclaimer must be in *writing* and *conspicuous.* Section 2–316(2); Section 2A–214(2).

All implied warranties, unless the circumstances indicate otherwise, are excluded by expressions like *as is, with all faults,* or other language plainly calling the buyer's attention to the exclusion of warranties. Section 2–316(3)(a); Section 2A–214(3)(a). Most courts require the "as is" clause to be conspicuous. Implied warranties also may be excluded by course of dealing, course of performance, or usage of trade. Section 2–316(3)(c); Section 2A–214(3)(c).

The courts will invalidate disclaimers they consider unconscionable. Sections 2–302 and 2A–108 of the Code, as discussed in Chapter 21, permit a court to limit the application of any contract or provision of a contract that it finds unconscionable.

◊ See Case 24-3

Buyer's Examination or Refusal to Examine If the buyer inspects the goods before entering into the contract, *implied warranties* do not apply to defects that are apparent upon examination. The particular buyer's skill and the normal method of examining goods in the circumstances determine what defects are excluded by examination. Section 2–316, Comment 8. Moreover, no implied warranty exists as to defects which an examination ought to have revealed, not only where the buyer has examined the goods as fully as she desired, but also where the buyer has *refused* to examine the goods. Section 2–316(3)(b); Section 2A–214(3)(b).

A mere failure or omission to examine the goods is not a refusal to examine them. It is not enough that the goods were available for inspection and the buyer did not see fit to inspect them. In order for the buyer to have "refused to examine the goods," the seller *must* first have demanded that the buyer examine them.

◊ See Case 24-3

--- C I S G ---

If at the time of entering into the sales contract the buyer knew or could not have been unaware of the lack of conformity, the seller is not liable for the warranty of particular purpose, ordinary purpose, or sale by sample or model.

Federal Legislation Relating to Warranties of Consumer Goods To protect purchasers of consumer goods (defined as "tangible personal property normally used for personal, family, or household purposes"), Congress enacted the **Magnuson-Moss Warranty Act**. The purpose of the act is to prevent deception and to make available to consumer purchasers adequate information with respect to warranties. Some courts have applied the act to leases.

The Federal Trade Commission administers and enforces the act. The commission's guidelines regarding the type of information a seller must set forth in warranties of consumer products are aimed at providing the consumer with clear and useful information. More significantly, the act provides that a seller who makes a written warranty cannot disclaim *any* implied warranty. For a complete discussion of the act, see Chapter 42.

♦ **SEE FIGURE 24-1** **Warranties**

Limitation or Modification of Warranties

Sometimes a seller is willing to give some warranty protection but wishes to limit the scope or type of protection she gives. For example, a seller who is willing to repair or replace a defective product may not be willing to pay consequential damages, such as the buyer's lost profits, arising from any product defects. Sections 2–719 and 2A–503 of the Code permit a seller to *limit* or *modify* the buyer's remedies for breach of warranty. Two important exceptions to the seller's right are Sections 2–719(3) and 2A–503(3), which prohibit "unconscionable" limitations or exclusions of consequential damages. Specifically, the limitation of consequential damages for injury to the person in the case of consumer goods is prima facie unconscionable.

♦ **FIGURE 24-1** **Warranties**

Type of Warranty	How Created	What Is Warranted	How Disclaimed
Title (Section 2-312)/ Use and Possession (2A-211)	• Seller contracts to sell goods	• Good title • Rightful transfer • Not subject to lien	• Specific language • Circumstances giving buyer reason to know that seller does not claim title
Express (Section 2-313; Section 2A-210)	• Affirmation of fact • Promise • Description • Sample or model	• Conform to affirmation • Conform to promise • Conform to description • Conform to sample or model	• Specific language (extremely difficult)
Merchantability (Section 2-314; Section 2A-212*)	• Merchant sells goods	• Fit for ordinary purpose • Adequately contained, packaged, and labeled	• Must mention "merchantability" • If in writing must be conspicuous/in lease must be in writing and conspicuous • As-is sale • Buyer examination • Course of dealing, course of performance, usage of trade
Fitness for a particular purpose (Section 2-315; Section 2A-213*)	• Seller knows buyer is relying upon seller to select goods suitable for buyer's particular purpose	• Fit for particular purpose	• No buzzwords necessary • Must be in writing and conspicuous • As-is sale • Buyer examination • Course of dealing, course of performance, usage of trade

*except in a finance lease

In some cases, a seller may choose not to limit the buyer's rights to seek damages for breach of warranty but to impose time limits within which the warranty is effective. Except for instances of unconscionability, the Code permits such clauses; it does not, however, permit any attempt to shorten to less than one year the time period for filing an action for personal injury.

Privity of Contract

Because of the association of warranties with contracts, a principle of law in the nineteenth century established that a plaintiff could not recover for breach of warranty unless he was in a contractual relationship with the defendant. This relationship is known as privity of contract.

Horizontal privity pertains to noncontracting parties who are injured by the defective goods; this group would include users, consumers, and bystanders who are not the contracting purchaser. Horizontal privity determines who benefits from a warranty and who may, therefore, sue for its breach.

Under this rule, a warranty by seller Ingrid to buyer Sylvester, who resells the goods to purchaser Lyle under a similar warranty, gives Lyle no rights against Ingrid. There is no privity of contract between Ingrid and Lyle. In the event of breach of warranty, Lyle may recover only from his seller, Sylvester, who in turn may recover from Ingrid.

The Code relaxes the requirement of horizontal privity of contract by permitting recovery on a seller's warranty, at a minimum, to members of the buyer's family or household or to guests in his home. Section 2–318 of the Code provides three alternative sections from which the States may select. *Alternative A*, the least comprehensive and most widely adopted, provides that a seller's warranty, whether express or implied, extends to any natural person who is in the family or household of the buyer or who is a guest in his home, if it is reasonable to expect that such person may use, consume, or be affected by the goods, and who is injured in person by breach of the warranty. *Alternative B* extends Alternative A to any natural person who may reasonably be expected to use, consume, or be affected by the goods. *Alternative C* further expands the coverage of the section to any person, not just natural persons, and to property damage as well as personal injury. (A natural person would not include artificial entities such as corporations.) A seller may not exclude or limit the operation of this section for injury to a person. Section 2A–216 provides the same alternatives with slight modifications.

Nonetheless, the Code merely sets a minimum standard that the States may expand through case law. Most States have judicially accepted the Code's invitation to relax the requirements of horizontal privity and, for all practical purposes, have *eliminated* horizontal privity in warranty cases.

Vertical privity, in determining who is liable for breach of warranty, pertains to remote sellers within the chain of distribution, such as manufacturers and wholesalers, with whom the consumer purchaser has not entered into a contract. Although the Code adopts a neutral position regarding vertical privity, the courts in most States have eliminated the requirement of vertical privity in warranty actions.

Notice of Breach of Warranty

When a buyer has accepted a tender of goods that are not as warranted by the seller, she is required to notify the seller of any breach of warranty within a reasonable time after she has discovered or should have discovered it. If the buyer fails to notify the seller of any breach within a reasonable time, she is barred from any remedy against the seller. Section 2–607(3)(a); Section 2A–516(3)(a).

The purpose of the reasonable notice requirement is (1) to enable the seller to cure the defect or to minimize the buyer's loss, (2) to provide the seller an opportunity to prepare for conflict resolution and litigation, and (3) to provide the seller with an end point to liability. In determining whether notice was provided within a reasonable time, commercial standards apply to a merchant buyer whereas standards designed to preserve a good faith consumer's right to his remedy apply to a retail consumer.

Plaintiff's Conduct

Because warranty liability developed in the law of sales and contracts, in most States contributory negligence of the buyer is no defense to an action against the seller for breach of warranty. In a number of States, however, comparative negligence statutes apply to warranty actions. (Comparative negligence is discussed more fully later in this chapter.)

If the buyer discovers a defect in the goods that may cause injury and then proceeds to make use of the goods, he will not be permitted to recover damages from the seller for loss or injuries caused by such use. This is not contributory negligence but **voluntary assumption** of a known risk.

Strict Liability in Tort

The most recent and far-reaching development in the field of products liability is that of strict liability in tort. All but a very few States have now accepted the concept, which is embodied in **Section 402A** of the Restatement, Second, of Torts. In 1997 a new Restatement of the Law, Third, Torts: Products Liability (the Restatement Third) was promulgated. It is far more comprehensive than the second Restatement in dealing with the liability of commercial sellers and distributors of goods for harm caused by their products (This revision will be discussed more fully later in this chapter).

Section 402A imposes **strict liability in tort** on merchant sellers for both personal injuries and property damage resulting from selling a product in a **defective condition, unreasonably dangerous** to the user or consumer. Section 402A applies even though "the seller has exercised all possible care in the preparation and sale of his product." Thus, negligence is not the basis of liability in strict liability cases. The essential distinction between the two doctrines is that actions in strict liability do not require the plaintiff to prove that the injury-producing defect resulted from any specific act of negligence of the seller. Strict liability actions focus on the product, not on the conduct of the manufacturer. Courts in strict liability cases are interested in the fact that a product defect arose—not in how it arose. Thus, even an "innocent" manufacturer—one who has not been negligent—may be liable if his product contains a defect that injures a consumer.

The reasons asserted in support of imposing strict liability in tort upon manufacturers and assemblers of products include the following: (1) consumers should be given maximum protection against dangerous defects in products; (2) manufacturers are in the best position to prevent or reduce the hazards to life and health in defective products; (3) manufacturers, who realize the most profit from the total sales of their goods, are best able to carry the financial burden of such liability by distributing it among the public as a cost of doing business; (4) manufacturers utilize wholesalers and retailers merely as conduits in the marketing of their products and should not be permitted to avoid liability simply because they have no contract with the user or consumer; and (5) because the manufacturer is liable to his purchaser who may be a wholesaler who in turn is liable to the retailer who in turn is liable to the ultimate purchaser, time and expense is saved by making liability direct rather than a chain reaction.

Although liability for personal injuries caused by a product in an unreasonably dangerous defective condition is usually associated with sales of goods, such liability also exists with respect to **leases** and **bailments** of defective goods. The extension of liability to lessors and bailors of goods is not surprising in view of the rationale the courts have developed in imposing strict liability in tort upon manufacturers and sellers of products. The danger to which the public is exposed by defectively manufactured cars and trucks traveling on the highways, for example, does not differ greatly from the hazards of defective cars and trucks leased to operators.

REQUIREMENTS OF STRICT LIABILITY

Section 402A imposes strict liability in tort on merchant sellers for both personal injuries and property damage that result from selling a product in a defective condition unreasonably dangerous to the user or consumer. Specifically, this section provides:

1. One who sells any product in a defective condition unreasonably dangerous to the user or consumer or to his property is subject to liability for physical harm thereby caused to the ultimate user or consumer, or to his property, if (a) the seller is engaged in the business of selling such a product, and (b) it is expected to and does reach the user or consumer without substantial change in the condition in which it is sold.
2. The rule stated in Subsection (1) applies although (a) the seller has exercised all possible care in the preparation and sale of his product, and (b) the user or consumer has not bought the product from or entered into any contractual relation with the seller.

Negligence, as previously stated, is not the basis of this liability; it applies even though "the seller has exercised all possible care in the preparation and sale of his product." The seller is not an insurer of the goods which he manufactures or sells, however; and the essential requirements for strict product liability are that (1) the defendant was engaged in the business of selling such a product; (2) the defendant sold the product in a defective condition; (3) the defective condition was one which made the product unreasonably dangerous to the user or consumer or to his property; (4) the defect in the product existed at the time it left the hands of the defendant; (5) the plaintiff sustained physical harm or property damage by use or consumption of the product; and (6) the defective condition was the proximate cause of such injury or damage.

This liability is imposed by law as a matter of public policy and does not depend upon contract, either express or implied. It does not require reliance by the injured user or consumer upon any statements made by the manufacturer or seller. The liability is not limited to persons in a buyer-seller relationship; thus, neither vertical nor horizontal privity is required. No notice of the defect is required to have been given by the injured user or consumer. The liability, furthermore, is generally not subject to disclaimer, exclusion, or modification by contractual agreement. Rather, the liability is solely in tort and arises out of the common law; it is not governed by the provisions of the Uniform Commercial Code.

The majority of courts considering the question have held that Section 402A imposes liability for injury to person and damage to property (the economic loss doctrine) but not for commercial loss (such as loss of bargain or profits), which is recoverable in an action for breach of warranty. A minority of States has held, however, that commercial loss may be recovered in tort where the defect creates an unreasonable risk of personal injury or property damage, even though the only damage resulting is to the defective goods themselves.

Merchant Sellers

Section 402A imposes liability only upon a person who is in the *business* of selling the product involved. It does *not* apply to an occasional seller, such as a person who trades in his used car or who sells his lawn mower to a neighbor. In this respect, the section is similar to the implied warranty of merchantability, which applies only to sales by a merchant with respect to goods of the type in which he deals. A growing number of jurisdictions recognize the applicability of strict liability in tort to merchant sellers of *used* goods.

Defective Condition

In an action against a defendant manufacturer or other seller to recover damages under the rule of strict liability in tort, the plaintiff must prove a defective condition in the product, but she is not required to prove how or why the product became defective. In an action based on Section 402A, the reason for or cause of the defect is not material, although it would be in an action based on negligence. Under a strict liability approach, a manufacturer will be held liable even though it did not act negligently. For example, if the Quality Bottling Company, despite its having the most stringent quality control program in the industry, through no negligence of its own manufactures a bottle that explodes in the hands of a consumer, the company would be liable to the consumer under Section 402A. Whether or not Quality Bottling Company acted negligently is irrelevant. The plaintiff, however, must show that at the time she was injured the condition of the product was not substantially changed from the condition in which the manufacturer or seller sold it. In general, defects may arise through faulty manufacturing, faulty product design, or inadequate warning, labeling, packaging, or instructions. Some States, however, and the Restatement Third do not impose strict liability for a design defect or a failure to provide proper warnings or instructions.

Manufacturing Defect A manufacturing defect occurs when the product is not properly made; that is, it fails to meet its own manufacturing specifications. For instance, suppose a chair is manufactured with legs designed to be attached by four screws and glue. If such a chair were produced without the required screws, this would constitute a manufacturing defect.

Design Defect A product contains a design defect when, despite its being produced as specified, the product is dangerous or hazardous because of inadequate design. Design defects can result from a number of causes, including poor engineering and poor choice of materials. An example of a design defect that received great notoriety was the Ford Pinto. A number of courts found the car to be inadequately designed because its fuel tank had been placed too close to its rear axle, causing the tank to rupture upon impact from the rear.

Section 402A provides no guidance in determining which injury-producing designs should give rise to strict liability and which should not; consequently, the courts have adopted widely varying approaches in applying 402A to defective design cases.

At one extreme, a few courts have taken a very literal approach to Section 402A by ruling that a manufacturer is strictly liable for injuries caused by a design that a reasonable person would not have produced had he known of the design's harmful character at the time it was made. Whether the manufacturer did or could have known of the risk associated with the design, or of an alternative design that could have avoided the risk, is deemed irrelevant for purposes of strict liability. Manufacturers, in effect, are held liable for hazards that were unknowable at the time they manufactured their products.

A slightly larger number of courts, although still a minority, have taken the opposite approach: recognizing no difference between negligence and strict liability principles in defective design cases, they apply negligence principles to such cases. Unless the plaintiff can demonstrate that the manufacturer knew, or should have known, of a safer, cost-effective design, these courts will not hold the manufacturer liable.

The majority of courts have ostensibly adopted a middle-of-the-road approach, stating that strict liability cases should be viewed differently from negligence cases. Beyond reciting that strict liability cases focus on the product, not on the manufacturer's conduct, these courts have yet to clarify what the different view implies. Nevertheless, virtually none of them has upheld a judgment in a strict liability case in which the defendant demonstrated that the "**state of the art**" was such that the manufacturer (1) neither knew nor could have known of a product hazard, or (2) if he knew of the product hazard, could have designed a safer product given existing technology. Thus, almost all courts evaluate the design of a product on the basis of the dangers that could have been known when the product was produced or sold.

In deciding design defect cases, courts identify any government safety standards applicable to the design involved in the product liability lawsuit. If such a standard exists and the manufacturer's failure to follow it caused the plaintiff's injury, the courts tend to impose liability automatically. On the other hand, a manufacturer's compliance with safety standards does not equal automatic relief from liability. If a plaintiff can demonstrate that a safer, cost-effective design was available to the manufacturer, the plaintiff can still prevail in a product liability lawsuit even though the manufacturer complied with a government safety standard.

Failure to Warn A seller is under a duty to provide adequate warning of possible danger, to provide appropriate directions for safe use, and to package the product safely. Warnings do not, however, always protect sellers from liability. A seller who could have designed or manufactured a product in a safe but cost-effective manner, but who instead chooses to produce the product cheaply and to provide a warning of the product's hazards, cannot escape liability simply through the warning.

Warnings usually will avoid liability only if there are no cost-effective designs or manufacturing processes available to reduce a risk of injury.

The duty to give a warning arises out of a foreseeable danger of physical harm resulting from the normal or probable use of the product and out of the likelihood that, unless warned, the user or consumer will not ordinarily be aware of such danger or hazard. For example, a seller may reasonably assume that those with allergies to products such as eggs or strawberries will know of their allergies and therefore need not be warned of this risk. On the other hand, if a product contains an ingredient to which a substantial number of persons are allergic, and the ingredient is one whose danger is not generally known or, if known, is one which the consumer would not reasonably expect to find in the product, the seller is required to give a warning about it. Under strict liability principles, sellers are generally required to provide warnings against uses for which a product is not marketed, including certain instances of consumer misuse, if such uses are foreseeable by the manufacturer and the consumer is unlikely to recognize the hazard.

Section 402A imposes liability in failure-to-warn cases only where the seller "has knowledge, or by the application of reasonable, developed human skill and foresight should have knowledge, of the . . . danger." Comment j. In effect, the seller is held to the knowledge and skill of an expert in the field. Some courts have ruled that this means a manufacturer not only must keep abreast of scientific knowledge, discoveries, and advances, but also must conduct research to determine whether his product contains hazards. Most courts today require proof that the manufacturer knew, or could have known, of a product hazard before imposing liability for a failure to warn.

◊ SEE CASE 24-4

Unreasonably Dangerous

Section 402A liability applies only if the defective product is **unreasonably dangerous** to the user or consumer. An unreasonably dangerous product is one which contains a danger beyond that which the ordinary consumer, who purchases the product with common knowledge of its characteristics, would contemplate. Thus, "good whiskey is not unreasonably dangerous merely because it will make some people drunk, and is especially dangerous to alcoholics; but bad whiskey, containing a dangerous amount of fuel oil, is unreasonably dangerous. Good tobacco is not unreasonably dangerous merely because the effects of smoking may be harmful; but tobacco containing something like marijuana may be unreasonably dangerous. Good butter is not unreasonably dangerous merely because, if such be the case, it deposits cholesterol in the arteries and leads to heart attacks; but bad butter, contaminated with poisonous fish oil, is unreasonably dangerous." Comment i to Section 402A. Most courts have left the question of reasonable consumer expectations to the jury.

◊ SEE CASE 24-5

OBSTACLES TO RECOVERY

Few of the obstacles to recovery in warranty cases present serious problems to plaintiffs in strict liability actions brought pursuant to Section 402A because this section was drafted largely to avoid such obstacles.

Disclaimers and Notice

Comment m to Section 402A provides that the basis of strict liability rests solely in tort and therefore is not subject to contractual defenses. The comment specifically states that strict product liability is not governed by the Code, that it is not affected by contractual limitations or disclaimers, and that it is not subject to any requirement that the injured party gives notice to the seller within a reasonable time. Nevertheless, most courts have allowed clear and specific disclaimers of Section 402A liability in *commercial* transactions between merchants of relatively equal economic power.

Privity

With respect to horizontal privity, the majority of States hold that the strict liability in tort of manufacturers and other sellers extends not only to buyers, users, and consumers, but also to injured bystanders. Bystanders to whom such liability has extended include the occupants of an automobile injured in a collision with another car due to the other car's having defective brakes; a golfer killed by a runaway golf cart that started due to a faulty transmission system; a bystander injured by a runaway truck started by a short circuit; a bystander injured by the explosion of a defective beer keg; a neighbor injured by the explosion of a propane gas tank; and a bystander injured by the explosion of a shotgun barrel caused by a defective shell. Some States, however, limit liability to foreseeable purchasers or users of the product.

In terms of **vertical privity**, strict liability in tort imposes liability on any seller who is engaged in the business of selling the product, including a wholesaler or distributor as well as the manufacturer and retailer. The rule of strict liability in tort also applies to the manufacturer of a defective component that has been incorporated into a larger product where the manufacturer of the finished product has made no essential change in the component.

Plaintiff's Conduct

Many product liability defenses relate to the conduct of the plaintiff. The contention common to all of them is that the plaintiff's improper conduct so contributed to the plaintiff's injury that it would be unfair to blame the product or its seller.

Contributory Negligence Contributory negligence is conduct on the part of the plaintiff that falls below the standard to which he should conform for his own protection and that is the legal cause of the plaintiff's harm. Under traditional negligence law principles, if the negligence of the plaintiff together with that of the defendant proximately caused the plaintiff's injury, the plaintiff could not recover *any* damages from the defendant. It did not matter whether the plaintiff's contributory negligence was slight or extensive. Because strict liability is designed to assess liability without fault, Section 402A rejects contributory negligence as a defense. Thus, a seller cannot defend a strict liability lawsuit on the basis of a plaintiff's negligent failure to discover a defect or to guard against its possibility. But, as discussed below, contributory negligence in the form of an assumption of the risk can bar recovery under Section 402A.

Comparative Negligence The harshness of the contributory negligence doctrine has caused all but a few States to reject the all-or-nothing rule of contributory negligence and to substitute the doctrine of comparative negligence. Under **comparative negligence**, damages are apportioned between the parties in proportion to the degree of fault or negligence found against them.

Despite Section 402A's bar of contributory negligence in strict liability cases, some courts apply comparative negligence to strict liability cases. (Some courts use the term **comparative responsibility** rather than *comparative negligence*.) There are two basic types of comparative negligence or comparative responsibility. One is **pure comparative responsibility**, which simply reduces the plaintiff's recovery in proportion to her fault, whatever that may be. Thus, the recovery of a plaintiff found to be 80 percent at fault in causing an accident in which she suffered a $100,000 loss would be limited to 20 percent of her damages, or $20,000. By comparison, under **modified comparative responsibility**, the plaintiff recovers according to the general principles of comparative responsibility *unless* she is more than 50 percent responsible for her injuries, in which case she recovers nothing. The majority of comparative negligence States follows the modified comparative responsibility approach.

Voluntary Assumption of the Risk Assumption of risk is a defense in an action based on strict liability in tort. Basically, **assumption of risk** is the plaintiff's express or implied consent to encounter a known danger. The user or consumer who voluntarily uses goods in an unusual, inappropriate, or improper manner for which they were not intended, such use being, under the circumstances, unreasonable, assumes the risk of injuries that result from such use. Thus, a person who drives an automobile after realizing that the brakes are not working or an employee who attempts to remove a foreign object from a high-speed roller press without shutting off the power has assumed the risk of his own injury. In a comparative negligence or comparative responsibility State, assumption of the risk would either reduce or bar recovery, depending on the degree to which it contributed to the plaintiff's injury.

To establish such a defense, the defendant must show that (1) the plaintiff actually knew and appreciated the particular risk or danger the defect created, (2) the plaintiff voluntarily encountered the risk while realizing the danger, and (3) the plaintiff's decision to encounter the known risk was unreasonable.

Misuse or Abuse of the Product Closely connected to voluntary assumption of the risk is the valid defense of misuse or abuse of the product by the injured party. **Misuse** or **abuse** occurs when the injured party knows, or should know, that he is using the product in a manner not contemplated by the seller. The major difference between misuse or abuse and assumption of the risk is that the former includes actions which the injured party does not know to be dangerous, whereas the latter does not. Instances of such misuse or abuse include standing on a rocking chair to change a light bulb or using a lawn mower to trim hedges.

The courts, however, have significantly limited this defense by requiring that the misuse or abuse not be foreseeable by the seller. If a use is foreseeable, then the seller must take measures to guard against it. For example, if William stands on a rocking chair to change a light bulb and is injured when the chair tilts and tips over, his misuse of the chair would bar his recovery. Similarly, if Jenny hammers a nail with a hair dryer and suffers an eye injury when a chip flies from the dryer, she will be unsuccessful in a claim against the manufacturer.

Subsequent Alteration

Section 402A provides that liability exists only if the product reaches "the user or consumer without substantial change in the condition in which it is sold." Accordingly, most, but not all, courts would not hold a manufacturer liable for a faulty oil pump if a car dealer were to remove the part and make significant changes in it prior to reinstalling it in an automobile.

Statute of Repose

Numerous lawsuits have been brought against manufacturers many years after a product was first sold. In one case, a manufacturer was successfully sued twenty-two years after a defective water meter was first purchased and fourteen years after it was installed in the plaintiff's home. In another case, Volkswagen of America was ordered to pay $1.8 million in damages in an accident case centering around a missing door latch costing 35 cents. The accident occurred ten years after the car had been manufactured and nine years after Volkswagen had informed its dealers about the defect.

In response, many States have adopted **statutes of repose**. These enactments limit the time period—typically to between six and twelve years—for which a manufacturer is liable for injury caused by a defective product. After the statutory period has elapsed, a manufacturer ceases to be liable for such harm.

Limitations on Damages

More than half of the States have limited the punitive damages that a plaintiff can collect in a product liability lawsuit. They have done this by a number of means including:

1. Placing caps on the amount of damages that can be awarded, with caps ranging from $50,000 to $5,000,000;
2. Providing for the State to receive all or a portion of any punitive damages awarded with the State's share ranging from 35 percent to 100 percent in order to reduce the plaintiff's incentive to bring products liability suits;
3. Providing for bifurcated trials; i.e. separate hearings to determine liability and punitive damages;
4. Increasing the plaintiff's burden of proof for recovery of punitive damages, with most states adopting the "clear and convincing" evidence standard;
5. Requiring proportionality between compensatory and punitive damages by specifying an acceptable ratio between the two types of damages.

◆**SEE FIGURE 24-2** Products Liabilities

RESTATEMENT OF TORTS (THIRD): PRODUCTS LIABILITY

The recently promulgated Restatement (Third) of Torts: Products Liability makes some significant changes in product liability. It is likely that the adoption of the new Restatement by the States will be a slow process and in the mean time the great majority of States will continue to follow Section 402A of the Second Restatement of Torts.

The new Restatement expands Section 402A into an entire treatise of its own, comprising more than twenty sections. The Restatement Third does not use the term strict liability but instead defines separate liability standards for each type of defect. The new Restatement continues to cover anyone engaged in the business of selling or distributing a defective product if the defect causes harm to persons or property. Its major provision (Section 2) defines a product as defective "when, at the time of sale or distribution, it contains a manufacturing defect, is defective in design, or is defective because of

◆**FIGURE 24-2**   **Products Liabilities**

Type of Warranty	Warranty of Merchantability*	Strict Liability in Tort (§ 402A)
Condition of Goods Creating Liability	Not fit for ordinary purposes	Defective condition, unreasonably dangerous
Type of Transaction Covered	Sales and leases (except finance leases); some courts apply to bailments of goods	Sales, leases, and bailments of goods
Disclaimer	Must mention "merchantability" If in writing, must be conspicuous (lease must be in writing) Must not be unconscionable Sales subject to Magnuson-Moss Act/ leases may be subject	Not possible in consumer transactions; may be permitted in commercial transactions
Notice to Seller	Required within reasonable time	Not required
Causation	Required	Required
Who May Sue	In some States, buyer and the buyer's family or guests in home; in other States, any person who may be expected to use, consume, or be affected by goods	Any user or consumer of product; also, in most States, any bystander
Compensable Harms	Personal injury, property damage, economic loss	Personal injury, property damage
Who May Be Sued	Seller or lessor who is a merchant with respect to the goods sold	Seller who is a merchant with respect to the goods sold

*The warranty of fitness for a particular purpose differs from the warranty of merchantability in the following respects: (1) the condition that triggers liability is the failure of the goods to perform according to the particular purpose of the warranty, (2) a disclaimer need not mention "fitness for a particular purpose" but must be in writing, and (3) applies to any seller.

inadequate instructions or warnings." Thus, Section 2 explicitly recognizes the three types of product defects discussed above: manufacturing defects, design defects, and failure to warn. However, as discussed below, strict liability is imposed only on the first of these, while liability for inadequate design or warning is imposed only for foreseeable risks of harm that could have been avoided by the use of an alternative *reasonable* design, warning, or instruction.

Manufacturing Defect

Section 2(a) provides that "A product . . . contains a manufacturing defect when the product departs from its intended design even though all possible care was exercised in the preparation and marketing of the product." Therefore, sellers and distributors of products remain strictly liable for manufacturing defects, although a plaintiff may seek to recover based upon allegations and proof of negligent manufacture. In actions against the manufacturer, the plaintiff ordinarily must prove that the defect existed in the product when it left the manufacturer.

Design Defect

Section 2(b) states: "A product . . . is defective in design when the foreseeable risks of harm posed by the product could have been reduced or avoided by the adoption of a reasonable alternative design by the seller or other distributor, or a predecessor in the commercial chain of distribution, and the omission of the reasonable alternative design renders the product not reasonably safe." This rule pulls back from a strict liability standard and imposes a negligence-like standard by requiring that the defect be reasonably foreseeable and that it could have been avoided by a reasonable alternative design. The Comments explain that this standard involves resolving "whether a reasonable alternative design would, at a reasonable cost, have reduced the foreseeable risk of harm posed by the product and, if so, whether the omission of the alternative design by the seller . . . rendered the product not reasonably safe." The burden rests upon the plaintiff to demonstrate the existence of a reasonable alternative safer design that would have reduced the foreseeable risks of harm. However, consumer expectations do not constitute an independent standard for judging the defectiveness of product designs.

Failure to Warn

Section 2(c) provides: "A product... is defective because of inadequate instructions or warnings when the foreseeable risks of harm posed by the product could have been reduced or avoided by the provision of reasonable instructions or warnings by the seller or other distributor, or a predecessor in the commercial chain of distribution and the omission of the instructions or warnings renders the product not reasonably safe." Commercial product sellers must provide reasonable instructions and warnings about risks of injury associated with their products. The omission of warnings sufficient to allow informed decisions by reasonably foreseeable users or consumers renders the product not reasonably safe at time of sale. A seller, however, is under a duty to warn only if it knew or should have known of the risks involved. Moreover, warning about risks is effective only if an alternative design to avoid the risk cannot reasonably be implemented. Whenever safer products can be reasonably designed at a reasonable cost, adoption of the safer design is required rather than using a warning or instructions.

— **C H A P T E R   S U M M A R Y** —

Warranties

Types of Warranties	**Definition of Warranty** an obligation of the seller to the buyer concerning title, quality, characteristics, or condition of goods
	Warranty of Title the obligation of a seller to convey the right to ownership without any lien (in a lease the warranty protects the lessee's right to possess and use the goods)
	Express Warranty an affirmation of fact or promise about the goods or a description, including a sample, of the goods that becomes part of the basis of the bargain
	Implied Warranty a contractual obligation, arising out of certain circumstances of the sale, imposed by operation of law and not found in the language of the sales contract
	• *Merchantability* warranty by a merchant seller that the goods are reasonably fit for the ordinary purpose for which they are manufactured or sold, pass without objection in the trade under the contract description, and are of fair, average quality

- *Fitness for Particular Purpose* warranty by any seller that goods are reasonably fit for a particular purpose if, at the time of contracting, the seller had reason to know the buyer's particular purpose and that the buyer was relying on the seller's skill and judgment to furnish suitable goods

Obstacles to Warranty Actions

Disclaimers of Warranties negations of warranties
- *Express Warranty* not usually possible to disclaim
- *Warranty of Title* may be excluded or modified by specific language or by certain circumstances, including judicial sale or a sale by a sheriff, executor, or foreclosing lienor
- *Implied Warranty of Merchantability* the disclaimer must mention "merchantability" and, in the case of a writing, must be conspicuous (in a lease the disclaimer must be in writing)
- *Implied Warranty of Fitness for a Particular Purpose* the disclaimer must be in writing and conspicuous
- *Other Disclaimers of Implied Warranties* the implied warranties of merchantability and fitness for a particular purpose may also be disclaimed (1) by expressions like "as is," "with all faults," or other similar language; (2) by course of dealing, course of performance, or usage of trade; or (3) as to defects an examination ought to have revealed where the buyer has examined the goods or where the buyer has refused to examine the goods
- *Federal Legislation Relating to Warranties of Consumer Goods* the Magnuson-Moss Warranty Act protects purchasers of consumer goods by providing that warranty information be clear and useful and that a seller who makes a written warranty cannot disclaim any implied warranty

Limitation or Modification of Warranties permitted as long as it is not unconscionable

Privity of Contract a contractual relationship between parties that was necessary at common law to maintain a lawsuit
- *Horizontal Privity* doctrine determining who benefits from a warranty and who therefore may bring a cause of action; the Code provides three alternatives
- *Vertical Privity* doctrine determining who in the chain of distribution is liable for a breach of warranty; the Code has not adopted a position on this

Notice of Breach if the buyer fails to notify the seller of any breach within a reasonable time, she is barred from any remedy against the seller

Plaintiff's Conduct
- *Contributory Negligence* is not a defense
- *Voluntary Assumption of the Risk* is a defense

Strict Liability in Tort

Nature

General Rule imposes tort liability on merchant sellers for both personal injuries and property damage for selling a product in a defective condition unreasonably dangerous to the user or consumer

Defective Condition
- *Manufacturing Defect* by failing to meet its own manufacturing specifications, the product is not properly made
- *Design Defect* the product, though made as designed, is dangerous because the design is inadequate
- *Failure to Warn* failure to provide adequate warnings of possible danger or to provide appropriate directions for use of a product

Unreasonably Dangerous contains a danger beyond that which would be contemplated by the ordinary consumer

---

Obstacles to Recovery

Contractual Defenses defenses such as privity, disclaimers, and notice generally do not apply to tort liability

Plaintiff's Conduct
- *Contributory Negligence* not a defense in the majority of States
- *Comparative Negligence* most States have applied the rule of comparative negligence to strict liability in tort
- *Voluntary Assumption of the Risk* is a defense
- *Misuse or Abuse of the Product* is a defense

Subsequent Alteration liability exists only if the product reaches the user or consumer without substantial change in the condition in which it is sold

Statute of Repose limits the time period for which a manufacturer is liable for injury caused by its product

Limitations on Damages many States have limited the punitive damages that a plaintiff can collect in a product liability lawsuit

---

Restatement (Third) of Torts: Products Liability

General Rule one engaged in the business of selling products who sells a defective product is subject to liability for harm to persons or property caused by the defect

Manufacturing Defect a seller is held to strict liability when the product departs from its intended design

Design Defect a product is defective when the foreseeable risks of harm posed by the product could have been reduced or avoided by the adoption of a reasonable alternative design

Failure to Warn a product is defective because of inadequate instructions or warnings when the foreseeable risks of harm posed by the product could have been reduced or avoided by the provision of reasonable instructions or warnings

---

━ C A S E S ━

Express Warranties
FELLEY v. SINGLETON
Appellate Court of Illinois, Second District, 1999
302 Ill.App.3d 248, 705 N.E.2d 930, 235 Ill.Dec. 747
http://caselaw.lp.findlaw.com/scripts/getcase.pl?court=IL&vol=app/1999/2980043&invol=3

Bowman, J.

Defendants, Thomas and Cheryl Singleton, appeal from an order entered by the circuit court of Boone County in this small claims action. Defendants contend that the trial court erred when it found that statements they made to plaintiff, Brian D. Felley, when he purchased a used car from them constituted an express warranty. We affirm.

The relevant facts are not in dispute. On June 8, 1997, plaintiff went to defendants' home to look at a used car that defendants had offered for sale by newspaper advertisement. The car was a 1991 Ford Taurus and had about 126,000 miles

on it. After test driving the car and discussing its condition with defendants, plaintiff purchased the car from defendants for $5,800.

At trial, plaintiff testified that he soon began experiencing problems with the car. On the second day after he bought the car, plaintiff noticed a problem with the clutch. Over the next few days, the clutch problem worsened to the point where plaintiff was unable to shift the gears no matter how far he pushed in the clutch pedal. Plaintiff presented an invoice dated June 18, 1997, showing that he paid $942.76 on that date for the removal and repair of the car's clutch.

Antitrust

The economic community is best served by free competition in trade and industry. It is in the public interest that quality, price, and service in an open, competitive market for goods and services be determining factors in the business rivalry for the customer's dollar. Nevertheless, in lieu of competing, businesses would prefer to eliminate their rivals and consequently gain a position from which they could dictate both the price of their goods and the quantity they produce. Although to eliminate competition by producing a better product is the goal of a business, some businesses try to effect this elimination through illegitimate means, such as fixing prices and allocating exclusive territories to certain competitors within an industry. The law of antitrust prohibits such activities and attempts to ensure free and fair competition in the marketplace.

The common law has traditionally favored competition and has held agreements and contracts in restraint of trade illegal and unenforceable. In addition, several States enacted antitrust statutes during the 1800s. The latter half of the nineteenth century, however, disclosed concentrations of economic power in the form of "trusts" and "combinations" that were too powerful and widespread to be effectively curbed by State action. In 1890, this awesome growth of corporate power prompted Congress to enact the Sherman Antitrust Act, which was the first Federal statute in this field. Since then, Congress has enacted other antitrust statutes, including the Clayton Act, the Robinson-Patman Act, and the Federal Trade Commission Act. These statutes prohibit anticompetitive practices and seek to prevent unreasonable concentrations of economic power that stifle or weaken competition.

SHERMAN ACT

Section 1 of the Sherman Act prohibits contracts, combinations, and conspiracies that restrain trade, while Section 2 prohibits monopolies and attempts to monopolize. Failure to comply with either section is a criminal felony and subjects the offender to fine or imprisonment, or both. As amended by the 1990 Antitrust Amendments, the Act subjects individual offenders to imprisonment of up to three years and fines up to $350,000, while corporate offenders are subject to fines of up to $10 million per violation. Moreover, the Sherman Act empowers the Federal district courts to issue injunctions restraining violations, and anyone injured by a violation is entitled to recover in a civil action **treble damages**, that is, three times the amount of the actual loss sustained. In addition, State Attorneys General may bring suit for treble damages on behalf of citizens of their States. The United States Justice Department and the Federal Trade Commission have the duty to institute appropriate enforcement proceedings other than treble damage actions.

The case the United States brought against Microsoft, Inc. may have a profound effect upon antitrust law. In June 2000, U.S. District Court Judge Thomas Penfield Jackson ordered the breakup of Microsoft for violating the Sherman Antitrust Act. The breakup order followed more than two years of litigation in which Microsoft was accused of illegally maintaining its monopoly over the personal computer operating system market and then attempting to extend it into the market for Internet browsers. The U.S. Court of Appeals upheld the district court's ruling that Microsoft used illegal conduct to retain its operating system monopoly, reversed the browser monopolization finding and the breakup order, and remanded the case to the district court to determine an appropriate remedy. After the appellate court decision the Department of Justice and a number of States settled with Microsoft, although some States are contesting the decision. The settlement allows Microsoft to remain as one company but includes the following provisions: (1) Microsoft may not "retaliate against" a computer maker in any way, including raising prices or withholding technical support, for dealing with Microsoft's competitors; (2) Microsoft must establish and follow a schedule of fixed prices; (3) Computer makers like Dell, Gateway, and IBM will be allowed to install non-Microsoft products and "desktop shortcuts of any size or shape" on its computers; (4) Microsoft will reveal previously confidential programming interfaces that its products rely on to link to Windows code; and (5) Microsoft "shall not retaliate" against other companies because their products compete with other Microsoft applications.

The Supreme Court previously stated the purpose of the Sherman Act as follows:

> The Sherman Act was designed to be a comprehensive charter of economic liberty aimed at preserving free and unfettered competition as the rule of trade. It rests on the premise that the unrestrained interaction of competitive forces will yield the best allocation of our economic resources, the lowest prices, the highest quality and the greatest material progress, while at the same time providing an environment conducive to the preservation of our democratic political and social institutions. *Northern Pacific Railway Co. v. United States*, 356 U.S. 1 (1958).

Moreover, the Justice Department has expanded its policy of enforcement regarding the Sherman Act to cover conduct by foreign companies that harms U.S. exports. Under this policy, the department examines conduct to determine whether it would violate the law if it occurred within the borders of the United States. The department has indicated that it will focus primarily on boycotts and cartels that injure the export of U.S. products and services.

`http:` **Federal Trade Commission, Antitrust/Competition Division:** http://www.ftc.gov/ftc/antitrust.htm
Department of Justice Antitrust Division: http://www.usdoj.gov/atr/index.html
United States v. Microsoft, Department of Justice Information: http://www.usdoj.gov/atr/cases/ms_index.htm
Sherman Act: http://www4.law.cornell.edu/uscode/15/1.html

Restraint of Trade

Section 1 of the Sherman Act provides that "[e]very contract, combination in the form of trust or otherwise, or conspiracy, in restraint of trade or commerce among the several states, or with foreign nations is hereby declared to be illegal." Because the language of the section is so broad, judicial interpretation has played a significant role in establishing the elements that constitute a violation.

Standards As noted above, Section 1 prohibits every contract, combination, or conspiracy in restraint of trade. Taken literally, this prohibition would invalidate every unperformed contract. For example, under a strict interpretation of the section, a contract in which a seller agrees to supply a buyer with 1,000 pounds of grapes, no one but the seller would be permitted to fulfill the buyer's need for those 1,000 pounds of grapes, and the seller would not be allowed to sell those grapes to any other buyer. This agreement would therefore restrain trade. To avoid such a broad and impractical application, the courts have interpreted this section to invalidate only *unreasonable* restraints of trade:

> The true test of legality is whether the restraint imposed is such as merely regulates and perhaps thereby promotes competition or whether it is such as may suppress or even destroy competition. To determine that question the courts must ordinarily consider the facts peculiar to the business to which the restraint is applied; its condition before and after the restraint was imposed; the nature of the restraint and its effect, actual or probable. The history of the restraint, the evil believed to exist, the reason for adopting the particular remedy, the purpose or end sought to be attained, are all relevant facts. This is not because a good intention will save an otherwise objectionable regulation or the reverse; but because knowledge of intent may help the court to interpret facts and to predict consequences. *Chicago Board of Trade v. United States*, 246 U.S. 231 (1918).

This flexible standard, known as the **rule of reason test**, requires the courts, in determining whether a challenged practice unreasonably restricts competition, to consider a variety of factors, including the makeup of the relevant industry, the defendants' positions within that industry, the ability of the defendants' competitors to respond to the challenged practice, and the defendants' purpose in adopting the restraint. After reviewing the various factors, a court determines whether the challenged restraint unreasonably restricts competition. By requiring courts to balance the anticompetitive effects of every questioned restraint against its procompetitive effects, this standard places a substantial burden upon the judicial system. The United States Supreme Court addressed this problem by declaring certain categories of restraints to be unreasonable by their very nature, that is, **illegal *per se***:

> [T]here are certain agreements or practices which because of their pernicious effect on competition and lack of any redeeming

virtue are conclusively presumed to be unreasonable and therefore illegal without elaborate inquiry as to the precise harm they have caused or the business excuse for their use. This principle of *per se* unreasonableness not only makes the type of restraints which are proscribed by the Sherman Act more certain to the benefit of everyone concerned, but it also avoids the necessity for an incredibly complicated and prolonged economic investigation into the entire history of the industry involved, as well as related industries, in an effort to determine at large whether a particular restraint has been unreasonable—an inquiry so often wholly fruitless when undertaken. *Northern Pacific Railway Co. v. United States*, 356 U.S. 1 (1958).

Characterizing a type of restraint as *per se* illegal therefore has a significant effect on the prosecution of an antitrust suit. In such a case, the plaintiff need only show that the type of restraint occurred; she does not need to prove that the restraint limited competition. Furthermore, the defendants may not defend on the basis that the restraint is reasonable. Additionally, as noted in *Northern Pacific Railway*, the court is not required to conduct extensive, and often difficult, economic analysis. Not surprisingly, the ease of applying the *per se* rule has helped to deter those restraints subject to the rule.

Over the last decade a third, intermediate test has been frequently used when the *per se* approach is not appropriate for the situation but the challenged conduct has obvious anticompetitive effects. Under this "quick look" rule of reason analysis, the courts will apply an abbreviated rule of reason standard rather than using the extensive analysis required by a full-blown rule of reason test. However, as shown by *California Dental Association v. Federal Trade Commission*, the extensiveness of the legal analysis required under the quick look test will vary based upon the circumstances, details, and logic of the restraint being reviewed.

❖ See Case 41-1

Horizontal and Vertical Restraints A restraint of trade may be classified as either horizontal or vertical. A **horizontal restraint** involves collaboration among competitors at the same level in the chain of distribution. For example, an agreement among manufacturers, among wholesalers, or among retailers would be horizontal.

On the other hand, an agreement made by parties that are not in direct competition at the same level of distribution is a **vertical restraint**. Thus, an agreement between a manufacturer and a wholesaler is vertical.

Although the distinction between horizontal and vertical restraints can become blurred, it often determines whether a restraint is illegal *per se* or should be judged by the rule of reason test. For instance, horizontal market allocations are illegal *per se*, whereas vertical market allocations are subject to the rule of reason test.

Concerted Action Section 1 does not prohibit unilateral conduct; rather, it forbids **concerted action**. Thus, one person or business by itself cannot violate the section. An organization has the "right to deal, or refuse to deal, with whomever it likes, as long as it does so independently." *Monsanto Co. v. Spray-Rite Service Corporation*, 465 U.S. 752 (1984). For example, if a manufacturer announces its resale prices in advance and refuses to deal with those who disagree with the pricing, there is no violation of Section 1 because the manufacturer has acted alone. On the other hand, if a manufacturer and its retailers together agree that the manufacturer will sell only to those retailers who agree to sell at a specified price, there may be a violation of Section 1.

For purposes of the concerted action requirement, a firm and its employees are viewed as one entity. The same rule is also true for a corporation and its wholly owned subsidiaries; thus, the Sherman Act is not violated when a parent and its wholly owned subsidiary agree to a restraint in trade. *Copperwald Corp. v. Independence Tube Corp.*, 467 U.S. 752 (1984). The Supreme Court has yet to decide, however, whether a parent and its partially owned subsidiary may violate Section 1.

The concerted action requirement may be established by an express agreement. Not surprisingly, however, an express agreement often is nonexistent, leaving the court to infer an agreement between the parties from circumstantial evidence:

No formal agreement is necessary to constitute an unlawful conspiracy. Often crimes are a matter of inference deduced from the acts of the person accused and done in pursuance of a criminal purpose. Where the conspiracy is proved, as here, from the evidence of the action taken in concert by the parties to it, it is all the more convincing proof of an intent to exercise the power of exclusion acquired through the conspiracy. The essential combination or conspiracy in violation of the Sherman Act may be found in a course of dealings or other circumstances as well as in any exchange of words. . . . Where the circumstances are such as to warrant a jury in finding that the conspirators had a unity of purpose or a common design and understanding, or a meeting of minds in an unlawful arrangement, the conclusion that a conspiracy is established is justified. *American Tobacco Co. v. United States*, 328 U.S. 781 (1946).

Nonetheless, similar patterns of conduct among competitors, called **conscious parallelism**, are not sufficient in themselves to suggest a conspiracy in violation of Section 1. Actual conspiracy requires an additional factor, such as complex action that, to benefit the competitors, requires the participation of each or indications of a traditional conspiracy, such as identical sealed bids from each competitor.

Joint ventures, which are discussed in Chapter 31, are a form of business association organized to carry out a particular business enterprise. Competitors frequently will pool their resources to share costs and to eliminate wasteful redundancy.

The validity under antitrust law of a joint venture generally depends on the competitors' primary purpose in forming it. A joint venture that was not formed to fix prices or divide markets will be judged under the rule of reason.

However, because uncertainty about the legality of joint ventures seemed to discourage their use for joint research and development, Congress passed the National Cooperative Research Act to facilitate such applications. The Act provides that joint ventures in the research and development of new technology are to be judged under the rule of reason test and that treble damages do not apply to ventures formed in violation of Section 1 if those forming the venture have notified the Justice Department and the Federal Trade Commission (FTC) of their intent to form the joint venture.

http: National Cooperative Research Act: http://www4.law.
cornell.edu/uscode/15/4301.html
**Department of Justice Antitrust Division and Federal
Trade Commission, Joint Venture Guidelines:**
http://www.usdoj.gov/atr/public/guidelines/jointindex.htm

Price Fixing Price fixing is an agreement with the purpose or effect of inhibiting price competition; such an agreement may attempt to raise, depress, fix, peg, or stabilize prices. Price fixing is the primary and most serious example of a *per se* violation under the Sherman Act. As held in *United States v. Socony-Vacuum Oil Co.*, 310 U.S. 150 (1940), all **horizontal** price-fixing agreements are illegal *per se*. This prohibition not only covers any agreement between sellers to establish the *maximum* prices at which certain commodities or services will be offered for sale but encompasses agreements establishing *minimum* prices as well.

The U.S. Supreme Court has condemned not only agreements among horizontal competitors that directly fix prices but also agreements whose effect on price is indirect. For example, in *Catalano, Inc. v. Target Sales, Inc.*, 446 U.S. 643 (1980), the Court held that an agreement among beer wholesalers to eliminate interest-free short-term credit on sales to beer retailers was illegal *per se*. The Court viewed the credit terms "as an inseparable part of price" and concluded that the agreement to eliminate interest-free short-term credit was equivalent to an agreement to eliminate discounts and was thus an agreement to fix prices.

Similarly, it is illegal *per se* for a seller to fix the price at which purchasers must resell its product. This **vertical** form of price fixing—usually called retail price maintenance—is considered a *per se* violation of Section 1.

Despite its early and consistent condemnation of resale price maintenance agreements, the U.S. Supreme Court has found no Section 1 violation when a manufacturer who announces in advance that it will not sell to dealers who cut prices then ceases to do business with dealers who actually do

so. Not surprisingly, courts sometimes have difficulty distinguishing between an illegal resale price maintenance agreement and a manufacturer's legal refusal to deal with a retailer who refuses to charge the manufacturer's dictated minimum price.

In a recent case, *State Oil Company v. Khan* (Case 41-2), the U.S. Supreme Court dealt with whether manufacturers' restrictions on the maximum resale price violate the antitrust laws. Overruling a thirty-year-old precedent, the Court held that vertical maximum price fixing is not *per se* illegal but instead is to be judged by a rule of reason standard.

◊ See Case 41-2

Market Allocations Direct price fixing is not the only way to control prices. Another method involves **market allocation**, whereby competitors agree not to compete with each other in specific markets, which may be defined by geographic area, customer type, or product class. All **horizontal** agreements to divide markets have been declared illegal *per se*, because they confer upon the firm remaining in the market a monopolistic control over price. Thus, if Suny and RGE, both manufacturers of color televisions, agree that Suny shall have the exclusive right to sell color televisions in Illinois and Iowa and that RGE shall have the exclusive right in Minnesota and Wisconsin, Suny and RGE have committed a *per se* violation of Section 1 of the Sherman Act. Likewise, if Suny and RGE agree that Suny shall have the exclusive right to sell color televisions to Sears and that RGE shall sell exclusively to JC Penney, or that Suny shall have the exclusive right to manufacture nineteen-inch color televisions while RGE alone manufactures fifteen-inch sets, they are also in *per se* violation of Section 1 of the Sherman Antitrust Act. Horizontal market allocations may be found not only on the manufacturing level but also on the wholesale or retail level.

No longer illegal *per se*, **vertical** territorial and customer restrictions are now judged by the rule of reason. This change in approach resulted from a U.S. Supreme Court decision that mandated the lower Federal courts to balance the positive effect of vertical market restrictions upon interbrand competition against the negative effects upon intrabrand competition. Consequently, in some situations, vertical market restrictions will be found legitimate if, on balance, they do not inhibit competition in the relevant market.

In 1985, the U.S. Department of Justice issued a "market structure screen," under which the Justice Department will not challenge restraints by a firm having less than 10 percent of the relevant market or a "Vertical Restraint Index" (a measure of relative market share) indicating that neither collusion nor exclusion is possible. The concept of relevant market is discussed later, in the section on monopolization.

Boycotts As noted above, Section 1 of the Sherman Act applies not to unilateral action but only to agreements or combinations.

Accordingly, a seller's refusal to deal with any particular buyer does not violate the act, and a manufacturer thus can refuse to sell to a retailer who persists in selling below the manufacturer's suggested retail price. On the other hand, when two or more firms agree not to deal with a third party, their agreement constitutes a **concerted refusal to deal**, or a group boycott, which may violate Section 1 of the Sherman Act. Such a boycott may be clearly anticompetitive, eliminating competition or reducing market entry.

Some group boycotts are illegal *per se*, while others are subject to the rule of reason. Group boycotts designed to eliminate a competitor or to force that competitor to meet a group standard are illegal *per se* if the group has market power. On the other hand, cooperative arrangements "designed to increase economic efficiency and render markets more, rather than less, competitive" are subject to the rule of reason.

Finally, most courts hold that the *per se* rule of illegality for concerted refusals to deal extends only to horizontal boycotts, not to vertical refusals to deal. Most courts have held that a rule of reason test should govern all nonprice vertical restraints, including concerted refusals to deal.

Tying Arrangements A tying arrangement occurs when the seller of a product, service, or intangible (the "tying" product) conditions its sale on the buyer's purchasing a second product, service, or intangible (the "tied" product) from the seller. For example, assume that Xerox, a major manufacturer of photocopying equipment, were to require that all purchasers of its photocopiers also purchase from Xerox all of the paper they would use with the copiers. Xerox thereby would tie the sale of its photocopier—the *tying* product—to the sale of paper—the *tied* product.

Because tying arrangements limit buyers' freedom of choice and may exclude competitors, the law closely scrutinizes such agreements. A tying arrangement exists where a seller exploits its economic power in one market to expand its empire into another market. When the seller has considerable economic power in the tying product and more than an insubstantial amount of interstate commerce is affected in the tied product, the tying arrangement will be *per se* illegal. The courts may establish a seller's economic power by showing that (1) the seller occupied a dominant position in the tying market, (2) the seller's product enjoys an advantage not shared by its competitors in the tying market, or (3) a substantial number of customers have accepted the tying arrangement, and the sole explanation for their willingness to comply is the seller's economic power in the tying market. If the seller lacks economic power, the tying arrangement is judged by the rule of reason test.

◆ SEE FIGURE 41-1　**Restraints of Trade under Sherman Act**

◊ SEE CASE 41-3

Monopolies

Economic analysis indicates that a monopolist will use its power to limit production and increase prices. Accordingly, a monopolistic market will produce fewer goods than a competitive market would and will sell those goods at higher prices. To address the problem of monopolization, Section 2 of the Sherman Act prohibits monopolies and all attempts or conspiracies to monopolize. Thus, Section 2 prohibits both agreements among businesses and, unlike Section 1, unilateral conduct by one firm.

Monopolization Although the language of Section 2 appears to prohibit without exception *all* monopolization, the courts have required that in addition to merely possessing market power, a firm must have either attained the monopoly power unfairly or abused that power, once attained. Possession of monopoly power is not in itself considered a violation of

◆ FIGURE 41-1　　　　**Restraints of Trade under Sherman Act**

Type of Restraint	Standard	
	Per Se Illegal	Rule of Reason
Price fixing	Horizontal Vertical (minimum)	Vertical (maximum)
Market allocations	Horizontal	Vertical
Group boycotts or refusals to deal	Horizontal, Vertical (minority)	Vertical (majority)
Tying arrangements	If seller has economic power in tying product and affects a substantial amount of interstate commerce in the tied product	If seller lacks economic power in tying product

Section 2 because a firm may have obtained such power through its skills in developing, marketing, and selling products; that is, through the very competitive conduct that the antitrust laws are designed to promote.

Because it is extremely rare to find an unregulated industry with only one firm, determining the presence of monopoly power involves defining the degree of market dominance that constitutes such power. **Monopoly power** is the ability to control prices or to exclude competitors from the marketplace. In grappling with this question of power, the courts have developed a number of criteria, but the prevalent test is market share. A market share greater than 75 percent generally indicates monopoly power, while a share less than 50 percent does not. A share between 50 percent and 75 percent share is inconclusive.

Market share is a firm's fractional share of the total relevant product and geographic markets, but defining these relevant markets is often a difficult and subjective task for the courts. The relevant *product market* includes products that are substitutable for the firm's product on the basis of price, quality, and elasticity. For example, although brick and wood siding are both used on building exteriors, they would not likely be considered part of the same product market. On the other hand, Coca-Cola and Pepsi are both soft drinks and would be considered part of the same product market.

The relevant *geographic market* is that territory in which the firm makes sales of its products or services. This may be at the local, regional, or national level. For instance, the relevant geographic market for the manufacture and sale of aluminum might be national whereas that of a taxicab operating company would be local. The scope of a geographic market depends upon factors such as transportation costs, the type of product or services, and the location of competitors and customers.

If sufficient monopoly power has been proved, the law then must show that the firm has engaged in **unfair conduct**. The courts, however, have yet to agree upon what constitutes such conduct. One judicial approach is to place upon a firm possessing monopoly power the burden of proving that it acquired such power passively or that the power was "thrust" upon it. An alternative view is that monopoly power, when coupled with conduct designed to exclude competitors, violates Section 2. A third approach requires monopoly power plus some type of predatory practice, such as pricing below marginal costs. For example, one case that adopted the third approach held that a firm does not violate Section 2 of the Sherman Act if it attained its market share through either (1) research, technical innovation, or a superior product, or (2) ordinary marketing methods available to all. *Telex Corp. v. IBM*, 510 F.2d 894 (10th Cir. 1975).

The U.S. Supreme Court decision in *Aspen Skiing Co. v. Aspen Highlands Skiing Corp.*, 472 U.S. 585 (1985), appears to combine these approaches. The Court held that "[i]f a firm has been attempting to exclude rivals on some basis other than efficiency, it is fair to characterize its behavior as predatory."

To date, however, the U.S. Supreme Court has yet to define the exact conduct, beyond the mere possession of monopoly power, that violates Section 2. To do so, the Court must resolve the complex and conflicting policies this most basic question regarding monopolies involves. On the one hand, condemning fairly acquired monopoly power—that acquired "merely by virtue of superior skill, foresight, and industry"—penalizes firms that compete effectively. On the other hand, permitting firms with monopoly power to continue provides them the opportunity to lower output and raise prices, thereby injuring consumers.

❧ **SEE CASE 41-3**

Attempts to Monopolize Section 2 also prohibits attempts to monopolize. As with monopolization, the courts have had difficulty developing a standard that distinguishes undesirable conduct likely to engender a monopoly from healthy competitive conduct. The standard test applied by the courts requires proof of a specific intent to monopolize plus a dangerous probability of success; however, this test neither defines an "intent" nor provides a standard of power by which to measure "success." Recent cases suggest that the greater the measure of market power a firm acquires, the less flagrant must its conduct be to constitute an attempt. These cases do not, however, specify any threshold level of market power.

Conspiracies to Monopolize Section 2 also condemns conspiracies to monopolize. Few cases involve this offense alone, as any conspiracy to monopolize would also constitute a combination in restraint of trade in violation of Section 1. Because of the overlap between these two provisions, some scholars have stated that the offense of conspiracy to monopolize is "redundant."

CLAYTON ACT

In 1914, Congress strengthened the Sherman Act by adopting the Clayton Act, which was expressly designed "to supplement existing laws against unlawful restraints and monopolies." The Act is intended to stop trade practices before they become restraints of trade or monopolies forbidden by the Sherman Act. The Clayton Act provides only for civil actions, not for criminal penalties. Private parties may bring civil actions in Federal court for treble damages and attorneys' fees. In addition, the Justice Department and the FTC are authorized to bring civil actions, including proceedings in equity, to prevent and restrict violations of the Act.

The substantive provisions of the Clayton Act deal with price discrimination, tying contracts, exclusive dealing, mergers, and interlocking directorates. Section 2, which deals with price discrimination, was amended and rewritten by the

Robinson-Patman Act, discussed later. In addition, the Clayton Act exempts labor, agricultural, and horticultural organizations from all antitrust laws.

http: **Clayton Act:** http://www4.law.cornell.edu/uscode/ 15/12.html

Tying Contracts and Exclusive Dealing

Section 3 of the Clayton Act prohibits tying arrangements and exclusive dealing, selling, or leasing arrangements which prevent purchasers from dealing with the seller's competitors and which *may* substantially lessen competition or *tend* to create a monopoly. This section is intended to attack incipient anticompetitive practices before they ripen into violations of Section 1 or 2 of the Sherman Act. Unlike the Sherman Act, however, Section 3 applies only to practices involving commodities, not to those that involve services, intangibles, or land.

Tying arrangements, which were discussed in the sections covering the Sherman Act, have been labeled by the Supreme Court as serving "hardly any purpose beyond the suppression of competition." Although the Court at one time indicated that different standards applied under the Sherman Act and the Clayton Act, recent lower court cases suggest that the same rules now govern both types of actions.

Exclusive dealing arrangements are agreements by which the seller or lessor of a product conditions the agreement upon the buyer's or lessor's promise not to deal in the goods of a competitor. For example, a manufacturer of razors might require retailers wishing to sell its line of shaving equipment to agree not to carry competing merchandise. Such conduct, although treated more leniently than tying arrangements, violates Section 3 if it tends to create a monopoly or may substantially lessen competition. The courts regard exclusive dealing arrangements more tolerantly because such arrangements may be procompetitive to the extent that they benefit buyers, and thus, indirectly, ultimate consumers, by ensuring supplies, deterring price increases, and enabling long-term planning on the basis of known costs.

Mergers

In the United States, corporate mergers have played a significant role in reshaping both the structure of corporations and our economic system. Mergers are horizontal, vertical, or conglomerate, depending upon the relationship between the acquirer and the acquired company. A **horizontal merger** involves the acquisition by a company of all or part of the stock or assets of a competing company. For example, if IBM were to acquire Apple, this would be a horizontal merger. A **vertical merger** is a company's acquisition of one of its customers or suppliers. A vertical merger is a *forward* merger if the acquiring company purchases a customer, such as the purchase of Revco Discount Drug Stores by Procter & Gamble. A vertical merger is a *backward* merger if the acquiring company purchases a supplier; for example, Circuit City's purchase of Maytag Appliance. The third type of merger, the **conglomerate merger**, is a catchall category that covers all acquisitions not involving a competitor, customer, or supplier.

Section 7 of the Clayton Act prohibits a corporation from merging or acquiring stock or assets of another corporation where such action would lessen competition substantially or would tend to create a monopoly.

> Section 7 of the Clayton Act was intended to arrest the anticompetitive effects of market power in their incipiency. The core question is whether a merger may substantially lessen competition, and necessarily requires a prediction of the merger's impact on competition, present and future. The section can deal only with probabilities, not with certainties. And there is certainly no requirement that the anticompetitive power manifest itself in anticompetitive action before § 7 can be called into play. If the enforcement of § 7 turned on the existence of actual anticompetitive practices, the congressional policy of thwarting such practices in their incipiency would be frustrated. *F.T.C. v. Procter & Gamble Co.*, 386 U.S. 568 (1967).

The principal objective of the antitrust law governing mergers is to maintain competition. Accordingly, horizontal mergers are scrutinized most stringently. Factors that the courts consider in reviewing the legality of a horizontal merger include the market share of each of the merging firms, the degree of industry concentration, the number of firms in the industry, entry barriers, market trends, the strength of other competitors in the industry, the character and history of the merging firms, market demand, and the extent of industry price competition. The leading Supreme Court cases on horizontal mergers date from the 1960s and early 1970s. Since then, lower Federal courts, the Department of Justice, and the FTC have emphasized antitrust's goal of promoting economic efficiency. Accordingly, while the Supreme Court cases remain the law of the land, recent lower court decisions reflect a greater willingness to tolerate industry concentrations. Nevertheless, the government continues to prosecute, and the courts continue to condemn, horizontal mergers that are likely to hurt consumers.

Though vertical mergers are far less likely to be challenged, the Justice Department and the FTC have attacked vertical mergers that threatened to raise entry barriers in the industry or to foreclose other firms in the acquiring firm's industry from competitively significant customers or suppliers. While the Supreme Court has not decided a vertical merger case since 1972, recent decisions indicate that at least some lower courts have been willing to condemn only those vertical mergers that clearly show anticompetitive effects.

Finally, conglomerate mergers have been challenged only (1) where one of the merging firms would be highly likely to enter the market of the other firm or (2) where the merged company would be disproportionately large as compared with the largest competitors in its industry.

The Justice Department and the FTC have both indicated that they will be primarily concerned with horizontal mergers in highly or moderately concentrated industries and that they question the benefits of challenging vertical and conglomerate mergers. Both the Justice Department and the FTC have justified this policy on the basis that the latter two types of mergers are necessary to transfer assets to their most productive use and that any challenge to such mergers would impose costs on consumers without corresponding benefits.

Antitrust law, as currently applied, focuses on the size of the merged firm in relation to the relevant market, not on the resulting entity's absolute size. In 1992 (subsequently revised in 1997), the Justice Department and the FTC jointly issued new Horizontal Merger Guidelines to replace their earlier and separate guidelines. In doing so, the two agencies sought to prevent market power that results in "a transfer of wealth from buyers to sellers or a misallocation of resources." The guidelines are designed to provide an analytical framework to judge the impact of potential mergers:

> The process of assessing market concentration, potential adverse competitive effects, entry, efficiency and failure is a tool that allows the Agency to answer the ultimate inquiry in merger analysis: whether the merger is likely to create or enhance market power or to facilitate its exercise.

Moreover, the guidelines clearly indicate that neither agency will apply them mechanically.

The 1992 and 1997 guidelines, like their earlier counterparts, quantify market concentration through the Herfindahl-Hirschman Index (HHI) and measure a horizontal merger's impact on the index. This concentration index is calculated by summing the squares of the individual market shares of all firms in the market. An industry with only one firm would have an HHI of 10,000 (100^2). With two firms of equal size, the index would be 5,000 ($50^2 + 50^2$); with five firms of equal size, the result would be 2,000 ($20^2 + 20^2 + 20^2 + 20^2 + 20^2$). The increase a merger would cause in the index is calculated by doubling the product of the merging firms' market shares. For example, the merger of two firms with market shares of 5 percent and 10 percent respectively would increase the index by 100 ($5 \times 10 \times 2 = 100$).

The guidelines use three categories of market concentration to analyze horizontal mergers and to determine the likelihood of governmental opposition, based on the increase the proposed merger would cause in the index. The three categories are classified according to the postmerger HHI. If the postmerger figure is below 1,000, the agencies are unlikely to challenge the merger without regard to the increase the merger would cause in the index. For postmerger HHIs between 1,000 and 1,800, the department will examine the increase in HHI due to the merger. Increases of less than 100 are unlikely to generate a challenge, but those greater than 100 raise significant competitive concerns that mandate an examination of

other factors. When the postmerger HHI is above 1,800, an increase of more than 50 points also will raise significant competitive concerns and thus force an examination of other factors; furthermore, the department is likely to challenge any merger contributing an increase of more than 100, for such a merger is presumed to enhance market power.

In 1987, the National Association of Attorneys General, composed of the Attorneys General of the fifty States and five U.S. territories and protectorates, promulgated its own set of guidelines for horizontal mergers. Intended to apply to enforcement actions brought by the State Attorneys General under Federal and State antitrust statutes, the State guidelines place a greater emphasis on preventing transfers of wealth from consumers to producers than do the Federal guidelines. Accordingly, the State Attorneys General would be more likely to challenge certain mergers than would the Federal government.

`http:` **Herfindahl-Hirschman Index:** http://www.usdoj.gov/atr/ public/guidelines/merger.txt

◆ SEE CASE 41-4

ROBINSON-PATMAN ACT

Section 2 of the Clayton Act originally prohibited only sellers from differentially pricing their products to injure local or regional competitors. In 1936, in an attempt to limit the power of large purchasers, Congress amended Section 2 of the Clayton Act by adopting the Robinson-Patman Act, which further prohibited **price discrimination** in interstate commerce involving commodities of like grade and quality. Thus, the Act prohibits buyers from inducing and sellers from granting discrimination in prices. To constitute a violation, the price discrimination must substantially lessen competition or tend to create a monopoly.

Under this Act, a seller of goods may not grant discounts to buyers, including allowances for advertisements, counter displays, and samples, unless the seller offers the same discounts to all other purchasers on proportionately equal terms. The Act also prohibits other types of discounts, rebates, and allowances and makes it unlawful to sell goods at unreasonably low prices for the purpose of destroying competition or eliminating a competitor. Furthermore, the Act makes it unlawful for a person knowingly to "induce or receive" an illegal discrimination in price, thus imposing liability on the buyer as well as the seller. Violation of the Robinson-Patman Act, with limited exceptions, is civil, not criminal, in nature. The Act does permit price differentials that are justified by proof of either a cost savings to the seller or a good-faith price reduction to meet the lawful price of a competitor.

`http:` Robinson-Patman Act: http://www4.law.cornell.edu/
uscode/15/13.html

Primary-Line Injury

In enacting Section 2 of the Clayton Act in 1914, Congress was concerned with sellers who sought to harm or eliminate their competitors through price discrimination. Injuries accruing to a seller's competitors are called "primary-line" injuries. Because the Act forbids price discrimination only where such discrimination may substantially lessen competition or tend to create a monopoly, the plaintiff in a Robinson-Patman primary-line injury case must either show that the defendant, with the intent to harm competition, has engaged in predatory pricing or present a detailed market analysis that demonstrates how the defendant's price discrimination actually harmed competition. To prove predatory intent, a plaintiff may rely either on direct evidence of such intent or, more commonly, on inferences drawn from the defendant's conduct, such as a significant period of below-cost or unprofitable pricing. A predatory pricing scheme also may be challenged under the Sherman Act.

Secondary- and Tertiary-Line Injury

In amending Section 2 of the Clayton Act in 1936 through the adoption of the Robinson-Patman Act, Congress was concerned primarily with small buyers, who were harmed by the discounts that sellers granted to large buyers. Injuries accruing to some buyers because of the lower prices granted to other buyers are called "secondary-line" injuries. To prove the required harm to competition, a plaintiff in a secondary-line injury case must either show substantial and sustained price differentials in a market or offer a detailed market analysis that demonstrates actual harm to competition. Because courts have been willing in secondary-line injury cases to infer harm to competition from a sustained and substantial price differential, proving a secondary-line injury generally is easier than proving a primary-line injury.

Tertiary-line injury occurs when the recipient of a favored price passes the benefits of the lower price on to the next level of distribution. Purchasers from other secondary-line sellers are injured in that they do not receive the benefits of the lower price; these purchasers may recover damages from the original discriminating seller.

Cost Justification

If a seller can show that it costs less to sell a product to a particular buyer, the seller may lawfully pass along the cost savings. Section 2(a) provides that the Act does not "prevent differentials which make only due allowance for differences in the cost of manufacture, sale, or delivery resulting from the differing methods or quantities in which . . . commodities are . . . sold or delivered." For example, if Retailer A orders goods from Seller X by the carload, whereas Retailer B orders in small quantities, Seller X, who delivers F.O.B. buyer's warehouse, may pass along the transportation savings to Retailer A. Nonetheless, although it is possible to pass along transportation savings, it is extremely difficult to pass along alleged savings in manufacturing or distribution because of the complexity involved in calculating and proving such savings. Therefore, sellers rarely rely upon the defense of cost justification.

Meeting Competition

A seller may lower his price in a good faith attempt to meet competition. To illustrate:

1. Manufacturer X sells its motor oil to retail outlets for 65 cents per can. Manufacturer Y approaches A, one of Manufacturer X's customers, and offers to sell a comparable type of motor oil for 60 cents per can. Manufacturer X will be permitted to lower its price to A to 60 cents per can and need not lower its price to its other retail customers—B, C, and D. Manufacturer X, however, may not lower its price to A to 55 cents unless it also offers this lower price to B, C, and D.
2. To allow A to meet the lower price that A's competitor, N, charges when selling Manufacturer Y's oil, Manufacturer X will not be permitted to lower its price to A without also lowering its price to B, C, and D.

A seller may beat its competitor's price, however, if it does not know the competitor's price, cannot reasonably determine the competitor's price, and acts reasonably in setting its own price.

◆ **See Figure 41-2** Meeting Competition Defense

FEDERAL TRADE COMMISSION ACT

In 1914, through the enactment of the Federal Trade Commission Act, Congress created the Federal Trade Commission and charged it with the duty to prevent "unfair methods of competition in commerce, and unfair or deceptive acts or practices in commerce." To this end, the five-member commission is empowered to conduct appropriate investigations and hearings and to issue against violators "cease and desist" orders enforceable in the Federal courts. Its broad power has been described by the U.S. Supreme Court:

The "unfair methods of competition," which are condemned by . . . the Act, are not confined to those that were illegal at common law or that were condemned by the Sherman Act. . . . It is also clear that the Federal Trade Commission Act was designed to supplement and bolster the Sherman Act and the Clayton Act . . . *to stop in their incipiency acts and practices*

◆ FIGURE 41-2   **Meeting Competition Defense**

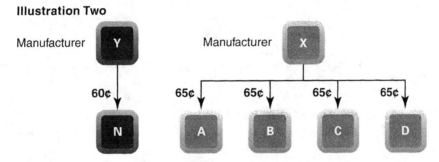

Illustration One

Result: Manufacturer **X** may lower its price to A to 60¢ without lowering its price to B, C, and D.

Illustration Two

Result: Manufacturer **X** may *not* lower its price to A to 60¢ without lowering its price to B, C, and D.

which, when full blown, would violate those Acts. F.T.C. v. Motion Picture Advertising Service Co., 344 U.S. 392 (1953). (Emphasis supplied.)

Complaints may be instituted by the commission, which, after a hearing, "has wide latitude for judgment and the courts will not interfere except where the remedy selected has no reasonable relation to the unlawful practices found to exist." Although the commission most frequently enters a cease and desist order having the effect of an injunction, it may order other relief, such as affirmative disclosure, corrective advertising, and the granting of patent licenses on a reasonable royalty basis. Appeals may be taken from orders of the commission to the U.S. Courts of Appeals, which have exclusive jurisdiction to enforce, set aside, or modify orders of the commission.

In performing its duties, the FTC investigates not only possible violations of the antitrust laws but also unfair methods of competition, such as false and misleading advertisements, false or inadequate product labeling, the passing or palming off of goods as those of a competitor, lotteries, gambling schemes, discriminatory rebate or discount offers, false disparagement of a competitor's goods, false or misleading descriptive names of products, the use of false testimonials, and other unfair trade practices. For a more detailed discussion of the FTC and its powers, see Chapter 42.

http: **Federal Trade Commission Act:** http://www4.law.cornell. edu/uscode/15/41.html

CHAPTER SUMMARY

Sherman Antitrust Act

Restraint of Trade Section 1 prohibits contracts, combinations, and conspiracies that restrain trade
- *Rule of Reason* standard that balances the anticompetitive effects against the procompetitive effects of the restraint
- Per se *Violations* conclusively presumed unreasonable and therefore illegal
- *Quick Look Standard* a modified or abbreviated rule of reason standard
- *Horizontal Restraints* agreements among competitors
- *Vertical Restraints* agreements among parties at different levels in the chain of distribution

Application of Section 1
- *Price Fixing* an agreement with the purpose or effect of inhibiting price competition; both horizontal and minimum vertical agreements are *per se* illegal, while maximum vertical price fixing is judged by the rule of reason
- *Market Allocation* division of markets by customer type, geography, or products; horizontal agreements are *per se* illegal, while vertical agreements are judged by the rule of reason standard
- *Boycott* agreement among competitors not to deal with a supplier or customer; *per se* illegal
- *Tying Arrangement* conditioning a sale of a desired product (tying product) on the buyer's purchasing a second product (tied product); *per se* illegal if the seller has considerable power in the tying product or affects a not-insubstantial amount of interstate commerce in the tied product

Monopolies Section 2 prohibits monopolization, attempts to monopolize, and conspiracies to monopolize
- *Monopolization* requires market power (ability to control price or exclude others from the marketplace) plus either the unfair attainment of the power or the abuse of such power
- *Attempt to Monopolize* specific intent to monopolize, plus a dangerous probability of success
- *Conspiracies to Monopolize*

Sanctions
- *Treble Damages* three times actual loss
- *Criminal Penalties*

Clayton Act

Tying Arrangement prohibited if it tends to create a monopoly or may substantially lessen competition

Exclusive Dealing arrangement by which a party has sole right to a market; prohibited if it tends to create a monopoly or may substantially lessen competition

Merger prohibited if it tends to create a monopoly or may substantially lessen competition
- *Horizontal Merger* one company's acquisition of a competing company
- *Vertical Merger* a company's acquisition of one of its suppliers or customers
- *Conglomerate Merger* the acquisition of a company that is not a competitor, customer, or supplier

Sanctions treble damages

Robinson-Patman Act

Price Discrimination the act prohibits buyers from inducing or sellers from giving different prices to buyers of commodities of similar grade and quality

Chapter 41   Antitrust

829

Injury plaintiff may prove injury to competitors of the seller (primary-line injury), to competitors of other buyers (secondary-line injury), or to purchasers from other secondary-line sellers (tertiary-line injury)
Defenses (1) cost justification, (2) meeting competition, and (3) functional discounts
Sanctions civil (treble damages); criminal in limited situations

---

Federal Trade Commission Act

Purpose to prevent unfair methods of competition and unfair or deceptive practices
Sanctions actions may be brought by the FTC, not by private individuals

---

CASES

CASE 41-1

Restraint of Trade: Standards
CALIFORNIA DENTAL ASSOCIATION v. FEDERAL TRADE COMMISSION
Supreme Court of the United States, 1999
526 U.S. 756, 119 S.Ct.1604, 143 L.Ed.2d 935
http://caselaw.lp.findlaw.com/cgi-bin/getcase.pl?court=US&navby=case&vol=000&invol=97-1625

Souter, J.

* * *

The [California Dental Association] CDA is a voluntary nonprofit association of local dental societies to which some 19,000 dentists belong, including about three-quarters of those practicing in the State. [Citation.] * * * CDA lobbies and litigates in its members' interests, and conducts marketing and public relations campaigns for their benefit. [Citation.]

The dentists who belong to the CDA through these associations agree to abide by a Code of Ethics (Code) including the following § 10:

> "Although any dentist may advertise, no dentist shall advertise or solicit patients in any form of communication in a manner that is false or misleading in any material respect. In order to properly serve the public, dentists should represent themselves in a manner that contributes to the esteem of the public. Dentists should not misrepresent their training and competence in any way that would be false or misleading in any material respect." [Citation.]

* * *

Responsibility for enforcing the Code rests in the first instance with the local dental societies, to which applicants for CDA membership must submit copies of their own advertisements and those of their employers or referral services to assure compliance with the Code. The local societies also actively seek information about potential Code violations by applicants or CDA members. Applicants who refuse to withdraw or revise objectionable advertisements may be denied membership; and

members who, after a hearing, remain similarly recalcitrant are subject to censure, suspension, or expulsion from the CDA.

The Commission brought a complaint against the CDA, alleging that it applied its guidelines so as to restrict truthful, nondeceptive advertising, and so violated § 5 of the FTC Act, [citation]. The complaint alleged that the CDA had unreasonably restricted two types of advertising: price advertising, particularly discounted fees, and advertising relating to the quality of dental services. An Administrative Law Judge (ALJ) * * * found that, although there had been no proof that the CDA exerted market power, no such proof was required to establish an antitrust violation * * * since the CDA had unreasonably prevented members and potential members from using truthful, nondeceptive advertising, all to the detriment of both dentists and consumers of dental services. He accordingly found a violation of § 5 of the FTC Act. [Citation.]

The Commission adopted the factual findings of the ALJ except for his conclusion that the CDA lacked market power, with which the Commission disagreed. The Commission treated the CDA's restrictions on discount advertising as illegal *per se*. In the alternative, the Commission held the price advertising (as well as the nonprice) restrictions to be violations of the Sherman and FTC Acts under an abbreviated rule-of-reason analysis. * * *

The Court of Appeals for the Ninth Circuit affirmed, * * *. The court thought it error for the Commission to have applied *per se* analysis to the price advertising restrictions, finding analysis under the rule of reason required for all the restrictions. But the Court of Appeals went on to explain that the Commission had properly

Consumer Protection

Consumer transactions have increased enormously since World War II, and today consumer debt amounts to more than one trillion dollars. Although the definition varies, a consumer transaction generally involves goods, credit, services, or land acquired for personal, household, or family purposes. Historically, consumers were subject to the rule of *caveat emptor*—let the buyer beware. In recent years, however, the law has largely abandoned this principle and now provides consumers greater protection. Most of this protection takes the form of statutory enactments at both the State and Federal levels, and a wide variety of governmental agencies are charged with enforcing these statutes. This enforcement varies enormously. In some cases, only government agencies may exercise enforcement rights, which they impose through criminal penalties, civil penalties, injunctions, and cease and desist orders. In other cases, in addition to the government's enforcement rights, consumers may privately seek the rescission of contracts and damages for harm resulting from violations of consumer protection laws. Finally, under certain consumer protection statutes such as State "lemon laws," consumers alone may exercise enforcement rights. This chapter examines State and Federal consumer protection agencies and consumer protection statutes.

STATE AND FEDERAL CONSUMER PROTECTION AGENGIES

Through the enactment of laws and regulations, legislatures and administrative bodies at the Federal, State, and local levels all actively seek to shield consumers from an enormous range of harm. The most common abuses in consumer transactions involve the extension of credit, deceptive trade practices, unsafe products, and unfair pricing.

State and Local Consumer Protection Agencies

The many consumer protection agencies at the State and local levels typically deal with fraudulent and deceptive trade practices and fraudulent sales practices, such as false statements about a product's value or quality. In most jurisdictions, consumer protection agencies also help to resolve consumer complaints about defective goods or poor service.

Most State Attorneys General play an active role in consumer protection by enforcing laws against consumer fraud through judicially imposed injunctions and restitution. In recent years, as the Federal government's role in consumer protection has diminished in response to the deregulatory movement, the States correspondingly have expanded their role. The National Association of Attorneys General (NAAG) has been active in coordinating lawsuits among the States. Under NAAG's guidance, several States often will simultaneously file lawsuits against a company that has been engaging in fraudulent acts involving more than one State.

In some instances, however, States have not coordinated their efforts and, as a consequence, have acted inconsistently with respect to consumer protection, especially in health and safety matters. This lack of coordination can present serious problems to companies that sell large numbers of products in interstate commerce. For example, assume that the Glueco Company, which makes and sells glue containing certain toxic chemicals, finds that Connecticut requires warning labels of a certain size and wording, while Indiana requires completely different labels. Glueco must incur the added expenses of placing different labels on different boxes and making sure that each State receives the correct label type. Should numerous States adopt inconsistent labeling requirements, the resulting increase in labeling costs could force Glueco to limit the number of States in which it sells or to raise its prices.

The Federal Trade Commission

At the Federal level, the most significant consumer protection agency is the **Federal Trade Commission** (FTC). Established in 1914, the FTC has two major functions: (1) Under its mandate to prevent "unfair methods of competition in commerce," it is responsible for roughly half of the antitrust enforcement at the Federal level (the FTC's role in antitrust enforcement is discussed in Chapter 41); and (2) under its mandate to prevent "unfair and deceptive" trade practices, it is responsible for stopping fraudulent sales techniques.

To address unfair and deceptive trade practices, the five-member commission (no more than three of whose members may be from the same political party) has the power to issue substantive "trade regulation rules" and to conduct appropriate investigations and hearings. Among the rules it has issued so far are those regulating used car sales, franchising and business opportunity ventures, funeral home services, and the issuance of consumer credit, as well as those requiring a "cooling-off" period for door-to-door sales (discussed later in this chapter).

When considering a deceptive trade practice, the agency often may seek a **cease and desist order** rather than issue a substantive trade rule. A cease and desist order directs a party to stop a certain practice or face punishment such as a fine. In a typical situation, the FTC staff discovers a potentially deceptive practice, investigates the matter, files a complaint against the alleged offender (usually referred to as the respondent), and after a hearing in front of an administrative law judge (ALJ) to determine whether a violation of the law has occurred, obtains a cease and desist order if the ALJ finds that one is necessary. The respondent may appeal to the FTC commissioners to reverse or modify the order. Appeals from orders issued by the commissioners go to the United States Courts of Appeals, which have exclusive jurisdiction to enforce, set aside, or modify orders of the commission.

`http:` **Federal Trade Commission:** http://www.ftc.gov/

Federal Trade Commission Act: http://www4.law. cornell.edu/uscode/15/41.html

Standards The FTC Act does not define the words *unfair* or *deceptive*, and for many years the Commission was criticized for its failure to do so. Partly in response to these criticisms and partly in response to congressional pressure, the Commission issued three policy statements. The first, which addresses the meaning of **unfairness**, provides the following:

> To justify a finding of unfairness the injury must satisfy three tests. It must be substantial; it must not be outweighed by any countervailing benefits to consumers or competition that the practice produces; and it must be an injury that consumers themselves could not reasonably have avoided. The standard, therefore, applies a cost-benefit analysis to the issue of unfairness.

`http:` **FTC Unfairness Policy:** http://www.ftc.gov/bcp/ menu-ads.htm#policy

The second policy statement deals with the meaning of **deception**—the basis of most FTC consumer protection actions. The controversy that the formulation of this statement generated among the commissioners led to its approval by a narrow 3–2 vote and prompted the dissenting commissioners to issue a minority statement. It is generally accepted that the minority position reflected previous FTC policy, whereas the majority position established new policy.

`http:` **FTC Deception Policy:** http://www.ftc.gov/bcp/ menu-ads.htm#policy

The majority position provides that "the Commission will find deception if there is a misrepresentation, omission, or practice that is likely to mislead the consumer acting reasonably in the circumstances, to the consumer's detriment." Thus, the Commission will find an act or practice deceptive if it meets a three-prong test:

> First, there must be a representation, omission, or practice that is likely to mislead the consumer. Second, we examine the practice from the perspective of a consumer acting reasonably in the circumstances. Third, the representation, omission, or practice must be a "material" one. The basic question is whether the act or practice is likely to affect the consumer's conduct or decision with regard to a product or service. If so, the practice is material, and consumer injury is likely because consumers are likely to have chosen differently but for the deception.

Perhaps the most controversial feature of the new policy is the notion that deception can occur only with respect to "consumers acting reasonably."

Deception may occur through either false representation or material omission. Examples of deceptive practices have included advertising that a certain product will save consumers 25 percent on their automotive motor oil, when the product simply replaced a quart of oil in the engine (which normally contains four quarts of oil) and was, in fact, more expensive than the oil it replaced; placing marbles in a bowl of vegetable soup to displace the vegetables from the bottom of the bowl and therefore make the soup appear thicker; and claiming that one drug provides greater pain relief than another, when the evidence was insufficient to prove the claim to the medical community. On the other hand, the FTC will not take action against **puffery** (sales talk composed of general bragging or overstatement that makes no specific factual representation) if the consumer would recognize it as puffery and not be deceived. For example, a statement by a salesperson that "this is one terrific deal" would likely be considered puffery.

Deception can also occur through a failure to disclose important product information if such disclosure is necessary to correct a false and material expectation created in the consumer's mind by the product or by the circumstances of sale. For example, the FTC has insisted that the failure to disclose a product's country of origin constitutes a deceptive omission, based on the agency's view that consumers assume the United States to be the country of origin of a product bearing no other country's name.

The third policy statement issued by the commission involves **ad substantiation**. This policy requires advertisers to have a reasonable basis for their claims at the time they make such claims. Moreover, in determining the reasonableness of a claim, the commission places great weight upon the cost and benefits of substantiation.

 FTC Ad Substantiation Policy: http://www.ftc.gov/bcp/ menu-ads.htm#policy

◆ SEE CASE 42-1

Remedies In addition to the remedies discussed above, the FTC has employed three other potent remedies: (1) affirmative disclosure, (2) corrective advertising, and (3) multiple product orders.

Affirmative disclosure, a remedy frequently employed by the FTC, requires an offender to provide certain information in its advertisement to prevent the ad from being considered deceptive.

Corrective advertising goes beyond affirmative disclosure by requiring an advertiser who has made a deceptive claim to disclose in future advertisements that such prior claims were in fact untrue. The theory behind this remedy is that the effects of a previous deception will continue until expressly corrected.

A **multiple product order** requires a deceptive advertiser to cease and desist from any future deception not only in regard to the product in question but in regard to all products sold by the company. This remedy is particularly useful in dealing with companies that have violated the law repeatedly.

In addition to these traditional remedies, the FTC recently has turned to direct court action in lieu of administrative proceedings. The FTC has the power to seek in a Federal district court a preliminary injunction, pending completion of administrative proceedings, whenever the agency had reason to believe that a person was violating FTC laws or rules. First used to stop mergers, this authority is now often invoked in consumer protection cases. The same provision also grants the agency authority to seek a permanent injunction "in proper cases" without a prior administrative finding that FTC law has been violated.

The Consumer Product Safety Commission

In 1967, President Lyndon Johnson, in accordance with a joint resolution of Congress, appointed a study group to examine the level of product safety in the United States. In a report issued in 1970, the study group, known as the National Commission on Product Safety, disclosed the following:

> Americans—20 million of them—are injured each year in the home as a result of incidents connected with consumer products. Of the total, 110,000 are permanently disabled and 30,000 are killed. A significant number could have been spared if more attention had been paid to hazard reduction. . . . The exposure of consumers to unreasonable consumer product hazards is excessive by any standard of measurement.

Two years later, Congress enacted the Consumer Product Safety Act (CPSA), which established an independent Federal regulatory agency, the Consumer Product Safety Commission (CPSC). The purposes of the CPSA were fourfold:

1. to protect the public against unreasonable risks of injury associated with consumer products;
2. to assist consumers in evaluating the comparative safety of consumer products;
3. to develop uniform safety standards for consumer products and to minimize conflicting State and local regulations; and
4. to promote research and investigation into the causes and prevention of product-related deaths, illnesses, and injuries.

Consisting of five commissioners, no more than three of whom can be from the same political party, the CPSC has authority to set safety standards for consumer products; ban unsafe products; issue administrative "recall" orders to compel repair, replacement, or refunds for products found to present substantial hazards; and seek court orders requiring the recall of "imminently hazardous" products. In addition, Congress requires businesses under CPSC jurisdiction to notify the agency of any information indicating that their products contain defects that "could create" substantial product hazards. By triggering investigations that may lead to product recalls, these reports play a major role in the agency's regulatory activities.

The CPSC also enforces four statutes previously enforced by other agencies. These acts, commonly referred to as the "transferred acts," are the Federal Hazardous Substances Act, the Flammable Fabrics Act, the Poison Prevention Packaging Act, and the Refrigerator Safety Act. Whenever the CPSC can regulate a product under one of these specific acts, rather than under the more general CPSA, the agency is directed to do so unless it finds specifically that regulating the product under the CPSA is in the public interest. Thus, many CPSC regulations, such as those for toys, children's flammable sleepwear, and hazard warnings on household chemical products, arise under the transferred acts rather than under the CPSA.

When first established, the CPSC promulgated a number of **mandatory safety standards**; manufacturers either must follow these rules, which regulate product design, packaging, and warning labels, or face legal sanctions. To save time and money, the agency began to rely on industry to establish **voluntary safety standards**—rules for which noncompliance does not violate the law—reserving mandatory standards for those instances in which voluntary standards proved inadequate. In 1981, Congress enacted legislation requiring the CPSC to rely on voluntary standards "whenever compliance with such voluntary standards would eliminate or adequately reduce the risk of injury addressed and there is substantial compliance with such voluntary standards." Although the 1981 amendments do not bar the CPSC from writing mandatory standards, the CPSC has promulgated few such standards since the law was amended.

http: **Consumer Product Safety Act:** http://www4.law.cornell.edu/uscode/15/2051.html
Consumer Product Safety Commission: http://www.cpsc.gov/

Other Federal Consumer Protection Agencies

Among the many other Federal agencies that play a major consumer protection role are the **National Highway Traffic Safety Administration (NHTSA)** and the **Food and Drug Administration (FDA)**.

Congress established the NHTSA to reduce the number of deaths and injuries resulting from automobile accidents. Highway crashes kill approximately 45,000 Americans each year (equal to 121 fatalities per day) and inflict disabling injuries on 1.6 million others. Under authority similar to that of the CPSC, the NHTSA sets motor vehicle safety standards that promote crash prevention (e.g., rules for safer tires and brakes) and crashworthiness (e.g., interior padding, safety belts, and collapsible steering columns). As with the CPSC, manufacturers are required to report possible safety

defects, and the agency may seek a recall if it determines that a particular automobile model presents a sufficiently great hazard. The NHTSA also is authorized to provide grants-in-aid for State highway safety programs and to conduct research on improving highway safety.

The Food and Drug Administration is the oldest Federal consumer protection agency, dating back to 1906. The FDA enforces the Food, Drug and Cosmetic Act, enacted in 1938, which authorizes the agency to regulate "adulterated and misbranded" products. The agency uses two basic methods of enforcement: it sets standards for products or requires their premarket approval. The products most often subject to premarket approval are drugs. Since 1976, the agency also has had the authority to require the premarket approval of medical devices such as pacemakers and intrauterine devices; the number of such devices required to undergo this approval process is large and increasing.

Although the FTC, CPSC, NHTSA, and FDA are perhaps the best known Federal consumer protection agencies, numerous other agencies also play important roles in this area. For example, the United States Postal Service (USPS) brings many cases every year to close down mail fraud operations and the Securities and Exchange Commission (SEC) protects consumers against fraud in the sale of securities. (The SEC is discussed in Chapter 44.) In addition, many other agencies assist consumers with specific types of problems that fall within the agency's scope.

http: **National Highway Traffic Safety Administration:** http://www.nhtsa.dot.gov/
Food and Drug Administration: http://www.fda.gov/
United States Postal Service: http://www.usps.gov/
Securities and Exchange Commission: http://www.sec.gov/

CONSUMER PURCHASES

Whenever a consumer purchases a product or obtains a service, certain rights and obligations arise. The extent to which these rights and obligations apply to all contracts is discussed more fully in Chapters 9 through 18; the extent to which they apply to a sale of goods under the Uniform Commercial Code (UCC) is discussed in Chapters 21 through 25. Although a number of consumer protection laws have been enacted in recent years, they still leave large areas of a consumer's rights and duties to State contract law. In particular, Article 2 of the UCC provides the basic rules governing when a contract for the sale of goods is formed, what constitutes a breach of contract, and what rights an innocent party has against a party who commits a breach. While many consumer protection laws provide for rights the UCC does not address, they still use its principles as building blocks. For example, the Magnuson-

Moss Warranty Act builds upon the perceived inadequacy of the UCC in permitting sellers to disclaim or modify warranties. Similarly, many States have passed so-called "lemon laws" to provide additional contract cancellation rights to dissatisfied automobile purchasers.

Federal Warranty Protection

A **warranty** creates a duty on the part of the seller to ensure that the goods or services she sells will conform to certain qualities, characteristics, or conditions. A seller, however, is not required to warrant what she sells; and in general she may, by appropriate words, disclaim (exclude) or modify a particular warranty or all warranties. Because a seller's power to disclaim or modify is so flexible, consumer protection laws have been enacted to ensure that consumers understand the warranty protection provided them.

To protect buyers and to prevent deception in selling, Congress enacted the **Magnuson-Moss Warranty Act**, which requires sellers of consumer products to provide adequate information about written warranties. The FTC administers and enforces the Act, which was enacted to alleviate certain reported warranty problems: (1) Most warranties were not understandable; (2) most warrantors disclaimed implied warranties; (3) most warranties were unfair; and (4) in some instances the warrantors did not live up to their warranties. Through the Magnuson-Moss Warranty Act, Congress attempted to make consumer product warranties more comprehensible and to facilitate the satisfactory enforcement of consumer remedies. To accomplish these purposes, the Act provides for:

1. clear and understandable disclosure of the warranty that is to be offered,
2. a description of the warranty as either "full" or "limited,"
3. a prohibition against disclaiming implied warranties if a written warranty is given, and
4. an optional informal settlement mechanism.

The Act applies to consumer products with **written warranties**. A consumer product is any item of tangible personal property that is normally used for family, household, or personal use and is distributed in commerce. The Act does not protect commercial purchasers, who are considered sufficiently knowledgeable, in terms of contracting, to protect themselves; better able to retain attorneys for their ongoing protection; and able to spread the cost of their injuries in the marketplace.

http: **Magnuson-Moss Warranty Act:** http://www4.law. cornell.edu/uscode/15/ch50.html

Presale Disclosure The Act contains presale disclosure provisions, which are calculated to avert confusion and deception

and to enable purchasers to make educated product comparisons. A warrantor must, "to the extent required by the rules of the [Federal Trade] Commission, fully and conspicuously disclose in simple and readily understood language the terms and conditions of such warranty." When it implemented this requirement, the FTC adopted a rule requiring that the text of a warranty be accessible to the consumer. Under that rule, the warranty could be attached to the package, placed on a visible sign, or maintained in a binder. In 1986, the FTC relaxed the rule by permitting stores simply to make warranties available to consumers upon request. Retailers using this option, however, must post signs informing the consumer that the warranties are available. Separate rules apply to mail order, catalog, and door-to-door sales.

Labeling Requirements The second major part of the Act provides for labeling requirements by first dividing written warranties into two categories—limited and full—one of which, for any product costing more than ten dollars, must be designated on the written warranty itself. The purpose of this provision is to enable the consumer to make an initial comparison of her legal rights under certain warranties. The Act provides that under a **full warranty** the warrantor must agree to repair the product to conform with the warranty, without charge; no limitation may be placed on the duration of any implied warranty; the consumer must be given the option of a refund or replacement if repair is unsuccessful; and consequential damages may be excluded only if the warranty conspicuously notes their exclusion. A **limited warranty** is any warranty not designated as full.

Limitations on Disclaimers Most significantly, the Act provides that a written warranty, whether full or limited, cannot disclaim any implied warranty. This provision strikes at the heart of the problems plaguing warranty protection, for, as revealed in an earlier presidential task force report, most written warranties provided limited protection but in return nullified the more valuable implied warranties. Hence, consumers believed—often mistakenly—that the warranties they received and the warranty registration cards they promptly returned to the manufacturer were to their benefit. The Act, on the other hand, provides that a full warranty must not disclaim, modify, or limit any implied warranty and that a limited warranty cannot disclaim or modify any implied warranty but can limit its duration to that of the written warranty, provided that such limitation is reasonable, conscionable, and conspicuously displayed. Some States, however, do not allow limitations in the duration of implied warranties.

For example, GE sells consumer goods to Barry for $150 and provides a written warranty regarding the quality of the goods. GE must designate the warranty as full or limited, depending on its characteristics, and cannot disclaim or modify any implied warranty. On the other hand, if GE had not provided Barry with a written warranty, the Magnuson-Moss Warranty Act would not apply, and GE could then disclaim any and all implied warranties.

◆**See Figure 42-1**   **Magnuson-Moss Act**

State "Lemon Laws"

With the enactment of the Magnuson-Moss Warranty Act, many consumers assumed that automobile manufacturers would feel compelled to offer full warranties to buyers of new cars, thereby giving such buyers the option to obtain a refund or replacement without charge for a defective automobile or defective parts. Automobile sellers, however, opted for limited warranties. In response, virtually all of the State legislatures enacted "**lemon laws**" that attempt to provide new car purchasers with rights that are similar to full warranties under the Magnuson-Moss Warranty Act. Some States have broadened their laws to cover used cars; some also cover motorcycles. There are many different lemon laws, but most define a *lemon* as a car that continues to have a defect that substantially impairs its use, value, or safety, even after the manufacturer has made reasonable attempts to correct the problem. In most States, the opportunity to repair a defect is considered sufficient if the manufacturer made four unsuccessful attempts to fix the problem or the car was out of service for more than thirty days during the year it was sold. If a consumer can prove that her car is a lemon, most lemon laws require the manufacturer either to replace the car or to refund its retail price, less an allowance for the consumer's use of the car. In addition, most lemon laws provide that the consumer may recover attorneys' fees and expenses if the case goes to litigation.

Consumer Right of Rescission

In most cases, a consumer is legally obligated once he has signed a contract. In many States, however, a consumer has by statute a brief time—generally two or three days—during which he may **rescind** an otherwise binding credit obligation if the sale was solicited in his home. Moreover, the FTC has promulgated a trade regulation applicable to door-to-door sales, leases, or rentals of goods and services for twenty-five dollars or more, whether the sale is for cash or on credit. The regulation permits a consumer to rescind a contract within three days of signing. To make the rule effective, the FTC requires sellers to provide a buyer with written notice of her cancellation rights. If the buyer properly cancels, she must make available to the seller, in a condition substantially as good as that in which they were received, any goods the seller has delivered. The seller in turn must, within ten business days of receiving notice of rescission, return any money paid or any negotiable instrument (such as a personal check or a promissory note) executed by the buyer and cancel any security interest arising out of the transaction. If the seller fails to comply, the FTC will consider the noncompliance to be a violation of the Federal Trade Commission Act and will seek appropriate sanctions, such as a cease and desist order and civil penalties. To the extent that State laws on door-to-door sales are directly inconsistent with the FTC rule (e.g., if a State provides only two days for rescission) they are unenforceable.

The right of rescission also exists under the **Federal Consumer Credit Protection Act** (discussed more fully later), which allows a consumer three days during which he may withdraw from any credit obligation secured by a mortgage on his home, unless the extension of credit was made to acquire the dwelling. This right of rescission exists whether the contract was the result of a door-to-door sale or not. If the consumer rescinds,

◆**Figure 42-1**   **Magnuson-Moss Act**

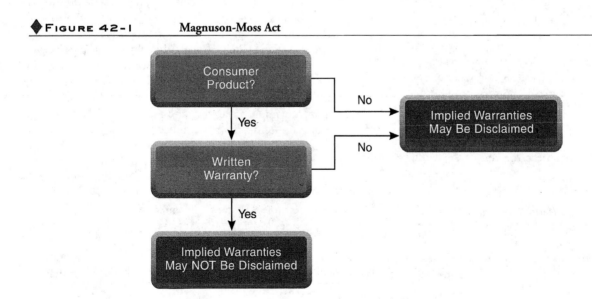

the creditor has twenty days to return any money or property he has received from the consumer.

http: Consumer Credit Protection Act: http://www4.law. cornell.edu/uscode/15/1601.html

The **Interstate Land Sales Full Disclosure Act** applies to sales or leases of 100 or more lots of unimproved land as part of a common promotional plan in interstate commerce. The Act requires a developer to file a detailed "statement of record" containing specified information about the subdivision and the developer with the Department of Housing and Urban Development (HUD) before offering the lots for sale or lease. The developer must provide a property report, which is a condensed version of the statement of record, to each prospective purchaser or lessee. The Act provides that a purchaser or lessee may revoke any contract or agreement for sale or lease at her option within seven days of signing the contract and that the contract must clearly provide this right. A purchaser or lessee who does not receive a property report before signing a contract may revoke the contract within two years from the date of signing.

http: Interstate Land Sales Full Disclosure Act: http://www4. law.cornell.edu/uscode/15/1701.html

◆**SEE FIGURE 42-2** Consumer Rescission Rights

CONSUMER CREDIT TRANSACTIONS

A **consumer credit transaction** is customarily defined as any credit transaction involving subject matter to be used by one of the parties for personal, household, or family purposes. The following are illustrative: Atkins borrows $600 from a bank to pay a dentist bill or to take a vacation; Bevins buys a refrigerator for her home from a department store and agrees to pay the purchase price in twelve equal monthly installments; Carpenter has an oil company credit card that he uses to purchase gasoline and tires for his family car.

Regulation of consumer credit has increased considerably because of the dramatic expansion of consumer credit since World War II and the numerous abuses in credit transactions, including misleading credit disclosures, unfair marketing practices, and oppressive collection methods. In 1968, in response to concerns about consumer credit, Congress passed the **Federal Consumer Credit Protection Act (FCCPA)**, which requires creditors to disclose finance charges (including interest and other charges) and credit extension charges, and sets limits on garnishment proceedings. Since 1968, Congress has added additional titles to this law. Today, it includes the following laws: (1) the Truth-in-Lending Act (including the Fair Credit Billing Act and the Consumer Leasing Act), (2) the Restriction on Garnishment, (3) the Fair Credit Reporting Act, (4) the Equal Credit Opportunity Act, (5) the Fair Debt Collection Practices Act, and (6) the Electronic Fund Transfer Act. Also in 1968, the National Conference of Commissioners on Uniform State Laws (the group that drafted the UCC) promulgated the **Uniform Consumer Credit Code (UCCC)**, which integrated into one recommended law the regulation of all consumer credit transactions—loans and purchases on credit. Though the UCCC has been adopted in only nine States, its impact on the development of consumer credit has extended well beyond their borders.

http: Federal Consumer Credit Protection Act: http://www4.law.cornell.edu/uscode/15/1601.html Uniform Consumer Credit Code: http://www. creditcode.gov.au

Access to the Market

The **Equal Credit Opportunity Act** prohibits all businesses that regularly extend credit from discriminating against any applicant for credit on the basis of sex, marital status, race,

◆**FIGURE 42-2** **Consumer Rescission Rights**

Law	Rescission Period	Door-to-Door Solicitation Required?	Credit or Cash
State "cooling-off" laws	Varies	Yes	Varies
FTC trade regulation	Within 3 days of signing the contract	Yes	Both
Consumer Credit Protection Act (CCPA)	Within 3 days of signing the contract	No	Credit only
Interstate Land Sales Full Disclosure Act	Within 7 days of signing the contract	No	Both

color, religion, national origin, or age. A major congressional goal in passing the Act was to eliminate the lenders' practice of refusing credit to women of childbearing age under the assumption that such women were apt to quit work to have children and thereby reduce their ability to repay credit. Under **Regulation B**, issued by the Federal Reserve Board to implement the Act, and the Women's Business Ownership Act, creditors who are determining an applicant's creditworthiness cannot inquire into or use information about the applicant's marital status or her likelihood of having children.

Under the Act, a creditor has thirty days after receiving a credit application to notify the applicant of action taken, and the creditor must give specific reasons for a denial of credit. Several Federal agencies administer and enforce the Act, under the overall enforcement authority of the FTC. Credit applicants aggrieved by a violation of the Act may recover actual and punitive damages plus attorneys' fees.

http: **Equal Credit Opportunity Act:** http://www4.law.cornell. edu/uscode/15/1691.html

The **Home Mortgage Disclosure Act (HMDA)** was enacted by Congress along with the **Community Reinvestment Act (CRA)** to emphasize to financial institutions the importance of their reinvesting funds in the communities that they serve. Through the HMDA, Congress outlawed geographic discrimination, or *redlining*, the process by which financial institutions refuse to provide reasonable home financing terms to qualified applicants whose homes are located in geographic areas of declining value. In addition, the HMDA requires public disclosure of the financial institution's geographic pattern of mortgage lending. The CRA, by comparison, was intended to encourage financial institutions to meet the credit needs of their local communities. In 1989, Congress adopted a major banking bailout bill, the **Financial Institutions Reform, Recovery, and Enforcement Act (FIRREA)**, which included amendments to the HMDA and the CRA. The amendments expanded the disclosure and reporting requirements for all mortgage lenders and mandated that Federal regulating agencies evaluate and rate CRA performance reports.

Disclosure Requirements

Title One of the FCCPA, also known as the **Truth-in-Lending Act**, has superseded State disclosure requirements relating to credit terms for both consumer loans and credit sales under $25,000. The Act does not cover credit transactions for business, commercial, or agricultural purposes. Creditors in every State not specifically exempted by the Federal Reserve Board must comply with Federal disclosure standards. The board exempts only those States that have disclosure requirements

substantially the same as the Federal requirements and that ensure enforcement of their requirements. The FCCPA does not, however, excuse creditors from compliance with State requirements not covered by, or more stringent than, the FCCPA requirements, so long as the State-required disclosure is not inconsistent with the FCCPA.

Before a consumer formally incurs a contractual obligation for credit, both State and Federal statutes require a creditor to present to the consumer a written statement containing certain information about contract terms. Generally, the required disclosure concerns the cost of credit, such as interest, sales charges, finder's fees, mortgage guarantee insurance, or any mandatory credit life insurance. An important requirement in the Truth-in-Lending Act is that sales finance charges and interest rates must be quoted in terms of an **annual percentage rate (APR)** and must be calculated on a uniform basis. Congress required disclosure of this information to encourage consumers to compare credit terms, to increase competition among financial institutions, and to facilitate economic stability. Enforcement and interpretation of the Truth-in-Lending Act was assigned to several agencies, the two most important being the FTC and the Federal Reserve Board, which issued **Regulation Z** to carry out this responsibility.

Many individuals have claimed that the interest rates charged for credit cards are unfairly excessive and should be limited by legislation. In 1988, statutes for this purpose were proposed in Congress, but none was enacted. Instead, Congress passed the **Fair Credit and Charge Card Disclosure Act** of 1988. The Act, which is consistent with other legislation in the field in that it emphasizes the disclosure of key items, adds to the Truth-in-Lending Act a new section requiring all credit and charge card applications and solicitations to include extensive disclosures whose requirements depend upon the type of card involved and whether the application or solicitation is by mail, telephone, or other means.

Credit Accounts Under the Truth-in-Lending Act a creditor must inform consumers who open revolving or open-end credit accounts about how the finance charge is computed and when it is charged, what other charges may be imposed, and whether the creditor retains or acquires a security interest. Moreover, the Federal Reserve Board in 2000 published a rule requiring marketing material to display clearly a table that shows the APR and other important information such as the annual fee. An **open-end** credit account is one that permits the debtor to enter into a series of credit transactions that he may pay off either in installments or in a lump sum. Examples of this type of credit include most department store credit cards, most gasoline credit cards, VISA cards, and MasterCards. With this type of credit, the creditor is also required to provide a statement of account for each billing period.

Closed-end credit is credit extended for a specified time, during which the debtor generally makes periodic payments in an amount and at a time agreed upon in advance. Examples of this type of credit include most automobile financing agreements, most real estate mortgages, and numerous other major purchases. For nonrevolving or closed-end credit accounts, the creditor must provide the consumer with information about the total amount financed; the cash price; the number, amount, and due date of installments; delinquency charges; and a description of the security, if any.

◆ **See Case 42-2**

ARMs The Federal Reserve Board has amended Regulation Z to deal with variable or adjustable rate mortgages (ARMs). The *ARM disclosure rules* apply to any loan that is (1) a closed-end consumer transaction, (2) secured by the consumer's principal residence, (3) longer than one year in duration, and (4) subject to interest rate variation. This coverage excludes open-end lines of credit secured by the consumer's principal dwelling. A creditor must make the disclosures when he furnishes an application to a prospective borrower or before the creditor receives payment of a nonrefundable fee, whichever occurs first. The ARM disclosure rules require that the creditor provide the consumer with a consumer handbook on ARMs and a loan program disclosure statement covering the terms of each ARM that the creditor offers.

Home Equity Loans In recent years a popular method of consumer borrowing has been the home equity loan. To regulate the disclosures and advertising of these loans, Congress enacted the **Home Equity Loan Consumer Protection Act (HELCPA)**. HELCPA amends the Truth-in-Lending Act to require that lenders provide a disclosure statement and consumer pamphlet at (or, in some limited instances, within three days of) the time they provide an application to a prospective consumer borrower. HELCPA applies to all open-end credit plans for consumer loans that are secured by the consumer's principal dwelling. Unlike other Truth-in-Lending statutes, HELCPA defines a principal dwelling to include second or vacation homes. The disclosure statement must include a statement that (1) a default on the loan may result in the consumer's loss of the dwelling, (2) certain conditions must be met, such as a time by which an application must be submitted to obtain the specified terms, and (3) the creditor, under certain circumstances, may terminate the plan and accelerate the outstanding balance, prohibit the further extension of credit, reduce the plan's credit limit, or impose fees upon the termination of the account. In addition, if the plan contains a fixed interest rate, the creditor must disclose each APR imposed. If the plan involves an ARM, it must include how the rate is computed, the manner in which rates will be changed, the initial rate and how it was determined, the maximum rate change that may occur in any one

year, the maximum rate that can be charged under the plan, the earliest time at which the maximum interest can be reached, and an itemization of all fees imposed by the plan. Regulation Z provides the consumer with the right to rescind such a plan until midnight of the third day following the opening of the plan, until delivery of a notice of the right to rescind, or until delivery of all material disclosures, whichever comes last.

Billing Errors The **Fair Credit Billing Act** went into effect to relieve some of the problems and abuses associated with credit card billing errors. The Act establishes procedures for the consumer to follow in making complaints about specified billing errors and requires the creditor to explain or correct such errors. Billing errors include (1) credit extensions that were never made or were not made in the amount indicated on the billing statement; (2) undelivered or unaccepted goods or services; (3) incorrect recording of payments or credits; and (4) accounting or computational errors. Until the creditor responds to the complaint, it may not take any action to collect the disputed amount, restrict the use of an open-ended credit account because the disputed amount is unpaid, or report the disputed amount as delinquent.

http: **Fair Credit Billing Act:** http://www4.law.cornell.edu/ uscode/15/1666.html

Settlement Charges Congress enacted the **Real Estate Settlement Procedures Act (RESPA)** to provide consumers who purchase a home with greater and more timely information on the nature and costs of the settlement process and to protect them from unnecessarily high settlement charges. The Act, which applies to all Federally related mortgage loans, requires advance disclosure to homebuyers and sellers of all settlement costs, including attorneys' fees, credit reports, title insurance, and, if relevant, an initial escrow account statement. Nearly all first mortgage loans fall within the scope of the Act. RESPA prohibits kickbacks and referral fees and limits the amount homebuyers must place in escrow accounts to insure payment of real estate taxes and insurance. RESPA was amended in 1990 by the National Affordable Housing Act of 1990 to require an annual analysis of escrow accounts. The Act is administered and enforced by the Secretary of Housing and Urban Development.

http: **Real Estate Settlement Procedures Act:** http://www4. law.cornell.edu/uscode/12/2601.html

Contract Terms

Consumer credit is marketed on a mass basis. Frequently, contract documents are printed forms containing blank spaces to accommodate the contractual details the creditor usually will negotiate at the time she extends credit. Standardization and uniformity of contract terms facilitate the transfer of the creditor's rights (in most situations, those of a seller) to a third party, usually a bank or finance company.

Almost all the States impose statutory ceilings on the amount that creditors may charge for the extension of consumer credit. Statutes regulating rates also specify what other charges may be made. For example, charges for insurance, official fees, and taxes usually are not considered part of the finance charge, whereas charges incidental to the extension of credit, such as a service charge or a commission for extending credit, usually are. Any charge that does not qualify as an authorized additional charge is treated as part of the finance charge and is subject to the statutory rate ceiling. Other special permitted charges include delinquency and default charges, charges incurred in connection with storing and repairing repossessed goods for sale, reasonable fees for a lawyer who is not a salaried employee of the creditor, and court costs.

Most statutes require a creditor to permit the debtor to pay her obligation in full at any time prior to the maturity date of the final installment. If the interest charge for the loan period was computed in advance and added to the principal of the loan, a debtor who prepays in full is entitled to a refund of the unearned interest already paid.

Aside from provisions relating to cost, the balance of a credit contract deals with repayment terms and the remedies available to the creditor if payments are delinquent. Usually, payments must be periodic and substantially equal in amount. Balloon payments (loans in which the final payment is much larger than the regular payments; for example, where the monthly installments are $50 and the final installment is $1,000) may be prohibited. Where they are not prohibited, the creditor may be required to refinance the loan at the same rate and with installments in the same amount as the original loan without penalty to the borrower.

In the past, certain purchases involving consumer goods were financed in such a manner that the consumer was legally obligated to make full payment of the price to a third party, even though the dealer from whom she bought the goods had committed fraud or the goods were defective. This occurred when the purchaser executed and delivered to the seller a negotiable promissory note which the seller negotiated to a holder in due course, a third party who purchased the note for value, in good faith, and without notice of its being overdue or of any defenses or claims to it. Though valid against the seller, the buyer's defense that the goods were defective or that the seller had committed fraud was not valid against a holder in due course of the note. To preserve the claims and defenses of consumer buyers and borrowers and to make such claims and defenses available against holders in due course, the FTC adopted a rule that limits the rights of a holder in due course of an instrument that evidences a debt arising out of a consumer

credit contract. The rule applies to sellers and lessors of goods. A discussion of the rule is in Chapter 28.

A similar rule applies to credit card issuers under the Fair Credit Billing Act. The Act preserves a consumer's defenses against the issuer (provided the consumer has made a good faith attempt to resolve the dispute with the seller), but only if (1) the seller is controlled by the card issuer or is under common control with the issuer; (2) the issuer has included the seller's promotional literature in the monthly billing statements sent to the card holder; or (3) the sale involves more than fifty dollars and the consumer's billing address is in the same State as, or within 100 miles of, the seller's place of business.

Consumer Credit Card Fraud

Consumer credit card fraud has become an increasingly serious problem and now totals approximately $200 million per year. In 1984, Congress enacted the **Credit Card Fraud Act**, which closed many of the loopholes in prior law. The Act prohibits the following practices: (1) possessing unauthorized cards, (2) counterfeiting or altering credit cards, (3) using account numbers alone, and (4) using cards obtained from a third party with his consent, even if the third party conspires to report the cards as stolen. It also imposes stiffer, criminal penalties for violation.

The FCCPA protects the credit card holder from loss by limiting to fifty dollars the card holder's liability for another's unauthorized use of the holder's card. The card issuer may collect up to that amount for unauthorized use only if (1) the holder has accepted the card; (2) the issuer has furnished adequate notice of potential liability to the card holder; (3) the issuer has provided the card holder with a statement describing the means by which the holder may notify the card issuer of the loss or theft of the credit card; (4) the unauthorized use occurs before the card holder has notified the card issuer of the loss or theft; and (5) the card issuer has provided a method by which the person using the card can be identified as the person authorized to use the card.

> **http:** **Credit Card Fraud Act:** http://www4.law.cornell.edu/ uscode/18/1029.html

Fair Reportage

Whenever an individual applies for credit, the lender is likely to run a credit check on the applicant, commonly by purchasing a credit report from a credit bureau—a private company that keeps files on consumers and their skill at paying their debts. An applicant whose file indicates that he fails to repay loans or pays them delinquently may have difficulty obtaining credit.

Before passage of the Fair Credit Reporting Act, certain unscrupulous creditors coerced consumers into paying questionable claims by preying on their fears of bad credit ratings.

For example, if today Barry bought an overpriced, malfunctioning vacuum cleaner from the Ajax Vacuum Company based on the false representations of Ajax's salesperson, Barry would have the right to rescind the sale and refuse to pay Ajax. Before the Act, however, if Barry withheld payments, Ajax might have threatened to report him to the credit bureau as being delinquent on his account. This would have been a significant threat because such a report might have ruined Barry's ability to obtain other credit. Accordingly, Barry might have paid Ajax simply to avoid future credit problems. Consumers faced other problems with credit bureaus. In some instances, a credit bureau might simply have made a mistake, such as listing Harry Jones instead of Larry Jones as delinquent, but then have no procedure for, or interest in, correcting the error. In other cases, outdated information concerning a consumer's conduct formed the basis for the denial of credit. These and other perceived credit abuses led Congress to enact the **Fair Credit Reporting Act**, which sets guidelines for credit reports used to secure employment, insurance, and credit.

The Act prohibits consumer reporting agencies from including inaccurate or obsolete information in consumer reports (most information is obsolete after seven years; bankruptcy information becomes obsolete after ten years) and requires consumer reporting agencies to give consumers written, advance notice before making investigative reports. Consumers may request and receive from any consumer reporting agency information regarding (1) the nature and substance of all information on the consumer in the agency's files, (2) the sources of the information, and (3) the names of all recipients to whom the agency has furnished the information for employment purposes within the preceding two years and for other purposes within the preceding six months.

If the consumer believes that the information in the file is inaccurate or incomplete, and so notifies the agency, the agency must then reinvestigate the matter within a reasonable period of time unless the complaint is frivolous or irrelevant. If reinvestigation proves that the information is inaccurate, it must be promptly deleted. If the dispute remains unresolved after reinvestigation, the consumer may submit a brief statement setting forth the nature of the dispute, which the agency must incorporate into the report.

In 1997, Congress amended the Act to restrict the use of credit reports by employers. An employer must now notify the job applicant or current employee that a report may be used and must obtain the applicant's consent prior to requesting an individual's credit report from a credit bureau. In addition, prior to taking an adverse action (refusal to hire, reassignment or termination, or denial of a promotion) against the applicant or employee, the employer must provide the individual with a "pre-adverse action disclosure," which must contain the credit report and a copy of the FTC's "A Summary of Your Rights Under the Fair Credit Reporting Act."

 Fair Credit Reporting Act: http://www4.law.cornell.edu/uscode/15/1681.html

❖ **SEE CASE 42-3**

CREDITORS' REMEDIES

A primary concern of creditors involves their rights should a debtor default or become tardy in payment. When the credit charge is precomputed, the creditor may impose a delinquency charge for late payments, subject to statutory limits for such charges. If, instead of being delinquent, the consumer defaults, the creditor may declare the entire balance of the debt immediately due and payable and may sue on the debt. The other courses of action to which the creditor may turn depend upon his security. Security provisions included in consumer credit contracts may require a cosigner, an assignment of wages, a security interest in the goods sold, a security interest in other real or personal property of the debtor, and a confession of judgment clause (i.e., an agreement by the debtor giving the creditor the authority to enter judgment against the debtor).

Wage Assignments and Garnishment

Wage assignments are prohibited by some States. In most States and under the FCCPA, a limitation is imposed on the amount that may be deducted from an individual's wages during any pay period. In addition, the FCCPA prohibits an employer from discharging an employee solely because of a creditor's exercise of an assignment of wages in connection with any one debt.

Even where wage assignments are prohibited, the creditor may still reach a consumer's wages through garnishment. But garnishment is available only in a court proceeding to enforce the collection of a judgment. The FCCPA and State statutes contain exemption provisions which limit the amount of wages subject to garnishment.

Security Interests

In the case of credit sales, the seller may retain a security interest in the goods sold. Many States impose restrictions on other security the creditor may obtain. Where the debt is secured by property as collateral, the creditor, upon default by the debtor, may take possession of the property and, subject to the provisions of the UCC, either retain it in full satisfaction of the debt or sell it and, if the proceeds are less than the outstanding debt, sue the debtor for the balance and obtain a deficiency judgment. The UCC provides that where a buyer of goods has paid 60 percent of the purchase price or 60 percent of a loan secured by consumer goods, the secured creditor may not retain the property in full satisfaction but must sell the goods and pay to the buyer that part of the sale proceeds in excess of the balance due. In addition, Federal regulation prohibits a credit seller or lender from obtaining a consumer's grant of a nonpossessory security interest in household goods. Household goods include clothing, furniture, appliances, kitchenware, personal effects, one radio, and one television; such goods specifically exclude works of art, other electronic entertainment equipment, antiques, and jewelry. This rule, which does not apply to purchase money security interests or to pledges, prevents a lender or seller from obtaining a non-purchase money security interest covering the consumer's household goods. Secured transactions are discussed in Chapter 38.

Debt Collection Practices

Abuses by some collection agencies led Congress to pass the **Fair Debt Collection Practices Act**, which makes abusive, deceptive, and unfair practices by debt collectors in collecting consumer debts illegal. The Act does not apply to creditors who use their own names in trying to collect debts themselves. Rather, it applies only to those who collect debts for others. This does not mean that creditors are free to use improper methods to collect debts. Most States have laws or common law decisions that prohibit unfair debt collection practices.

Before the Act, many debt collectors contacted third parties, such as relatives, neighbors, or employers, to inquire about the whereabouts or financial condition of the debtor. In doing so, the collectors made sure to tell the third parties who they were and why they were calling. To avoid the embarrassment resulting from such contacts, many debtors would hasten to pay their debts, even questionable ones. To prevent these often unfair and unnecessary disclosures, the Act bars, except in certain narrow circumstances, debt collectors from communicating with third parties about a consumer's debt. The Act does permit debt collectors to contact a third party to ascertain the location of the consumer, but it prohibits them from disclosing that they are debt collectors and from stating that the consumer owes any debt.

The Act forbids other abusive collection practices, including (1) communication with the consumer at unusual or inconvenient hours; (2) communication with the consumer if he is represented by an attorney; (3) harassing, oppressive, or abusive conduct, such as threats of violence or the use of obscene language; (4) false, deceptive, or misleading representations, such as false claims that the debt collector is an attorney or a government official, or that the consumer has committed a crime; or (5) other unfair or unconscionable means to collect or attempt to collect a debt, such as a false threat of a lawsuit.

The Act requires a debt collector, within five days of the initial communication with a consumer, to provide the consumer with a written notice that includes (1) the amount of the debt; (2) the name of the current creditor; and (3) a statement informing the consumer that she can request verification of the alleged debt.

The Act gives consumers one extremely powerful right in dealing with debt collectors. If a consumer notifies a debt collector in writing that the consumer refuses to pay a debt or that the consumer wishes the debt collector to cease further communication with the consumer, the debt collector must stop further communication except to notify the consumer that the creditor or collector may invoke specified remedies such as filing a lawsuit to collect the debt. Consumers have the right to seek damages from debt collectors for violations of the Act. In addition, the FTC has authority for administrative enforcement of its provisions.

 Fair Debt Collection Practices Act: http://www4.law. cornell.edu/uscode/15/1692.html

❖ **See Case 42-4**

CHAPTER SUMMARY

Federal Trade Commission

Purpose to prevent unfair methods of competition and unfair or deceptive acts or practices

Standards
- *Unfairness* requires injury to be (1) substantial, (2) not outweighed by any counter-vailing benefit, and (3) unavoidable by reasonable consumer action
- *Deception* misrepresentation, omission, or practice that is likely to mislead the consumer acting reasonably in the circumstances
- *Ad Substantiation* requires advertisers to have a reasonable basis for their claims

Remedies
- *Cease and Desist Order* command to stop doing the act in question
- *Affirmative Disclosure* requires an advertiser to include certain information in its ad so that the ad is not deceptive

- *Corrective Advertising* requires an advertiser to disclose that previous ads were deceptive
- *Multiple Product Order* requires an advertiser to cease and desist from deceptive statements regarding all products it sells

---

Consumer Health and Safety

Consumer Product Safety Act Federal statute enacted to
- *Protect public against unsafe products*
- *Assist consumers in evaluating products*
- *Develop uniform safety standards*
- *Promote safety research*

Other Federal Consumer Protection Agencies

Consumer Purchases

Federal Warranty Protection applies to sellers of consumer goods who give written warranties
- *Presale Disclosure* requires terms of warranty to be simple and readily understood and to be made available before the sale
- *Labeling Requirement* requires warrantor to inform consumers of their legal rights under a warranty (full or limited)
- *Disclaimer Limitation* prohibits a written warranty from disclaiming any implied warranty

State "Lemon Laws" State laws that attempt to provide new car purchasers with rights similar to full warranties under the Magnuson-Moss Warranty Act

Consumer Right of Rescission in certain instances a consumer is granted a brief period of time during which she may rescind (cancel) an otherwise binding obligation

---

Consumer Credit Transactions

Definition any credit transaction involving goods, services, or land for personal, household, or family purposes

Access to the Market discrimination in extending credit on the basis of gender, marital status, race, color, religion, national origin, or age is prohibited

Truth-in-Lending Act requires creditor to provide certain information about contract terms, including annual percentage rate (APR), to the consumer before he formally incurs the obligation

Contract Terms statutory and judicial limitations have been imposed on consumer obligations

Consumer Credit Card Fraud Act prohibits certain fraudulent practices and limits a card holder's liability for unauthorized use of a credit card to $50

Fair Credit Reporting consumer credit reports are prohibited from containing inaccurate or obsolete information

---

Creditors' Remedies

Wage Assignments and Garnishment most States limit the amount that may be deducted from an individual's wages through either assignment or garnishment

Security Interest seller may retain a security interest in goods sold or other collateral of the buyer, although some restrictions are imposed

Debt Collection Practices abusive, deceptive, and unfair practices by debt collectors in collecting consumer debts are prohibited by the Fair Debt Collection Practices Act

Employment Law

Though in general the common law governs the relationship between employer and employee in terms of tort and contract duties (rules that are part of the law of agency; see Chapter 19), this common law has been supplemented—and in some instances replaced—by statutory enactments, principally at the Federal level. In fact, government regulation now affects the balance and working relationship between employers and employees in three areas. First, the general framework in which management and labor negotiate the terms of employment is regulated by Federal statutes designed to promote both labor–management harmony and the welfare of society at large. Second, Federal law prohibits employment discrimination based upon race, sex, religion, age, disability, or national origin. Finally, Congress, in response to the changing nature of American industry and the tremendous number of industrial accidents, has mandated that employers provide their employees with a safe and healthy work environment. Moreover, all of the States have adopted workers' compensation acts to provide compensation to employees injured during the course of employment.

This chapter will focus upon these three categories of government regulation of the employment relationship: (1) labor law, (2) employment discrimination law, and (3) employee protection.

LABOR LAW

Traditionally, labor law opposed concerted activities by workers, such as strikes, picketing, and refusals to deal, to obtain higher wages and better working conditions. At various times, such activities were found to constitute criminal conspiracy, tortious conduct, and violation of antitrust law. As subjecting union workers to criminal sanctions became publicly unpopular, employers began to resort to civil remedies in an attempt to halt unionization. The primary tool in this campaign was the injunction. Eventually, public pressure opposing such action forced Congress to intervene.

Norris–La Guardia Act

Congress enacted the **Norris–La Guardia Act** in 1932 in response to the growing criticism of the use of injunctions in peaceful labor disputes. The Act withdrew from the Federal courts the power to issue injunctions in nonviolent labor disputes. Section 1. The term **labor dispute** was broadly defined to include any controversy concerning terms or conditions of employment or union representation, regardless of whether the parties stood in an employer–employee relationship or not. Section 13(c). More significantly, the Act declared it to be United States policy that labor was to have full freedom to form unions without employer interference. Section 2. Accordingly, the Act prohibited the so-called yellow dog contracts through which employers coerced their employees into promising that they would not join a union.

http: **Norris-La Guardia Act:** http://www4.law.cornell.edu/uscode/29/101.html

National Labor Relations Act

Enacted in 1935, the **National Labor Relations Act (NLRA)**, or the *Wagner Act*, embodied the Federal government's effort to support collective bargaining and unionization. The Act provides that "the right to self-organization, to form, join or assist labor organizations, to bargain collectively through representatives of their own choosing, and to engage in concerted activities for the purpose of collective bargaining or other mutual aid or protection" is, for workers, a Federally protected right. Thus, the Act gave employees the right to union representation when negotiating employment terms with their employers. Section 7. The Supreme Court upheld the Act against constitutional challenge in *NLRB v. Jones & Laughlin Steel Corp.*, 301 U.S. 1 (1937).

> [The right of employees to bargain collectively] is a fundamental right. Employees have as clear a right to organize and select their representatives for lawful purposes as the respondent [employer] has to organize its business and select its own officers and agents. Discrimination and coercion to prevent the free exercise of the right of employees to self-organization and representation is a proper subject for condemnation by competent legislative authority. Long ago we stated the reason for labor organizations. We said that they were organized out of the necessities of the situation; that a single employee was helpless in dealing with an employer; that he was dependent ordinarily on his daily wage for the maintenance of himself and family; that if the employer refused to pay him the wages that he thought fair, he was nevertheless unable to leave the employ and resist arbitrary and unfair treatment; that union was essential to give laborers opportunity to deal on an equality with their employer. . . . Fully recognizing the legality of collective action on the part of employees in order to safeguard their proper interests, we said that Congress was not required to ignore this right but could safeguard it. Congress could seek to make appropriate collective action of employees an instrument of peace rather than of strife. We said that such collective action would be a mockery if representation were made futile by interference with freedom of choice. Hence the prohibition by Congress of interference with the selection of representatives for the purpose of negotiation and conference between employers and employees, "instead of being an invasion of the constitutional right of either, was based on the recognition of the rights of both."

The Act sought to enforce the collective bargaining right by prohibiting certain employer conduct deemed to constitute unfair labor practices. Under the Act, the following employer activities are **unfair labor practices**: (1) to interfere with the employees' rights to unionize and bargain collectively; (2) to dominate the union; (3) to discriminate against union members; (4) to discriminate against an employee who has filed charges or testified under the NLRA; and (5) to refuse to bargain in good faith with duly established employee representatives. Section 8(a). The U.S. Supreme Court has interpreted this section to include as an unfair labor practice employer conduct that improves employment conditions or benefits in an attempt to undermine a union's efforts to organize:

> The danger inherent in well-timed increases in benefits is the suggestion of a fist inside the velvet glove. Employees are not likely to miss the inference that the source of benefits now conferred is also the source from which future benefits must flow and which may dry up if it is not obliged. *NLRB v. Exchange Parts Co.*, 375 U.S. 405 (1964).

Moreover, the Act established the **National Labor Relations Board (NLRB)** to monitor and administer these employee rights. The NLRB is empowered to order employers to remedy their unfair labor practices and to supervise elections by secret ballot so that employees can freely select a representative organization.

http: **National Labor Relations Act:** http://www4.law.cornell.edu/uscode/29/151.html

Labor-Management Relations Act

Following the passage of the National Labor Relations Act, union membership and labor unrest increased tremendously in the United States. In response to this trend, Congress passed the **Labor-Management Relations Act** (the **LMRA**, or **Taft-Hartley Act**) in 1947. The Act prohibits certain unfair union practices and separates the NLRB's prosecutorial and adjudicative functions. More specifically, the Act amended the NLRA by declaring the following seven *union* activities to be **unfair labor practices**: (1) coercing an employee to join a union, (2) causing an employer to discharge or discriminate against a nonunion employee, (3) refusing to bargain in good faith, (4) levying excessive or discriminatory dues or fees, (5) causing an employer to pay for work not performed ("featherbedding"), (6) picketing an employer to require it to recognize an uncertified union, and (7) engaging in secondary activities. NLRA Section 8(b). A **secondary activity** is a boycott, strike, or picketing of an employer with whom a union has no labor dispute to persuade the employer to cease doing business with the company that is the target of the labor dispute. For example, assume that a union is engaged in a labor dispute with Adams Company. To coerce Adams into resolving the dispute in the union's favor, the union organizes a strike against Brookings Company, with which the union has no labor dispute. The union agrees to cease striking Brookings Company if Brookings agrees to cease doing business with Adams. The strike against Brookings Company is a secondary activity prohibited as an unfair labor practice.

In addition to prohibiting unfair union practices, the Act also fosters *employer* free speech by declaring that no employer unfair labor practice could be based on any statement of opinion or argument that contains no threat of reprisal. NLRA Section 8(c).

The LMRA also prohibits the closed shop, although it permits union shops if such are not prohibited by a State right-to-work law. A **closed shop** contract requires the employer to hire only union members. A **union shop** contract permits the employer to hire nonunion members but requires them to become union members within a specified time and to remain members in good standing as a condition of employment. Although a State may prohibit union shop contracts through a **right-to-work law**, most States permit the existence of union shops.

Finally, the Act reinstates the availability of civil injunctions in labor disputes, if requested of the NLRB to prevent an unfair labor practice. The Act also empowers the president of the United States to obtain an injunction for an eighty-day cooling-off period for a strike that is likely to endanger the national health or safety.

http: **Labor-Management Relations Act:** http://www4.law. cornell.edu/uscode/29/141.html
National Labor Relations Board: http://www.nlrb.gov/

◆ SEE FIGURE 43-1 **Unfair Labor Practices**

Labor-Management Reporting and Disclosure Act

The **Labor-Management Reporting and Disclosure Act**, also known as the **Landrum-Griffin Act**, is aimed at eliminating corruption in labor unions. Section 2(b) of the Act provides the following statement in support of the passage of the Act:

The Congress further finds, from recent investigations in the labor and management fields, that there have been a number of instances of breach of trust, corruption, disregard of the rights of

individual employees, and other failures to observe high standards of responsibility and ethical conduct which require further and supplementary legislation that will afford necessary protection of the rights and interests of employees and the public generally as they relate to the activities of labor organizations, employers, labor relations consultants, and their officers and representatives.

The Act attempts to eradicate corruption through an elaborate reporting system and a union "bill of rights" designed to make unions more democratic. Section 101. The latter provides union members with the right to nominate candidates for union offices, to vote in elections, to attend membership meetings, to participate in union business, to express themselves freely at union meetings and conventions, and to be accorded a full and fair hearing before the union takes any disciplinary action against them.

EMPLOYMENT DISCRIMINATION LAW

A number of Federal statutes prohibit discrimination in employment on the basis of race, sex, religion, national origin, age, and disability. The cornerstone of Federal employment discrimination law is Title VII of the 1964 Civil Rights Act, but other statutes and regulations also are significant, including two recently enacted discrimination laws: the Civil Rights Act of 1991 and the Americans with Disabilities Act of 1990. In addition, most States have enacted similar laws prohibiting discrimination based on race, sex, religion, national origin, and disability. The Civil Rights Act of 1991 extended the coverage of both Title VII and the Americans with Disabilities Act to include United States citizens working for U.S.-owned or controlled companies in foreign countries.

Equal Pay Act

The **Equal Pay Act** prohibits an employer from discriminating between employees on the basis of sex by paying unequal

◆ FIGURE 43-1 **Unfair Labor Practices**

Unfair Employer Practices	Unfair Union Practices
• Interfering with right to unionize	• Coercing an employee to join the union
• Refusing to bargain in good faith	• Refusing to bargain in good faith
• Discriminating against union members	• Causing employer to discriminate against a nonunion employee
• Dominating the union	• Featherbedding
• Discriminating against an employee	• Picketing an employer to require recognition of an uncertified union
	• Engaging in secondary activity
	• Levying excessive or discriminatory dues

wages for the same work. The Act forbids an employer from paying wages at a rate less than the rate at which he pays wages to employees of the opposite sex for equal work at the same establishment. Most courts define *equal work* to mean "substantially equal" rather than identical. The burden of proof is on the claimant to make a *prima facie* showing that the employer pays unequal wages for work requiring equal skill, effort, and responsibility under similar working conditions. Once the employee has demonstrated that the employer pays members of the opposite sex unequal wages for equal work, the burden shifts to the employer to prove that the pay differential is based on:

1. a seniority system,
2. a merit system,
3. a system that measures earnings by quantity or quality of production, or
4. any factor except sex.

Remedies include the recovery of back pay, an award of liquidated damages (an additional amount equal to back pay), and enjoining the employer from further unlawful conduct. Although the Department of Labor is the Federal agency designated by the statute to interpret and enforce the Act, these functions were transferred to the Equal Employment Opportunity Commission in 1979.

Civil Rights Act of 1964

Title VII of the **Civil Rights Act of 1964** prohibits **employment discrimination** on the basis of race, color, sex, religion, or national origin in hiring, firing, compensating, promoting, training, and other employment-related processes. The definition of *religion* includes all aspects of religious observance and practice, and the statute provides that an employer must make reasonable efforts to accommodate an employee's religious belief. The Act applies to employers engaged in an industry affecting commerce and having fifteen or more employees.

The Act also covers Federal, State and local governments, as well as labor organizations with fifteen or more members.

 Civil Rights Act of 1964: http://assembler.law.cornell.edu/ uscode/html/uscode42/usc_sec_42_00002000---a000-notes.html

When Congress passed the **Pregnancy Discrimination Act of 1978**, it extended the benefits of Title VII to pregnant women. Under the Act, an employer cannot refuse to hire a pregnant woman, fire her, or force her to take maternity leave unless the employer can establish a *bona fide* occupational qualification defense (discussed later in this chapter). The Act, which protects the job reinstatement rights of women returning from maternity leave, requires employers to treat pregnancy like any other temporary disability.

The enforcement agency for Title VII is the Equal **Employment Opportunity Commission (EEOC)**. The EEOC is empowered (1) to file legal actions in its own name or to intervene in actions filed by third parties; (2) to attempt to resolve alleged violations through informal means prior to bringing suit; (3) to investigate all charges of discrimination; and (4) to issue guidelines and regulations concerning enforcement policy.

Equal Employment Opportunity Commission: http://www.eeoc.gov/

◆ **SEE CASE 43-1**

◆ **SEE FIGURE 43-2** Charges Filed in 2003 with the EEOC

Proving Discrimination Each of the following constitutes discriminatory conduct prohibited by the Act:

1. **Disparate Treatment.** An individual shows that an employer used a prohibited criterion in making an employ-

◆ **FIGURE 43-2** Charges Filed in 2003 with the EEOC

Category	Number of Charges
Race	28,526
Sex	24,362
National Origin	8,450
Religion	2,532
Retaliation	22,690
Age	19,124
Disability	15,377
Equal Pay	1,167

Source: The U.S. Equal Employment Opportunity Commission, March 8, 2004, http://www.eeoc.gov/stats/charges.html

ment decision by treating some people less favorably than others. Liability is based on proving that the employer's decision was motivated by the protected characteristic or trait. *Raytheon Co. v. Hernandez*, 537 U.S. 1187 (2003). The Supreme Court held in *McDonnell Douglas Corp. v. Green*, 411 U.S. 792 (1973), that a *prima facie* case of discrimination would be shown if the plaintiff (a) is within a protected class, (b) applied for an open position, (c) was qualified for the position, (d) was denied the job, and (e) the employer continued to try to fill the position from a pool of applicants with the complainant's qualifications or gave it to someone with similar qualifications from a different class. Once the plaintiff establishes a *prima facie* case, the burden of proof shifts to the defendant to "articulate legitimate and nondiscriminatory reasons for the plaintiff's rejection." If the defendant so rebuts, the plaintiff then has the opportunity to demonstrate that the employer's stated reason was merely a pretext.

If the employer's decision was based on a "mixed motive" (the employer used both lawful and unlawful reasons in making its decision) the courts employ a shifting burden of proof standard. First, the plaintiff must prove by a preponderance of the evidence that the employer used the protected characteristic as a motivating factor. The defendant, however, can limit the remedies available to the plaintiff by proving by a preponderance of the evidence that the defendant would have made the same decision even without the forbidden motivating factor. If the defendant sustains its burden of proof, under the Civil Rights Act of 1991 the remedies are limited to declaratory relief, certain types of injunctive relief, and attorney's fees and costs.

2. **Present Effects of Past Discrimination.** An employer engages in conduct that on its face is "neutral," that is, nondiscriminatory, but that actually perpetuates past discriminatory practices. For example, it has been held illegal for a union that had previously limited its membership to whites to adopt a requirement that new members be related to or recommended by existing members. *Local 53 of International Association of Heat and Frost Insulators and Asbestos Workers v. Vogler*, 407 F.2d 1047 (5th Cir. 1969).

3. **Disparate Impact.** An employer adopts "neutral" rules that adversely affect a protected class and that are not justified as being necessary to the business. *Raytheon Co. v. Hernandez*, 537 U.S. 1187 (2003). Despite the employee's proof of disparate impact, the employer may prevail if it can demonstrate that the challenged practice is "job related for the position in question and consistent with business necessity." *Wards Cove Packing Co. v. Antonio*, 490 U.S. 642, 109 S.Ct. 2115 (1989). Thus, all requirements that might have a disparate impact upon women, such as height and weight requirements, must be shown to be job related. Nevertheless, under the **Civil Rights Act of 1991**, even if the employer can demonstrate the business

necessity of the questioned practice, the complainant will still prevail if she shows that a nondiscriminatory alternative practice exists.

❧ **See Case 43-2**

Defenses The Act provides several basic defenses: (1) a *bona fide* seniority or merit system; (2) a professionally developed ability test; (3) a compensation system based on performance results, and (4) a *bona fide* occupational qualification (BFOQ). The BFOQ defense does not apply to discrimination based on race. A fifth defense, business necessity, is available in a disparate impact case. In addition, a defendant can reduce damages in a "mixed motive" case by showing that it would have discharged the plaintiff for legal reasons.

❧ **See Case 43-1**

Remedies Remedies for violation of the Act include enjoining the employer from engaging in the unlawful behavior, appropriate affirmative action, and reinstatement of employees to their rightful place (which may include promotion) and award of back pay from a date not more than two years prior to the filing of the charge with the EEOC. First employed by Executive Order, as discussed below, **affirmative action** generally means the active recruitment of minority applicants, although courts also have used the remedy to impose numerical hiring ratios (quotas) and hiring goals based on race and sex. In 1985, the EEOC defined affirmative action in employment as "actions appropriate to overcome the effects of past or present practices, policies, or other barriers to equal employment opportunity."

Prior to 1991, only victims of *racial* discrimination could recover compensatory and punitive damages from the courts. Today, however, under the Civil Rights Act of 1991, *all* victims of *intentional* discrimination—whether based on race, sex, religion, national origin, or disability—can recover compensatory and punitive damages, except in cases involving disparate impact. In cases not involving race, the Act limits the amount of recoverable damages according to the number of persons the defendant employs. Companies with 15 to 100 employees are required to pay no more than $50,000; companies with 101 to 200 employees, no more than $100,000; those with 201 to 500 employees, no more than $200,000; and those with 501 or more employees, no more than $300,000. Either party may demand a jury trial. Victims of racial discrimination are still entitled to recover unlimited compensatory and punitive damages.

Reverse Discrimination A major controversy has arisen over the use of reverse discrimination in achieving affirmative action. In this context, **reverse discrimination** refers to affirmative action that directs an employer to remedy the underrepresentation of a given race or sex in a traditionally segregated job by considering an individual's race or gender when hiring or promoting. An example would be an employer who discriminates against white males to increase the proportion of females or members of a racial minority in a company's workforce. This question was presented in *United Steelworkers of America v. Weber*, 443 U.S. 193 (1979). In *Weber*, the employer and union were implementing a collectively bargained affirmative action plan that granted preference to blacks even though the employer had engaged in no proven racial discrimination. There was, however, a conspicuous racial imbalance in the employer's skilled labor force. The Supreme Court upheld the affirmative action plan against a challenge under Title VII, even though the plan favored black employees with less seniority than white employees. The Court held,

> We need not today define in detail the line of demarcation between permissible and impermissible affirmative action plans [under Title VII]. It suffices to hold that the challenged Kaiser-USWA affirmative action plan falls on the permissible side of the line. The purposes of the plan mirror those of the statute. Both were designed to break down old patterns of racial segregation and hierarchy. Both were structured to "open employment opportunities for Negroes in occupations which have been traditionally closed to them." [Citation.]
>
> At the same time, the plan does not unnecessarily trammel the interests of the white employees. The plan does not require the discharge of white workers and their replacement with new black hires. [Citation.] Nor does the plan create an absolute bar to the advancement of white employees; half of those trained in the program will be white. Moreover, the plan is a temporary measure; it is not intended to maintain racial balance, but simply to eliminate a manifest racial imbalance.

Due to the absence of State action, challenges to affirmative action plans adopted by private employers—those that are not governmental units at the local, State, or Federal level—are tested under Title VII of the Civil Rights Act of 1964, not under the Equal Protection Clause of the U.S. Constitution.

In *Johnson v. Transportation Agency*, 480 U.S. 616 (1987), also an action under Title VII, the Supreme Court upheld the employer's right to promote a female employee rather than a white male employee who had scored higher on a qualifying examination:

> In making our decision, we find that the employment decision was justified by the existence of a "manifest imbalance" that reflected underrepresentation of women in "traditionally segregated job categories." The Agency's [employer's] Plan did not authorize such blind hiring but expressly directed that numerous factors be taken into account in making employment decisions. Furthermore, the Plan did not trammel male employees' rights or create a bar to their advancement as it set aside no positions for women. Substantial evidence shows that the Agency has sought to take a moderate, gradual approach to eliminating the imbalance in its work force, one which establishes realistic guidance for employment decisions. Given this fact, as well as the

Agency's express commitment to "attain" a balanced work force, there is ample assurance that the Agency does not seek to use its Plan to "maintain" a permanent racial and sexual balance. Thus, we do not find the Agency in violation of Title VII.

When a State or local government adopts an affirmative action plan that is challenged as constituting illegal reverse discrimination, the plan is subject to strict scrutiny under the **Equal Protection Clause** of the Fourteenth Amendment. Under the strict scrutiny test, the subject classification must (1) be justified by a compelling governmental interest and (2) be the least intrusive means available. (For a fuller discussion of the Equal Protection Clause and the standards of review, see Chapter 4.) With regard to racial discrimination, the U.S. Supreme Court, in 1995, placed significant constraints upon the ability of governments to create programs favoring minorities over whites: benign and invidious discrimination are both held to the standard under which the government must show a compelling interest that is as narrowly tailored as feasible. Following this decision, the EEOC issued a statement which provided that "affirmative action is lawful only when it is designed to respond to a demonstrated and serious imbalance in the work force, is flexible, time-limited, applies only to qualified workers, and respects the rights of non-minorities and men."

Sexual Harassment In 1980, the EEOC issued a definition of sexual harassment:

> Unwelcome sexual advances, requests for sexual favors, and other verbal or physical conduct of a sexual nature constitute sexual harassment when
> (1) submission to such conduct is made either explicitly or implicitly a term or condition of an individual's employment,
> (2) submission to or rejection of such conduct by an individual is used as the basis for employment decisions affecting such individual, or
> (3) such conduct has the purpose or effect of reasonably interfering with an individual's work performance or creating an intimidating, hostile or offensive working environment.

The courts, including the Supreme Court, have held that sexual harassment may constitute illegal sexual discrimination in violation of Title VII. Moreover, an employer will be held liable for sexual harassment committed by one of its employees if it does not take reasonable action when it knows or should have known of the harassment. When the employee engaging in sexual harassment is an agent of the employer or holds a supervisory position over the victim, the employer may be liable without knowledge or reason to know.

In 1998, the U.S. Supreme Court held that sex discrimination consisting of same-sex harassment is actionable under Title VII.

❖ **See Case 43-3**

Comparable Worth Industrial statistics indicate that women earn approximately two-thirds as much as men do. Studies have suggested that between one-third and one-half of this disparity in earnings results from sexual discrimination. Other probable causes for the gap include (1) the differing educational backgrounds and job skills of males and females, (2) the tendency for females to be employed in lower-paying occupations, and (3) the idea that females are more likely to interrupt their careers to raise families.

Because the Equal Pay Act requires equal pay for equal work only, it does not apply to different jobs even if they are comparable. Thus, that statute provides no remedy for women who have been systematically undervalued and underpaid in "traditional" occupations, such as secretary, teacher, or nurse. As a result, women have sought redress under Title VII by arguing that the failure to pay comparable worth is discrimination on the basis of sex. The concept of **comparable worth** provides that employers should measure the relative values of different jobs through a job evaluation rating system that is free of any potential sex bias. Theoretically, the consistent application of objective criteria (including factors such as skill, effort, working conditions, responsibility, and mental demands) across job categories will ensure fair payment for all employees. For example, if under such a system the jobs of truck driver and nurse were evaluated at the same level, then workers in both jobs would receive the same pay.

In 1981, the Supreme Court held that a claim of discriminatory undercompensation based on sex may be brought under Title VII, even where the plaintiffs (women, in the 1981 case) were performing jobs different from those of their opposite-sex counterparts. As the Court noted, however, the case involved a situation in which the defendant intentionally discriminated in wages; and the defendant, not the courts, had compared the jobs in terms of value. *County of Washington v. Gunther*, 452 U.S. 161 (1981). The Court also held that the four defenses available under the Equal Pay Act would apply to a Title VII claim. Since *Gunther*, the concept of comparable worth has met with limited success in the courts. Nonetheless, a number of States have adopted legislation requiring public and private employers to pay equally for comparable work.

Executive Order

In 1965, President Johnson issued an executive order that prohibits discrimination by Federal contractors on the basis of race, color, sex, religion, or national origin in employment on any work the contractor performs during the period of the Federal contract. Federal contractors are also required to implement affirmative action in recruiting. The Secretary of Labor, **Office of Federal Contract Compliance Programs (OFCCP)**, enforces compliance with the program.

The program applies to all contractors (and all of their subcontractors in excess of $10,000) who enter into a Federal contract to be performed in the United States. Compliance with the affirmative action requirement differs for construction and nonconstruction contractors. All **nonconstruction** contractors with fifty or more employees or with contracts for more than $50,000 must have a written affirmative action plan to be in compliance. The plan must include a workforce analysis; planned corrective action, if necessary, with specific goals and timetables; and procedures for auditing and reporting. The Director of the OFCCP periodically issues goals and timetables for each segment of the construction industry for each region of the country. As a condition precedent to bidding on a Federal contract, a contractor must agree to make a good faith effort to achieve current published goals.

Age Discrimination in Employment Act of 1967

The **Age Discrimination in Employment Act (ADEA)** prohibits discrimination in hiring, firing, compensating, or other employment-related processes on the basis of age when the employee or applicant is over forty years old. The Act applies to private employers having twenty or more employees and to all governmental units regardless of size. The Act also prohibits the mandatory retirement of most employees, no matter what their age, though it provides employers a limited exception regarding *bona fide* executives and high policymaking employees. In 2004 the United States Supreme Court held that the ADEA does not prevent an employer from favoring an older employee over a younger employee.

The major statutory defenses include (1) a *bona fide* occupational qualification; (2) a *bona fide* seniority system; and (3) any other reasonable action, including the voluntary retirement of an individual. Remedies include back pay, injunctive relief, affirmative action, and liquidated damages equal to the amount of the award for "willful" violations. Furthermore, an ADEA claimant is entitled to a jury trial.

http: Age Discrimination in Employment Act of 1967:
http://www4.law.cornell.edu/uscode/29/621.html

Disability Law

The **Rehabilitation Act of 1973** attempts to assist the handicapped in obtaining rehabilitation training, access to public facilities, and employment. The Act requires Federal contractors and Federal agencies to take affirmative action to hire qualified handicapped persons. It also prohibits discrimination on the basis of handicap in Federal programs and programs receiving Federal financial assistance.

A **handicapped person** is defined as an individual who (1) has a physical or mental impairment that substantially affects one or more of her major life activities; (2) has a history of major life activity impairment; *or* (3) is regarded as having such an impairment. Major life activities include such functions as caring for oneself, seeing, speaking, or walking.

Alcohol and drug abuses are not considered handicapping conditions for the purposes of this statute.

http: **Rehabilitation Act of 1967:** http://www4.law.cornell.edu/ uscode/29/701.html

The **Americans with Disabilities Act (ADA) of 1990** forbids an employer from discriminating against any person with a disability with regard to "hiring or discharge..., employee compensation, advancement, job training and other terms, conditions and privileges of employment." In addition, businesses must make special accommodations, such as installing wheelchair-accessible bathrooms, for handicapped workers and customers unless the cost is unduly burdensome. An employer may use qualification standards, tests, or selection criteria that screen out handicapped workers if these measures are job related and consistent with business necessity *and* if no reasonable accommodation is possible. The ADA took effect on July 26, 1992, for employers with twenty-five or more employees and on July 26, 1994, for employers with fifteen or more employees. Remedies for violation of the ADA are those generally allowed under Title VII and include injunctive relief, reinstatement, back pay, and, for intentional discrimination, compensatory and punitive damages (capped according to company size by the Civil Rights Act of 1991).

http: **Americans with Disabilities Act:** http://www.usdoj.gov/ crt/ada/statute.html

In addition, the **Vietnam Veterans Readjustment Act of 1974** requires firms having $10,000 or more in Federal contracts to take affirmative action regarding handicapped veterans and Vietnam era veterans.

◆ **See Figure 43-3** Federal Employment Discrimination Laws

◊ **See Case 43-4**

EMPLOYEE PROTECTION

Employees are accorded a number of job-related protections. These include a limited right not to be unfairly dismissed, a right to a safe and healthy workplace, compensation for injuries sustained in the workplace, and some financial security upon retirement or loss of employment. This section discusses (1) employee termination at will, (2) occupational safety and health, (3) employee privacy, (4) workers' compensation, (5) Social Security and unemployment insurance, (6) the Fair Labor Standards Act, (7) employee notice of termination or layoff, and (8) family and health leave.

Employee Termination at Will

Under the common law, a contract of employment is terminable at will by either party unless the employment is for other than a definite term or the employee is represented by a labor union. Accordingly, under the common law, employers may "dismiss their employees at will for good cause, for no cause or even for cause morally wrong, without being thereby guilty of legal wrong." In recent years, however, the courts have delineated a growing number of judicial exceptions to the rule, based on implied contract, tort, and public policy. A number of Federal and State statutes enacted in the last sixty years further limit the rule, which also may be restricted by contractual agreement between employer and employee. In particular, most collective bargaining agreements negotiated through union representatives contain a provision prohibiting dismissal "without cause."

Statutory Limitations In 1934, as previously discussed, Congress enacted the National Labor Relations Act, which provided employees with the right to unionize free of intimidation or coercion from their employers, including freedom from dismissal for engaging in union activities. Since the enactment of the NLRA, additional Federal legislation, such as ADEA, ADA, ERISA, and Fair Labor Standards Act has limited the employer's right to discharge. These statutes fall into three categories: (1) those protecting certain employees from discriminatory discharge; (2) those protecting certain employees in their exercise of statutory rights; and (3) those protecting certain employees from discharge without cause.

At the State level, statutes protect workers from discriminatory discharge for filing workers' compensation claims. Also, many State statutes parallel Federal legislation. Some States have adopted statutes similar to the NLRA, and many States prohibit discrimination in employment on the basis of factors such as race, creed, nationality, sex, or age. In addition, some States have statutes prohibiting employers from discharging employees or taking other punitive actions in order to influence voting or, in some States, political activity.

Judicial Limitations Judicial limitations on the employment-at-will doctrine have been based on contract law, tort law, and public policy. Cases founded in contract theory have relied on arguments contending, among other things, (1) that the dismissal was improper because the employee had detrimentally relied on the employer's promise of work for a reasonable time; (2) that the employment was not at will because of implied-in-fact promises of employment for a specific duration, which meant that the employer could not terminate the employee without just cause; (3) that the employment contract implied or provided expressly that the employee would not be dismissed so long as he satisfactorily performed his work; (4) that the employer had assured the employee that he would not be

◆ **FIGURE 43-3**   **Federal Employment Discrimination Laws**

	Protected Characteristics	Prohibited Conduct	Defenses	Remedies
Equal Pay Act	Sex	Wages	Seniority Merit Quality or quantity measures Any factor other than sex	Back pay Injunction Liquidated damages Attorneys' fees
Title VII of Civil Rights Act	Race Color Sex Religion National origin	Terms, conditions, or privileges of employment	Seniority Ability test BFOQ (except for race) Business necessity (disparate impact only)	Back pay Injunction Reinstatement Compensatory and punitive damages for intentional discrimination • unlimited for race • limited for all others Attorneys' fees
Age Discrimination in Employment Act	Age	Terms, conditions, or privileges of employment	Seniority BFOQ Any other reasonable act	Back Pay Injunction Reinstatement Liquidated damages for willful violation Attorneys' fees
Americans with Disabilities Act	Disability	Terms, conditions, or privileges of employment	Undue hardship Job-related criteria and business necessity Risk to public health and safety	Back pay Injunction Reinstatement Compensatory and punitive damages for intentional discrimination (limited) Attorneys' fees

dismissed except for cause; or (5) that, upon entering into the employment contract, the employee gave consideration over and above the performance of services to support a promise of job security.

Some courts have circumvented the common law at-will doctrine under implied contract theories by finding that employment contracts contain an implied promise to deal in good faith, including a duty on the part of the employer to terminate only in good faith. These cases provide a remedy for an employee whose discharge was motivated by bad faith, malice, or retaliation.

Courts have also created exceptions to the employment-at-will doctrine by imposing tort obligations on employers, particularly the torts of intentional infliction of emotional distress and of interference with employment relations.

A majority of States now consider a discharge as wrongful if it violates a statutory or other established public policy. In general, this public policy exception renders a discharge wrongful if it involves a dismissal for (1) refusing to violate a statute, (2) exercising a statutory right, (3) performing a statutory obligation, or (4) reporting an alleged violation of a statute that is of public interest ("whistle-blowing").

◆ SEE CASE 43-5

Occupational Safety and Health Act

In 1970, Congress enacted the **Occupational Safety and Health Act** to ensure, as far as possible, a safe and healthful working environment for every worker. The Act established the *Occupational Safety and Health Administration* (OSHA) to develop standards, conduct inspections, monitor compliance, and institute enforcement actions against those who are not in compliance.

Upon each employer engaged in a business affecting interstate commerce, the Act imposes a general duty to provide a work environment that is "free from recognized hazards that are causing or likely to cause death or serious physical harm to his employees." Section 119. In addition to this general duty, the employer must comply with specific OSHA-promulgated safety rules. The Act also requires employees to comply with all OSHA rules and regulations. Finally, the Act prohibits any employer from discharging or discriminating against an employee who exercises her rights under the Act. Section 11(c)(1).

Enforcing the Act generally involves OSHA inspections and citations of employers, as appropriate, for (1) breach of the general duty obligation; (2) breach of specific safety and health standards; or (3) failure to keep records, make reports, or post notices required by the Act.

When a violation is discovered, the offending employer receives a written citation, a proposed penalty, and a date by which the employer must remedy the breach. A citation may be contested, in which case the Occupational Safety and Health Review Commission assigns an administrative law judge to hold a hearing. The commission, at its discretion, may grant review of an administrative law judge's decision; review is not a matter of right. If no such review occurs, the judge's decision becomes the final order of the commission thirty days after its receipt by the aggrieved party, who then may appeal the order to the appropriate United States Circuit Court of Appeals.

Penalties for violations are both civil and criminal. In cases involving civil penalties, serious violations require that a penalty be proposed; in contrast, for nonserious violations, penalties are discretionary and rarely proposed. The Act further empowers the Secretary of Labor to obtain temporary restraining orders when regular OSHA procedures are insufficient to halt imminently hazardous or deadly business operations.

One stated purpose of the Act is to encourage State participation in regulating safety and health. The Act therefore permits a State to regulate the safety and health of the work environment within its borders, provided that OSHA approves the plan. The Act sets minimum acceptable standards for the States to impose, but it does not require that a State plan be identical to OSHA guidelines. More than half of the States regulate workplace health and safety through State-promulgated plans.

 Occupational Safety and Health Act: http://www4.law.cornell.edu/uscode/29/651.html
Occupational Safety and Health Administration: http://www.osha.gov/

Employee Privacy

Over the last decade, employee privacy has become a major issue. The fundamental right to privacy is a product of common law protection, discussed in Chapter 7. Thus, employee protection from unwanted searches, electronic monitoring and other forms of surveillance, and disclosure of confidential records is safeguarded by the tort of invasion of privacy, which actually consists of four different torts: (1) unreasonable intrusion into the seclusion of another; (2) unreasonable public disclosure of private facts; (3) unreasonable publicity that places another in a false light; and (4) appropriation of a person's name or likeness. In addition, the Federal government and some States have legislatively supplemented the common law in certain areas.

Drug and Alcohol Testing Although no Federal legislation deals comprehensively with drug and alcohol tests, legislation in a number of States either prohibits such tests altogether or prescribes certain scientific and procedural standards for conducting them. In the absence of a State statute, *private* sector employees have little or no protection from such tests. The NLRB has held, however, that drug and alcohol testing in a union setting is a mandatory subject of collective bargaining.

In 1989, the U.S. Supreme Court ruled that the employer of a *public* sector employee whose position involved public health or safety or national security could subject the employee to a drug or alcohol test without either first obtaining a search warrant or having reasonable grounds to believe the individual had engaged in any wrongdoing. Based on Supreme Court and lower court decisions, it appears that a government employer may use (1) random or universal testing where the public health or safety or national security is involved and (2) selective drug testing where there is sufficient cause to believe an employee has a drug problem.

Lie Detector Tests The **Federal Employee Polygraph Protection Act of 1988** prohibits private employers from requiring employees or prospective employees to undergo a lie detector test, inquiring about the results of such a test, or using the results of such a test or the refusal to be thus tested as grounds for an adverse employment decision. The Act exempts government employers and, in certain situations, Energy Department contractors or persons providing consulting services for Federal intelligence agencies. In addition, security firms and manufacturers of controlled substances may use a polygraph to test prospective employees. Moreover, an employer, as part of an ongoing investigation of economic loss or injury to its business, may utilize a polygraph test. Nevertheless, the use of the test must meet the following requirements: (1) it must be designed to investigate a specific incident or activity, not to document a chronic problem; (2) the employee to be tested must have had access to the property that is the subject of the investigation; and (3) the employer must have reason to suspect the particular employee.

Employees and prospective employees tested under any of these exemptions cannot be terminated, disciplined, or denied employment solely as a result of the test. The Act further provides that those subjected to a polygraph test (1) cannot be asked intrusive or degrading questions regarding topics such as their religious beliefs, opinions as to racial matters, political views, or sexual preferences or behaviors; (2) must be given the right to review all questions before the test and to terminate the test at any time; and (3) must receive a complete copy of the test results.

Workers' Compensation

At common law, the basis of most actions by an injured employee against his employer was the employer's failure to use reasonable care under the circumstances to ensure the employee's safety. In such an action, however, the employer could make use of several well-established defenses, including the fellow servant rule, contributory negligence on the part of the employee, and the doctrine of assumption of risk by the employee. By establishing any of these defenses, the employer was not liable to the injured employee.

The **fellow servant rule** relieved an employer from liability for injuries an employee sustained through the negligence of a fellow employee. Under the common law defense of **contributory negligence**, if an employer established that an employee's negligence contributed to the injury he sustained in the course of his employment, in many jurisdictions the employee could not recover damages from the employer. Additionally, at common law, an employer was not liable to an employee for harm or injury caused by the unsafe condition of the premises if the employee, with knowledge of the facts and an understanding of the risks involved, voluntarily entered into or continued in the employment. This was regarded as a **voluntary assumption of risk** by the employee.

To provide speedier and more certain relief to injured employees, all States have adopted statutes providing for workers' compensation. (Several States, however, exempt specified employers from such statutes.) Workers' compensation statutes create commissions or boards that determine whether an injured employee is entitled to receive compensation and, if so,

how much. The basis of recovery under workers' compensation is strict liability: the employee does not have to prove that the employer was negligent. The common law defenses discussed previously are not available to employers in proceedings under these statutes. Such defenses are abolished. The only requirement is that the employee be injured and that the injury arises out of and in the course of his employment. The amounts recoverable are fixed by statute for each type of injury and are lower than the amounts a court or jury would probably award in an action at common law. The courts, therefore, do not have jurisdiction over such cases, except to review decisions of the board or commission; even then, the courts may determine only whether such decisions are in accordance with the statute. If a third party causes the injury, however, the employee may bring a tort action against that third party.

Early workers' compensation laws did not provide coverage for occupational disease, and most courts held that occupational injury did not include disease. Today, virtually all States provide general compensation coverage for occupational diseases, although the coverage varies greatly from State to State.

 U.S. Department of Labor: Employment Standards Administration Office of Workers' Compensation Programs: http://www.dol.gov/esa/owcp_org.htm

Social Security and Unemployment Insurance

Social Security was enacted in 1935 in an attempt to provide limited retirement and death benefits to certain employees. Since then, the benefits have increased greatly; the Federal Social Security system, which has expanded to cover almost all employees, now contains four major benefit programs: (1) Old-Age and Survivors Insurance (OASI) (providing retirement and survivor benefits), (2) Disability Insurance (DI), (3) Hospitalization Insurance (Medicare), and (4) Supplemental Security Income (SSI).

The system is financed by contributions (taxes) paid by employers, employees, and self-employed individuals. Employees and employers pay matching contributions. These contributions are calculated by multiplying the Social Security tax (a fixed percentage) times the employee's wages up to a specified maximum. Both the base tax rate and the maximum dollar amount are subject to change by Congress. It is the employer's responsibility to withhold the employee's contribution and to forward the full amount of the tax to the Internal Revenue Service. Contributions made by the employee are not tax deductible by the employee, while those made by the employer are tax deductible.

http: Social Security Administration: http://www.ssa.gov/

The Federal **unemployment insurance** system was initially created by Title IX of the Social Security Act of 1935. Subsequently, Title IX was supplemented by the Federal Unemployment Tax Act and by numerous other Federal statutes. This complex system depends upon cooperation between State and Federal entities. Federal law provides the general guidelines, standards, and requirements for the program, while the States administer the program through their employment laws. The system is funded by employer taxes: Federal taxes generally pay the administrative costs of the program, and State contributions pay for the actual benefits.

Under the Federal Unemployment Tax Act, unemployment compensation is provided to workers who have lost their jobs, usually through no fault of their own. The Act is meant to help workers who are temporarily out of work and who need to support themselves while they search for jobs. Unemployed workers usually receive weekly payments in an amount based on each State's particular formula. Employees who voluntarily quit without good cause, who have been dismissed for misconduct, or who fail to look for or who refuse suitable work are not eligible for unemployment benefits.

Fair Labor Standards Act

The **Fair Labor Standards Act (FLSA)** regulates the employment of child labor outside of agriculture. The Act prohibits the employment of anyone under fourteen years of age in all nonfarm work except newspaper delivery and acting. Fourteen- and fifteen-year-olds may work for a limited number of hours outside of school hours, under specific conditions, in certain nonhazardous occupations. Sixteen- and seventeen-year-olds may work in any nonhazardous job, while persons eighteen years old or older may work in any job, whether it is hazardous or not. The Secretary of Labor determines which occupations are considered hazardous.

In addition, the FLSA imposes wage and hour requirements upon covered employers. With certain exceptions, the Act provides for a minimum hourly wage and overtime pay of time-and-a-half for hours worked in excess of forty hours per week; those workers exempted from both the FLSA's minimum wage and overtime provisions include professionals, managers, and outside salespersons.

 Fair Labor Standards Act: http://www4.law.cornell.edu/uscode/29/201.html

Worker Adjustment and Retraining Notification Act

The **Worker Adjustment and Retraining Notification Act (WARN)** requires an employer to provide sixty days' advance notice of a plant closing or mass layoff. A "plant closing" is defined as the permanent or temporary shutting down of a single site or units within a site if the shutdown results in fifty or more employees losing employment during any thirty-day period. A "mass layoff" is defined as a loss of employment during a thirty-day period either for 500 employees or for at least one-third of the employees at a given site, if that one-third equals or exceeds fifty employees. WARN requires that notification be given to specified State and local officials as well as to the affected employees or their union representatives. The Act, which reduces the notification period with regard to failing companies and emergency situations, applies to employers with a total of 100 or more employees who in the aggregate work at least 2,000 hours per week, not including overtime.

 Worker Adjustment and Retraining Notification Act: http://www4.law.cornell.edu/uscode/29/2101.html

Family and Medical Leave Act of 1993

The **Family and Medical Leave Act of 1993** requires employers with fifty or more employees and governments at the Federal, State, and local levels to grant employees up to twelve weeks of leave during any twelve-month period for the birth of a child; adopting or gaining foster care of a child; or the care of a spouse, child, or parent who suffers from a serious health condition. A "serious health condition" is defined as an "illness, injury, impairment or physical or mental condition" that involves inpatient medical care at a hospital, hospice, or residential care facility or continuing medical treatment by a health care provider. Employees are eligible for such leave if they have been employed by their present employer for at least twelve months and have worked at least 1,250 hours for their employer during the twelve months preceding the leave request. The requested leave may be paid, unpaid, or a combination of both.

Family and Medical Leave Act of 1993: http://www4.law.cornell.edu/uscode/29/2601.html

— CHAPTER SUMMARY —

Labor Law

Purpose to provide the general framework in which management and labor negotiate terms of employment

Norris–La Guardia Act established as United States policy the full freedom of labor to form labor unions without employer interference and withdrew from the Federal courts the power to issue injunctions in nonviolent labor disputes (any controversy concerning terms or conditions of employment or union representation)

National Labor Relations Act
- *Right to Unionize* declares it a Federally protected right of employees to unionize and to bargain collectively
- *Prohibits Unfair Employer Practices* the Act identifies five unfair labor practices by an employer
- *National Labor Relations Board (NLRB)* created to administer these rights

Labor-Management Relations Act
- *Prohibits Unfair Union Practices* the Act identifies seven unfair labor practices by a union
- *Prohibits Closed Shops* which are agreements that mandate that employers can hire only union members
- *Allows Union Shops* an employer can hire nonunion members, but the employee must join the union

Labor-Management Reporting and Disclosure Act aimed at eliminating corruption in labor unions

Employment Discrimination Law

Equal Pay Act prohibits an employer from discriminating between employees on the basis of gender by paying unequal wages for the same work

Civil Rights Act of 1964 prohibits employment discrimination on the basis of race, color, gender, religion, or national origin
- *Pregnancy Discrimination Act of 1978* extends the benefits of the Civil Rights Act to pregnant women
- *Equal Employment Opportunity Commission (EEOC)* enforcement agency for the Act
- *Affirmative Action* the active recruitment of a designated group of applicants
- *Discrimination* prohibited by the Act; includes (1) using proscribed criteria to produce disparate treatment, (2) engaging in nondiscriminatory conduct that perpetuates past discrimination, and (3) adopting neutral roles that have a disparate impact
- *Reverse Discrimination* affirmative action that directs an employer to consider an individual's race or gender when hiring or promoting for the purpose of remedying underrepresentation of that race or gender in traditionally segregated jobs
- *Defenses* four defenses are provided by the Act (1) a *bona fide* seniority or merit system, (2) a professionally developed ability test, (3) a compensation system based on performance results, and (4) a *bona fide* occupational qualification
- *Remedies* remedies for violation of the Act include injunctions, affirmative action, reinstatement, back pay, and compensatory and punitive damages
- *Sexual Harassment* an illegal form of sexual discrimination that includes unwelcome sexual advances, requests for sexual favors, and other verbal or physical conduct of a sexual nature
- *Comparable Worth* equal pay for jobs that are of equal value to the employer

Executive Order prohibits discrimination by Federal contractors on the basis of race, color, gender, religion, or national origin on any work the contractors perform during the period of the Federal contract

Age Discrimination in Employment Act of 1967 prohibits discrimination on the basis of age in hiring, firing, or compensating

Disability Law several Federal acts, including the Americans with Disabilities Act, provide assistance to the disabled in obtaining rehabilitation training, access to public facilities, and employment

---

Employee Protection

Employee Termination at Will under the common law, a contract of employment for other than a definite term is terminable at will by either party
- *Statutory Limitations* have been enacted by the Federal government and some States
- *Judicial Limitations* based on contract law, tort law, or public policy
- *Limitations Imposed by Union Contract*

Occupational Safety and Health Act enacted to assure workers of a safe and healthful work environment

Employee Privacy
- *Drug and Alcohol Testing* some States either prohibit such tests or prescribe certain scientific and procedural safeguards
- *Lie Detector Tests* Federal statute prohibits private employers from requiring employees or prospective employees to take such tests

Workers' Compensation compensation awarded to an employee who is injured in the course of his employment

Social Security measures by which the government provides economic assistance to disabled or retired employees and their dependents

Unemployment Compensation compensation awarded to workers who have lost their jobs and cannot find other employment

Fair Labor Standards Act regulates the employment of child labor outside of agriculture

Worker Adjustment and Retraining Notification Act Federal statute that requires an employer to provide sixty days' advance notice of a plant closing or mass layoff

Family and Medical Leave Act of 1993 requires some employers to grant employees leave for serious health conditions or certain other events

---

CASES

CASE

43-1

Civil Rights Act of 1964 and
Pregnancy Discrimination Act: Defenses

INTERNATIONAL UNION, UNITED AUTOMOBILE, AEROSPACE AND AGRICULTURAL IMPLEMENT WORKERS OF AMERICA, UAW v. JOHNSON CONTROLS, INC.

Supreme Court of the United States, 1991
499 U.S. 187, 111 S.Ct. 1196, 113 L.Ed.2d 158
http://supct.law.cornell.edu/supct/html/89-1215.ZS.html

Blackmun, J.
In this case we are concerned with an employer's gender-based fetal-protection policy. May an employer exclude a fertile female employee from certain jobs because of its concern for the health of the fetus the woman might conceive?

Respondent Johnson Controls, Inc., manufactures batteries. In the manufacturing process, the element lead is a primary ingredient. Occupational exposure to lead entails health risks, including the risk of harm to any fetus carried by a female employee.

Before the Civil Rights Act of 1964, [citation], became law, Johnson Controls did not employ any woman in a battery-manufacturing job. In June 1977, however, it announced its first official policy concerning its employment of women in lead-exposure work:

Securities Regulation

The primary purpose of Federal securities regulation is to foster public confidence in the securities market by preventing fraudulent practices in the sale of securities. Federal securities law consists principally of two statutes: the Securities Act of 1933, which focuses on the issuance of securities, and the Securities Exchange Act of 1934, which deals mainly with trading in issued securities. These "secondary" transactions greatly exceed in number and dollar value the original offerings by issuers.

Both statutes are administered by the Securities and Exchange Commission (SEC), an independent, quasi-judicial agency consisting of five commissioners. In 1996 Congress enacted legislation requiring the SEC, when making rules under either of the securities statutes, to consider, in addition to the protection of investors, whether its action will promote efficiency, competition, and capital formation. The SEC has the power to seek in a Federal district court civil injunctions against violations of the statutes, to recommend that the Justice Department bring criminal prosecutions, and to issue orders censuring, suspending, or expelling broker-dealers, investment advisers, and investment companies. The Securities Enforcement Remedies and Penny Stock Reform Act of 1990 granted the SEC the power to issue cease-and-desist orders and to impose administrative, civil penalties up to $600,000. Congress enacted the Private Securities Litigation Reform Act of 1995 (Reform Act), which amends both the 1933 Act and the 1934 Act. One of its provisions grants authority to the SEC to bring civil actions for specified violations of the 1934 Act against aiders and abettors (those who knowingly provide substantial assistance to a person who violates the statute).

The Reform Act sought to prevent abuses in private securities fraud lawsuits. To prevent certain State private securities class action lawsuits alleging fraud from being used to frustrate the objectives of the Reform Act, Congress enacted the Securities Litigation Uniform Standards Act of 1998. The Act sets national standards for securities class action lawsuits involving nationally traded securities, while preserving the appropriate enforcement powers of State securities regulators and leaving unchanged the current treatment of individual lawsuits. The Act amends both the 1933 Act and the 1934 Act by prohibiting any private class action suit in State or Federal court by any private party based upon State statutory or common law alleging: (1) an untrue statement or omission in connection with the purchase or sale of a covered security; or (2) that the defendant used any manipulative or deceptive device in connection with such a transaction.

In response to the business scandals involving companies such as Enron, WorldCom, Global Crossing, Adelphia, and Arthur Andersen, in 2002 Congress passed the Sarbanes-Oxley Act, which amends the securities acts in a number of significant respects. The Act allows the SEC to add civil penalties to a disgorgement fund for the benefit of victims of violations of the 1933 Act or the 1934 Act. Other provisions of the Act are discussed later in this chapter.

The 1933 Act has two basic objectives: (1) to provide investors with material information concerning securities offered for sale to the public and (2) to prohibit misrepresentation, deceit, and other fraudulent acts and unfair practices in the sale of securities generally, whether or not they are required to be registered.

The 1934 Act extends protection to investors trading in securities that are already issued and outstanding. The 1934 Act also imposes disclosure requirements on publicly held corporations and regulates tender offers and proxy solicitations.

Effective October 6, 1995, the SEC provided interpretive guidance for the use of electronic media for the delivery of information required by the Federal securities laws. The SEC defined *electronic media* to include audiotapes, videotapes, facsimiles, CD-ROM, electronic mail, bulletin boards, Internet Web sites, and computer networks. Basically, electronic delivery must provide notice, access, and evidence of delivery comparable to that provided by paper delivery.

The SEC has established the EDGAR (Electronic Data Gathering, Analysis, and Retrieval) computer system, which performs automated collection, validation, indexing, acceptance, and dissemination of reports required to be filed with the SEC. Its primary purpose is to increase the efficiency and fairness of the securities market for the benefit of investors, corporations, and the economy by speeding up the receipt, acceptance, dissemination, and analysis of corporate information filed with the SEC. The SEC now requires all public domestic companies to make their filings on EDGAR, except filings exempted for hardship. EDGAR filings are posted at the SEC's Web site twenty-four hours after the date of filing.

In addition to the Federal laws regulating the sale of securities, each State has its own laws regulating such sales within its borders. Commonly called **blue sky laws**, these statutes all contain provisions prohibiting fraud in the sale of securities. In addition, most States require the registration of securities and also regulate brokers and dealers.

Any person who sells securities must comply with the Federal securities laws as well as with the securities laws of each State in which he intends to offer his securities. However, in 1996 Congress enacted the National Securities Markets Improvements Act, preempting State regulation of many offerings of securities. Because the State securities laws vary greatly, this chapter will discuss only the 1933 Act and the 1934 Act.

| http: | **Securities Exchange Commission:** http://www.sec.gov
State enactments of the Uniform Securities Act
http://www.law.cornell.edu/uniform/vol7.html#secur |

"Truth in Securities Act"

Securities Act of 1933

The 1933 Act, also called the "Truth in Securities Act," requires that a registration statement be filed with the Securities and Exchange Commission and that it become effective before any securities may be offered for sale to the public, unless either the securities or the transaction in which they are offered is exempt from registration. The purpose of registration is to disclose financial and other information about the issuer and those who control it, so that potential investors may appraise the merits of the securities. The 1933 Act also requires that potential investors be furnished with a **prospectus** (a document offering the securities for sale) containing the important data set forth in the registration statement. The 1933 Act prohibits fraud in all sales of securities involving interstate commerce or the mails, even if the securities are exempt from the registration and disclosure requirements of the 1933 Act. Civil and criminal liability may be imposed for violations of the 1933 Act.

The National Securities Markets Improvements Act of 1996 broadly authorized the SEC to issue regulations or rules exempting any person, security, or transaction from any of the provisions of the 1933 Act or the SEC's rules promulgated under that Act. This authorization extends so far as such exemption is necessary or appropriate in the public interest and is consistent with the protection of investors.

| http: | **Securities Act of 1933:** http://www4.law.cornell.edu/
uscode/15/ch2A.html
http://www.law.uc.edu/CCL/33Act/index.html |

DEFINITION OF A SECURITY

Section 2(1) of the 1933 Act defines a security as

> any note, stock, treasury stock, bond, debenture, evidence of indebtedness, certificate of interest or participation in any profit-sharing agreement, collateral-trust certificate, preorganization certificate or subscription, transferable share, investment contract, voting-trust certificate, certificate of deposit for a security, fractional undivided interest in oil, gas, or other mineral rights, any put, call, straddle, option, or privilege on any security . . . or, in general, any interest or instrument commonly known as a "security," or any certificate of interest or participation in, temporary or interim certificate for, receipt for, guarantee of, or warrant or right to subscribe to or purchase, any of the foregoing.

This definition broadly incorporates the many types of instruments that fall within the concept of a security. Furthermore, the courts generally have interpreted the statutory definition to include nontraditional forms of investments. In *Landreth*

Timber Co. v. Landreth, 471 U.S. 681 (1985), the Supreme Court adopted a two-tier analysis of what constitutes a security. Under this analysis, the Court will presumptively treat as a security a financial instrument designated as a note, stock, bond, or other instrument specifically named in the Act.

On the other hand, if a financial transaction lacks the traditional characteristics of an instrument specifically named in the statute, the Court has used a three-part test, derived from *Securities and Exchange Commission v. W.J. Howey Co.*, 328 U.S. 293 (1946), to determine whether that financial transaction constitutes an investment contract and thus a security. Under the *Howey* test, a financial instrument or transaction that involves (1) an investment in a common venture (2) premised on a reasonable expectation of profit (3) to be derived from the entrepreneurial or managerial efforts of others constitutes an investment contract. Thus, limited partnership interests are usually considered securities because limited partners may not participate in management or control of the limited partnership. On the other hand, general partnership interests are usually held not to be securities because general partners have the right to participate in management of the general partnership. Similarly, interests in limited liability companies are considered securities where the members do not take part in management (manager-managed LLCs) but are not deemed securities when the members exercise control of the company (member-managed LLCs). In certain circumstances, investments in citrus groves, whiskey warehouse receipts, real estate condominiums, cattle, franchises, and pyramid schemes have been held to be securities under the *Howey* test.

◆ **See Case 44-1**

REGISTRATION OF SECURITIES

The 1933 Act prohibits the offer or sale of any security through the use of the mails or any means of interstate commerce unless a registration statement for the securities being offered is in effect or the issuer secures an exemption from registration. Section 5. The purpose of registration is to adequately and accurately disclose financial and other information upon which investors may appraise the merits of the securities. Registration does not, however, insure investors against loss—the SEC does not judge the financial merits of any security. Moreover, the SEC does not guarantee the accuracy of the information presented in a registration statement.

Disclosure Requirements

In general, registration (Form S–1) calls for disclosure of such information as (1) a description of the registrant's properties, business, and competition, (2) a description of the significant provisions of the security to be offered for sale and

its relationship to the registrant's other capital securities, (3) information about the management of the registrant, and (4) financial statements certified by independent public accountants. In 1992, the SEC imposed new disclosure requirements regarding compensation paid to senior executives and directors. The registration statement must be signed by the issuer, its chief executive officer, its chief financial officer, its chief accounting officer, and a majority of its board of directors.

A registration statement and prospectus become public immediately on filing with the SEC. The effective date of a registration statement is the twentieth day after filing, although the commission, at its discretion, may advance the effective date or require an amendment to the filing, which will begin a new twenty-day period.

Before the filing of the registration statement, it is unlawful to sell, offer to sell, or offer to buy the securities, though the issuer may give notice that it proposes to make a public offer. Furthermore, although it is unlawful to sell the securities until the effective date, the issuer may, after filing the registration statement, *offer* the securities (1) orally; (2) by certain summaries of the information in the registration statement, as permitted by SEC rules; (3) by a "tombstone advertisement" that identifies the security, its price, and by whom orders will be executed; or (4) by a preliminary prospectus, called a "red herring," which may contain substantially the same information as a final prospectus but must bear a legend in red ink stating that the registration statement has not become effective. After the effective date, the issuer may make sales, provided the purchaser has received a final prospectus.

◆ **See Figure 44-1** **Permissible Sales Activities**

In 1998 the SEC issued a rule requiring issuers to write and design the cover page, summary, and risk factors section of their prospectuses in plain English. In these sections issuers must use short sentences; definite, concrete, everyday language; tabular presentation of complex information; no legal or business jargon; and no multiple negatives. Issuers will also have to design these sections to make them inviting to the reader and free from legalese and repetition that blur important information.

Integrated Disclosure

The disclosure system under the 1933 Act developed independently of that required by the 1934 Act, which is discussed later in this chapter. As a result, issuers subject to both statutes were compelled to provide duplicative or overlapping disclosure. In an effort to reduce or eliminate unnecessary duplication of corporate reporting, the SEC in 1982 adopted an integrated system that provides for three levels of disclosure, depending on the issuer's reporting history and market following. All issuers may use the detailed form (S–1) described previously. Corporations that have reported continuously under the 1934

◆ **FIGURE 44-1**   **Permissible Sales Activities**

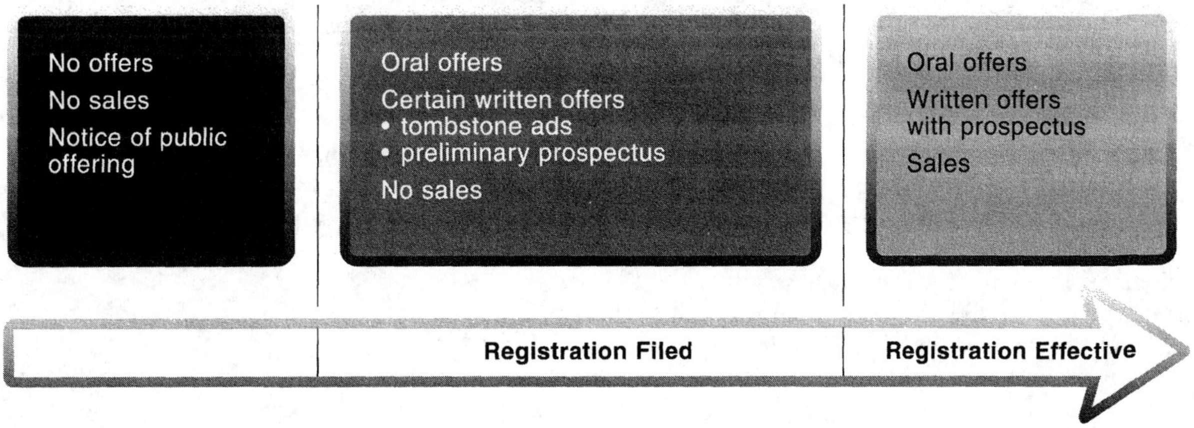

No offers No sales Notice of public offering	Oral offers Certain written offers • tombstone ads • preliminary prospectus No sales	Oral offers Written offers with prospectus Sales
	Registration Filed	**Registration Effective**

Act for at least three years are permitted to disclose less detailed information in the 1933 Act registration statement (S–2) and to incorporate by reference certain information from reports filed under the 1934 Act. Those corporations that have filed continuously under the 1934 Act for at least one year and that have a minimum market value of publicly held voting and non-voting stock of $75 million are permitted to disclose even less detail in the 1933 Act registration (S–3) and to incorporate even more information by reference to 1934 Act reports.

In 1992, the SEC issued new rules establishing an integrated registration and reporting system for small business issuers. These rules are intended to facilitate access to the public financial markets for start-up and developing companies and to reduce costs for small business issuers wishing to have their securities traded in public markets. The rules define a small business issuer as a noninvestment company whose annual revenues total less than $25 million and whose voting and non-voting common stock has a market value of less than $25 million. A new form (SB–2) has been designated as the registration form for small business issuers, although, if eligible, they may use Forms S–2 or S–3. Form SB–2 has no dollar limit. In 1993 the SEC adopted another new form (SB–1), which small business issuers may use to sell up to $10 million of securities in any twelve-month period. Form SB–1 is a streamlined disclosure document permitting either a narrative or a question-and-answer format.

`http:` **1933 Act registration forms:** http://www.law.uc.edu/ CCL/33forms/index.html

Shelf Registrations

Shelf registrations permit certain qualified issuers to register securities that are to be offered and sold "off the shelf" on a delayed or continuous basis in the future. This is a departure from the requirement that an issuer must file a registration for *every* new distribution of nonexempt securities. **Rule 415** of the SEC, which governs shelf registrations, requires that the information in the original registration be kept accurate and current. Only companies eligible to use the S–3 short form for registration qualify for shelf registrations. The issuer must reasonably expect that the securities will be sold within two years of the effective date of the registration. Shelf registrations allow issuers to respond more quickly to market conditions such as changes in stock prices and interest rates.

EXEMPT SECURITIES

The 1933 Act exempts a number of specific securities from its registration requirements. Because these exemptions apply to the securities themselves, the securities also may be resold without registration.

Short-Term Commercial Paper

The Act exempts any note, draft, or bankers' acceptance (a draft accepted by a bank) issued for working capital that has a maturity of not more than nine months when issued. Section 3(a)(3). This exemption is not available, however, if the proceeds are to be used for permanent purposes, such as the acquisition of a plant, or if the paper is of a type not ordinarily purchased by the general public.

Other Exempt Securities

The 1933 Act also exempts the following kinds of securities from registration:

1. securities issued or guaranteed by domestic governmental organizations, such as municipal bonds;
2. securities of domestic banks and savings and loan associations;

3. securities of not-for-profit, charitable organizations;
4. certain securities issued by Federally regulated common carriers; and
5. insurance policies and annuity contracts issued by State-regulated insurance companies.

EXEMPT TRANSACTIONS FOR ISSUERS

In addition to exempting specific types of securities, the 1933 Act also exempts *issuers* from the registration requirements for certain kinds of transactions. These exempt transactions include (1) private placements (Rule 506), (2) limited offers not exceeding $5 million (Rule 505), (3) limited offers not exceeding $1 million (Rule 504), and (4) limited offers solely to accredited investors (Section 4(6)). Except for some issuances under Rule 504, these exemptions from registration apply only to the transaction in which the securities are issued; therefore, any resale must be made by registration, unless the resale qualifies as an exempt transaction.

In addition, the 1933 Act provides a number of securities exemptions that are in effect transaction exemptions. These include intrastate issues, exchanges between an issuer and its security holders, and reorganization securities issued and exchanged with court or other governmental approval. Moreover, the Bankruptcy Act exempts securities issued by a debtor if they are offered under a reorganization plan in exchange for a claim or interest in the debtor. Bankruptcy Act,

Section 1145(a). These exemptions apply only to the original issuance; resales may be made only by registration unless the resale qualifies as an exempt transaction.

Another transaction exemption is Regulation A, which permits an issuer to sell a limited amount of securities in an unregistered public offering if certain conditions are met. Unlike other transaction exemptions, Regulation A places no restrictions upon the resale of securities issued pursuant to it.

◆ **See Figure 44-2**   Registration and Exemptions under the 1933 Act

Limited Offers

The 1933 Act exempts, or authorizes the SEC to exempt, transactions that do not require the protection of registration because they either involve a small amount of money or are made in a limited manner. Sections 3(b) and 4(2). Promulgated in 1982 to simplify and clarify the transaction exemptions relating to small issues and small issuers, Regulation D contains three separate exemptions (Rules 504, 505, and 506), each involving limited offers. Section 4(6), also aimed at small issues, is a companion section to the exemptions under Regulation D.

Securities sold pursuant to these exemptions (with the exception of some sold pursuant to Rule 504) are considered **restricted securities** and may be resold only by registration or in another transaction exempt from registration. An issuer who uses these exemptions must take reasonable care to prevent nonexempt, unregistered resales of restricted securities.

◆ **Figure 44-2**   **Registration and Exemptions under the 1933 Act**

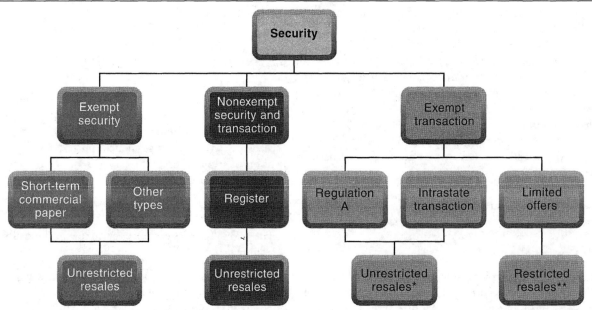

* Under intrastate exemption, resales to nonresidents may only be made nine months after the last sale in the initial issuance.
** Except some issuances under Rule 504.

Reasonable care includes, but is not limited to, the following: (a) making a reasonable inquiry to determine if the purchaser is acquiring the securities for herself or for other persons; (b) providing written disclosure prior to the sale to each purchaser that the securities have not been registered and therefore cannot be resold unless they are registered or unless an exemption from registration is available; and (c) placing a legend on the securities certificate stating that the securities have not been registered and that they are restricted securities.

`http:` **Regulation D:** http://www.law.uc.edu/CCL/33ActRls/regD.html

Private Placements The most important transaction exemption for issuers is the so-called private placement provision of the Act, which exempts "transactions by an issuer not involving any public offering." Section 4(2). SEC **Rule 506** establishes for all issuers a nonexclusive safe harbor for limited offers and sales without regard to the dollar amount of the offering. While compliance with the rule ensures the exemption, the exemption is not presumed to be unavailable for noncomplying transactions.

Securities sold under this exemption are restricted securities and may be resold only by registration or in a transaction exempt from registration. General advertising or general solicitation is not permitted. The issue may be purchased by an unlimited number of "accredited investors" and by no more than thirty-five other purchasers. **Accredited investors** include banks, insurance companies, investment companies, executive officers or directors of the issuer, savings and loan associations, registered broker-dealers, certain employee benefit plans with total assets in excess of $5 million, any person whose net worth exceeds $1 million, and any person whose income exceeded $200,000 in each of the two preceding years and who reasonably expects an income in excess of $200,000 in the current year. Before a sale involving any nonaccredited investors, such purchasers must receive specified material information about the issuer, its business, and the securities being offered. If the sale involves only accredited investors, such disclosure is not mandatory. The issuer must reasonably believe that each purchaser who is not an accredited investor has sufficient knowledge regarding and experience in financial and business matters to evaluate capably the merits and risks of the investment or has the services of a representative possessing such knowledge and experience. The issuer must notify the SEC of sales made under the exemption and must take precautions against nonexempt, unregistered resales.

Limited Offers Not Exceeding $5 Million SEC **Rule 505** exempts from registration those offerings by noninvestment company issuers that do not exceed $5 million over twelve months. Securities sold under this exemption are restricted securities and may be resold only by registration or in a transaction exempt from registration. General advertising or general solicitation is not permitted. The issue may be purchased by an unlimited number of accredited investors and by no more than thirty-five other purchasers. Before a sale involving any nonaccredited investors, such purchasers must receive specified material information about the issuer, its business, and the securities being offered; in the absence of nonaccredited investors, such disclosure is unnecessary. Unlike the issuer under Rule 506, however, the issuer under Rule 505 is *not* required to believe reasonably that each nonaccredited investor, either alone or with his representative, has sufficient knowledge and experience regarding financial matters to be capable of evaluating the merits and risks of the investment. Like its counterpart under Rule 506, the issuer must take precautions against nonexempt, unregistered resales and must notify the SEC of sales made under the exemption.

Limited Offers Not Exceeding $1 Million As amended in 1999, SEC **Rule 504** provides private, noninvestment company issuers with an exemption from registration for issues not exceeding $1 million within twelve months. Issuers required to report under the 1934 Act and investment companies may not use Rule 504. The issuer is to notify the SEC of sales under the rule, which permits sales to an unlimited number of investors and does not require the issuer to furnish any information to them.

If the issuance meets certain conditions, Rule 504 permits general solicitations, and acquired shares are freely transferable. The conditions are that the issuance is either (1) registered under State law requiring public filing and delivery of a disclosure document to investors before sale or (2) exempted under State law permitting general solicitation and advertising so long as sales are made only to accredited investors.

If the issuance does not meet these conditions, general solicitation and advertising is not permitted. Moreover, the securities issued are restricted, and the issuer must take precautions against nonexempt, unregistered resales.

Limited Offers Solely to Accredited Investors In 1980, Congress added **Section 4(6)**, which provides an exemption for offers and sales of $5 million made by an issuer solely to accredited investors. General advertising or public solicitation is not permitted. As with Rules 505 and 506, an unlimited number of accredited investors may purchase the issue; however, unlike these rules, Section 4(6) allows no unaccredited investors to purchase. No information is required to be furnished to the purchasers. Securities sold under this exemption are restricted securities and may be resold only by registration or in a transaction exempt from registration. The issuer must notify the SEC of sales made under the exemption and must take precautions against nonexempt, unregistered resales.

Regulation A

As amended in 1992, Regulation A permits an issuer to offer up to $5 million of securities in any twelve-month period without registering them, provided that the issuer files an offering statement with the SEC prior to the sale of the securities. An offering circular must also be provided to offerees and purchasers. The issuer may make offers upon filing the offering statement but may make sales only after the SEC has qualified it. Issuers required to report under the 1934 Act and investment companies may not use Regulation A. Regulation A filings are less detailed and time-consuming than full registration statements, and the required financial statements are simpler and need not be audited unless the issuer has audited financial statements prepared for other purposes. Issuers now may use an optional, simplified question-and-answer disclosure document.

Regulation A sets no restrictions regarding the number or qualifications of investors who may purchase securities under its provisions. Furthermore, securities sold under Regulation A may be resold freely after they are issued.

http: **Regulation A:** http://www.law.uc.edu/CCL/33ActRls/
regA.html

Intrastate Issues

The 1933 Act also exempts from registration any security that is part of an issue offered and sold only to persons resident within a single State where the issuer of such security is resident and doing business. Section 3(a)(11). This exemp-

tion is intended to apply to local issues representing local financing carried out by local persons through local investments. The exemption does not apply if *any* offeree, who need not become a purchaser, is not a resident of the State in which the issuer is resident.

The courts and the SEC have interpreted the exemption narrowly. **Rule 147**, promulgated by the SEC, provides a nonexclusive safe harbor for securing the intrastate exemption. Rule 147 requires that:

1. the issuer be incorporated or organized in the State in which the issuance occurs;
2. the issuer be principally doing business in that State, which means that the issuer must derive 80 percent of its gross revenues from that State, 80 percent of its assets must be located in that State, and 80 percent of its net proceeds from the issue must be used in that State;
3. all of the *offerees* and purchasers be residents of that State;
4. no resales to nonresidents be made during the period of sale and for nine months after the last sale; and
5. the issuer take precautions against interstate distributions. Such precautions include (a) placing on the security certificate a legend stating that the securities have not been registered and that resales can be made only to residents of the State and (b) obtaining a written statement of residence from each purchaser.

◆ **SEE FIGURE 44-3** **Exempt Transactions for Issuers under the 1933 Act**

◆ **FIGURE 44-3**   **Exempt Transactions for Issuers under the 1933 Act**

Exemption	Price Limitation	Information Required	Limitations on Purchasers	Resales
Regulation A	$5 million	Offering circular	None	Unrestricted
Intrastate Rule 147	None	None	Intrastate only	Only to residents before 9 months
Rule 506	None	Material information to unaccredited purchasers	Unlimited accredited; 35 unaccredited	Restricted
Rule 505	$5 million	Material information to unaccredited purchasers	Unlimited accredited; 35 unaccredited	Restricted
Rule 504	$1 million	None	None	Restricted*
Section 4(6)	$5 million	None	Only accredited	Restricted

* Unrestricted if under State law the issuance is either (1) registered or (2) exempted with sales only to accredited investors.

EXEMPT TRANSACTIONS FOR NON-ISSUERS

The 1933 Act requires registration for any sale by any person (including non-issuers) of any nonexempt security unless a statutory exemption can be found for the transaction. The Act, however, provides a transaction exemption for any person other than an issuer, underwriter, or dealer. Section 4(1). In addition, the Act exempts most transactions by dealers and brokers. Sections 4(3) and 4(4). These three provisions exempt from the registration requirements of the 1933 Act most secondary transactions; that is, the numerous resales that occur on an exchange or in the over-the-counter market. Nevertheless, these exemptions do not extend to some situations involving resales by non-issuers, in particular to (1) resales of restricted securities acquired under Regulation D (Rules 506 or 505) or Sections 4(6) and (2) sales of restricted or nonrestricted securities by affiliates. Such sales must be made pursuant to registration, Rule 144, or Regulation A. An **affiliate** is a person who controls, is controlled by, or is under common control with the issuer. **Control** is the direct or indirect possession of the power to direct the management and policies of a person through ownership of securities, by contract, or otherwise. Rule 405.

Rule 144

Rule 144 of the SEC sets forth conditions that, if met by an affiliate or any person selling restricted securities, exempt her from registering those securities. The rule requires that there be adequate current public information about the issuer, that the person selling under the rule have owned the securities for at least one year, that she sell them only in limited amounts in unsolicited brokers' transactions, and that notice of the sale be provided to the SEC. A person who is not an affiliate of the issuer when the restricted securities are sold and who has owned the securities for at least two years may, however, sell them in unlimited amounts and is not subject to any of the other requirements of Rule 144. Sales by an affiliate are subject to Rule 144 whether the securities are restricted or nonrestricted; however, an affiliate who sells nonrestricted securities need not comply with the one-year holding period.

Rule 144A

While Rule 144 permits sales of restricted securities, the requirements of the rule have hampered the liquidity of privately placed securities. To improve the liquidity of such securities, in 1990 the SEC adopted Rule 144A, which provides an additional, nonexclusive safe harbor from registration for resales of restricted securities. Only securities that at the time of issue are not of the same class as securities listed on a national securities exchange or quoted in a U.S. automated interdealer quotation system ("nonfungible securities") may be sold under Rule 144A. Such nonfungible securities may be sold only to a qualified institutional buyer, defined generally as an institution that in the aggregate owns and invests on a discretionary basis at least $100 million in securities. Rule 144A also requires the seller of the nonfungible securities to take reasonable steps to ensure that the buyer knows that the seller is relying on Rule 144A. In addition, special requirements apply to securities issued by foreign companies. Securities acquired pursuant to Rule 144A are restricted securities.

Regulation A

In addition to providing issuers an exemption from registration for securities up to $5 million, Regulation A provides an exemption for non-issuers. Use of this exemption, which places a $1.5 million limit on the total amount of securities sold in any twelve-month period by all non-issuers, requires compliance with all of the conditions Regulation A imposes upon issuers, as discussed above.

LIABILITY

To implement the statutory objectives of providing full disclosure and preventing fraud in the sale of securities, the 1933 Act imposes a number of sanctions for noncompliance with its requirements. These sanctions include administrative remedies by the SEC, civil liability to injured investors, and criminal penalties.

The Reform Act provides "forward-looking" statements (predictions) a "safe harbor" under the 1933 Act from civil liability based on an untrue statement of material fact or an omission of a material fact necessary to make the statement not misleading. The safe harbor applies only to issuers required to report under the 1934 Act. The safe harbor eliminates civil liability if a forward-looking statement is (1) immaterial, (2) made without actual knowledge that it was false or misleading, or (3) identified as a forward-looking statement and is accompanied by meaningful cautionary statements identifying important factors that could cause actual results to differ materially from those predicted. "Forward-looking statements" include projections of revenues, income, earnings per share, capital expenditures, dividends, or capital structure; management's plans and objectives for future operations; and statements of future economic performance. The safe harbor provision, however, does not cover statements made in connection with an initial public offering, a tender offer, a going private transaction, or offerings by a partnership or a limited liability company.

Unregistered Sales

The Act imposes express civil liability for the sale of an unregistered security that is required to be registered, the sale of a registered security without delivery of a prospectus, the sale of a security by use of an outdated prospectus, or the offer of a sale prior to the filing of the registration statement. **Section 12(a)(1)**. Liability is strict or absolute because there are no defenses. The person who purchases a security sold in violation of this provision has the right to tender it back to the seller and recover the purchase price. If the purchaser no longer owns the security, he may recover monetary damages from the seller.

False Registration Statements

When securities have been sold subject to a registration statement, **Section 11** of the Act imposes express liability upon those who have included any untrue statement in the registration statement or who omit from the statement any material fact. **Material** matters are those to which a reasonable investor would be substantially likely to attach importance in determining whether to purchase the security registered. SEC Rule 405. Usually, proof of reliance upon the misstatement or omission is not required. The section imposes liability upon (1) the issuer; (2) all persons who signed the registration statement, including the principal executive officer, principal financial officer, and principal accounting officer; (3) every person who was a director or partner; (4) every accountant, engineer, appraiser, or expert who prepared or certified any part of the registration statement; and (5) all underwriters. These persons are generally jointly and severally liable for the amount paid for the security, less either its value at the time of suit or the price for which it was sold, to any person who acquires the security without knowledge of the untruth or omission. A defendant is not liable for any or the entire amount otherwise recoverable under Section 11 that the defendant proves was caused by something other than the defective disclosure. The court may award attorneys' fees against any party who brings suit or asserts a defense without merit.

An expert is liable only for misstatements or omissions in the portion of the registration that he prepared or certified. Moreover, any defendant, other than the issuer (who has strict liability), may assert the affirmative defense of due diligence. This **due diligence** defense generally requires the defendant to show that she had reasonable grounds to believe, and did believe, that there were no untrue statements or material omissions. In some instances, due diligence requires a reasonable investigation to determine grounds for belief. The standard of reasonableness for such investigation and such grounds is that required of a prudent person in the management of his own property. Section 11(c).

◆ SEE CASE 44-2

Antifraud Provisions

The 1933 Act also contains two antifraud provisions: Section 12(a)(2) and Section 17(a). In addition, Rule 10b–5 of the 1934 Act applies to the issuance or sale of all securities, even those exempted by the 1933 Act. Rule 10b–5 is discussed later in this chapter.

Section 12(a)(2) Section 12(a)(2) imposes express liability upon any person who offers or sells a security by means of a prospectus or oral communication that contains an untrue statement of material fact or omits a material fact. That liability extends only to the immediate purchaser, provided she did not know of the untruth or omission. The seller may avoid liability by proving that he did not know and in the exercise of reasonable care could not have known of the untrue statement or omission. The seller is liable to the purchaser for the amount paid upon tender of the security. If the purchaser no longer owns the security, she may recover damages from the seller. A defendant is not liable for any or the entire amount otherwise recoverable under Section 12(a)(2) that the defendant proves was caused by something other than the defective disclosure.

Section 17(a) Section 17(a) makes it unlawful for any person in the offer or sale of any securities, whether registered or not, to do any of the following when using any means of transportation or communication in interstate commerce or the mails:

1. employ any device, scheme, or artifice to defraud;
2. obtain money or property by means of any untrue statement of a material fact or any statement that omits a material fact, without which the information is misleading; or
3. engage in any transaction, practice, or course of business that operates or would operate as a fraud or deceit upon the purchaser.

There is considerable doubt whether the courts may imply a private right of action for persons injured by violations of this section. The Supreme Court has reserved this question, and most lower courts have denied the existence of a private remedy. The SEC may, however, bring enforcement actions under Section 17(a).

Criminal Sanctions

The 1933 Act imposes criminal sanctions upon any person who willfully violates any of its provisions or the rules and regulations the SEC promulgates pursuant to the Act. Section 24. Conviction may carry a fine of not more than $10,000 or imprisonment of not more than five years, or both.

◆ SEE FIGURE 44-4   **Registration and Liability Provisions of the 1933 Act**

◆ FIGURE 44-4 **Registration and Liability Provisions of the 1933 Act**

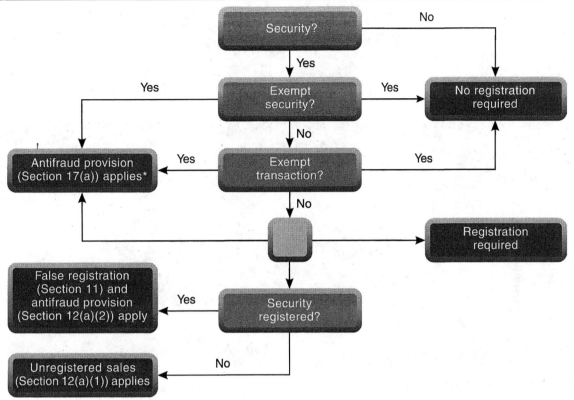

* Section 12(a)(2) *may* apply to some of these issuances.

Securities Exchange Act of 1934

The Securities Exchange Act of 1934 deals principally with the secondary distribution (resale) of securities. The definition of a security in the 1934 Act is substantially the same as the definition in the 1933 Act. The 1934 Act seeks to ensure fair and orderly securities markets by prohibiting fraudulent and manipulative practices and by establishing rules for market operations. It provides protection for holders of all securities listed on national exchanges, as well as for those holders of equity securities of companies traded over the counter whose corporate assets exceed $10 million and whose equity securities include a class with five hundred or more shareholders. Companies must register such securities and are also subject to the 1934 Act's periodic reporting requirements, short-swing profits provision, tender offer provisions, and proxy solicitation provisions, as well as the internal control and recordkeeping requirements of the Foreign Corrupt Practices Act. An over-the-counter issuer may terminate its registration when the holders of its registered equity securities number fewer than

three hundred or when the issuer has had fewer than five hundred shareholders *and* assets totaling less than $10 million on the last day of each of the past three years. In addition, issuers of securities, whether registered under the 1934 Act or not, must comply with the antifraud and antibribery provisions of the Act.

◊ SEE CASE 44-1

◆ SEE FIGURE 44-5 **Applicability of the 1934 Act**

The National Securities Markets Improvements Act of 1996 broadly authorized the SEC to issue regulations, rules, or orders exempting any person, security, or transaction from any of the provisions of the 1934 Act or the SEC's rules promulgated under that Act. This authorization extends so far as such exemption is necessary or appropriate in the public interest and is consistent with the protection of investors. This exemptive authority does not, however, extend to the regulation of government securities broker-dealers.

 Securities Exchange Act of 1934: http://www4.law. cornell.edu/uscode/15/ch2B.html
http://www.law.uc.edu/CCL/34Act/index.html

◆ **FIGURE 44-5**   Applicability of the 1934 Act

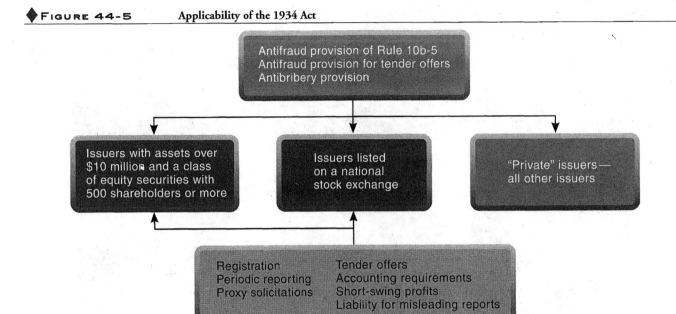

DISCLOSURE

The 1934 Act imposes significant disclosure requirements upon reporting companies. These include the filing of securities registrations, periodic reports, disclosure statements for proxy solicitations, and disclosure statements for tender offers, as well as compliance with the accounting requirements imposed by the Foreign Corrupt Practices Act. As part of its integrated registration and reporting system for small business issuers, in 1992 the SEC developed a new series of forms for qualifying issuers to use for registration and periodic reporting under the 1934 Act. Also in 1992, the SEC imposed new disclosure requirements for registration statements, periodic reports, and proxy statements that contain information regarding the compensation paid to senior executives and directors. The compensation disclosure rules are designed to provide shareholders with a lucid presentation of both annual and long-term compensation for senior executives over the previous three years. In addition, the issuer must inform the shareholders of their cumulative return over the previous five years and how that figure compares with the Standard and Poor's 500 Composite Stock Price Index *and* any recognized industry index. Effective in 2000, a plain English summary term sheet is required in all tender offers, mergers, and going private transactions.

◆ **SEE FIGURE 44-6**   Disclosure under the 1934 Act

http: **Forms prescribed under the Securities Exchange Act of 1934:** http://www.law.uc.edu/CCL/34forms/index.html

Registration Requirements for Securities

The 1934 Act requires all regulated publicly held companies to register with the SEC. Section 12. These one-time registrations apply to an entire class of securities. Thus, they differ from registrations under the Securities Act of 1933, which relate only to the securities involved in a specific offering. Registration requires disclosure of information such as the organization, financial structure, and nature of the business; the terms, positions, rights, and privileges of the different classes of outstanding securities; the names of the directors, officers, and underwriters and of each security holder owning more than 10 percent of any class of nonexempt equity security; bonus and profit-sharing arrangements; and balance sheets and profit-and-loss statements for the three preceding fiscal years.

Periodic Reporting Requirements

Following registration, an issuer must file specified annual (10–K) and periodic (10–Q and 8–K) reports to update the information contained in the original registration. Also subject to the periodic reporting requirements are issuers who have filed a 1933 Act registration statement with respect to any security. Section 15. This duty is suspended, however, in any subsequent year during which the securities registered under the 1933 Act are held by fewer than three hundred persons.

The SEC has adopted rules under the Sarbanes-Oxley Act requiring an issuer's chief executive and chief financial officers to *certify* the financial and other information contained in the issuer's annual and quarterly reports. Moreover, the Act requires that each periodic report shall be *accompanied* by a

◆ FIGURE 44-6   Disclosure under the 1934 Act

	Initial Registration	Periodic Reporting	Insider Reporting	Proxy Statement	Tender Offer
Registrant	Issuer if regulated, publicly held company	Issuer if regulated, publicly held company	Statutory insiders (directors, officers, and principal stockholders)	Issuer and other persons soliciting proxies	5 percent stockholder, tender offeror, or issuer
Information	Nature of business; Financial structure; Directors and executive officers; Financial statements	Annual, quarterly, or current report updating information in initial registration	Initial statement of beneficial ownership of equity securities; Changes in beneficial ownership	Details of solicitation; Legal terms of proxy; Annual report (if directors to be elected)	Identity and background; Terms of transaction; Source of funds; Intentions
Filing Date	Within 120 days after becoming a reporting company	Annual: within 90 days after year's end; Quarterly: within 45 days after quarter's end; Current: within 15 days after any material change	Within 10 days of becoming a statutory insider; Within 2 days after a change in ownership takes place	10 days before final proxy statement is distributed	5 percent stockholder: within 10 days after acquiring more than 5 percent of a class of registered securities; Tender offeror: before tender offer is made; Issuer: before offer to repurchase
Purpose of Disclosure	Adequate and accurate disclosure of material facts regarding securities listed on a national exchange or traded publicly over the counter	Update information contained in initial registration	Prevent unfair use of information which may have been obtained by statutory insider	Full disclosure of material information; Facilitation of shareholder proposals	Adequate and accurate disclosure of material facts; Opportunity to reach uncoerced decision

written statement by the chief executive officer and the chief financial officer of the issuer certifying that the periodic report fully complies with the requirements of the 1934 Act and that information contained in the periodic report fairly presents, in all material respects, the financial condition and results of operations of the issuer. A CEO or CFO who certifies while *knowing* that the report does not comply with the Act is subject to a fine of not more than $1 million or imprisonment of not more than ten years, or both. A CEO or CFO who *willfully* certifies a statement knowing it does not comply with the Act shall be fined not more than $5 million or imprisoned not more than twenty years, or both.

The Sarbanes-Oxley Act requires that issuers disclose in plain English to the public on a rapid and current basis such additional information concerning material changes in the financial condition or operations of the issuer as the SEC determines is necessary or useful for the protection of investors and in the public interest.

The Act also requires that each director, each officer, and any person who owns more than 10 percent of a registered equity security file reports with the SEC for any month during which changes in his ownership of such equity securities have occurred. Previously, such transactions were required to be reported within ten days after the end of that month. The Sarbanes-Oxley Act now requires that these reports be filed before the end of the second business day following the day on which the transaction was executed, unless the SEC establishes a different deadline. The Act also requires that these filings be made electronically on EDGAR, that the SEC make them publicly available on its Internet site, and that the issuers make them available on their corporate Web sites, if they maintain one.

Proxy Solicitations

A **proxy** is a writing signed by a shareholder authorizing a named person to vote his shares of stock at a specified shareholders' meeting. To ensure that shareholders have adequate information with which to vote, the 1934 Act regulates the proxy solicitation process. The Act makes it unlawful for any person to solicit any proxy with respect to any registered security "in contravention of such rules and regulations as the Commission may prescribe." Section 14. **Solicitation** includes any request for a proxy, any request not to execute a proxy, or any request to revoke a proxy. The SEC has issued comprehensive and detailed rules prescribing the solicitation process and the disclosure of information about the issuer.

http: Proxy solicitation rules: http://www.law.uc.edu/CCL/ 34ActRls/reg14A.html

Proxy Statements Rule 14a–3 prohibits the solicitation of a proxy unless each person solicited has been furnished with a written proxy statement containing specified information. An issuer making solicitations must furnish security holders with a *proxy statement* describing all material facts concerning the matters being submitted to their vote, together with a *proxy form* on which the security holders can indicate their approval or disapproval of each proposal to be presented. Even a company that submits a matter to a shareholder vote rather than solicit proxies must provide its shareholders with information substantially equivalent to what would appear in a proxy statement. With few exceptions, the issuer must file preliminary copies of a proxy statement and proxy form with the SEC at least ten days prior to the first date they are to be sent. In addition, in an election of directors, solicitations of proxies by a person other than the issuer are subject to similar disclosure requirements. The issuer in such an election also must include an annual report with the proxy statement.

Shareholder Proposals Where management makes a solicitation, any security holder entitled to vote has the opportunity to communicate with other security holders. Upon written request, the corporation must mail the communication at the security holder's expense or, at its option, promptly furnish to that security holder a current list of security holders.

If an eligible security holder entitled to vote submits a timely and appropriate proposal for action at a forthcoming meeting, management must include the proposal in its proxy statement and provide security holders with an opportunity to vote for or against it. To be eligible, the holder must own the lesser of 1 percent or $2,000 in market value of the security for at least one year prior to submitting the proposal. If management opposes the proposal, it must include in its proxy materials a statement by the security holder in support of the proposal. The aggregate length of the proposal and the supporting statement may not exceed five hundred words. A security holder is limited to submitting one proposal to an issuer each year.

Management may omit a proposal if, among other things, (1) under State law it is not a proper subject for shareholder action, (2) it would require the company to violate any law, (3) it is beyond the issuer's power or authority to effectuate, (4) it relates to the conduct of the ordinary business operations of the issuer, or (5) it relates to an election to office.

Tender Offers

A **tender offer** is a general invitation by a buyer (bidder) to the shareholders of a target company to tender their shares for sale at a specified price for a specified time. In 1968, Congress enacted the Williams Act, which amended the 1934 Act to extend reporting and disclosure requirements to tender offers and other block acquisitions. The purpose of the Williams Act is to provide public shareholders with full disclosure by both the bidder and the target company, so that the shareholders may make an informed decision.

http: Tender offer rules: http://www.law.uc.edu/CCL/34ActRls/ reg14D.html

Disclosure Requirements The 1934 Act imposes disclosure requirements in three situations: (1) when a person or group acquires more than 5 percent of a class of voting securities registered under the 1934 Act, (2) when a person makes a tender offer for more than 5 percent of a class of registered equity securities, or (3) when the issuer makes an offer to repurchase its own registered shares. Although each situation is governed by different rules, the disclosure required is substantially the same. A statement must be filed with the SEC containing (1) the acquisitor's background; (2) the source of the funds used to acquire the securities; (3) the purpose of the acquisition, including any plans to liquidate the company or to make major changes in the corporate structure; (4) the number of shares owned; (5) the terms of the transaction; and (6) any relevant contracts, arrangements, or understandings. Sections 13(d) and 14(d). This disclosure is also required of anyone soliciting shareholders to accept or reject a tender offer. A copy of the statement must be furnished to each offeree and sent to the issuer.

The target company has ten days in which to respond to the bidder's tender offer by (1) recommending acceptance or rejection, (2) expressing no opinion and remaining neutral, or (3) stating that it is unable to take a position. The target company's response must include the reasons for the position taken.

Required Practices A tender offer by either a third party or the issuer is subject to the following rules. The initial tender offer must be kept open for at least twenty business days and for at least ten days after any change in terms. Shareholders who tender their shares may withdraw them at any time during the offering period. The tender offer must be open to all holders of the class of shares subject to the offer, and all shares tendered must be purchased for the same price; thus, if an offering price is increased, both those who have tendered and those who have yet to tender will receive the benefit of the increase. A tender offeror who offers to purchase less than all of the outstanding securities of the target must accept, on a *pro rata* basis, securities tendered during the offer. During the tender offer, the bidder may buy shares of the target only through that tender offer. Effective in 2000, in a tender offer for all outstanding shares of a class, a tender offeror may provide a subsequent offering period of three to twenty days after completion of a tender offer, during which security holders can tender shares without withdrawal rights.

Defensive Tactics When confronted by an uninvited takeover bid—or by a potential, uninvited bid—management of the target company may decide either to oppose the bid or seek to prevent it. The defensive tactics management employs to prevent or defend against undesired tender offers have developed (and are still evolving) into a highly ingenious, and metaphorically named, set of maneuvers, some of which require considerable planning and several of which are of questionable legality.

State Regulation More than forty States have enacted statutes regulating tender offers. Although they vary greatly, most of these statutes tend to protect a target company from an unwanted tender offer. Some empower the State to review the merits of an offer or the adequacy of disclosure. Many impose waiting periods before the tender offer becomes effective. The State statutes generally require disclosures more detailed than those the Williams Act requires, and many of them exempt tender offers supported by the target company's management. A number of States have adopted fair price statutes, which require the acquisitor to pay to all shareholders the highest price paid to any shareholder. Some States have enacted business combination statutes prohibiting transactions with an acquisitor for a specified time after change in control, unless disinterested shareholders approve.

Foreign Corrupt Practices Act

In 1977, Congress enacted the Foreign Corrupt Practices Act (FCPA) as an amendment to the 1934 Act. Amended in 1988, the Act imposes internal control requirements upon companies with securities registered under the 1934 Act and, as discussed later in this chapter, prohibits all domestic concerns from bribing foreign governmental or political officials.

The accounting requirements of the FCPA reflect the ideas that accurate recordkeeping is essential to managerial responsibility and that investors should be able to rely on the financial reports they receive. Accordingly, the accounting requirements were enacted (1) to assure that an issuer's books accurately reflect financial transactions, (2) to protect the integrity of independent audits of financial statements, and (3) to promote the reliability of financial information required by the 1934 Act.

The FCPA requires every issuer that has a class of registered securities to:

1. make and keep books, records, and accounts which, in reasonable detail, accurately and fairly reflect the transactions and disposition of the assets of the issuer, and
2. devise and maintain a system of internal controls to assure that transactions are executed as authorized and recorded in conformity with generally accepted accounting principles, thereby establishing accountability with regard to assets and assuring that access to those assets is permitted only with management's authorization. Section 13(b).

LIABILITY

To implement its objectives, the 1934 Act imposes a number of sanctions for noncompliance with its disclosure and antifraud requirements. These sanctions include civil liability to injured investors and issuers, civil penalties, and criminal penalties.

The Reform Act contains several provisions that affect civil liability under the 1934 Act. First, the Reform Act imposes on a plaintiff in any private action under the 1934 Act the burden of proving that the defendant's alleged violation of the 1934 Act caused the loss for which the plaintiff seeks to recover damages. Second, the Reform Act imposes a limit on the amount of damages a plaintiff can recover in any private action under the 1934 Act based on a material misstatement or omission in which she seeks to establish damages by reference to the market price of a security. The plaintiff may not recover damages in excess of the difference between the purchase or sale price she paid or received for the security and the mean trading price of that security during the ninety-day period beginning on the date when the information correcting the misstatement or omission is disseminated to the market. Third, the Reform Act provides a "safe harbor" under the 1934 Act from civil liability based on an untrue statement of material fact or an omission of a material fact necessary to make the statement not misleading. The safe harbor applies to issuers required to report under the 1934 Act and who make "forward-looking" statements (predictions) if the statements meet specified requirements. The requirements of the safe harbor and the transactions to which it does not apply were discussed earlier in this chapter.

Misleading Statements in Reports

Section 18 imposes express civil liability upon any person who makes or causes to be made any false or misleading statement with respect to any material fact in any application, report, document, or registration filed with the SEC under the 1934 Act. Any person who purchased or sold a security in reliance upon a false or misleading statement without knowing that it was false or misleading may recover under Section 18. Nevertheless, a person who made such a statement or who caused one to be made is not liable if she proves that she acted in good faith and had no knowledge that such statement was false or misleading. The court may award attorneys' fees against either the plaintiff or the defendant.

Short-Swing Profits

Section 16(b) of the 1934 Act imposes express liability upon insiders—directors, officers, and any person owning more than 10 percent of the stock of a corporation listed on a national stock exchange or registered with the SEC—for all profits resulting from their "short-swing" trading in such stock. If any insider sells such stock within six months from the date of its purchase or purchases such stock within six months from the date of a sale of the stock, the corporation is entitled to recover any and all profit the insider realizes from these transactions. The "profit" recoverable is calculated by matching the highest sale price against the lowest purchase price within the relevant six-month period. Losses cannot be offset against profits. Suit to recover such profit may be brought by the issuer or by the owner of any security of the issuer in the name and on behalf of the issuer if the issuer fails or refuses to bring such suit within sixty days of the owner's request.

Antifraud Provision

Section 10(b) of the 1934 Act and SEC **Rule 10b–5** make it unlawful for any person to do any of the following when using the mails or facilities of interstate commerce in connection with the purchase or sale of any security:

1. employ any device, scheme, or artifice to defraud;
2. make any untrue statement of a material fact;
3. omit to state a material fact necessary to make the statements made not misleading; or
4. engage in any act, practice, or course of business that operates or would operate as a fraud or deceit upon any person.

Rule 10b–5 applies to any purchase or sale of any security, whether it is registered under the 1934 Act or not, whether it is publicly traded or closely held, whether it is listed on an exchange or sold over the counter, or whether it is part of an initial issuance or a secondary distribution. There are *no* exemptions. The implied liability under Rule 10b–5 applies to purchaser as well as seller misconduct and allows both defrauded sellers and buyers to recover.

Requisites of Rule 10b–5   Recovery of damages under Rule 10b–5 requires proof of (1) a misstatement or omission (2) that is material, (3) made with *scienter*, and (4) relied upon (5) in connection with the purchase or sale of a security. This rule differs from common law fraud in that Rule 10b–5 imposes an affirmative duty of disclosure. A misstatement or omission is **material** if there is a substantial likelihood that a reasonable investor would consider it important in deciding whether to purchase or sell the security. Examples of material facts include substantial changes in dividends or earnings, significant misstatements of asset value, and the fact that the issuer is about to become a target of a tender offer. In an action for damages under Rule 10b–5, it must be shown that the violation was committed with **scienter**, or intentional misconduct. Negligence is not sufficient. Although the Supreme Court has yet to decide whether reckless conduct is sufficient to satisfy the requirement of *scienter*, the vast majority of circuit and district courts have held recklessness to be sufficient.

Direct reliance may be difficult to prove in a 10b–5 action because the buyer and seller usually do not negotiate their deal face-to-face. Recognizing the special nature of securities market transactions, the Supreme Court adopted the fraud-on-the-market theory, which establishes a rebuttable presumption of reliance based on the premise that the market price of a stock reflects any misstatement or omission and that the fraudulently affected market price has injured the plaintiff.

Remedies for violations of Rule 10b–5 include rescission, damages, and injunctions. The courts are divided over the measure of damages to impose.

Insider Trading   Rule 10b–5 applies to sales or purchases of securities made by an "insider" who possesses material information that is not available to the general public. An insider who fails to disclose the material, nonpublic information before trading on the information will be liable under Rule 10b–5 unless he waits for the information to become public. Under SEC Rule 10b5-1, a purchase or sale of an issuer's security is based on material nonpublic information about that security or issuer if the person making the purchase or sale was *aware* of the information when the person entered into the transaction. **Insiders**, for the purpose of Rule 10b–5, include directors, officers, employees, and agents of the security issuer, as well as those with whom the issuer has entrusted information solely for corporate purposes, such as underwriters, accountants, lawyers, and consultants. In some instances, the rule also precludes persons who receive material, nonpublic information from insiders—tippees—from trading on that information. A tippee who knows or should know that an insider has breached his fiduciary duty to the shareholders by disclosing inside information to the tippee is under a duty not to trade on such information.

◆SEE FIGURE 44-7 Parties Forbidden to Trade on Inside Information

The U.S. Supreme Court has upheld the misappropriation theory as an additional and complementary basis for imposing liability for insider trading. Under this theory, a person may be held liable for insider trading under Rule 10b–5 if she trades in securities for personal profit using confidential information misappropriated in breach of a fiduciary duty to the source of the information. This liability applies even though the source of information is not the issuer of the securities that were traded. SEC Rule 10b5-2 adopts the misappropriation theory of liability: A violation of Section 10(b) includes the purchase or sale of a security of an issuer on the basis of material nonpublic information about that security or issuer in breach of trust or confidence that is owed to the issuer, the shareholders of that issuer *or any other person who is the source of the material nonpublic information.* Under SEC Rule 10b5-2, a person has a duty of trust or confidence for purposes of the misappropriation theory of liability when: (1) a person agrees to maintain information in confidence; (2) two people have a history, pattern, or practice of sharing confidences such that the recipient of the information knows or reasonably should know that the person communicating the material nonpublic information

expects that the recipient will maintain its confidentiality; *or* (3) a person receives or obtains material nonpublic information from his or her spouse, parent, child, or sibling.

Under SEC Regulation FD, regulated issuers who disclose material nonpublic information to specified persons (primarily securities market professionals such as analysts and mutual fund managers) must make public disclosure of that information. If the selective disclosure was intentional or reckless, the issuer must make public disclosure simultaneously; for a non-intentional disclosure, the issuer must make public disclosure promptly, usually within 24 hours. With a few exceptions, Regulation FD does not apply to disclosures made in connection with a securities offering registered under the 1933 Act. The SEC can enforce this rule by bringing an administrative action seeking a cease-and-desist order or a civil action seeking an injunction and/or civil money penalties.

◊ SEE CASE 44-3

Although both Section 16(b) and Rule 10b–5 address the problem of insider trading and both may apply to the same transaction, they differ in several respects. First, Section 16(b) applies only to transactions involving registered equity securities; Rule 10b–5 applies to all securities. Second, the definition of *insider* under Rule 10b–5 extends beyond directors, officers, and owners of more than 10 percent of a company's stock, whereas the definition under Section 16(b) is limited to these persons. Third, Section 16(b) does not require that the insider possess material, nonpublic information; liability is strict. Rule 10b–5 applies to insider trading only where such information is not disclosed. Fourth, Section 16(b) applies only to transactions occurring within six months of each

◆FIGURE 44-7   **Parties Forbidden to Trade on Inside Information**

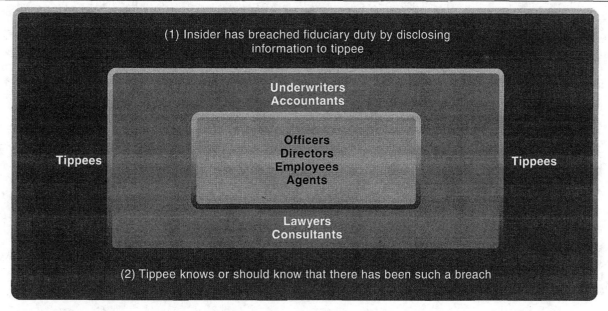

other; Rule 10b–5 has no such limitation. Fifth, under Rule 10b–5, injured investors may recover damages on their own behalf; under Section 16(b), although shareholders may bring suit, any recovery is on behalf of the corporation.

Express Insider Trading Liability

In 1988, Congress amended the 1934 Act by adding **Section 20A**, which imposes express civil liability upon any person who violates the Act by purchasing or selling a security while in possession of material, nonpublic information. Any person who contemporaneously sold or purchased securities of the same class as those improperly traded may bring a private action against the traders to recover damages for the violation. The total amount of damages may not exceed the profit gained or loss avoided by the violation, diminished by any amount the violator disgorges to the SEC pursuant to a court order. The action must be brought within five years after the date of the last transaction that is the subject of the violation. Tippers are jointly and severally liable with tippees who commit a violation by trading on the inside information.

Civil Penalties for Insider Trading

In addition to the remedies discussed above, the SEC is authorized by legislation enacted in 1984 and 1988 to bring an action in a U.S. district court to have a civil penalty imposed upon any person who purchases or sells a security while in possession of material, nonpublic information. Liability also extends to any person who by communicating material, non-public information aids and abets another in committing such a violation. Liability may also be imposed on any person who directly or indirectly controlled a person who ultimately committed a violation if the controlling person knew or recklessly disregarded the fact that the controlled person was likely to commit a violation and consequently failed to take appropriate steps to prevent the transgression. Under this provision law firms, accounting firms, issuers, financial printers, news media, and others must implement policies to prevent insider trading. The violating transaction must be on or through the facilities of a national securities exchange or from or through a broker or dealer. Purchases that are part of a public offering by an issuer of securities are not subject to this provision.

The civil penalty for a person who trades on inside information is determined by the court in light of the facts and circumstances but may not exceed three times the profit gained or loss avoided as a result of the unlawful purchase or sale. The maximum amount that may be imposed upon a controlling person is the greater of $1.2 million or three times the profit gained or loss avoided as a result of the controlled person's violation. If that violation consists of tipping inside information, the court measures the controller's liability by the profit gained or loss avoided by the person to whom the controlled person directed

the tip. For the purpose of this provision, "profit gained" or "loss avoided" is "the difference between the purchase or sale price of the security and the value of that security as measured by the trading price of the security a reasonable period after public dissemination of the nonpublic information."

Civil penalties for insider trading are payable into the United States Treasury. The SEC is authorized to award bounties of up to 10 percent of a recovered penalty to informants who provide information leading to the imposition of the penalty. An action to recover a penalty must be brought within five years after the date of the purchase or sale.

Misleading Proxy Statements

Any person who distributes a materially false or misleading proxy statement may be liable to a shareholder who relies upon the statement in purchasing or selling a security and thereby suffers a loss. In this context, a misstatement or omission is material if there is a substantial likelihood that a reasonable shareholder would consider it important in deciding how to vote. A number of courts have held that negligence is sufficient for an action under the proxy rule's antifraud provisions. In addition, when the proxy disclosure or filing requirement has been violated, a court may, if appropriate, enjoin a shareholder meeting or any action taken at that meeting. Other remedies are rescission, damages, and attorneys' fees. Since a proxy statement is filed with the SEC, a materially false or misleading proxy statement may also give rise to liability under Section 18, discussed above. In addition, Rule 10b–5 also applies to misstatements in proxy statements.

Fraudulent Tender Offers

It is unlawful for any person to make any untrue statement of material fact, to omit to state any material fact, or to engage in any fraudulent, deceptive, or manipulative practices in connection with any tender offer. Section 14(e). This provision applies even if the target company is not subject to the 1934 Act's reporting requirements. Insider trading during a tender offer is prohibited by Rule 14e–3, which has been upheld by the U.S. Supreme Court in *United States v. O'Hagan* (Case 44-3).

Some courts have implied civil liability for violations of Section 14(e). Because relatively few cases have involved such violations, however, the requirements for such an action are not entirely clear. At present, a target company may seek an injunction, and a shareholder of the target may be able to recover damages or obtain rescission. Furthermore, it appears likely that the courts will require *scienter*.

◆ **See Case 44-4**

◆ **See Figure 44-8**   **Civil Liability under the 1933 and 1934 Acts**

◆ **Figure 44-8**   Civil Liability under the 1933 and 1934 Acts

Provision	Conduct	Plaintiffs	Defendants	Standard of Culpability	Reliance Required	Type of Liability	Remedies
Section 12a(1) 1933 Act	Unregistered sale or sale without prospectus	Purchasers from a violator	Sellers in violation	Strict liability	No	Express	Rescission Damages
Section 11 1933 Act	Registration statement containing material misstatement or omission	Purchasers of registered security	Issuer Directors Signers Underwriters Experts	Strict liability for issuer; Negligence for others	No	Express	Damages Attorneys' fees
Section 12(a)(2) 1933 Act	Material misstatement or omission	Purchasers from a violator	Sellers in violation	Negligence	No	Express	Rescission Damages
Section 18 1934 Act	False or misleading statements in a document filed with SEC	Purchasers or sellers	Persons making filing in violation	Knowledge or bad faith	Yes	Express	Damages Attorneys' fees
Section 16(b) 1934 Act	Short-swing profit by insider	Issuer; Shareholder of issuer	Directors; Officers; 10 percent shareholders	Strict liability	No	Express	Damages
Rule 10b–5 1934 Act	Deception or material misstatement or omission	Purchasers or sellers	Purchasers or sellers in violation	Scienter	Yes	Implied	Rescission Damages Injunction
Section 20A 1934 Act	Insider trading	Contemporaneous purchasers or sellers	Inside traders	Scienter	No	Express	Damages
Section 14(a) 1934 Act	Materially false or misleading proxy solicitation	Shareholders	Persons making proxy solicitation in violation	Negligence (probably)	Probably	Implied	Rescission Damages Injunction Attorneys' fees
Section 14(e) 1934 Act	Tender offer with: Deception or Manipulation or Material misstatement or omission	Target company; Shareholders of target	Persons making tender offer in violation	Scienter (probably)	Probably	Implied	Rescission Damages Injunction

Antibribery Provision of FCPA

The FCPA makes it unlawful for any domestic concern or any of its officers, directors, employees, or agents to offer or give anything of value directly or indirectly to any foreign official, political party, or political official for the purpose of (1) influencing any act or decision of that person or party in his or its official capacity, (2) inducing an act or omission in violation of his or its lawful duty, or (3) inducing such person or party to use his or its influence to affect a decision of a foreign government in order to assist the domestic concern in obtaining or retaining business. An offer or promise to make a prohibited payment is a violation even if the offer is not accepted or the promise is not performed. The 1988 amendments to the Act explicitly excluded routine governmental actions not involving the official's discretion, such as obtaining permits or processing applications. They also added an affirmative defense for payments that are lawful under the written laws or regulations of the foreign official's country.

Violations can result in fines of up to $2 million for companies; individuals may be fined a maximum of $100,000 or be imprisoned for up to five years, or both. Section 32(c). Fines imposed upon individuals may not be paid directly or indirectly by the domestic concern on whose behalf they acted. In addition, the courts may impose civil penalties of up to $11,000.

In 1997 the United States and thirty-three other nations signed the Organization for Economic Cooperation and Development Convention on Combating Bribery of Foreign Public Officials in International Business Transactions (OECD Convention). In 1998 Congress enacted the International Anti-Bribery and Fair Competition Act of 1998 to conform the FCPA to the Convention. The 1998 Act expands the FCPA to include (1) payments made to "secure any improper advantage" from foreign officials, (2) all foreign persons who commit an act in furtherance of a foreign bribe while in the United States, and (3) officials of public international organizations within the definition of a "foreign official." A public international organization is defined as either an organization designated by executive order pursuant to the International Organizations Immunities Act, or any other international organization designated by executive order of the president.

 OECD Convention: http://www.oecd.org/daf/ nocorruption/instruments.htm

Criminal Sanctions

Section 32 of the 1934 Act imposes criminal sanctions on any person who willfully violates any provision of the Act (except the antibribery provision) or the rules and regulations the SEC promulgates pursuant to the Act. As amended by the Sarbanes-Oxley Act, for individuals, conviction may carry a fine of not more than $5 million or imprisonment for not more than twenty years, or both, with one exception: a person who proves she had no knowledge of the rule or regulation is not subject to imprisonment. If the person, however, is not a natural person (e.g., a corporation), a fine not exceeding $25 million may be imposed.

CHAPTER SUMMARY

Securities Act of 1933

Definition of a Security	**Security** includes any note, stock, bond, preorganization subscription, and investment contract **Investment Contract** any investment of money or property made in expectation of receiving a financial return solely from the efforts of others
Registration of Securities	**Disclosure Requirements** disclosure of accurate material information required in all public offerings of nonexempt securities unless offering is an exempt transaction **Integrated Disclosure and Shelf Registrations** permitted for certain qualified issuers
Exempt Securities	**Definition** securities not subject to the registration requirements of the 1933 Act **Types** exempt securities include short-term commercial paper, municipal bonds, and certain insurance policies and annuity contracts
Exempt Transactions for Issuers	**Definition** issuance of securities not subject to the registration requirements of the 1933 Act

Types exempt transactions include limited offers under Regulation D and Section 4(6), Regulation A, and intrastate issues

Exempt Transactions for Non-issuers	**Definition** resales by persons other than the issuer that are exempted from the registration requirements of the 1933 Act **Types** exempt transactions include Rule 144, Regulation A, and Rule 144A
Liability	**Unregistered Sales** Section 12(a)(1) imposes absolute civil liability as there are no defenses **False Registration Statements** Section 11 imposes liability on the issuer, all persons who signed the statement, every director or partner, experts who prepared or certified any part of the statement, and all underwriters; defendants other than issuer may assert the defense of due diligence **Antifraud Provisions** Section 12(a)(2) imposes liability upon the seller to the immediate purchaser, provided the purchaser did not know of the untruth or omission, but the seller is not liable if he did not know and, in the exercise of reasonable care could not have known, of the untrue statement or omission; Section 17(a) broadly prohibits fraud in the sale of securities **Criminal Sanctions** willful violations are subject to a fine of not more than $10,000 and/or imprisonment of not more than five years

Securities Exchange Act of 1934

Disclosure	**Registration and Periodic Reporting Requirements** apply to all regulated publicly held companies and include one-time registration as well as annual, quarterly, and monthly reports **Proxy Solicitations** • *Definition of a Proxy* a signed writing by a shareholder authorizing a named person to vote her stock at a specified meeting of shareholders • *Proxy Statements* proxy disclosure statements are required when proxies are solicited or an issuer submits a matter to a shareholder vote **Tender Offers** • *Definition of a Tender Offer* a general invitation to shareholders to purchase their shares at a specified price for a specified time • *Disclosure Requirements* a statement disclosing specified information must be filed with the SEC and furnished to each offeree **Foreign Corrupt Practices Act** imposes internal control requirements on companies with securities registered under the 1934 Act
Liability	**Misleading Statements in Reports** Section 18 imposes civil liability for any false or misleading statement made in a registration or report filed with the SEC **Short-Swing Profits** Section 16(b) imposes liability on certain insiders (directors, officers, and shareholders owning more than 10 percent of the stock of a corporation) for all profits made on sales and purchases within six months of each other, with any recovery going to the issuer **Antifraud Provision** Rule 10b–5 makes it unlawful to (1) employ any device, scheme, or artifice to defraud; (2) make any untrue statement of a material fact; (3) omit to state a material fact; or (4) engage in any act that operates as a fraud

- *Requisites of Rule 10b–5* recovery requires (1) a misstatement or omission, (2) materiality, (3) scienter (intentional and knowing conduct), (4) reliance, and (5) connection with the purchase or sale of a security
- *Insider Trading* "insiders" are liable under Rule 10b–5 for failing to disclose material, nonpublic information before trading on the information

Express Insider Trading Liability is imposed on any person who sells or buys a security while in possession of inside information

Civil Penalties for Inside Trading may be imposed on inside traders in an amount up to three times the gains they made or losses they avoided

Misleading Proxy Statements any person who distributes a false or misleading proxy statement is liable to injured investors

Fraudulent Tender Offers Section 14(e) imposes civil liability for false and material statements or omissions or fraudulent, deceptive, or manipulative practices in connection with any tender offer

Antibribery Provision of FCPA prohibited bribery can result in fines and imprisonment

Criminal Sanctions individuals who willfully violate the 1934 Act are subject to a fine of not more than $5 million and/or imprisonment of not more than twenty years

---

CASES

CASE

44-1

Definition of a Security
SEC v. EDWARDS
Supreme Court of the United States, 2004
540 U.S. 389, 124 S.Ct. 892, 157 L.Ed.2d 813
http://caselaw.lp.findlaw.com/cgi-bin/getcase.pl?court=US&navby=case&vol=000&invol=02-1196

O'Connor, J.

"Opportunity doesn't always knock * * * sometimes it rings." [Citation.] And sometimes it hangs up. So it did for the 10,000 people who invested a total of $300 million in the payphone sale-and-leaseback arrangements touted by respondent under that slogan. The Securities and Exchange Commission (SEC) argues that the arrangements were investment contracts, and thus were subject to regulation under the federal securities laws. In this case, we must decide whether a moneymaking scheme is excluded from the term "investment contract" simply because the scheme offered a contractual entitlement to a fixed, rather than a variable, return.

I

Respondent Charles Edwards was the chairman, chief executive officer, and sole shareholder of ETS Payphones, Inc. (ETS). ETS, acting partly through a subsidiary also controlled by respondent, sold payphones to the public via independent distributors. The payphones were offered packaged with a site lease, a 5-year leaseback and management agreement, and a buyback agreement. All but a tiny fraction of purchasers chose this package, although other management options were offered. The purchase price for the payphone packages was approximately $7,000. Under the leaseback and management agreement, purchasers received $82 per month, a 14% annual return. Purchasers were not involved in the day-to-day operation of the

payphones they owned. ETS selected the site for the phone, installed the equipment, arranged for connection and long-distance service, collected coin revenues, and maintained and repaired the phones. Under the buyback agreement, ETS promised to refund the full purchase price of the package at the end of the lease or within 180 days of a purchaser's request.

In its marketing materials and on its website, ETS trumpeted the "incomparable pay phone" as "an exciting business opportunity," in which recent deregulation had "open[ed] the door for profits for individual pay phone owners and operators." According to ETS, "[v]ery few business opportunities can offer the potential for ongoing revenue generation that is available in today's pay telephone industry." [Citation.]

The payphones did not generate enough revenue for ETS to make the payments required by the leaseback agreements, so the company depended on funds from new investors to meet its obligations. In September 2000, ETS filed for bankruptcy protection. The SEC brought this civil enforcement action the same month. It alleged that respondent and ETS had violated the registration requirements of §§ 5(a) and (c) of the Securities Act of 1933, [citation], the antifraud provisions of both § 17(a) of the Securities Act of 1933, [citation], and § 10(b) of the Securities Exchange Act of 1934, [citation], and Rule 10b–5 thereunder, [citation]. The District Court concluded that the payphone sale-and-leaseback arrangement was an investment

Environmental Law

As technology has advanced and people have become more urbanized, their effect on the environment has increased. Our air has become dirtier; our waters have become more polluted. While individuals and environmental groups have brought private actions against some polluters, the common law has proved unable to control environmental damage. Because of this inadequacy, the Federal and State governments have enacted a variety of statutes designed to promote environmental concerns and prevent environmental harm. Although in recent years certain developed countries, such as the United States, have made significant progress in controlling pollutants, such is not the case worldwide. Moreover, even as we have enjoyed some success in controlling some pollutants, a new generation of environmental problems has arisen. In this chapter, we will discuss both common law causes of action for environmental damage and Federal regulation of the environment.

Common Law Actions for Environmental Damage

Private tort actions may be used to recover for harm to the environment. For example, if Alice's land is polluted by the mill next door, Alice may sue the mill in tort for the damage to her land. In suing to recover for environmental damage, plaintiffs generally have relied on the theories of nuisance, trespass, and strict liability.

NUISANCE

The term *nuisance* encompasses two distinct types of wrong: private nuisance and public nuisance. A private nuisance involves an interference with a person's use and enjoyment of his land, while a public nuisance is an act that interferes with a public right.

Private Nuisance

To establish a private nuisance, a plaintiff must show that the defendant has substantially and unreasonably interfered with the use and enjoyment of the plaintiff's land. In an action for damages, the plaintiff need not prove that the defendant's conduct was unreasonable, only that the interference was unreasonable. Thus, assuming all other requirements are met, the question in a private nuisance suit for damages is whether the defendant should pay for the harm it caused the plaintiff, even if the defendant's action was not unreasonable. For example, in one case, an electric utility using a coal-burning electric generator which employed the latest scientific methods for reducing emissions was held liable for the harm it caused its neighbor's alfalfa crops, even though the utility was performing the socially useful function of creating electric power.

Although a plaintiff need not prove the defendant's conduct is unreasonable to recover in a private nuisance action for damages, such reasonableness is an issue when the plaintiff sues for an injunction. In determining whether an injunction against a nuisance is appropriate, a court will "balance the equities" by considering a number of factors, including the gravity of the harm to the plaintiff, the social value of the defendant's activity that is causing the harm, the feasibility and costs of avoiding the harm, and the public interest, if any.

The need to balance the equities has meant that courts often deny injunctions when the defendant is engaged in a socially useful activity. Additionally, injunctions are frequently denied because the defendant successfully raises an equitable defense. Consequently, private nuisance actions have been of limited value in controlling environmental damage.

Public Nuisance

To be treated as a public nuisance, an activity must somehow interfere with the health, safety, or comfort of the public. For example, the actions of an industrial plant in polluting a stream will be treated as a private nuisance if such actions inconvenience only the owners of land downstream but will be treated as a public nuisance if they kill the stream's marine life. Generally, only a public representative, such as the attorney general, may sue to stop a public nuisance. If, however, the nuisance inflicts upon an individual some unique harm that the general populace does not suffer, that individual may also sue to halt the nuisance. Out of concern about the economic impact of closing an industrial operation, public representatives frequently are unwilling to sue to abate a public nuisance. Consequently, because these representatives often will not, and private parties may not, sue, relatively few public nuisance actions have been brought against polluters.

TRESPASS TO LAND

To establish trespass to land, a plaintiff must show an invasion that interferes with the plaintiff's right of exclusive possession of the property and that is the direct result of an action by the defendant. For example, entering or throwing trash on someone else's land without permission constitutes a trespass. Trespass differs from private nuisance in that trespass requires an interference with the plaintiff's possession of the land. Thus, sending smoke or gas onto another's property may constitute a private nuisance but does not constitute a trespass.

Trespass often is difficult to establish in actions for environmental damage, either because the plaintiff is not in possession of the property or because the injury does not stem from an invasion of the property. Trespass actions have thus been of limited benefit in halting environmental damage. For a more complete discussion of trespass, see Chapter 7.

STRICT LIABILITY FOR ABNORMALLY DANGEROUS ACTIVITIES

While they generally base tort liability on fault, the courts may hold **strictly liable**, that is, liable without fault, a person engaged in an abnormally dangerous activity. To establish such strict liability, a plaintiff must show that the defendant is carrying on an unduly dangerous activity in an inappropriate location and that the plaintiff has suffered damage because of this activity. For example, a person who operates an oil refinery in a densely populated area may be held strictly liable for any damage the refinery causes. The requirement that the activity engaged in be (1) ultrahazardous and (2) inappropriate for its locale has limited the number of strict liability actions brought against polluters.

PROBLEMS COMMON TO PRIVATE CAUSES OF ACTION

In addition to the shortcomings of each tort theory discussed above, using a private cause of action to control environmental damage presents its own problems. The costs associated with private litigation (including the payment of one's own legal fees) are high, and although overall the environmental damage may be considerable, the extent of any particular injury may not warrant pursuing a private lawsuit. Furthermore, tort actions generally do not provide relief for aesthetic, as opposed to physical, injury. Additionally, in many tort actions a significant issue of causation arises. For example, if a landowner lives near several plants, each of which emits pollution and none of which, by itself, would cause the amount of damage the landowner's property has suffered, the landowner may have difficulty recovering from any of the plant owners. Finally, even if a private plaintiff is successful, her recovery may be limited to monetary damages, leaving the defendant free to continue to pollute.

Federal Regulation of the Environment

Because private causes of action have proved inadequate to recompense and prevent environmental damage, the Federal, State, and some local governments have enacted statutes designed to protect the environment. In this chapter, we will consider some of the more important Federal environmental laws. In addition, the Environmental Protection Agency (EPA) has encouraged companies to conduct voluntary environmental audits. One of the key issues surrounding such self-audits is whether these audits are discoverable by State or Federal prosecutors.

 Environmental Protection Agency: http://www.epa.gov/
State Environmental Protection Agencies:
http://www.epa.gov/epahome/state.htm

THE NATIONAL ENVIRONMENTAL POLICY ACT

In 1969, Congress enacted the **National Environmental Policy Act** (NEPA) to establish environmental protection as a goal of Federal policy. The NEPA's declaration of national environmental policy states the following:

> The Congress, recognizing the profound impact of man's activity on the interrelations of all components of the natural environment, particularly the profound influences of population growth, high-density urbanization, industrial expansion, resource exploitation, and new and expanding technological advances, and recognizing further the critical importance of restoring and maintaining environmental quality to the overall welfare and development of man, declares that it is the continuing policy of the Federal Government, in cooperation with State and local governments . . . to use all practicable means and measures . . . in a manner calculated to foster and promote the general welfare, to create and maintain conditions under which man and nature can exist in productive harmony, and fulfill the social, economic and other requirements of present and future generations of Americans.

Thus, NEPA imposes the responsibility for maintaining the environment on all Federal agencies. It is the responsibility of the Federal government to consider the environmental consequences of all of its actions and to administer all of its programs in an environmentally sound manner.

The NEPA has two major substantive sections, one creating the Council on Environmental Quality (CEQ) and the other requiring that each Federal agency, when recommending or reporting on proposals for legislation or other major Federal action, prepare an **environmental impact statement** (EIS) if the legislation or Federal action will have a significant environmental effect.

 National Environmental Policy Act: http://www4.law.
cornell.edu/uscode/42/4321.html
Council on Environmental Quality: http://www.
whitehouse.gov/ceq/

The Council on Environmental Quality

The Council on Environmental Quality (CEQ), a three-member advisory group, is not a separate administrative agency but rather is part of the Executive Office of the President; as such, it makes recommendations to the President on environmental matters and prepares annual reports on the condition of the environment. Although not expressly authorized to do so by statute, the CEQ, acting under a series of executive orders, has issued regulations regarding the content and preparation of environmental impact statements. The Federal courts generally have deferred to these regulations.

Environmental Impact Statements

Unlike most Federal environmental statutes, the NEPA does not focus on a particular type of environmental damage or harmful substance but instead expresses the Federal government's continuing concern with protection of the environment. The NEPA's promotion of environmental considerations is effected through the EIS requirement. An environmental impact statement (EIS) is required if the proposed action (1) is Federal, (2) is considered "major," and (3) has a significant environmental impact.

Procedure for Preparing an EIS When proposing legislation or considering a major Federal action, the CEQ regulations require that a Federal agency initially make an "environmental assessment," which is a short analysis of the need for an EIS. If the agency decides that no EIS is required, it must make this decision available to the public. If, on the other hand, the agency concludes that an EIS is required, the agency must engage in "scoping," which consists of consulting other relevant Federal agencies and the public to determine the significant issues the EIS will address and the statement's appropriate scope. After scoping, the agency prepares a draft EIS, for which there is a comment period. After the comment period ends and revisions, if necessary, are made, a final EIS is published.

Scope of EIS Requirement The EIS requirement of the NEPA applies to a broad range of projects:

> [T]here is "Federal action" within the meaning of the statute not only when an agency proposes to build a facility itself, but also whenever an agency makes a decision which permits action by other parties which will affect the quality of the environment. NEPA's impact statement procedure has been held to apply where a federal agency approves a lease of land to private parties, grants licenses and permits to private parties, or approves and funds state highway projects. In each of these instances the federal agency took action affecting the environment in the sense that the agency made a decision which permitted some other party—private or governmental—to take action affecting the environment.

The NEPA's EIS requirement applies not only to a broad range of projects but also to a broad range of environmental effects. The NEPA has been held to apply not only to the natural environment but also to the urban environment, including impact on crime, esthetics, and socioeconomics.

> The Act [NEPA] must be construed to include protection of the quality of life for city residents. Noise, traffic, overburdened mass transportation systems, crime, congestion and even availability of drugs all affect the urban "environment" and are surely results of the "profound influences of . . . high-density urbanization [and] industrial expansion."

While effects on health, including psychological health, are considered environmental effects under the NEPA, the Supreme Court has held that an effect is environmental only if it has a reasonably close causal relation to an impact on the physical environment.

Content of an EIS The NEPA requires that an EIS describe in detail the environmental impact of a proposed action, any adverse environmental effects which could not be avoided if the proposal were implemented, alternatives to the proposed action, the relationship between local short-term uses of the environment and the maintenance and enhancement of long-term productivity, and any irreversible and irretrievable commitments of resources the proposed action would involve if it were implemented. Impact statements provide a basis for evaluating the benefits of a proposed project in light of its environmental risks and for comparing its environmental risks with those of alternatives. The Supreme Court has held that a Federal agency is required to consider all *reasonable* alternatives in its EIS (a rule of reason standard). One reasonable alternative that always must be considered is doing nothing.

Nature of EIS Requirement Whether the NEPA was solely procedural or whether it had a substantive component was initially unclear. The Supreme Court resolved the issue by holding that the NEPA's requirements are primarily procedural and that the NEPA does not require that the relevant Federal agency attempt to mitigate the adverse effects of a proposed Federal action. Rather, NEPA attempts to prohibit uninformed decisions, not unwise agency actions.

THE CLEAN AIR ACT

Initially, the Federal government's role in controlling air pollution was quite limited. The States had primary responsibility for air pollution control, and the Federal government merely supervised their efforts and offered technical and financial assistance. When State efforts proved inadequate to alleviate the problem, Congress enacted the Clean Air Act Amendments of 1970, greatly expanding the Federal role in

antipollution efforts. Major revisions to the Clean Air Act were enacted in 1977 and 1990.

The Act establishes two regulatory schemes, one for existing sources and one for new stationary sources. The States retain primary responsibility for regulating existing stationary sources and motor vehicles then in use (i.e., in use when the Act, or its subsequently enacted amendments, took effect), while the Federal government regulates new sources, new vehicles, and hazardous air pollutants.

Under the Act, the Environmental Protection Agency (EPA) may impose civil penalties of up to $25,000 per day of violation. Criminal penalties, which depend on the type of violation, vary greatly, providing for a maximum fine of $1 million per violation and/or fifteen years' imprisonment for a knowing violation that endangers a person. For repeat convictions, the Act doubles the maximum punishments.

http: **Clean Air Act:** http://www4.law.cornell.edu/uscode/ 42/7401.html

Existing Stationary Sources and Motor Vehicles Then in Use

Because the States had not managed adequately to control air pollution, the 1970 amendments provided that, with respect to existing stationary sources and motor vehicles then in use, the Federal government would set national air quality standards that the States would be primarily responsible for achieving.

National Ambient Air Quality Standards Under the Act, the EPA administrator is required to establish **national ambient air quality standards (NAAQSs)** for air pollutants that endanger the public health and welfare. The EPA administrator must establish "primary" standards to protect the public health, allowing for an adequate safety margin, and "secondary" standards to protect elements relating to the public welfare, such as animals, crops, and structures. The NAAQS for a particular pollutant specifies the concentration of that pollutant that will be allowed in the outside air over designated periods of time.

The EPA administrator established quality standards for seven major classes of pollutants—carbon monoxide, particulates, sulfur dioxide, nitrogen dioxide, hydrocarbons, ozone, and lead, although the hydrocarbon NAAQS was subsequently withdrawn as no longer being necessary. Recognizing that many areas would not meet the 1977 NAAQS deadline, Congress, in the 1977 amendments to the Act, extended the deadline to December 1982 and further provided that States demonstrating the impossibility of meeting the 1982 deadline "despite the implementation of all reasonably available measures" could obtain an extension until December 1987. In 1987, Congress extended the deadline for another eight months. The August 1988 deadline expired without extension, but the EPA has not vigorously enforced it.

The 1990 amendments sought to hasten attainment of the standards and provided that the EPA must establish new standards for major pollutants every five years. The amendments also imposed tighter standards with regard to ozone pollution, due to the lack of progress in this area.

◆ SEE CASE 46-1

State Implementation Plans   Once the EPA promulgates a new NAAQS, each State must submit to the agency a **State implementation plan (SIP)** detailing how the State will implement and maintain the NAAQS within the State. If the State adopted the SIP after public hearings and the SIP meets certain statutory conditions, the EPA is required to approve it. Foremost among the statutory conditions is the requirement that under the SIP the State will attain primary standards as soon as practicable but in any case within three years after the EPA approves the SIP. If the EPA determines that under an SIP a State will not attain an NAAQS within the designated time and the State fails to make the necessary amendments, the EPA is authorized to make amendments that will be binding on the State.

Under the 1990 amendments, the EPA also must decide whether an SIP is complete. If it is not, the EPA may treat the plan as a nullity in whole or in part. If it is complete, the EPA must approve or disapprove the plan within a year. Once the EPA approves an SIP, the plan is regarded as both State and Federal law, enforceable by either its State of implementation or the Federal government.

Prevention of Significant Deterioration Areas   Prior to the 1977 amendments, an issue arose as to whether air that was cleaner than required by an applicable NAAQS would be allowed to deteriorate to the NAAQS level. This issue was significant because much of the United States, particularly land in the Southwest, had air whose quality was higher than that required by applicable standards. Responding to this issue, Congress, in the 1977 amendments, established a policy to prevent the quality of such air from deteriorating. To effectuate this policy, Congress established rules for areas whose air quality was higher than the applicable NAAQS required it to be or for which information was insufficient to determine the air quality (so-called **prevention of significant deterioration [PSD] areas**). Because the rules classified an area on a pollutant-by-pollutant basis, a particular area might be a PSD area with respect to one pollutant and an area that had not met the applicable NAAQS with respect to another pollutant.

In PSD areas, only limited increases in air pollution are allowed. Before a major stationary source in a PSD area may be constructed or modified, the owner or operator of the source must receive a permit from the applicable State regulator. To

receive a permit, the owner/operator must demonstrate that the source will not increase pollution beyond permitted levels and must show that the source will utilize the best control technology available.

Nonattainment Areas   The 1977 and 1990 amendments also established special rules for areas that did not meet applicable NAAQSs, so-called **nonattainment areas**. Before a major stationary source may be constructed or modified in a nonattainment area, the owner/operator of the source must receive a permit from the applicable State regulator. To receive a permit, the owner/operator must show that the source will comply with the lowest achievable emission rate, which is the more stringent of either the most stringent emission limitation contained in any SIP or the most stringent emission limitation actually achieved. Additionally, total emissions from existing stationary sources and the proposed new or modified source together must be less than the total emissions allowed from existing sources at the time the permit is sought. Thus, to obtain a permit in a nonattainment area, an owner/operator must in some way reduce total emissions from all sources (existing and new/modified).

Under the 1990 amendments, the reduction required varies with the severity of the area's nonattainment problem. One way to reduce total emissions from all sources is to pay the owner/operator of another source to reduce its emissions by either installing more advanced emission control technology or closing its source. Alternatively, an owner/operator may reduce its own total emissions by altering the mix of emission controls at its plant. Under the EPA's "**bubble concept**," an entire plant is viewed as one source; consequently, the permit process applies only if total emissions from the plant increase. If, instead, the EPA treated each unit at a plant as a separate source, the owner/operator would be required to obtain a permit whenever it made a change to one unit. The bubble concept thus enables an owner/operator to bypass the permit process in some instances. Though environmental groups challenged the concept on this basis, in 1984 the Supreme Court upheld the bubble concept, finding the regulation to be a reasonable exercise of the EPA's discretion.

New Source Standards

The scheme of Federal NAAQSs and State SIPs applies to existing stationary sources and to motor vehicles then in use. In contrast, the Clean Air Act authorizes the Federal government to establish national emission standards for new stationary sources, new vehicles, and hazardous air pollutants.

New Stationary Sources   The Act requires the EPA administrator to establish performance standards for stationary sources that are constructed or modified after the publication of applicable regulations. The standard of performance must "reflect the degree of emission limitation and percentage reduction achievable through application of the best technological system of continuous emission reduction which . . . has been adequately demonstrated." As Case 46-1 indicates, the standard governing new sources is more stringent than the standard governing existing sources; accordingly, it is, from industry's perspective, better to be considered an existing source than a new or modified one.

New Vehicles The Clean Air Act requires the EPA administrator to establish emission standards for new motor vehicles and new motor vehicle engines. The Act also requires the use of reformulated automotive fuels to reduce ozone and carbon monoxide pollution. The reformulated gasoline must contain more oxygen and less in terms of volatile organic compounds.

Hazardous Air Pollutants The Act authorizes the EPA administrator to establish national emission standards for hazardous or toxic air pollutants, defined as "air pollutant[s] . . . caus[ing], or contribut[ing] to, air pollution which may reasonably be anticipated to result in an increase in mortality or an increase in serious irreversible, or incapacitating reversible, illness." The standard must be set at a level that "provides an ample margin of safety to protect the public health."

Acid Rain The 1990 amendments attempt to halt environmental destruction caused by **acid rain**, precipitation that contains high levels of sulfuric or nitric acid. Because sulfur dioxide (which forms sulfuric acid in the atmosphere and comes back as acid rain) is released into the atmosphere primarily by electric utilities, the 1990 amendments regulate such utilities by allotting them emission allowances with regard to the amount of sulfur dioxide they may release into the atmosphere, based upon past emissions and fuel consumption. The amendments establish an allowance schedule that should significantly reduce emissions of sulfur dioxide and nitrous oxides. The amendments also permit each utility to bank or sell its emission allowances.

THE CLEAN WATER ACT

As with air pollution control, the primary responsibility for controlling water pollution fell initially to the States. When their efforts proved inadequate, Congress fundamentally revised the nation's water pollution laws in its 1972 amendments to the Federal Water Pollution Control Act (subsequently renamed the Clean Water Act). Substantially amended again in 1977, 1981, and 1987, the Act attempts comprehensively to restore and maintain the chemical, physical, and biological integrity of the nation's waters.

The EPA may impose civil penalties of up to $25,000 per day for each violation. Maximum criminal penalties for knowing violations are $50,000 per day of violation and/or three years' imprisonment. For repeat convictions, the maximum punishments are doubled.

Like the Clean Air Act, the Clean Water Act establishes different schemes for existing sources and new sources. Additionally, the Act provides different programs for point and nonpoint sources of pollution. A **point source** is "any discernible, confined and discrete conveyance . . . from which pollutants are or may be discharged." A **nonpoint source**, in contrast, is a land use that causes pollution, such as a pesticide runoff from farming operations.

The scope of the Act is extremely broad, applying not only to all navigable waters in the United States but also to tributaries of navigable waters, interstate waters and their tributaries, the use of nonnavigable intrastate waters, if their misuse could affect interstate commerce, and freshwater wetlands.

http: **Clean Water Act:** http://www4.law.cornell.edu/uscode/ 33/1251.html

Point Sources

The Act mandates that the EPA administrator establish effluent limitations for categories of existing point sources. An **effluent limitation** is a technology-based standard that limits the amount of a pollutant that a point source may discharge into a body of water. The Act effectuates such limitations through the **National Pollutant Discharge Elimination System (NPDES)**, a permit system.

Effluent Limitations Under the 1972 amendments, effluent limitations for existing point sources, other than publicly owned treatment works, required application of the **best practicable control technology (BPT)** currently available by 1977 and application of the **best available technology (BAT)** economically achievable by 1983. According to the EPA, BPT is "the average of the best existing performance by well-operated plants within each industrial category or subcategory," while BAT is "the very best control and treatment measures that have been or are capable of being achieved." Somewhat different standards apply to publicly owned treatment works.

The National Pollutant Discharge Elimination System The National Pollutant Discharge Elimination System (NPDES), the permit system through which effluent limitations are to be achieved, requires that any person responsible for the discharge from a point source of a pollutant into U.S. waters must obtain a discharge permit from the EPA, the Army Corps of Engineers, or, in some circumstances, the relevant State. An NPDES permit incorporates the applicable effluent limitations and establishes a schedule for compliance. The holder of an NPDES permit is required to notify the appropriate authority if the holder will not meet its obligations under the permit. A discharge not in compliance with a permit is unlawful. With limited exceptions, new permits for existing facilities cannot be less stringent than current permits.

◆ See Case 46-2

The 1977 Amendments Recognizing that the application deadlines it had set in the 1972 amendments would not be met, Congress extended and modified the deadlines in 1977. The 1977 amendments to the Clean Water Act divided pollutants into three categories—toxic, conventional, and nonconventional (any pollutants that are neither toxic nor conventional)—and established different deadlines and standards for each category. For toxic pollutants, the 1983 BAT deadline was extended to 1984; for nonconventional pollutants, this standard was to be achieved by 1984 or within three years after the effluent limitation was established, whichever was later. For conventional pollutants, a new standard, **best conventional pollution control technology (BCT)**, was to be achieved by 1984. These deadlines were subsequently extended to 1989.

Nonpoint Source Pollution

Controlling nonpoint source pollution—such as agricultural and urban runoff—is inherently more difficult than controlling point source pollution.

> There is no effective way as yet, other than land use control, by which you can intercept that runoff and control it in a way that you do a point source. We have not yet developed technology to deal with that kind of a problem. We need to find ways to deal with it, because a great quantity of pollutants [are] discharged by runoff, not only from agriculture but from construction sites, from streets, from parking lots, and so on, and we have to be concerned with developing controls for them.

Although Congress tried to address the problem of nonpoint source pollution in the 1972 amendments, little effective control of nonsource pollution occurred before 1987. The 1987 amendments require States to identify State waters that will not meet the Act's requirements without the management of nonpoint sources of pollution and to institute "best management practices" to control such sources. The EPA must approve each State's management plan.

New Source Performance Standards

The Act requires the EPA administrator to establish Federal performance standards for new sources. A performance standard should "reflect the greatest degree of effluent reduction . . . achievable through application of the best available demonstrated control technology." The preferred standard for new sources is one "permitting no discharge of pollutants." Violation of a standard by an owner/operator of a new source is unlawful.

HAZARDOUS SUBSTANCES

Technological advances have enabled human beings to produce numerous artificial substances, some of which have proven extremely hazardous to health. As the potential and actual harm from these latter substances became clear, Congress responded by enacting various hazardous substances-related statutes. In this section, we will consider some of the most important Federal statutes governing hazardous substances: the Federal Insecticide, Fungicide and Rodenticide Act (FIFRA), the Toxic Substances Control Act (TSCA), the Resource Conservation and Recovery Act (RCRA), the Comprehensive Environmental Response, Compensation and Liability Act (CERCLA, or the Superfund), and the Superfund Amendments and Reauthorization Act of 1986 (SARA).

The Federal Insecticide, Fungicide and Rodenticide Act

The Federal government began regulating pesticides in 1910 and greatly expanded its control over such substances in 1947 with the passage of the Federal Insecticide, Fungicide and Rodenticide Act (FIFRA). Concern about pesticides increased dramatically after the publication in 1962 of *Silent Spring*, by Rachel Carson, and Congress has amended the FIFRA several times in the last thirty years.

The FIFRA requires that a pesticide be registered with the EPA before any person in any State may distribute it. Such registration is legal only if the pesticide's composition warrants the claims its manufacturer proposes for it, the pesticide will perform its intended function without "unreasonable adverse effects on the environment," the pesticide generally will not cause unreasonably adverse environmental effects when used in accordance with widespread and commonly recognized practice, and the pesticide complies with FIFRA labeling requirements. The FIFRA defines "unreasonable adverse effects on the environment" as any unreasonable risk to humans or the environment, taking into account the economic, social, and environmental costs and benefits of the use of any pesticide. Thus, unlike many environmental statutes, the FIFRA expressly requires the EPA to consider the costs of the action it takes under the statute.

If a pesticide is registered and subsequent data reveals additional hazards, the EPA may cancel the registration after an administrative hearing. The 1988 amendments placed upon industry the cost of disposing of canceled pesticides. Cancellation proceedings typically take years, both because of the numerous stages of the administrative process and because of the required use of a scientific advisory committee. While the cancellation process is in progress, the pesticide may be manufactured and sold. If additional hazard is imminent, however, the product's registration may be suspended until the cancellation proceeding is completed. Once its registration has been suspended, the pesticide may not be manufactured or distributed.

Until recently, the FIFRA did not adequately address the problem of old pesticides that had been registered under earlier and less strict standards. Concerned that these pesticides did not meet current standards, Congress in 1988 amended the FIFRA to require the re-registration of pesticides registered before 1984. U.S. exports are not subject to most of the Act's requirements, though an exported pesticide not registered under the FIFRA must bear a label stating "Not Registered for Use in the United States of America."

The EPA may impose civil penalties of up to $5,000 for each offense. Maximum criminal penalties for knowing violations are a $50,000 fine and/or one year imprisonment.

| http: | Federal Insecticide, Fungicide and Rodenticide Act: http://www4.law.cornell.edu/uscode/7/136.html |

The Toxic Substances Control Act

Congress passed the **Toxic Substances Control Act (TSCA)** in 1976 in an effort to provide a comprehensive scheme for regulating toxic substances. The TSCA contains provisions on the manufacture of new chemicals, the testing of suspect chemicals, the regulation of chemicals that present an unreasonable risk of injury to health and the environment, and the inventorying of all chemicals.

Under the Act, a manufacturer must notify the EPA before it manufactures a new chemical or makes a significant new use of an existing chemical. If the EPA administrator concludes that the information submitted is insufficient to permit a reasoned evaluation of the health and environmental effects of the chemical and the chemical may present an unreasonable risk of injury to health or the environment, the administrator may limit or prohibit the chemical's manufacture or distribution.

The Act authorizes the EPA to require the testing of any substance, whether existing or new, if (1) the manufacture or distribution of the substance may present an unreasonable risk of injury to health or the environment, (2) the data on the effects of the substance on health and the environment is insufficient, and (3) testing is necessary to develop such data.

Because of the many substances that might be subject to testing under the statutory standard, the TSCA mandates that the EPA establish a priority list for testing that contains no more than fifty substances at any time. This list is established by a committee whose members come from eight specified agencies.

Once the EPA determines, either through its testing program or through the premanufacturing notice process, that a substance "presents or will present an unreasonable risk of injury to health or the environment," the agency may restrict or prohibit use of the substance.

If the EPA administrator believes that a substance presents an imminent hazard, he is authorized to bring an action in Federal district court for seizure of the substance or other appropriate relief. The statute defines an "imminently hazardous chemical substance or mixture" as one that presents an unreasonable risk of serious or widespread injury to health or the environment.

The TSCA requires the EPA to compile and keep current a list of each chemical substance manufactured or processed in the United States. The EPA's initial inventory of existing chemicals, completed in 1980, listed approximately 55,000 substances. A chemical not listed on the inventory is subject to premanufacture review, even if it was in fact previously manufactured. Although not explicitly required to do so by the TSCA, the EPA reviews the substances on the inventory to determine their safety.

The EPA may impose civil penalties of up to $20,000 per day for a violation of the TSCA. Maximum criminal penalties for knowing violations are $25,000 fines for each day of violation and/or one year's imprisonment.

| http: | Toxic Substances Control Act: http://www4.law.cornell. edu/uscode/15/2601.html |

The Resource Conservation and Recovery Act

In 1976, Congress enacted the **Resource Conservation and Recovery Act (RCRA)** to provide a comprehensive scheme for the treatment of solid waste, particularly hazardous waste. The statute provides that the States are primarily responsible for nonhazardous waste, while the EPA regulates all phases of hazardous waste: generation, transportation, and disposal. Under the Act, the Federal government must establish criteria for identifying hazardous waste, taking into account factors that include toxicity, persistence, degradability, flammability, and corrosiveness.

The Act prescribes for generators (entities that produce hazardous waste) standards concerning recordkeeping, labeling, the use of appropriate containers, and reporting. The statute requires the EPA to establish a **manifest system** to be used by generators. A manifest is a form on which the generator must specify the quantity, composition, origin, routing, and destination of hazardous waste. On the manifest the generator also must certify that the volume and toxicity of the waste have been reduced to the greatest degree economically practicable and that the method of treatment, storage, and disposal minimizes the threat to health and the environment.

Transporters must maintain records and properly label the waste they transport. Furthermore, they must comply with manifests and may transport hazardous waste only to facilities holding an RCRA hazardous waste facility permit.

Owners/operators of hazardous waste treatment, storage, and disposal sites must maintain records and comply with generator manifests. Facilities for hazardous waste treatment, storage, and disposal must obtain an RCRA hazardous waste facility permit. To obtain a permit, a facility must comply with relevant EPA standards. Failure to comply may subject the owner/operator to civil or criminal penalties.

The Act authorizes the EPA administrator to sue in Federal court for an injunction if the administrator has evidence that "the past or present handling, storage, treatment, transportation or disposal of any solid waste or hazardous waste may present an imminent and substantial endangerment to health or the environment." Moreover, the EPA may impose civil penalties of up to $25,000 per day of violation. Maximum criminal penalties for knowing violations are $50,000 for each day of violation and/or five years' imprisonment. Where a knowing violation endangers a person, the maximum criminal penalty is a $1 million fine and/or fifteen years' imprisonment.

> **http:** The Resource Conservation and Recovery Act: http://www4.law.cornell.edu/uscode/42/6901.html

The Superfund

Although the RCRA regulates current and future generation, transportation, and disposal of hazardous waste, the Act provides only limited authority for the cleanup of abandoned or inactive hazardous waste sites. To fill this gap, Congress in 1980 enacted the Comprehensive Environmental Response, Compensation and Liability Act (CERCLA, or the Superfund). By 1986, the EPA, working under the Act, had spent $1.6 billion and had begun the cleanup of only eight sites. This record and other problems with the initial legislation prompted Congress to amend the CERCLA by enacting the Superfund Amendments and Reauthorization Act of 1986 (SARA). As of early 1998, the EPA had cleaned up 509 National Priorities List sites and had 470 still under construction. Nevertheless, it is predicted that if Congress does not provide additional funds the Superfund will run out of money in the near future.

CERCLA requires the Federal government to establish a National Contingency Plan (NCP) prescribing procedures and standards for responding to hazardous substance releases. The NCP specifies criteria for determining the priority of sites to be cleaned. The plan also identifies, on at least an annual basis, the sites that most require immediate cleanup.

Under the Act, the Federal government has authority to take either removal or remedial actions in response to a release or threatened release of hazardous substances, as long as such removal or remedial actions are consistent with the NCP. Removal typically is an immediate response to control a specific release of a hazardous substance. Remedial actions, on the other hand, consist of efforts to prevent or reduce the release of hazardous substances; such actions are intended to be long-term solutions. The President may impose a civil penalty of up to $25,000 per day of violation; for repeat violations, the penalty may reach up to $75,000 per day of violation.

States and private parties also may engage in response actions, although such actions must meet certain conditions

for the responder to recover its costs from either the governmental trust fund or the parties responsible under CERCLA for the release or threatened release of hazardous substances.

CERCLA establishes a trust fund to pay for hazardous waste removal and other remedial actions. The trust fund is financed in part by a surtax on businesses with annual incomes over $2 million, a tax on petroleum, and a tax on chemical feedstocks. An additional part of the trust fund comes from money recovered from persons responsible for the release of hazardous substances. These parties include the owners and operators of a hazardous waste disposal facility from which there has been a release, as well as any generator of hazardous wastes that were disposed of at that facility.

Because CERCLA initially imposed liability on all owners of contaminated property, some parties were held liable even though they had acquired the land either involuntarily or without knowledge of the hazardous wastes stored there. For example, after foreclosing on a mortgage of $335,000 and taking title to a piece of property, a bank was held liable for Superfund costs of more than $555,000. Responding to the inequity of such situations, Congress in SARA established a new defense to CERCLA liability for "innocent landowners." To qualify as an innocent landowner, one "must have undertaken, at the time of acquisition, all appropriate inquiry into the previous ownership and uses of the property consistent with good commercial or customary practice in an effort to minimize liability." In addition, under the Superfund Recycling Act of 1999, recyclers are exempt from liability to third parties, although they remain liable in suits brought by the federal or state governments.

> **http:** Comprehensive Environment Response, Compensation, and Liability Act: http://www4.law. cornell.edu/uscode/42/9601.html

In 2002, President Bush signed into law the Small Business Liability Relief and Brownfields Revitalization Act. The purpose of the Act is to promote the purchase, development, and use of brownfields (industrially polluted property which are not sufficiently contaminated as to be classified as a priority by either the EPA or state environmental agencies). The Act attempts to accomplish this purpose by providing protection from liability under CERCLA to any purchaser of contaminated property, to owners and developers who clean up property under state voluntary cleanup programs, and to owners of property that have become contaminated by migrating pollutants.

> **http:** Small Business Liability Relief and Brownfields Revitalization Act: http://www.epa.gov/brownfields/ sblrbra.htm

◆ **SEE FIGURE 46-1**   **Major Federal Environmental Statutes**

◆ **SEE CASE 46-3**

◆ **FIGURE 46-1**   **Major Federal Environmental Statutes**

Act	Major Purpose	Maximum Civil Penalty	Maximum Criminal Penalty
National Environmental Policy Act (NEPA)	• Establish environmental protection as a major national goal • Mandate environmental impact statements prepared prior to Federal action having a significant environmental effect	None	None
Clean Air Act	• Control and reduce air pollution • Establish National Ambient Air Quality Standards	$32,500 per day of violation	$1,000,000 fine per violation and/or 15 years' imprisonment*
Clean Water Act	• Protect against water pollution • Establish effluent limitations	$32,500 per day of violation	$50,000 per day of violation and/or 3 years' imprisonment*
Federal Insecticide, Fungicide and Rodenticide Act (FIFRA)	• Regulate the sale and distribution of pesticides • Prevent pesticides having an unreasonably adverse effect on the environment	$6,500 per offense	$50,000 fine and/or 1 year's imprisonment
Toxic Substances Control Act (TSCA)	• Regulate toxic substances • Prevent unreasonable risk of injury to health and the environment from toxic substances	$32,500 per day of violation	$25,000 fine per day of violation and/or 1 year's imprisonment
Resource Conservation and Recovery Act (RCRA)	• Regulate the disposal of solid waste • Establish standards to protect human health and the environment from hazardous wastes	$32,500 per day of violation	$1,000,000 fine and/or 15 years' imprisonment
Comprehensive Environmental Response, Compensation and Liability Act (CERCLA, or the Superfund) and Superfund Amendments and Reauthorization Act (SARA)	• Establish a national contingency plan for responding to releases of hazardous substances. • Establish a trust fund to pay for removal of hazardous waste and other remedial actions	$32,500 per day of violation; $97,500 for repeat violations	None

* Doubled for repeat convictions.

INTERNATIONAL PROTECTION OF THE OZONE LAYER

In 1987, the United States and twenty-three other countries entered into the Montreal Protocol on Substances that Deplete the Ozone Layer, a treaty designed to prevent pollution that harms the ozone layer. The treaty requires all signatories to reduce their production and consumption of all chemicals, in particular chlorofluorocarbons (CFCs, more commonly called freon), that deplete the ozone layer by 50 percent. Although excessive ozone in the air we breathe can be hazardous, the ozone layer in the stratosphere helps to protect the earth from harmful ultraviolet radiation. By 1985, scientists believed that the release of CFCs into the atmosphere had caused a hole to develop in the ozone layer over Antarctica.

Chlorofluorocarbons, halocarbons, carbon dioxide, methane, and nitrous oxide are extremely potent "greenhouse gases," which trap heat and thereby warm the earth. Human activities, however, have increased the release of greenhouse gases, resulting in the serious threat of global warming. Scientists warn that the earth's temperature could rise by as much as 6 degrees over the next century due to global warming. If this occurs, the levels of the seas will rise and the climate will change over most of the earth, causing severe flooding and disruptions of agricultural production.

To combat this predicted climate change, 165 nations in 1992 negotiated a treaty at the UN Convention on Climate Change (FCCC) in Rio de Janeiro. The treaty's ultimate objective was to stabilize the "greenhouse gas concentration in the atmosphere at a level that would prevent dangerous anthropogenic [human-induced] interference with the climate system." More than 160 countries eventually ratified the treaty, which went into effect on March 21, 1994. The FCCC calls for all signatory countries to develop and update national inventories of all greenhouse gases not otherwise covered by the Montreal Protocol. The treaty, however, is voluntary, and most nations, including the United States, will not meet its objectives. At a subsequent FCCC, held in Kyoto, Japan in December 1997, the participating nations proposed the Kyoto Protocol, which is a set of binding emission targets for developed nations. Under this Protocol, the United States is to reduce by the years 2008–2012 its emissions of greenhouse gases (carbon dioxide, methane, nitrous oxide, and synthetic substitutes for CFCs) to a level 7 percent below 1990 emission standards. Japan agreed to reduce its level to 6 percent below 1990 levels, and the European Union agreed to a level 8 percent below 1990 emission levels. The United States has not ratified this treaty. However, in 2001, President Bush stated that he does not support the Kyoto Treaty and saw no hope to salvage it. This followed a 95-0 vote in the Senate against its ratification.

 United Nations Environment Programme: http://www.unep.org

CHAPTER SUMMARY

Common Law Actions for Environmental Damage

Nuisance	**Private Nuisance** substantial and unreasonable interference with the use and enjoyment of a person's land **Public Nuisance** interference with the health, safety, or comfort of the public
Other Common Law Actions	**Trespass** an invasion of land that interferes with the right of exclusive possession of the property **Strict Liability for Abnormally Dangerous Activities** liability without fault for an individual who engages in an unduly dangerous activity in an inappropriate location

Federal Regulation of the Environment

National Environmental Policy Act (NEPA)	**Purpose** to establish environmental protection as a goal of Federal policy **Council on Environmental Quality** three-member advisory group in the Executive Office of the President that makes recommendations to the President on environmental matters **Environmental Impact Statement** a detailed statement concerning the environmental impact of a proposed Federal action • *Scope* NEPA applies to a broad range of activities, including direct action by a Federal agency as well as any action by a Federal agency that permits action by other parties that will affect the quality of the environment • *Content* the EIS must contain, among other items, a detailed statement of the environmental impact of the proposed action, any adverse environmental effects that cannot be avoided, and alternative proposals
Clean Air Act	**Purpose** to control and reduce air pollution **Existing Sources** • *National Ambient Air Quality Standards (NAAQSs)* the EPA administrator must establish NAAQSs for air pollutants that endanger the public health and welfare • *State Implementation Plan* each State must submit a plan for each NAAQS detailing how the State will implement and maintain the standard **New Sources** • *New Stationary Sources* owner/operator must employ the best technological system of continuous emission reduction that has been adequately demonstrated • *New Vehicles* extensive emission standards are established • *Hazardous Air Pollutants* to protect the public health, the EPA administrator must establish for hazardous air pollutants standards that provide ample safety margins • *Acid Rain* standards are established to protect against acid rain (precipitation that contains high levels of sulfuric or nitric acid)
Clean Water Act	**Purpose** protect against water pollution **Point Sources Act** establishes the National Pollutant Discharge Elimination System (NPDES), a permit system, to control the amounts of pollutants that may be discharged by point sources into U.S. waters **Nonpoint Sources Act** requires the States to use best management practices to control water runoff from agricultural and urban areas
Hazardous Substances	**FIFRA** the Federal Insecticide, Fungicide and Rodenticide Act regulates the sale and distribution of pesticides **TSCA** the Toxic Substances Control Act provides a comprehensive scheme for regulation of toxic substances **RCRA** the Resource Conservation and Recovery Act provides a comprehensive scheme for treatment of solid waste, particularly hazardous waste **Superfund** the Comprehensive Environmental Response, Compensation and Liability Act (CERCLA) establishes (1) a national contingency plan for responding to releases of hazardous substances and (2) a trust fund to pay for removal and cleanup of hazardous waste

International Protection of the Ozone Layer

Montreal Protocol treaty by which countries agreed to cut production of chlorofluoro-carbons (CFCs) by 50 percent

Kyoto Protocol reduction of greenhouse gases

CASES

CASE 46-1

National Ambient Air Quality Standards

WHITMAN v. AMERICAN TRUCKING ASSOCIATIONS, INC.

Supreme Court of the United States, 2001
531 U.S. 457, 121 S.Ct. 903, 149 L.Ed.2d 1
http://laws.findlaw.com/us/000/99-1257.html

Scalia, J.

These cases present the following questions: (1) Whether § 109(b)(1) of the Clean Air Act (CAA) delegates legislative power to the Administrator of the Environmental Protection Agency (EPA). (2) Whether the Administrator may consider the costs of implementation in setting national ambient air quality standards (NAAQS) under § 109(b)(1). * * *

I

Section 109(a) of the CAA, [citation], requires the Administrator of the EPA to promulgate NAAQS for each air pollutant for which "air quality criteria" have been issued under § 108, [citation]. Once a NAAQS has been promulgated, the Administrator must review the standard (and the criteria on which it is based) "at five-year intervals" and make "such revisions * * * as may be appropriate." [Citation.] These cases arose when, on July 18, 1997, the Administrator revised the NAAQS for particulate matter (PM) and ozone. [Citation.] American Trucking Associations, Inc., and its co-respondents * * * —which include, in addition to other private companies, the States of Michigan, Ohio, and West Virginia—challenged the new standards in the Court of Appeals for the District of Columbia Circuit, * * *.

The District of Columbia Circuit accepted some of the challenges and rejected others. It agreed with the * * * respondents that § 109(b)(1) delegated legislative power to the Administrator in contravention of the United States Constitution, Art. I, § 1, because it found that the EPA had interpreted the statute to provide no "intelligible principle" to guide the agency's exercise of authority. [Citation.] The court thought, however, that the EPA could perhaps avoid the unconstitutional delegation by adopting a restrictive construction of § 109(b)(1), so instead of declaring the section unconstitutional the court remanded the NAAQS to the agency * * *. On the second issue that the Court of Appeals addressed, it unanimously rejected respondents' argument that the court should depart from the rule of *Lead Industries*

Assn., Inc. v. EPA, [citation], that the EPA may not consider the cost of implementing a NAAQS in setting the initial standard. It also rejected respondents' argument that the implementation provisions for ozone found [citation], were so tied to the existing ozone standard that the EPA lacked the power to revise the standard. * * *

* * * We granted certiorari. * * *

II

In *Lead Industries Assn., Inc. v. EPA*, [citation], the District of Columbia Circuit held that "economic considerations [may] play no part in the promulgation of ambient air quality standards under Section 109" of the CAA. In the present cases, the court adhered to that holding, [citation], as it had done on many other occasions. [Citations.] Respondents argue that these decisions are incorrect. We disagree; * * *.

Section 109(b)(1) instructs the EPA to set primary ambient air quality standards "the attainment and maintenance of which * * * are requisite to protect the public health" with "an adequate margin of safety." [Citation.] * * * The language, as one scholar has noted, "is absolute." [Citation.] The EPA, "based on" the information about health effects contained in the technical "criteria" documents compiled under § 108(a)(2), [citation], is to identify the maximum airborne concentration of a pollutant that the public health can tolerate, decrease the concentration to provide an "adequate" margin of safety, and set the standard at that level. Nowhere are the costs of achieving such a standard made part of that initial calculation.

* * *

Even so, respondents argue, many more factors than air pollution affect public health. In particular, the economic cost of implementing a very stringent standard might produce health losses sufficient to offset the health gains achieved in cleaning the air—for example, by closing down whole industries and thereby impoverishing the workers and consumers

International Business Law

Today every aspect of business, including business law, requires some understanding of international business practices. Since World War II, the global economy has become increasingly interconnected. Many U.S. corporations now have investments or manufacturing facilities in other countries, while an increasing number of foreign corporations are conducting business operations in the United States. Furthermore, whether a domestic corporation exports goods or not, it competes with imports from many other countries. For example, U.S. firms face competition from Japanese electronics and automobiles, French wines and fashions, German machinery, and Taiwanese textiles. To compete effectively, U.S. firms need to be aware of international business practices and developments.

Laws vary greatly from country to country: what one nation requires by law, another may forbid. To complicate matters, there is no single authority in international law that can compel countries to act. When the laws of two or more nations conflict, or when one party has violated an agreement and the other party wishes to enforce it or recover damages, establishing who will adjudicate the matter, which laws will be applied, what remedies will be available, or where the matter will be decided often is very confusing. Nonetheless, given the growing impact of the global economy, a basic understanding of international business law is essential.

THE INTERNATIONAL ENVIRONMENT

International law deals with the conduct and relations between nation-states and international organizations, as well as some of their relations with persons. Unlike domestic law, international law generally cannot be enforced. Nevertheless, although international courts do not have compulsory jurisdiction to resolve international disputes, they do have authority to resolve an international dispute if the parties to the dispute *accept* the court's jurisdiction over the matter. Furthermore, a sovereign nation that has adopted an international law will enforce that law to the same extent as all of its domestic laws. This section of the chapter examines some of the sources and institutions of international law.

International Court of Justice

The United Nations, which is probably the most famous international organization, has a judiciary branch called the International Court of Justice (ICJ). The ICJ consists of fifteen judges, no two of whom may be from the same sovereign state, elected for nine-year terms by a majority of both the U.N. General Assembly and the U.N. Security Council. The usefulness of the ICJ is limited, however, because only nations (not private individuals or corporations) may be parties to an action before the court. Furthermore, the ICJ has contentious jurisdiction only over nation-parties who agree not only to allow the ICJ to decide the case but also to be bound by its decision. Moreover, because the ICJ cannot enforce its rulings, countries displeased with an ICJ decision may simply ignore it. Consequently, few nations submit their disputes to the ICJ.

The ICJ also has advisory jurisdiction if requested by a U.N. organ or specialized U.N. agency. Neither sovereign states nor individuals may request an advisory opinion. These opinions are nonbinding, and the U.N. agency requesting the opinion usually decides by vote whether to follow it.

http: United Nations: http://www.un.org
United Nations charter: http://www.un.org/aboutun/charter/
International Court of Justice: http://www.icj-cij.org/

Regional Trade Communities

Of much greater significance are international organizations, conferences, and treaties that focus on business and trade regulation. Regional trade communities, such as the European Union (EU), promote common trade policies among member nations. Other important regional trade communities include the Central American Common Market (CACM), the Caribbean Community (CARICOM), the Association of Southeast Asian Nations (ASEAN), the Andean Common Market (ANCOM), the Common Market for Eastern and Southern Africa (COMESA), the Asian Pacific Economic Cooperation (APEC), Mercado Comun del Cono Sur (Latin American Trading Group, MERCO-SUR), the Gulf Cooperation Council (GCC), and the Economic Community of West African States (ECOWAS).

European Union (EU) The European Community (EC), the predecessor to the European Union, was formed in 1967 through a merger between the European Economic Community (better known as the Common Market), the European Coal and Steel Community, and the European Atomic Energy Community (Euratom). The EC worked to remove trade barriers between its member nations and to unify their economic policies. The EC had the power to make rules that bound member nations and that preempted their domestic laws.

In 1993 the Treaty on European Union (popularly called the Maastricht Treaty) took effect. It changed the name of the EC to the European Union (EU) and stated the Union's objectives to include (1) promoting economic and social progress by creating an area without internal borders and by establishing an economic and monetary union (the euro); (2) asserting its identity on the international scene by implementing a common foreign and security policy; (3) strengthening the protection of the rights and interests of citizens of its member states; and (4) developing close cooperation on justice and home affairs. Until May 2004, the EU had fifteen members: Austria,

Belgium, Denmark, Finland, France, Germany, Greece, Ireland, Italy, Luxembourg, the Netherlands, Portugal, Spain, Sweden, and the United Kingdom. In May 2004, ten eastern and southern European countries joined the European Union, bringing the EU's total population to nearly 500 million. The new members are Cyprus, the Czech Republic, Estonia, Hungary, Latvia, Lithuania, Malta, Poland, the Slovak Republic, and Slovenia.

http: European Union: http://europa.eu.int/index-en.htm

NAFTA The North American Free Trade Agreement, which took effect in 1994, established a free trade area among the United States, Canada, and Mexico. Its objectives are to (1) eliminate trade barriers to the movement of goods and services across the borders, (2) promote conditions of fair competition in the free trade area, (3) increase investment opportunities in the area, and (4) provide adequate and effective enforcement of intellectual property rights. Over fifteen years, the treaty will gradually eliminate all tariffs between the three countries.

http: NAFTA: http://www.sice.oas.org/trade/nafta/naftatce.asp

International Treaties

A **treaty** is an agreement between or among independent nations. As discussed in Chapter 1, the U.S. Constitution authorizes the president to enter into treaties with the advice and consent of the Senate "providing two-thirds of the Senators present concur." The Constitution provides that all valid treaties are "the law of the land," having the legal force of a Federal statute.

Nations have entered into bilateral and multilateral treaties to facilitate and regulate trade and to protect their national interests. In addition, treaties have been used to serve as constitutions of international organizations, to establish general international law, to transfer territory, to settle disputes, to secure human rights, and to protect investments. The Treaty Section of the Office of Legal Affairs within the United Nations Secretariat is responsible for registering and publishing treaties and agreements among member nations. Since its inception in 1946, the U.N. Secretariat has registered and published more than 30,000 treaties that expressly or indirectly concern international business.

Probably the most important multilateral trade treaty is the General Agreement on Tariffs and Trade (GATT), which is now called the World Trade Organization (WTO) and has more than 145 members accounting for over 97% of world trade. (Approximately thirty other countries are negotiating membership.) Its basic purpose is to facilitate the flow of trade by establishing agreements on potential trade barriers such as import quotas, customs, export regulations, antidumping restrictions (the prohibition against selling goods for less than their fair market value), subsidies, and import fees. The WTO administers trade agreements, acts as a forum for trade negotiations, handles trade disputes, monitors national trade policies, and provides technical assistance and training for developing countries.

Under GATT's **most-favored nation provision**, all signatories must treat each other as favorably as they treat any other country. Thus, any privilege, immunity, or favor given to one country must be given to all. Nevertheless, nations may give preferential treatment to developing nations and also may enter into free trade areas with one or more other nations. A free trade area permits countries to discriminate in favor of their free trade partners, provided that the agreement covers substantially all trade among the partners. A second important principle adopted by GATT is that the protection accorded domestic industries should take the form of a customs tariff, rather than other more trade-inhibiting measures.

The most recent set of accords, adopted in 1994, included multilateral trade agreements on such matters as agricultural products, textiles and clothing, technical barriers to trade, trade-related investment measures, customs valuation, subsidies and countervailing measures, trade in services, antidumping measures, and protection of intellectual property rights. It also created the Dispute Settlement Body and increased the scope of GATT's dispute resolution process.

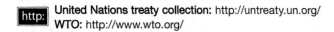 **United Nations treaty collection:** http://untreaty.un.org/
WTO: http://www.wto.org/

JURISDICTION OVER ACTIONS OF FOREIGN GOVERNMENTS

This section will focus on the power, and the limits on that power, of a sovereign nation to exercise jurisdiction over a foreign nation or to take over property owned by foreign citizens. More specifically, it will examine state immunities (the principle of sovereign immunity and the act of state doctrine) and the power of a state to take foreign investment property.

Sovereign Immunity

One of the oldest concepts in international law is that each nation has absolute authority over the events occurring within its territory. It also has been long recognized, however, that to maintain international relations and trade, a host country must refrain from imposing its laws on a foreign sovereign nation present within its borders. This absolute immunity from the courts of a host country is known as **sovereign immunity**. Originally, all acts of a foreign sovereign nation within a host country were considered immune from the host country's laws. In modern times, however, international law distinguishes between the public and commercial acts of a for-

eign nation. Only public acts, such as those concerning diplomatic activity, internal administration, or armed forces, will be granted sovereign immunity. When engaging in trade or commercial activities, a foreign nation subjects itself to the jurisdiction of the host country's courts with respect to disputes arising out of those commercial activities.

In 1976, Congress enacted the Foreign Sovereign Immunities Act in order to establish the circumstances under which the United States would extend immunity to foreign nations. The Act specifically provides that a foreign state shall be immune from neither Federal nor State court jurisdiction if the suit is based upon (1) a commercial activity conducted in the United States by the foreign state, (2) an act that the foreign state performed in the United States in connection with a commercial activity it carried on elsewhere, or (3) a commercial activity performed outside U.S. borders that directly affects the United States. If an activity is one that a private party could normally carry on, it is commercial and a foreign government engaging in that activity is not immune. On the other hand, if the activity is one that only governments can undertake, it is noncommercial under the Act. Examples of commercial activities include a contract by a foreign government to buy provisions or equipment for its armed forces; a contract by a foreign government to construct or repair a government building; and a sale of a service or a product by a foreign government or its leasing of property, borrowing of money, or investing in a security of a U.S. corporation. Examples of public (noncommercial) activities to which sovereign immunity would extend include nationalizing a corporation, determining limitations upon the use of natural resources, and granting licenses to export a natural resource.

◆ **See Case 47-1**

Act of State Doctrine

The act of state doctrine provides that a nation's judicial branch should not question the validity of the actions a foreign government takes within its own borders. In 1897, the U.S. Supreme Court described the act of state doctrine in terms that remain valid today: "Every sovereign State is bound to respect the independence of every other sovereign State, and the courts of one country will not sit in judgment on the acts of the government of another done within its own territory."

In the United States, there are several possible exceptions to the act of state doctrine. Some courts hold (1) that a sovereign may waive its right to raise the act of state defense and (2) that the doctrine may be inapplicable to commercial activities of a foreign sovereign. In addition, by Federal statute, the courts will not apply the act of state doctrine to claims to property based on the assertion that a foreign state confiscated the property in violation of the principles of international law, unless the president of the United States determines that the doctrine should be applied in a particular case.

Taking of Foreign Investment Property

Investing in foreign states involves the risk that the host nation's government may take the investment property. An **expropriation** or nationalization occurs when a government seizes foreign-owned property or assets for a public purpose and pays the owner just compensation for what is taken. In contrast, **confiscation** occurs when a government offers no payment (or a highly inadequate payment) in exchange for seized property or seizes it for a nonpublic purpose. Confiscations violate generally observed principles of international law, whereas expropriations do not. In either case, few remedies are available to injured parties.

One precaution that U.S. firms can take is to obtain insurance from a private insurer or from the Overseas Private Investment Corporation (OPIC), an agency of the U.S. government. In 2003 Congress reauthorized OPIC through September 30, 2007, provided the agency with enhancements to its political risk insurance program, and authorized a new local currency guaranty program.

The World Bank established the Multilateral Investment Guarantee Agency (MIGA) to encourage increased investment in developing nations. The MIGA has approximately 165 member countries. It offers foreign investment risk insurance for noncommercial risks, including deprivation of ownership or control by governmental actions, breach of contract by a government where there is no judicial recourse, and loss from military action or civil disturbance.

TRANSACTING BUSINESS ABROAD

Transacting business abroad may involve activities such as selling goods, information, or services; investing capital; or arranging for the movement of labor. Because these transactions may affect the national security, economy, foreign policy, and interests of both the exporting and importing countries, nations have imposed measures to restrict or encourage such transactions. This section examines the legal controls imposed upon the flow of trade, labor, and capital across national borders.

Flow of Trade

Advances in modern technology, communication, transportation, and production methods have greatly increased the flow of goods across national boundaries. The governments within each country thereby face a dilemma. On the one hand, they wish to protect and stimulate domestic industry. On the other hand, they want to provide their citizens with the best quality goods at the lowest possible prices and to encourage exports from their own countries.

Governments have used a variety of trade barriers to protect domestic businesses and to achieve other social and political goals. A frequently applied device is the **tariff**, which is a duty or tax imposed on goods moving into or out of a country. Tariffs raise the price of imported goods, prompting some consumers to purchase less expensive, domestically produced items. Governments can also use **nontariff barriers** to give local industries a competitive advantage. Examples of nontariff barriers include unilateral or bilateral import quotas; import bans; overly restrictive safety, health, or manufacturing standards; environmental laws; complicated and time-consuming customs procedures; and subsidies to local industry.

Dumping is the sale of exported goods from one country to another country at less than normal value. Under the WTO's Antidumping Code, "normal value" is the price that would be charged for the same or a similar product in the ordinary course of trade for domestic consumption in the exporting country. Dumping violates the GATT "if it causes or threatens material injury to an established industry in the territory of a contracting party or materially retards the establishment of a domestic industry."

Governments also control the flow of goods out of their countries by imposing quotas, tariffs, or total prohibitions. **Export controls** or restrictions usually result from important policy considerations, such as national defense, foreign policy, or the protection of scarce national resources. For example, the United States passed the Export Administration Act of 1979, amended in 1985 and 1988, which restricts the flow of technologically advanced goods and data from the United States to other countries. (The Act has been in lapse since August 21, 2001, but the President has extended control over exports by invoking his emergency powers under the International Emergency Economic Powers Act.) Nonetheless, to assist domestic businesses, countries generally encourage exports through the use of **export incentives** and **export subsidies**.

Flow of Labor

The flow of labor across national borders generates policy questions involving the employment needs of local workers. Each country has immigration policies and regulations. Almost all countries require that foreigners obtain valid passports before entering their borders; citizens, in turn, often must have passports to leave or reenter the country. In addition, a country may issue foreign citizens visas that permit them to enter the country for identified purposes or for specific periods of time. For example, the U.S. Immigration and Naturalization Service issues various types of visas to persons who are temporarily visiting the United States for pleasure or business, to persons who enter the United States to perform services that the unemployed in this country cannot perform, and to persons who are transferred to the United States by their employers.

Flow of Capital

Multinational businesses frequently need to transfer funds to, and receive money from, operations in other countries. Because there is no international currency, nations have sought to ease the flow of capital among themselves. In 1945, the International Monetary Fund (IMF) was established to promote international monetary cooperation, to facilitate the expansion and balanced growth of international trade, to assist in the elimination of foreign exchange restrictions that hamper such growth, and to shorten the duration and lessen the disequilibrium in the international balance of payments between the members of the fund. Currently, more than 180 countries are members of the IMF.

Many nations have laws regulating foreign investment. Restrictions on the establishment of foreign investment tend to limit the amount of equity and the amount of control allowed foreign investors. They may also restrict the way in which the investment is created, such as limiting or prohibiting investment by acquiring an existing locally owned business. Approximately 150 nations have signed the Convention on the Settlement of Investment Disputes Between States and Nationals of Other States. The Convention created the International Centre for the Settlement of Investment Disputes, which offers conciliation and arbitration for investment disputes between governments and foreign investors to promote increased flows of international investment.

Nations also have joined to form international and regional banks to facilitate the flow of capital and trade. Such banks include the International Bank for Reconstruction and Development (part of the World Bank), the African Development Bank, the Asian Development Bank, the European Investment Bank, and the Inter-American Development Bank.

> **http:** **International Monetary Fund:** http://www.imf.org/
> **World Bank:** http://www.worldbank.org/

International Contracts

The legal issues inherent in domestic commercial contracts also arise in international contracts. Moreover, certain additional issues, such as differences in language, customs, legal systems, and currency, are peculiar to international contracts. Such a contract should specify its official language and define all of the significant legal terms it incorporates. In addition, it should specify the acceptable currency (or currencies) and payment method. The contract should include a choice of law clause designating what law will govern any breach or dispute

regarding the contract, and a choice of forum clause designating whether the parties will resolve disputes through one nation's court system or through third-party arbitration. (The United Nations Committee on International Trade Law and the International Chamber of Commerce have promulgated arbitration rules that have won broad international acceptance.) Finally, the contract should include a *force majeure* (unavoidable superior force) clause apportioning the liabilities and responsibilities of the parties in the event of an unforeseeable occurrence, such as a typhoon, tornado, flood, earthquake, war, or nuclear disaster.

The United Nations Commission on International Trade Law (UNCITRAL) was established by the U.N. General Assembly to further the progressive harmonization and unification of the law of international trade. The Commission is composed of sixty member states elected by the General Assembly and is structured to be representative of the world's various geographic regions and its principal economic and legal systems. One of its primary functions is to develop conventions, model laws, and rules that are acceptable worldwide. One example is the CISG (discussed below and in Chapters 21 through 25) and the arbitration rules mentioned above. Another is the UNCITRAL Model Law on Electronic Commerce, adopted in 1996, which is intended to facilitate the use of modern means of communications and storage of information. Legislation based on it has been adopted in about twenty nations, and in the United States, it has influenced the Uniform Electronic Transactions Act, adopted in 1999 by the National Conference of Commissioners on Uniform State Law. See Chapter 48. In 2001 the UNCITRAL Model Law on Electronic Signatures was adopted to bring additional legal certainty regarding the use of electronic signatures. Following a technology-neutral approach, the Act establishes a presumption that electronic signatures, which meet certain criteria of technical reliability, shall be treated as equivalent to handwritten signatures.

CISG The United Nations Convention on Contracts for the International Sales of Goods (CISG), which has been ratified by the United States and more than sixty other countries, governs all contracts for the international sale of goods between parties located in different nations that have ratified the CISG. Because treaties are Federal law, the CISG supersedes the Uniform Commercial Code in any situation to which either could apply. The CISG includes provisions dealing with interpretation, trade usage, contract formation, obligations and remedies of sellers and buyers, and risk of loss. Parties to an international sales contract may, however, expressly exclude CISG governance from their contract. The CISG specifically excludes sales of (1) goods bought for personal, family, or household use; (2) ships or aircraft; and (3) electricity. In addition, it does not apply to contracts in which the primary obligation of the party furnishing the goods consists of supplying labor or services. The CISG is discussed in Chapters 21 through 25.

http: **CISG:** http://cisgw3.law.pace.edu/cisg/text/cisg-toc.html

Letters of Credit International trade involves a number of risks not usually encountered in domestic trade, particularly the threat of governmental controls over the export or import of goods and currency. The most effective means of managing these risks—as well as the ordinary trade risks of nonperformance by seller and buyer—is the irrevocable documentary letter of credit. Most international letters of credit are governed by the Uniform Customs and Practices for Documentary Credits, a document drafted by commercial law experts from many countries and adopted by the International Chamber of Commerce. A **letter of credit** is a promise by a buyer's bank to pay the seller, provided certain conditions are met. The letter of credit transaction involves three or four different parties and three underlying contracts. To illustrate: a U.S. business wishes to sell computers to a Belgian company. The U.S. and Belgian firms enter into a sales agreement that includes details such as the number of computers, the features they will have, and the date they will be shipped. The buyer then enters into a second contract with a local bank, called an *issuer*, committing the bank to pay the agreed price upon receiving specified documents. These documents normally include a bill of lading (proving that the seller has delivered the goods for shipment), a commercial invoice listing the purchase terms, proof of insurance, and a customs certificate indicating that customs officials have cleared the goods for export. The buyer's bank's commitment to pay is the irrevocable letter of credit. Typically, a **correspondent** or **paying bank** located in the seller's country makes payment to the seller. Here, the Belgian issuing bank arranges to pay the U.S. correspondent bank the agreed sum of money in exchange for the documents. The issuer then sends the U.S. computer firm the letter of credit. When the U.S. firm obtains all the necessary documents, it presents them to the U.S. correspondent bank, which verifies the documents, pays the computer company in U.S. dollars, and sends the documents to the Belgian issuing bank. Upon receiving the required documents, the issuing bank pays the correspondent bank and then presents the documents to the buyer. In our example, the Belgian buyer pays the issuing bank in Belgian francs for the letter of credit when the buyer receives the specified documents from the bank.

Antitrust Laws

Section 1 of the Sherman Act provides that U.S. antitrust laws shall have a broad, extraterritorial reach. As discussed in Chapter 41, contracts, combinations, or conspiracies that restrain trade with foreign nations, as well as among the domestic States, are deemed illegal. Therefore, agreements among competitors to increase the cost of imports, as well as arrangements to exclude imports from U.S. domestic markets in exchange for agreements not to compete in other countries, clearly violate U.S. antitrust laws. The antitrust provisions are also designed to protect U.S. exports from privately imposed restrictions seeking to exclude U.S. competitors from foreign markets. Amendments to the Sherman Act and the Federal Trade Commission Act limit their application to unfair methods of competition that have a direct, substantial, and reasonably foreseeable effect on U.S. domestic commerce, U.S. import commerce, or U.S. export commerce.

◆ **See Case 47-2**

Securities Regulation

The securities markets have become increasingly internationalized, thereby raising questions regarding which country's law governs a particular transaction in securities. (U.S. Federal securities laws are discussed in Chapter 44.) Foreign issuers who issue securities in the United States must register them under the 1933 Act unless an exemption is available. Foreign issuers whose securities are sold in the secondary market in the United States must register under the 1934 Act unless the issuer is exempt. Some nonexempt foreign issuers may avoid registration under the 1934 Act by providing the Securities and Exchange Commission (SEC) with copies of all information material to investors that they have made public in their home country. Regulation S provides a safe harbor from the 1993 Act registration requirements for offshore sales of equity securities of U.S. issuers. The antifraud provisions of the U.S. securities laws apply to securities sold by the use of any means or instrumentality of interstate commerce. In determining the extraterritorial application of these provisions, the courts have generally found jurisdiction where there is either *conduct* or *effects* in the United States relating to a violation of the Federal securities laws.

◆ **See Case 47-3**

Protection of Intellectual Property

The U.S. laws protecting intellectual property (discussed in Chapter 40) do not apply to transactions in other countries. Generally, the owner of an intellectual property right must comply with each country's requirements to obtain from that country whatever protection is available. The requirements vary substantially from country to country, as does the degree of protection. The United States belongs to multinational treaties that try to coordinate the application of member nations' intellectual property laws. The principal treaties for patent protection are the Paris Convention for the Protection of Industrial Property and the Patent Cooperation Treaty. International treaties protecting trademarks are the Paris Convention, the Trademark Law Treaty, the Arrangement of Nice Concerning the International Classification of Goods and Services, and the Vienna Trademark Registration Treaty. In 2002 Congress enacted legislation implementing the Madrid Protocol, a procedural agreement allowing U.S. trademark owners to file for registration in any number of over sixty-five member countries by filing a single application in English and paying a single fee. Copyrights are covered by the Universal Copyright Convention and the Berne Convention for the Protection of Literary and Artistic Works. The Trade-Related Aspects of Intellectual Property Rights (TRIPS) portion of the World Trade Organization Agreement state how the range of intellectual property should be protected when trade is involved. The World Intellectual Property Organization (WIPO), one of the specialized agencies of the United Nations, attempts to promote—through cooperation among nations—the protection of intellectual property throughout the world. WIPO administers twenty-one international treaties dealing with intellectual property protection and includes more than 175 nations as member states.

http: **TRIPS:** http://www.wto.org/english/tratop_e/trips_e/trips_e.htm

World Intellectual Property Organization: http://www.wipo.org/eng/main.htm

Foreign Corrupt Practices Act

In 1977, Congress enacted the Foreign Corrupt Practices Act (FCPA), prohibiting all domestic concerns from bribing foreign governmental or political officials. The FCPA makes it unlawful for any domestic concern or any of its officers, directors, employees, or agents to offer or give anything of value directly or indirectly to any foreign official, political party, or political official for the purpose of (1) influencing any act or decision of that person or party in his or its official capacity, (2) inducing an act or omission in violation of his or its lawful duty, or (3) inducing such person or party to use his or its influence to affect a decision of a foreign government to assist the domestic concern in obtaining or retaining business. An offer or promise to make a prohibited payment is a violation even if the offer is not accepted or the promise is not performed. The 1988 amendments to the FCPA explicitly excluded routine governmental actions not involving the discretion of the official, such as obtaining permits or processing applications. This exclusion does *not* cover any decision by a foreign official whether, or on what terms, to award new business or to continue business with a particular party. The amendments also added an affirmative defense for payments

that are lawful under the written laws or regulations of the foreign officials' country.

Violations can result in fines of up to $2 million for companies; individuals may be fined a maximum of $100,000 or imprisoned up to five years, or both. Section 32(c). Fines imposed upon individuals may not be paid directly or indirectly by the domestic concern on whose behalf they acted. In addition, the courts may impose civil penalties of up to $11,000.

In 1997 the United States and thirty-three other nations signed the Organization for Economic Cooperation and Development Convention on Combating Bribery of Foreign Public Officials in International Business Transactions (OECD Convention). In 1998 Congress enacted the International Anti-Bribery and Fair Competition Act of 1998 to conform the FCPA to the Convention. The 1998 Act expands the FCPA to include (1) payments made to "secure any improper advantage" from foreign officials, (2) all foreign persons who commit an act in furtherance of a foreign bribe while in the United States, and (3) officials of public international organizations within the definition of a "foreign official." A public international organization is defined as either an organization designated by executive order pursuant to the International Organizations Immunities Act, or any other international organization designated by executive order of the president.

http: **OECD Convention:** http://www.oecd.org/department/0,2688,en_2649_34859_1_1_1_1_1,00.html

Employment Discrimination

Title VII of the Civil Rights Act of 1964, the Americans with Disabilities Act, and the Age Discrimination in Employment Act, discussed in Chapter 43, apply to U.S. citizens employed abroad by U.S. employers or by foreign companies controlled by U.S. employers. Employers, however, are not required to comply with these employment discrimination laws if compliance would violate the law of the foreign country in which the workplace is located.

FORMS OF MULTINATIONAL ENTERPRISES

The term *multinational enterprise* refers to any business that engages in transactions involving the movement of goods, information, money, people, or services across national borders. Such an enterprise may conduct its business in any of several forms: direct sales, foreign agents, distributorships, licensing, joint ventures, and wholly owned subsidiaries. A number of considerations determine the form of business organization that would be best for conducting international transactions. These factors include financing, tax consequences, legal restrictions imposed by the host country, and the degree to which the multinational enterprise wishes to control the business.

Direct Export Sales

Under a direct export sale, the seller contracts directly with the buyer in the other country. This is the simplest and least involved multinational enterprise.

Foreign Agents

An agency relationship often is used by multinational enterprises seeking limited involvement in an international market. The principal firm will appoint a local agent, who may be empowered to enter into contracts in the agent's country on behalf of the principal or who may be authorized only to solicit and take orders. The agent generally does not take title to the merchandise.

 Convention on Agency in the International Sale of Goods: http://www.unidroit.org/english/conventions/c-ag.htm

Distributorships

A commonly used form of multinational enterprise is the distributorship, in which a producer of goods appoints a foreign distributor. Unlike an agent, a distributor takes title to the merchandise it receives; consequently, the distributor, not the producer, bears many of the risks connected with commercial sales. By its very format, the distributorship is especially susceptible to antitrust violations. Therefore, both the producer and the distributor must take special care to ensure that the arrangement does not violate the antitrust laws of their respective governments.

Licensing

A multinational enterprise wishing to exploit an intellectual property right, such as a patent, trademark, trade secret, or an unpatented but innovative production technology, may choose to sell the right to use such property to a foreign company rather than enter the foreign market itself. The sale of such rights, called licensing, is one of the major means by which technology and information are transferred among nations. Normally, the foreign firm will pay royalties in exchange for the information, technology, or patent. Franchising is a form of licensing in which the owner of intellectual property grants permission to a foreign business under carefully specified conditions.

Joint Ventures

In a joint venture, two or more independent businesses from different countries agree to coordinate their efforts to achieve a common result. The sharing of profits and liabilities, as well as the delegation of responsibilities, is fixed by contract. One advantage of the joint venture is that each company can be assigned responsibility for that which it does best. To promote local ownership of investments, a number of developing nations and regional groups have enacted legislation that prohibits foreign businesses from owning more than forty-nine percent of any business enterprise in those countries. In addition, each country may require that its citizens comprise a majority of the management of an enterprise.

Wholly Owned Subsidiaries

By far, wholly owned subsidiaries require the most active participation by a parent firm. Nevertheless, creating a foreign wholly owned subsidiary corporation can offer a business numerous advantages, most significantly the ability to retain authority and control over all phases of operation. This is especially attractive to businesses wishing to safeguard their technology.

CHAPTER SUMMARY

The International Environment

International Law includes law that deals with the conduct and relations of nation-states and international organizations as well as some of their relations with persons; such law is enforceable by the courts of a nation that has adopted the international law as domestic law

International Court of Justice judicial branch of the United Nations having voluntary jurisdiction over nations

Regional Trade Communities international organizations, conferences, and treaties focusing on business and trade regulation; the EU (European Union) is the most prominent of these

International Treaties agreements between or among independent nations, such as the General Agreement on Tariffs and Trade (GATT), now called the World Trade Organization

Jurisdiction over Actions of Foreign Governments	**Sovereign Immunity** foreign country's freedom from a host country's laws **Act of State Doctrine** rule that a court should not question the validity of actions taken by a foreign government in its own country **Taking of Foreign Investment Property** • *Expropriation* governmental taking of foreign-owned property for a public purpose and with payment of just compensation • *Confiscation* governmental taking of foreign-owned property without payment (or for a highly inadequate payment) or for a nonpublic purpose
Transacting Business Abroad	**Flow of Trade** controlled by trade barriers on imports and exports • *Tariff* duty or tax imposed on goods moving into or out of a country • *Nontariff Barriers* include quotas, bans, safety standards, and subsidies **Flow of Labor** controlled through passport, visa, and immigration regulations **Flow of Capital** International Monetary Fund facilitates the expansion and balanced growth of international trade, assists in eliminating foreign exchange restrictions, and smooths the international balance of payments **International Contracts** involve additional issues beyond those in domestic contracts, such as differences in language, legal systems, and currency • *CISG* United Nations Convention on Contracts for the International Sales of Goods governs all contracts for international sales of goods between parties located in different nations that have ratified the CISG • *Letter of Credit* bank's promise to pay the seller, provided certain conditions are met; used to manage the payment risks in international trade **Antitrust Laws** U.S. antitrust laws apply to unfair methods of competition that have a direct, substantial, and reasonably foreseeable effect on the domestic, import, or export commerce of the United States **Securities Regulation** foreign issuers who issue securities, or whose securities are sold in the secondary market, in the United States must register them unless an exemption is available; the antifraud provisions apply where there is either *conduct* or *effects* in the United States relating to a violation of the Federal securities laws **Protection of Intellectual Property** the owner of an intellectual property right must comply with each country's requirement to obtain from that country whatever protection is available **Foreign Corrupt Practices Act** prohibits all U.S. companies from bribing foreign governmental or political officials **Employment Discrimination** Title VII of the Civil Rights Act of 1964, the Americans with Disabilities Act, and the Age Discrimination in Employment Act apply to U.S. citizens employed in foreign countries by U.S.-owned or -controlled companies
Forms of Multinational Enterprises (MNE)	**Definition** any business that engages in transactions involving the movement of goods, information, money, people, or services across national borders **Forms of MNE** the choice of form depends on a number of factors, including financing considerations, tax consequences, and degree of control • *Direct Export Sales* seller contracts directly with the buyer in the other country • *Foreign Agents* a local agent in the host country is used to provide limited involvement for an MNE • *Distributorship* MNE sells to a foreign distributor who takes title to the merchandise • *Licensing* MNE sells a foreign company the right to use technology or information • *Joint Ventures* two independent businesses from different countries share profits, liabilities, and duties • *Wholly Owned Subsidiary* enables an MNE to retain control and authority over all phases of operation

CHAPTER 12

The Employment Agreement

INTRODUCTION

EMPLOYEE RIGHTS, POWERS, AND PROTECTION

Over the past seventy-five years, there has been an explosion in laws regulating the employment relationship. As a result of the union movement, employees acquired economic and political power in their dealings with employers. With the emergence of the civil rights movement and the antidiscrimination legislation of the 1960s, employers began to examine their hiring and other employment practices more closely with respect to the treatment of women, minorities, and other protected groups. New laws concerning worker safety challenged employers to make the workplace safer. Federal and state whistle-blower statutes prohibited retaliation against employees who complained to a governmental agency about working conditions that they believed violated the law.

The courts developed new doctrines that limit a U.S. employer's traditional right to discharge an employee for any reason. These judicial decisions moved U.S. employment law closer to the European model, which requires an employer to show just cause for a discharge. Indeed, under the current law, an employer may be bound by contracts with its employees without even knowing it. Managers must devote an ever-increasing amount of attention and resources to complying with the sometimes bewildering array of statutes, regulations, and common law principles that bear upon their relations with their employees.

CHAPTER OVERVIEW

This chapter discusses the traditional U.S. rule that employees can be terminated at will and the exceptions to this rule that have developed in recent years, including wrongful termination based on a violation of public policy, breach of an implied contract, and breach of the implied covenant of good faith and fair dealing. It also examines the common law doctrine of fair procedure, the tort of fraudulent inducement, and the enforceability of covenants not to compete. The laws relating to drug testing, genetic testing, lie detector tests, and certain hiring practices are also addressed. The chapter explains the employer's responsibility for worker safety and the system of workers' compensation, including the minimum wage and overtime payments. It also briefly discusses the coverage and application of the National Labor Relations Act (NLRA), which governs union activities in the United States. In addition, the chapter examines how U.S. immigration law affects domestic employment of foreign citizens and how foreign employment laws generally require just cause for the termination of workers.

At-Will Employment

Most nonunionized American workers have no written employment contract. They are hired for a job without any express agreement as to how long the job will last. For at least the last hundred years, the American rule has been that an employment agreement of indefinite duration is an *at-will contract;* that is, the employee can quit at any time, and the employer can discharge the employee at any time, for any or no reason, with or without advance notice. Whether by statute or judicial decision, all states originally followed this rule. The courts reasoned that denying the employer the right to discharge its employee, while the employee was at liberty to quit at any time for any reason, would deprive the employer of property without due process of law.

Today, however, in many states, the at-will rule has been largely buried under its exceptions. Although some courts have declined to recognize these exceptions to the at-will doctrine, the trend is toward some level of protection against discharge in certain circumstances. Employers are well advised to consider whether the reasons for any termination will pass muster as "good" or "just" cause.

EMPLOYEES NOT SUBJECT TO THE AT-WILL RULE

Public employees, employees who negotiated express contracts for a fixed term with their employers, and unionized workers have generally not been subject to the at-will rule.

Public Employees

Most employees of federal, state, and local government agencies have long worked under civil service or merit systems that provide for tenure, require just cause for discharge, and guarantee administrative procedures to determine whether there is just cause for discharge.

Employees with Individual Contracts

A private-sector employee can avoid at-will status by negotiating a contract that provides for a specific term of employment and defines how the contract can be terminated. Employers will almost always reserve the right to fire an employee, but the employment contract will usually require the employer to provide some level of severance pay if the termination was without cause. For example, a contract might give an employee with a three-year contract, who is fired without cause at the end of the first year, the right to salary and benefits for the remaining two years. In some cases, but not all, the amount due is reduced by any monies the employee receives from another employer. Negotiated contracts requiring just cause for termination by the employer may also provide some level of payment and benefits if the employee quits "for good reason." This is often defined to include being required to move more than fifty miles from the original place of employment or having one's duties and responsibilities substantially changed or reduced. Persons in professional or managerial positions are more likely to be able to negotiate individual contracts with such provisions.

Union Contracts

Other employees rely on union contracts, which almost universally require just cause for termination and establish grievance procedures whereby an employee can challenge his or her discharge.

WRONGFUL DISCHARGE

Beginning in the early 1970s, courts in a number of states began to recognize exceptions to the at-will doctrine in new causes of action for *wrongful discharge,* that is, termination of employment without good cause. Wrongful discharge is a common-law-based claim supported by three theories: public policy, implied contract, and implied covenant of good faith and fair dealing.

These causes of action are based on both contract and tort law. Although the line between wrongful discharge and fraud is not always clear, each claim receives different damages. Wrongful discharge gives rise only to contract damages, whereas fraud gives rise to personal-injury and punitive damages. Even this distinction is hazy, however. Thus, some wrongful-discharge plaintiffs may be able to collect damages for emotional distress and punitive damages, not simply lost wages.

The Public Policy Exception

One of the earliest exceptions to the at-will rule was the *public policy exception.* Even if an individual is an at-will employee, in most states the employer is prohibited from discharging the employee for a reason that violates public policy. The greatest protection is given to an employee discharged due to a refusal to commit an unlawful act, such as perjury or price-fixing, at the employer's request. Indeed, an employer's request that an employee violate a criminal statute—or even a noncriminal regulation—is almost always deemed to be against public policy and would give rise to damages for discharge.

Although most states recognize a public policy exception to at-will employment, several states do not.[1]

Remedies In *Tameny v. Atlantic Richfield,*[2] the California Supreme Court held that an employee may maintain both tort and contract actions if the employee's discharge violated fundamental principles of public policy. As a result, damages for pain and suffering and possibly punitive damages were available.

Sources of Public Policy Different jurisdictions recognize different sources of public policy.

State Sources Jurisdictions are split as to whether to recognize an exception to the at-will rule for nonlegislative sources of public policy. Some jurisdictions, including

1. Alabama, Florida, Georgia, Louisiana, Maine, New York, Rhode Island. *See, e.g.,* Kiddler v. AmSouth Bank, N.A., 639 So. 2d 1361 (Ala. 1994); Smith v. AVSC Inking, Inc., 148 F. Supp. 2d 302 (S.D.N.Y. 2001).
2. 610 P.2d 1330 (Cal. 1980).

California and Georgia, limit the sources of public policy to statutory or constitutional provisions designed to protect society at large.[3] For example, the Georgia Supreme Court held in *Reilly v. Alcan Aluminum Corp.*[4] that an at-will employee could not sue in tort for wrongful discharge based on age discrimination because only the state legislature can create a public policy exception to the at-will doctrine. The court ruled that since the Georgia age discrimination law provided no civil remedy and another state statute merely set forth general principles of tort law, the court had no authority to create an exception to the state's at-will doctrine.

Other jurisdictions permit courts to find that a termination violates public policy even where no state statute prohibits the discharge. For example, an employee claimed she was discharged by the Central Indiana Gas Company for filing a workers' compensation claim. Although no state statute prohibiting such a discharge existed, the Indiana Supreme Court recognized that employees should be able to sue an employer in tort because "retaliatory discharge for filing a workmen's compensation claim is a wrongful, unconscionable act and should be actionable in a court of law."[5] The court further stated that an employee must be able to exercise his or her right under the Indiana workers' compensation statute without fear of reprisal in order for the public policy of the statute to be actualized.

The Oregon Supreme Court created a public policy exception for termination of an employee for performing jury duty.[6] The court reasoned that jury duty was an important civic duty and that the will of the community and the effectiveness of the jury system would be thwarted if employers were allowed to discharge employees for fulfilling such an obligation.

Federal Sources Many federal statutes expressly prohibit termination of employees who report violations of, or exercise rights under, the statutes. For example, the National Labor Relations Act prohibits discharge for union or other concerted activities or for filing charges under the Act.[7] In addition, the Occupational Health and Safety Act prohibits discharge of employees in retaliation for exercising rights under the Act, such as complaining about work procedures or about health and safety violations in the workplace.[8] Many state statutes contain similar provisions.

The Fair Labor Standards Act (FLSA) prohibits discharge for exercising rights guaranteed by its minimum-wage and overtime provisions.[9] In *Valerio v. Putnam Associates*,[10] the U.S. Court of Appeals for the First Circuit extended the antiretaliation provisions of the FLSA to retaliatory discharge as a result of internal complaints lodged by employees with employers as well as legal proceedings commenced by an employee. In that case, the court held that a worker, who was fired after complaining to her employer that it was not properly paying her overtime pursuant to the FLSA, could sue under the antiretaliation provisions of the FLSA. The U.S. courts of appeals are split on this issue, however: the majority allow employees to sue if they are discharged after filing internal complaints with their employers, but a minority of the courts require the employee to have initiated a formal, legal proceeding.

Nongovernmental Sources Some jurisdictions have recognized that nongovernmental sources of public policy, including professional ethical codes, may provide the basis for a public policy exception to the at-will doctrine.[11] For example, in *General Dynamics Corp. v. Rose*,[12] the California Supreme Court held that an attorney could base a claim of retaliatory discharge on allegations that he was terminated for refusing to violate a mandatory ethical duty embodied in the rules of attorney professional conduct. Andrew Rose, former in-house counsel at General Dynamics, had filed a claim for retaliatory discharge, alleging that he had been fired because he had (1) spearheaded an investigation of drug use at the company that resulted in the termination of more than sixty employees; (2) protested the company's failure to investigate the bugging of the office of the chief of security, a criminal offense; and (3) advised company officials that General Dynamics' salary policy might be in violation of the FLSA, which could potentially expose the company to several hundred million dollars in backpay claims.

In contrast, in *Jacobson v. Knepper & Moga*,[13] the Illinois Supreme Court held that an attorney, who had

---

3. *See, e.g.,* Phillips v. St. Mary's Reg'l Med. Ctr., 96 Cal. App. 4th 218 (2002); Reilly v. Alcan Aluminum Corp., 528 S.E.2d 238 (Ga. 2000).
4. 528 S.E.2d 238 (Ga. 2000).
5. Frampton v. Cent. Ind. Gas Co., 297 N.E.2d 425 (Ind. 1973).
6. Nees v. Hocks, 536 P.2d 512 (Or. 1975).
7. 29 U.S.C. §§ 158(a) (1), (3), and (4).
8. 29 U.S.C. § 660(c).
9. 29 U.S.C. §§ 215(a) (3), 216(b).
10. 173 F.3d 35 (1st Cir. 1999).
11. *See, e.g.,* Winkelman v. Beloit Mem'l Hosp., 483 N.W.2d 211 (Wis. 1992) (administrative rules); Pierce v. Ortho Pharm. Corp., 417 A.2d 505 (N.J. 1980) (legislation; administrative rules, regulations, or decisions; judicial decisions; and, in certain instances, a professional code of ethics).
12. 876 P.2d 487 (Cal. 1994).
13. 706 N.E.2d 491 (Ill. 1998).

been fired by his firm after complaining that it was violating federal law, could not recover for retaliatory discharge. Alan Jacobson, an associate at the law firm, Knepper & Moga, discovered that the firm was filing consumer debt collection actions in violation of the Fair Debt Collection Practices Act. He was terminated after he complained about these activities several times to one of the principal partners of the firm. Jacobson filed a claim against the firm, alleging that he had been discharged in retaliation for his insistence that the firm comply with the rules of attorney professional conduct and cease violating the federal law. The court found that the public policy to be protected by the Fair Debt Collection Practices Act (protecting debtors' property and ensuring them due process) was already adequately safeguarded by the ethical obligations imposed by the rules of attorney professional conduct, making it unnecessary to expand the tort of retaliatory discharge to protect discharged employee attorneys.

Whistleblower Statutes A more recent development has been the adoption of *whistleblower statutes* that protect employees who report illegal activities going on within their company. The rationale behind protecting whistleblowers is that it is in the public interest to promote compliance with the law. It would be irresponsible to blindly protect all employee disclosures, however, because some disclosures may be intended merely to harass the employer. Hence, courts must balance the public interest in the enforcement of laws, the whistleblower's interest in being protected from reprisal, and the employer's interest in managing its workforce.

A number of states have statutes that provide whistleblower protection for terminated employees. For example, the New York state statute[14] protecting private-sector whistleblowers provides:

An employer shall not take any retaliatory personnel action against an employee because such employee does any of the following:

14. N.Y. LAB. LAW § 740 (McKinney 2002).

(a) discloses, or threatens to disclose to a supervisor or to a public body an activity, policy or practice of the employer that is in violation of law, rule or regulation which violation creates and presents a substantial and specific danger to the public health or safety;
(b) provides information to, or testifies before, any public body conducting an investigation, hearing or inquiry into any such violation of a law, rule or regulation by such employer; or
(c) objects to, or refuses to participate in any such activity, policy or practice in violation of a law, rule or regulation.

California's whistleblower statute is similar to New York's but is broader in that it does not limit its protection to violations of law that create a danger to public health or safety.[15] In addition, the California attorney general maintains a "whistleblower" hotline to receive telephone reports of violations of laws by corporations.[16]

In addition to state whistleblower provisions, there are a number of federal whistleblower statutes, many of which apply only to federal employees who report violations by governmental agencies or employees. The Sarbanes-Oxley Act of 2002 (SOX)[17] includes several whistleblower provisions that apply to all public companies and one that applies to private companies as well.[18] In the following case, the U.S. District Court for the Northern District of Georgia considered whether an employee of a public company was terminated in violation of the whistleblower provision set forth in Section 806 of SOX.

15. CAL. LAB. CODE § 1102.5 (West 2004).
16. CAL. LAB. CODE § 1102.7 (West 2004).
17. 18 U.S.C. § 1514A.
18. The SOX whistleblower provision provides criminal penalties for public and private company employers who retaliate against a person who provides truthful information relating to the commission of a federal offense to a law enforcement officer. 18 U.S.C. § 1514A.

A CASE IN POINT	**Summary**

CASE 12.1

Collins v. Beazer Homes USA, Inc.

United States District Court for the Northern District of Georgia

334 F. Supp. 2d 1365 (N.D. Ga. 2004).

> FACTS Judy Collins was offered and accepted a position as director of marketing for the Jacksonville, Florida division of Beazer Homes Corporation. According to the offer, Collins would be subject to a ninety-day assessment review period during which "either [Collins] or the Company may decide to terminate employment without giving a reason."

Soon after starting with Beazer, Collins began having conflicts with her manager, Bill Mazar, and another coworker stemming from Collins's disagreement with Mazar's use of the Montello Advertising Agency for advertising services. Collins found Montello's

(Continued)

(Case 12.1 *continued*)

services to be unsatisfactory and terminated the agency's contract with Beazer's Jacksonville division. Collins alleged that Mazar continued to use and pay Montello behind her back simply because the president of Montello and the Jacksonville division president, Marty Schaffer, were friends. Collins also suspected that employees in the Jacksonville division were providing kickbacks on lumber purchases and that marketing costs were being categorized incorrectly in an attempt to hide certain information. In addition, Collins believed that the director of sales was providing more favorable sales commissions to her friends.

In early August 2002, Collins raised her concerns to Beazer's vice president of sales and marketing, the vice president of human resources, and the company's CEO. In a subsequent meeting between Schaffer and Collins on August 19, 2002, Schaffer terminated Collins's employment.

Collins filed a complaint in the U.S. District Court for the Northern District of Georgia, alleging that Beazer retaliated against her in violation of SOX because she was terminated soon after she raised concerns about violations of securities laws. Beazer moved for summary judgment, arguing that the court should dismiss the case because no genuine issue of material fact existed regarding whether Collins's termination was retaliatory. Beazer also contended that Collins had not engaged in a protected activity and that she was terminated during her ninety-day probationary period because of personality conflicts with her coworkers.

> **ISSUE PRESENTED** Does a genuine issue of material fact exist regarding whether Beazer violated SOX by terminating Collins soon after she raised concerns about violations of securities laws?

> **SUMMARY OF OPINION** The court noted that Section 806 of SOX provides "whistle-blower" protection to employees of publicly traded companies. Pursuant to that section, an employer may not discriminate against any employee in the terms and conditions of employment because of any lawful act done by the employee "to provide information . . . regarding any conduct which the employee reasonably believes constitutes a violation of section 1341, 1343, 1344, or 1348, any rule or regulation of the Securities and Exchange Commission, or any provision of Federal law relating to fraud against shareholders."[19]

The court found that the evidentiary framework for a claim under SOX required that Collins show by a preponderance of the evidence that (1) she had engaged in a protected activity, (2) Beazer knew of the protected activity, (3) she suffered an unfavorable personnel action, and (4) circumstances exist to suggest that the protected activity was a contributing factor to the unfavorable action. Assuming that Collins met her burden of proof, Beazer could still avoid liability if it could demonstrate by clear and convincing evidence that it "would have taken the same unfavorable personnel action in the absence of [the protected] behavior."

Applying the above framework, the court found that Collins had engaged in a protected activity despite Beazer's assertions that she never specifically alleged securities or accounting fraud and that her complaints were too vague to constitute protected activity. Comparing Collins with Sherron Watkins, the former Enron vice president, Beazer argued that Watkins had outlined specific accounting procedures and transactions about which she was concerned and had expressed concerns that specific securities laws were being violated whereas Collins expressed only vague concerns that amounted to "nothing more than personality conflicts and differences in marketing strategies." The court concluded:

> Though this is a close case, . . . the Court finds that there is a genuine issue of material
> fact whether Plaintiff engaged in protected activity. It is evident that Plaintiff's complaints

19. 18 U.S.C. § 1514A(a)(1).

(Continued)

(Case 12.1 *continued*)

do not rise to the level of complaints that were raised by Sherron Watkins. . . . However, the mere fact that the severity or specificity of her complaints does not rise to the level of action that would spur Congress to draft legislation does not mean that the legislation it did draft was not meant to protect her. In short if Congress had intended to limit the protection of Sarbanes-Oxley to accountants, or to have required complaints to specifically identify the code section they believe was being violated, it could have done so. It did not.

The court also found that Beazer knew of Collins's protected activity and that she suffered an unfavorable personnel action when she was terminated. Finally, the court found that the fact that Collins was fired fourteen days after making her complaint established circumstances sufficient to demonstrate causation.

Because Collins had met her burden of proof, the court found that Beazer would be entitled to summary judgment only if it could establish by clear and convincing evidence that it would have fired her even if she had not participated in the protected activity. The court concluded that Beazer had not met this burden of proof. Although Beazer contended that Schaffer fired Collins based on her personality conflicts with her coworkers and Mazar's dissatisfaction with her performance, Mazar testified that he did not believe he had a personality conflict with Collins. In addition, none of Collins's superiors had ever met with her to discuss the alleged personality conflicts or her job performance. Finally, Collins's short employment history with Beazer made it more difficult to determine whether the alleged problems would have ultimately resulted in her termination without her participation in the protected activity or whether they could have been addressed and resolved.

> **RESULT** The court found that there was a genuine issue of material fact as to whether Beazer terminated Collins in violation of SOX and therefore denied Beazer's motion for summary judgment.

Implied Contracts

The second judicial exception to the at-will rule arises out of the willingness of courts to interpret the parties' conduct as implying a contract that limits the employer's right to discharge, even though no written or express oral contract exists. Such a contract is known as an *implied contract*. Some factors that can give rise to an implied obligation to discharge the employee only for good cause are that the person (1) has been a long-term employee; (2) has never been formally criticized or warned about his or her conduct; (3) has received raises, bonuses, and promotions throughout his or her career; (4) has been assured that his or her employment would continue if he or she did a good job or that the company did not terminate employees at his or her level except for good cause; and (5) has been assured by the company's management that he or she was doing a good job. Other relevant factors include the personnel policies or practices of the employer and the practices of the industry in which the employee is engaged.

A personnel manual stating that it was the employer's policy to release employees for just cause only, together with oral assurances that the employee would be with the company as long as he or she did his or her job properly, can give rise to a reasonable expectation that an employee will not be terminated except for good cause. In so holding in *Toussaint v. Blue Cross & Blue Shield of Michigan*,[20] the Michigan Supreme Court stated that there could be a contractual obligation binding on the employer without negotiations or any meeting of the minds, or even any communication of the policies to the employee:

No pre-employment negotiations need take place and the parties' minds need not meet on the subject; nor does it matter that the employee knows nothing of the particulars of the employer's policies and practices or that the employer may change them unilaterally. It is enough that the employer chooses, presumably in its own interest, to create an

20. 292 N.W.2d 880 (Mich. 1980).

environment in which the employee believes that, whatever the personnel policies and practices, they are established and official at any given time, purport to be fair, and are applied consistently and uniformly to each employee. The employer has then created a situation "instinct with an obligation."

Although few courts have been willing to go as far as the Michigan Supreme Court went in *Toussaint*, some courts have agreed that a personnel manual given to employees may give rise to contractual obligations. For example, the Oklahoma Court of Appeals held that a manual constitutes an offer of terms and conditions and that the employee's continuing to work is deemed an acceptance of the offer.[21]

In *Havill v. Woodstock Soapstone Co.*,[22] the Vermont Supreme Court ruled that Woodstock's failure to follow the discipline policy set forth in its personnel manual amounted to a breach of its implied contract with its employee, Lois Havill. Woodstock's personnel policy stated that an employee was entitled to two written warnings in a twelve-month period prior to termination for "willful or repeated violations, or exaggerated behavior not in the best interest of the company or its employees." Prior to her termination, Havill continually clashed with a corporate reorganization consultant hired by Woodstock to redefine employment duties. The consultant complained to Woodstock's management about Havill's "rude" and "insubordinate" behavior. Forty-one days after the consultant's initial complaint, Woodstock fired Havill without providing her with any formal written warning. The court ruled that the personnel manual required Woodstock to provide Havill with two written warnings before terminating her; thus, Woodstock was liable for damages arising out of its breach of the implied promise of "just cause" termination and progressive discipline.

Other courts have been unwilling to treat written personnel policies as contracts. For example, an employee of Citibank based his claim that he was entitled not to be discharged except for cause on provisions of a personnel manual. A New York appellate court rejected this argument and held that the manual did not create any legal obligation upon the employer because the employee was still free to terminate the relationship at will.[23] Similarly, in a case involving Westinghouse Electrical Corporation, the North Carolina Court of Appeals held that unilaterally implemented employment policies are not part of the employment contract unless expressly included in it.[24]

Even when there is an implied contract not to terminate except for good cause, an employer may legally terminate an employee suspected of misconduct if, acting in good faith and following an investigation that is appropriate under the circumstances, the employer has reasonable grounds for believing that the employee did engage in misconduct. For example, in one case,[25] a male manager was terminated following charges of sexual harassment by two female employees. The employer conducted a thorough investigation, which included interviews with the manager, the two accusers, and twenty-one other people who had worked with the manager. The investigation was inconclusive, however; the employer could not determine with certainty whether the acts of harassment had actually taken place. The company felt that the accusers were credible, and its investigator concluded that, more likely than not, the harassment had occurred. Fearing a suit by the two women, the company terminated the male manager. He sued for wrongful termination; the jury awarded him $1.78 million, after apparently finding that the charges against him were false. The California Supreme Court reversed and sent the case back for retrial so that the jury could determine whether the company had a good faith belief, following a reasonable investigation, that the manager had engaged in sexual harassment. If so, the company would not be liable for wrongful termination.

Implied Covenant of Good Faith and Fair Dealing

The third prong in the developing law of wrongful discharge is the recognition of an *implied covenant of good faith and fair dealing* in the employment relationship. For example, the Supreme Judicial Court of Massachusetts held that a twenty-five-year employee of National Cash Register Company, with a written contract providing for at-will employment, could sue for wrongful termination when the employer discharged him to deprive him of $46,000 in commissions.[26]

Courts in Texas, New Mexico, Florida, and Wisconsin have expressly declined to recognize an implied covenant of good faith and fair dealing in employment cases. About a dozen states[27] have recognized the covenant in the employment context. California, like Massachusetts,

21. Langdon v. Saga Corp., 569 P.2d 524 (Okla. Ct. App. 1976).
22. 2004 WL 1801776 (Vt. 2004).
23. Edwards v. Citibank, N.A., 74 A.D.2d 553 (N.Y. App. Div. 1980).
24. Walker v. Westinghouse Elec. Corp., 335 S.E.2d 79 (N.C. Ct. App. 1985).
25. Cotran v. Rollins Hudig Hall Int'l, 948 P.2d 412 (Cal. 1998).
26. Fortune v. Nat'l Cash Register Co., 364 N.E.2d 1251 (Mass. 1977).
27. Alaska, Arizona, California, Connecticut, Delaware, Idaho, Massachusetts, Montana, New Hampshire, New Jersey, Utah, and Wyoming.

recognizes such an implied covenant but provides only contract remedies for breach of the implied covenant; tort remedies, such as damages for pain and suffering and punitive damages, are not available.[28]

Right to Fair Procedure

The California courts have acknowledged the common law right of fair procedure, a right that is related to the doctrine of wrongful discharge. *Fair procedure* protects individuals from arbitrary exclusion or expulsion from private organizations that control important economic interests. Individuals having this right must be given notice of the charges against them and an opportunity to

28. Foley v. Interactive Data Corp., 765 P.2d 373 (Cal. 1988).

IN BRIEF

Limits on At-Will Employment

The employer's right to terminate an employee without cause may be subject to and restricted by:

- Express statutory abrogation of terminable at-will employment[29]
- Statutory prohibition of discrimination on specified characteristic (e.g., race, sex, age)
- Statutory prohibition of discrimination for protected activity (e.g., NLRA, protected leaves of absence, off-duty lawful conduct)
- Civil service systems
- Union contracts
- Express employment contracts (oral or written)
- The public policy exception
- Whistleblower statutes
- Implied contracts
- The implied covenant of good faith and fair dealing

29. *See, e.g.*, MONT. CODE ANN. §§ 39-2-901 to 39-2-915, as amended.

respond to those charges. They cannot be expelled from membership for reasons that are arbitrary, capricious, or contrary to public policy, even though the organization's bylaws contain provisions to the contrary. Organizations can exercise their sound business judgment when establishing standards for membership, but any removal must be "both substantively rational and procedurally fair."[30] This right has become increasingly important for healthcare providers belonging to managed care networks.

For example, the California Supreme Court applied the doctrine of fair procedure to an insurance company's decision to remove a physician from its preferred provider lists even though the contract between the physician and the insurer provided that the listing could be terminated by either party at any time with or without cause.[31] The court declined to extend its holding to every insurer wishing to remove a doctor from one of its preferred provider lists, however: "The [fair procedure] obligation . . . arises only when the insurer possesses power so substantial that the removal significantly impairs the ability of an ordinary, competent physician to practice medicine or a medical specialty in a particular geographic area, thereby affecting an important, substantial economic interest."[32]

Fraudulent Inducement

During difficult economic times, a business may engage in puffery and exaggeration to keep and attract highly qualified personnel. The following case serves as a warning that a company may be held liable for overzealous sales pitches under a theory of fraudulent inducement.

30. Pinsker v. Pacific Coast Soc'y. of Orthodontists, 526 P.2d 253 (Cal. 1974).
31. Potvin v. Metro. Life Ins. Co., 997 P.2d 1153 (Cal. 2000). *See also* Harper v. Healthsource New Hampshire, Inc., 674 A.2d 962, 966 (N.H. 1996) ("The public has a substantial interest in the relationship between health maintenance organizations and their preferred provider physicians.").
32. *Potvin*.

A CASE IN POINT	In the Language of the Court

CASE 12.2

Lazar v. Rykoff-Sexton, Inc.
Supreme Court of California
909 P.2d 981 (Cal. 1996).

> **FACTS** Andrew Lazar was employed as president of a family-owned restaurant equipment company in New York where he lived with his wife and two children. In September 1989, a vice president of Rykoff-Sexton, Inc. (Rykoff) contacted Lazar and asked him to move to Los Angeles to work as Rykoff's West Coast general manager for contract design. The company intensively recruited Lazar through February 1990. During this

(Continued)

(Case 12.2 *continued*)

process, Lazar expressed concern to Rykoff about relinquishing a secure job with a family business, moving his children far away from their friends, and leaving his home of forty years. As a condition of agreeing to relocate, Lazar required Rykoff's assurance that his job would be secure and would involve significant pay increases.

Rykoff represented that Lazar would become part of Rykoff's "family," would enjoy continued advancement, and would have security and a long-term relationship with the company. The company told Lazar that it would employ him as long as he performed his job and achieved goals. Rykoff also implied that the current head of the department in which Lazar would work had plans to retire and that Lazar would be groomed for that position. In addition, Rykoff represented that the company was very strong financially and anticipated profits and growth in the future. Lazar was assured that he would receive annual reviews and raises.

In fact, Rykoff's representations were false, as the company had just experienced its worst economic performance in recent history and its financial outlook was pessimistic. Rykoff was planning an operational merger that would eliminate Lazar's position, and the company had no intention of retaining him. The company also knew that the promised compensation increases would not be forthcoming as company policy limited increases to only 3 percent a year.

Based on Rykoff's false representations, in May 1990, Lazar resigned from his job in New York, relocated his family to Los Angeles, and commenced employment at Rykoff. He performed his job in an exemplary manner, obtaining sales increases for his assigned regions and lowering operating costs within his department. In April 1992, Rykoff failed to pay Lazar bonus compensation to which he was entitled. Several months later, Rykoff told Lazar his job was being eliminated owing to management reorganization. After being terminated, Lazar was unable to find comparable employment.

Lazar sued Rykoff on a number of theories, including fraudulent inducement, for inducing his relocation to Los Angeles by making false representations. The trial court dismissed most of Lazar's claims, but the appeals court vacated this order. Rykoff appealed.

> ISSUE PRESENTED Can an employer be held liable to an employee for promissory fraud for statements that it made to induce the employee to come to work for it?

> OPINION WERDEGAR, J., writing for the California Supreme Court:

An action for promissory fraud may lie where a defendant fraudulently induces the plaintiff to enter into a contract. . . . In such cases, the plaintiff's claim does not depend upon whether the defendant's promise is ultimately enforceable as a contract. "If it is enforceable, the [plaintiff] . . . has a cause of action in tort as an alternative at least, and perhaps in some instances in addition to his cause of action on the contract.". . . Recovery, however, may be limited by the rule against double recovery of tort and contract compensatory damages. . . .

Lazar's allegations, if true, would establish all the elements of promissory fraud. As detailed above, Lazar alleges that, in order to induce him to come to work in California, Rykoff intentionally represented to him that he would be employed by the company so long as he performed his job, he would receive significant increases in salary, and the company was strong financially. Lazar further alleges that Rykoff's representations were false, and he justifiably relied on them in leaving secure New York employment, severing his connections with the New York employment market, uprooting his family, purchasing a California home and moving here.
      . . .

(Continued)

(Case 12.2 *continued*)

. . . Lazar's reliance on Rykoff's misrepresentations was truly detrimental, such that he may plead all the elements of fraud. Lazar's employer, Rykoff, did not have the power to compel Lazar to leave his former employment. Rykoff's misrepresentations were made before the employment relationship was formed, when Rykoff had no coercive power over Lazar and Lazar was free to decline the offered position. Rykoff used misrepresentations to induce Lazar to change employment, a result Rykoff presumably could not have achieved truthfully (because Lazar had required assurances the Rykoff position would be secure and would involve significant increases in pay). Moreover, Lazar's decision to join Rykoff left Lazar in worse circumstances than those in which he would have found himself had Rykoff not lied to him. (Allegedly, Lazar's secure living and working circumstances were disrupted, and Lazar became the employee of a financially troubled company, which intended to treat him as an at-will employee.)

. . .

. . . Because of the extra measure of blameworthiness inhering in fraud, and because in fraud cases we are not concerned about the need for "predictability about the cost of contractual relationships," fraud plaintiffs may recover "out-of-pocket" damages. . . .

. . .

Consistent with the foregoing, as to his fraud claim Lazar may properly seek damages for the costs of uprooting his family, expenses incurred in relocation, and the loss of security and income associated with his former employment in New York. On the facts as pled, however, Lazar must rely on his contract claim for recovery of any loss of income allegedly caused by wrongful termination of his employment with Rykoff. Moreover, any overlap between damages recoverable in tort and damages recoverable in contract would be limited by the rule against double recovery.

> RESULT   The court affirmed the appeals court's decision, finding that Lazar had stated a cause of action for fraudulent inducement.

> COMMENTS   In reaching its decision, the court distinguished *Hunter v. Up-Right, Inc.,*[33] an earlier case in which the California Supreme Court had held that an at-will employee who was induced to resign by being falsely told that his job was being eliminated could not state a valid tort claim for fraud. The *Lazar* court reasoned that the employer in *Hunter* had used deception when it could have directly fired the employee. In contrast, the employer in *Lazar* did not have the power to force the executive to leave his company in New York. As a result, the executive's reliance on the employer's representations was truly detrimental.

> CRITICAL THINKING QUESTIONS

1. What is the difference between breach of contract and fraudulent inducement?
2. Why was it necessary for the plaintiff to couch his claim in terms of fraudulent inducement?

33. 864 P.2d 88 (Cal. 1993).

In *Rodowicz v. Massachusetts Mutual Life Insurance Co.,*[34] certain retired MassMutual employees sued the company, alleging that it had failed to reveal that a more

34. 192 F.3d 162 (1st Cir. 1999).

favorable retirement option was forthcoming at the time they were considering retiring. As a result, they retired under terms that were less favorable than those in a special offer made to employees shortly after they retired. Under Massachusetts fraud law, the plaintiffs had to

> ▶ **ETHICAL CONSIDERATION**
>
> What role, if any, should the law play in penalizing an employer who lies to its employee about the reason for termination in order to persuade the employee to resign? What role do ethics play in this situation?

demonstrate that (1) MassMutual made false statements of material fact to induce them to retire when they did and (2) they reasonably relied on those statements to their detriment. In contrast, the Employee Retirement Income Security Act (ERISA) requires employers to disclose information to employees about possible changes in benefits only if those changes reach a level of "serious consideration." The U.S. Court of Appeals for the First Circuit ruled that the retired employees could sue for fraudulent inducement under state law based upon MassMutual's misrepresentation that its board of directors was not considering changing its retirement package.

◆ Noncompete Agreements

A *covenant not to compete* is a device, ancillary to another agreement (such as an employment contract), that is designed to protect a company's interests by limiting a former employee's ability to use trade secrets in working for a competitor or setting up a competing business. Enforcing a noncompete agreement can be difficult because rules vary by jurisdiction. For example, California, Texas, and Georgia severely limit the enforceability of noncompetes.

Due to these differences in state laws, disputes can arise regarding which law to apply to noncompete agreements. In a recent case, an employee working in Ohio signed a noncompete with his employer, Convergys, which included an Ohio choice-of-law provision. When the employee resigned to work for a competitor in Georgia, he filed a lawsuit in Georgia seeking a declaration that the noncompete was unenforceable and an injunction restraining Convergys from enforcing the noncompete. The district court concluded that it could not follow "a contractual selection of law of a foreign state where such chosen law would contravene the public policy of Georgia," declared the noncompete void, and granted an injunction against Convergys that prohibited the company from seeking to enforce the noncompete in any court nationwide. On appeal, the U.S. Court of Appeals for the Eleventh Circuit found that

although Georgia was entitled to enforce its public policy interests within its borders, "Georgia cannot in effect apply its public policy decisions nationwide—the public policy of Georgia is not that everywhere [sic]. To permit a nationwide injunction would in effect interfere both with parties' ability to contract and their ability to enforce appropriately derived expectations." As a result, the court modified the injunction to preclude Convergys only from enforcing the noncompete in Georgia.[35]

Even if an employment agreement does not contain an express noncompetition clause, any provisions having a similar effect will be unenforceable in a jurisdiction banning noncompetes. For example, Dean Witter's employment agreement forced brokers in Los Angeles to repay training costs if they left the company within two years. In a settlement of a class-action suit in October 1997, Dean Witter agreed to return $540,000 collected from thirty-four former brokers and to pay another $1.2 million in legal fees for "involuntary servitude" in violation of California's ban on noncompetes unrelated to the sale of a business.[36]

Even in states permitting noncompete agreements, courts will enforce only reasonable restrictions on competition. Unreasonableness can be found on many grounds, including duration of limitation, geographic extent, scope of activities prohibited, and the employer's relation to the interests being protected. For example, the Nevada Supreme Court invalidated a noncompete agreement that restricted a lighting-retrofitting employee from competing with his former employer within a 100-mile radius of the former employer's site for five years.[37] The duration placed a great hardship on the employee and was not necessary to protect the former employer's interests.

Thus, care must be taken when drafting noncompete agreements to ensure that they are not unduly restrictive. Corporate managers should keep the following guidelines in mind:[38]

- Know the relevant state laws. Given that different states apply different standards for reviewing noncompetes, be sure to structure each agreement in a way that courts will recognize and uphold.

---

35. Keener v. Convergys Corp., 342 F.3d 1264 (11th Cir. 2003).
36. Patrick McGeehan, *Attempting to Dun a Former Broker Costs Dean Witter $1.8 Million*, WALL ST. J., Oct. 23, 1997, at B12.
37. Jones v. Deeter, 913 P.2d 1272 (Nev. 1996). See also Rollins Burdick Hunter of Wis., Inc. v. Hamilton, 304 N.W.2d 752 (Wis. 1981).
38. See Christopher Caggiano, *Think All Noncompetes Stink? Think Again*, INC., Oct. 1997, at 114.

- Be specific. Clarify the specific roles and responsibilities of a given employee so that the noncompete is not overly restrictive, thereby reducing the risk of judicial invalidation.
- Provide consideration for the noncompete. The noncompete may be a condition of employment; but for existing employees, be sure to provide something in exchange, such as a bonus or a promotion.[39]

To protect trade secrets, a New York court imposed noncompete obligations in the absence of a written agreement. Former employees of DoubleClick, Inc. who had not signed noncompete agreements were enjoined from

working in the same industry for six months.[40] The court reasoned that the similarity in the two businesses and positions made it inevitable that the employees would use the former employer's trade secrets in their work for the new company. Trade secret protection and the inevitable disclosure doctrine are discussed further in Chapter 11.

The majority of states recognize an employer's investment of time and money to develop customer and client relationships as a legitimate employer interest that can justify a noncompete agreement. In the following case, the New York Court of Appeals considered whether the protection of customer and client relationships was a justification for enforcing a noncompete agreement.

---

39. Some jurisdictions state that a continued at-will employment relationship amounts to consideration for a noncompetition agreement. *See* Lake Land Employment Group of Akron v. Columber, 804 N.E.2d 27 (Ohio 2004).

40. Frances A. McMorris, *Judge Restricts Two Executives Despite Lack of Noncompete Pacts,* WALL ST. J., Nov. 25, 1997, at B10.

| A CASE IN POINT | In the Language of the Court |

CASE 12.3

BDO Seidman v. Hirshberg
Court of Appeals of New York
712 N.E.2d 1220
(N.Y. 1999).

› FACTS Jeffrey Hirshberg was employed in the Buffalo, New York office of BDO Seidman, a national accounting firm. As a condition of receiving a promotion to the position of manager, Hirshberg was required to sign a "Manager's Agreement." Paragraph SIXTH of the agreement provided that if, within eighteen months following the termination of his employment, Hirshberg served any former client of BDO Seidman's Buffalo office, he would be required to compensate BDO Seidman "for the loss and damages suffered" in an amount equal to one-and-a-half times the fees BDO Seidman had charged that client over the last fiscal year of the client's patronage.

After Hirshberg resigned from BDO Seidman, the accounting firm claimed that it lost to Hirshberg 100 former clients who were billed a total of $138,000 in the year he left the firm. Hirshberg denied serving some of the clients; claimed that a substantial number of them were personal clients he had brought to the firm through his own contacts; and claimed, with respect to some clients, that he had not been the primary BDO Seidman employee working on their accounts.

The trial court invalidated the reimbursement clause on the grounds that it constituted an overbroad and unenforceable anticompetitive agreement. BDO Seidman appealed.

› ISSUE PRESENTED Is an agreement requiring a former employee to reimburse the employer for any loss sustained by losing clients to the employee enforceable?

› OPINION LEVINE, J., writing for the New York Court of Appeals:

The modern, prevailing common-law standard of reasonableness for employee agreements not to compete applies a three-pronged test. A restraint is reasonable only if it: (1) is no greater than is required for the protection of the legitimate interest of the employer, (2) does not impose undue hardship on the employee, and (3) is not injurious to the public. . . . A violation of any prong renders the covenant invalid.

. . .

. . . Close analysis of paragraph SIXTH of the agreement under the first prong of the common-law rule, to identify the legitimate interest of BDO and determine

(Continued)

(Case 12.3 *continued*)

whether the covenant is no more restrictive than is necessary to protect that interest, leads us to conclude that the covenant as written is overbroad in some respects. BDO claims that the legitimate interest it is entitled to protect is its entire client base, which it asserts a modern, large accounting firm expends considerable time and money building and maintaining. However, the only justification for imposing an employee agreement not to compete is to forestall unfair competition. . . . If the employee abstains from unfair means in competing for those clients, the employer's interest in preserving its client base against the competition of the former employee is no more legitimate and worthy of contractual protection than when it vies with unrelated competitors for those clients.

. . . Protection of customer relationships the employee acquired in the course of employment may indeed be a legitimate interest. . . . "The risk to the employer reaches a maximum in situations in which the employee must work closely with the client or customer over a long period of time, especially when his services are a significant part of the total transaction.". . . The employer has a legitimate interest in preventing former employees from exploiting or appropriating the goodwill of a client or customer, which had been created and maintained at the employer's expense, to the employer's competitive detriment. . . .

. . .

To the extent, then that paragraph SIXTH of the Manager's Agreement requires defendant to compensate BDO for lost patronage of clients with whom he never acquired a relationship through the direct provision of substantive accounting services during his employment, the covenant is invalid and unenforceable. . . . Indeed, enforcement of the restrictive covenant as to defendant's personal clients would permit BDO to appropriate goodwill created and maintained through defendant's efforts, essentially turning on its head the principal justification to uphold any employee agreement not to compete based on protection of customer or client relationships.

Except for the overbreadth in the foregoing two respects, the restrictions in paragraph SIXTH do not violate the tripartite common-law test for reasonableness. The restraint on serving BDO clients is limited to eighteen months, and to clients of BDO's Buffalo office. The time constraint appears to represent a reasonably brief interlude to enable the firm to replace the client relationship and goodwill defendant was permitted to acquire with some of its clients. Defendant is free to compete immediately for new business in any market and, if the overbroad provisions of the covenant are struck, to retain his personal clients and those clients of BDO's that he had not served to any significant extent while employed at the firm. . . .

Moreover, given the likely broad array of accounting services available in the greater Buffalo area, and the limited remaining class of BDO clientele affected by the covenant, it cannot be said that the restraint, as narrowed, would seriously impinge on the availability of accounting services in the Buffalo area from which the public may draw, or cause any significant dislocation in the market or create a monopoly in accounting services in that locale. These factors militate against a conclusion that a reformed paragraph SIXTH would violate the third prong of the common-law test, injury to the public interest.

❯ RESULT The New York Court of Appeals found that the agreement was reasonable and enforceable except to the extent that it required Hirshberg to compensate BDO Seidman for fees paid by his personal clients or by clients with whom he had never acquired a relationship through his employment at BDO Seidman.

(Continued)

(Case 12.3 *continued*)

> **COMMENTS** Six weeks before *BDO Seidman v. Hirshberg* was decided, the U.S. Court of Appeals for the Second Circuit reached a similar conclusion on the issue of recognizing relationships with customers as a basis to enforce a noncompete agreement. In *Ticor Title Insurance Co. v. Cohen,*[41] the Court of Appeals for the Second Circuit affirmed the enforcement of a noncompete agreement between a title insurance company and one of its most successful salespeople. The noncompete agreement prohibited the salesman from competing for six months after leaving Ticor to afford the company an opportunity to fairly compete to retain the business of the customers with whom the former employee had maintained relationships on Ticor's behalf. The salesman's relationships with Ticor clients qualified as unique services because competition for title insurance business relied heavily on personal relationships with salespeople. In addition, because Ticor's potential clients were limited and well known throughout the industry, maintaining current clients from this established group was crucial to the company.

> **CRITICAL THINKING QUESTIONS**

1. Could Hirshberg be required to reimburse BDO for fees paid by a client for whom he had not worked while at BDO if the firm could prove that he was aware of the client only because the name was on BDO's client list?

2. Should Hirshberg be excused from paying fees to BDO in connection with a client that testifies that it was dissatisfied with BDO's services and had planned to move its account elsewhere even before knowing that Hirshberg had left?

41. 173 F.3d 63 (2d Cir. 1999).

Employers may attempt to prevent other companies from poaching employees. In *Reeves v. Hanlon,*[42] the California Supreme Court held that although competition between companies for at-will employees is encouraged, inducing the termination of an at-will employment relationship may be tortious intentional interference with prospective economic advantage if the new employer engages in "independently wrongful acts" when inducing the employee to join its ranks. The court defined "independently wrongful acts" as acts "proscribed by constitutional, statutory, regulatory, common law, or other determinable legal standard." When the defendants in *Reeves* left their former employer, an immigration law firm, they induced six other employees to leave to join their new law practice. The court found that the defendants were liable for damages suffered by Reeves because they had also mounted "a campaign to deliberately disrupt plaintiff's business," including having employees resign without notice, leaving no status reports of outstanding matters or deadlines, destroying the firm's computer files and forms, taking confidential information, and improperly soliciting Reeves's clients.

42. 33 Cal. 4th 1140 (2004).

ETHICAL CONSIDERATION

Companies can require their employees to sign a noncompete agreement as a condition of employment. In *Tatge v. Chambers & Owen, Inc.,*[43] a company asked an at-will employee to sign a noncompete agreement that provided that he would not work for one of the company's competitors for a period of six months after termination of his employment. Tatge refused to sign the agreement, and the company terminated him. He sued the company, alleging several claims including wrongful discharge. The Supreme Court of Wisconsin dismissed his claim, after concluding that the company's requirement that he sign the noncompete agreement was not a violation of public policy. The court noted that signing the agreement would not have prevented Tatge from arguing that its terms were unreasonable if the company had tried to enforce it. California law reaches a different outcome. An employer's termination of an employee for refusing to sign an unenforceable noncompete agreement constitutes a wrongful termination in violation of public policy.[44] Although it was legal for the employer to fire Tatge for failing to sign the noncompete agreement, was it ethical? Does it matter whether the employer knows the agreement is overbroad?

43. 579 N.W.2d 217 (Wis. 1998).
44. D'sa v. Playhut, 85 Cal. App. 4th 927, 929 (2000).

◆ Preserving At-Will Employment Status

In deciding whether there is an express or implied contractual right not to be fired except for cause, a court may consider statements made during preemployment interviews or performance review meetings, or language on application forms or in offer letters, bonus plans, or policy manuals. Consequently, if an employer wants to preserve the traditional legal right to discharge employees at will, it should take steps to ensure that it does not inadvertently limit this right.

To illustrate, an application form might include the following language above the employee signature line: "I understand that, if hired, my employment can be terminated at any time, with or without cause, at either my employer's or my option." Inclusion of such language reminds the employee that his or her employment is at will—and verifies that he or she was so informed—and lessens the likelihood that the employee will be able to establish an implied contractual right to be discharged only for cause. Additionally, no statements should be made during interviews that could create an impression that the applicant will not be fired without good cause. "Employees are never fired from here without good reason," "Your job will be secure, as long as you do your work," and "We treat our employees like family" are examples of such statements. In short, the employer should not mislead an applicant about the security of the job offered.

In some states, it may be difficult to maintain an at-will relationship except by an express contract or by a disclaimer in the employment application or the personnel manual stating that nothing in the employment relationship and no personnel policy or benefit shall create a right to continued employment or to employment for a specified duration. If such a disclaimer is plainly contrary to the company's stated policy, however, it may be rejected by a court. For example, a statement on an application form that employment is at will probably will not be upheld if the company's written personnel policy expressly provides that employees will be given progressive discipline and will not be fired without just cause.

Employers should also have a system of checks and balances in place to ensure that the company's policies and managers do not promise more job security than the company intends. Appropriate policies should be properly communicated and followed. To avoid disputes, discharges should be well documented whenever possible, handled in accordance with these policies, and employees should be treated in a fair and consistent manner. Nevertheless, a written policy requiring extensive documentation for termination, or promising fairness and consistency, may undermine at-will employment and invite second-guessing by a court and jury.

These guidelines can help to avoid suits for wrongful discharge:

- If an employer chooses to have a written personnel policy, care should be taken to see that the language expressly reserves those rights that the employer wishes to maintain, especially with respect to discharge. Also, if employees are given handbooks that purport to summarize the official personnel manuals, the handbook and the manuals must be consistent. Otherwise, courts and juries are likely to uphold the policy that is most favorable to the employee.

- If an employer chooses to have a policy of progressive discipline, it is essential that the policy explain that the policy does not alter at-will employment, and that all decisions on progressive discipline—whether to apply it, what steps to take or skip—are within the sole discretion of the company. If specific rules of conduct are listed, the manual should describe them as examples, not an exhaustive list, and inform employees that violation of a stated rule is not required for termination because employment remains terminable at will. Supervisors and managers, as well as the human resources staff, must be trained to administer the policy. In particular, they should be trained to document performance problems and to counsel employees about the need to improve, but not to portray the policy as an entitlement.

- An employer can enter into an agreement with the employee that any dispute shall be subject to arbitration. Most courts will enforce an evenhanded arbitration clause in a fairly negotiated written contract; however, a *boilerplate clause*—that is, standardized, nonnegotiable language—in an employment application form may be found invalid. As discussed in Chapter 4, mandatory arbitration of discrimination claims can pose special concerns.

- An employer should decide whether to establish an internal grievance procedure. Such a procedure can result in fewer lawsuits. If established, however, a grievance procedure must be followed. Otherwise, the employer may face claims for failure to follow its own procedure, especially when the procedure is elaborate.

Recommendations for Former Employees

Employers are often asked to give references regarding former employees to prospective employers. An employee always hopes that a reference will be favorable, but that is not always the case. At any rate, the employee expects the reference to be fair. If the reference is not fair and the employer has impugned the individual's reputation, he or she can sue the employer for defamation.

In *Deutsch v. Chesapeake Center*,[45] a reverend, who was hired as director of an overnight lodging and meeting facility for church groups, was terminated as a result of accusations of racism and sexual harassment. When he applied for a position as a church pastor in another community, his former employer told the prospective employer of the charges that had resulted in termination of his employment. The reverend sued his former employer for defamation, but the U.S. District Court for the District of Maryland dismissed his claim, finding that the former employer's statements were protected by a conditional privilege to communicate information concerning a former employee to a prospective employer.

In contrast, in *MacCord v. Christian Academy*,[46] the U.S. District Court for the Eastern District of Pennsylvania concluded that a principal's comments regarding a teacher's poor performance during a faculty meeting were not protected by the privilege. The principal had abused the privilege by publishing the defamatory statements to the entire faculty and including allegedly defamatory matter not reasonably believed to be necessary for the purpose of informing the faculty that some teachers' contracts would not be renewed.

Traditionally, defamation law requires publication, meaning that the communicator of the defamatory information tells the information to a third party, such as a prospective employer. A few jurisdictions, however, recognize an exception in the employment context. Under the *doctrine of self-publication*, a defamatory communication by an employer to an employee may constitute publication if the employer could foresee that the employee would be required to repeat the communication, for instance, to a prospective employer. The doctrine is designed to provide a cause of action to the job-seeking employee who is forced to self-publicize a former employer's defamatory statement. Although as many as seven state appellate courts have adopted the doctrine of self-publication, the highest courts of only two states, Colorado and Minnesota, have adopted it, and the legislatures of both these states responded by eliminating or restricting it. The majority of the other states have concluded that public policy concerns favor the rejection of the doctrine. As the Connecticut Supreme Court stated in a recent decision rejecting the doctrine:

> The most compelling public policy consideration against recognition of the doctrine is that acceptance of the doctrine would have a chilling effect on communication in the workplace, thereby contradicting society's fundamental interest in encouraging the free flow of information. . . . Recognition of compelled self-publication defamation . . . would encourage employers to curtail communications with employees, and the employees' prospective employers, for fear of liability. As one commentator noted, recognition of the doctrine could create a perpetual "culture of silence," negatively affecting not only employers, but employees in numerous ways.[47]

An employer may be protected against liability for defamation claims by a former employee if the employee signs a waiver and release form releasing potential claims. In *Bardin v. Lockheed Aeronautical Systems Co.*,[48] Bethany Bardin had worked for Lockheed from 1987 until 1993. After she was laid off by the company, she applied for a job as a police officer with the Los Angeles Police Department. As part of the application process, she signed a "Release and Waiver" form, which authorized a background investigation and provided that former employers were cleared "from any and all liability for damage of whatever kind." The police department notified Bardin that her application was suspended because she had failed to disclose employment problems at Lockheed, including a complaint related to her drinking. Bardin sued Lockheed, but the court found the language in the waiver and release form sufficiently broad to protect Lockheed from liability.

In general, employers should be cautious when giving recommendations for former employees. A growing number of job applicants are hiring third-party companies to investigate what their former employers are saying about them.[49] Companies should have a written policy outlining who may provide references and what

---

45. 27 F. Supp. 2d 642 (Md. 1998).
46. 1998 U.S. Dist. LEXIS 19412 (E.D. Pa. Dec. 4, 1998).
47. Cweklinksy v. Mobil Chem. Co., 837 A.2d 759 (Conn. 2004).
48. 82 Cal. Rptr. 2d 726 (Cal. Ct. App. 1999).
49. Marci Alboher Nusbaum, *When a Reference Is a Tool for Snooping*, N.Y. Times, Oct. 19, 2003, BU12.

information can be provided to companies seeking a reference. Although fear of a defamation claim may tempt an employer to give an overly positive recommendation, this is not prudent. As explained in Chapter 9, an employer giving an untrue assessment of a former employee may be liable not only to the new employer who relies on the recommendation but also to third parties physically harmed as a foreseeable result of the recommendation.

◈ Employer Testing and Surveillance

Employers often administer tests to employees in an effort to increase productivity, manage legal risks, and cut costs. However, such testing and surveillance activities may conflict with an employee's right to privacy.

DRUG TESTING

Many employers have adopted drug-screening programs for their employees and applicants to avoid the decreased productivity, quality control problems, absenteeism, on the job accidents, and employee theft that can result from drug and alcohol abuse. According to the American Management Association, 62 percent of companies in the United States test their employees for drugs.[50] Some employers use drug testing in conjunction with a comprehensive drug program that provides education and assistance to an employee with a drug or an alcohol problem.

The issue of drug testing generally comes before the courts in the context of discipline or discharge of an employee for refusing to take a test. An employee may challenge a drug test in many ways. The employee may claim that (1) the test breached his or her employment contract; (2) there was no justification for the test; (3) it violated the public policy that protects privacy; (4) he or she was defamed by false accusations of drug use based on an erroneous test; (5) he or she suffered emotional distress, especially if the test result was in error; or (6) the testing disproportionately affected employees of one race or gender and therefore was discriminatory.

Whether testing will be deemed permissible in a particular situation depends on four factors: (1) the scope of the testing program, (2) whether the employer is a public or private employer, (3) any state constitutional guarantees of a right to privacy, and (4) any state statutes regulating drug testing.

The first major factor, scope, concerns who is being tested: all employees (random testing); only employees in a specific job where the employer believes there is a legitimate job-related need (for example, nuclear power plant employees); groups of employees (for example, all employees in one facility because there is a general suspicion of drug use within that group); or specific individuals who are believed to be using drugs. The smaller the group to be tested and the more specific the reason for testing, the more likely a court will uphold the test. Random testing is the most difficult to defend. The final three factors are discussed in more detail below.

Public Employees

Because public employees are protected by the U.S. Constitution's Fourth Amendment prohibition against unreasonable searches and seizures and by the right to privacy, there are greater limitations on testing public employees than on testing private-sector employees. It has long been recognized that urine tests and blood tests are a substantial intrusion upon bodily privacy and are therefore searches subject to regulation. With some exceptions, there is no federal constitutional limitation on drug testing in the private sector.

In *Skinner v. Railway Labor Executives' Ass'n*,[51] the U.S. Supreme Court held that railroads can be required to test public employees involved in a major train accident and have the authority to test employees who violate certain safety rules. The Court reasoned that any intrusion upon individual privacy rights in the railroad context was outweighed by the government's compelling interest in public and employee safety.

The Supreme Court also upheld mandatory drug testing of U.S. Customs Service employees in line for transfer or promotion to certain sensitive positions involving drug interdiction or the handling of firearms.[52] Although there was no perceived drug problem among Customs employees, the Court held that the program was justified by the need for national security and by the extraordinary safety hazards attendant to the positions involved.

In *Knox County Education Ass'n v. Knox County Board of Education*,[53] the U.S. Court of Appeals for the Sixth Circuit held that subjecting public school teachers

---

50. American Management Association, *2004 Workplace Testing Survey: Medical Testing* (2004), at http://www.amanet.org/research/pdfs/Medical_testing_04.pdf.

51. 489 U.S. 602 (1989).
52. Nat'l Treasury Employees Union v. Von Raab, 489 U.S. 656 (1989).
53. 158 F.3d 361 (6th Cir. 1998).

to drug and alcohol testing was not an unconstitutional violation of their right to privacy. Of primary importance in the court's decision was the unique role teachers play by accepting *in loco parentis* (in place of the parents) obligations to ensure the safety of children and to serve as role models. The court commented that "teachers must expect with this extraordinary responsibility, they will be subject to scrutiny to which other civil servants or professionals might not be subjected, including drug testing."[54]

Constitutional Protection

The right to privacy guaranteed by the U.S. Constitution protects against invasions of privacy by public actors (i.e, state and federal governments or agencies) but does not protect against invasions by private (i.e., nongovernmental) actors. Similarly, the Fourth Amendment ban on unreasonable searches and seizures applies only to governmental activity. Many state constitutions also guarantee the right to privacy, however, and some states extend this right to private invasions of privacy.

In *Luddtke v. Nabors Alaska Drilling, Inc.*,[55] the Alaska Supreme Court held that the right to privacy in the state constitution applied only to governmental intrusions, not to alleged violations by private entities. Therefore, the state constitution did not shield its citizens from drug tests by a private employer. Moreover, even if there was a right to privacy, the company's interest in maintaining the health, safety, and welfare of its workers would outweigh any privacy interest.

In contrast, the California Court of Appeal held that a pupillary-reaction test given to all employees of Kerr–McGee Corporation at its chemical plant in Trono, California, might violate the California Constitution's right to privacy, depending on the intrusiveness of the test and the employer's safety needs.[56] The test consisted of shining a light in the person's eye and observing how much the pupil contracted. Although the court acknowledged that the pupillary test was less intrusive than urine, blood, or breath tests, it held that the trial court needed more facts to determine just how intrusive the test was.

Statutory Regulation

A number of states have enacted legislation regarding drug testing of private employees. Such legislation often sets forth the notice procedures an employer must follow before asking an employee to submit to a drug test. In Vermont, for example, before administering the test, the employer must give the employee a copy of a written policy setting forth the circumstances under which persons may be tested, the drugs that will be screened, the procedures involved, and the consequences of a positive result.

A number of states have comprehensive drug- and alcohol-testing laws that require reasonable suspicion or probable cause before an employer may test. The requirements for establishing reasonable suspicion or probable cause vary from state to state. For instance, Connecticut's law permits testing when "the employer has reasonable suspicion that the employee is under the influence of drugs or alcohol which adversely affects or could adversely affect such employee's job performance."[57] Other states take the opposite approach and encourage fair and consistent testing in order to promote drug-free workplaces. For example, Alabama permits discounted workers' compensation insurance premiums for employers that follow fair testing procedures, including random testing.[58]

Although private employers, as well as public employers, may face some limits on implementing a drug-testing program, it should be noted that employers have the right to make and enforce rules prohibiting drug use or possession on work premises, as well as rules prohibiting employees from being under the influence of drugs while at work. When an employee exhibits visible signs of intoxication or impairment or inadequate performance, the employer may take disciplinary action. Because of the inadequacy of drug tests and the uncertainty about the scope of employees' rights, the employer may wish instead to develop programs that provide assistance and drug education and to counsel employees about the performance problems that drug abuse can cause.

HEALTH SCREENING AND GENETIC TESTING

Health screening and genetic testing have become important issues and raise many of the same questions that arise in the context of drug testing. Genetic testing predicts whether a person has a genetic predisposition for developing a certain disease, although the accuracy of such tests is unproven.[59] Employers may be motivated to perform

---

54. *Id.* at 384.
55. 768 P.2d 1123 (Alaska 1989).
56. Semore v. Pool, 217 Cal. App. 3d 1087 (Cal. Ct. App. 1990).
57. CONN. GEN. STAT. ANN. § 31-51x (West 1993).
58. Alabama seeks to maximize productivity, enhance competitive positions of its companies in the marketplace, and reach companies' "desired levels of success without experiencing the costs, delays, and tragedies associated with work related accidents resulting from substance abuse by employees." ALA. CODE § 25–5–330 *et seq.*
59. American Civil Liberties Union, *Genetic Discrimination in the Workplace Fact Sheet* (Mar. 12, 2002), *at* http://www.aclu.org/workplacerights/workplacerights.cfm?ID=9918&c=34.

genetic tests to (1) decrease exposure to tort liability for negligent hiring of an employee who, for example, has a propensity toward dangerous behavior or (2) reduce costs by lowering absenteeism rates and health insurance premiums kept high by unhealthy workers.[60]

A survey of U.S. companies in 2004 found that 15 percent of the surveyed companies inquired into their employees' family medical history.[61]

In February 2000, President Bill Clinton signed an executive order prohibiting the federal government from using genetic testing in hiring or promotion decisions.[62] As of January 2005, no federal legislation had passed relating to genetic discrimination in the workplace, although several bills were introduced in Congress during the past decade.[63] However, at least thirty-one states have enacted laws outlawing genetic discrimination in the workplace.[64] These state laws generally fit within one of three types of legislation: (1) laws prohibiting discrimination in employment based on genetic characteristics, (2) laws prohibiting employers from requiring applicants or employees to undergo genetic testing, and (3) laws banning discrimination based on genetic test results or the refusal to take a genetic test.[65] Private employers may also have liability under state constitutions that provide protection from private invasions of privacy.

Although no federal statute regulates genetic testing, employees may be able to sue for violation of their constitutional right to privacy if a public employer tests them for medical conditions without their knowledge or consent. In *Norman-Bloodsaw v. Lawrence Berkeley Laboratory*,[66] employees sued their government employer when they discovered that it had tested them for syphilis, sickle-cell anemia, and pregnancy without their knowledge or consent. The district court granted the laboratory's motion for summary judgment, but the U.S. Court of Appeals for the Ninth Circuit reversed, stating:

> The constitutionally protected privacy interest in avoiding disclosure of personal matters clearly encompasses medical

information and its confidentiality. Although cases defining the privacy interest in medical information have typically involved its disclosure to "third" parties, rather than the collection of information by illicit means, it goes without saying that the most basic violation possible involves the performance of unauthorized tests—that is, the non-consensual retrieval of previously unrevealed medical information that may be unknown even to plaintiffs. These tests may also be viewed as searches in violation of Fourth Amendment rights that require Fourth Amendment scrutiny. The tests at issue in this case thus implicate rights protected under both the Fourth Amendment and the Due Process Clause of the Fifth or Fourteenth Amendments.

The court also found that genetic testing may violate Title VII when employees or applicants are singled out for testing based on race or gender. For example, the laboratory singled out black and female employees for additional nonconsensual testing and thus selectively invaded the privacy of certain employees on the basis of race, gender, or pregnancy. As a result, the Ninth Circuit found that the district court had erred in dismissing the plaintiffs' Title VII claims because "it was error to rule that as a matter of law no 'adverse effect' could arise from a classification that singled out particular groups for unconstitutionally invasive, non-consensual medical testing."

The Americans with Disabilities Act (ADA) may also provide employees with a cause of action for genetic testing. A person is protected by the ADA only if he or she is disabled. The ADA defines "disability" as "(A) a physical or mental impairment that substantially limits one or more of the major life activities . . . (B) a record of such an impairment; or (C) being regarded as having such an impairment."[67] Since 1995 the Equal Employment Opportunity Commission (EEOC) has argued that genetically predisposed individuals possess an "impairment" under section C and thereby qualify for ADA protection. In 2002, the EEOC brought suit against the Burlington Northern Santa Fe Railroad on behalf of Burlington employees who were secretly tested after they complained of carpal tunnel syndrome (CTS) stemming from work-related activities. The EEOC attempted to include the employees under its definition of those suffering from an "impairment" under section C, although it conceded that Burlington had taken no action to discriminate against the employees based on the results of the genetic testing and that no employees tested were

60. Human Genome Project Information, *Genetics Privacy and Legislation* (Sept. 16, 2004), *at* http://www.ornl.gov/sci/techresources/Human_Genome/elsi/lesislat.shtml.
61. American Management Association, *supra* note 50.
62. Francine Kiefer, *Amid Genetic Discoveries, a Nod to Privacy. As Science Advances, Clinton Bars Use of Genetic Information in Hiring for Federal Jobs*, CHRISTIAN SCI. MONITOR, Feb. 10, 2000, at 2.
63. Human Genome Project Information, *supra* note 60.
64. Public Broadcast System, *Bloodlines* (Apr. 2003), http://www.pbs.org/bloodlines/mapping_the_future/map.html.
65. Samantha French, *Genetic Testing in the Workplace: The Employer's Coin Toss*, 2002 DUKE L. & TECH. REV. 15 (Sept. 5, 2002).
66. 135 F.3d 1260 (9th Cir. 1998).
67. 42 U.S.C. § 12102(2).

found to possess the CTS genetic disorder. Nevertheless, Burlington agreed to pay $2.2 million to settle the case.[68]

Although efforts to conduct genetic testing may lead to suits for invasion of privacy, an employer may also be concerned that its failure to use genetic testing could result in possible tort liability under theories of employer negligence. Because employers have a duty of good faith and due care to prevent unnecessary work-related injuries, an employer could be sued by a third party who is injured by an employee with an undiscovered genetic condition that caused a lapse of consciousness or incapacity. An employee who is injured as a result of an undiscovered genetic condition might also sue his or her employer for failure to implement genetic testing.

Where employees are exposed to dangerous chemicals or conditions as part of their jobs, regular health monitoring is encouraged and in some instances required in standards adopted by the Occupational Safety and Health Administration.[69] Presumably, even where regulations do not require monitoring, an employer may choose to require participation in the health monitoring program as a condition of employment in positions affected by hazardous exposure.

POLYGRAPH TESTING OF EMPLOYEES

Polygraph testing is another area where an employee's right to privacy may limit an employer's investigative rights. The Employee Polygraph Protection Act of 1988 (EPPA)[70] generally makes it unlawful for employers to (1) ask an applicant or employee to take a polygraph exam or other lie detector test; (2) rely on or inquire about the results of a lie detector test that an applicant or employee has taken; (3) take or threaten to take any adverse action against an applicant or employee because of a refusal to take a lie detector test or on the basis of the results of such a test; or (4) take or threaten to take any adverse action against an employee or applicant who has filed a complaint or participated in a proceeding relating to the polygraph law.

These rights cannot be waived by the employee in advance. For example, a federal district court held that a bartender could still sue for violation of the EPPA even though she had signed a release form stating that her employer had reasonable suspicion of theft before the employer requested that she take a polygraph test.[71] The

court held that an employee can waive rights or procedures under the EPPA only pursuant to a written settlement of a pending lawsuit.

The EPPA does not completely ban the use of polygraph exams. Employers may test employees who are reasonably suspected of conduct injurious to the business, as well as applicants or employees in certain businesses involving security services or the handling of drugs. In addition, the EPPA does not restrict federal, state, or local government employers from administering polygraph exams.

Several states have laws that restrict or prohibit the use of polygraph examinations, however. For example, in Massachusetts, an employer cannot request that an applicant or employee take a lie detector test as a condition of employment.[72] Rhode Island,[73] Delaware,[74] and Pennsylvania[75] have similar statutes. Even when lie detector tests are permitted, no question should be asked during the test that could not lawfully be asked on an application form or during an interview.

EMPLOYEE SURVEILLANCE

According to a 2001 survey by the American Management Association, 82 percent of surveyed businesses in the United States check up on their employees by using various strategies such as listening in on employees' phone calls, inspecting their computer files, and conducting video surveillance. Of those companies, 12 percent indicated that they conducted these activities without the consent or awareness of employees.

Companies engage in employee surveillance for several reasons. Regulated industries, such as telemarketing, may conduct surveillance to show their compliance with regulations; other industries may do so to satisfy due diligence requirements. Another reason is to limit legal liability; for example, employees unwittingly exposed to offensive material on a colleague's computer may sue the employer for allowing a hostile workplace environment. Surveillance is also used to gain information for performance reviews and productivity measures and to promote security, including the protection of trade secrets and other confidential information.[76]

---

68. French, *supra* note 65.
69. *See, e.g.,* 29 C.F.R. § 1910.1450 & Apps. A and B.
70. 29 U.S.C. §§ 2001–2009.
71. Long v. Mango's Tropical Cafe, Inc., 958 F. Supp. 612 (S.D. Fla. 1997).

72. MASS. GEN. LAWS ANN. ch. 149, § 19B (West 1996).
73. R.I. GEN. LAWS § 28-6.1-1 (1996).
74. DEL. CODE ANN. tit. 19, § 704 (1997).
75. 18 PA. CONS. STAT. ANN. § 7321 (West 1998).
76. American Management Association, *2001 AMA Survey: Workplace Monitoring & Surveillance* (2001), *at* http://www.amanet.org/research/pdfs/ems_short2001.pdf.

Employers have a legitimate interest in observing their employees, but under certain circumstances surveillance may transgress the employees' privacy rights. The watershed case in this area was *O'Connor v. Ortega*.[77] In that case, the U.S. Supreme Court ruled that a public employee may, in certain circumstances, enjoy a reasonable expectation of privacy in the workplace. However, the employee's privacy interest is to be balanced by the "operational realities" of the workplace. Since *Ortega*, lower courts have looked to (1) whether the employee was provided exclusive working space, (2) the nature of the employment, and (3) whether the employee was on notice that parts of the workplace were subject to

employer intrusions. For example, in *Vega-Rodriguez v. Puerto Rico Telephone Co.*,[78] the U.S. Court of Appeals for the First Circuit held that governmental security operators, sitting in an open, undifferentiated work area, who monitored computer banks to detect alarm-system signals, had no reasonable expectation of privacy. As a result, the public employer's soundless video surveillance of the workplace did not violate the employees' Fourth Amendment rights.

The following case examines whether an employee has a legitimate expectation of privacy in personal information stored on an employer's computer.

77. 480 U.S. 709 (1987).

78. 110 F.3d 174 (1st Cir. 1997).

A CASE IN POINT	**Summary**

CASE 12.4

TBG Insurance Services Corp. v. Superior Court of Los Angeles County
Court of Appeal of California
96 Cal. App. 4th 443
(Cal. Ct. App. 2002).

> **FACTS** Robert Zieminski worked as a senior executive for TBG Insurance Services Corporation. In the course of his employment, Zieminski used two computers owned by TBG, one at the office, the other at his residence. Zieminski signed TBG's "electronic and telephone equipment policy statement" in which he agreed, among other things, that he would use the computers "for business purposes only and not for personal benefit or non-company purposes, unless such use [was] expressly approved. Under no circumstances [could the] equipment or systems be used for improper, derogatory, defamatory, obscene or other inappropriate purposes." Zieminski consented to have his computer use "monitored by authorized company personnel" on an "as needed" basis and agreed that communications transmitted by computer were not private. He acknowledged that he understood that his improper use of the computers could result in disciplinary action, including discharge.

Zieminski was terminated when TBG discovered that he had "violated TBG's electronic policies by repeatedly accessing pornographic sites on the Internet while he was at work." According to Zieminski, the pornographic websites were not accessed intentionally but simply "popped up" on his computer. Zieminski sued TBG for wrongful termination. In its answer, TBG asked Zieminski to return his home computer so that TBG could corroborate evidence that Zieminski accessed sexually explicit websites using its computers. Zieminski objected, claiming an invasion of his constitutional right to privacy. Zieminski and his entire family had used the home computer for personal purposes, and it contained details of his personal finances and his family's personal correspondence. Zieminski stated that he had a privacy interest in the information stored on the computer and that TBG had no right to access such information because it was "universally accepted and understood by all that the home computers would also be used for personal purposes as well."

The trial court denied TBG's demand that Zieminski return its computer. It concluded that TBG already had extensive evidence supporting its claim that Zieminski accessed sexually explicit material from his TBG office computer, and "any additional evidence that the home computer may disclose does not outweigh the fact that the computer contains personal information." TBG then filed a petition for a writ of mandate, asking the California Court of Appeal to intervene.

(Continued)

(Case 12.4 *continued*)

➤ ISSUE PRESENTED   Does an employee have a protectable privacy interest in the information stored on a computer owned by his employer?

➤ SUMMARY OF OPINION   The California Court of Appeal began by defining what constitutes a reasonable expectation of privacy. The court concluded that "[a] 'reasonable' expectation of privacy is an objective entitlement founded on broadly based and widely accepted community norms," and "the presence or absence of opportunities to consent voluntarily to activities impacting privacy interests obviously affects the expectations of the participant."

The court then noted that a party who seeks affirmative relief to prevent a constitutionally prohibited invasion of privacy must establish "(1) a legally protected privacy interest; (2) a reasonable expectation of privacy in the circumstances; and (3) conduct by [the other party] constituting a serious invasion of privacy." The court stated:

> We are concerned in this case with the "community norm" within 21st Century computer-dependent businesses. In 2001, the 700,000 member American Management Association (AMA) reported that more than three-quarters of this country's major firms monitor, record, and review employee communications and activities on the job, including their telephone calls, e-mails, Internet connections, and computer files.

The court concluded that the evidence was "insufficient to support the trial court's implied finding that Zieminksi had a reasonable expectation of privacy." The court stated that TBG's electronic and telephone equipment policy statement gave Zieminski the opportunity to consent to or reject use of the home computer. No one at TBG compelled Zieminski or his family to use the home computer for personal matters, and no one prevented Zieminski from purchasing his own computer for personal use. As a result of signing the equipment policy, Zieminski was aware that TBG would monitor the files and messages stored on the employer-owned computers that he used at home and at the office. Thus, Zieminski fully and voluntarily relinquished his privacy rights in the information he stored on his employer-owned home computer.

➤ RESULT   The court granted TBG's petition and commanded the trial court to vacate its order denying TBG's demand that Zieminski return the employer-owned home computer. The court stated that on remand, it would be up to Zieminski to identify with particularity the information that should be excluded from TBG's inspection and up to the trial court to determine whether to issue a protective order excluding such information from TBG's inspection.

🔳 Responsibility for Worker Safety

Both federal and state laws require employers to provide a reasonably safe workplace.

OCCUPATIONAL SAFETY AND HEALTH ACT

The Occupational Safety and Health Act of 1970 (OSHA)[79] was enacted to require employers to establish safe and healthful working environments. The federal

agency responsible for enforcing the provisions of OSHA is the Occupational Safety and Health Administration (also called OSHA). This agency is authorized by Congress to govern additional workplace issues, including exposure to hazardous chemicals, protective gear, fire protection, and workplace temperatures and ventilation. About half of the states have enacted similar legislation and established enforcement agencies at the state level. Typically, in states with approved employment health and safety programs, federal OSHA defers to the state agency for enforcement activities.

An employer governed by OSHA has a general duty to provide a safe workplace, which includes the obligation to abate workplace hazards that are causing or are

---

79. Pub. L. No. 91-596, 84 Stat. 1590 (1970) (codified as amended at 29 U.S.C. §§ 651–678).

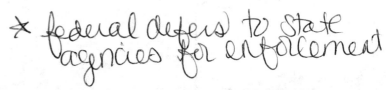
✻ federal defers to state agencies for enforcement

View from Cyberspace

BIG BROTHER IS READING YOUR E-MAIL

A 2000 survey of over a thousand U.S. employees by The Vault.com found that electronic mail had become the primary business communication tool: 80 percent of respondents used e-mail as their primary form of business correspondence.[a] By 2004, instant messaging (IM) had also become an important tool of communication. According to another survey, 31 percent of employees surveyed were using IM at work.[b] Employee use of the Internet, e-mail, and IM has raised a number of new issues in the workplace. Employers are increasingly concerned that employees are wasting company time by using the Internet for personal reasons during working hours. In addition, employees' improper use of the Internet, e-mail, and IM could (1) subject their employers to various forms of liability, such as potential discrimination claims due to inappropriate e-mails or liability for copyright and trademark violations due to unauthorized downloading of materials, and (2) disrupt business by allowing viruses to enter the employer's computer systems or disclosing the employer's confidential information and trade secrets.[c] Despite employers' concerns, a survey by the American Management Association (AMA) revealed that 46 percent of surveyed companies do not train their employees on the proper and improper use of e-mail (although 78 percent have formal written policies addressing its use)[d]

and only 20 percent have a written policy governing use of IM.

Nearly three-quarters of employers monitored employee e-mail in 2004, up from 27 percent in 1999, but only 10 percent monitored employee IMs.[e] In 1999, the New York Times Company fired more than twenty employees for sending e-mail that was "inappropriate and offensive"; Xerox Corporation fired forty workers, including those who visited pornographic websites from office computers, for violating its company policy on Internet use; and investment firm Edward Jones & Co. terminated nineteen employees when it discovered they were using the company's e-mail system to send inappropriate material.[f] Despite such incidents, the 2004 AMA survey revealed that most companies have never terminated an employee for violating an e-mail policy.[g]

Most courts have upheld the right of employers to monitor and regulate workplace e-mail and use of computers on the grounds that the employees could not prove that they had a reasonable expectation of privacy in workplace e-mails or computer use.[h] In 2004, the U.S. Court of Appeals for the Third Circuit ruled that an employer may read and access employees' e-mails without violating the Electronic Communications Privacy Act, which bars the interception of any electronic communication or the unauthorized access of stored communications, as long as the employer reads only e-mail messages that were already sent and stored on the company's own e-mail system.[i]

Because the Internet and e-mail can be used for union-organizing and other protected concerted activities, the General Counsel of the National Labor Relations Board has imposed more restrictions than the courts on employers' monitoring and regulation of employee use of the Internet and e-mail.[j]

An employer's control of its e-mail systems may not extend to former employees, however. In 2003, the Supreme Court of California ruled that a former employee of Intel Corporation, Kenneth Hamidi, did not trespass on Intel property when he sent seven mass e-mailings criticizing the company to as many as 30,000 Intel employees.[k] After Hamidi was fired by Intel, he began a campaign of criticizing its human resource policies; in addition to his mass e-mailings, he established a website critical of the company. The court stated that Hamidi's e-mails neither damaged Intel's computer system nor impaired its functioning, as was required by Intel's trespass claim. The court ultimately rejected Intel's plea for a permanent injunction against Hamidi.

To avoid problems and resolve conflicts with employees, companies should draft Internet, e-mail, IM, and computer use policies.[l] These policies should prohibit the sending of unlawful, offensive, or defamatory statements, or unauthorized disclosures of trade secrets, via the corporate e-mail system. They should also eliminate employees' expectations of privacy in use of the electronic resources, and advise employees of the company's right to monitor use and contents without notice. In addition, companies should establish security measures and educate their employees about the policies and the manner in which the employer will enforce them.

a. The Vault.com, *Email Behavior in the Workplace*, THE VAULT (May 2000), *at* http://www.vault.com/surveys/email_behavior/email_behavior.jsp.
b. American Management Association, *2004 Workplace E-mail & Instant Messaging Survey Summary*, (2004), *at* http://www.amanet.org/research/pdfs/IM_2004_Summary.pdf.
c. Lou Licata, *An Employer's Right to Read an Employee's Email*, CLEV. B.J. (Apr. 2004), http://www.clevelandbar.org/new/right_to_email.php.
d. American Management Association, *supra* note b.

e. *Id.*; Nick Wingfield, *More Companies Monitor Employees' E-Mail*, WALL ST. J., Dec. 2, 1999, at B8.
f. Wingfield, *supra* note e.
g. American Management Association, *supra* note b.
h. Susan E. Gindin, *Employee E-Mail and Internet Use Raises Many Legal Issues*, CORP. COUNS. WKLY., Sept. 15, 1999, at 8.
i. *See* Fraser v. Nationwide Mut. Ins. Co., 352 F.3d 107 (3d Cir. 2004).

j. Gindin, *supra* note h.
k. *See* Intel v. Hamidi, 30 Cal. 4th 1342 (Cal. 2003).
l. Gindin, *supra* note h.

likely to cause death or serious physical harm to employees.[80] Conditions that are obviously dangerous or are regarded by the employer or other employers in the industry as dangerous are considered to be *recognized hazards.* What constitutes a recognized hazard is not entirely clear. However, its reach is broad and includes anything from sharp objects to radiation to repetitive stress injuries.[81]

In February 2004, OSHA announced that approximately 13,000 employers needed to correct workplace safety and health hazards or face comprehensive safety and health inspections.[82] OSHA identified the employers based on data reported in a 2002 OSHA survey of injuries resulting in lost workdays and illness rates at 80,000 workplaces. The identified employers had seven or more injuries and illnesses resulting in lost workdays for every 100 workers, substantially higher than the national average of 2.8 incidents per 100 workers.

OSHA inspectors are allowed to conduct surprise inspections at work sites when (1) OSHA believes an imminent danger is present, (2) an employee has filed a complaint, or (3) a fatality or catastrophe has occurred. During the inspection, the OSHA investigator may review company records, check for compliance with the relevant OSHA standards, inspect fire-protection and other safety equipment, examine the company's safety and health-management programs, interview employees, and walk through the facility.

When the inspection has been completed, the inspector meets with the employer and the employee representative, if any. The inspector discusses the results of the inspection and, if appropriate, issues a written citation for violations. There are five types of violations: (1) *de minimis* (that is, unimportant) violations, for which no notice is posted and no penalty is imposed; (2) nonserious violations, which present hazards that are not likely to cause death or serious bodily harm, for which a fine of up to $7,000 for each violation may be imposed; (3) serious violations, which have a substantial likelihood of

resulting in death or serious bodily harm, for which a fine of up to $7,000 for each violation may be imposed; (4) willful violations, which are deliberate or intentional, for which a fine of at least $5,000 and up to $70,000 may be imposed for each violation; and (5) repeated violations, which occur within three years of a previously cited violation, for which a fine of up to $70,000 for each violation may be imposed. Failure to correct a prior violation may result in civil penalties of up to $7,000 per day for each day the violation continues beyond the prescribed abatement date. Inspectors may also decide to criminally prosecute employers for misdemeanors for "willful violations" by sending the case to the Department of Justice (see Chapter 14).

For purposes of sanctioning violations, the U.S. Court of Appeals for the Fifth Circuit held that the hazardous condition is the proper unit of prosecution, rather than the number of employees exposed to the hazardous condition.[83] Thus, if eighty-seven employees are threatened by a chemical explosion, then one violation (the explosion), rather than eighty-seven (the number of individuals exposed to the risk of heat, burns, and flying debris as a result of the explosion), may be cited.

If OSHA finds a violation, the employer is required to remedy the problem immediately. If remedial action is not taken, OSHA will seek a court order to ensure compliance. The employer may either settle the violation or seek review of the OSHA decision by the Occupational Safety and Health Review Commission. OSHA may penalize egregious violations by imposing a separate fine for each violation rather than an overall fine for a group of violations. Additionally, punitive damages are available, and the courts have upheld their application in extreme cases. For example, a federal district court permitted punitive damages in a suit against a nursing home that "blatantly" retaliated against a nurse for filing a complaint with OSHA regarding the lack of latex gloves at the site.[84]

In September 2000, OSHA imposed a fine of $2.5 million—its largest in recent years—on Chevron Phillips Chemical Company, a Texas petrochemical company, for an explosion that killed one plant worker and injured sixty-nine others.[85] The company had failed to properly train workers to recognize when certain chemical reactions amount to a hazard. OSHA issued citations alleging thirty willful violations for failure to train plant

80. Reich v. Pepperidge Farm, 66 U.S.L.W. 2095 (1997).

81. In 2001 President Bush signed legislation that repealed OSHA's controversial ergonomics rule, which was aimed at repetitive stress injuries. It would have compensated employees who suffered such injuries on the job and required employers to fix workplace hazards after receiving a report of a repetitive stress injury. Businesses and labor groups opposed the rules on the basis that they were too onerous and expensive. President Bush said that the administration would pursue a comprehensive approach to ergonomics that addressed the concerns surrounding the repealed rule.

82. Occupational Safety and Health Administration, *13,000 High Rate Workplaces Receiving OSHA Letters* (Feb. 2004), *at* http://www.osha.gov/as/opa/foia/hot_10.html.

83. Reich v. Arcadian Corp., 110 F.3d 1192 (5th Cir. 1997).

84. Reich v. Skyline Terrace, Inc., 977 F. Supp. 1141 (N.D. Okla. 1997).

85. Ruth Rendon, *Phillips Facing Fine for Fatal Plant Blast,* CNN.COM, Sept. 22, 2000, *at* http://archives.cnn.com/2000/LOCAL/southwest/09/22/hci.phillips.blast/ (last visited Dec. 8, 2004).

operators and four willful violations of process safety management. OSHA records revealed that it had inspected the facility forty-six times since 1974, including three inspections in 1999. Three of the inspections occurred after explosions. Chevron Phillips had previously been fined in both 1989 and 1999 for blasts that killed a total of twenty-five people.

OSHA also requires employers to maintain certain records, including the OSHA Form 300, which lists and summarizes all work-related injuries and illnesses. (Certain industries, such as retail, finance, and insurance, are exempt from this record-keeping requirement.) A summary of these records must be posted annually at the job site. In addition, employers must post in a conspicuous place (1) OSHA's official Job Safety Poster; (2) any OSHA citations for violations; and (3) notices of imminent danger to employees, including exposure to toxic substances.

A 1999 OSHA survey revealed that more than 85 percent of employers conduct voluntary self-audits of safety and health conditions at their work sites as part of an effort to reduce workplace injury and illness rates, to ensure compliance with OSHA regulations, and because it is the "right thing" to do.[86] California requires employers of at least ten employees to maintain a written Injury and Illness Prevention Program, calling for regular safety inspections, safety training for employees, and hazard abatement provisions.[87]

Criminal Prosecutions

OSHA makes it a misdemeanor to cause the death of a worker by willfully violating safety laws. The maximum penalty is six months in jail and a $500,000 fine. By law, a willful violation means the employer demonstrated either "intentional disregard" or "plain indifference" toward safety laws. Safety violations that result in workplace deaths may also be prosecuted under state manslaughter and reckless homicide statutes.

An eight-month examination of workplace deaths by the *New York Times,* however, found that such deaths seldom result in prosecution, conviction, or jail time because state and federal OSHA inspectors rarely refer cases to law enforcement authorities. "A company official who willfully and recklessly violates federal OSHA laws stands a greater chance of winning a state lottery

than being criminally charged," according to a 1988 congressional report.

Since 1982, more than 170,000 American workers have been killed on the job, but federal and state workplace safety regulators investigated less than 25 percent of these cases. Of those they examined, they found that 2,197 were caused by "willful" safety violations. The 2,197 deaths were the result of 1,798 different incidents, more than two-thirds of which were investigated by OSHA (the rest were investigated by states that administer their own versions of OSHA). Of these 2,197 deaths, 1,798 cases were eligible for prosecution, but only 104 were prosecuted. In 2003, OSHA's former administrator, John L. Henshaw, acknowledged that the agency had referred few cases to prosecutors, but he insisted that OSHA sought criminal sanctions "to the fullest extent that the law provides." According to Henshaw, OSHA did not seek more prosecutions because officials concluded that most cases lacked enough evidence for conviction.[88]

State Analogues to OSHA

Many states have enacted laws similar to OSHA to ensure employees' safety in the workplace. In 2002, after two workers drowned in sewage while repairing a sewer line, the state of Iowa fined Insituform Technologies, Inc. $808,250 for safety violations under Iowa's OSHA.[89] The workers were not wearing or using the required protective equipment. The fine was the largest monetary sanction ever levied by the state of Iowa under its OSHA statute. California has one of the strongest safety violation penalties in the nation, with a maximum penalty of up to three years in prison and a $1.5 million fine for worker deaths.[90]

STATE CRIMINAL PROSECUTIONS

Many states enforce workplace safety laws independently of OSHA by empowering state prosecutors to charge employers for crimes ranging from assault and battery to reckless homicide for ignoring warnings to correct workplace safety hazards.[91] In addition, Maine and California

86. *More Than 85 Percent of Employers Do Self-Audits of Work Site Safety, Health Conditions, OSHA Says,* Corp. Couns. Wkly., Dec. 1, 1999, at 4, *available at* http://pubs.bna.com/ip/BNA/CCW.NSF/ 0fe6b3166851874585256d0c004c4ca3/ dfe30577a91bf0d9852568390005c5b4?OpenDocument.

87. Cal. Lab. Code § 6401.7.

88. David Barstow, *U.S. Rarely Seeks Charges for Deaths in Workplace,* N.Y. Times, Dec. 22, 2003, at A1.

89. Sandy Smith, *Iowa OSHA Issues $808,000 Fine Following Des Moines Drownings,* Occupational Hazards, Sept. 12, 2002, *at* http://www.occupationalhazards.com/articles/4646.

90. David Barstow, *California Leads in Making Employers Pay for Job Deaths,* N.Y. Times, Dec. 23, 2003, at A1.

91. Ann Davis, *Treating On-the-Job Injuries as True Crimes,* Wall St. J., Feb. 26, 1997, at B1.

have enacted laws specifically providing for criminal penalties for employers who endanger their employees.

Prosecutors have criminally charged a number of managers and officers of corporations in connection with serious violations that led to the death of employees. These prosecutions have had mixed results. For example, in 1990, the Michigan Court of Appeals held that a supervisor was not guilty of involuntary manslaughter because he did not own the equipment that caused the accident.[92] In 1992, after twenty-five workers died in a fire at a chicken plant in North Carolina because fire-exit doors were locked, allegedly to prevent employees from stealing chickens, the plant owner pled guilty to involuntary manslaughter and was sentenced to nearly twenty years, the stiffest prison term to date.[93]

In 2004, a New York district attorney charged the owner of Tri-State Scaffolding & Equipment Supplies with five counts of manslaughter in the second degree and five counts of assault in the second degree when the scaffolding he designed collapsed on five workers who were attempting to erect it.[94] New York law requires that scaffolding over seventy-five feet high be designed and built by a licensed architect or engineer; the defendant was neither. The defendant, who admitted the scaffolding was dangerous, was sentenced to three-and-a-half to ten-and-a-half years in prison. The New York State Supreme Court Justice who heard the cases stated: "This sentence will, I trust, serve as a warning to others who, in pursuit of their own economic interests, care to be cavalier about the lives of others."

LIABILITY FOR TERRORIST ATTACKS

As a result of the terrorist attack on the World Trade Center on September 11, 2001, OSHA has encouraged employers to implement emergency action plans to ensure employee safety in the event of another terrorist attack.[95] OSHA recommends that employers have plans for evacuation, anthrax risk management, and tightened security at building entrances and exits. As of 2004, 43 percent of the businesses surveyed by the American Management Association had implemented such a

plan.[96] Some employers, such as the U.S. military, have terminated employees for refusing to cooperate with such plans.[97]

TORT LIABILITY FOR VIOLENCE IN THE WORKPLACE

Employers also face potential liability for violence in the workplace perpetrated by employees or their former lovers or spouses. A survey of security professionals for Fortune 1000 companies, released in June 2002, revealed that workplace violence was the most significant security concern for U.S. businesses.[98] Workplace violence is the third leading cause of fatal occupational injuries in the United States,[99] resulting in three deaths daily and thousands of injuries yearly, as well as costing employers $36 billion annually.[100]

According to a survey conducted in 2004 regarding crisis management and security issues by the American Management Association, 50 percent of businesses surveyed have a crisis prevention and management plan addressing workplace violence.[101] To help prevent domestic violence from spilling over into the workplace, some companies hold seminars on domestic-violence issues on company time, provide a twenty-four-hour telephone counseling service for employees and their partners, and tap the phones of women who fear an attack and provide them with escorts to and from parking lots. Sometimes, the employer seeks restraining orders in its name to keep alleged abusers from potential victims' work sites.[102]

Once an employer is informed about the risk of violence or takes an interest in the case, it exposes itself to liability for negligence if it fails to take reasonable steps to prevent injury. For example, in 1995, both the employer of a woman killed in her Houston office by a former

92. Michigan v. Hegedus, 451 N.W.2d 861 (Mich. Ct. App. 1990).
93. Davis, *supra* note 91.
94. Karen Freifeld, *Punishment for "Cavalier" Act: Prison Time in Scaffold Deaths,* NEWSDAY, Jan. 15, 2004, *available at* http://www.nynewsday.com/news/local/manhattan/nyc-nysent153637070jsn25,0,3773583.story?coll=nyc-topheadlines-left.
95. OSHA, *How Should I Prepare if My Company Has a Credible Risk of Anthrax Exposure?* (2001), http://www.osha.gov/SLTC/etools/anthrax/credible_risk.html.

96. American Management Association, *2004 AMA Survey: Crisis Management and Security Issues* (2004), http://www.amanet.org/research/pdfs/CMSI_04.pdf.
97. *See* Mazares v. Dep't of the Navy, 302 F.3d 1382 (Fed. Cir. 2002).
98. Press Release, Pinkerton Consulting & Investigations, Fortune 1000 Rate Workplace Violence Top Security Threat, (June 4, 2002), http://www.ci-pinkterton.com/news/prTST6.4.html.
99. OSHA, *Workplace Violence* (Mar. 15, 2004), http://www.osha.gov/SLTC/workplaceviolence/.
100. Pinkerton Consulting & Investigations, *supra* note 98.
101. American Management Association, *supra* note 96.
102. U.S. FEDERAL BUREAU OF INVESTIGATION, WORKPLACE VIOLENCE: ISSUES IN RESPONSE 44–45 (Mar. 1, 2004), http://www.fbi.gov/page2/march04/violence030104.htm.

boyfriend and the office-building manager agreed to pay more than $350,000 to settle a case brought by the woman's family. The woman had told them that the former boyfriend was subject to a restraining order and that she feared he would kill her. According to her mother, "They didn't believe her story."[103]

In contrast, in *Jarrell v. Englefield*,[104] the Ohio Court of Appeals did not hold a gas station/convenience store operator responsible when a cashier was murdered at one of its stores. The court found that the company did not know of the existence of a dangerous condition or of a high probability that an employee would be injured there because there was no history of violence at the store. In addition, the store contained security devices (including a closed-circuit camera, a silent alarm, and signs indicating there was a camera), and the employee had been trained in handling himself during a robbery. Thus, the court concluded that the employer had taken adequate measures to protect its employees.

◆ Workers' Compensation

State workers' compensation statutes provide for coverage of income and medical expenses for employees[105] who suffer work-related accidents or illnesses.[106] The statutes are based on the principle that the risks of injury in the workplace should be borne by industry. The system is no-fault, and an employee is entitled to monetary benefits from the employer regardless of the level of safety in the work environment and the degree to which the employee's carelessness contributed to the incident. Workers receive medical treatment and benefits sooner and with more certainty, as a trade-off for receiving smaller total compensation than civil litigation might bring.

Monetary awards paid through the workers' compensation system are generally lower than those that might be awarded in lawsuits for negligence or other torts. The amount of workers' compensation received by an employee is determined by a definite schedule, based on the employee's loss of earning power. The usual provision is for payment of a specified amount at regular intervals over a definite period of time. In most cases, benefits include medical, surgical, hospital, nursing, and burial

services in addition to payment of compensation.[107] Workers' compensation can be provided through (1) self-insurance, (2) insurance purchased through a state fund, or (3) insurance purchased through a private company.

Generally, workers' compensation benefits paid by the employer are the employee's sole remedy for workplace injuries. Some courts have recognized exceptions to this general rule, however, and allow employees to sue employers in tort for their injuries, in addition to collecting workers' compensation, for the following: (1) nonphysical injuries resulting from the tort of intentional infliction of emotional distress; (2) mental distress, indignity, or loss of wages or promotion opportunities due to sexual harassment; (3) injury to reputation caused by an employer's defamatory statements; and (4) both physical and nonphysical injuries as a result of an employer's intentional tort or misconduct.[108]

For example, the Washington Supreme Court held that a suit involving employee exposure to toxic chemicals in a fiberglass cloth used in airplane construction was not barred by the workers' compensation remedy because the employer's conduct amounted to deliberate intent to injure.[109] On the other hand, the California Supreme Court ruled that a firefighter's claim of intentional infliction of emotional distress was barred by the workers' compensation statutes.[110]

◆ Minimum Wage, Overtime, and Child Labor

The federal Fair Labor Standards Act (FLSA),[111] enacted in 1938 and amended many times thereafter, was established primarily to regulate the minimum wage, overtime pay, and the use of child labor. Many, if not all, states have established wage and hour regulations as well. In general, when the federal and state laws vary, employers must abide by the stricter law. Because of the wide variance in state laws, this discussion focuses on the federal law.

WHO IS COVERED

The FLSA applies to employees who individually are engaged in interstate commerce or in the production of goods for interstate commerce, or who are employed by

---

103. *As Reports of Workplace Violence Rise, Employers Step Up Security Measures, Training,* CORP. COUNS. WKLY., Nov. 24, 1999.
104. 2000 Ohio App. LEXIS 1076 (Ohio Ct. App. Mar. 17, 2000).
105. Independent contractors are generally excluded from workers' compensation.
106. See CONSTANCE E. BAGLEY & CRAIG E. DAUCHY, THE ENTREPRENEUR'S GUIDE TO BUSINESS LAW 291–92 (2d ed. 2003).

107. 82 AM. JUR. 2D *Workers' Compensation* § 6 (2004).
108. 82 AM. JUR. 2D *Workers' Compensation* §§ 62, 58, 73, 74 (2004).
109. Birklid v. Boeing Co., 904 P.2d 278 (Wash. 1995).
110. Cole v. Fair Oaks Fire Prot. Dist., 729 P.2d 743 (Cal. 1987).
111. 29 U.S.C. §§ 201–219.

employers that engage in interstate commerce. In other words, employers of any size that participate in interstate commerce or in the production of goods for interstate commerce are covered by the FLSA.

The FLSA does not apply to independent contractors. Proper characterization of workers as employees or independent contractors can be hotly contested. Chapter 5 outlines the factors courts use in deciding whether a worker is an employee or an independent contractor.

Who Is Liable for Violations

Individuals as well as corporations may be held liable for violations under the FLSA. In *Herman v. RSR Security Services,*[112] the U.S. Court of Appeals for the Second Circuit ruled that Murray Portnoy, a principal in a labor relations firm, exercised enough control over a security company's employees to be held liable as an employer for violations of the FLSA's minimum-wage, overtime, and record-keeping requirements. Portnoy partially owned the security company, funded its start-up costs, and chaired its board of directors. The appeals court affirmed a judgment of $160,000 against Portnoy.

In contrast, in *Luder v. Endicott,*[113] the U.S. Court of Appeals for the Seventh Circuit held that individual employees of a state government could not be liable under the FLSA. In this case, hourly employees at a Wisconsin state penitentiary brought a claim alleging that the warden and other supervisors violated the FLSA by altering time sheets and not compensating them for their work. The court ruled that the plaintiffs, who were suing the supervisors in their individual capacities because a suit against the state of Wisconsin was barred by the Eleventh Amendment, could not bring a suit against the supervisors because the effect of suing the supervisors was the same as suing the state.

HOURS WORKED

The FLSA does not limit the number of hours that an employee may work in a workweek or workday, as long as the employee is paid appropriate overtime. (But, as noted in Chapter 9, if an employer forces an employee to work too many hours, the employer may be liable under common law negligence for injury to a third party resulting from the employee's fatigue.) The FLSA requires that, with some exceptions, every employee be paid one and one-half times the regular rate of pay for hours worked in excess of forty in a workweek. The "regular rate" is not necessarily the hourly wage, but includes all cash compensation for the workweek. In most cases, employers can exclude profits from certain employer-provided stock options, stock appreciation rights, and bona fide stock purchases from the calculation of regular pay rates when calculating overtime pay.[114]

In 1985, Congress amended the FLSA to permit state and local governments to comply with the statute's overtime provisions by giving employees compensatory time (comp time) in lieu of overtime pay. *Comp time* is extra paid vacation time granted instead of extra pay for overtime work.

In the following case, the U.S. Supreme Court considered whether public employers can require employees to use their accrued comp time when the amount reaches a certain level.

---

112. 172 F.3d 132 (2d Cir. 1999).
113. 253 F.3d 1020 (7th Cir. 2001).

114. Simon J. Nadel, *FLSA: The Law Employers Love to Hate Is Scrutinized in Light of the New Economy,* 68 U.S.L.W. 49, June 27, 2000, at 2771.

A CASE IN POINT	Summary

CASE 12.5

Christensen v. Harris County
*Supreme Court of the
United States
529 U.S. 576 (2000).*

> **FACTS** Sheriff Tommy B. Thomas of Harris County, Texas, and 127 deputy sheriffs agreed to accept compensatory time, instead of cash, as compensation for overtime. As they accumulated comp time, Harris County became concerned that it lacked the financial resources to pay employees who (1) worked overtime after reaching the statutory cap on comp time accrual or (2) left their jobs with large amounts of accrued time.

To address these concerns, Harris County implemented a policy setting the maximum number of hours of comp time that could be accumulated. After an employee's hours had reached the maximum, the employee was asked to reduce his or her comp time; if the employee did not do so, a supervisor could order the employee to use the comp time at specified times. The sheriffs sued, claiming that the policy violated the FLSA.

(Continued)

(Case 12.5 *continued*)

> **ISSUE PRESENTED**   Can a state or its subdivision require employees to use accrued comp time?

> **SUMMARY OF OPINION**   The U.S. Supreme Court began its analysis by noting that both parties conceded that nothing in the FLSA expressly prohibits a state or subdivision thereof from compelling employees to use accrued comp time. The sheriffs argued, however, that the FLSA implicitly prohibits this practice in the absence of an agreement authorizing compelled use, because the statute requires an employer to reasonably accommodate employee requests to use comp time. The Court found this argument unpersuasive. The Court read this provision as a safeguard to ensure that an employee will receive timely compensation for working overtime rather than as setting forth the exclusive method by which compensatory time can be used. Thus, the statute imposes a restriction upon an employer's efforts to prohibit the use of comp time when employees request to do so, but it says nothing about restricting an employer's efforts to require employees to use comp time.

> **RESULT**   The Supreme Court upheld Harris County's policy requiring use of comp time.

COMPENSATION

The FLSA requires that employees be compensated for all hours worked. In general, the hours that an employer knows or has reason to know that an employee has worked, even though the employee has not been requested to work, are deemed hours worked. If an employee is asked to be on standby—that is, available to return to work while off duty—the hours spent on standby will not be counted as hours worked if the employee is generally free to use the time for his or her own purposes.

Workers will also not be compensated for their time spent traveling to or from the job. In *Kavanagh v. Grand Union Co.,*[115] a supermarket employee who worked as a mechanic traveling to different job sites sought overtime compensation for his commute. Although the U.S. Court of Appeals for the Second Circuit held that he was entitled to compensation for travel between the different sites during his workday between 8:00 A.M. and 4:30 P.M., he was not entitled to overtime compensation for time spent traveling between his home and the first job of the day or the time between the last job of the day and home.

MINIMUM WAGE

In 1938, the FLSA established the first minimum wage at 25 cents per hour. The federal minimum wage in December 2004 was $5.15 per hour. States often impose higher minimum wages. For example, the California minimum wage in December 2004 was $6.75 per hour. During the 1990s, as many full-time, minimum-wage workers were unable to support their families' basic needs, various localities around the country began requiring employers to provide wages and employee benefits higher than either federal or state minimum wages.[116] Called *living wage ordinances,* these programs require employers to pay their employees wages approximating the real cost of living in the locality, which is often significantly higher than the applicable state or federal minimum wage.

Such living wage ordinances, unlike their state and federal counterparts, often target only certain businesses, such as recipients of city contracts or lessees of city property, or larger businesses with more employees and higher earnings. For example, RUI One Corporation, which owned and operated a restaurant located on an open space preserve held in public trust by the City of Berkeley, California, challenged Berkeley's living wage ordinance, arguing that it violated the Equal Protection Clause of the U.S. and California Constitutions. The ordinance applied only to five employers that (1) were located on the open space preserve, (2) had a minimum number of employees, and (3) earned an annual revenue of more than $350,000.[117] The U.S. Court of Appeals

---

115. 192 F.3d 269 (2d Cir. 1999).

116. RUI One Corp. v. City of Berkeley, 371 F.3d 1137 (9th Cir. 2004).

117. *Id.*

for the Ninth Circuit determined that RUI was not unfairly targeted by the ordinance because RUI operated its restaurant on the highly desirable open space preserve under a privilege granted by the City. The court also stated that, ultimately, cities should be allowed leeway to approach the problem of their working poor by implementing their living wage ordinances incrementally.

OVERTIME

Certain types of employees are exempt from the minimum-wage and overtime requirements of the FLSA, including employees classified as executive, administrative, professional, computer, and outside sales employees. The regulations of the Wage and Hour Division of the Department of Labor define the characteristics of these exempt employees in terms of salary and work duties. These regulations were updated for the first time in decades in August 2004 to more accurately reflect the realities of the contemporary workplace.[118]

To qualify as an *exempt employee,* generally three requirements must be met. First, the employee must be paid a minimum salary amount. Second, the employee must be paid on a "salary basis." Third, the employee must meet the "duties test" for the particular exemption. All other employees are *nonexempt employees* and must be paid both minimum wage and overtime as required by the FLSA. The regulations also provide that certain types of jobs do not qualify for the exemptions from the FLSA minimum-wage and overtime requirements; these workers include manual laborers and other blue-collar workers, as well as police officers, firefighters, paramedics, and other public safety "first responders."

Minimum Salary

Employees who earn less than $455 per week ($23,660 annualized) are automatically considered nonexempt. The Labor Department has also adopted a "bright-line" test for highly paid employees—those employees who earn an annual salary of at least $100,000 per year (including commissions and nondiscretionary bonuses). Highly paid employees are considered exempt as long as the employer can show that they regularly perform at least one of the exempt duties or responsibilities of an executive, administrative, or professional employee. For employees earning between $23,660 and $100,000, the FLSA provides a test based on the types of duties the employee performs to determine whether the employee will be classified as exempt or nonexempt.

118. *See generally* 29 C.F.R. pt. 541 (2004).

Salary Basis Test

The salary basis test requires that an employee regularly receive a predetermined amount of compensation for each pay period in which work is performed, without reduction because of variations in the quality or quantity of work performed. Thus, an employee must be paid his or her full weekly salary for any week within which he or she performs work and is ready, willing, and able to perform additional work, subject to certain exceptions. Employers may, however, make deductions from an exempt employee's pay for personal or sick days off, or for certain disciplinary suspensions, without violating the salary basis test. Also, certain computer employees paid on an hourly basis will still qualify for exemption if he or she is paid at a rate not less than $27.63 per hour.

If an employer is found to have an actual practice of making improper deductions, it will lose the exemption during the time period in which the deductions were made for all employees in the same job classification who are working for the manager responsible for the improper deductions. Inadvertent or isolated improper deductions will not result in a loss of the exemption, however, if the employer reimburses the employee for the improper deductions. The regulations also provide a safe harbor that allows an employer to retain the exemption despite improper deductions if the employer complies with the safe harbor requirements.

Duties Test

For each exemption category, the FLSA sets forth the "primary duty", the performance of which will qualify the employee as exempt. Although the FLSA notes that the amount of time spent performing exempt duties may indicate whether the exempt work is the employee's primary duty, there is no requirement that the employee spend more than 50 percent of his or her time in exempt work.

To qualify as an *executive,* an employee must (1) have the primary duty of management of the enterprise or a customarily recognized department or subdivision; (2) customarily and regularly direct the work of two or more other employees, and (3) have authority to hire or fire other employees or be an employee whose suggestions and recommendations as to the hiring, firing, advancement, promotion, or any other change of status of other employees are given particular weight. The executive exemption also includes an employee who owns at least a 20 percent interest in the business, so long as the employee is actively engaged in the management of the company.

To qualify as an *administrative employee,* an employee must (1) have the primary duty of the performance of office or nonmanual work directly related to the management or general business operations of the employer or the employer's customers and (2) have a primary duty that includes the exercise of discretion and independent judgment with respect to matters of significance. For example, the U.S. Court of Appeals for the First Circuit held that insurance company marketing representatives qualify as administrative employees. The court rejected the Department of Labor's argument that the representatives were not given discretion in "matters of consequence."[119] Instead, the court looked to the nature of the work and held that the discretion and independent judgment involved, in addition to its substantial economic consequences, satisfied the requirements of an administrative employee.

For a person to qualify as a *professional employee,* he or she must be either a "learned" professional or a "creative" professional. The test for the *learned professional* requires that the employee's primary duty be the performance of work requiring advanced knowledge in a field of science or learning customarily acquired by a prolonged course of specialized intellectual instruction; "work requiring advanced knowledge" is defined as work that (1) is predominantly intellectual in character and (2) includes work requiring the consistent exercise of discretion and judgment. The FLSA permits some of the advanced knowledge to be acquired through a combination of work experience and intellectual instruction. *Creative professionals,* on the other hand, must have the primary duty of performance of work requiring invention, imagination, originality, or talent in a recognized field of artistic or creative endeavor.

The *computer employee* exemption is available to computer systems analysts, computer programmers, software engineers, and other similarly skilled workers in the computer field. This exemption does not cover employees who are engaged in the manufacture or repair of computer hardware or related equipment, nor does it cover employees whose work is highly dependent upon computers or computer software (such as engineers, drafters, and employees who work with computer-aided design), but who are not primarily engaged in systems analysis and programming or similarly skilled jobs.

The *outside sales employee* exemption requires that the employee have the primary duty of either making sales or obtaining orders or contracts for services or for the use of facilities. In addition, the employee must be customarily and regularly engaged away from the employer's place of business in performing such duty.

119. Reich v. John Alden Life Ins. Co., 126 F.3d 1 (1st Cir. 1997).

> ## ETHICAL CONSIDERATION
>
> In November 2003, lawyers representing a group of thousands of immigrant janitors filed a lawsuit in federal court accusing Wal-Mart of violating federal racketeering laws by conspiring with cleaning contractors to cheat the janitors out of overtime wages.[a] According to the suit, the janitors, who were hired by the cleaning contractors, generally earned $325 to $500 per week for waxing and washing floors seven nights a week in Wal-Mart department stores, usually for 56 hours or more each week. The contractors did not pay the janitors the required overtime of time and a half for hours worked over a forty-hour workweek. Wal-Mart allegedly shielded itself from liability for paying overtime by hiring the corporate contractors, to whom Wal-Mart was not required to pay overtime; the contractors in turn hired the janitors to work at Wal-Mart stores. The plaintiff janitors, however, say that they were actually supervised and controlled by Wal-Mart managers; thus, Wal-Mart should be responsible for the overtime payments because the contractors and Wal-Mart were acting as joint employers. Is it ethical for a company to shield itself from liability for violations of the Fair Labor Standards Act by employing workers indirectly through contractors rather than directly?
>
> **a.** Steven Greenhouse, *Suit by Wal-Mart Cleaners Asserts Rackets Violation,* N.Y. TIMES, Nov. 11, 2003, at A12.

CHILD LABOR

The FLSA child-labor provisions were enacted to stop the early twentieth-century abuses of many employers who employed children at minimal wages. Under federal law, it is illegal to employ anyone under the age of fourteen, except in specified agricultural occupations. Children aged fourteen or fifteen may work in some occupations, but only if the employment occurs outside school hours and does not exceed daily and weekly hour limits. Individuals aged sixteen to eighteen may work in manufacturing occupations, but they may not work in jobs that the secretary of labor has declared to be particularly hazardous, such as operating a power-driven woodworking machine, a hoisting apparatus, a metal-forming machine, or a circular or band saw. Jobs entailing exposure to radioactive materials are also deemed to be hazardous.

MODERN-DAY SLAVERY

Trafficking in persons, which often involves the recruitment and smuggling of foreign nationals into the United States to force them to work in factories, fields, or homes, amounts to "modern-day slavery." In one case, Mexican farm workers were smuggled into the United States and then forced to work for their captors to pay their smuggling fees. In another case, Russian women, who were recruited and transported to the United States as folk dancers, were subsequently forced to work as exotic dancers and turn their earnings over to their captors. The Victims of Trafficking and Violence Protection Act of 2000, which became effective October 28, 2000, amended the slavery statute to make prosecutions more effective and to increase the statutory maximum sentences that traffickers faced. From January 2001 to July 2001, the Criminal Section of the Civil Rights Division of the U.S. Department of Justice, working with the U.S. Attorneys' offices, charged 150 human traffickers, more than triple the number charged during the preceding three-year period, and achieved a 100 percent conviction rate.[120]

◆ Immigration Law

On October 23, 2003, Immigration and Customs Enforcement officials arrested approximately 250 to 300 alien workers at sixty-one Wal-Mart stores across the country and searched the office of one of the retail chain's corporate executives.[121] The workers were arrested for working without proper authorization and were threatened with immediate deportation.[122] Wal-Mart was also threatened with fines for employing such workers. In March 2005 Wal-Mart agreed to pay $11 million, the largest fine ever imposed for employing illegal immigrants, to settle the federal charges.

Under the Immigration and Reform and Control Act of 1986,[123] employers may hire only persons who may legally work in the United States, that is, citizens and nationals of the United States and aliens authorized to work in the United States. Employers that violate this rule are subject to penalties.

OBTAINING AUTHORIZATION

The primary way by which aliens become authorized to work in the United States is by obtaining a work visa. The U.S. government offers a number of visas based on different classifications including, for example, as (1) a student, (2) an educational or cultural exchange visitor,

(3) a professional worker from Canada or Mexico authorized to work in the United States under the North American Free Trade Agreement, or (4) a foreign employee of an overseas company who is temporarily transferred to the United States.

Many U.S. employers, especially those in Silicon Valley, rely on the employment of foreign workers with an *H-1B visa*, which is available only for workers in professional and specialty occupations (generally those requiring a bachelor's degree or its equivalent), such as computer programmers, engineers, doctors, or fashion models,[124] where the employer can show an inability to recruit qualified workers in the United States. Employers generally apply for the visa on behalf of the foreign worker; it authorizes the worker to work in the United States for up to six years (with some exceptions). During a worker's tenure, he or she is entitled to the same wages, benefits, and working conditions as other similarly situated employees. The U.S. government caps the number of H1-B visas granted each year in the United States. As of January 2005, this cap was set at 65,000 workers, with an exemption from the cap for up to 20,000 master's and Ph.D. graduates from U.S. universities.

VERIFYING AUTHORIZATION

To ensure that only authorized workers are hired, the U.S. government requires that all employers verify the identity and employment eligibility of all persons they hire.[125] This includes completing the Employment Eligibility Verification Form, also called the *I-9*, which must be kept on file by the employer for at least three years for purposes of government audits. Employers may also ask a potential employee questions regarding his or her work status. The questions should not identify a candidate by his or her national origin or citizenship status, however, because doing so could expose the employer to an employment-discrimination claim.[126] Questions that may be asked include "Can you, if hired, show that you are legally authorized to work in the United States?"

120. AAG R. Alexander Costa, Keynote Address at National Conference on Trafficking in Persons (July 15, 2004), *at* http://www.usdoj.gov/crt/crim/acosta_tp_071504.htm.

121. CBS News, *INS Agents Raid Wal-Mart Stores,* CBSNEWS.COM, Oct. 23, 2003 *at* http://www.cbsnews.com/stories/2003/10/24/national/printable579798.shtml.

122. Press Release, U.S. Immigration and Customs Enforcement, ICE Employment Investigation Yields Hundreds of Arrests (Oct. 23, 2003), *at* http://www.ice.gov/graphics/news/newsreleases/articles/arrests102303.htm.

123. 8 U.S.C. § 1101.

124. U.S. Department of Labor, *Employment Law Guide: Workers in Professional and Specialty Occupations (H-1B Visas)* (Jan. 5, 2005), http://www.dol.gov/asp/programs/guide/h1b.htm.

125. U.S. Department of Labor, *Employment Law Guide: Authorized Workers* (Jan. 4, 2005), http://www.dol.gov/asp/programs/guide/aw.htm.

126. Letter from Nguyen Van Hanh, Director of the Office of Refugee Resettlement, and Juan Carlos Benitez, Special Counsel to the Office of Special Counsel for Immigration-Related Unfair Employment Practices, Civil Rights Division, U.S. Department of Justice, to State Refugee Coordinators, National Voluntary Agencies and Other Interested Parties (Nov. 21, 2001), *at* http://www.acf.dhhs.gov/programs/orr/policy/oscj_lt.htm.

AMNESTY PROPOSAL

As of January 2005, approximately ten million illegal aliens were working in the United States,[127] even though an employer can be fined up to $11,000 and imprisoned for up to six months for each illegal alien it has knowingly hired.[128] In 2004, President George W. Bush proposed a plan that would grant amnesty to all illegal alien workers.

127. Aaron Bernstein, et al., *This Plan May Not Get a Green Card*, BUS. WK. ONLINE, Jan. 8, 2004, http://www.businessweek.com:/pring/bwdaily/dnflash/jan2004/nf2004018_7637_db038.html.
128. Memorandum from the U.S. Citizenship and Immigration Services Office of Business Liaison, Employer Sanctions (Dec. 7, 2004), http://uscis.gov/graphics/services/employerinfo/EIB111.pdf.

Under Bush's plan, illegal aliens would be allowed to apply for a three-year temporary-worker permit, renewable for at least another three years. They could also apply for a green card to obtain permanent residency status. Bush said that his proposal would allow illegal workers to live without constant fear of deportation. Many employers applauded the proposal because they would no longer have to worry about federal raids and lawsuits alleging that they hire undocumented workers. Companies would also have a more stable supply of low-wage labor, with fewer hiring problems and less turnover.

Opponents of the proposal argued that bringing ten million illegal residents into the mainstream would increase labor costs by raising wages and benefits for formerly illegal

ECONOMIC PERSPECTIVE

OUTSOURCING

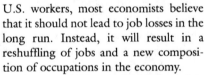

Between 1987 and 1997, the share of imported components used in U.S. manufacturing increased from 10.5 percent to 16.2 percent overall and from 26 percent to 38 percent in high-tech manufacturing, such as computers and electronics. As these statistics demonstrate, in its early years, foreign outsourcing largely affected U.S. manufacturing and was associated with the loss of blue-collar jobs in many industrial sectors. The outsourcing of manufactured parts resulted in a shift of demand, and hence jobs, from blue-collar to white-collar workers and from manufacturing to services. It also increased wage inequality between blue-collar and white collar workers and increased the profitability of U.S. firms.

Since the late 1990s, however, white-collar jobs have been moving overseas as well. Nonmanufacturing sectors, such as information technology, telecommunications, retail trade, and finance (including banking and insurance), have seen the most outsourcing to countries such as India, Malaysia, the Philippines, South Africa, Russia, and Israel. Companies find outsourcing an attractive cost-cutting

measure because wages and health-care costs for employees are generally lower overseas.

White-collar outsourcing has become a viable option for many companies due to (1) the rapid dissemination of the Internet; (2) the liberalization of emerging market economies; (3) the widespread acceptance of English as a medium of education, business, and communication; (4) the emergence of a common legal and accounting system (at least in some countries); (5) the 24/7 capability and overnight turnaround time made possible by the time differential between the United States and other geographic locations; and (6) the abundant supply of technically savvy graduates in other countries.

Data on the number of U.S. jobs moving overseas are generally scattered and unreliable. The U.S. Chamber of Commerce claims that 200,000 jobs a year are going abroad, whereas a bipartisan congressional commission found that 406,000 U.S. jobs are migrating overseas each year. Although outsourcing may cause pain and dislocation for many

U.S. workers, most economists believe that it should not lead to job losses in the long run. Instead, it will result in a reshuffling of jobs and a new composition of occupations in the economy.

Many managers may feel the need to outsource jobs to foreign countries as a result of their perceived duty to maximize profits for shareholders. At the same time, however, these managers may also have an obligation to provide U.S. workers terminated as a result of outsourcing with transparency regarding the layoffs and access to retraining programs.

Sources: This discussion is based on (1) Ashok Deo Bardhan & Cynthia A. Kroll, *The New Wave of Outsourcing*, RESEARCH REPORT OF THE FISHER CENTER FOR REAL ESTATE AND URBAN ECONOMICS AT THE UNIVERSITY OF CALIFORNIA, BERKELEY (Fall 2003), *at* http://repositories.cdlib.org/iber/fcreue/reports/1103/; (2) Kimberly Blanton, *Outsourcing of Jobs Is Accelerating in U.S.*, INT'L HERALD TRIB. ONLINE, Nov. 18, 2004, *at* http://www.iht.com/bin/print/ipub.php?file=/articles/2004/11/17/business/jobs.html.

workers. In addition, they claimed it would cause an influx of illegal immigrants. As of January 2005, Congress was debating the issue, which was viewed by many as a key step in the reform of U.S. immigration policy that the Bush administration had started prior to September 11, 2001.[129]

◆ Labor–Management Relations

Before the mid-1930s, attempts by employees to band together and demand better wages and working conditions were largely ineffective. Organized economic actions, such as strikes and picketing, were enjoined as unlawful conspiracies. Employers squelched attempts to organize by lawfully discharging union organizers. Starting in the 1930s, Congress has attempted to equitably balance the economic power of employers, individual employees, and unions by comprehensively regulating labor–management relations.

NATIONAL LABOR RELATIONS ACT

Since 1932, Congress has enacted a series of legislation aimed at both providing employees with greater economic bargaining power and curbing union excess and corruption.[130] The central statute governing labor relations in most private industries is the National Labor Relations Act (NLRA). An earlier similar law governing railroads, and later airlines, is the Railway Labor Act.[131] Pubic sector employees have since been granted similar rights under both federal and state laws.

Section 7 of the NLRA grants rights only to employees. It does not grant rights to independent contractors or to supervisors. The NLRA defines *supervisor* to mean:

> Any individual having authority, in the interest of the employer, to hire, transfer, suspend, lay off, recall, promote, discharge, assign, reward or discipline other employees, or responsibility to direct them, or to adjust their grievances, or effectively to recommend such action, if in connection with the foregoing the exercise of such authority is not of a merely routine or clerical nature, but requires the use of independent judgment.

UNION REPRESENTATION

The five-member National Labor Relations Board (NLRB) oversees *representation elections,* that is, elections among employees to decide whether they want a union to represent them for collective bargaining. The procedure for conducting a representation election is initiated by filing a petition with a regional office of the NLRB. The NLRB will hold an election only in an *appropriate collective bargaining unit* of employees. To form such a unit, the group of employees must share a community of interest, meaning that they have similar compensation, working conditions, and supervision and work under the same general employer policies.

Following an agreement between the parties for an election or a decision from the regional director over disputed unit issues, the regional office of the NLRB will conduct an election. The party losing the election may file objections to it. If the objections are deemed to be without merit, the NLRB will certify the election. If the objections are meritorious, the NLRB will conduct a new election. Once a union is elected, it is the employees' exclusive bargaining representative and has a statutory duty under Section 8(b)(1) of the NLRA to represent all employees fairly when engaging in collective bargaining (without regard to their union affiliation) and when enforcing the collective bargaining agreement.[132]

UNFAIR LABOR PRACTICES BY EMPLOYERS

Section 8(a) of the NLRA prohibits employers from engaging in specified activities against employees or their unions. Such activities, known as *unfair labor practices,* are investigated and prosecuted by the general counsel of the NLRB and his or her representatives.

Section 8(a)(1) of the NLRA makes it illegal for an employer to interfere with, restrain, or coerce employees in the exercise of their Section 7 rights to organize and bargain collectively and to engage in other protected, concerted activities. This prohibition covers a wide range of employer conduct, including (1) threatening employees with any adverse action for organizing or supporting a union, (2) promising employees any benefits if they abandon support for a union, (3) interrogating employees about union sentiment or activity, and (4) engaging in surveillance of employees' union activities.

Section 8(a)(1) also prohibits an employer from enforcing an overly broad rule against soliciting other employees (perhaps for union support) or distributing

129. Tom Raum, *Bush Faces GOP Fight over Guest Workers,* ABCNEWS.COM, Dec. 27, 2004, *at* http://abcnews.go.com/Politics/print?id=362524.
130. *See generally* Norris–La Guardia Act, 29 U.S.C. §§ 101–115; Wagner Act, 29 U.S.C. §§ 151–169; Taft–Hartley Act, 29 U.S.C. §§ 141–144.
131. 45 U.S.C. §§ 151 *et seq.* (enacted 1926).

132. Vaca v. Sipes, 386 U.S. 171 (1967).

literature on company premises and protects employees who engage in concerted activities for mutual aid and protection. For example, an employer may not retaliate against a group of employees who approach management and complain about some aspect of their working conditions, such as poor lighting or uncomfortable temperatures in the workplace. For an activity to be a *concerted activity*, it must be "engaged in with or on the authority of other employees, and not solely by and on behalf of the employee himself."[133]

Under Section 8(a)(2) of the NLRA, an employer may not dominate or assist a labor organization. The employer may not instigate, encourage, or directly participate in the formation of a labor organization, nor may it give financial support to a labor organization. These provisions were enacted to prevent employers from assisting compliant organizations in becoming representatives of their employees and then imposing "sweetheart" collective bargaining contracts—that is, contracts unduly favorable to the employer.

Section 8(a)(3) prohibits employers from discriminating against any employee to encourage or discourage membership in any labor organization. If an employee has been unlawfully discharged, the NLRB may order that the employee be reinstated and given full back pay.

Under Section 8(a)(4) of the NLRA, it is an unfair labor practice for an employer to discharge or otherwise discriminate against an employee because he or she has filed charges with, or given testimony to, the NLRB, either in a representation proceeding or pursuant to an unfair labor practice charge.

Section 8(a)(5) of the NLRA imposes upon unionized employers a duty to bargain collectively. A related provision, Section 8(d), requires employers to bargain in good faith, that is, to approach negotiations with an honest and serious intent to engage in give-and-take bargaining in an attempt to reach an agreement. The obligation to bargain in good faith does not, however, compel either party to agree to a proposal or to make concessions. If an employer does not bargain in good faith, a union may seek redress through the NLRB. Remedies may include damages payable to employees, or injunctive relief.

Lawful and Unlawful Strikes and Economic Action

Labor law permits both employers and labor organizations to engage in certain tactics against each other, known as "economic action," to influence the other party to reach agreement in collective bargaining. Strikes

133. Meyers Indus., Inc., 268 N.L.R.B. 493, 497 (1984).

and related publicity tactics such as picketing form an important part of the economic actions available to labor organizations.

Lawful strikes are of two kinds: economic strikes and unfair labor practice strikes. An *economic strike* occurs when a union is unable to extract acceptable terms and conditions of employment through collective bargaining. An employer subjected to an economic strike is permitted to hire permanent replacements for the positions vacated by the striking employees. If it does so, the employer is not required to reinstate striking employees who offer to return to work unless the departure of replacements creates vacancies. An *unfair labor practice strike* occurs when workers strike an employer wholly or partly to protest an unfair labor practice and the employer's conduct is in fact found to violate the NLRA. For example, a union may strike to protest the employer's bad faith bargaining. Workers who engage in an unfair labor practice strike have a right to be reinstated upon an unconditional offer to return to work.

Striking employees may have no legal protection or reinstatement rights if they conduct a "wildcat" strike by violating a "no-strike" provision in their collective bargaining agreements. Slowdowns, intermittent strikes, and work stoppages likewise are unprotected activity. Strikes otherwise lawful under the labor laws may incur liability for employees if striker tactics violate local safety or public peace ordinances or the state penal code (e.g., assault and battery).

The NLRA prohibits unduly lengthy *recognitional* picketing (whose purpose is to force the employer to recognize the union as a collective bargaining agent for its employees). It also outlaws *secondary boycotts*, which are certain threats or tactics against an outside company to induce the third party to put pressure (usually by withholding business) on the employer with whom the union has a dispute.

Non-Strike-Related Unfair Labor Practices by Unions

Section 8(b)(1)(A) of the NLRA prohibits unions from coercing employees to join the union or to support its activities. A union is also prohibited from coercing employees to join, or refrain from abandoning, a strike. Unions are prohibited from discriminating against represented employees on the basis of race, sex, national origin, union membership, or internal union political affiliations.

Under Section 8(b)(2) of the NLRA, a union may not cause or attempt to cause an employer to discriminate against an employee on the basis of union affiliation or activities. Section 8(b)(3) requires the union to bargain in good faith with the employer.

Global View

THE RIGHT TO CONTINUED EMPLOYMENT

Most foreign countries do not share the U.S. concept of "employment at will" and instead provide employees with certain rights to continued employment.

THE EUROPEAN UNION

Although the European Union (EU) has worked on harmonizing many employment laws of its member states, it has not attempted to harmonize the laws related to termination of employment.[a] No member states recognize the U.S. concept of employment at will. Instead, each country has specific laws on unfair dismissal and/or general civil code provisions that apply to the termination of employment contracts. Although the specifics of these laws vary, they all provide employees with a basis for challenging a dismissal on the grounds that it is unfair and a mechanism for adjudicating such claims. The laws of the United Kingdom and France are summarized here to demonstrate how individual EU members differ in terms of the right to vested employment.

United Kingdom The employment laws of the United Kingdom are largely based on contract law and thus have more similarities with U.S. law than the employment laws of other EU countries.[b] The employee's contract of employment governs his or her contract rights, whether these are contained in an express, written or oral agreement or by terms that are implied by common law, custom, or practice.

In general, employers are free to agree with their employees to whatever employment relationship suits them both, subject to certain statutory restrictions. These restrictions are set forth in various statutes, the most important of which is the Employee Rights Agreement 1996 (ERA 1996). The restrictions are superimposed on the contract rights and are generally enforced by a claim for unfair dismissal.

A fixed-term employment contract ends on the expiration of that term. Unless a contract specifies a fixed term, it is considered to be for an indefinite term and can be terminated in accordance with the contract's notice and termination provisions. In addition, the Fixed Term Employees (Prevention of Less Favorable Treatment) Regulations 2002 place a four-year limit on the use of successive fixed-term contracts and provide that an employment contract becomes a permanent contract after four years unless the employer can objectively justify continued employment on a fixed-term basis.

Section 86 of the ERA 1996 provides that an employee who is employed for an indefinite term, or pursuant to a permanent contract, and who has been continuously employed for one month or more is entitled to one week's notice of termination. This is the applicable notice period until the employee has two years of continuous service; from that time, he or she is entitled to one week's notice for each completed year of service up to a maximum of twelve weeks' notice. Subject to these statutory requirements, the notice period may be expressly stated in the contract. If the notice period is not stated in the contract, termination is subject to an implied requirement of "reasonable notice," although no notice is required if the employee is terminated for gross misconduct. An employer can pay the employee an amount in lieu of notice only if the employment contract contains an express provision that allows the employer to do so. If an employer provides a terminated employee with the correct notice, no claim for wrongful termination arises.

Wrongful dismissal occurs when an employer dismisses an employee in breach of its contractual obligations. An employee's normal remedy for breach of contract is to sue for damages, which are limited to the amount required to put the employee in the position he or she would have been in had the contract been performed.

Unfair dismissal is a statutory concept embodied in the ERA 1996. To bring a claim for unfair dismissal, an employee must show that his or her dismissal was for a reason listed in Section 95 of the ERA 1996, which applies to terminations for, among others, a union-related reason, the assertion of a statutory right, a health- and safety-related reason, a reason related to working time or the assertion of rights under the national minimum-wage law, a reason connected with trade union recognition or bargaining arrangements, and taking part in protected industrial action in certain circumstances. The three remedies for unfair dismissal are reinstatement (which treats the employee as if he or she had never been dismissed); reengagement (which involves returning to the same or a similar job); or compensation (which consists of a basic award calculated on a strict formula and a compensatory award, which is based on what the tribunal considers just and equitable according to the loss sustained by the employee as a result of the dismissal).

France French workers are entitled to significantly more benefits and legal protection than their counterparts in the United States or the United Kingdom. French law recognizes the concept of "just cause" dismissal, in that an employer must

a. *See generally* INTERNATIONAL LABOR AND EMPLOYMENT LAWS 1-1–1-187 (Timothy J. Dorby & William L. Keller eds., 2003).
b. *Id.*

(Continued)

(Global View *continued*)

justify an employee's dismissal and will be subject to legal sanctions if it is unable to do so.[c] During any agreed-on trial period, a French employee can be dismissed without formalities or particular reasons. Once the trial period has elapsed, however, the employer must prove that any dismissal is for legitimate reasons (either for cause or as a result of a reduction in force due to economic factors). Case law has accepted that "just cause" includes professional incompetence, insufficient results, professional shortcomings, loss of confidence in the employee, and sexual harassment.

Regardless of the reason, the employer must provide the employee with a written notice of a conciliatory meeting before confirming any termination decision. Only after the meeting is the employer entitled to notify the employee of his or her dismissal. The employer must also provide notice to French labor authorities. After notice of dismissal is given, the employment still remains in force during the notice period. The length of the notice period depends on the seniority of the employee and the position he or she held, but it generally ranges from one to three months. An employee is not entitled to any notice period if he or she is terminated for "gross negligence" (which has been defined as behavior that makes it impossible for the employer to keep the employee performing his or her functions, such as unauthorized and unjustified absence, damage caused to the employer, or assault and battery) or "willful misconduct" (which requires an intentional element similar to that involved in theft).

Unless terminated for gross negligence or willful misconduct, the employee is entitled to a payment, or indemnity, set by statute, if he or she has at least two years of uninterrupted seniority and any accrued, but unused vacation pay and if the employer wants to pay the employee, in lieu of providing the required notice, an indemnity equal to the salary he or she would have received during the notice period. In addition, if the employee is dismissed without legitimate reason, he or she is entitled to receive compensation and damages for abusive breach of the employment contract. Although this indemnity is based on the prejudice suffered by the employee, French labor courts have tended to grant a minimum of six months' salary if the employee has two years of seniority. An employer's failure to

c. *See generally id.* at 3-1-3-78.

comply with the statutory dismissal procedure also gives rise to damages even if the dismissal was justified.

JAPAN

Employers in Japan must give a minimum of either thirty days' prior notice of dismissal or thirty days' wages in lieu of notice.[d] An employer may apply to the Labor Standards' Inspection Office for prior recognition that the employee's dismissal is for cause based on the employee's conduct or is due to natural calamity. If this recognition is granted, neither prior notice of dismissal nor payment of wages in lieu of notice is required.

Although Japanese law contains no statutory provision requiring cause for the termination of employees, an employer's freedom to dismiss is restricted by its work rules and by established case law that requires just cause. If an employee challenges a termination on these grounds, the employer must demonstrate just cause. A wrongfully terminated employee may recover his or her wages for the period of dismissal plus 5 percent interest and may also seek reinstatement and reimbursement of the costs of litigation (exclusive of attorneys' fees). Generally, no further penalties or compensation will be awarded.

INDIA

India views the employment relationship as a contract that is subject to judicial intervention. Thus, the courts have implemented procedural safeguards shielding employees from indiscriminate termination by employers.[e] According to Indian law, termination is to be used solely as punishment for employee misconduct, which must be proved under very stringent procedural and evidentiary requirements. In addition, employers are required to provide some form of compensation to a terminated employee, and most employers with more than 100 employees must seek permission from the labor department of the government before dismissing or laying off a worker, or shutting down, irrespective of financial condition. Such approval is very hard to obtain.

d. *See generally id.* at 32-1-32-57.
e. Jaivir Singh, The Law, Labour and Development in India, paper presented at the Annual World Bank Conference on Development Economics in Oslo, Norway (June 24–26, 2002), *at* http://wbln0018.worldbank.org/eurup/web.nsf/pages/paper+by+Jaivir+Singh/$File/SINGH.PDF.

THE RESPONSIBLE MANAGER

AVOIDING WRONGFUL-DISCHARGE SUITS AND OTHER EMPLOYEE PROBLEMS

Many courts appear to be moving toward providing all employees the protection against discharge without good cause that traditionally was offered only by union contracts or by individually negotiated contracts. As a result,

employers often find themselves in costly litigation, attempting to convince a jury that a discharge was justified. A survey released by Chubb Group of Insurance

(Continued)

(The Responsible Manager *continued*)

Companies in 2004 revealed that 26 percent of Chubb insureds were named as a defendant in at least one employment-related suit during the past few years.[134]

An employer needs to develop a human resource approach that takes into account its own business needs and the laws of the state or country in which its employees are located.[135] This need is particularly acute in the new economy where busy employers, under pressure from rapidly changing conditions and intense competition, may neglect to devote sufficient attention to compliance with employment laws and regulations.

An employer can do many things to limit its exposure to unwanted contractual obligations.[136] First, the employer should articulate the kind of contractual relationship it wishes to have with its employees. That relationship may not be the same for every employee or job classification. In some instances, it may be appropriate to maintain an at-will relationship documented in a simple offer letter and clear policy statements. For other employees, the employer may prefer to have a more elaborate written contract that specifies the circumstances under which the employment relationship may be terminated, including a definition of "Cause", and a specific severance agreement in the event of termination without cause. Restrictive covenants may be available and desired by the employer as a fair exchange for the severance obligation.

If the company has a code of conduct (as discussed in Chapter 1), violations of the code may be good cause for termination, particularly if the employee has signed an agreement to comply with it. For example, American Express Company requires each of its approximately 15,000 managers to sign an agreement to abide by the policies set forth in the company's code of conduct.

Recently, companies have been exploring the viability of peer review of employment conflicts rather than judicial review. For example, Darden Restaurants (the company that owns the Red Lobster and Olive Garden chains of restaurants) has been using peer review of employee complaints since 1994.[137] The company has found that peer review (1) reduces the quantity, and therefore the costs, of litigation; (2) reduces tensions in

the workplace; and (3) often avoids the costs of hiring and training a new person by facilitating reconciliation rather than conflict. Red Lobster takes peer review seriously. Employees who have been fired or disciplined may seek a peer review. The decision of the peer review panel is binding and can overturn management's decision. The panels can even award damages. The program has reduced annual legal fees by $1 million.

There are numerous issues that employers should consider with respect to the FLSA.[138] Most importantly, an employer must carefully classify its employees as exempt or nonexempt to ensure that it is paying overtime to all employees who do not qualify for one of the FLSA exemptions. Employers should make sure that nonexempt employees required to work through lunch are compensated. Employers cannot dock salary for late arrivals or partial-day absences of exempt employees. Employers should factor in bonus payments, prorated to a weekly rate of pay, when calculating overtime payments to nonexempt employees. Although commuting time to and from work is not compensable, employers must consider whether they should compensate for commuting time if the employee travels from home directly to a client's site rather than to the employer's site. Although outside salespeople are exempt, salespeople who work at the employer's place of business are not exempt. Perhaps the best defense against a lawsuit is to create a corporate culture where employees feel appreciated, which includes compensating them fairly and providing honest feedback about job requirements and performance.

Most managers in the United States have a visceral negative reaction to attempts to unionize their workers, believing that unions interfere with management control in the workplace and hinder efforts to achieve competitive levels of costs, quality, and productivity. Nevertheless, some academics argue that there is systemic empirical evidence indicating that unions are positively associated with higher training expenditures, successful employee involvement, and successful quality-improvement programs and organizational innovation. Indeed, many of the best-known examples of high-performance production systems occur at unionized plants, such as those at Saturn, Xerox, Corning, Levi-Strauss, NUMMI, and AT&T.[139] These and other benefits of a well-regulated workforce—and the assistance of a labor organization to achieve that objective—may become apparent to management faced with organizing desires in its workforce.

134. Press Release, Chubb Group of Insurance Companies, Employment Practices Liability Survey Findings (May 25, 2004), *at* http://www.chubb.com/news/pr20040525.html.

135. See Jeffrey Pfeffer, COMPETITIVE ADVANTAGE THROUGH PEOPLE 137–48 (1994).

136. See Bagley & Dauchy, *supra* note 106, at 321–24.

137. Margaret A. Jacobs, *Red Lobster Tale: Peers Decide Fired Waitress's Fate*, WALL ST. J., Jan. 20, 1998, at B1.

138. Nadel, *supra* note 114.

139. JEFFREY PFEFFER, THE HUMAN EQUATION: BUILDING PROFITS BY PUTTING PEOPLE FIRST 226 (1998).

INSIDE STORY

WORKING "OFF THE CLOCK"

The FLSA requires all nonexempt employees working more than forty hours per week to receive overtime, that is, pay for one and one-half times the hours worked. Many businesses, however, are finding ways to avoid this requirement by having their employees work "off the clock" so that they will not be compensated for the time they put in. Companies avoid paying overtime by (1) not marking the hours employees work on their time cards, (2) having employees come to work at different hours, (3) rolling one week's overtime to another week, (4) encouraging a work atmosphere where everyone puts in extra time, and (5) even making promotions and social acceptance dependent upon working the extra hours without pay.

The practice is surprisingly pervasive. The Department of Labor estimated that 288,296 workers were owed more than $196 million in overtime pay in 2004.[140] Off-the-clock work is most often found at workplaces that employ immigrants, like farms and poultry-processing plants, but the phenomenon has spread, especially among low-wage companies in the service sector. Analysts attribute the rise in off-the-clock work to middle managers facing greater pressure to lower labor costs and workers' ignorance and fear that they will lose their jobs if they complain. But as workers learn their rights and news about the practice spreads, more lawsuits are appearing.

For example, the U.S. Court of Appeals for the Second Circuit held that workers required to remain at outdoor work sites over their lunch break were providing a valuable service and were entitled to compensation for that time.[141] The court upheld the lower court's award of $5 million in overtime pay and almost $10 million in damages for 1,500 telecommunications employees. Similarly, Wal-Mart has been sued in a class-action lawsuit brought on behalf of 100,000 California employees, who allege that Wal-Mart routinely asked

workers to work "off the clock" without pay. The work allegedly included times when workers were told to shorten, skip, or interrupt lunch and other breaks.[142]

Many other cases have been settled. In November 2003, the Labor Department announced a $4.8 million back-wages settlement with T-Mobile, the wireless telephone company, after finding that it had forced 20,500 call-center employees to work off the clock by making them show up ten to fifteen minutes before their scheduled clock-in time.[143] Nordstrom's department stores also settled a suit that alleged that the company required employees to deliver packages to customers' homes off the clock. The Department of Labor settled a case with Kinko's Copies, a chain of photocopy centers, after finding that store managers in Ithaca, New York, and Hyannis, Massachusetts, had erased time on thirteen employees' time cards.[144]

Not all claims of off-the-clock work have been successful, however. The U.S. Court of Appeals for the Eleventh Circuit rejected a claim by police officers that physical training necessary to pass mandatory physical fitness tests constitutes work under the FLSA.[145] The court reasoned that the officers' exercise time was not compensable because it was undertaken outside regular working hours and was neither compulsory nor productive work. Moreover, the court found that the exercise provided benefits that transcended the employment requirements and, as a result, the exercise was not directly related to the police officers' jobs. Thus, although claims of off-the-clock work are increasingly brought by disgruntled employees, courts do not blindly accept the plaintiffs' charges.

---

140. Department of Labor, *Wage and Hour Maintains High Enforcement Levels in Fiscal Year 2004* (2004), *at* http://www.dol.gov/esa/whd/statistics/200411.htm.

141. Reich v. Southern New Eng. Telecomm. Corp., 121 F.3d 58 (2d Cir. 1997).

142. Savaglio v. Wal-Mart Stores, Inc., 2004 WL 20434092 (Cal. Super. Ct. 2004).

143. Steven Greenhouse, *Forced to Work Off the Clock, Some Fight Back,* N.Y. TIMES, Nov. 19, 2004, at A1.

144. Steven Greenhouse, *Altering of Worker Time Cards Spurs Growing Number of Suits,* N.Y. TIMES, Apr. 4, 2004, http://www.nytimes.com/2004/04/04/national/04WAGE.html?th=&pagewanted=print&posi.

145. Dade County v. Alvarez, 124 F.3d 1380 (11th Cir. 1997), *cert. denied,* 523 U.S. 1122 (1998).

CHAPTER 13

Civil Rights and Employment Discrimination

INTRODUCTION

LAWS DESIGNED TO ELIMINATE EMPLOYMENT DISCRIMINATION

The abolition of slavery after the Civil War and the civil rights movement of the 1960s were two great forces behind modern civil rights legislation. From the Civil Rights Act of 1866 to that of 1991, the law has been moving in a direction to eliminate discrimination based on race, gender, color, religion, national origin, age, or disability. Civil rights laws help ensure that every member of society has the opportunity to reach his or her full potential.

Managers who fail to enact and enforce policies to ensure compliance with federal legislation prohibiting employment discrimination put their companies at risk of being penalized by large fines and judgments. In 2003 and 2004, corporations paid millions of dollars in settlements or judgments as a result of discrimination lawsuits brought by their employees: as described further in the "Inside Story" for this chapter, Merrill Lynch agreed to pay more than $100 million to settle charges that it paid women employees less than men and did not promote them as often; Abercrombie & Fitch paid $50 million to a class of job applicants claiming that Abercrombie's recruitment program excluded women and minorities; Home Depot paid $5.5 million for a suit alleging a hostile work environment based on gender, race, and national origin; and Foot Locker settled a class-action age discrimination lawsuit brought by hundreds of workers terminated in a nationwide layoff for $3.5 million.[1]

1. EEOC, *EEOC Litigation Settlements Monthly Reports,* at http://www.eeoc.gov/litigation/settlements/index.html (last modified Jan. 10, 2005).

CHAPTER OVERVIEW

This chapter provides an overview of federal legislation barring employment discrimination, with special attention to Title VII, the Age Discrimination in Employment Act, the Americans with Disabilities Act, and the Family and Medical Leave Act. It illustrates the various legal theories pursued under each piece of legislation and shows how those theories relate to legal and appropriate behavior by managers in a business environment. It also discusses how discrimination laws apply to affirmative action and the hiring of contingent or temporary workers. The chapter concludes with an overview of the ways that other countries approach workplace discrimination and diversity.

◆ Overview of Civil Rights Legislation

The federal statutes that forbid various kinds of discrimination in employment are summarized in Exhibit 13.1. Many states have passed their own fair employment acts, which in some instances provide greater protection than their federal counterparts. The federal statutes apply only to employees, not independent contractors (see Chapter 5 for a discussion of the difference between employees and contractors).

Although the statutes described in Exhibit 13.1 have created a far more level playing field for all workers, progress can be slow. For example, the Equal Pay Act was enacted in 1963, but as of 2000, women earned 80 percent of what men earned annually.[2]

2. U.S. General Accounting Office, *U.S. General Accounting Office Report to Congressional Requestors, Women's Earnings* (Oct. 2003), http://www.gao.gov/new.items/d0435.pdf.

EXHIBIT 13.1	Major Pieces of Federal Civil Rights Legislation		
Statute	**Major Provisions**	**Employers Subject to Statute**	**Comments**
Civil Rights Act of 1866[a] (Section 1981)	Prohibits racial discrimination by employers of any size in the making and enforcement of contracts, including employment contracts.	All public and private employers.	The bar against racial discrimination applies not only to hiring, promotion, and termination but also to working conditions, such as racial harassment, and to breaches of contract occurring during the term of the contract.
Equal Pay Act of 1963[b]	Mandates equal pay for equal work without regard to gender.	All public and private employers with twenty or more employees (including federal, state, and local governments).	
Title VII of the Civil Rights Act of 1964[c] (Title VII)	Prohibits discrimination in employment on the basis of race, color, religion, national origin, or sex. Later amended to provide that discrimination on the basis of sex includes discrimination on the basis of pregnancy, childbirth, or related medical conditions.	All public and private employers with fifteen or more employees (including federal, state, and local governments).	
Age Discrimination in Employment Act of 1967[d] (ADEA)	Protects persons forty years and older from discrimination on the basis of age. The ADEA was amended in 1990 by the Older Workers' Benefit Protection Act, which prohibits age discrimination in providing employee benefits and establishes minimum standards for waiver of one's rights under the ADEA.	All public and private employers with twenty or more employees (including federal, state, and local governments).	
Vietnam Era Veterans' Readjustment Assistance Acts of 1972 and 1974[e]	Require affirmative action to employ disabled Vietnam-era veterans.	Employers holding federal contracts of $10,000 or more.	Enforced by U.S. Department of Labor.
Vocational Rehabilitation Act of 1973[f]	Prohibits discrimination against the physically and mentally disabled. Imposes affirmative-action obligations on employers having contracts with the federal government in excess of $2,500.	Employers receiving federal financial assistance of any amount.	Enforced by U.S. Department of Labor. This legislation was the precursor to and guided the development of the Americans with Disabilities Act.

a. 42 U.S.C. § 1981.
b. 29 U.S.C. § 206(d).
c. 42 U.S.C. §§ 2000e–2000e-17.
d. 29 U.S.C. §§ 621–634.
e. 38 U.S.C. §§ 4100 *et seq.*
f. 29 U.S.C. §§ 701–797.

(Continued)

EXHIBIT 13.1	Major Pieces of Federal Civil Rights Legislation—continued		
Statute	**Major Provisions**	**Employers Subject to Statute**	**Comments**
Veterans Re-Employment Act of 1974[g]	Gives employees who served in the military at any time the right to be reinstated in employment without loss of benefits and the right not to be discharged without cause for one year following such reinstatement.	All public and private employers.	
Immigration Reform and Control Act of 1986[h] (IRCA)	Prohibits discrimination against applicants or employees based on national origin or citizenship status.	All private employers with four or more employees.	If employer has fifteen or more employees, plaintiff must file national origin discrimination claims under Title VII.
Americans with Disabilities Act of 1990[i] (ADA)	Prohibits discrimination in employment on the basis of a person's disability. Also requires businesses to provide "reasonable accommodation" to the disabled, unless such an accommodation would result in "undue hardship" on business operations.	All private employers with fifteen or more employees.	The ADA is the most sweeping civil rights measure since the Civil Rights Act of 1964.
Civil Rights Act of 1991[j]	Legislatively overruled several parts of recent Supreme Court rulings that were unfavorable to the rights of plaintiffs in employment-discrimination cases. Also extended coverage of the major civil rights statutes to the staffs of the president and the Senate.	Varies.	
Family and Medical Leave Act of 1993[k]	Designed to allow employees to take time off from work to handle domestic responsibilities, such as the birth or adoption of a child or the care of an elderly parent. Employees are guaranteed job security despite familial responsibilities.	Private employers with fifty or more employees at work sites within seventy-five miles of each other.	Part-time employees are excluded from the Act's coverage and are not to be counted in calculating the fifty employees necessary for an employer to be covered by the Act.

g. 38 U.S.C. §§ 4301–4307.
h. Pub. L. No. 99-603, 100 Stat. 3359 (codified as amended in scattered sections of the U.S.C.) (1986).
i. 42 U.S.C. §§ 12101–12213.
j. Pub. L. No. 102–106, 105 Stat. 1071 (codified in scattered sections of the U.S.C.) (1991).
k. 29 U.S.C. §§ 2601–2654.

DEFINITION OF ADVERSE EMPLOYMENT ACTION

[handwritten: employee has burden of proof]

In most discrimination and retaliation cases, the employee must establish that his or her employer subjected him or her to an adverse employment action. The federal appeals courts are split as to what constitutes an adverse employment action. Seven of the circuits have taken an expansive view.[3] Under this interpretation, demotions, refusals to hire or promote, unwarranted negative job evaluations, disadvantageous transfers or assignments, depriving an employee of support services, cutting off challenging assignments, moving an employee from a spacious office to a dingy closet, forcing an employee to jump through hoops in order to obtain severance benefits, making and soliciting from coworkers negative comments about an employee, needlessly delaying authorization for medical treatment, requiring an employee to work without a lunch break, and changing an employee's schedule without notification have all been characterized as adverse employment actions.[4] Two circuits have held that an adverse action is something that materially affects the terms and conditions of employment, such as employee compensation or privileges.[5] The remaining two circuits have adopted the most restrictive test, holding that only actions affecting hiring, firing, promoting, and demoting are adverse employment actions.[6]

◆ Enforcement

The Equal Employment Opportunity Commission (EEOC) is the primary enforcer of civil rights legislation in the United States. A part of the Department of Justice, the EEOC processes hundreds of complaints, investigating and evaluating their merit. If a claim is unfounded, it is dismissed. If the claim withstands initial inquiry and the EEOC is unable to pursue the case due to staff and resource constraints, the agency will provide a right-to-sue letter to the private party. Without this administrative permission, private litigants cannot initiate suits under various statutes, including Title VII and the ADA.

The EEOC has become more proactive in its approach to enforcing antidiscrimination laws. In early 1998, the EEOC began contracting with private organizations to use "testers" to identify employers that discriminate.[7] In employment-discrimination testing, pairs of individuals who are equally qualified are sent to apply for entry-level positions in an effort to determine whether impermissible factors such as race, gender, national origin, or disability influence employment decisions. In 2000, the U.S. Court of Appeals for the Seventh Circuit held that testers had standing to bring employment-discrimination cases under Title VII even though they had no real desire to work for the companies to which they applied.[8]

Although an individual employee can be required to agree to arbitrate civil rights' disputes, this does not preclude the EEOC from suing the employer in a court of law for damages payable to the aggrieved employee. See Chapter 4 for further information on the arbitration of discrimination claims.

◆ Title VII

SCOPE

Title VII bans discrimination based on an individual's race, color, religion, national origin, or sex. Title VII claims generally fall within one of four broad categories: traditional discrimination, harassment, failure to accommodate religious beliefs, and retaliation.

TRADITIONAL DISCRIMINATION CLAIMS

Litigation in traditional Title VII actions has produced two distinct legal theories of discrimination: (1) disparate treatment and (2) disparate impact.

Disparate Treatment

A plaintiff claiming *disparate treatment* must prove that the employer intentionally discriminated against him or her by denying a benefit or privilege of employment (such as a promotion or pay raise) because of his or her race, color, religion, sex, or national origin. The U.S.

---

3. The U.S. Courts of Appeals for the First, Fourth, Seventh, Ninth, Tenth, Eleventh, and D.C. Circuits have defined adverse employment action broadly. *See, e.g.,* Ray v. Henderson, 217 F.3d 1234 (9th Cir. 2000); Von Gunten v. Maryland, 243 F.3d 858 (4th Cir. 2001).
4. *E.g.,* Ray.
5. The U.S. Courts of Appeals for the Second and Third Circuits have adopted this intermediate test.
6. The U.S. Courts of Appeals for the Fifth and Eighth Circuits have adopted the most restrictive test. *But see* Fierros v. Tex. Dep't of Health, 274 F.3d 187 (5th Cir. 2001) (upholding a narrow standard of adverse employment action while applying a broader standard).

7. *EEOC Contracts with Private Testers to Uncover Employers' Discriminatory Hiring,* 66 U.S.L.W. 2391–92 (Jan. 8, 1998).
8. Kyles v. J.K. Guardian Sec. Servs., Inc., 222 F.3d 289 (7th Cir. 2000).

Supreme Court has established a systematic approach for proving these claims.[9] First, the employee must prove a *prima facie* case, which entails proving that (1) he or she is a member of a class of persons protected by Title VII and (2) he or she was denied a position or benefit that he or she sought, for which he or she was qualified, and that was available. If the employee proves the *prima facie* case, the employer then must present evidence, but need not prove, that it had legitimate, nondiscriminatory grounds for its decision, such as the employee's lack of qualifications or poor job performance. If the employer meets this burden of producing evidence, the employee then must prove that the grounds offered by the employer were merely a pretext for the employer's actions and that intentional discrimination was the true reason.

In a disparate treatment case, for example, an African-American employee might claim that he was fired because of his race. To prove his *prima facie* case, he might introduce evidence that he is an African American, was fired, and possessed at least the minimum qualifications for the job. Some courts may require that he also show that his job was not eliminated but was filled by someone else after his termination. Once he proves this, his employer must present evidence that the employee was terminated for a legitimate, nondiscriminatory reason, for example, excessive absenteeism. The employer might produce the employee's attendance records and a supervisor's testimony that his attendance was unacceptable. The employee could attempt to prove pretext in a number of ways. He might show that his employer's attendance policy requires a written warning about poor attendance before the employee can be terminated on that ground, and that he received no such warning. He might show that white employees with similar attendance records were not fired. He might show that his supervisor uttered racial slurs from time to time. In any event, the employee has the burden of proving that his employer fired him because of his race.

In *Frank v. United Airlines, Inc.*,[10] the U.S. Court of Appeals for the Ninth Circuit held that United Airlines' use of different weight policies for male and female flight attendants was illegal disparate treatment on the basis of sex. The airline required female flight attendants to meet weight limits based on suggested weights for medium body frames but permitted male flight attendants to meet weight limits based on large body frames. The court held that United failed to show that having thinner female than male flight attendants affected the flight attendants'

ability to greet passengers, move luggage, push carts, or provide physical assistance in emergencies. The court found that the plaintiffs had successfully established that United's reasons were a pretext and that the different weight limits for male and female flight attendants constituted illegal discrimination. In fact, the court concluded, the discriminatory weight requirement may have actually hindered female employees' job performance.

Disparate Impact

The *disparate impact* theory arose out of Title VII class actions brought in the 1970s against large employers. These suits challenged testing and other selection procedures, claiming that they systematically excluded women or particular ethnic groups from certain types of jobs. It is not necessary to prove intentional discrimination to prevail in a disparate impact case. Discrimination can be established by proving that an employment practice, although neutral on its face, disproportionately affected a protected group in a negative way.

For example, suppose an employer has a policy of hiring for security guard positions only persons who are at least 5 feet 8 inches tall, weigh at least 150 pounds, and can pass certain agility tests. This policy would seem to be neutral, in that it does not expressly exclude women or some Asian males. However, if the number of qualified women or Asian males who are refused employment is proportionately greater than the number of white males refused employment, then that policy has a disparate impact.

To prove disparate impact, the plaintiff must demonstrate that the specific employment practice, policy, or rule being challenged has caused a statistically significant disproportion between the racial or other composition of the persons holding the jobs at issue and the racial or other composition of the *qualified* persons in the relevant labor market.[11] The employer then has the burden of demonstrating that the challenged practice is job related for the position in question and consistent with business necessity.

If a job requires no special skills, then all members of the labor pool are considered when doing the statistical analysis necessary to determine whether a facially neutral policy has a disparate impact. For example, in *EEOC v. Steamship Clerks Union, Local 1066*,[12] a labor union representing the individuals who check cargo passing through the port of Boston against inventory lists had adopted a membership sponsorship policy (MSP) that

---

9. *See* McDonnell Douglas Corp. v. Green, 411 U.S. 792 (1973).
10. 216 F.3d 845 (9th Cir. 2000).

11. Wards Cove Packing Co. v. Atonio, 490 U.S. 642 (1989).
12. 48 F.3d 594 (1st Cir. 1995).

required union applicants to be sponsored by an existing member. When the union adopted the MSP, it had no African-American or Hispanic members. Over the next six years, the union accepted thirty new members, all of whom were Caucasian. After 1986, the union closed its membership rolls.

In 1991, the EEOC sued the union for disparate impact discrimination. Although African Americans and Hispanics constituted between 8 and 27 percent of the relevant labor pool in the Boston area, none had been hired by the union. Because the jobs required no special skills, all members of the labor pool were deemed qualified and therefore included in the calculation of qualified applicants. The union claimed that its MSP was merely a form of nepotism, not racial discrimination, because every member admitted between 1980 and 1986 was closely related to an existing member of the union. The U.S. Court of Appeals for the First Circuit disagreed, holding that the union's membership policy was discriminatory: by its very nature, it created a strong likelihood that no nonwhite face would ever appear in the union's ranks.

Historically, disparate impact analysis has been limited to objective selection criteria, such as tests and degree requirements. This analysis may also apply to subjective bases for decisions, such as interviews and supervisor evaluations.[13]

The business justification offered by the employer to justify the disparate impact must relate to job performance. Inconvenience, annoyance, or expense to the employer will not suffice. For example, a Latina applicant who is denied employment because she failed an English-language test might challenge the language requirement. If she has applied for a sales job, the employer might be able to justify the requirement on the ground that ability to communicate with customers is an indispensable qualification. On the other hand, if she has applied for a job on the production line, that justification would probably not suffice unless her duties included communicating with others in English. As under disparate treatment analysis, the ultimate burden of persuasion rests with the plaintiff.

HARASSMENT

Employees can bring claims for harassment in violation of Title VII on the basis of sex, race, color, religion, or national origin. The most prevalent type of harassment claim is sexual harassment, and thus the law regarding harassment has been developed in the context of sexual harassment claims.[14] Nevertheless, the analysis used in sexual harassment cases is applied to claims of harassment on the basis of race, color, religion, and national origin as well.

Sexual Harassment

As more women have entered the workforce and risen to positions previously dominated by men, courts have recognized sexual harassment as a form of sexual discrimination. Sexual harassment, which can be asserted by male or female employees, is one of the more complex and emotional issues in antidiscrimination law. Sexual harassment law is based on language in Title VII that prohibits discrimination "because of sex."

Quid Pro Quo Harassment
Early on, the courts recognized that a specific, job-related adverse action, such as denial of a promotion, in retaliation for a person's refusal to respond to his or her supervisor's sexual advances is a violation of Title VII. Such retaliation, which is referred to as *quid pro quo harassment,* is a theory unique to sexual harassment claims.

Hostile Environment Harassment
A threat of adverse job action in retaliation for rebuffing sexual advances does not constitute *quid pro quo* harassment, however, if the threat is not carried out. Instead, it is a form of *hostile environment harassment.*[15] Claims for hostile environment harassment can be brought under Title VII on the basis of race, religion, and national origin as well.

In *Meritor Savings Bank v. Vinson,*[16] the U.S. Supreme Court first ruled that creation of a hostile environment by sexual harassment is a form of sex discrimination barred by Title VII, even if the employee cannot show a concrete economic effect on employment, such as discharge or denial of a raise or promotion, to establish a violation. Not every sexually offensive comment or act constitutes actionable sexual harassment; there must be sufficient offensive conduct to give rise to a pervasively hostile atmosphere. This determination should be based upon the totality of the circumstances.

In *Harris v. Forklift Systems, Inc.,*[17] the U.S. Supreme Court held that a showing of a serious effect on an employee's psychological well-being, or other injury, is not necessary for a hostile work environment claim under Title VII, reasoning that "Title VII comes into

---

13. *See* Allen v. City of Chicago, 351 F.3d 306 (7th Cir. 2003).

14. EMPLOYMENT DISCRIMINATION LAW 749 (Barbara Lindemann and Paul Grossman eds., 1996).
15. Burlington Indus. v. Ellerth, 524 U.S. 742 (1998).
16. 477 U.S. 51 (1986).
17. 510 U.S. 17 (1993).

play before the harassing conduct leads to a nervous breakdown." The Court ruled in favor of a female manager of an equipment-rental company who was harassed for two years by its president. In the presence of other employees, the president said such things as, "You're a woman, what do you know?" and "We need a man as the rental manager," and called her "a dumb-ass woman." The president also made sexual innuendos, suggesting that they "go to the Holiday Inn to negotiate her raise," and occasionally asked female employees to get coins from his front pants pocket. Despite the employee's complaints, the sexual comments continued.

Defining a Hostile Work Environment To determine whether there is a hostile or abusive environment, courts must look at all the circumstances, including (1) the frequency and severity of the discriminatory conduct; (2) whether it is physically threatening or humiliating, or merely an offensive utterance; and (3) whether it unreasonably interferes with an employee's work performance.

To be actionable under Title VII, sexual harassment must be so severe or pervasive as to alter the conditions of the victim's employment and create an abusive work environment. The U.S. Supreme Court has ruled that "'simple teasing,' offhand comments, and isolated incidents (unless extremely serious) will not amount to discriminatory changes in the terms and conditions of employment.'"[18] The conduct must be "extreme." The standards for judging hostility are sufficiently demanding to prevent plaintiffs from converting Title VII into a "general civility code"; they are intended to filter out "complaints attacking 'the ordinary tribulations of the workplace, such as the sporadic use of abusive language, gender-related jokes, and occasional teasing.'"

For example, the U.S. Court of Appeals for the Seventh Circuit ruled that a supervisor's multiple and direct propositions for sex during a business meeting were sufficiently severe to create a hostile work environment.[19] In *Duncan v. General Motors*,[20] however, the U.S. Court of Appeals for the Eighth Circuit concluded that a male supervisor did not create a hostile work environment when he showed three-dimensional models of sexual organs and a picture of a naked woman to a female subordinate. The court stated that such action, while "boorish, chauvinistic, and decidedly immature," did not create an objectively hostile work environment where the plaintiff's employment had been altered. Similarly, in

Brooks v. San Mateo, California,[21] the U.S. Court of Appeals for the Ninth Circuit held that a single incident in which a male coworker touched a female employee's breast and stomach while she was answering a 911 emergency call was not sufficient to establish a hostile work environment. The employee suffered no physical injury, and the employer took prompt steps to remove the male employee from the workplace. The court noted that a single incident involving a supervisor was more likely to result in employer liability for hostile environment than comparable conduct by a coworker.

In *Schmitz v. ING Securities, Futures & Options, Inc.*,[22] however, the court considered whether repeated comments made by the employer's chief financial officer to the receptionist regarding her risqué clothing constituted sexual harassment. The CFO told her that her skirts and blouses were too tight, too short, and too revealing. He called her an "exhibitionist" and once summoned her into his office to reprimand her for dressing so provocatively that any "hot-blooded male" in the office would be aroused and distracted from his work. After she complained to ING's director of human resources, her workload increased, and the CFO became openly hostile to her. Six weeks later, she was terminated for inadequate work performance. The court dismissed her claim for sexual discrimination and retaliation, and the U.S. Court of Appeals for the Seventh Circuit affirmed on the grounds that the receptionist failed to establish that she was subject to sexual advances or requests for sexual favors. The court also held that the receptionist had failed to show that her work environment was hostile or abusive. Commenting on the CFO's behavior, the court said that "[his] failings 'to treat a female employee with sensitivity, tact, and delicacy'" are "too commonplace . . . to be classified as discriminatory."[23]

A majority of the federal courts of appeals have struck down claims for hostile work environment in so-called paramour cases where coworkers have claimed that an employee has received preferential treatment by a supervisor as a result of having sexual relations with the supervisor.[24] For example, in *Ackel v. National Communications, Inc.*,[25] the plaintiff complained that she was replaced by her supervisor's paramour as a result of favoritism based on their sexual relationship. The U.S. Court of Appeals for the Fifth Circuit stated that "'courts have held that when an employer discriminates in favor of a paramour, such an

---

18. Faragher v. City of Boca Raton, 524 U.S. 775 (1998).
19. Quantock v. Shared Mktg. Servs., 32 F.3d 899 (7th Cir. 2002).
20. 300 F.3d 928 (8th Cir. 2002).
21. 229 F.3d 917 (9th Cir. 2000).
22. 191 F.3d 456 (7th Cir. 1999).
23. *Id.* (quoting Minor v. Ivy Tech State Coll., 174 F.3d 855, 858 (7th Cir. 1999)).
24. Riggs v. County of Banner, 159 F. Supp. 2d 1158 (D. Neb. 2001).
25. 339 F.3d 376 (5th Cir. 2003).

action is not sex-based discrimination, as the favoritism, while unfair, disadvantages both sexes alike for reasons other than gender.'"[26]

Same-Sex Sexual Harassment In 1988, in *Oncale v. Sundowner Offshore Services, Inc.*, the U.S. Supreme Court held that Title VII prohibits same-sex harassment; in other words, it prohibits harassment where the harasser is the same sex as the employee being harassed.[27] Acknowledging that same-sex harassment was not the evil Congress sought to remedy when it passed Title VII, the Court nevertheless saw "no justification in the statutory language or our precedents for a categorical rule excluding same-sex harassment claims from the coverage of Title VII." However, the Court was careful to explain that to be actionable, the harassment must be tied to some type of gender discrimination: it must be "discrimination because of sex." "The critical issue is whether members of one sex are exposed to disadvantageous terms or conditions of employment to which members of the other sex are not exposed." The Supreme Court called on courts and juries to use "common sense" to differentiate sex discrimination from horseplay, saying that a pat on the bottom by a football coach to a player running onto the field may not constitute sex discrimination, but similar touching of a secretary might.[28]

Applying the standard set forth in *Oncale,* the U.S. Court of Appeals for the Fifth Circuit found that obnoxious comments by a male supervisor about a male employee's sexuality, inappropriate touching of the employee's private body parts, and spitting tobacco juice on him could constitute sex discrimination if the plaintiff could show that the same-sex harasser's actions were "explicit or implicit proposals of sexual activity" and that there was "credible evidence that the harasser was homosexual."[29] Such evidence would prove that the same-sex employee would not have been harassed if he had been a member of the opposite sex.

The EEOC reported that sexual harassment charges brought by men accounted for 13.5 percent of all sexual harassment charges brought to the commission in 2003, up from 9.1 percent in 1992.[30] The vast majority of such charges involve harassment by other men.

26. *Id.* (quoting Green v. Adm'rs of the Tulane Educ. Fund, 284 F.3d 642 (5th Cir. 2002)).
27. 523 U.S. 75 (1988).
28. *Id.*
29. La Day v. Catalyst Technology, 302 F.3d 474 (5th Cir. 2002).
30. EEOC, *Sexual Harassment Charges,* at http://www.eeoc.gov/stats/harass.html (last modified Mar. 8, 2004); see also Reed Abelson, *Men Are Claiming Harassment by Men,* N.Y. Times, June 10, 2001, *available at* http://www.nytimes.com/2001/06/10/business/10SAME.html?pagewanted=print.

Sexual Orientation Harassment The *Oncale* decision did not extend Title VII protection to harassment based on a person's sexual orientation. Although legislation to amend Title VII to include sexual orientation has been introduced in every term of Congress since 1975, it has not been enacted.

As a result, lower courts have had to decide (1) whether claims are based on sex or sexual orientation and (2) whether sexual orientation claims are actionable under Title VII. In *Simonton v. Runyan*[31] the U.S. Court of Appeals for the Second Circuit held that harassment on the basis of sexual orientation is not actionable under Title VII. Dwayne Simonton sued the U.S. Postal Service for abuse and harassment he suffered because of his sexual orientation. The court noted that the abuse that Simonton allegedly incurred—which included repeated verbal assaults, notes, pornographic photographs, demeaning posters, and repeated statements that he was a "f—— faggot"—was "morally reprehensible whenever and in whatever context it occurs, particularly in the modern workplace." However, the court concluded that "[w]hen interpreting a statute, the role of a court is limited to discerning and adhering to legislative meaning. The law is well settled in this circuit . . . that Simonton has no cause of action under Title VII because Title VII does not prohibit harassment or discrimination because of sexual orientation."

In contrast, the U.S. Court of Appeals for the Ninth Circuit's broad definition of what constitutes harassment "because of sex" appears to permit claims based on sexual orientation to be brought under Title VII. In *Rene v. MGM Grand Hotel*[32] a gay male alleged that his harassers grabbed and poked at his genitals, but there was no evidence that any of his harassers had expressed any interest in engaging in sexual activity with Rene. The court found that harassment that included touching body parts was "inescapably [harassment] because of sex." The court held that an employee's sexual orientation is irrelevant for purposes of Title VII and neither provides nor precludes a cause of action for sexual harassment. "That the harasser is, or may be, motivated by hostility based on sexual orientation is similarly irrelevant. . . . It is enough that the harasser engaged in severe or pervasive unwelcome physical conduct of a sexual nature."

More recently, the U.S. Court of Appeals for the Sixth Circuit held that a self-identified transsexual could sue for sex discrimination under Title VII on the basis of discrimination due to nonstereotypical behavior and

31. 232 F.3d 33 (2d Cir. 2000).
32. 305 F.3d 1061 (9th Cir. 2002).

appearance. Smith, a biological male, was employed by the City of Salem, Ohio, as a lieutenant in the fire department. After he informed his supervisor that he had been diagnosed as a transsexual and began treatment, which involved expressing a more feminine appearance, a plan was devised to require Smith to undergo a series of psychological evaluations in the hope that he would either resign or refuse to comply and be terminated for insubordination. The court held that Title VII's protection is available for transsexuals because its prohibition against sex discrimination applies to males as well as females and Smith had sufficiently stated a claim of sexual stereotyping and sex discrimination.[33] Several courts have also allowed homosexual employees to state sexual stereotyping claims under Title VII against employers who discriminated against them because they were not "manly" enough men or "womanly" enough women.

Racial, National Origin, and Religious Harassment

Similar to claims of hostile environment harassment on the basis of sex, claims of racial, national origin, or religious harassment are evaluated according to the rule in

33. Smith v. City of Salem, 378 F.3d 566 (6th Cir. 2004).

IN BRIEF

Elements of a Sexual Harassment Claim

Unwelcome sexual advances, requests for sexual favors, and other verbal or physical conduct of a sexual nature constitute sexual harassment when:

1. An individual's employment depends on submission to such conduct;
2. Submission to or rejection of such conduct is used as the basis of employment decisions; or
3. Such conduct unreasonably interferes with the individual's work performance or creates an intimidating, hostile, or offensive working environment.

To establish a claim of hostile environment sexual harassment under Title VII, the plaintiff must show that:

1. The harassment created an abusive working environment;
2. The harassment was based on sex; and
3. The harassment was so severe or pervasive as to alter the conditions of the victim's employment.

Harris v. Forklift Systems, Inc.[34] Courts examine the totality of the circumstances to determine whether an employee was exposed to a hostile environment. In *Bowen v. Missouri Department of Social Services,*[35] the U.S. Court of Appeals for the Eighth Circuit found that Bowen's exposure to racial epithets, such as "white bitch," coupled with physically threatening behavior by her supervisor were sufficiently severe and pervasive to constitute a racially hostile work atmosphere.

Although some courts have held that a onetime incident is not enough to create a hostile environment, the trend in both sexual harassment suits and other claims of harassment appears to be to find a hostile environment if the incident is severe enough and involves a supervisor. For example, in *Taylor v. Metzger,*[36] an African-American female county employee alleged that while she was training at a police academy firing range, her direct supervisor turned to a deputy and said, "There's the jungle bunny." The New Jersey Supreme Court identified several factors that made the incident severe enough to create actionable hostile environment discrimination under the New Jersey Law Against Discrimination (patterned after Title VII): (1) the derogatory term used by the sheriff was "patently a racial slur, and [was] ugly, stark and raw in its opprobrious connotation"; (2) the sheriff was the plaintiff's ranking supervisor, effectively closing her avenue for redress; (3) the sheriff was a chief law enforcement officer; and (4) the remark was made not only in the plaintiff's presence but in front of the deputy.

Liability for Hostile Environment

As explained in Chapter 5, employers are vicariously liable under the doctrine of *respondeat superior* for all torts committed by employees acting within the scope of employment. As a result, if a supervisor fails to promote an employee because of his or her national origin, the employer is liable for discrimination because the supervisor was acting within the scope of employment when deciding whom to promote. But when a supervisor harasses an employee (either by demanding sexual favors or by creating a hostile environment), the supervisor is rarely acting within the scope of his or her employment.

The U.S. Supreme Court reviewed general principles of agency law to determine when an employer is liable for the creation of a hostile environment. Under Section 219(2) of the Restatement (Second) of Agency, an

34. 510 U.S. 17 (1993).
35. 311 F.3d 878 (8th Cir. 2002).
36. 706 A.2d 685 (N.J. 1998).

employer is liable for torts of employees not acting in the scope of employment if (1) the employer intended the conduct, (2) the employee's high rank makes him or her the employer's alter ego, (3) the employer was negligent, or (4) the employee was aided in accomplishing the tort by the existence of the agency relation.[37]

Negligence The employer is negligent with respect to harassment if it knew or should have known of the harassment but failed to stop it by taking appropriate corrective measures. This negligence standard governs

hostile environment by coworkers (and probably customers with whom the employee must deal as part of his or her job). For example, in *Ferris v. Delta Air Lines*,[38] the U.S. Court of Appeals for the Second Circuit found that Delta was responsible for a sexually hostile work environment that allowed the plaintiff flight attendant to be raped by a male coworker. Delta was on notice that the male employee had previously raped three other flight attendants, yet it failed to take any action against him. The court stated that Delta had a "responsibility to warn or protect likely future victims."

37. *See* Burlington Indus. v. Ellerth, 524 U.S. 742 (1998).

38. 277 F.3d 128 (2d. Cir. 2001).

View from Cyberspace

HARASSMENT IN THE VIRTUAL OFFICE

In December 1989, Tammy Blakey became the first female captain at Continental to fly an Airbus 300 widebody jet.[a] Soon thereafter, she began complaining to Continental about a hostile working environment, based on conduct and comments directed at her by male coworkers. Among other things, they placed pornographic photographs in her plane's cockpit and other work areas and directed vulgar gender-based comments at her. After she sued Continental for sexual discrimination in 1993, a number of Continental's male pilots posted derogatory and insulting remarks about Blakey on the Crew Members Forum, the pilots' online computer bulletin board. Although employees using the Forum, not Continental, paid the Internet service provider (CompuServe) an hourly fee to access the Forum, the Forum was an option on the Continental Airlines Home Access program, which crew members were required to access to learn their flight schedules.

In analyzing Continental's potential liability for the retaliatory comments posted on the Forum, the New Jersey Supreme Court began by stating that if a bulletin board in an airport lounge used exclusively by the pilots and crew members of an airline contained similar comments by the pilots, there would be "little doubt" that if management had notice of the messages that created a hostile environment, the airline would be liable for hostile environment harassment, if it failed to take prompt corrective action. Similarly, if senior management, pilots, and crew members frequented some nearby place where one of the crew was subjected to sexually offensive insults that continued a pattern of harassment in the workplace, then an employer with notice of the harassment "would not be entirely free to ignore it." The court then reasoned that the fact that an electronic bulletin board is located outside the workplace does not mean that the employer has no duty to correct off-site harassment by coworkers.[b] The court

noted the importance of extensions of the workplace where "the relations among employees are cemented or sometimes sundered" and asked "what exactly is the outsider (whether black, Latino, or woman) to do" when the belittling conduct continues in an after-hours setting: "Keep swallowing the abuse or give up the chance to make the team?"

The court was careful to explain that employers have no duty to monitor employees' mail, given the "[g]rave privacy concerns" implicated. But, the court suggested, employers may not disregard the posting of offensive messages on company or state agency e-mail systems when the employer knows or has reason to know that this is part of a pattern of harassment that is taking place in the workplace and in settings related to the workplace. Otherwise, the employer "sends the harassed employee the message that the harassment is acceptable and that the management supports the harasser."

a. Blakey v. Cont'l Airlines, Inc., 751 A.2d 538 (2000).

b. *See, generally,* Diana J.P. McKenzie, *Information Technology Policies: Practical Protection in Cyberspace,* 3 STAN. J. L. BUS. & FIN. 84 (1997).

Aided-in-the-Agency Relation and Supervisor Harassment In *quid pro quo* sexual harassment cases and hostile environment cases, the employer is always vicariously liable under the aided-in-the-agency-relation standard when a supervisor takes a tangible employment action against a subordinate (such as firing, failing to promote, reassigning with significantly different responsibilities, or reducing benefits). Thus, in such cases, the employer is vicariously liable for the hostile environment created by a supervisor with immediate (or successively higher) authority over the victimized employee regardless of whether the employer knew or should have known about the supervisor's conduct.

In *Faragher v. City of Boca Raton*,[39] the U.S. Supreme Court applied the aided-in-the-agency-relation standard to a case involving the creation of a hostile environment by a supervisor who threatened to take tangible adverse employment action but did not do so. The Court acknowledged that in a sense a harassing supervisor is always assisted in his or her conduct by the supervisory relationship: "When a fellow employee harasses, the victim can walk away or tell the offender where to go, but it may be difficult to offer such responses to a supervisor" with the power to hire, fire, and set work schedules and pay raises.

Even so, the Court felt constrained by its prior holding in *Meritor* that the employer is not automatically liable for harassment by a supervisor. It also noted that the primary

39. 524 U.S. 775 (1998).

objective of Title VII is to avoid harm. To implement that statutory policy, the Court considered it appropriate "to recognize the employer's affirmative obligation to prevent violations and give credit here to employers who make the reasonable efforts to discharge their duty." At the same time, the Court acknowledged an employee's duty to avoid or mitigate harm. If the employee unreasonably failed to avail himself or herself of the employer's preventive or remedial apparatus, the employee should not recover damages that could have been avoided if he or she had done so.

Accordingly, the Court held that if the supervisor's harassment does not culminate in a tangible employment action, then the employer may raise an affirmative defense to liability or damages. To establish the defense, the employer must prove two things: (1) it exercised reasonable care to prevent and correct promptly any harassing behavior, and (2) the employee unreasonably failed to take advantage of any preventive or corrective opportunities provided by the employer or to avoid harm otherwise. For example, if an employer has provided a proven, effective mechanism for reporting and resolving complaints of sexual harassment that is available to the employee without undue risk or expense, then the employee's unreasonable failure to use that complaint procedure will normally suffice to satisfy the employer's burden under the second element of the defense.

In the following case, the court considered whether the employer had taken adequate steps to prevent and correct harassing behavior and was, therefore, able to establish the affirmative defense provided in *Faragher*.

A CASE IN POINT	**Summary**

CASE 13.1

Hill v. American General Finance, Inc.

United States Court of Appeals for the Seventh Circuit
218 F.3d 639
(7th Cir. 2000).

> FACTS Louise Hill worked as a lending/collection administrator in the Alton, Illinois office of American General Finance, Inc. (AGF). She was the only African American working in the office. Within a month of her arrival, her supervisor Darin Brandt started to racially and sexually harass her. For example, he said, "I like a woman with a big ass, like Louise's," and he made reference to the size of his penis. On one occasion, he rubbed his pelvis against her buttocks and said, "Boy that feels good." He also said, "Once you go black, you never go back." In addition to the sexual comments, he made offensive racial comments such as, "Don't come into this office talking black, because this ain't no Aunt Jemima office." He also told her that he was "sick of black people getting food stamps and having those black babies."

On two separate occasions, Hill wrote a letter to AGF's chief executive officer complaining about Brandt's behavior. Rather than signing her own name, she signed the letters with a pseudonym, pretending to be a customer. AGF's human resources officer conducted an investigation, including an interview with Hill. Although no other employees confirmed the harassment, some said that conversations of a sexual nature did occur in the office. Gary English, the director of operations, issued Brandt a letter warning him for allowing these conversations to occur.

(Continued)

(Case 13.1 *continued*)

Subsequently, Hill wrote a letter to English describing the harassment, but this time she signed her name. The company's human resources attorney and outside counsel promptly commenced an investigation and decided to issue a written warning to Brandt, provide him with additional training, transfer and demote him with a $10,000 reduction in salary, and transfer Hill to prevent retaliation from her coworkers.

Hill complained that her transfer was to a high-crime area and claimed that the company was retaliating against her. She resigned and filed a claim for sexual and racial harassment under Title VII. The district court dismissed the case after finding both that the plaintiff had failed to take advantage of her employer's policies and procedures regarding harassment and that the company had promptly taken appropriate corrective action after learning of the harassment. Hill appealed.

> ISSUE PRESENTED   What actions constitute reasonable care by an employer to prevent and correct sexually harassing behavior?

> SUMMARY OF OPINION   The U.S. Court of Appeals for the Seventh Circuit began by stating that a defendant employer can raise an affirmative defense to a charge of harassment by establishing that (1) the employer exercised reasonable care to prevent and correct promptly any sexually harassing behavior, and (2) the plaintiff employee unreasonably failed to take advantage of any corrective or preventive opportunities provided by the employer.

With respect to the first prong of the defense, the court found that the company took immediate corrective action after receiving Hill's letter by launching an investigation regarding the allegations. As a result of this investigation, the company punished Brandt for his conduct and transferred him so that he could no longer harass Hill.

In determining whether the company took corrective action, the court also considered whether the company had policies or procedures to help employees deal with harassment. AGF had several policies in place at the time of these incidents. It had an equal employment policy and a sexual harassment policy. In addition, the company had established a complaint procedure with four levels. Employees could report to their immediate supervisor or manager. Alternatively, the employee could speak with the field relations consultant, the associate director of employee relations and benefits, or the director of human resources and systems management. The third level of a complaint was to the fair employment practices compliance officer. Employees were provided with a phone number so that they could communicate complaints. Finally, the fourth level was the Personnel Administration Committee through the director of human resources and system management.

Although Hill claimed that she did not receive AGF's policies, the policies were kept in a set of notebooks available to the public within each branch office. In addition, Hill testified that she knew that the human resources group in the company had the responsibility to prevent sexual and racial harassment. She testified that she knew that she could talk to that group or English about any complaints she had.

The court stated that Hill's signed letter reporting Brandt's conduct was a reasonable step taken to correct the situation, but it found that she did not notify the company of the harassment until sending this letter. The two previous letters signed with false names of customers were not a reasonable form of notice.

> RESULT   The court of appeals affirmed the lower court's decision. The adequacy of AGF's policies and procedures and Hill's failure to take reasonable steps to notify the company of the harassment established a defense against her discrimination claims.

Personal Liability As a general rule, the U.S. courts of appeals have ruled that a supervisor cannot be held personally liable for discrimination in violation of Title VII against a subordinate employee.[40] There are exceptions to this rule, however. The U.S. Court of Appeals for the Second Circuit has held that supervisors may be held personally liable for harassment under other federal statutes.[41] In addition, supervisors may be held personally liable under some state antidiscrimination statutes.[42]

DUTY TO ACCOMMODATE RELIGIOUS BELIEFS

The EEOC reported in 2003 that the number of religious discrimination claims under Title VII had increased 75 percent since 1993.[43] These claims include not just refusals to

hire or promote based on religious prejudice, but also allegations that employers would not give employees flexible schedules so that they could attend religious ceremonies or flexibility in workplace dress codes to accommodate clothing mandated by the employee's religion.

A growing number of these religious discrimination cases involve Christian employees who bring their religious views into the workplace.[44] In the following case, the U.S. Court of Appeals for the Seventh Circuit considered whether an employer engaged in religious discrimination when it failed to reassign an employee whose job description violated his religious beliefs.

40. *E.g.*, Little v. BP Exploration & Oil Co., 265 F.3d 357 (6th Cir. 2001).
41. Patterson v. County of Oneida, New York, 375 F.3d 206 (2d Cir. 2004).
42. Dantz v. Apple Ohio, LLC, 277 F. Supp. 2d 794 (N.D. Ohio 2003).
43. EEOC, *Religion-Based Charges, at* http://www.eeoc.gov/stats/religion.html (last modified Mar. 4, 2004).

44. Jason Hoppin, *Cubicle Postings Merited Firing*, THE RECORDER, Jan. 7, 2004, at 1.

A CASE IN POINT	Summary

CASE 13.2

Endres v. Indiana State Police

United States Court of Appeals for the Seventh Circuit
349 F.3d 922
(7th Cir. 2003).

> **FACTS** Endres was an officer in the Indiana State Police. Soon after Indiana began licensing casinos, Endres was assigned by lottery to a full-time position as a Gaming Commission agent at the Blue Chip Casino in Michigan City, Indiana. Gaming Commission agents certify gambling revenue, investigate complaints from the public about the gaming system, and conduct licensing investigations for the casinos and their employees. Endres, a Baptist, believed that he must neither gamble nor help others to do so because games of chance are sinful.

Endres told the State Police that he was willing to enforce general vice laws at casinos, but that providing the specialized services required of Gaming Commission agents would violate his religious beliefs because it would facilitate gambling. When the State Police refused his request for a different assignment, Endres refused to report for duty and was fired for insubordination.

Endres sued under Title VII, contending that the State of Indiana had discriminated against him on account of his religion by failing to reasonably accommodate his religious beliefs. The district court denied Indiana's motion to dismiss, and the State appealed. The U.S. Court of Appeals for the Seventh Circuit ruled for the State, and Endres moved for a rehearing en banc.

> **ISSUE** Is the State of Indiana required to reassign an employee who objects to working as a Gaming Commission agent on the basis that facilitating gambling violates his religious beliefs?

> **SUMMARY OF OPINION** The court began by stating that Section 701(j) of Title VII requires an employer to offer reasonable accommodations for an employee's religious beliefs unless doing so would cause "undue hardship on the conduct of the employer's business." Though Endres contended that Section 701(j) should give law enforcement

(Continued)

(Case 13.2 *continued*)

personnel a right to choose which laws they enforce and whom they will protect from crime, the court concluded that this argument was not practical:

> Many officers have religious scruples about particular activities: to give just a few examples, Baptists oppose liquor as well as gambling, Roman Catholics oppose abortion, Jews and Muslims oppose the consumption of pork, and a few faiths include hallucinogenic drugs in their worship and thus oppose legal prohibitions on these drugs. If Endres is right, all of these faiths . . . must be accommodated by assigning believers to duties compatible with their principles. Does Section 701(j) require the State Police to assign Unitarians to guard the abortion clinic, Catholics to prevent thefts from liquor stores, and Baptists to investigate claims that supermarkets misweigh bacon and shellfish? Must prostitutes be left exposed to slavery or murder at the hands of pimps because protecting them from crime would encourage them to ply their trade and thus offend almost every religious faith?

The court stated that juggling law enforcement assignments to make each compatible with the varying religious beliefs of a heterogeneous police force would be daunting to managers and difficult for other officers who would be called on to fill in for the objector. Even if it were possible to swap assignments on one occasion, another could arise when personnel were not available to cover for selective objectors, or when seniority systems or limits on overtime curtailed the options for shuffling personnel.

The court held that Title VII did not require the State Police to make an accommodation for Endres, stating that "Endres has made a demand that . . . would be unreasonable to require any police or fire department to tolerate."

> **RESULT** The court denied Endres's motion to rehear the case en banc, reversed the district court's decision, and remanded the case with instructions to enter judgment on the merits for the Indiana State Police.

RETALIATION

Title VII states that it is unlawful for any employer to retaliate against an employee for complaining to the employer or the EEOC about discrimination banned by Title VII. To prove a case of retaliation, an employee must demonstrate that (1) the employee's activity was protected by Title VII; (2) the employer knew of the employee's exercise of protected rights; (3) the employer took some adverse employment action against the employee, or the employee was subjected to severe or pervasive retaliatory harassment by a supervisor; and (4) there was a causal connection between the protected activity and the adverse employment action or harassment. Generally, plaintiffs file a retaliation claim in conjunction with an underlying claim of discrimination. To succeed on a claim for retaliation, however, a plaintiff does not need to prevail on his or her Title VII discrimination claim.[45]

In *Fine v. Ryan International Airlines,*[46] the U.S. Court of Appeals for the Seventh Circuit found that Ryan retaliated against Fine by firing her a day after she submitted a letter outlining her multiple experiences of sexual discrimination at the company. In reaching its decision, the court noted that Ryan claimed Fine was fired because she "routinely missed work and was always hard to get along with." The court found that there were no written complaints about either Fine's attendance or her interpersonal skills in her personnel file, and thus Fine had adequately demonstrated that her dismissal was a retaliatory act by Ryan.

In contrast, in *Hill v. Lockheed Martin,*[47] Ethel Hill, an airline mechanic, was unable to prove that her employer terminated her in retaliation for reporting that Lockheed's safety inspector, Ed Fultz, often called her a "useless old lady" who needed to be retired. Hill claimed

45. Fine v. Ryan Int'l Airlines, 305 F.3d 746 (7th Cir. 2002).

46. *Id.*
47. Hill v. Lockheed Martin Logistics Mgmt., Inc., 354 F.3d 277 (4th Cir. 2004).

that after she complained about Fultz's comments, Fultz issued Hill several safety violations. The court found that although reporting evidence of discriminatory conduct is a protected activity, Hill's evidence was insufficient to establish a retaliation claim. Fultz held no disciplinary authority over Hill and he was neither the actual decision maker nor otherwise principally responsible for the decision to terminate Hill, which Lockheed claimed was predicated on Hill's shoddy performance.

Actions allegedly taken to prevent further harassment may be deemed a retaliation under Title VII if they harm the employee's employment situation. For example, in *White v. Burlington Northern & Santa Fe Railway Co.,*[48] the U.S. Court of Appeals for the Sixth Circuit found that transferring an employee from a forklift operator to a track laborer was an adverse employment action because the track laborer position, though involving equal pay, was more arduous than the forklift operator position, which was considered prestigious. Similarly, in *DiIenno v. Goodwill Industries of Mid-Eastern Pennsylvania,*[49] the Third Circuit found that transferring an employee to a job that the employer knew she could not perform was retaliation for her complaint that her manager was sexually harassing her. The plaintiff was transferred from her job of tagging and pricing clothing to a job requiring her to sort through clothes contributed to Goodwill. The employee's phobia of "critters," such as mice, insects, and bugs found in these bags of clothing, prevented her from performing the job. The court explained that "[i]t is important to take a plaintiff's job-related attributes into account when determining whether a lateral transfer was an adverse employment action."

In 1997, the U.S. Supreme Court unanimously ruled that both current and former employees can sue for retaliation. The case involved an employer who allegedly gave a former employee a negative reference because he had filed a claim of racial discrimination against the company.[50] In addition, the U.S. Court of Appeals for the Second Circuit has held that even involuntary participation in Title VII proceedings by an employee accused of sexual harassment qualifies as protected activity. As a result, it found that it would violate Title VII for an employer to retaliate against an employee who had successfully defended himself against harassment charges.[51]

SPECIAL APPLICATIONS OF TITLE VII

Civil rights legislation was founded on the fundamental premise that people should not be denied a job or an opportunity on the job because of their race, color, religion, national origin, or sex. The law has expanded beyond that basic premise to reach more subtle forms of discrimination.

Pregnancy Discrimination

The Pregnancy Discrimination Act provides that discrimination on the basis of pregnancy is, on its face, a form of sex discrimination under Title VII.[52] For example, employers must provide the same compensation for disabilities related to pregnancy and childbirth as they provide for any other disability. Many states have enacted similar laws, and, as in other areas of discrimination law, these state laws provide greater protection than required under federal law.

These protections are not absolute, however. The U.S. Court of Appeals for the First Circuit, for example, ruled that an employer could discharge a manager who was on maternity leave when it realized that the company could function effectively without her.[53] The court reasoned that discharge is an ordinary risk of employment, whether or not one is pregnant, and it ruled that the employer had demonstrated that it would have eliminated her position regardless of her pregnancy. Likewise, the U.S. Court of Appeals for the Fifth Circuit held that an employer with a strict probationary attendance policy, which provided that any employee who was absent more than three days within the first ninety days of employment would be terminated, was not liable for pregnancy discrimination when it terminated a probationary employee who was absent for more than two weeks due to a miscarriage.[54] The court stated that the Pregnancy Discrimination Act does not require employers to treat pregnancy-related absences more leniently than other absences.

Fetal-Protection Policies

Certain substances used in manufacturing are harmful to the fetus being carried by a pregnant woman. In an effort to avoid such harm, and related lawsuits for unsafe working environments, some companies adopted so-called fetal-protection policies. A *fetal-protection policy* bars a woman from certain jobs unless her inability to

48. 364 F.3d 789 (6th Cir. 2004).
49. 162 F.3d 235 (3d Cir. 1998).
50. Robinson v. Shell Oil Co., 519 U.S. 377 (1997).
51. Deravin v. Kerik, 335 F.3d 195 (2d Cir. 2003).

52. 42 U.S.C. § 2000e(k).
53. Smith v. F.W. Morse & Co., 76 F.3d 413 (1st Cir. 1996); *accord* Rhett v. Carnegie Ctr. Assoc., 129 F.3d 290 (3d Cir. 1997).
54. Stout v. Baxter Healthcare Corp., 282 F.3d 856 (5th Cir. 2002).

bear children is medically documented. In *Automobile Workers v. Johnson Controls, Inc.,*[55] the Supreme Court struck down Johnson Controls' policy, which precluded women with childbearing capacity from working at jobs in which lead levels were defined as excessive.

The Court held that the fetal-protection policy was a facially discriminatory policy forbidden under Title VII and that women cannot be excluded from certain jobs because of their childbearing capacity. The Court stated that "[d]ecisions about the welfare of future children must be left to the parents who conceive, bear, support, and raise them rather than to the employers who hire those parents." The Court went on to say that "[i]t is no more appropriate for the courts than it is for individual employers to decide whether a woman's reproductive role is more important to herself and her family than her economic role."

In the wake of *Johnson Controls,* employers have been forced to walk a fine line between avoiding discrimination related to pregnancy and limiting or reducing potential workplace hazards. For example, in *Asad v. Continental Airlines,*[56] Asad sued Continental under state tort laws claiming that Continental was responsible for her newborn son's cerebral palsy. Asad had requested a job transfer for the duration of her pregnancy to escape exposure to carbon monoxide fumes. Continental refused the transfer, citing *Johnson Controls* and other cases holding that the Pregnancy Discrimination Act does not require employers to "accommodate" pregnant women.[57] The U.S. District Court for the Northern District of Ohio acknowledged the confusion caused by *Johnson Controls.*

> For the employer, the question involves whether compliance with the mandates of the Pregnancy Discrimination Act could potentially subject them to liability for fetal injuries. Pregnant women, on the other hand, face the uncertainty of their legal rights in a potentially hazardous workplace and the legal rights of their children who turn out to be born with injuries allegedly caused, at least in part, by employer negligence.

The court deviated from prior court rulings when it held that although *Johnson Controls* demonstrated that employers could not prevent women who are or who may become pregnant from working in an environment that may be hazardous to a fetus, "the PDA and Title VII should not prevent an employer from temporarily transferring a pregnant woman, at her request, for the protection of her fetus."

English-Only Laws

The national origin provisions of Title VII have been used to challenge workplace rules that prohibit employees from speaking any language other than English at work. The EEOC has taken the position that language is closely linked with national origin, so English-only policies can have a disparate impact on Hispanic employees and others whose native language may not be English.[58] Federal courts have agreed with the EEOC. For example, in 2000, a federal court in Texas ruled that an employer's English-only policy barred Hispanic workers from speaking the language in which they were best able to communicate, causing them to face a disproportionate risk of termination for violating the policy.[59] The court concluded:

> [P]rohibiting employees at all times, in the workplace, from speaking their primary language or the language they speak most comfortably, disadvantages an individual's employment opportunities on the basis of national origin. It may also create an atmosphere of inferiority, isolation and intimidation based on national origin which could result in a discriminatory working environment.

Dress Codes

Although employers have the right to enact and enforce dress codes, they can result in legal claims involving religious and sexual discrimination and harassment. The trend by employers to allow employees to wear casual clothing has the potential to further complicate this matter.

Employees have based claims of religious discrimination on their employer's refusal to let them wear turbans rather than protective headgear. In response, the Occupational Health and Safety Administration amended its regulations to exempt persons wearing turbans from its hard-hat requirements.

DEFENSES UNDER TITLE VII

Title VII sets forth several statutory defenses to claims of discriminatory treatment. Of these defenses, the one most frequently cited is the defense of bona fide occupational qualification.

55. 499 U.S. 187 (1991).
56. 328 F. Supp. 2d 772 (N.D. Ohio 2004).
57. *See Johnson Controls,* 499 U.S. 187; Spivey v. Beverly Enters., Inc., 196 F.3d 1309 (11th Cir. 1999); Armstrong v. Flowers, 33 F.3d 1308 (11th Cir. 1994); Duncan v. Children's Nat'l Med. Ctr., 702 A.2d 207 (D.C. 1997).
58. *At Panel Discussion on National Origin Bias EEOC Says English-Only Challenges Are Rising,* 66 U.S.L.W. 2375 (Dec. 23, 1997).
59. EEOC v. Premier Operator Servs., Inc., 113 F. Supp. 2d 1066 (N.D. Tex. 2000).

Bona Fide Occupational Qualification

Title VII provides that an employer may lawfully hire an individual on the basis of religion, sex, or national origin if religion, sex, or national origin is a *bona fide occupational qualification (BFOQ)* reasonably necessary to the normal operation of that particular business. This is known as the *BFOQ defense*. The BFOQ defense is not available when discriminatory treatment is based on a person's race or color. Because BFOQ is an affirmative defense, the employer has the burden of showing a reasonable basis for believing that the category of persons (for example, women) excluded from a particular job was unable to perform that job.

The BFOQ defense has been narrowly construed. EEOC regulations provide that gender will not qualify as a BFOQ where a gender-based restriction is based on (1) assumptions of the comparative employment characteristics of women in general (such as the assumption that women have a higher turnover rate than men); (2) stereotyped characterizations of the sexes (for example, that men are less capable of assembling intricate equipment than women); or (3) the preferences of coworkers, employers, or customers for one gender or the other.[60] Gender will be considered a BFOQ when physical attributes are important for authenticity (as with actors) or when a gender-based restriction is necessary to protect the rights of others to privacy (as with restroom attendants).

Seniority and Merit Systems

Title VII states that it is not unlawful for employers to apply different standards of compensation, or different terms, conditions, or privileges of employment pursuant to a bona fide seniority or merit system, provided that such differences are not the result of an intention to discriminate because of race, color, religion, sex, or national origin. This is considered an exemption from Title VII rather than an affirmative defense. Consequently, the plaintiff has the burden of proving the employer had a discriminatory intent or illegal purpose in implementing the seniority or merit system. Moreover, although a disproportionate impact may be used as evidence of discriminatory intent, such an impact is not, in itself, sufficient to establish discriminatory intent.

After-Acquired Evidence

When an employee initiates a suit under Title VII, sometimes over the course of discovery the employer will learn that the individual violated company rules. Under these circumstances, employers have argued that the plaintiff's discrimination claim should fail because, had the employer known of the employee misconduct, the employee would have been discharged anyway.

In *McKennon v. Nashville Banner Publishing Co.*,[61] the U.S. Supreme Court held that after-acquired evidence of misconduct does not bar a discrimination claim. But the employee misconduct is not ignored: remedies available to plaintiffs in cases involving misconduct should be limited to back pay and should not include reinstatement or front pay.

REMEDIES UNDER TITLE VII

Remedies available under Title VII include compensation for lost salary and benefits ("back pay"), reinstatement or "front pay" equal to what the employee would have received had he or she not been discharged, and injunctive relief to stop prohibited discriminatory actions. Front pay is generally awarded when reinstatement is inappropriate because the position is unavailable or hostility raises a practical barrier.

The plaintiff may also recover compensatory damages for future pecuniary losses, emotional pain and suffering, inconvenience, mental anguish, loss of enjoyment of life, and other nonpecuniary losses. While front pay is limited in duration because it compensates for the immediate effects of discrimination, lost future earnings compensate an employee for a lifetime of diminished earnings resulting from the reputational harm suffered as a result of discrimination. Therefore, an employee may be awarded both front pay and damages for lost future earnings.[62]

Punitive Damages

In *Kolstad v. American Dental Ass'n*,[63] the Supreme Court considered the circumstances under which punitive damages may be awarded under Title VII. The Court began by noting that punitive damages awards are available only in cases of "intentional discrimination," that is, cases that do not rely on the disparate impact theory of discrimination. To recover punitive damages, the complaining party must demonstrate that the employer engaged in a discriminatory practice or practices *with malice or with reckless indifference to the federally protected rights of an aggrieved individual.* (Punitive damages are not available in suits against a government, governmental agency, or political subdivision.) To prevail in obtaining punitive damages, the employee is not required to show

---

60. 29 C.F.R. pts. 1604.2(a)(1)(i)–1604.2(a)(1)(iii).
61. 513 U.S. 352 (1995).
62. Williams v. Pharmacia, Inc., 137 F.3d 944 (7th Cir. 1998).
63. 527 U.S. 526 (1999).

that the employer engaged in egregious misconduct. Rather, the employee must show that the employer had the requisite discriminatory mental state. Punitive damages are also available and can be awarded even if the jury awarded no compensatory damages.[64]

Even if the employee can show the requisite malice or indifference, the employer may still not be liable for punitive damages. The Court held that if the employer has engaged in "good-faith efforts" to comply with Title VII, then it is not vicariously liable for punitive damages based on discriminatory employment decisions by managerial agents when those decisions are contrary to those good faith efforts. To hold otherwise, the Court reasoned, would reduce the incentive for employers to implement antidiscrimination programs.

In *EEOC v. Wal-Mart Stores, Inc.*,[65] the U.S. Court of Appeals for the Tenth Circuit held that Wal-Mart's written antidiscrimination policy was not sufficient to establish a "good faith" defense preventing an award of punitive damages for discriminatory conduct prohibited under the Americans with Disabilities Act. The appeals court highlighted the language in *Kolstad* requiring employers both to adopt antidiscrimination policies and to educate employees on federal discrimination laws. Although Wal-Mart did establish a written policy, it did not "demonstrate an implemented good faith policy of educating employees on the Act's accommodation and nondiscrimination requirements."

Caps on Liability

The compensatory and punitive damages available for discrimination based on sex or religion are capped by the Civil Rights Act of 1991 at $50,000 for employers of 100 or fewer employees, $100,000 for employers with 101 to 200 employees, $200,000 for employers with 201 to 500 employees, and $300,000 for employers with more than 500 employees.[66] However, the compensatory caps do not apply to intentional racial or ethnic discrimination. In addition, the Supreme Court has stated that front pay is not considered compensatory damages and thus is not subject to the cap on compensatory awards.[67]

Courts may also decide to limit the amount of compensatory damages awarded a plaintiff. For example, the Supreme Court of Michigan threw out a $21 million jury award to a sexual harassment plaintiff on the basis that it was excessive.[68] Employees claiming discrimination frequently sue under state employment-discrimination laws, which often do not include caps on damages.

Age Discrimination

As the baby boomers, who comprise a substantial percentage of the American workforce, grow older, the issue of age discrimination in employment has become more visible. In fact, the number of workers above the age of fifty-five is expected to grow by more than 10.2 million by 2012, making this the fastest-growing age group in the workforce.[69] The Age Discrimination in Employment Act (ADEA) prohibits age discrimination in employment with respect to individuals aged forty years or older. Individuals under age forty have no protection from discrimination based on age. Courts have held that the employer, not the individual making the discriminatory decision, is liable for age discrimination.[70]

The substantive provisions of the ADEA are similar to those of Title VII. The ADEA generally prohibits age discrimination with respect to employee hiring, firing, and compensation, as well as with respect to the terms, conditions, and privileges of employment. As with Title VII, creation of a hostile environment because of age is a form of age discrimination.[71] The ADEA also prohibits retaliation against an individual aged forty or older because of the individual's opposition to unlawful age discrimination or because he or she has made a charge or testified or assisted in an investigation, proceeding, or litigation under the ADEA.

Although the ADEA protects individuals over the age of forty, a unanimous Supreme Court explained in *O'Connor v. Consolidated Coin Caterers Corp.*[72] that age discrimination cannot be inferred simply because the replacement employee is outside the protected class. In other words, replacing a 40-year-old employee with a 39-year-old employee does not give rise to a stronger infer-

64. Timm v. Progressive Steel Treating, Inc., 137 F.3d 1008 (7th Cir. 1998); Cush-Crawford v. Adchem Corp., 271 F.3d 352 (2d Cir. 2001); Corti v. Storage Tech. Corp., 304 F.3d 336 (4th Cir. 2002).
65. 187 F.3d 1241 (10th Cir. 1999).
66. Civil Rights Act of 1991, Pub. L. 102–106, § 1977(a)(b)(3), 105 Stat. 1071 (1991).
67. Pollard v. E.I. du Pont de Nemours & Co., 532 U.S. 843 (2001). *But see* Peyton v. diMario, 287 F.3d 1121 (D.C. Cir. 2002) (stating that awards of front pay may be considered too speculative, and thus reduced, if the length of time for which the front pay was awarded is considered too great).

68. Gilbert v. DaimlerChrysler, 685 N.W.2d 391 (Mich. 2004).
69. William C. Martucci & Carrie A. McAtee, *Is "Overqualified" a Pretext for Age Discrimination?*, NAT'L L.J., Sept. 20, 2004, at S3.
70. Stults v. Conoco, Inc., 76 F.3d 651 (5th Cir. 1996).
71. Crawford v. Medina Gen. Hosp., 96 F.3d 830 (6th Cir. 1996) (finding the hostile work environment claim a "relatively uncontroversial proposition").
72. 517 U.S. 308 (1996).

ence of discrimination than replacing a 52-year-old employee with a 40-year-old employee. Rather, "the fact that a replacement is substantially younger than the plaintiff is a far more reliable indicator of age discrimination."

Even so, the ADEA prohibits unlawful age discrimination among persons within the protected age group. Thus, for example, if two individuals aged 41 and 53 apply for the same position, the employer may not lawfully reject either applicant on the basis of age. On the other hand, an employer may still have engaged in age discrimination against the 53-year-old individual if it hires the 41-year-old applicant.

However, the U.S. Supreme Court has held that the ADEA does not protect younger workers over forty against older workers. In *General Dynamics Land Systems, Inc. v. Cline*,[73] a collective bargaining agreement between Land Systems and a union eliminated the company's obligation to provide health benefits to subsequently retired employees, except for then-current workers who were at least fifty years old. Employees who were at least forty and therefore protected under the ADEA, but under fifty, filed a complaint claiming that the agreement violated the ADEA because it discriminated against them because of their age. The district court dismissed the action, calling the claim one of "reverse age discrimination" on which no court had ever granted relief. The U.S. Court of Appeals for the Sixth Circuit reversed, but the Supreme Court held that "[w]e see the text, structure, purpose and history of the ADEA, along with its relationship to other federal statutes, as showing that the statute does not mean to stop an employer from favoring an older employee over a younger one."

To establish a *prima facie* case of age discrimination under the ADEA, the employee must prove that he or she (1) was within the protected age group, (2) was qualified for the position at issue, (3) suffered an adverse employment action, and (4) was replaced by a sufficiently younger person.[74]

In *Reeves v. Sanderson Plumbing Products, Inc.*,[75] the Supreme Court established that a finding of liability for intentional discrimination under the ADEA could be based solely on the plaintiff's *prima facie* case of discrimination together with sufficient evidence for a reasonable fact finder to reject the employer's nondiscriminatory explanation for its decision. In *Reeves*, a fifty-seven-year-old worker established a *prima facie*

"Do you think now that we're doing fewer illegal things we can scale back the legal department?"

case and offered evidence showing that he had properly maintained attendance records to dispute the employer's claim that he was fired for failing to discipline late and absent employees due to shoddy record keeping. Reeves also introduced evidence that the supervisor responsible for his firing was motivated by age-based animus. The supervisor told Reeves that he was old enough to have come over on the *Mayflower* and said that he was just "too damn old" for the job. The Court found that this was sufficient evidence for the jury to conclude that the employer had intentionally discriminated and reinstated the jury verdict in favor of Reeves.

In contrast, the U.S. Court of Appeals for the First Circuit held that Ramon Suarez, the fifty-nine-year-old president of CaribAd (a subsidiary of Pueblo International), was not constructively discharged based on age when Pueblo was restructured and most of CaribAd's employees were relocated to corporate headquarters, leaving Suarez alone in an office with a receptionist.[76] Although Suarez was told that the in-house advertising for which he had been responsible was being transferred to someone else and that he would be responsible for bringing in new clients, he maintained his position as president and continued to be paid his salary of $190,000 a year. The court stated that "[i]n that rarified financial atmosphere . . . an increase in work

---

73. 124 S. Ct. 1236 (2004).
74. Anderson v. Consol. Rail Corp., 297 F.3d 242 (3d Cir. 2002).
75. 530 U.S. 133 (2000).

76. Suarez v. Pueblo Int'l, Inc., 229 F.3d 49 (1st Cir. 2000).

requirements that does not surpass reasonable expectations" cannot sustain a constructive discharge claim. Even if Pueblo was attempting to marginalize Suarez, the "unpleasantness, hurt feelings, and wounded pride" that resulted did not create working conditions that were "so onerous, abusive or unpleasant that a reasonable person in the employee's position would have felt compelled to resign." In short, the ADEA does not guarantee workplaces "free from the ordinary ebb and flow of power relations and inter-office politics."

In *Smith v. City of Jackson, Mississippi*,[77] the U.S. Supreme Court held that employer actions which on their face do not discriminate based on age may still violate the ADEA if they have a statistically significant impact on workers over forty. Nonetheless, the Court held that the scope of disparate-impact liability under the ADEA is narrower than under Title VII. Recognizing that "age, unlike race or other classifications protected by Title VII, not uncommonly has relevance to an individual's capacity to engage in certain types of employment," the Court ruled that employees must identify the specific test, requirement, or practice that is responsible for any observed statistical disparities. It is not enough to point to a generalized policy that leads to such an impact.[78] Moreover, even if the employee identifies the relevant practice, the employer has a defense if the employer bases its discussion on a "reasonable factor other than age" (the *RFOA defense*). The employer is not required to show business necessity.

OLDER WORKERS' BENEFIT PROTECTION ACT

The Older Workers' Benefit Protection Act[79] (OWBPA) prohibits age discrimination in providing employee benefits. It also establishes minimum standards for employees who waive their rights under the ADEA.

To meet the minimum standards, the waiver must be "knowing and voluntary." The employee must be given at least twenty-one days to consider whether to enter into an agreement waiving rights under the ADEA. This period is extended to forty-five days when the waiver is in connection with an early retirement or exit-incentive plan offered to a group or class of employees. The agreement must also give the employee a period of at least seven days following execution of the agreement during which the employee may revoke it. An employee who has accepted a severance payment in exchange for waiving his or her rights under the ADEA can still sue the employer for violation of the ADEA without having to return the payment if the waiver was not made in accordance with the OWBPA.[80]

Employers may revoke a proposed early retirement agreement during the time frame that the OWBPA gives employees to act on it. For example, in *Ellison v. Premier Salons International, Inc.*,[81] the Eighth Circuit held that an employer could revoke a separation agreement containing a waiver of claims under the ADEA and provide a new, less valuable agreement, after learning that the employee had made defamatory statements about the company.

DEFENSES

An employer faced with an age discrimination claim may assert in its defense that (1) age is a BFOQ reasonably necessary to the normal operation of the business (extremely difficult to prove); (2) the differential treatment is based on reasonable factors other than age; (3) the employer's action is based on a bona fide seniority system or employee benefit plan—such as a retirement, pension, or insurance plan—that is not invoked as a subterfuge to evade the purposes of the ADEA; or (4) the discharge or discipline of a protected individual was for good cause.[82] Although these defenses are set forth in the ADEA itself, employers should proceed with caution because the courts construe them strictly.

REMEDIES UNDER THE ADEA

Employees who bring successful claims under the ADEA are entitled to both equitable relief, which includes hiring, wage adjustments, promotion, or reinstatement, and monetary relief.[83] Monetary remedies include back pay, front pay, and liquidated damages. Back pay consists of wages, salary, and fringe benefits the employee would have earned during the period of discrimination. Front pay is awarded to restore employees to their "rightful place" and compensates the employees for anticipated future losses. Liquidated damages equal to the amounts owing to a person as a result of the violation are provided only in the event of willful violations by the employer. Compensatory damages and punitive damages are available under the ADEA.

77. 125 S. Ct. 1536 (2005).

78. This is the standard of proof the Supreme Court had imposed in *Wards Cove Packing Co. v. Atonio*, 490 U.S. 642 (1986), for disparate-impact cases under Title VII before Congress expanded the coverage of Title VII in the Civil Rights Act of 1991 (§ 2, 105 Stat. 1071 (1991).

79. 29 U.S.C. § 623(f) (1994).

80. Oubre v. Entergy Operations, Inc., 522 U.S. 422 (1998).

81. 164 F.3d 1111 (8th Cir. 1999).

82. 29 U.S.C. § 623(f) (1998).

83. EEOC, *When a Charge Is Filed Against My Company*, at http://www.eeoc.gov/employers/chargesfiled.html#if%20my%20company (last modified Dec. 17, 2001).

🔷 Disability Discrimination

Title I of the Americans with Disabilities Act (ADA) prohibits employers from discriminating against a qualified individual because of a disability in regard to job-application procedures, hiring, advancement, discharge, compensation, job training, and other terms, conditions, and privileges of employment. Such discrimination includes the use of selection criteria to screen out individuals with disabilities unless the criteria are job related and consistent with business necessity. The employer may not exclude a disabled individual if that individual, with some "reasonable accommodation," could perform the essential functions of the position, unless the accommodation would impose an "undue hardship" upon the employer. The EEOC has indicated that employers may ask preemployment questions about reasonable accommodations but are barred from asking about disabilities.[84]

The employee must be able to attend work to be considered a "qualified individual" within the meaning of the ADA. In *Corder v. Lucent Technologies*,[85] the court found that an employee diagnosed with depression who was unable to attend work could not qualify for protection under the ADA.

The ADA also extends to employee benefit packages. In March 2000, however, the U.S. Court of Appeals for the Second Circuit agreed with six other federal circuits in holding that the ADA does not bar employers from providing less coverage for mental and emotional disabilities than for physical disabilities under long-term disability plans.[86] The court reasoned that "[s]o long as every employee is offered the same plan regardless of that employee's contemporary or future disability status, then no discrimination has occurred even if the plan offers different coverage for various disabilities."

IMPERMISSIBLE DISCRIMINATION

Under the ADA, employers are prohibited from intentionally discriminating against disabled persons and from engaging in employment practices that are not intentionally discriminatory, but have the effect of discriminating against disabled persons or perpetuating the past effects of such discrimination. The term "discriminate" as construed by the ADA includes the following prohibited practices:

1. Limiting, segregating, or classifying an applicant or employee because of his or her disability so as to adversely affect his or her opportunities or status.
2. Entering into a contractual relationship with an employment or referral agency, union, or other organization that has the effect of subjecting employees or applicants with a disability to prohibited discrimination.
3. Utilizing standards, criteria, or methods of administration that have the effect of discriminating or perpetuating the effects of discrimination because of disability.
4. Denying equal job benefits to a qualified individual because of the known disability of a person with whom the qualified individual is known to have a relationship or association.
5. Not making reasonable accommodations to the known physical or mental limitations of an otherwise qualified employee or applicant with a disability unless to do so would impose undue hardship on the employer.
6. Denying job opportunities to an otherwise qualified employee or applicant with a disability in order to avoid having to make reasonable accommodations for that disability.
7. Using qualification standards or employment tests that tend to screen out individuals with disabilities, unless the qualification standards or employment tests are shown to be job related and are consistent with business necessity.
8. Failing to select and conduct job testing in such a way as to ensure that when the test is administered to an applicant or employee with a disability that impairs his or her sensory, manual, or speaking skills, the results of the test accurately reflect the skills or aptitude that test is designed to measure, rather than reflecting the sensory, manual, or speaking impairment.

Recently, the U.S. Courts of Appeals for the Fourth, Fifth, and Eighth Circuits have determined that employees can bring a claim for a hostile work environment under the ADA.[87]

DEFINITION OF DISABILITY

The ADA codifies existing law developed under the Vocational Rehabilitation Act of 1973 by defining a "person with a disability" as (1) a person with a physical

---

84. Asra Q. Nomani, *EEOC Eases Question Limits for Disabled*, WALL ST. J., Oct. 11, 1995, at A5.
85. 162 F.3d 924 (7th Cir. 1998).
86. EEOC v. Staten Island Sav. Bank, 207 F.3d 144 (2d Cir. 2000).

87. Fox v. Gen. Motors, 247 F.3d 169 (4th Cir. 2001); Flowers v. S. Reg'l Physician Servs., Inc., 247 F.3d 229 (5th Cir. 2001); Shaver v. Indep. Stave Co., 350 F.3d 716 (8th Cir. 2003).

or mental impairment that substantially limits one or more of that person's major life activities, (2) a person with a record of a physical or mental impairment that substantially limits one or more of that person's major life activities, or (3) a person who is regarded as having such an impairment.

Physical or Mental Impairment

The first and second prongs of the ADA's definition of a disability focus on whether the individual has, or has a record of, a disability. The individual must have a physical or mental impairment. The Code of Federal Regulations defines a physical or mental impairment as:

> Any physiological disorder, or condition, cosmetic disfigurement, or anatomical loss affecting one or more of the following body systems: neurological, musculoskeletal, special sense organs, respiratory (including speech organs), cardiovascular, reproductive, digestive, genito-urinary, hemic and lymphatic, skin, and endocrine; or [a]ny mental or psychological disorder, such as mental retardation, organic brain syndrome, emotional or mental illness, and specific learning disabilities.[88]

Neither the ADA nor the Code of Federal Regulations lists all of the diseases or conditions that qualify as a "physical or mental" impairment. The ADA states generally, however, that an impairment is a physiological or mental disorder.[89] As a result, physical characteristics, such as skin color, weight, or height within the normal range, are not physical impairments, and personality traits like rudeness, irresponsible behavior, or a short temper are not themselves impairments either. In addition, environmental, cultural, or economic disadvantages, such as lack of education or a prison record, are not impairments. For example, a person who cannot read due to dyslexia, which is a learning disability, has an impairment and is thus disabled. In contrast, a person who cannot read because he or she did not go to school does not have a disability because failure to attend school is not an impairment.

Substantially Limits a Major Life Activity
An impairment is a disability under the ADA only if it causes the individual to be unable to perform, or to be significantly limited in the ability to perform, an activity compared to an average person in the general population. Courts will

consider the impairment's nature and severity, how long it will last or is expected to last, and its expected impact.[90]

A major life activity is one that an average person can perform with little or no difficulty. For example, the U.S. Supreme Court resolved a split in the circuits when it ruled in *Bragdon v. Abbott*[91] that reproduction is a major life activity. The Ninth Circuit ruled that an employee who took medication for an anxiety disorder that made him drowsy and sexually impotent was entitled to relief under the ADA on the grounds that sleeping, engaging in sexual relations, and interacting with others were major life activities.[92] In contrast, in *Furnish v. SVI Systems*,[93] the U.S. Court of Appeals for the Seventh Circuit held that an employee with cirrhosis of the liver caused by chronic hepatitis B had no claim under the ADA because lack of a fully functioning liver did not limit the ability to perform a "major life activity." Likewise, in *Pack v. Kmart Corp.*,[94] the U.S. Court of Appeals for the Tenth Circuit held that although a pharmacy technician's depression was a mental impairment that limited her ability to concentrate at work, concentration was not a "major life activity" under the ADA.

The U.S. Courts of Appeals for the Seventh, Eighth, and Ninth Circuits recently held that eating is considered a major life activity because it is integral to daily existence.[95] The U.S. Court of Appeals for the Seventh Circuit found that severe diabetes substantially limited an employee's major life activity of eating because he was required to perpetually and constantly monitor his food and sugar intake to avoid "debilitating, and potentially life-threatening, symptoms."[96]

In *Toyota Motor Manufacturing, Kentucky, Inc. v. Williams*,[97] an employee who claimed that she was unable to perform her automobile assembly-line job because she was disabled due to carpal tunnel syndrome and related impairments sued Toyota for failing to provide her with a reasonable accommodation as required by the ADA. The district court granted Toyota's motion for summary judgment, holding that the employee's impairment did not qualify as a "disability" under the

88. 29 C.F.R. pt. 1630.2.
89. ADA & IT Technical Assistance Centers, *What Is the ADA: Definition of Disability* (2004), *at* http://www.adata.org/whatsada-definition.html.
90. *Id.*
91. 524 U.S. 624 (1998).
92. McAlindin v. County of San Diego, 192 F.3d 1226 (9th Cir. 1999).
93. 270 F.3d 445 (7th Cir. 2001).
94. 166 F.3d 1300 (10th Cir. 1999).
95. *See* Lawson v. CSX Transp., Inc., 245 F.3d 916 (7th Cir. 2001); Land v. Baptist Med. Ctr., 164 F.3d 423 (8th Cir. 1999); Fraser v. Goodale, 342 F.3d 1032 (9th Cir. 2003).
96. *Lawson.*
97. 534 U.S. 184 (2001).

ADA because it had not "substantially limit[ed]" any "major life activit[y]." The U.S. Court of Appeals for the Sixth Circuit reversed, finding that her impairments substantially limited the employee in the major life activity of performing manual tasks. The Supreme Court faulted the appeals court for failing to ask whether the employee's impairments prevented or restricted her from performing tasks that were of central importance to most people's daily lives. The Court concluded that an employee is not considered to be substantially limited from performing manual tasks if he or she simply cannot perform tasks associated with his or her job. Accordingly, the Court reversed the Sixth Circuit's judgment and remanded the case for further proceedings.

Doctors can play a large role in deciding whether an impairment substantially limits a major life activity. For example, in *Blockel v. J.C. Penney Co.*,[98] the U.S. Court of

Appeals for the First Circuit did not question whether an employee, who was fired after she was required to limit the number of hours she worked per week by her doctor due to a seizure disorder, depression, and post-traumatic stress disorder, was disabled. In contrast, in *McKenzie v. Dovala*,[99] the U.S. Court of Appeals for the Tenth Circuit stated that an employee, who had a prior record of a variety of psychological afflictions, including post-traumatic stress disorder related to childhood sexual abuse by her father, was not protected by the ADA because her doctors had cleared her for all work-related activities at the time her employment application was denied.

In the following case, the Supreme Court considered whether correctable myopia is a "disability" under the ADA.

---

98. 337 F.3d 17 (1st Cir. 2003).

99. 242 F.3d 967 (10th Cir. 2001).

A CASE IN POINT	In the Language of the Court

CASE 13.3

Sutton v. United Air Lines, Inc.

Supreme Court of the United States
527 U.S. 471 (1999).

› FACTS Karen Sutton and Kimberly Hinton were twin sisters who had severe myopia. Although their myopia prevented them from conducting numerous activities, they could, with the help of glasses or contact lenses, function in the same way as individuals with normal vision. They applied to United Air Lines to become commercial airline pilots but were told that they did not meet the airline's minimum vision requirements (uncorrected vision of 20/100 or better). The sisters filed a suit, alleging that United had discriminated against them on the basis of their disability in violation of the ADA.

› ISSUE PRESENTED Is myopia that is correctable with glasses or contact lenses a "disability" under the ADA?

› OPINION O'CONNOR, J., writing for the U.S. Supreme Court:

A "disability" exists only where an impairment "substantially limits" a major life activity, not where it "might," "could," or "would" be substantially limiting if mitigating measures were not taken. A person whose physical or mental impairment is corrected by medication or other measures does not have an impairment that presently "substantially limits" a major life activity. To be sure, a person whose physical or mental impairment is corrected by mitigating measures still has an impairment, but if the impairment is corrected it does not "substantially limit" a major life activity.

. . .

. . . Had Congress intended to include all persons with corrected physical limitations among those covered by the Act, it undoubtedly would have cited a much higher number of disabled persons in the findings. That it did not is evidence that the ADA's coverage is restricted to only those whose impairments are not mitigated by corrective measures.

. . .

. . . Under subsection (C), individuals who are "regarded as" having a disability are disabled within the meaning of the ADA. . . .

. . .

(Continued)

(Case 13.3 *continued*)

Assuming without deciding that working is a major life activity and that the EEOC regulations interpreting the term "substantially limits" [to mean "unable to perform" or "significantly restricted"] are reasonable, petitioners have failed to allege adequately that their poor eyesight is regarded as an impairment that substantially limits them in the major life activity of working. They allege only that respondent regards their poor vision as precluding them from holding positions as a "global airline pilot." Because the position of global airline pilot is a single job, this allegation does not support the claim that respondent regards petitioners as having a *substantially limiting impairment*. Indeed, there are a number of other positions utilizing petitioners' skills, such as regional pilot and pilot instructor to name a few, that are available to them. Even under the EEOC's Interpretative Guidance, to which petitioners ask us to defer, "an individual who cannot be a commercial airline pilot because of a minor vision impairment, but who can be a commercial airline co-pilot or a pilot for a courier service, would not be substantially limited in the major life activity of working."

> RESULT The appeals court's decision dismissing the case was affirmed. The sisters were not disabled and therefore were not protected by the ADA.

> CRITICAL THINKING QUESTIONS

1. Would a person with diabetes that can be controlled with insulin be disabled if he or she elected not to take insulin and, as a result, could not work?
2. Could an employer terminate an employee with high cholesterol to avoid having to pay for expensive cholesterol-lowering drugs? Would the result be the same if the employee were HIV-positive and was taking very expensive drugs to control the condition?

Regarded as Disabled

The third prong of the definition of a disability provides that a person is protected under the ADA if he or she is regarded as having an impairment that substantially limits one or more major life activities. This is based on the notion that societal stereotypes and prejudices may constrain individuals more than their actual limitations. As a result, the ADA prohibits an employer from discriminating against an individual based on its perception that the individual is disabled because the employer's reactions may be based on stereotypes, misinformation, and long-held misconceptions of handicapped individuals. In other words, an individual might be "regarded as" disabled even if he or she does not actually have a disability, if the employer treats him or her as if the condition constituted a disability.

Exclusions

Although the definition of a disability under the ADA is relatively vague, the statute does clearly exclude many things. For example, the ADA specifically excludes homosexuality, bisexuality, sexual-behavior disorders, compulsive gambling, kleptomania, and pyromania from the definition of a disability.

Psychoactive-substance-use disorders resulting from current illegal use of drugs, including the use of alcohol in the workplace against the employer's policies, are also excluded from the ADA's definition of a disability. Although "current use" is not specifically defined in the statute, it has been interpreted to include drug use weeks or months before discharge.[100] However, an employee or applicant who no longer actively uses drugs or alcohol on the work site, but who is involved in or has completed a supervised rehabilitation program, may be regarded as a disabled person.[101] Also, although an individual may not be fired on the basis of his or her alcoholism, an employer may discharge the person based on behavior related to the alcoholism.[102] In 2000, the EEOC issued an informal guidance letter stating that an employer that

100. Shafer v. Preston Mem'l Hosp. Corp., 107 F.3d 274 (4th Cir. 1997).
101. *See* Brown v. Lucky Stores, Inc., 246 F.3d 1182 (9th Cir. 2001).
102. James Podgers, *Disability and DUIs: ADA Claims by Fired or Demoted Alcoholic Employees Fail*, A.B.A. J., Feb. 1996, at 46.

excludes injuries or diseases that result from chronic alcoholism or drug addiction from its disability retirement plan could be required to justify the exclusion by the risks or costs of coverage or as necessary for the viability of the plan.[103]

REASONABLE ACCOMMODATION

The ADA requires employers to make reasonable accommodations to an employee's disability, as long as doing so does not cause the employer "undue hardship." Thus, even if a disability precludes an individual from performing the essential functions of the position or presents a safety risk, the employer is required to assess whether there is a reasonable accommodation that will permit the individual to be employed despite the disability.

Title I sets forth a nonexhaustive list of what might constitute "reasonable accommodation." It includes (1) making work facilities accessible; (2) restructuring jobs or modifying work schedules; (3) reassigning the individual to another job; (4) acquiring or modifying equipment or devices; (5) modifying examinations, training materials, or policies; and (6) providing qualified readers or interpreters or other similar accommodations for individuals with disabilities.

To establish liability under the ADA, the employee must have requested an accommodation from the employer; it is the employee's initial request for an accommodation that triggers the employer's obligation to provide one.[104] An employee who fails to provide the employer with necessary medical information is precluded from claiming that the employer failed to provide reasonable accommodation.[105] Employers must train supervisors to recognize when a reasonable request for accommodation has been made.[106]

At least six federal appeals courts have found that once a request for accommodation is made, an employer must be proactive and make a reasonable effort to determine the appropriate accommodation.[107] A minimum

requirement seems to be that the employer should discuss potential accommodations with the disabled employee and not make unilateral decisions regarding the adequacy of potential accommodations.[108] Courts have not been receptive to claims that a reasonable accommodation includes transferring the individual to a new supervisor.[109]

Reassignment, however, may be considered a reasonable accommodation. In *Smith v. Midland Brake, Inc.,*[110] the U.S. Court of Appeals for the Tenth Circuit found that the employer, Midland Brake, could have reassigned employee Robert Smith to another job within the company after he became unable to perform his job because of a chronic skin condition. The court argued that the ADA's reasonable accommodation requirement would be transformed into a "hollow promise" if it merely extended the right "to compete equally with the rest of the world for a vacant position" to disabled workers.

In contrast, in *EEOC v. Humiston-Keeling, Inc.,*[111] the U.S. Court of Appeals for the Seventh Circuit held that the employer did not violate the ADA by refusing to reassign a warehouse picker to a vacant clerical position for which she was minimally qualified when there were other applicants for the position who were better qualified. The court ruled that the ADA does not require an employer to reassign a disabled employee to a job for which a better qualified applicant exists, provided the employer's consistent and honest policy is to hire the best applicant for the job. The court rejected the argument that a disabled employee is entitled to more consideration than a nondisabled employee, saying that would amount to a policy of requiring employers to give bonus points to people with disabilities.

An employer does not have to accommodate a disabled employee if doing so would conflict with seniority rules under the employer's collective bargaining agreement.[112] In *U.S. Airways, Inc. v. Barnett,*[113] however, the Supreme Court held that an employer's unilaterally imposed seniority system (not embodied in a collective bargaining agreement) that conflicts with a reassignment that is a reasonable accommodation under the ADA will

103. *EEOC Says Alcohol-Related Disabilities May Not Be Excluded from Employer Plan,* 69 U.S.L.W. 2089 (Aug. 15, 2000).
104. Jovanovic v. In-Sink-Erator Div. of Emerson Elec. Co., 201 F.3d 894 (7th Cir. 2000).
105. Templeton v. Neodata Servs., 162 F.3d 617 (10th Cir. 1998).
106. *Employers Should Train Supervisors in ADA Accommodation Duty, EEOC Official Advises,* 69 U.S.L.W. 2254–5 (Oct. 31, 2000).
107. *See, e.g.,* Loulseged v. Akz. Nobel, Inc., 178 F.3d 731 (5th Cir. 1999) (an interactive process is a "means to the end of forging reasonable accommodation"); Mengine v. Runyon, 114 F.3d 415 (3d Cir. 1997) (an employer that fails to work with the employee requesting accommodation "may not discover a way in which the employee's disability could have been reasonably accommodated, thereby risking violation").

108. Bultemeyer v. Fort Wayne Cmty. Schs., 100 F.3d 1281 (7th Cir. 1996).
109. Frances A. McMorris, *Employee's Transfer Plea Rejected in Another Disabilities-Act Ruling,* WALL ST. J., Jan. 21, 1997, at B5.
110. 180 F.3d 1154 (10th Cir. 1999).
111. 227 F.3d 1024 (7th Cir. 2000).
112. *See, e.g.,* Davis v. Fla. Power & Light Co., 205 F.3d 1301 (11th Cir. 2000).
113. 535 U.S. 391 (2002).

not necessarily serve to bar the reassignment. In this case, an employee who suffered a serious back injury while working had asked his employer to reassign him to another job in the company's mail room. Two employees with greater seniority planned to exercise their seniority right to transfer to jobs in the mail room, thereby preventing the disabled employee from working there. The Court found that while a seniority system is ordinarily sufficient to show that accommodation is not reasonable under the ADA, the employee may present evidence of special circumstances that make exception to the seniority rule reasonable under particular facts. The Court stated that "the plaintiff might show, for example, that the employer, having retained the right to change the system unilaterally, exercises the right fairly frequently, reducing employee expectations that the system will be followed—to the point where the requested accommodation will not likely make a difference."

DEFENSES UNDER THE ADA

Defenses available to an employer under the ADA include undue hardship, business necessity, and permissible exclusion.

Undue Hardship

A reasonable accommodation is not required if it would impose an undue hardship on the employer. The ADA defines "undue hardship" to mean an activity requiring significant difficulty or expense when considered in light of (1) the nature and cost of the accommodation needed; (2) the overall financial resources of the facility, the number of persons employed at the facility, the effect on expenses and resources, or any other impact of the accommodation on the facility; (3) the overall financial resources of the employer and the overall size of the business with respect to the number of employees and the type, number, and location of its facilities; and (4) the type of operation of the employer, including the composition, structure, and functions of the workforce, and the geographic separateness and administrative or fiscal relationship of the facility in question to the employer.

An example of an accommodation that was deemed unreasonable involved an employee with various mental impairments that made it impossible for him to work in an unduly stressful environment. The employee asked for a transfer out of the stressful work environment and later sued when the employer did not honor his request. The U.S. Court of Appeals for the Third Circuit ruled that transferring the employee away from the stressful work environment was not a reasonable accommodation because it would impose extraordinary administrative costs on the employer.[114]

Business Necessity

Employers may also argue that they had to discriminate against an applicant or employee with a disability due to a business necessity. In *Belk v. Southwestern Bell Telephone Co.*,[115] the U.S. Court of Appeals for the Eighth Circuit ruled that employment tests, qualification standards, and other selection criteria are acceptable under the ADA if they are related to the job and consistent with business necessity. Southwestern Bell had argued that it had job-related reasons for not accommodating a worker who wore a leg brace during a physical performance test for a technician job.

In *EEOC v. Exxon Corp.*,[116] the U.S. Court of Appeals for the Fifth Circuit analyzed Exxon's policy, adopted in response to the 1989 *Exxon Valdez* oil spill disaster, of permanently removing any employee who had undergone treatment for substance abuse from certain safety-sensitive positions. The EEOC sued, arguing that Exxon had to prove that the class of individuals posed a "direct threat" to the health or safety of others. The court rejected this argument, stating that Exxon could justify its policy as a business necessity. Whereas the "direct threat" test focuses on the individual employee and the specific risk posed by the employee's disability, the "business necessity" defense concerns whether a safety policy is addressed to all employees of a given class. The court further ruled that in evaluating whether a safety policy constitutes a business necessity, both the magnitude of possible harm and the probability of harm must be evaluated.

In *Tice v. Centre Area Transportation Authority*,[117] the U.S. Court of Appeals for the Third Circuit held that a transportation authority did not violate the ADA by ordering a post-hiring physical examination of a bus driver who had repeatedly taken medical leave due to a back injury because the examination was job related and consistent with the business necessity of determining whether the employee was physically fit to perform his job.

Permissible Exclusion

An applicant or employee who is disabled may be excluded from the employment opportunity only if, by reason of the disability, he or she (with or without rea-

114. Gaul v. Lucent Techs., Inc., 134 F.3d 576 (3d Cir. 1998).
115. 194 F.3d 946 (8th Cir. 1999).
116. 203 F.3d 871 (5th Cir. 2000).
117. 247 F.3d 506 (3d Cir. 2001).

sonable accommodation) cannot perform the essential functions of the job or if the employment of the individual poses a significant risk to the health or safety of others.

Inability to Perform Essential Functions In determining whether a job function is essential, the ADA requires that consideration be given to the employer's judgment as to which functions are essential, but it also looks to any written job description prepared *before* advertising or interviewing for the job commenced. The applicant or employee does not have to prove his or her ability to perform all the functions of the job, only the essential functions.[118]

Direct Threat An employer cannot deny a job due to risk of future injury unless, given the person's current condition, there is a probability of substantial harm. For example, the U.S. Court of Appeals for the Eleventh

118. Deane v. Pocono Med. Ctr., 142 F.3d 138 (3d Cir. 1998).

Circuit ruled that a dental office acted lawfully when it laid off an HIV-positive hygienist after concluding that he posed a direct threat to the health and safety of others. His job included engaging in invasive, exposure-prone activities, such as cleaning teeth, on a frequent basis.[119] The presence of sharp instruments on which the hygienist could prick his hand increased the risk of HIV transmission. Employers cannot rely on their own physician's opinion, however; risk of injury must be based upon generally accepted medical opinion.

In the following case, the Supreme Court considered whether the "direct threat" defense under the ADA applies to employees who pose a direct threat to their own health or safety, but not to other persons in the workplace.

119. Waddell v. Valley Forge Dental Assoc., 276 F.3d 1275 (11th Cir. 2001).

A CASE IN POINT	Summary

CASE 13.4

Echazabal v. Chevron USA, Inc.

Supreme Court of the United States
536 U.S. 73 (2002).

> FACTS Mario Echazabal worked for various maintenance contractors at Chevron's oil refinery in El Segundo, California. In 1992, he applied to work directly for Chevron. Chevron offered him a job contingent on his passing a physical examination. The exam revealed that Echazabal's liver was releasing certain enzymes at an abnormally high level. Chevron concluded that his liver might be damaged by exposure to solvents and chemicals in the refinery, so it rescinded the offer. Echazabal continued to work for a maintenance contractor operating at the refinery.

Subsequently, Echazabal was diagnosed with asymptomatic chronic active hepatitis C. His physicians did not advise him to stop working at the refinery because of his medical condition. In 1995, Echazabal applied again to Chevron for a position in the refinery. After making him an offer, Chevron again rescinded it after learning about Echazabal's liver disease. Chevron also wrote to the maintenance contractor who employed him and requested that it remove Echazabal from the refinery or place him in a position where he would not be exposed to solvents or chemicals. As a result, Echazabal could no longer work at the refinery. He filed a complaint against Chevron, alleging that it had violated the ADA. The district court dismissed his claim, and he appealed to the U.S. Court of Appeals for the Ninth Circuit, which reversed the summary judgment. Chevron then appealed to the U.S. Supreme Court.

> ISSUE PRESENTED Does the "direct threat" defense apply to employees who pose a direct threat to their own health or safety, but not to the health or safety of other persons?

> SUMMARY OF OPINION The U.S. Supreme Court began by examining the language of the ADA, which states that an employer's defense to alleged discrimination against a disabled individual may include denying employment to individuals who pose a "direct threat to the health or safety of *other* individuals in the workplace." The Court then pointed out that the EEOC expands upon this language by stating that an individual shall not pose a direct threat to the health or safety *of the individual* or others in the workplace.

(Continued)

(Case 13.4 *continued*)

The Supreme Court rejected Echazabal's argument that the EEOC's regulation is wrong in light of the language of the ADA. The Court pointed out that although Congress did not include a reference to individuals in the language of the ADA, the language does not specifically exclude individuals from the regulation either. Thus, it can be inferred that the EEOC was free to recognize threats to self in its regulations.

The Court further stated that employers can make a statutory defense against violations of the ADA by claiming that denying employment to threatened individuals was "job-related and consistent with business necessity." The Court found that Chevron's reasons for denying employment to Echazabal were reasonable: Chevron wished to avoid time lost to sickness, excessive turnover from medical retirement or death, litigation under state tort law, and the risk of violating the Occupational Safety and Health Act (OSHA). Even though Echazabal argued that there is no known instance of OSHA being enforced against an employer that relied on the ADA to hire a worker willing to accept a risk to himself from his disability on the job, the Court said that the text of OSHA itself mandates that employers provide a workplace free from recognized hazards to *each and every* worker. Hence, the Court stated, if an employer hires an individual who knowingly consents to the particular dangers the job would pose to him, "there is no denying that the employer would be asking for trouble." The employer's decision to hire "would put Congress's policy in the ADA, a disabled individual's right to operate on equal terms within the workplace, at loggerheads with the competing policy of OSHA, to ensure the safety of all workers."

> RESULT   The Supreme Court reversed the judgment of the U.S. Court of Appeals for the Ninth Circuit, holding that the EEOC regulation authorizing an employer to refuse to hire an individual because his performance on the job would endanger his own health owing to a disability did not exceed the scope of permissible rulemaking under the ADA.

HIV DISCRIMINATION

A major issue today is the employer's relationship with an employee who has HIV disease, that is, an individual who has been infected with the human immunodeficiency virus (HIV). Due to advances in drug treatments, more individuals are living healthy, productive lives while infected with HIV. This is called asymptomatic HIV disease. When an individual's immune system is compromised and the person becomes ill due to HIV-related complications, the individual is considered symptomatic. Acquired immune deficiency syndrome (AIDS) refers to the most serious stage of symptomatic HIV disease.

Although the ADA does not specifically list HIV disease as a disability, in *Bragdon v. Abbott*,[120] the Supreme Court held that asymptomatic HIV-positive individuals are disabled within the meaning of the ADA.[121] The Court concluded that infection with HIV constitutes a physiological disorder that substantially limits the major life activity of reproduction. Although the HIV infection did not make it impossible for Abbott to reproduce, it substantially limited her ability to reproduce by (1) imposing on the man a significant risk of becoming infected and (2) creating a risk that the child would be infected during gestation and childbirth. The Court rejected the defendant's attempt to limit the phrase "major life activity" to those aspects of a person's life that have a public, economic, or daily character.

Applying *Bragdon*, the U.S. Court of Appeals for the Fifth Circuit found that an HIV-positive employee was not disabled under the ADA because he and his wife did not want more children. Thus, his major life activity of reproduction was not substantially limited.[122]

In the context of HIV disease, courts have narrowly construed the direct threat defense in accordance with medical evidence that HIV cannot be transmitted through casual contact. Thus, only those professions that

---

120. 524 U.S. 624 (1998).
121. John Gibeaut, *Filling a Need*, A.B.A. J., July 1997, at 48.

122. Blanks v. Southwestern Bell Communications, 310 F.3d 398 (5th Cir. 2002).

could lead to the transmission of bodily fluids, such as health-care workers, are given closer analysis under the direct threat exception.

Dealing with HIV Disease in the Workplace

An employer cannot justify discrimination against a person with AIDS on the basis of coworker or customer preference. Similarly, the fact that the employment of someone with AIDS will increase group health insurance costs or cause absenteeism does not make discrimination permissible.

Many states recognize either a common law or a constitutional right to privacy. This protects individuals from improper communication of their HIV status, even though the information is true and was properly obtained for a specific purpose. Communication of such personal information might be protected by the qualified-privilege defense as long as it is confined only to those people who have a legitimate need to know. General communication of someone's HIV status among coworkers is probably not protected by the privilege. Statutes prohibiting disclosure of medical information, specifically HIV-related information, may also be a source of employer liability. Thus, HIV-related information should be kept in confidence among individuals who need to know.

The employer also runs the risk of being sued for libel or slander if careless statements are made about employees. For example, falsely accusing an employee of having AIDS could be grounds for a defamation suit. Truth, however, is a complete defense.

GENETIC DISCRIMINATION

Approximately eighteen states have enacted laws banning genetic discrimination by insurers and employers. In 2000, President Clinton signed an executive order prohibiting federal departments and agencies from using genetic information in personnel decisions. In April 2000, the EEOC Commissioner announced that the ADA prohibits genetic discrimination pursuant to a 1995 policy guidance adopted by the EEOC. Although the ADA does not specifically refer to genetic discrimination, the statute's "regarded as disabled" prong includes discrimination on the basis of a diagnosed genetic predisposition toward an asymptomatic condition or illness.[123] Further information on genetic testing can be found in Chapter 12.

123. *EEOC Commissioner Says ADA Bans Genetic Discrimination,* CORP. COUNS. WKLY., Apr. 12, 2000, at 7.

ENFORCEMENT AND REMEDIES

Title I of the ADA is enforced in the same manner as Title VII of the Civil Rights Act of 1964, and the same remedies are available. Compensatory and punitive damages are subject to the same caps as those applicable to discrimination based on sex or religion.

Claims of disability discrimination are frequently enforced. Disability-related claims now account for about 19 percent of all discrimination charges filed by the EEOC.[124] The EEOC received 15,377 charges of disability discrimination in 2003.[125] That same year, it collected $45 million from parties charged with such discrimination (not including awards from litigation).

◆ Family and Medical Leave Act of 1993

The Family and Medical Leave Act (FMLA) of 1993[126] states that eligible employees are entitled to twelve weeks of unpaid leave per year. An employee may use leave under the Act in four situations: (1) the birth of a child; (2) the placement of an adopted or foster-care child with the employee; (3) care of a child, a parent, or a spouse; or (4) a serious health condition that renders the employee unable to do his or her job.

The FMLA has a number of specific guidelines regarding employee eligibility and employer obligations. To be eligible for a family leave, the employee must have worked at the place of employment for at least twelve months and have completed at least 1,250 hours of service to the employer during that twelve-month period.

To vindicate rights under the FMLA, a plaintiff may sue both the employer and his or her supervisor individually.[127] This interpretation is distinctive because a supervisor generally cannot be sued in his or her individual capacity under Title VII, the ADEA, or the ADA. In addition, despite states' immunity from private actions under the Eleventh Amendment, the U.S. Supreme

124. EEOC, *EEOC Issues Fiscal Year 2003 Enforcement Data* (Mar. 8, 2004).
125. EEOC, *Disability Discrimination* (Dec. 10, 2004), *at* http://www.eeoc.gov/types/ada.html.
126. Pub. L. No. 103-3, 107 Stat. 6 (codified at 5 U.S.C. § 6381 *et seq.* and 29 U.S.C. § 2601 et seq.) (1993).
127. Freeman v. Foley, 911 F. Supp. 326 (N.D. Ill. 1995). *But see* Mitchell v. Chapman, 343 F.3d 811 (6th Cir. 2003) (holding that the FMLA does not impose individual liability on public agency employees).

Court has held that employees can sue state employers for FMLA violations.[128]

The FMLA's requirements should be considered a floor, not a ceiling, for what employers can provide their employees in terms of leave. Even if employers provide for more generous leave, however, they must give employees notice regarding the consequences of taking the extra leave.[129]

An employee cannot contract out of his or her right to leave time under the FMLA. But the employer may require, or an employee may choose, to substitute any or all accrued paid leave for the leave time that is provided for under the Act. Employers have no obligation to give employees advance notice that their paid leave will be counted toward the unpaid leave provided by the FMLA.[130]

In general, the employer is required to restore the employee to the same position, or one with equivalent benefits, pay, and other terms and conditions of employment, following the expiration of the leave. But the employer is not required to reinstate key employees to their previous position if the employer determines that "such denial is necessary to prevent substantial and grievous economic injury to the operations of the employer." "Key employee" is defined as a salaried employee who is among the highest-paid 10 percent of the employees located within seventy-five miles of the facility at which the subject employee is employed. The EEOC regulations require the employer to notify an employee, at the time the leave is requested, of his or her status as a key employee and of the consequence of taking a leave.[131]

In *O'Connor v. PCA Family Health Plan, Inc.*,[132] the U.S. Court of Appeals for the Eleventh Circuit held that an employee taking leave under the FMLA does not have an absolute right to reinstatement if his or her employment is terminated during the leave as part of a general reduction in force (RIF) by the employer. The court explained: "An employee has no greater right to reinstatement or to other benefits and conditions of employment than if the employee had been continuously employed during the FMLA leave period." The burden of proof is on the employer denying reinstatement to show that it would have discharged the employee even if he or she had not been on FMLA leave.

Increasingly, employees are suing under the FMLA rather than the ADA to protect their rights.[133] The focus of the ADA is to demonstrate that an employee can work despite a disability, whereas one of the objectives of the FMLA is to provide time off to an employee who cannot work due to a serious health condition. In *Byrne v. Avon Products, Inc.*,[134] the U.S. Court of Appeals for the Seventh Circuit reinstated the FMLA claim of an employee who was terminated for repeatedly sleeping on the job after years of exemplary service. The court found that the ADA did not protect the employee because he could not do the job and was, as a result, not "qualified as an individual with a disability" who could "perform essential functions of the job." But, the court stated, Byrne's sudden behavior shift created a jury question as to whether he was entitled to FMLA leave.

◆ Affirmative Action

Affirmative-action programs are generally viewed as a means of remedying past acts of discrimination. Such programs are usually established pursuant to court orders, court-approved consent decrees, or federal and state laws that impose affirmative-action obligations on government contractors.

Executive Order 11246 requires federal government contractors to include in every government contract not exempted by the order provisions whereby the contractor agrees (1) not to discriminate in employment on the basis of race, color, religion, sex, or national origin; (2) to take affirmative steps to prevent discrimination; and (3) to file equal opportunity surveys every other year.[135] In some cases, a contractor's affirmative-action plan must be put in writing. Although individuals have no private right of action based on an alleged violation of the order, the Department of Labor, through its Office of Federal Contract Compliance Programs, can impose a wide range of sanctions, including terminating a government contract and disqualifying the contractor from entering into any future government contracts.[136] Government contractors are subject to affirmative-action obligations under other federal laws as well, including the Vocational Rehabilitation

128. Nev. Dep't of Human Res. v. Hibbs, 538 U.S. 721 (2003).
129. *See* Kosakow v. New Rochelle Radiology Assocs., P.C., 274 F.3d 706 (2d Cir. 2001).
130. *See* Ragsdale v. Wolverine World Wide, Inc., 535 U.S. 81 (2002).
131. Panza v. Grappone Cos., Civil No. 99-221-M, Opinion No. 2000 DNH 224 (D.N.H. Oct. 20, 2000).
132. 200 F.3d 1349 (11th Cir. 2000).

133. David L. Hudson Jr., *Changing Act: Family Leave Law Taking Center Stage from Disabilities Act in Litigation*, A.B.A. J., Sept. 2003, at 15.
134. 328 F.3d 379 (7th Cir. 2003).
135. Exec. Order No. 11,246, 3 C.F.R. 339 (1964–1965), *reprinted in* 42 U.S.C. § 2000e (1994).
136. The Office of Federal Contract Compliance Programs' new regulations overhauling the thirty-year-old requirements for affirmative action under Executive Order 11,246 were published in the November 13, 2000 issue of the *Federal Register,* 65 Fed. Reg. 68,021, and took effect on December 13, 2000.

Act of 1973 and the Vietnam Era Veterans' Readjustment Assistance Act of 1972.

As explained in Chapter 2, the U.S. Supreme Court held in *Adarand Constructors, Inc. v. Peña*[137] that government-mandated affirmative-action plans are subject to strict scrutiny under the Equal Protection Clause. In reinstating a reverse-discrimination claim by a white-owned construction company that lost a contract to a minority-owned business, the Court held that benign and invidious racial classifications should be subject to the same standards. This ruling was significant because it required the government to show a specific history of discrimination in order to justify preferential treatment of minority-owned businesses in government contracts.

In 1998, in *Lutheran Church–Missouri Synod v. FCC*,[138] the U.S. Court of Appeals for the District of Columbia Circuit struck down the Federal Communications Commission's affirmative-action requirements for radio and television broadcast licenses. The court held that *Adarand's* requirement of strict scrutiny applied not just to racial preferences in hiring but to any race-conscious decision making that affects employment opportunities even if it does not establish preferences, quotas, or set-asides. The court explained:

> [W]e do not think it matters whether a government hiring program imposes hard quotas, soft quotas, or goals. Any one of these techniques induces an employer to hire with an eye toward meeting the numerical target. As such, they can and surely will result in individuals being granted a preference because of their race.

The court also held that the FCC's interest in fostering diverse programming was not compelling. Even if the diversity goal could be deemed a compelling state interest, the court concluded that the FCC's equal employment opportunity rules were not narrowly tailored to foster diverse programming.

In January 2000, in response to *Lutheran Church,* the FCC adopted new rules to promote employment of women and minorities in the broadcast and cable television industries.[139] The rules require broadcast licensees to disseminate information about job openings to all members of the community to ensure that all applicants have the opportunity to compete for jobs. The FCC chair stated that the rules were designed to advance the goals of prohibiting discrimination in hiring and promoting diversity in broadcasting.[140]

Although government programs have been struck down by the courts, some affirmative-action programs by private employers have been accepted. For example, the U.S. Supreme Court upheld a collective bargaining agreement containing an affirmative-action plan giving preference to African-American employees entering skilled-craft training positions.[141] Concluding that Title VII did not preclude all private, voluntary, race-conscious affirmative-action programs, the Court noted that the plan (1) like Title VII, was designed to break down patterns of racial segregation and hierarchy; (2) "did not unnecessarily trammel the interests of white employees"; and (3) was a temporary measure intended to attain rather than maintain racial balance. The EEOC has promulgated regulations regarding voluntary affirmative-action plans.[142]

In *Taxman v. Board of Education*,[143] the U.S. Court of Appeals for the Third Circuit struck down a school board's affirmative-action plan as a violation of Title VII. The plan gave preference to minority teachers over nonminority teachers in layoff decisions when teachers were equally qualified. The court read the Supreme Court's ruling in *United Steelworkers v. Weber* as permitting race-based employment decisions only when they are necessary to remedy past discrimination. A mere desire to promote diversity in education was not sufficient to warrant a discriminatory policy. The U.S. Supreme Court granted the petition for certiorari and heard oral arguments, but the parties settled the case before the Court ruled. Several civil rights groups feared that the Supreme Court would use this case as an occasion to ban all affirmative-action programs, so they contributed the bulk of the money paid in the settlement.[144]

The Civil Rights Act of 1991 limited the ability of persons to challenge affirmative-action litigated judgments and consent decrees. A person cannot challenge a judgment or consent decree if any of the following three conditions is applicable: (1) the person had actual notice of the proposed judgment or order sufficient to let that person know that the judgment or decree might adversely affect the interests and legal rights of that person and had an opportunity to present objections; (2) the person had a reasonable opportunity to present objections to the judgment or order; or (3) the person's interests were adequately represented by another person who had previously challenged the judgment or order on the same legal grounds and with a similar factual situation.

137. 515 U.S. 200 (1995).
138. 141 F.3d 344 (D.C. Cir. 1998).
139. 47 C.F.R. pt. 73.2080 (2000).
140. *FCC Votes to Adopt New Rule on Equal Employment Opportunity,* 68 U.S.L.W. 2443 (Feb. 1, 2000).

141. United Steelworkers of Am. v. Weber, 443 U.S. 193 (1979).
142. *See* 29 C.F.R. § 1608.1–12 (1997).
143. 91 F.3d 1547 (3d Cir. 1996).
144. Eva M. Rodriguez, *Rights Group's Settlement Settles Little,* WALL ST. J., Nov. 24, 1997, at A3.

▶ ETHICAL CONSIDERATION

In *Grutter v. Bollinger*,[a] the Supreme Court upheld the University of Michigan Law School's admission policy, which took race and ethnicity into account in an effort to achieve student body diversity. The Law School's policy did not define diversity solely in terms of racial and ethnic status, although it reaffirmed the Law School's commitment to diversity with reference to the inclusion of African-American, Hispanic, and Native American students. It did not use numerical quotas, however. The policy had been challenged by a white applicant who claimed that it discriminated against her on the basis of race in violation of the Fourteenth Amendment. In an amicus curiae brief submitted in support of the Law School, the U.S. military asserted that a racially diverse officer corps was essential to its national security mission. The Court ruled that, at least for law schools, diversity was a compelling state interest.

Yet, in a companion case,[b] the Supreme Court invalidated the University of Michigan's undergraduate admissions policy, which used mechanistic numerical formulas to admit more applicants of color. Unlike the Law School—which included race and ethnicity as just two of many factors used to make admissions decisions—the undergraduate programs specified one set of required grade point averages and board scores for whites granted automatic admission and another, lower set of grades and board scores for non-whites granted automatic admission.

Many U.S. employers actively recruit and hire minority candidates. Is it ethical for employers to make hiring decisions based on race in order to promote workplace diversity? For example, should an employer choose a qualified minority candidate over a more qualified nonminority candidate to promote diversity? What if the two candidates are equally qualified for a particular job?

a. 539 U.S. 306 (2003) (Case 2.6).
b. Gratz v. Bollinger, 539 U.S. 244 (2003).

◆ Applicability of Civil Rights Laws to Temporary Workers

The EEOC has responded to the growth in the number of temporary or contingent workers by extending potential liability for discrimination against such workers to both the employment agencies or temporary staffing firms and their client-employers.[145] If both the staffing firm and its client have the right to control the worker, then they are treated as joint employers, and both are

subject to liability for both back and front pay as well as compensatory and punitive damages.

If the staffing firm learns that one of its clients has discriminated against a temporary employee, the firm should not assign other workers to that work site unless the client has taken the necessary corrective and preventive measures to ensure that the discrimination will not recur. Otherwise, the staffing firm will be liable along with the client if a worker later assigned to that client is subjected to similar misconduct.

◆ The Extraterritorial Reach of American Law

In 1991, Congress amended Title VII to protect U.S. citizens employed in a foreign country by a U.S. employer or a U.S.-controlled employer. The ADEA and the ADA also apply extraterritorially to the same extent as Title VII.

The EEOC has provided guidance on how to determine whether an entity is a U.S. employer.[146] The nationality of an entity is determined on a case-by-case basis, taking into consideration the following factors: (1) the entity's place of incorporation, (2) the principal place of business, (3) contacts within the United States, (4) the nationality of dominant shareholders and/or those holding voting control, and (5) the nationality and location of management. An entity that is incorporated in the United States will generally be deemed a U.S. entity.

Even if a foreign entity is not deemed to be a U.S. entity, it will still be covered if it is "controlled by" a U.S. entity. Title VII provides that the determination of whether a U.S. employer controls an entity is based on the interrelation of the companies' operations, common management, centralized control of labor relations, and common ownership or financial control of the U.S. employer and the foreign entity.[147]

Section 109 makes it clear, however, that "it shall not be unlawful," under either Title VII or the ADA, for an employer to act in violation of either statute if compliance would cause the employer to violate the law of the foreign country in which the employee's workplace is located. For example, an employer may be permitted to deny employment to women in a country that prohibits women from working, even though this practice is in violation of Title VII.

---

145. The text of the EEOC's guidance on the application of the employment-discrimination laws to contingent workers is available at http://www.eeoc.gov/policy/docs/conting.html (last modified July 6, 2000).

146. EEOC, *Enforcement Guidance on Application of Title VII and the Americans with Disabilities Act*, at http://www.eeoc.gov/policy/docs/extraterritorial-vii-ada.html (last modified Apr. 24, 2003).
147. 42 U.S.C. § 2000e-1(c)(3).

ECONOMIC PERSPECTIVE

GLOBALIZATION, CULTURAL NORMS, AND WORKPLACE DISCRIMINATION

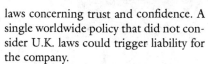

In 2004, Infosys Technologies, India's largest software exporter, settled its second sexual harassment lawsuit against one of its former officers and directors, Phaneesh Murthy. Murthy was accused of harassing two American women employed in Infosys's Fremont, California office. The suit sent shockwaves through Indian software companies with U.S. operations. In India, sexual harassment is widespread, but the Infosys suits caused Indian companies to realize that sexual harassment is taken seriously in the United States and that the possibility of lawsuits is very real.

In the current era of globalization, the interaction between the culture of a company's country of origin and the local culture and laws of its foreign branch offices is becoming more important. How multinational corporations should address this interaction as they create, implement, and maintain workplace diversity and antidiscrimination policies is the subject of much debate.

For example, many U.S. corporations, instilled with strong and well-established diversity and antidiscrimination views and practices, feel that it is important to implement a single global policy that applies to all employees in every country in order to create a corporate culture that clearly defines acceptable and unacceptable social norms. This worldwide approach may be based on the idea that certain sets of behaviors and practices are simply unacceptable for all people everywhere.

This global approach may encounter resistance from foreign employees who may view it as yet another way for Americans to impose their cultural standards on the rest of the world. For instance, kissing a work acquaintance may be the social norm in France and Italy. A corporate ban on displays of affection in the workplace could be viewed as offensive in these countries, even though its purpose is to prevent sexual harassment.

In Japan, it is generally acceptable to make distinctions based on such characteristics as age, gender, family, place of birth, ancestry, and education. Similarly, in Mexico, it is rare to find an indigenous Mexican manager or professional because individuals of European descent, who dominate the upper and middle classes, openly use family, social, and business ties to maintain advantages. As a result, a U.S.-mandated workplace policy that prohibits all decisions based on these characteristics may cause resentment and friction within the organization.

Because of these cultural differences, some companies have elected to create a single set of broad corporate values, but they implement these values differently at the local level based on the cultural norms and laws of each country in which the company operates. For example, a U.S. corporation could have a company-wide policy prohibiting sexual harassment and mandating investigation of all complaints. Yet this policy might be implemented differently in the United Kingdom, where an employer who questions employees and managers about alleged sexual harassment might violate laws concerning trust and confidence. A single worldwide policy that did not consider U.K. laws could trigger liability for the company.

In the wake of the Infosys lawsuits, Indian software companies have implemented this hybrid approach. For example, Indian multinational software giant Wipro, Ltd. instituted a company-wide discrimination policy including a sexual harassment policy, increased its focus on cross-cultural sensitivity training, and began to hire senior managers in its foreign offices to serve as workplace role models for Indian employees located there. "Today, geographic barriers are disappearing, and the way we do business is changing," said Nandan Nilekani, Infosys's chief executive. "Multicultural interaction is becoming a very important part of our work environment."

Sources: This discussion is based on *Discrimination Laws Vary from Country to Country*, CORP. COUNS. WKLY., Aug. 28, 2002, *at* http://pubs.bna.com/ip/bna/ccw.nsf/searchallviews/875e47bb58c936a085256c21007; Peggy Hazard, *Diversity: Think Locally for Global Success*, STRATEGIC HR REV., Aug. 2004, *available at* http://www.simonsassoc.com/html/new.html; Saritha Rai, *Harassment Suit in U.S. Shifts India's Work Culture*, N.Y. TIMES, Sept. 5, 2002, *available at* http://www.globalpolicy.org/globaliz/cultural/2002/0906india.htm.

Global View

DISCRIMINATION AND DIVERSITY

When engaging in business overseas, managers should familiarize themselves with the employment-discrimination laws of the foreign countries in which they are doing business.

EUROPEAN UNION

In the early 2000s, the European Commission, Parliament, and Council of Ministers adopted various directives aimed at preventing workplace discrimination on the basis of sex, religion, age, race, national origin, disability, and sexual orientation.[a] One directive was also modified to ban harassment as a form of discrimination on any of these grounds.[b] Although many of the European Union (EU) member states already had legislation prohibiting some types of discrimination, the new directives brought all of the varying national antidiscrimination laws together to ensure that antidiscrimination law was applied evenly in all EU countries. The EU Commissioner for Employment and Social Affairs commented that the new directives send a strong signal that the EU is not concerned simply with economics but "is also a community of values."[c]

Under the new directives, EU member states are required to (1) ban all forms of discrimination by 2006, (2) establish judicial or administrative bodies to enforce equal treatment in the workplace, and (3) remove any caps on awards for discrimination cases (although each member state is permitted to establish its own system of remedies). Any EU citizen claiming to be the victim of discrimination can also file a claim in the European Court of Justice in Luxembourg.

In trying discrimination cases, EU member states are required to utilize a burden of proof mechanism similar to the U.S. concepts of disparate treatment and disparate impact. "Disparate treatment" is called "direct discrimination," and "disparate impact" is called "indirect discrimination" in the EU. Direct discrimination analysis ensures that the burden of proof shifts if the complainant establishes "facts [from] which it may be presumed that there has been direct or indirect evidence of discrimination." The burden of proof for indirect discrimination states that indirect discrimination occurs "where a provision, criterion, or practice would put persons of a racial or ethnic origin at a particular disadvantage compared with other persons, unless that

provision, criterion, or practice is objectively justified by a particular aim." Like U.S. courts, European courts look at percentages to determine whether a protected class has been disadvantaged by a particular employment practice.

However, the Burden of Proof Directive, which became effective in October 2001, has caused the European system of analysis to differ from the U.S. system by shifting the burden of proof from employees to employers in cases of sex discrimination. Other European Commission directives have implemented similar rules regarding discrimination on the basis of race. For example, in the United Kingdom, if the facts indicate that there has been discrimination of some kind, then the employer is asked to give an explanation. Without a clear and specific explanation, unlawful discrimination will be inferred from the facts. If an employer hires a man, rather than a woman who is better qualified, then a tribunal can infer that the employer discriminated against the woman on grounds of gender unless the employer can show that its decision was based on other grounds. It might, for instance, have chosen the man because he appeared better motivated at the interview. This burden of proof method makes it easier for employees to prove direct discrimination in a court of law.

Even though the European Commission has mandated that all member states have uniform laws regarding employment discrimination, each member state implements and utilizes these directives in different ways.

JAPAN

Article 14 of the Japanese Constitution provides that "all of the people are equal under the law and there shall be no discrimination in political, economic or social relations because of race, creed, sex, social status, or family origin."[d] Despite this provision, Japanese antidiscrimination law is not very developed. Japan has no statutes prohibiting discrimination on the basis of race or national origin (most likely because Japan is generally a racially homogeneous society), and its laws regarding age, disability, and sex discrimination do not contain substantial enforcement provisions.

For example, although Japanese employers are required to maintain a certain ratio of disabled employees in the workplace,[e]

a. Equal Treatment Directive, European Parliament and Council Directive 2002/73/EC, 2002 O.J. (L 269); Equal Treatment Framework Directive, Council Directive 2000/78/EC, 2000 O.J. (L 308) (Nov. 27); Race Equality Directive, Council Directive 2000/43/EC, 2000 O.J. (L 180) 22 (June 29).
b. Council Directive 2002/73/EC, 2002 O.J. (L 269) 15 (Oct. 5).
c. Vikram Dodd & Andrew Osborn, *New Laws for EU on Bias in Workplace*, GUARDIAN, Oct. 19, 2000.

d. *See generally* INTERNATIONAL LABOR AND EMPLOYMENT LAWS 32-50–32-52 (Timothy J. Dorby & William L. Keller eds., 2003).
e. Japanese law does protect disabled workers from discrimination in termination, hiring, or harassment, however.

(Continued)

(Global View *continued*)

employers who violate this law are simply required to pay a nominal penalty to the government. In addition, Japanese law prohibits age discrimination in hiring or recruiting (but not termination), but the punishment for a violation is limited to posting the employer's name in the local newspaper.

Laws regarding sex discrimination are the most highly developed discrimination laws in Japan. There was a surge in the number of sexual harassment claims in Japan in the 1990s. Most of these cases were tort claims resulting from physical contact or sexual assaults. One Japanese district court has held that a hostile work environment can also constitute an actionable tort because it infringes on the employee's human dignity and causes working conditions to deteriorate.

In June 1997, Japan's Equal Employment Opportunity Law of 1985 (EEOL) was drastically revised to provide more protection for women in the workplace. The 1997 amendment includes a provision imposing on employers a duty to prevent sexual harassment. The EEOL also prohibits discrimination against women in employment recruitment, hiring, assignment, promotion, training, education, fringe benefits, and termination. The 1997 amendment includes sanctions, which were not present in the original law, to enforce these new provisions. In addition, when an employer violates the EEOL, the Labor Minister can publicize that fact.

Although twelve women were successful in procuring a court order upholding a $1.6 million award against a company for systematically discriminating against them in pay and promotions, most recent Japanese job seekers, labor lawyers, economists, and women's rights advocates interviewed by the *New York Times* said that the new law has "had little real impact, and the old patterns of consignment of women to noncareer positions [has] continued unabated."[f]

INDIA

Indian antidiscrimination law has developed slowly since the implementation of the Indian constitution in 1950. The constitution prohibits discrimination in employment on the basis of religion, race, caste, sex, descent, place of birth, or residence.[g]

Perhaps the greatest struggle for equal rights has involved members of the Dalit caste (formerly called "untouchables").

These people occupy India's lowest caste and are viewed as unclean by higher-caste Hindus. In an effort to end the caste system, India passed the Protection of Civil Rights Act, 1955.[h] One purpose of this Act was to enable Dalits to obtain jobs other than the low-paying and undesirable occupations to which they were traditionally relegated. As a result, the Indian government started an affirmative-action system for Dalits by implementing hiring quotas and special training programs in employment.[i] Christian Dalits, however, are not eligible for this program, although Buddhist and Sikh Dalits maintain eligibility. Some Indian states also reserve special government jobs for Muslim Dalits.[j]

The Indian government has started an affirmative-action program for citizens with disabilities as well. The Persons with Disabilities Act of 1995 mandates that 3 percent of government jobs be reserved for the disabled.[k]

The Indian government passed its first law regarding rights for women in the workplace in 1948. The law prohibited women from cleaning certain machinery in factories and granted female factory workers maternity leave for up to twelve weeks.[l] Since then, other laws mandating equal pay, maternity benefits, and equal opportunity in hiring have been passed. Sexual harassment is perhaps the most recent area of gender antidiscrimination law to be developed. In 1997, the Indian Supreme Court recognized sexual harassment in the workplace as not only a personal injury to the affected woman but also a violation of her fundamental human rights. In its ruling, the Supreme Court issued guidelines making employers responsible for both preventive and remedial measures to make the workplace safe for women.[m]

f. Howard W. French, *Diploma in Hand, Japanese Women Find Glass Ceiling Reinforced with Iron*, N.Y. TIMES, Jan. 1, 2001.
g. Unesco, *India—Constitution, available at* http://www.unesco.org/most/rr3indi.htm (last visited Jan. 16, 2005). Note that Indian law does not prohibit discrimination based on age.

h. Hillary Mayel, *India's "Untouchables" Face Violence, Discrimination*, NAT'L GEOGRAPHIC NEWS, July 2, 2003, http://news.nationalgeographic.com/news/2003/06/0602_030602_untouchables.html.
i. Andre Beteille, *Discrimination at Work*, THE HINDU, Nov. 7, 2002, http://www.thehindu.com/2002/07/11/stories/2002071100101000.htm.
j. Minority Rights Group, *India's Dalit Christians Face Caste Discrimination and Loss of Government Assistance* (Mar. 15, 2004), *at* http://www.minorityrights.org/news_detail.asp?ID=230.
k. Sugita Katyal, *India's Disabled Struggle for Survival* (Jan. 29, 2003), http://www.accessibility.com.au/news/articles/india.htm.
l. The Mines Act of 1952. *See* Ajmal Edappagath, *Gender Sensitive Legislative Legislation and Policies in India* (2001), http://www.unescap.org/esid/GAD/Events/EGMICT2001/edappagath.pdf.
m. Laxmi Murthy, *The Cost of Harassment*, INDIANEST.COM, Aug. 11, 2002, *at* http://www.boloji.com/wfs/wfs066.htm.

THE RESPONSIBLE MANAGER

HONORING EMPLOYEES' CIVIL RIGHTS

Managers must be diligent in preventing and correcting any unlawful discrimination either in the preemployment process or during employment. Management should develop a written policy, which (1) clearly outlines discriminatory acts prohibited by federal, state, and local statutes and (2) prohibits retaliation against employees who complain about discrimination. Employees should be advised that any form of discrimination is inappropriate. The policy should have an enforcement mechanism and should clearly state that violations of the policy will result in poor performance reviews or termination. Such a policy will not only curb discriminatory acts but will also demonstrate that management diligently attempted to prevent such behavior in the event that litigation should arise.

The firm should also create a working environment in which employees feel comfortable bringing complaints against fellow workers and supervisors. There should be at least two individuals in the company, a male and a female, to whom such complaints may be brought. Because supervisors are often the discriminators, an employee should not be required to first complain to his or her supervisor. Managers should not keep reports of harassment confidential, even if requested to do so by the employee. Each complaint should be thoroughly investigated, and, if necessary, the violator should be punished.

Although the establishment of a comprehensive policy is one way to prevent unlawful discriminatory practices, it is not sufficient in itself. Managers must also abide by the policy and comply with all federal, state, and local statutes prohibiting unlawful discrimination; supervisors should undergo training regarding such laws.[148] If management participates in discriminatory acts, the firm's employees will have little incentive to abide by its policy against discrimination and will hesitate to bring a claim for discriminatory treatment.

It is crucial that employers make sure that they do not retaliate against employees who have filed discrimination claims. Although employers often perceive discrimina-

tion claims by an employee as an act of disloyalty, retaliation for these claims will make it more likely that they will be found liable by a jury or judge even if the initial claim would not have supported liability.

Employers should also create nondiscriminatory policies and procedures for hiring new employees. The employer should avoid relying on word-of-mouth recruitment practices, which tend to reach a disproportionate number of persons of the same race or ethnicity as the employer's current employees and should utilize media designed to reach people in both minority and nonminority communities. When advertising vacant positions, employers should use a job posting system that allows for an open and fair application process. The job advertisements themselves should not express a preference or limitation based on race, color, religion, gender, national origin, or age, unless such specifications are based on bona fide occupational qualifications.

Employers should also train employees in interviewing to ensure that interviewers ask proper questions and use objective hiring criteria. Although federal laws do not expressly prohibit preemployment inquiries concerning an applicant's race, color, national origin, sex, marital status, religion, or age, such inquiries are disfavored because they create an inference that these factors will be used as selection criteria. These inquiries may also be expressly prohibited under state law. As a general rule, recruitment personnel should ask themselves, "What information do I really need to decide whether an applicant is qualified to perform this job?"

With respect to the ADA, employers should be proactive and engage in an interactive process with employees requesting accommodation. According to David Fram, director of equal employment opportunities and ADA services at the National Employment Law Institute, "Lack of communication is a big cause of lawsuits. If you share with someone how hard you're trying, he or she is likely to be less mad."[149] If an employer explores every option but still cannot find a way to provide an accom-

---

148. California codified this recommendation in 2004 by requiring that all supervisors employed in companies of more than fifty employees undergo harassment training every two years. CAL. GOV'T CODE § 12950.1 (West 2004).

149. *Interactive Process Helps Employers Prevail, but Isn't Required,* CORP. COUNS. WKLY., Jan. 10, 2001, at 12.

(Continued)

(The Responsible Manager *continued*)

modation, the employer should inform the individual and ask if he or she has any advice.[150] Employers should create a paper trail to document the actions they took to find an accommodation. While focusing on finding an accommodation, the employer should refrain from determining whether the employee is actually disabled and allow the courts to make that determination.

Employers may also want to purchase employment practice liability insurance (EPLI) to protect against discrimination claims. Although these insurance plans were expensive, did not have broad coverage, and excluded punitive damages when they were introduced in the early

150. *Id.*

1990s, by the late 1990s, more carriers had entered the market, resulting in lower prices and expanded coverage.

Dating and romantic relationships between employees at a company can lead to discrimination and sexual harassment claims, particularly when there is a significant power and age gap between partners. Such relationships are very perilous. If the parties have a falling out, the subordinate may claim that the relationship was not consensual and say that he or she feared adverse employment consequences for rebuffing the manager's advances. To address this problem, IBM instituted a policy that a manager may become involved with a subordinate as long as the manager transfers to another job within or outside the company so that he or she is not supervising or evaluating the performance of the subordinate involved.

INSIDE STORY

FROM WALL STREET TO MAIN STREET, WOMEN DEMAND EQUAL OPPORTUNITY

In 1973, Helen O'Bannon, who had graduated with honors from Wellesley College and received a Master's degree in economics from Stanford University, applied for a job as a stockbroker at Merrill Lynch. The firm gave O'Bannon a test that included the question, "When you meet a woman, what interests you the most about her: (a) her beauty; (b) her intellect." She later learned that applicants received more points for choosing "beauty" than "intellect." When Merrill Lynch turned down her application, O'Bannon filed a class-action sex discrimination lawsuit against Merrill, which resulted in Merrill's 1976 agreement to comply with U.S. civil rights laws and to hire applicants based on their qualifications instead of their gender.[151]

Twenty-one years later, eight women filed another class-action sex discrimination lawsuit against Merrill. The women alleged that they received lower compensation and had fewer opportunities for advancement than men. The *Cremin v. Merrill Lynch* lawsuit was settled in 1998 when the class representatives accepted a dispute resolution process that, under certain circumstances, led to arbitration. Since that time, almost one thousand women have filed claims against Merrill, most of which were resolved privately through negotiation and mediation.

151. *Now ACTS: Join Us!, at* http://www.nownyc.org/news/julyaug00news/nowacts2.htm (last visited Feb. 16, 2005).

In April 2004, a panel of arbitrators found that Merrill had engaged in a "pattern and practice of discrimination" and ordered it to pay $2.2 million to Hydie Sumner, a broker who had worked in Merrill's San Antonio, Texas office.[152] This decision was the largest award to date stemming from the *Cremin* dispute resolution process.

In August 2004, the *New York Times* published an article about claims filed early on by Valery and Janine Craane, a high-revenue generating mother-daughter stockbroker team known as the Craane Group, that sex discrimination at Merrill had cost them tens of millions of dollars in lost compensation.[153] Valery Craane, who started at Merrill in the early 1970s, claims that she and Janine did not receive big accounts, were passed over when Merrill allotted shares of new stocks and initial public offering shares to brokers, and did not receive the same type of administrative and emotional support as their male colleagues. The Craanes asserted that sex

152. Susan Antilla, *Merrill's Woman Problem—What Men Didn't Know,* Nov. 29, 2004, *at* http://www.bloomberg.com/apps/news?pid=10000039&sid=aLk_rlImn86Y&refer=columnist_antilla.
153. Patrick McGreehan, *What Merrill's Women Want,* N.Y. TIMES, Aug. 22, 2004, available at http://www.nytimes.com/2004/08/02/business/yourmoney/22sex.html.

(Continued)

(Inside Story *continued*)

discrimination at Merrill continued because "it was like a fraternity," with Merrill managers regularly going to strip clubs with male brokers.[154] According to Janine Craane, "You have your boys, your soldiers, the guys that you trust. Whether they're not so talented is maybe not so important as their loyalty to the group."[155] The men simply feel that "women don't belong."[156]

The women at Merrill Lynch are not the only women on Wall Street who believe they have been treated unfairly by their employer. In the late 1990s, a class action was filed against Smith Barney on behalf of more than 20,000 current and former female employees who alleged that they were subjected to a hostile work environment. Smith Barney settled this action by agreeing to allow female employees to bring their claims before a selected arbitrator.[157] In July 2004, Morgan Stanley announced a $54 million settlement of a class-action sex discrimination lawsuit brought by its women employees.[158]

At about the same time, a federal district court judge in California certified a class of approximately 1.6 million current and former female Wal-Mart employees in a class-action lawsuit claiming that Wal-Mart failed to promote women to management and to pay them the same wages as similarly situated men.[159] This class action against the nation's largest employer is the largest workplace sex discrimination lawsuit in U.S. history.

The lawyers who brought the class-action lawsuit say their goal is to pressure Wal-Mart to change the way that it behaves toward its more than 700,000 female employees. Wal-Mart stores generally did not advertise openings for managerial trainees, and male managers frequently pinpointed men for "the management track."[160]

Although women comprise almost 90 percent of Wal-Mart's cashiers, only 15.5 percent of its store managers are women. In addition, men at all levels are generally paid more. Stephanie Odle, an assistant store manager in Riverside, California, was surprised to learn that a male assistant manager at the same store was making approximately $25,000 per year more than she did. When she confronted the district manager about the salary difference, he replied that the other "assistant manager has a family and two children to support."[161] Stephanie is a single mother.

Like the women of Wall Street, the Wal-Mart plaintiffs assert that the Wal-Mart culture "did not take them seriously" and included "visits to strip clubs for managers and clients."[162] A store manager told one plaintiff: "Men are here to make a career and women aren't. Retail is for housewives who just need to earn extra money."[163]

With such a large class, any settlement by Wal-Mart could cost the company billions of dollars, even if individual plaintiffs receive small awards. The day after the class was certified, shares of Wal-Mart's stock fell 1.8 percent on the New York Stock Exchange. Wal-Mart opposed the class-action certification, claiming that it does not have a "centralized employment policy and that individual stores and district managers, rather than headquarters, make decisions on pay and promotions."[164] The plaintiffs, however, disproved these claims. As Judge Jenkins, who certified the Wal-Mart class, noted:

> The plaintiffs' request for class certification is being ruled upon in a year that marks the 50th anniversary of the Supreme Court's decision in *Brown v. Board of Education*. This anniversary serves as a reminder of the importance of the courts in addressing the denial of equal treatment under the law wherever and by whomever it occurs.[165]

To help improve its image, Wal-Mart has spent millions of dollars on television advertisements showing that it treats women well. It also announced that all senior managers would lose 7.5 percent of their bonuses in the next year if women were not promoted in direct proportion to the numbers that applied for management jobs.

154. *Id.*
155. *Id.*
156. *Id.*
157. Richard H. Block & M. Alexis Pennotti, *Reducing Sex Bias Liability on Wall Street*, NAT'L L. J., Jan. 21, 2005, available at http://www.law.com/jsp/article.jsp?id=1105364095728.
158. Betsy Morris, *How Corporate America Is Betraying Women*, FORTUNE, Jan. 10, 2005, at 66, 67.
159. Associated Press, *Judge Approves Wal-Mart Class Action Case*, Forbes.com, June 22, 2004, *at* http://www.forbes.com/feeds/ap/2004/06/22/ap1426888.html.
160. Steven Greenhouse & Constance L. Hays, *Wal-Mart Sex-Bias Suit Given Class Action Status*, N.Y. TIMES, June 23, 2004, at A-1.

161. William Rodamor, *The Class of '04*, CAL. LAW., Sept. 2003, at 22.
162. Greenhouse and Hays, *supra* note 160.
163. *Id.*
164. *Id.*
165. Rodamor, *supra* note 161.

KEY WORDS AND PHRASES

bona fide occupational qualification (BFOQ) 477
BFOQ defense 477
disparate impact 465

disparate treatment 464
fetal-protection policy 475
hostile environment harassment 466
quid pro quo harassment 466

reasonable factor other than age (RFOA) defense 480

46

STRATEGY FOR ETHICAL DECISION MAKING

When confronted with a problem, a person can take any number of actions. Some actions may be useful, whereas others may create more problems. Philosophers have developed various ethical decision-making models to help a person resolve a dilemma. Some models are more complex than others.

The following is a decision-making model that can be used to resolve the ethical problems related to business that begin each chapter of this book.[10] This model has the following six steps:

1. *FACTS.* Gather all the necessary facts, including whether any state or federal statutes apply. Once you have examined the facts, you will be able to define the problem you are facing.

2. *STAKEHOLDERS.* List all the stakeholders that may be affected by the decision.

3. *VALUES.* List all the personal and work-related values involved in the particular case. These values may include one or more of the following:

    a. *Religious values.*

    b. *Citizenship*, such as respect for law or social consciousness.

    c. *Honesty*, such as truth telling, candidness, or openness.

    d. *Integrity*, such as acting on convictions, courageous acts, advocacy, or leadership by example.

    e. *Promise keeping*, such as fulfilling the spirit of commitments.

    f. *Loyalty*, such as fidelity or confidentiality;

    g. *Fairness*, such as justice, equal treatment, diversity, or independence.

    h. *Caring*, such as compassion or kindness.

    i. *Respect*, such as human dignity or uniqueness.

    j. *Excellence*, such as quality of work.

    k. *Accountability*, such as responsibility or independence.

4. *ALTERNATIVE ACTIONS.* List all the possible alternative actions that you could choose to do.

5. *PRIORITIZATION.* Choose and prioritize in answering the following questions:

    a. Which stakeholder do you believe is the most important in this situation?

---

10. Created by Dr. Arthur Gross Schaefer, Loyola Marymount University, Los Angeles, California.

b. Which of the likely consequences do you believe will cause the greatest good or the least harm?

6. *POTENTIAL ACTION.* Make a decision as to which stakeholder should prevail and determine a strategy (course of action) to carry out that decision.

A SAMPLE CASE: USING THE MODEL FOR ETHICAL DECISION MAKING

A secretary has worked for your corporation for fifteen years. She is involved in a car accident in which she permanently loses the use of her right hand. Thus, she can no longer effectively type, file, or perform many of the other functions that she previously had performed and that are included in her job description. Your corporation has a very tight budget and does not have sufficient funds to pay for an additional secretary without reallocating budget items. The injured secretary has been very loyal to your corporation, and you have been very satisfied with her work and dedication. She wants to stay in her job. Moreover, she does not believe she could find other employment at this time. Should your corporation fire her, lay her off with compensation, or find a way to retain her? The following is an example of how to apply the model to a case.

1. FACTS. Gather all the necessary facts, including whether any state or federal statutes apply. Once you have examined the facts, you will be able to define the problem you are facing.

Three things need to be reviewed: the statutes, the secretary, and the budget. First, the Americans with Disabilities Act may apply. Second, review with the injured secretary exactly what duties she can and cannot do under the job description. Third, review to see if the budget can be modified by allocating funds from another category to the secretarial category if you decide to retain the worker.

In your interview with the secretary, you must find out if there are any rehabilitation or treatment programs that would allow her to regain the use of her right hand. Find out if there are technological devices that would allow her to type using a computer and to do other things with one hand. Ascertain her current financial position and what she would like to do. It is important to learn how the remaining secretarial staff feels about performing the additional duties once performed by the injured secretary.

After reviewing the above, based on the medical facts, you determine that the secretary cannot physically perform many of the essential duties of her job description. There is no way to accommodate her in their performance. If you terminate her, you would not violate the Americans with Disabilities Act, because she cannot perform the essential functions of her job and no way exists to reasonably accommodate her.

The budget is very tight but would allow a shift of funds among some categories. The problem is whether to retain the secretary, even though she cannot perform many of the required duties. You may resolve this problem by using the rest of the decision-making model.

2. STAKEHOLDERS. List all the stakeholders that may be affected by the decision:

a. Your corporation.
b. The injured secretary.
c. The secretarial staff.
d. The management staff.
e. The general community.

3. VALUES. List all the personal and work-related values involved in the particular case:

a. *Loyalty.* As the secretary has given her loyalty to your corporation, so should the corporation show its loyalty to her.

b. *Fairness.* The rest of the secretarial staff will have to perform many of the secretary's old duties.

c. *Respect.* Although disabled, the secretary is still a very talented individual who has contributed a great deal to your corporation.

d. *Integrity.* Your corporation should be in the forefront of making room for long-term loyal employees who have become disabled.

e. *Accountability.* The managerial staff is responsible for using corporate funds wisely and for providing essential services within the financial resources of the corporation.

4. ALTERNATIVE ACTIONS. List all the possible alternative actions that you could choose to do:

a. Do not retain the injured secretary because of the budget.

b. Do not retain the injured secretary because of the budget, but offer her an attractive severance package.

c. Retain the secretary even though the budget does not accommodate the salary of an additional secretary. Restructure the duties so that the remaining secretarial staff will assume many of her previous duties.

d. Retain the secretary by changing the budgetary priorities to accommodate the salary of an additional secretary.

5. PRIORITIZATION. Choose and prioritize in answering the following questions:

a. Which stakeholder do you believe is the most important in this situation? The injured secretary.

b. Which value do you believe to be the highest value in this situation? Integrity that includes leadership by example.

c. Which of the choices do you believe will cause the greatest good or the least harm? Finding a means to increase or restructure the budget in order to be able to retain the injured secretary and to hire additional secretarial help.

6. POTENTIAL ACTION. Retaining the secretary by increasing or restructuring the budget. Consider working with rehabilitation specialists from an insurance company, a health care provider, or from the state's workers compensation office. This action will create an affirmative atmosphere among the employees, who will see the corporation treating a fellow employee with respect when she is confronted with the potentially devastating combination of paralysis and unemployment. This action also will provide stability in the workplace.

The above solution represents one analysis of an ethical problem. Another decision with different results could be reached, for example, if the budget were not able to accommodate the retention of the secretary. No perfect answer exists.

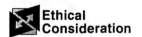
**Ethical
Consideration**

To Play or Not to Play Hardball

You are the president of an insurance company that insures a new company called Women Helping Women. This company heavily advertises that its products are designed to be especially safe because they are made by women for women.

One of the products is a hair dye that from its introduction sells very well and has a projected net income of $25 million for the first year. After the product is on the market for a period of time, you begin to hear scattered reports and read magazine accounts that this hair dye may have caused unhealthy side effects, such as severe hair loss, burned scalps, and permanent facial disfigurement. The number of persons who may be injured is projected to be between six and thirteen users per 100,000.

As a routine matter, you receive copies of all complaints of $1 million or more filed against your insureds. You receive a copy of a complaint filed by a woman seeking $5 million in damages for injuries suffered from using the hair dye. You are concerned that if representative from Women Helping Women or anyone from your company makes public acknowledgment that the hair dye is not perfectly safe, others will be encouraged to bring similar claims. Your insurance company will end up paying these claims.

You call in your chief legal counsel,. who has reviewed the complaint. He informs you that the law office handling the lawsuit against Women Helping Women is quite small and not experienced. He suggests that he assign a group of attorneys to the case. These attor-

neys will generate so many motions, requests to produce documents, requests for physical and mental examinations, depositions, and interrogatories that the plaintiff and her attorneys will be overwhelmed. They will be forced to give up or to take a small settlement. If this approach does not work, your counsel will be able to intentionally postpone the trial for several years. This tactic will wear the plaintiff out financially, if not emotionally. It also will deter anyone else from trying to bring a legal action against your client.

Even though you believe that the hair dye may have caused the alleged injuries, what course of action should you follow? Use the ethical model in Chapter 2 to develop your answer.

Ethical Consideration

FULL DISCLOSURE IN ARBITRATION?

A homeowner signed a contract with a builder to build a new home. A dispute arose between the homeowner and the building contractor. Among the many items under dispute, she is claiming that the contractor failed to install below-surface drains as specified in the building plans. She comes to you because she wants to file a lawsuit against the contractor.

You review the contract between the builder and your client. A clause in the contract requires that all disputes will be resolved by arbitration. Arbitration is a formal procedure used by parties to a dispute. The matter is submitted by the parties to an impartial third party called an arbitrator. Arbitra-tion is used in place of a lawsuit as a way to quickly and inexpensively resolve disputes.

As you prepare for the arbitration hearing, you come across an old memorandum in the homeowner's handwriting that could be interpreted as acknowledging that she knew the drains had not been installed and that she had relieved the contractor of liability for the drainage system in exchange for some additional work on the new house. When you talk with the homeowner, she states that it is the only copy, and she is sure that the contractor has forgotten about it because it was written during a particularly hectic part of the construction project.

You are aware that discovery procedures prior to arbitration hearings are either nonexistent or are so limited in scope that you will probably not have to involuntarily provide this document to the other side. If this matter were before a regular court, you most likely would be required to turn over a copy of this document to the attorney representing the contractor. Do you have any duty to supply this document to the other side prior to the hearing, or at least to present it at the proceeding? Use the ethical model in Chapter 2 to develop your answer.

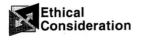

Ethical Consideration

GOOD ADVERTISING?

You are the advertising manager for a local television station. You decide which commercials will be aired and when. You have just received a commercial for a lawyer in town. The commercial depicts a casually dressed man who looks into the television camera and announces firmly that he was an accident victim and that this lawyer "got me $155,000, even though the police report said that I was totally at fault." The next scene in the commercial shows another accident victim relaxing around a pool. This person states that the same lawyer recovered a million dollars "from an insurance company that said I didn't even have a claim." Although you are aware that freedom of speech is an important right, you are personally disgusted by these types of advertisements, which you believe have an insidious negative effect on the image of lawyers and on the judicial system as a whole. Should you reject or air the commercials? Use the ethical model in Chapter 2 to develop your answer.

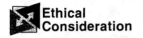
Ethical Consideration

CONFLICTS BETWEEN FREEDOM OF SPEECH AND ETHICS

You are a government employee working for the Nuclear Regulatory Agency. Already overwhelmed with requests for various reports, you have received still another request. A congressional committee needs information on the level of training required for personnel who work in the various reactors around the country. You have no idea when you will have time to write this report. The agency requires all congressional inquiries to be answered within ten working days. You do not even know how to obtain this information, because the agency does not require that it be kept.

As often happens, you are visited by a lobbyist from a company involved in the manufacture of nuclear power plants. She wants to discuss some pending legislation. In the course of the conversation, you explain your dilemma, and she volunteers to find out the information for you. You know that it is a common practice to obtain information from lobbyists and that their information generally is reliable.

Should you accept or decline this offer? Use the ethical model in Chapter 2 to develop your answer.

Ethical Consideration

BEYOND THE INSURANCE POLICY

You are the president of Shop'n Serve Mini Markets, a regional chain of all-night minimarkets. Several months ago, an armed robber threatened the clerk's life in one of your stores. Although the clerk was not harmed physically, he was severely traumatized. The company's medical policy allows for 20 hours of psychological counseling. Since the robbery the employee has already used the 20 hours and still is too afraid to return to work. The therapist has recommended a regimen of treatment that will exceed 100 additional hours. The employee does not have the money for the supplementary sessions. Should the company pay for the additional treatment? Please use the ethical model in Chapter 2 to develop your answer.

Ethical Consideration

MEDIA'S RESPONSIBILITY WHEN REPORTING ABOUT FAMILIES OF PUBLIC FIGURES

Senator Big Success had a teenage son, Small Success. The son, who otherwise had a spotless record, recently was arrested for shoplifting some small items in a grocery store. When he was arrested, Small Success had ample money in his wallet to pay for the items. He told the police that he had come into the store without the intent to steal. He said he was tired of the pressure to live up to the many expectations placed on him because of his father's prominence and that while in the store, he had a sudden whim to do something "bad." The items he took were of an insignificant monetary value. The city attorney decided not to prosecute, out of respect for the senator and because the store was paid in full for the items.

You are the editor of the *Morning Glory,* the local newspaper. One of your reporters wants to write up this story with a focus on how celebrities and politicians do not take the time to be good parents who teach their children right from wrong. Although you have no problem running stories about Senator Big Success, who is a public figure, you wonder if it is fair to put such a public spotlight on the actions of his young son. In addition, the story also might bring up the decision not to prosecute. It might then force the city attorney to prosecute Small Success, which would create negative publicity and blemish his record. Do you let your reporter go ahead with the story or assign her to another project? Use the ethical model in Chapter 2 to develop your answer.

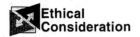
Ethical Consideration

FINDERS KEEPERS: IS THERE AN OBLIGATION TO DISCLOSE WHEN A DEAL IS NOT FAIR?

You love to shop at garage sales and have found many good bargains in the process. You stop at one home that has many items on the lawn. A young boy greets you and tells you that these items were from an old trunk found in the attic. He tells you that he is earning money to spend when the family takes their summer vacation.

As you browse through the various items, you pick up a small box that has a variety of items in it, including an old baseball. As you idly finger the baseball, you turn it over and cannot believe what you see. Trying not to act too excited, you take a second look and now are sure that this baseball was signed by Babe Ruth.

You know that this baseball is worth a lot of money. When you ask how much the boy wants for the junk in the box, he asks you if five dollars would be too much. Do you tell him about the Babe Ruth baseball or simply pay the five dollars and walk away? Use the ethical model in Chapter 2 to develop your answer.

Ethical Consideration

The Value of a Handshake: The Statute of Frauds as a Sword

You have been graduated from college and have landed your first job. After working for a while, you have saved enough money for a down payment on a new sports car and decide to sell your old Peugeot, which served you well while you were in college. You place an advertisement in the newspaper asking $3,000 for the car. You expect to sell the car for around $2,500. The advertisement generates interest, and you invite a prospective buyer to your home to examine the car. After the buyer looks at the car, she offers you $2,700. She recently was divorced, and as a single mother of four children, she needs the car for her family. As you shake her hand in acceptance of her offer, you hear the telephone ring. The person on the telephone tells you that he is calling from his car telephone across the street. He came to buy the car, and as he drove up, he saw you shake hands with the first buyer. He wants the car and offers you $3,000 in cash. When you tell him that you have already agreed to sell the car, he reminds you that the agreement is not legally binding, because you have not put anything in writing or signed over the owner's certificate of title. He then says that he will pay an extra $200 above the $3,000 if you sell the car to him. He needs it for a movie. To whom should you sell the car? Use the ethical model in Chapter 2 to develop your answer.

Ethical Consideration

SAFE PRODUCTS, AT WHAT COST?

You are the president of a company that manufactures a popular motorcycle called Distance Runner. Although you compete with several giant corporations in the motorcycle market, your highly successful innovative designs, including a gas tank with double the normal capacity, have made your company very profitable. Although your bike is relatively safe, you are aware that in case of an accident, the large-capacity gas tank is more likely than a normal gas tank to rupture, leading to spilled gas that could cause a fire. This danger is disclosed in bold print in the owner's manual.

A confidential internal report states that 5 percent of your motorcycles will probably be involved in accidents in which the fire from the ruptured gas tank will cause death to the cyclist. Generally, these accidents are caused when the driver exceeds the speed limit and loses control. The report suggests that the tank could be reduced in size and made safer, thus reducing the risk of rupture to 1 percent. The increased cost of the motorcycle and the loss of the double-sized gas tank, however, would probably reduce your sales by well over 20 percent. This large reduction would force you to lay off a significant number of your employees and might jeopardize the future of your company. Do you continue to make Distance Runner with its large-capacity tank, or do you change the construction of the gas tank? Use the ethical model in Chapter 2 to develop your answer.

Ethical Consideration

LEGALLY RIGHT BUT MORALLY WRONG: THE DILEMMA OF THE HDC

You are the branch manager of Bell Savings Bank and Trust. The bank stock is owned by local people in the community, some of whom rely on the dividends for a major portion of their income. Bell Savings is over 100 years old and has a good reputation in the community.

As the manager you look for ways to generate income for Bell. On behalf of Bell Savings, you purchase 20 promissory notes from Rosta's Computer Services, Inc. This company is in the business of selling computers to small businesses. The manager of Rosta's Computer Services informs you that these promissory notes represent good paying accounts from its business customers that have purchased computer equipment. You examine the notes and find them in proper order. Bell Savings purchases the notes at the usual discounted price, that is, an amount less than the principal on the note.

Bell Savings receives payments on a regular basis for two months. Within four months, however, your collection manager informs you that many of the notes are in default. When various customers were contacted for the reason they were not making payments, they told the collection manager that the promised computer equipment had not been received, and they were refusing to pay. The customers were contacted individually, and there does not appear to be any collusion among the disappointed customers. You try to contact Rosta's Computer Services but find its telephone disconnected. The post office has no forwarding address.

Bell Savings is a holder in due course (HDC) on the notes. To be a HDC means that the holder has the legal right to enforce payment on the notes through a lawsuit. The only defense the person who signed the notes, here the customers, has is that something is physically wrong with the note itself. In this case, the notes are in proper order and do not have anything wrong with them.

You are aware that the customers have received nothing of value, and the bank, unknowingly, may be part of a scam. Rosta's Computer Services apparently has committed a fraud. Both the bank and the consumers, however, are the innocent parties. Under the HDC doctrine Bell Savings has the right to collect on the principal and interest on the notes from the customers by filing a lawsuit. The court will order them to pay the principal and interest as they promised in their respective notes, even though they have not received anything in return. Some of these small businesses may be forced out of business if they have to pay the principal and interest.

Is the HDC doctrine ethical in this situation? Should the bank enforce collection on the notes? Use the ethical model in Chapter 2 to develop your answer.

MONITORING CONDITIONS OF FOREIGN EMPLOYEES

You are the president of a large clothing manufacturer. You recently returned from visiting several suppliers in Asia. Some of the suppliers treated their workers well. Others, however, seemed to be taking unfair advantage of their employees. In some locations, you saw young children and pregnant women doing heavy work and working long hours. The plants were filthy and inadequately ventilated. The smell of strong dyes and other pungent odors permeated the air. Foreign workers are paid much less than workers in the United States. Often their earnings do not provide a living wage for them.

You discuss the situation with upper-level management at your firm. They agree that the conditions are terrible. The company, however, needs to have the products made as cheaply as possible to keep competitive in the global marketplace. Management also argues that it is up to each nation to develop its own standards of employment protection, minimum wage, and child labor laws.

Should you try to control the working conditions of your suppliers or simply look for the cheapest manufacturing costs of your products? Use the ethical model in Chapter 2 to develop your answer.

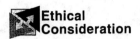

**Ethical
Consideration**

CAN YOU BE REQUIRED TO HAVE CREDIT LIFE INSURANCE?

You are the sole owner of both Fine Automobiles Dealership and Cheap Rates Insurance Company. When Fine Automobiles Dealership sells an automobile on credit, it requires all purchasers to acquire credit life, credit disability, and credit unemployment insurance. This type of insurance guarantees the monthly automobile payment in case of death, disability, or unemployment. Fine Automobiles Dealership has a serious, legitimate concern regarding continued payment of the automobile

loan in case of death, disability, or unemployment.

The Fine Automobiles Dealership sales force is required to recommend only Cheap Rates Insurance Company. Cheap Rates Insurance Company earns a substantial premium from selling this insurance. In fact, Cheap Rates Insurance Company has a low claim rate and a high income over expenses. Thus, Cheap Rates Insurance Company is able to pay its shareholders high dividends.

Is it ethical for Fine Automobiles

Dealership to require such insurance from its credit customers? Is it ethical that Fine Automobiles Dealership recommends to its customers only Cheap Rates Insurance Company rather than advising them to shop around to see if Cheap Rates Insurance Company actually does provide the best coverage for the lowest rates? Please use the ethical model in Chapter 2 to develop your answer.

Ethical Consideration

WHAT YOU DO NOT KNOW CAN BOTHER YOU: SHARING INFORMATION FROM WARRANTY CARDS

You own Global Electronics, a maker of electronic equipment. When Global Electronics sells a product, such as a television, it includes a warranty card. The card requests information regarding the purchaser's hobbies, salary, profession, age, marital status, number of persons in the household, income, and other personal information. Global Electronics uses some of the information for its own purposes. This information also is placed into a database, which is sold. This information will be used by direct-mail businesses and for other purposes. Customers who fill out the warranty cards do not know that their personal information will be sold. Is it ethical that this information is requested on the warranty card and the data sold without informing the customer? Would your answer change if the customer were informed? Use the ethical model in Chapter 2 to develop your answer.

Ethical Consideration

JOINT TENANCY: SHOULD THE PROPERTY ALWAYS GO TO THE SURVIVOR?

Your grandmother has just passed away. You were close to your grandmother, and you know that she trusted you and was proud of your many civic activities. You also are aware that she loved all of her ten grandchildren. You call your grandmother's attorney, Ms. Rubio, who informs you and your family that your grandmother has left a will naming the ten grandchildren as the beneficiaries to share her property equally. Ms. Rubio also discloses that several years before, your grandmother had heard in a lecture that the best way to avoid probate and reduce attorney's fees was to hold property in joint tenancy. Probate is a court proceeding that gathers the property of the deceased and redistributes the property in accordance with a will or if no will, then according to the state's statutes. Probate can be an expensive proceeding.

Based on this information, your grandmother placed her home, the main asset in her estate, in joint tenancy with you as the other joint tenant. You were unaware of what your grandmother had done. You are not totally surprised though, because you are the oldest and are more mature than the other grandchildren.

Legally, the home passed to you at the moment of your grandmother's death. The other grandchildren are quite upset and believe that the value of the home should be placed in the estate. Do you keep the home as your sole property, or do your sell it and divide the proceeds equally among your cousins? Use the ethical model in Chapter 2 to develop your answer. Disregard any tax issues that may arise.

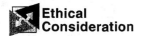

Ethical Consideration

THE HARD DECISIONS SURROUNDING MEDICAL INSURANCE

You are the owner of Sam's Clothing Store. You have a very loyal workforce, including several employees who have worked for you for over twenty years. One of your longtime employees is having severe medical problems that require very expensive procedures. Although he has been absent a little more than normal, he still is able to perform his job. The cost of his medical bills, however, are beginning to affect the cost of your medical plan.

You are advised by your medical insurance broker that if this employee continues on the medical plan, the rates for next year will increase significantly. Your broker advises you to replace this employee, to stop offering medical insurance as a guaranteed benefit, or to provide each employee a specific sum of money and let each find his or her own insurance. Although the broker's idea of letting each person find his or her own insurance appeals to your business sense, you know that individual medical insurance is very expensive. You believe that the employee who is ill will not be able to purchase insurance. What course of action should you take? Use the ethical model in Chapter 2 to develop your answer.

Ethical Consideration

If I Am Only for Myself, What Am I Getting Out of a Limited Partnership?

You are a limited partner in High Return Real Estate Partnership. High Returns owns several apartment buildings and is paying, as promised, a high rate of return to all the limited partners. You become suspicious of the lofty return, however, at a time when there appears to be a high vacancy rate in most apartment buildings. You do some investigation and find that many of the apartments owned by High Return are vacant. You also determine that the buildings are in need of significant repair. Neither the exteriors nor the interiors of the apartment buildings are being maintained. You talk with several of the tenants, who complain that basic plumbing and electrical repairs are being neglected. You conclude that High Return, to keep up its image, has decided to forgo making repairs and use its cash to pay investors. You believe that it is only a matter of time before this policy ruins the properties being held by High Return and jeopardizes the value of the partnership.

You approach the general partner and demand a return of your limited partnership investment. The general partner is willing to return your money on the condition that you do not disclose the information you know to anyone else. Do you take your money on that condition? Use the ethical model in Chapter 2 to develop your answer.

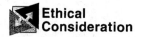

Ethical Consideration

CORPORATE GIVING: WHOSE MONEY IS IT? THE CORPORATION'S OR THE SHAREHOLDERS'?

You are the president of a highly successful corporation. You believe that business leaders have a civic duty to take significant leadership roles in community affairs. Involvement as a community leader helps to promote the corporation, although you have no way to measure this benefit. In addition to taking time away from your corporate duties to attend meetings and appear at functions, you use your office staff and management team to support the community activities. Significant donations to public programs are made in the name of the corporation.

At a recent shareholders' meeting, several shareholders questioned your right as the president to use work time, corporate staff, and corporate funds to assist the community endeavors. They believe that you should use your "free time" for your community work and donate to charities from your own assets. These shareholders believe that rather than the corporation donating time and money, it should pay larger dividends. They also believe that each shareholder should decide what charities, if any, they prefer the corporation to support. Do you continue your community involvement on corporate time and keep the corporate giving programs? Use the ethical model in Chapter 2 to develop your answer.

Ethical Consideration

SECURITIES DISCLOSURE REQUIREMENTS: DO THE CONSUMERS REALLY GET THE INFORMATION THEY NEED?

You are a staff attorney assigned to prepare material for prospective investors in a limited partnership that will be building and managing an office building. After putting all the material together, you are confident that you have satisfied the legal requirements for appropriate disclosure. You believe, however, that the documents are so complicated that few of the prospective investors will be able to understand what they are reading. The market for office space is soft, and you, personally, would never invest in such a project.

You carefully bring your concerns to your supervising attorney. He reminds you, however, that your obligation is to make sure that the legal requirements are met. When you question him about the financial soundness of building an office building in this economy, he explains that the deal allows for the general partners to receive their money up front and, therefore, to benefit whether or not the deal is successful. The general partners are the clients, and it is their interest that is to be protected. Because this initial payout to the general partners is fully disclosed, all the legal requirements have been met.

You are not satisfied and perceive that the law firm is participating in a rather shady deal that will benefit the general partners at the expense of the innocent investors. Do you insist on a meeting with the senior partner of the law firm in the hope that the firm does not want to be a party to such a practice, or do you simply certify that the documents meet all legal requirements and keep silent? Use the ethical model in Chapter 2 to develop your answer.

Ethical Consideration

ANTITRUST LAWS AND MEDICAL COSTS: A HELP OR A HINDRANCE?

You are a high-level administrator at one of the three large hospitals in a metropolitan area. The physicians on the hospital's staff are pressuring you to purchase a specialized laser surgery unit. If the hospital purchases this unit, the other two hospitals will purchase a similar unit in order to stay competitive. A feasibility study shows that one unit will service the needs of the community. One of the reasons for high-health care costs is the duplication of expensive, but often underutilized, high-tech equipment and services that the administration of each hospital believes it must provide to remain competitive.

If you could, you would have the administrators from the three hospitals in your area meet and work out a program in which distinct specialties and services would be allocated among the various hospitals. Units that earn money (such as a maternity ward) and units that lose money (such as a burn unit) would be distributed so that each hospital would have a financial base to earn income. This system would reduce the need for each of the competing hospitals to acquire all the latest equipment, would help ensure that the equipment purchased would be better utilized, and would reduce duplication of services.

You know that such a scheme is in violation of the antitrust laws. Your local congresswoman is involved with health-care reform issues and favors hospitals working together to reduce the multiplicity of services and equipment. In a recent conversation with your congresswoman, you told her of your dilemma. She confidently told you that she is sure that hospitals will be exempted from the antitrust laws within a very short period of time. This exemption is included in proposed legislation.

You would like to meet with the other hospital administrators to study the feasibility of dividing up the specialties. If the study were completed in time, it would contain the type of information that could be submitted to U.S. House and Senate committees studying the problem of antitrust exemption for hospitals. Because no exemption now exists, however, if you meet with the other hospital administrators, you may be in violation of the antitrust laws. Do you wait until hospitals legally are exempted from antitrust laws, or do you meet with the other hospital administrators to conduct a study? Use the ethical model in Chapter 2 to develop your answer.

 **Ethical Consideration**

SHOULD A BUSINESS HAVE A PENSION PLAN?

You own a small business that manufactures a commercial grade of carpeting. Most of your employees are paid hourly or they are on a commission basis. You always have been concerned about the welfare of your employees and their families. Because of this concern, you have provided a pension plan. As you review your financial statements, you realize that the expense of the pension plan is five percent of the business's gross sales. This cost will impede your ability to remain competitive. You consider whether to increase the pay of your employees and eliminate the pension benefits.

Many of your employees believe that they will retire comfortably with income from Social Security and they are not concerned with retirement benefits. Most of your employees are under the age of forty. What they do not realize, however, is that in 1995 the maximum benefit paid by Social Security was $12,804. This amount is received only by persons who paid the maximum amount into Social Security. The average Social Security benefit was far less and was not sufficient to support a person beyond a very minimum standard of living. As a result, as economic costs have increased, many senior citizens have been forced onto welfare programs. Thus, they have become an economic drain on taxpayers.

Today, as the population ages, the average number of years between retirement and death increases. In 1934, when Social Security was enacted, the retirement age was set at 65. At that time less than four percent of the population was 65 or older. If the Social Security benefits were to be paid to the same percentage of aged population today, benefits would not start until 90 years of age. Predictions have been made that the Social Security system will run out of money by the time people who are in their twenties or thirties in 1995 reach the age of retirement.

The 1980s saw a major decrease in the amount of benefits offered by businesses to their employees. Pension plans have been cut or eliminated. By the mid-1980s, over half of all workers were not covered by any pension plan. When these plans were abolished, the employers normally increased the hourly rate paid to employees. You have read studies that show that the employees did not take the increase in pay and set it aside in a retirement plan.

You take into consideration what you know about the Social Security system in deciding whether to end the pension plan and increase your employees' wages. What ethical responsibilities do you have for making provisions for the retirement of your youthful employees? Use the ethical model in Chapter 2 to develop your answer.

Ethical Consideration

THE GLASS CEILING: A RELIC OF THE PAST OR A REALITY OF THE PRESENT?

You are Bill Paper, the owner of Office Haven, a manufacturer of fine wooden office furniture. You recently hired Sue Sure as a trainee in the marketing department. She is very successful and well liked in spite of her outspoken position that men generally treat women poorly in the work environment.

When the director of marketing has a heart attack, Sure's name is proposed to take his place. Although you know that Sure is very capable, you are worried about bringing a woman into upper management, which until now has been exclusively male. You believe that your management team likes the current all-male atmosphere that allows for sexual jokes, strong language, drinks, and easy companionship—in other words, the old boy network. In addition, the past behavior of some members of the upper management team, in terms of language and actions, may be viewed by Sure as harassing. Do you promote Sure or do you conduct a search that will most likely result in a strong male executive's filling the vacancy? Use the ethical model in Chapter 2 to develop your answer.

Ethical Consideration

Who Is Right: Balancing the Needs to Protect the Environment and to Meet Current Exigencies

Your company produces a variety of pesticides, including one that eradicates virtually all insects. This particular product, called Life Protector, is banned in the United States because it is highly toxic and poses dangers to farm workers, the general environment, and consumers who ingest the toxic residue. In spite of these dangers, many developing nations are willing to use this highly efficient product that allows crops to grow in insect-infested locations.

Although your company has placed warning labels on the product that list specific rules for its proper handling and application, environmental organizations inform your company that poor, illiterate farm workers are applying Life Protector without wearing gloves, breathing apparatuses, or other protective devices required for safety. Your company also has information that the pesticide is being overapplied in many areas and is seeping into the groundwater creating the potential for severe and long-lasting damage to the environment.

You are disturbed by the many reports of the product's misuse. You are considering either stopping production or demanding proof that Life Protector is being used correctly before you distribute it in a particular country. When you raise these concerns with foreign buyers, however, they assure you that they are aware of the dangers and are doing the best they can to regulate the pesticide's use. They also contend that the potential for harm, especially in the future, is greatly outweighed by the current needs to feed their vast numbers of citizens. They even say that it is better that a few people die from Life Protector than that many starve if sufficient crops cannot be grown. Do you continue to manufacture Life Protector and distribute it as you have done in the past, or do you attempt to control its use? Use the ethical model in Chapter 2 to develop your answer.

Appendix F
Dictionary of Legal Terms

abatement Reduction or elimination of gifts by category upon the reduction in value of the estate.

absolute surety Surety liable to a creditor immediately upon the default of the principal debtor.

acceptance *Commercial paper* Acceptance is the drawee's signed engagement to honor the draft as presented. It becomes operative when completed by delivery or notification. UCC § 3–410.

    Contracts Compliance by offeree with terms and conditions of offer.

    Sale of goods UCC § 2–606 provides three ways a buyer can accept goods: (1) by signifying to the seller that the goods are conforming or that he will accept them in spite of their nonconformity, (2) by failing to make an effective rejection, and (3) by doing an act inconsistent with the seller's ownership.

acceptor Drawee who has accepted an instrument.

accession An addition to one's property by increase of the original property or by production from such property. *E.g.,* A innocently converts the wheat of B into bread. UCC § 9–315 changes the common law where a perfected security interest is involved.

accident and health insurance Provides protection from losses due to accident or sickness.

accommodation An arrangement made as a favor to another, usually involving a loan of money or commercial paper. While a party's intent may be to aid a maker of a note by lending his credit, if he seeks to accomplish thereby legitimate objects of his own and not simply to aid the maker, the act is not for accommodation.

accommodation indorser Signer not in the chain of title.

accommodation party A person who signs commercial paper in any capacity for the purpose of lending his name to another party to an instrument. UCC § 3–415.

accord and satisfaction A method of discharging a claim whereby the parties agree to accept something in settlement, the "accord" being the agreement and the "satisfaction" its execution or performance. It is a new contract that is substituted for an old contract, which is thereby discharged, or for an obligation or cause of action and that must have all of the elements of a valid contract.

account Any account with a bank, including a checking, time, interest or savings account. UCC § 4–194. Also, any right to payment, for goods or services, that is not evidenced by an instrument or chattel paper. *E.g.,* account receivable.

accounting Equitable proceeding for a complete settlement of all partnership affairs.

Many of the definitions are abridged and adapted from *Black's Law Dictionary*, 5th edition, West Publishing Company, 1979.

act of state doctrine Rule that a court should not question the validity of actions taken by a foreign government in its own country.

actual authority Power conferred upon agent by actual consent given by principal.

actual express authority Actual authority derived from written or spoken words of principal.

actual implied authority Actual authority inferred from words or conduct manifested to agent by principal.

actual notice Knowledge actually and expressly communicated.

actus reas Wrongful or overt act.

ademption The removal or extinction of a devise by act of the testator.

adequacy of consideration Not required where parties have freely agreed to the exchange.

adhesion contract Standard "form" contract, usually between a large retailer and a consumer, in which the weaker party has no realistic choice or opportunity to bargain.

adjudication The giving or pronouncing of a judgment in a case; also, the judgment given.

administrative agency Governmental entity (other than courts and legislatures) having authority to affect the rights of private parties.

administrative law Law dealing with the establishment, duties, and powers of agencies in the executive branch of government.

administrative process Entire set of activities engaged in by administrative agencies while carrying out their rulemaking, enforcement, and adjudicative functions.

administrator A person appointed by the court to manage the assets and liabilities of an intestate (a person dying without a will). A person named in the will of a testator (a person dying with a will) is called the executor. Female designations are administratrix and executrix.

adversary system System in which opposing parties initiate and present their cases.

adverse possession A method of acquiring title to real property by possession for a statutory period under certain conditions. The periods of time may differ, depending on whether the adverse possessor has color of title.

affidavit A written statement of facts, made voluntarily, confirmed by oath or affirmation of the party making it, and taken before an authorized officer.

affiliate Person who controls, is controlled by, or is under common control with the issuer.

affirm Uphold the lower court's judgment.

affirmative action Active recruitment of minority applicants.

affirmative defense A response that attacks the plaintiff's legal right to bring an action as opposed to attacking the truth of the claim. *E.g.,* accord and satisfaction; assumption of risk; contributory negligence; duress; estoppel.

affirmative disclosure Requirement that an advertiser include certain information in its advertisement so that the ad is not deceptive.

after-acquired property Property the debtor may acquire at some time after the security interest attaches.

agency Relation in which one person acts for or represents another by the latter's authority.

Actual agency Exists where the agent is really employed by the principal.

Agency by estoppel One created by operation of law and established by proof of such acts of the principal as reasonably lead to the conclusion of its existence.

Implied agency One created by acts of the parties and deduced from proof of other facts.

agent Person authorized to act on another's behalf.

allegation A statement of a party setting out what he expects to prove.

allonge Piece of paper firmly affixed to the instrument.

annuity contract Agreement to pay periodic sums to insured upon reaching a designated age.

annul To annul a judgment or judicial proceeding is to deprive it of all force and operation.

answer The answer is the formal written statement made by a defendant setting forth the ground of his defense.

antecedent debt Preexisting obligation.

anticipatory breach of contract (or **anticipatory repudiation**) The unjustified assertion by a party that he will not perform an obligation that he is contractually obligated to perform at a future time. See UCC §§ 610 & 611.

apparent authority Such principal power that a reasonable person would assume an agent has in light of the principal's conduct.

appeal Resort to a superior (appellate) court to review the decision of an inferior (trial) court or administrative agency.

appeal by right Mandatory review by a higher court.

appellant A party who takes an appeal from one court to another. He may be either the plaintiff or defendant in the original court proceeding.

appellee The party in a cause against whom an appeal is taken; that is, the party who has an interest adverse to setting aside or reversing the judgment. Sometimes also called the "respondent."

appropriation Unauthorized use of another person's name or likeness for one's own benefit.

appurtenances Things appurtenant pass as incident to the principal thing. Sometimes an easement consisting of a right of way over one piece of land will pass with another piece of land as being appurtenant to it.

APR Annual percentage rate.

arbitration The reference of a dispute to an impartial (third) person chosen by the parties, who agree in advance to abide by the arbitrator's award issued after a hearing at which both parties have an opportunity to be heard.

arraignment Accused is informed of the crime against him and enters a plea.

articles of incorporation (or **certificate of incorporation**) The instrument under which a corporation is formed. The contents are prescribed in the particular state's general incorporation statute.

articles of partnership A written agreement by which parties enter into a partnership, to be governed by the terms set forth therein.

as is Disclaimer of implied warranties.

assault Unlawful attempted battery; intentional infliction of apprehension of immediate bodily harm or offensive contact.

assignee Party to whom contract rights are assigned.

assignment A transfer of the rights to real or personal property, usually intangible property such as rights in a lease, mortgage, sale agreement, or partnership.

assignment of rights Voluntary transfer to a third party of the rights arising from a contract.

assignor Party making an assignment.

assumes Delegatee agrees to perform the contractual obligation of the delegator.

assumes the mortgage Purchaser of mortgaged property becomes personally liable to pay the debt.

assumption of risk Plaintiff's express or implied consent to encounter a known danger.

attachment The process of seizing property, by virtue of a writ, summons, or other judicial order, and bringing the same into the custody of the court for the purpose of securing satisfaction of the judgment ultimately to be entered in the action. While formerly the main objective was to coerce the defendant debtor to appear in court, today the writ of attachment is used primarily to seize the debtor's property in the event a judgment is rendered.

Distinguished from execution See **execution**.

Also, the process by which a security interest becomes enforceable. Attachment may occur upon the taking of possession or upon the signing of a security agreement by the person who is pledging the property as collateral.

authority Power of an agent to change the legal status of his principal.

authorized means Any reasonable means of communication.

automatic perfection Perfection upon attachment.

award The decision of an arbitrator.

bad checks Issuing a check with funds insufficient to cover it.

bailee The party to whom personal property is delivered under a contract of bailment.

Extraordinary bailee Absolutely liable for the safety of the bailed property without regard to the cause of loss.

Ordinary bailee Must exercise due care.

bailment A delivery of personal property in trust for the execution of a special object in relation to such goods, beneficial either to the bailor or bailee or both, and upon a contract to either redeliver the goods to the bailor or otherwise dispose of the same in conformity with the purpose of the trust.

bailor The party who delivers goods to another in the contract of bailment.

bankrupt The state or condition of one who is unable to pay his debts as they are, or become, due.

Bankruptcy Code The Act was substantially revised in 1978, effective October 1, 1979. Straight bankruptcy is in the nature of a liquidation proceeding and involves the collection and distribution to creditors of all the bankrupt's nonexempt property by the trustee in the manner provided by the Act. The debtor rehabilitation provisions of the Act (Chapters 11 and 13) differ from straight bankruptcy in that the debtor looks to rehabilitation and reorganization, rather than liquidation, and the creditors look to future earnings of the bankrupt, rather than to property held by the bankrupt, to satisfy their claims.

bargain Negotiated exchange.

bargained exchange Mutually agreed-upon exchange.

basis of the bargain Part of the buyer's assumption underlying the sale.

battery Unlawful touching of another; intentional infliction of harmful or offensive bodily contact.

bearer Person in possession of an instrument.

bearer paper Payable to holder of the instrument.

beneficiary One who benefits from act of another. See also **third-party beneficiary**.

Incidental A person who may derive benefit from performance on contract, though he is neither the promisee nor the one to whom performance is to be rendered. Since the incidental beneficiary is not a donee or creditor beneficiary (see **third-party beneficiary**), he has no right to enforce the contract.

Intended beneficiary Third party intended by the two contracted parties to receive a benefit from their contract.

Trust As it relates to trust beneficiaries, includes a person who has any present or future interest, vested or contingent, and also includes the owner of an interest by assignment or other transfer and, as it relates to a charitable trust, includes any person entitled to enforce the trust.

beyond a reasonable doubt Proof that is entirely convincing and satisfying to a moral certainty; criminal law standard.

bilateral contract Contract in which both parties exchange promises.

bill of lading Document evidencing receipt of goods for shipment issued by person engaged in business of transporting or forwarding goods; includes airbill. UCC § 1–201(6).

Through bill of lading A bill of lading which specifies at least one connecting carrier.

bill of sale A written agreement, formerly limited to one under seal, by which one person assigns or transfers his right to or interest in goods and personal chattels to another.

binder A written memorandum of the important terms of a contract of insurance which gives temporary protection to an insured pending investigation of risk by the insurance company or until a formal policy is issued.

blue law Prohibition of certain types of commercial activity on Sunday.

blue sky laws A popular name for state statutes providing for the regulation and supervision of securities offerings and sales, to protect citizen-investors from investing in fraudulent companies.

bona fide Latin. In good faith.

bond A certificate or evidence of a debt on which the issuing company or governmental body promises to pay the bondholders a specified amount of interest for a specified length of time and to repay the loan on the expiration date. In every case, a bond represents debt—its holder is a creditor of the corporation, not a part owner, as the shareholder is.

boycott Agreement among parties not to deal with a third party.

breach Wrongful failure to perform the terms of a contract.

Material breach Nonperformance which significantly impairs the aggrieved party's rights under the contract.

bribery Offering property to a public official to influence the official's decision.

bulk transfer Transfer not in the ordinary course of the transferor's business of a major part of his inventory.

burglary Breaking and entering the home of another at night with intent to commit a felony.

business judgment rule Protects directors from liability for honest mistakes of judgment.

business trust A trust (managed by a trustee for the benefit of a beneficiary) established to conduct a business for a profit.

but for rule Person's negligent conduct is a cause of an event if the event would not have occurred in the absence of that conduct.

buyer in ordinary course of business Person who buys in ordinary course, in good faith, and without knowledge that the sale to him is in violation of anyone's ownership rights or of a security interest.

by-laws Regulations, ordinances, rules, or laws adopted by an association or corporation for its government.

callable bond Bond that is subject to redemption (reacquisition) by the corporation.

cancellation One party's putting an end to a contract because of a breach by other party.

capital Accumulated goods, possessions, and assets, used for the production of profits and wealth. Owners' equity in a business. Also used to refer to the total assets of a business or to capital assets.

capital surplus Surplus other than earned surplus.

carrier Transporter of goods.

casualty insurance Covers property loss due to causes other than fire or the elements.

cause of action The ground on which an action may be sustained.

caveat emptor Latin. Let the buyer beware. This maxim is more applicable to judicial sales, auctions, and the like than to sales of consumer goods, where strict liability, warranty, and other laws protect.

certificate of deposit A written acknowledgment by a bank or banker of a deposit with promise to pay to depositor, to his order, or to some other person or to his order. UCC § 3–104(2)(c).

certificate of title Official representation of ownership.

certification Acceptance of a check by a drawee bank.

certification of incorporation See **articles of incorporation**.

certification mark Distinctive symbol, word, or design used with goods or services to certify specific characteristics.

certiorari Latin. To be informed of. A writ of common law origin issued by a superior to an inferior court requiring the latter to produce a certified record of a particular case tried therein. It is most commonly used to refer to the Supreme Court of the United States, which uses the writ of certiorari as a discretionary device to choose the cases it wishes to hear.

chancery Equity; equitable jurisdiction; a court of equity; the system of jurisprudence administered in courts of equity.

charging order Judicial lien against a partner's interest in the partnership.

charter An instrument emanating from the sovereign power, in the nature of a grant. A charter differs from a constitution in that the former is granted by the sovereign, while the latter is established by the people themselves.

Corporate law An act of a legislature creating a corporation or creating and defining the franchise of a corporation. Also a corporation's constitution or organic law; that is to say, the articles of incorporation taken in connection with the law under which the corporation was organized.

chattel mortgage A pre-Uniform Commercial Code security device whereby the mortgagee took a security interest in personal property of the mortgagor. Such security device has generally been superseded by other types of security agreements under UCC Article 9 (Secured Transactions).

chattel paper Writings that evidence both a debt and a security interest.

check A draft drawn upon a bank and payable on demand, signed by the maker or drawer, containing an unconditional promise to pay a sum certain in money to the order of the payee. UCC § 3–104(2)(b).

Cashier's check A bank's own check drawn on itself and signed by the cashier or other authorized official. It is a direct obligation of the bank.

C. & F. Cost and freight; a shipping contract.

C.I.F. Cost, insurance, and freight; a shipping contract.

civil law Laws concerned with civil or private rights and remedies, as contrasted with criminal laws.

The system of jurisprudence administered in the Roman empire, particularly as set forth in the compilation of Justinian and his successors, as distinguished from the common law of England and the canon law. The civil law (Civil Code) is followed by Louisiana.

claim A right to payment.

clearinghouse An association of banks for the purpose of settling accounts on a daily basis.

close corporation See **corporation**.

closed-ended credit Credit extended to debtor for a specific period of time.

closed shop Employer can only hire union members.

C.O.D. Collect on delivery; generally a shipping contract.

code A compilation of all permanent laws in force consolidated and classified according to subject matter. Many states have published official codes of all laws in force, including the common law and statutes as judicially interpreted, which have been compiled by code commissions and enacted by the legislatures.

codicil A supplement or an addition to a will; it may explain, modify, add to, subtract from, qualify, alter, restrain, or revoke provisions in an existing will. It must be executed with the same formalities as a will.

cognovit judgment Written authority by debtor for entry of judgment against him in the event he defaults in payment. Such provision in a debt instrument on default confers judgment against the debtor.

collateral Secondarily liable; liable only if the party with primary liability does not perform.

collateral (security) Personal property subject to security interest.

Banking Some form of security in addition to the personal obligation of the borrower.

collateral promise Undertaking to be secondarily liable, that is, liable if the principal debtor does not perform.

collecting bank Any bank, except the payor bank, handling the item for collection. UCC § 4–105(d).

collective mark Distinctive symbol used to indicate membership in an organization.

collision insurance Protects the owner of an automobile against damage due to contact with other vehicles or objects.

commerce power Exclusive power granted by the U.S. Constitution to the federal government to regulate commerce with foreign countries and among the states.

commercial bailment Bailment in which parties derive a mutual benefit.

commercial impracticability Performance can only be accomplished with unforeseen and unjust hardship.

commercial law A phrase used to designate the whole body of substantive jurisprudence (*e.g.,* Uniform Commercial Code; Truth in Lending Act) applicable to the rights, intercourse, and relations of persons engaged in commerce, trade, or mercantile pursuits. See **Uniform Commercial Code**.

commercial paper Bills of exchange (*i.e.,* drafts), promissory notes, bank checks, and other negotiable instruments for the payment of money, which, by their form and on their face, purport to be such instruments. UCC Article 3 is the general law governing commercial paper.

commercial reasonableness Judgment of reasonable persons familiar with the business transaction.

commercial speech Expression related to the economic interests of the speaker and its audience.

common carrier Carrier open to the general public.

common law Body of law originating in England and derived from judicial decisions. As distinguished from statutory law created by the enactment of legislatures, the common law comprises the judgments and decrees of the courts recognizing, affirming, and enforcing usages and customs of immemorial antiquity.

community property Rights of a spouse in property acquired by the other during marriage.

comparable worth Equal pay for jobs of equal value to the employer.

comparative negligence Under comparative negligence statutes or doctrines, negligence is measured in terms of percentage, and any damages allowed shall be diminished in proportion to amount of negligence attributable to the person for whose injury, damage, or death recovery is sought.

complainant One who applies to the courts for legal redress by filing a complaint (*i.e.,* plaintiff).

complaint The pleading which sets forth a claim for relief. Such complaint (whether it be the original claim, counterclaim, cross-claim, or third-party claim) shall contain (1) a short, plain statement of the grounds upon which the court's jurisdiction depends, unless the court already has jurisdiction and the claim needs no new grounds of jurisdiction to support it, (2) a short, plain statement of the claim showing that the pleader is entitled to relief, and (3) a demand for judgment for the relief to which he deems himself entitled. Fed.R. Civil P. 8(a). The complaint, together with the summons, is required to be served on the defendant. Rule 4.

composition Agreement between debtor and two or more of her creditors that each will take a portion of his claim as full payment.

compulsory arbitration Arbitration required by statute for specific types of disputes.

computer crime Crime committed against or through the use of a computer or computer/services.

concealment Fraudulent failure to disclose a material fact.

conciliation Nonbinding process in which a third party acts as an intermediary between disputing parties.

concurrent jurisdiction Authority of more than one court to hear the same case.

condition An uncertain event which affects the duty of performance.
  Concurrent conditions The parties are to perform simultaneously.
  Express condition Performance is contingent on the happening or non-happening of a stated event.

condition precedent An event which must occur or not occur before performance is due; event or events (presentment, dishonor, notice of dishonor) which must occur to hold a secondary party liable to commercial paper.

condition subsequent An event which terminates a duty of performance.

conditional acceptance An acceptance of an offer contingent upon the acceptance of an additional or different term.

conditional contract Obligations are contingent upon a stated event.

conditional guarantor of collection Surety liable to creditor only after creditor exhausts his legal remedies against the principal debtor.

confession of judgment Written agreement by debtor authorizing creditor to obtain a court judgment in the event debtor defaults. See also **cognovit judgment**.

confiscation Governmental taking of foreign-owned property without payment.

conflict of laws That branch of jurisprudence, arising from the diversity of the laws of different nations, states, or jurisdictions, that reconciles the inconsistencies, or decides which law is to govern in a particular case.

confusion Results when goods belonging to two or more owners become so intermixed that the property of any of them no longer can be identified except as part of a mass of like goods.

consanguinity Kinship; blood relationship; the connection or relation of persons descended from the same stock or common ancestor.

consensual arbitration Arbitration voluntarily entered into by the parties.

consent Voluntary and knowing willingness that an act should be done.

conservator Appointed by court to manage affairs of incompetent or to liquidate business.

consideration The cause, motive, price, or impelling influence which induces a contracting party to enter into a contract. Some right, interest, profit, or benefit accruing to one party or some forbearance, detriment, loss, or responsibility given, suffered, or undertaken by the other.

consignee One to whom a consignment is made. Person named in bill of lading to whom or to whose order the bill promises delivery. UCC § 7–102(b).

consignment Ordinarily implies an agency; denotes that property is committed to the consignee for care or sale.

consignor One who sends or makes a consignment; a shipper of goods. The person named in a bill of lading as the person from whom the goods have been received for shipment. UCC § 7–102(c).

consolidation In *corporate law,* the combination of two or more corporations into a newly created corporation. Thus, A Corporation and B Corporation consolidate to form C Corporation.

constitution Fundamental law of a government establishing its powers and limitations.

constructive That which is established by the mind of the law in its act of *construing* facts, conduct, circumstances, or instruments. That which has not in its essential nature the character assigned to it, but acquires such character in consequence of the way in which it is regarded by a rule or policy of law; hence, inferred, implied, or made out by legal interpretation; the word "legal" being sometimes used here in lieu of "constructive."

constructive assent An assent or consent imputed to a party from a construction or interpretation of his conduct; as distinguished from one which he actually expresses.

constructive conditions Conditions in contracts which are neither expressed nor implied but rather are imposed by law to meet the ends of justice.

constructive delivery Term comprehending all those acts which, although not truly conferring a real possession of the vendee, have been held by construction of law to be equivalent to acts of real delivery.

constructive eviction Failure by the landlord in any obligation under the lease that causes a substantial and lasting injury to the tenant's enjoyment of the premises.

constructive notice Knowledge imputed by law.

constructive trust Arising by operation of law to prevent unjust enrichment. See also **trustee**.

consumer goods Goods bought or used for personal, family, or household purposes.

consumer product Tangible personal property normally used for family, household, or personal purposes.

contingent remainder Remainder interest, conditional upon the happening of an event in addition to the termination of the preceding estate.

contract An agreement between two or more persons which creates an obligation to do or not to do a particular thing. Its essentials are competent parties, subject matter, a legal consideration, mutuality of agreement, and mutuality of obligation.
  Destination contract Seller is required to tender delivery of the goods at a particular destination; seller bears the expense and risk of loss.

Executed contract Fully performed by all of the parties.

Executory contract Contract partially or entirely unperformed by one or more of the parties.

Express contract Agreement of parties that is expressed in words either in writing or orally.

Formal contract Agreement which is legally binding because of its particular form or mode or expression.

Implied-in-fact contract Contract where agreement of the parties is inferred from their conduct.

Informal contract All oral or written contracts other than formal contracts.

Installment contract Goods are delivered in separate lots.

Integrated contract Complete and total agreement.

Output contract A contract in which one party agrees to sell his entire output and the other agrees to buy it; it is not illusory, though it may be indefinite.

Quasi contract Obligation not based upon contract that is imposed to avoid injustice.

Requirements contract A contract in which one party agrees to purchase his total requirements from the other party; hence, such a contract is binding, not illusory.

Substituted contract An agreement between the parties to rescind their old contract and replace it with a new contract.

Unconscionable contract One which no sensible person not under delusion, duress, or in distress would make, and such as no honest and fair person would accept. A contract the terms of which are excessively unreasonable, overreaching, and one-sided.

Unenforceable contract Contract for the breach of which the law does not provide a remedy.

Unilateral and bilateral A unilateral contract is one in which one party makes an express engagement or undertakes a performance, without receiving in return any express engagement or promise of performance from the other. Bilateral (or reciprocal) contracts are those by which the parties expressly enter into mutual engagements.

contract clause Prohibition against the states' retroactively modifying public and private contracts.

contractual liability Obligation on a negotiable instrument, based upon signing the instrument.

contribution Payment from cosureties of their proportionate share.

contributory negligence An act or omission amounting to a want of ordinary care on the part of the complaining party, which, concurring with defendant's negligence, is proximate cause of injury.

The defense of contributory negligence is an absolute bar to any recovery in some states; because of this, it has been replaced by the doctrine of comparative negligence in many other states.

conversion Unauthorized and wrongful exercise of dominion and control over another's personal property, to exclusion of or inconsistent with rights of the owner.

convertible bond Bond that may be exchanged for other securities of the corporation.

copyright Exclusive right granted by federal government to authors of original works including literary, musical, dramatic, pictorial, graphic, sculptural, and film works.

corporation A legal entity ordinarily consisting of an association of numerous individuals. Such entity is regarded as having a personality and existence distinct from that of its several members and is vested with the capacity of continuous succession, irrespective of changes in its membership, either in perpetuity or for a limited term of years.

Closely held or close corporation Corporation that is owned by few shareholders and whose shares are not actively traded.

Corporation de facto One existing under color of law and in pursuance of an effort made in good faith to organize a corporation under the statute. Such a corporation is not subject to collateral attack.

Corporation de jure That which exists by reason of full compliance with requirements of an existing law permitting organization of such corporation.

Domestic corporation Corporation created under the laws of a given state.

Foreign corporation Corporation created under the laws of any other state, government, or country.

Publicly held corporation Corporation whose shares are owned by a large number of people and are widely traded.

Subchapter S corporation A small business corporation which, under certain conditions, may elect to have its undistributed taxable income taxed to its shareholders. I.R.C. § 1371 et seq. Of major significance is the fact that Subchapter S status usually avoids the corporate income tax, and corporate losses can be claimed by the shareholders.

Subsidiary and parent Subsidiary corporation is one in which another corporation (called parent corporation) owns at least a majority of the shares and over which it thus has control.

corrective advertising Disclosure in an advertisement that previous ads were deceptive.

costs A pecuniary allowance, made to the successful party (and recoverable from the losing party), for his expenses in prosecuting or defending an action or a distinct proceeding within an action. Generally, "costs" do not include attorneys' fees unless such fees are by a statute denominated costs or are by statute allowed to be recovered as costs in the case.

cosureties Two or more sureties bound for the same debt of a principal debtor.

co-tenants Persons who hold title concurrently.

counterclaim A claim presented by a defendant in opposition to or deduction from the claim of the plaintiff.

counteroffer A statement by the offeree which has the legal effect of rejecting the offer and of proposing a new offer to the offeror. However, the provisions of UCC § 2–207(2) modify this principle by providing that the "additional terms are to be construed as proposals for addition to the contract."

course of dealing A sequence of previous acts and conduct between the parties to a particular transaction which is fairly to be regarded as establishing a common basis of understanding for interpreting their expressions and other conduct. UCC § 1–205(1).

course of performance Conduct between the parties concerning performance of the particular contract.

court above—court below In appellate practice, the "court above" is the one to which a cause is removed for review, whether by appeal, writ of error, or certiorari, while the "court below" is the one from which the case is being removed.

covenant Used primarily with respect to promises in conveyances or other instruments dealing with real estate.

Covenants against encumbrances A stipulation against all rights to or interests in the land which may subsist in third persons to the diminution of the value of the estate granted.

Covenant appurtenant A covenant which is connected with land of the grantor, not in gross. A covenant running with the land and binding heirs, executors, and assigns of the immediate parties.

Covenant for further assurance An undertaking, in the form of a covenant, on the part of the vendor of real estate to do such further acts for the purpose of perfecting the purchaser's title as the latter may reasonably require.

Covenant for possession A covenant by which the grantee or lessee is granted possession.

Covenant for quiet enjoyment An assurance against the consequences of a defective title, and against any disturbances thereupon.

Covenants for title Covenants usually inserted in a conveyance of land, on the part of the grantor, and binding him for the completeness, security, and continuance of the title transferred to the grantee. They comprise covenants for seisin, for right to convey, against encumbrances, or quiet enjoyment, sometimes for further assurance, and almost always of warranty.

Covenant in gross Such as do not run with the land.

Covenant of right to convey An assurance by the covenantor that the grantor has sufficient capacity and title to convey the estate which he by his deed undertakes to convey.

Covenant of seisin An assurance to the purchaser that the grantor has the very estate in quantity and quality which he purports to convey.

Covenant of warranty An assurance by the grantor of an estate that the grantee shall enjoy the same without interruption by virtue of paramount title.

Covenant running with land A covenant which goes with the land, as being annexed to the estate, and which cannot be separated from the land or transferred without it. A covenant is said to run with the land when not only the original parties or their representatives, but each successive owner of the land, will be entitled to its benefit, or be liable (as the case may be) to its obligation. Such a covenant is said to be one which "touches and concerns" the land itself, so that its benefit or obligation passes with the ownership. Essentials are that the grantor and grantee must have intended that the covenant run with the land, the covenant must affect or concern the land with which it runs, and there must be privity of estate between the party claiming the benefit and the party who rests under the burden.

covenant not to compete Agreement to refrain from entering into a competing trade, profession, or business.

cover Buyer's purchase of goods in substitution for those not delivered by breaching seller.

credit beneficiary See **third-party beneficiary**.

creditor Any entity having a claim against the debtor.

crime An act or omission in violation of a public law and punishable by the government.

criminal duress Coercion by threat of serious bodily injury.

criminal intent Desired or virtually certain consequences of one's conduct.

criminal law The law that involves offenses against the entire community.

cure The right of a seller under the UCC to correct a nonconforming delivery of goods to buyer within the contract period. § 2–508.

curtesy Husband's estate in the real property of his wife.

cy-pres As near (as possible). Rule for the construction of instruments in equity, by which the intention of the party is carried out *as near as may be*, when it would be impossible or illegal to give it literal effect.

damage Loss, injury, or deterioration caused by the negligence, design, or accident of one person, with respect to another's person or property. The word is to be distinguished from its plural, "damages," which means a compensation in money for a loss or damage.

damages Money sought as a remedy for breach of contract or for tortious acts.

Actual damages Real, substantial, and just damages, or the amount awarded to a complainant in compensation for his actual and real loss or injury, as opposed, on the one hand, to "nominal" damages and, on the other, to "exemplary" or "punitive" damages. Synonymous with "compensatory damages" and "general damages."

Benefit-of-the-bargain damages Difference between the value received and the value of the fraudulent party's performance as represented.

Compensatory damages Compensatory damages are such as will compensate the injured party for the injury sustained, and nothing more; such as will simply make good or replace the loss caused by the wrong or injury.

Consequential damages Such damage, loss, or injury as does not flow directly and immediately from the act of the party, but only from some of the consequences or results of such act. Consequential damages resulting from a seller's breach of contract include any loss resulting from general or particular requirements and needs of which the seller at the time of contracting had reason to know and which could not reasonably be prevented by cover or otherwise, and injury to person or property proximately resulting from any breach of warranty. UCC § 2–715(2).

Exemplary or punitive damages Damages other than compensatory damages which may be awarded against a person to punish him for outrageous conduct.

Expectancy damages Calculable by subtracting the injured party's actual dollar position as a result of the breach from that party's projected dollar position had performance occurred.

Foreseeable damages Loss of which the party in breach had reason to know when the contract was made.

Incidental damages Under UCC § 2–710, such damages include any commercially reasonable charges, expenses, or commissions incurred in stopping delivery, in the transportation, care, and custody of goods after the buyer's breach, in connection with the return or resale of the goods, or otherwise resulting from the breach. Also, such damages, resulting from a seller's breach of contract, include expenses reasonably incurred in inspection, receipt, transportation, and care and custody of goods rightfully rejected, any commercially reasonable charges, expenses, or commissions in connection with effecting cover, and any other reasonable expense incident to the delay or other breach. UCC § 2–715(1).

Irreparable damages In the law pertaining to injunctions, damages for which no certain pecuniary standard exists for measurement.

Liquidated damages and penalties Damages for breach by either party may be liquidated in the agreement but only at an amount which is reasonable in the light of the anticipated or actual harm caused by the breach, the difficulties of proof of loss, and the inconvenience or nonfeasibility of otherwise obtaining an adequate remedy. A term fixing unreasonably large liquidated damages is void as a penalty. UCC § 2–718(1).

Mitigation of damages A plaintiff may not recover damages for the effects of an injury which she reasonably could have avoided or substantially ameliorated. This limitation on recovery is generally denominated as "mitigation of damages" or "avoidance of consequences."

Nominal damages A small sum awarded where a contract has been breached but the loss is negligible or unproven.

Out-of-pocket damages Difference between the value received and the value given.

Reliance damages Contract damages placing the injured party in as good a position as he would have been in had the contract not been made.

Treble damages Three times actual loss.

de facto In fact, in deed, actually. This phrase is used to characterize an officer, a government, a past action, or a state of affairs which must be accepted for all practical purposes but which is illegal or illegitimate. See also **corporation**, *corporation de facto.*

de jure Descriptive of a condition in which there has been total compliance with all requirements of law. In this sense it is the contrary of *de facto.* See also **corporation**, *corporation de jure.*

de novo Anew; afresh; a second time.

debenture Unsecured bond.

debt security Any form of corporate security reflected as debt on the books of the corporation in contrast to equity securities such as stock; *e.g.,* bonds, notes, and debentures are debt securities.

debtor Person who owes payment or performance of an obligation.

deceit A fraudulent and cheating misrepresentation, artifice, or device used to deceive and trick one who is ignorant of the true facts, to the prejudice and damage of the party imposed upon. See also **fraud; misrepresentation.**

decree Decision of a court of equity.

deed A conveyance of realty; a writing, signed by a grantor, whereby title to realty is transferred from one party to another.

deed of trust Interest in real property which is conveyed to a third person as trustee for the creditor.

defamation Injury of a person's reputation by publication of false statements.

default judgment Judgment against a defendant who fails to respond to a complaint.

defendant The party against whom legal action is sought.

definite term Lease that automatically expires at end of the term.

delectus personae Partner's right to choose who may become a member of the partnership.

delegatee Third party to whom the delegator's duty is delegated.

delegation of duties Transferring to another all or part of one's duties arising under a contract.

delegator Party delegating his duty to a third party.

F.A.S. Free alongside. Term used in sales price quotations indicating that the price includes all costs of transportation and delivery of the goods alongside the ship. See UCC § 2–319(2).

federal preemption First right of the federal government to regulate matters within its powers to the possible exclusion of state regulation.

federal question Any case arising under the Constitution, statutes, or treaties of the United States.

fee simple

Absolute A fee simple absolute is an estate that is unlimited as to duration, disposition, and descendibility. It is the largest estate and most extensive interest that can be enjoyed in land.

Conditional Type of transfer in which grantor conveys fee simple on condition that something be done or not done.

Defeasible Type of fee grant which may be defeated on the happening of an event. An estate which may last forever, but which may end upon the happening of a specified event, is a "fee simple defeasible."

Determinable Created by conveyance which contains words effective to create a fee simple and, in addition, a provision for automatic expiration of the estate on occurrence of stated event.

fee tail An estate of inheritance, descending only to a certain class or classes of heirs; *e.g.,* an estate is conveyed or devised "to A. and the heirs of his body," or "to A. and the heirs male of his body," or "to A., and the heirs female of his body."

fellow servant rule Common law defense relieving employer from liability to an employee for injuries caused by negligence of fellow employee.

felony Serious crime.

fiduciary A person or institution who manages money or property for another and who must exercise in such management activity a standard of care imposed by law or contract; *e.g.,* executor of estate; receiver in bankruptcy; trustee.

fiduciary duty Duty of utmost loyalty and good faith, such as that owed by a fiduciary such as an agent to her principal.

field warehouse Secured party takes possession of the goods but the debtor has access to the goods.

final credit Payment of the instrument by the payor bank.

financing statement Under the Uniform Commercial Code, a financing statement is used under Article 9 to reflect a public record that there is a security interest or claim to the goods in question to secure a debt. The financing statement is filed by the security holder with the secretary of state or with a similar public body; thus filed, it becomes public record. See also **secured transaction.**

fire (property) insurance Provides protection against loss due to fire or other related perils.

firm offer Irrevocable offer to sell or buy goods by a merchant in a signed writing which gives assurance that it will not be rescinded for up to three months.

fitness for a particular purpose Goods are fit for a stated purpose, provided that the seller selects the product knowing the buyer's intended use and that the buyer is relying on the seller's judgment.

fixture An article in the nature of personal property which has been so annexed to realty that it is regarded as a part of the land. Examples include a furnace affixed to a house or other building, counters permanently affixed to the floor of a store, and a sprinkler system installed in a building. UCC § 9–313(1)(a).

Trade fixtures Such chattels as merchants usually possess and annex to the premises occupied by them to enable them to store, handle, and display their goods, which generally are removable without material injury to the premises.

F.O.B. Free on board at some location (for example, F.O.B shipping point; F.O.B destination); the invoice price includes delivery at seller's expense to that location. Title to goods usually passes from seller to buyer at the F.O.B location. UCC § 2–319(1).

foreclosure Procedure by which mortgaged property is sold on default of mortgagor in satisfaction of mortgage debt.

forgery Intentional falsification of a document with intent to defraud.

four unities Time, title, interest, and possession.

franchise A privilege granted or sold, such as to use a name or to sell products or services. The right given by a manufacturer or supplier to a retailer to use his products and name on terms and conditions mutually agreed upon.

fraud Elements include false representation; of a present or past fact; made by defendant; action in reliance thereon by plaintiff; and damage resulting to plaintiff from such misrepresentation.

fraud in the execution Misrepresentation that deceives the other party as to the nature of a document evidencing the contract.

fraud in the inducement Misrepresentation regarding the subject matter of a contract that induces the other party to enter into the contract.

fraudulent misrepresentation False statement made with knowledge of its falsity and intent to mislead.

freehold An estate for life or in fee. It must possess two qualities: (1) immobility, that is, the property must be either land or some interest issuing out of or annexed to land; and (2) indeterminate duration.

friendly fire Fire contained where it is intended to be.

frustration of purpose doctrine Excuses a promisor in certain situations when the objectives of contract have been utterly defeated by circumstances arising after formation of the agreement, and performance is excused under this rule even though there is no impediment to actual performance.

full warranty One under which warrantor will repair the product and, if unsuccessful, will replace it or refund its cost.

fungibles With respect to goods or securities, those of which any unit is, by nature or usage of trade, the equivalent of any other like unit. UCC § 1–201(17); *e.g.,* a bushel of wheat or other grain.

future estate See **estate**.

garnishment A statutory proceeding whereby a person's property, money, or credits in the possession or control of another are applied to payment of the former's debt to a third person.

general intangible Catchall category for collateral not otherwise covered.

general partner Member of either a general or limited partnership with unlimited liability for its debts, full management powers, and a right to share in the profits.

gift A voluntary transfer of property to another made gratuitously and without consideration. Essential requisites of "gift" are capacity of donor, intention of donor to make gift, completed delivery to or for donee, and acceptance of gift by donee.

gift causa mortis A gift in view of death is one which is made in contemplation, fear, or peril of death and with the intent that it shall take effect only in case of the death of the giver.

good faith Honesty in fact in conduct or in a transaction.

good faith purchaser Buyer who acts honestly, gives value, and takes the goods without notice or knowledge of any defect in the title of his transferor.

goods A term of variable content and meaning. It may include every species of personal property, or it may be given a very restricted meaning. Sometimes the meaning of "goods" is extended to include all tangible items, as in the phrase "goods and services."

All things (including specially manufactured goods) which are movable at the time of identification to a contract for sale other than the money in which the price is to be paid, investment securities, and things in action. UCC § 2–105(1).

grantee Transferee of property.

grantor A transferor of property. The creator of a trust is usually designated as the grantor of the trust.

gratuitous promise Promise made without consideration.

group insurance Covers a number of individuals.

guaranty A promise to answer for the payment of some debt, or the performance of some duty, in case of the failure of another person who, in the first instance, is liable for such payment or performance.

The terms *guaranty* and *suretyship* are sometimes used interchangeably; but they should not be confounded. The distinction between contract of suretyship and contract of guaranty is whether or not the undertaking is a joint undertaking with the principal or a separate and distinct contract; if it is the former, it is one of "suretyship," and if the latter, it is one of "guaranty." See also **surety**.

guardianship The relationship under which a person (the guardian) is appointed by a court to preserve and control the property of another (the ward).

heir A person who succeeds, by the rules of law, to an estate in lands, tenements, or hereditaments, upon the death of his ancestor, by descent and right of relationship.

holder Person who is in possession of a document of title or an instrument or an investment security drawn, issued, or indorsed to him or to his order, or to bearer, or in blank. UCC § 1–201(20).

holder in due course A holder who takes an instrument for value, in good faith, and without notice that it is overdue or has been dishonored or of any defense against or claim to it on the part of any person.

holograph A will or deed written entirely by the testator or grantor with his own hand and not witnessed (attested). State laws vary with respect to the validity of the holographic will.

homicide Unlawful taking of another's life.

horizontal privity Who may bring a cause of action.

horizontal restraints Agreements among competitors.

hostile fire Any fire outside its intended or usual place.

identified goods Designated goods as a part of a particular contract.

illegal per se Conclusively presumed unreasonable and therefore illegal.

illusory promise Promise imposing no obligation on the promisor.

implied-in-fact condition Contingencies understood but not expressed by the parties.

implied-in-law condition Contingency that arises from operation of law.

implied warranty Obligation imposed by law upon the transferor of property or contract rights; implicit in the sale arising out of certain circumstances.

implied warranty of habitability Leased premises are fit for ordinary residential purposes.

impossibility Performance that cannot be done.

in personam Against the person. Action seeking judgment against a person involving his personal rights and based on jurisdiction of his person, as distinguished from a judgment against property (*i.e.*, in rem).

in personam jurisdiction Jurisdiction based on claims against a person, in contrast to jurisdiction over his property.

in re In the affair; in the matter of; concerning; regarding. This is the usual method of entitling a judicial proceeding in which there are no adversary parties, but merely some res concerning which judicial action is to be taken, such as a bankrupt's estate, an estate in the probate court, a proposed public highway, etc.

in rem A technical term used to designate proceedings or actions instituted *against the thing*, in contradistinction to personal actions, which are said to be *in personam*.

   Quasi in rem A term applied to proceedings which are not strictly and purely *in rem*, but are brought against the defendant personally, though the real object is to deal with particular property or subject property to the discharge of claims asserted; for example, foreign attachment, or proceedings to foreclose a mortgage, remove a cloud from title, or effect a partition.

in rem jurisdiction Jurisdiction based on claims against property.

incidental beneficiary Third party whom the two parties to a contract have no intention of benefiting by their contract.

income bond Bond that conditions payment of interest on corporate earnings.

incontestability clause The prohibition of an insurer to avoid an insurance policy after a specified period of time.

indemnification Duty owed by principal to agent to pay agent for losses incurred while acting as directed by principal.

indemnify To reimburse one for a loss already incurred.

indenture A written agreement under which bonds and debentures are issued, setting forth maturity date, interest rate, and other terms.

independent contractor Person who contracts with another to do a particular job and who is not subject to the control of the other.

indicia Signs; indications. Circumstances which point to the existence of a given fact as probable, but not certain.

indictment Grand jury charge that the defendant should stand trial.

indispensable paper Chattel paper, instruments, and documents.

indorsee The person to whom a negotiable instrument, promissory note, bill of lading, etc., is assigned by indorsement.

indorsement The act of a payee, drawee, accommodation indorser, or holder of a bill, note, check, or other negotiable instrument, in writing his name upon the back of the same, with or without further or qualifying words, whereby the property in the same is assigned and transferred to another. UCC § 3–202 *et seq.*

   Blank indorsement No indorsee is specified.

   Qualified indorsement Without recourse, limiting one's liability on the instrument.

   Restrictive indorsement Limits the rights of the indorser in some manner.

   Special indorsement Designates an indorsee to be paid.

infliction of emotional distress Extreme and outrageous conduct intentionally or recklessly causing severe emotional distress.

information Formal accusation of a crime brought by a prosecutor.

infringement Unauthorized use.

injunction An equitable remedy forbidding the party defendant from doing some act which he is threatening or attempting to commit, or restraining him in the continuance thereof, such act being unjust and inequitable, injurious to the plaintiff, and not such as can be adequately redressed by an action at law.

innkeeper Hotel or motel operator.

inquisitorial system System in which the judiciary initiates, conducts, and decides cases.

insider Relative or general partner of debtor, partnership in which debtor is a partner, or corporation in which debtor is an officer, director, or controlling person.

insiders Directors, officers, employees, and agents of the issuer as well as those the issuer has entrusted with information solely for corporate purposes.

insolvency Under the UCC, a person is insolvent who either has ceased to pay his debts in the ordinary course of business or cannot pay his debts as they fall due or is insolvent within the meaning of the Federal Bankruptcy Law. UCC § 1–201(23).

   Insolvency (bankruptcy) Total liabilities exceed total value of assets.

   Insolvency (equity) Inability to pay debts in ordinary course of business or as they become due.

inspection Examination of goods to determine whether they conform to a contract.

instrument Negotiable instruments, stocks, bonds, and other investment securities.

insurable interest Exists where insured derives pecuniary benefit or advantage by preservation and continued existence of property or would sustain pecuniary loss from its destruction.

insurance A contract whereby, for a stipulated consideration, one party undertakes to compensate the other for loss on a specified subject by specified perils. The party agreeing to make the compensation is usually called the "insurer" or "underwriter"; the other, the "insured" or "assured"; the written contract, a "policy"; the events insured against, "risks" or "perils"; and the subject, right, or interest to be protected, the "insurable interest." Insurance is a contract whereby one undertakes to indemnify another against loss, damage, or liability arising from an unknown or contingent event.

   Co-insurance A form of insurance in which a person insures property for less than its full or stated value and agrees to share the risk of loss.

   Life insurance Payment of a specific sum of money to a designated beneficiary upon the death of the insured.

   Ordinary life Life insurance with a savings component that runs for the life of the insured.

   Term life Life insurance issued for a limited number of years that does not have a savings component.

intangible property Protected interests that are not physical.

intangibles Accounts and general intangibles.

intent Desire to cause the consequences of an act or knowledge that the consequences are substantially certain to result from the act.

inter alia Among other things.

inter se or **inter sese** Latin. Among or between themselves; used to distinguish rights or duties between two or more parties from their rights or duties to others.

interest in land Any right, privilege, power, or immunity in real property.

interest in partnership Partner's share in the partnership's profits and surplus.

interference with contractual relations Intentionally causing one of the parties to a contract not to perform the contract.

intermediary bank Any bank, except the depositary or payor bank, to which an item is transferred in the course of collection. UCC § 4–105(c).

intermediate test Requirement that legislation have a substantial relationship to an important governmental objective.

international law Deals with the conduct and relations of nation-states and international organizations.

interpretation Construction or meaning of a contract.

interpretative rules Statements issued by an administrative agency indicating its construction of its governing statute.

intestate A person is said to die intestate when he dies without making a will. The word is also often used to signify the person himself. *Compare* **testator**.

intrusion Unreasonable and highly offensive interference with the seclusion of another.

inventory Goods held for sale or lease or consumed in a business.

invitee A person is an "invitee" on land of another if (1) he enters by invitation, express or implied, (2) his entry is connected with the owner's business or with an activity the owner conducts or permits to be conducted on his land, and (3) there is mutual benefit or a benefit to the owner.

joint liability Liability where creditor must sue all of the partners as a group.

joint and several liability Liability where creditor may sue partners jointly as a group or separately as individuals.

joint stock company A general partnership with some corporate attributes.

joint tenancy See **tenancy**.

joint venture An association of two or more persons to carry on a single business transaction for profit.

judgment The official and authentic decision of a court of justice upon the respective rights and claims of the parties to an action or suit therein litigated and submitted to its determination.

judgment in personam A judgment against a particular person, as distinguished from a judgment against a thing or a right or *status*.

judgment in rem An adjudication pronounced upon the status of some particular thing or subject matter, by a tribunal having competent authority.

judgment n. o. v. Judgment non obstante veredicto in its broadest sense is a judgment rendered in favor of one party notwithstanding the finding of a verdict in favor of the other party.

judgment notwithstanding the verdict A final binding determination on the merits made by the judge after and contrary to the jury's verdict.

judgment on the pleadings Final binding determination on the merits made by the judge after the pleadings.

judicial lien Interest in property that is obtained by court action to secure payment of a debt.

judicial review Power of the courts to determine the constitutionality of legislative and executive acts.

jurisdiction The right and power of a court to adjudicate concerning the subject matter in a given case.

jurisdiction over the parties Power of a court to bind the parties to a suit.

jury A body of persons selected and summoned by law and sworn to try the facts of a case and to find according to the law and the evidence. In general, the province of the jury is to find the facts in a case, while the judge passes upon pure questions of law. As a matter of fact, however, the jury must often pass upon mixed questions of law and fact in determining the case, and in all such cases the instructions of the judge as to the law become very important.

justifiable reliance Reasonably influenced by a misrepresentation.

labor dispute Any controversy concerning terms or conditions of employment or union representation.

laches Based upon maxim that equity aids the vigilant and not those who slumber on their rights. It is defined as neglect to assert a right or claim which, taken together with a lapse of time and other circumstances causing prejudice to the adverse party, operates as a bar in a court of equity.

landlord The owner of an estate in land, or a rental property, who has leased it to another person, called the "tenant." Also called "lessor."

larceny Trespassory taking and carrying away of the goods of another with the intent to permanently deprive.

last clear chance Final opportunity to avoid an injury.

lease Any agreement which gives rise to relationship of landlord and tenant (real property) or lessor and lessee (real or personal property).

The person who conveys is termed the "lessor," and the person to whom conveyed, the "lessee"; and when the lessor conveys land or tenements to a lessee, he is said to lease, demise, or let them.

Sublease, or *underlease* One executed by the lessee of an estate to a third person, conveying the same estate for a shorter term than that for which the lessee holds it.

leasehold An estate in realty held under a lease. The four principal types of leasehold estates are the estate for years, periodic tenancy, tenancy at will, and tenancy at sufferance.

leasehold estate Right to possess real property.

legacy "Legacy" is a gift or bequest by will of personal property, whereas a "devise" is a testamentary disposition of real estate.

Demonstrative legacy A bequest of a certain sum of money, with a direction that it shall be paid out of a particular fund. It differs from a specific legacy in this respect: that, if the fund out of which it is payable fails for any cause, it is nevertheless entitled to come on the estate as a general legacy. And it differs from a general legacy in this: that it does not abate in that class, but in the class of specific legacies.

General legacy A pecuniary legacy, payable out of the general assets of a testator.

Residuary legacy A bequest of all the testator's personal estate not otherwise effectually disposed of by his will.

Specific legacy One which operates on property particularly designated. A legacy or gift by will of a particular specified thing, as of a horse, a piece of furniture, a term of years, and the like.

legal aggregate A group of individuals not having a legal existence separate from its members.

legal benefit Obtaining something to which one had no legal right.

legal detriment Doing an act one is not legally obligated to do or not doing an act one has a legal right to do.

legal entity An organization having a legal existence separate from that of its members.

legal sufficiency Benefit to promisor or detriment to promisee.

legislative rules Substantive rules issued by an administrative agency under the authority delegated to it by the legislature.

letter of credit An engagement by a bank or other person made at the request of a customer that the issuer will honor drafts or other demands for payment upon compliance with the conditions specified in the credit.

letters of administration Formal document issued by probate court appointing one an administrator of an estate.

letters testamentary The formal instrument of authority and appointment given to an executor by the proper court, empowering him to enter upon the discharge of his office as executor. It corresponds to letters of administration granted to an administrator.

levy To assess; raise; execute; exact; tax; collect; gather; take up; seize. Thus, to levy (assess, exact, raise, or collect) a tax; to levy an execution, *i.e.*, to levy or collect a sum of money on an execution.

liability insurance Covers liability to others by reason of damage resulting from injuries to another's person or property.

liability without fault Crime to do a specific act or cause a certain result without regard to the care exercised.

libel Defamation communicated by writing, television, radio, or the like.

liberty Ability of individuals to engage in freedom of action and choice regarding their personal lives.

license License with respect to real property is a privilege to go on premises for a certain purpose, but does not operate to confer on or vest in the licensee any title, interest, or estate in such property.

licensee Person privileged to enter or remain on land by virtue of the consent of the lawful possessor.

lien A qualified right of property which a creditor has in or over specific property of his debtor, as security for the debt or charge or for performance of some act.

lien creditor A creditor who has acquired a lien on the property by attachment.

life estate An estate whose duration is limited to the life of the party holding it or of some other person. Upon the death of the life tenant, the property will go to the holder of the remainder interest or to the grantor by reversion.

limited liability Liability limited to amount invested in a business enterprise.

limited partner Member of a limited partnership with liability for its debts only to the extent of her capital contribution.

limited partnership See **partnership.**

limited partnership association A partnership which closely resembles a corporation.

liquidated Ascertained; determined; fixed; settled; made clear or manifest. Cleared away; paid; discharged.

liquidated damages See **damages**.

liquidated debt Obligation that is certain in amount.

liquidation The settling of financial affairs of a business or individual, usually by liquidating (turning to cash) all assets for distribution to creditors, heirs, etc. To be distinguished from dissolution.

loss of value Value of promised performance minus value of actual performance.

lost property Property with which the owner has involuntarily parted and which she does not know where to find or recover, not including property which she has intentionally concealed or deposited in a secret place for safekeeping. Distinguishable from mislaid property, which has been deliberately placed somewhere and forgotten.

main purpose rule Where object of promisor/surety is to provide an economic benefit for herself, the promise is considered outside of the statute of frauds.

maker One who makes or executes; as the maker of a promissory note. One who signs a check; in this context, synonymous with drawer. See **draft.**

mala in se Morally wrong.

mala prohibita Wrong by law.

mandamus Latin, we command. A legal writ compelling the defendant to do an official duty.

manslaughter Unlawful taking of another's life without malice.

    Involuntary manslaughter Taking the life of another by criminal negligence or during the course of a misdemeanor.

    Voluntary manslaughter Intentional killing of another under extenuating circumstances.

manufacturing defect Not produced according to specifications.

mark Trade symbol.

market allocations Division of market by customers, geographic location, or products.

marketable title Free from any defects, encumbrances, or reasonable objections to one's ownership.

marshaling of assets Segregating the assets and liabilities of a partnership from the assets and liabilities of the individual partners.

master See **principal**.

material Matters to which a reasonable investor would attach importance in deciding whether to purchase a security.

material alteration Any change that changes the contract of any party to an instrument.

maturity The date at which an obligation, such as the principal of a bond or a note, becomes due.

maxim A general legal principle.

mechanic's lien A claim created by state statutes for the purpose of securing priority of payment of the price or value of work performed and materials furnished in erecting or repairing a building or other structure; as such, attaches to the land as well as buildings and improvements erected thereon.

mediation Nonbinding process in which a third party acts as an intermediary between the disputing parties and proposes solutions for them to consider.

mens rea Criminal intent.

mentally incompetent Unable to understand the nature and effect of one's acts.

mercantile law An expression substantially equivalent to commercial law. It designates the system of rules, customs, and usages generally recognized and adopted by merchants and traders that, either in its simplicity or as modified by common law or statutes, constitutes the law for the regulation of their transactions and the solution of their controversies. The Uniform Commercial Code is the general body of law governing commercial or mercantile transactions.

merchant A person who deals in goods of the kind involved in a transaction or who otherwise by his occupation holds himself out as having knowledge or skill peculiar to the practices or goods involved in the transaction or to whom such knowledge or skill may be attributed by his employment of an agent or broker or other intermediary who by his occupation holds himself out as having such knowledge or skill. UCC § 2–104(1).

merchantability Merchant seller guarantees that the goods are fit for their ordinary purpose.

merger The fusion or absorption of one thing or right into another. In corporate law, the absorption of one company by another, the latter retaining its own name and identity and acquiring the assets, liabilities, franchises, and powers of the former, which ceases to exist as separate business entity. It differs from a consolidation, wherein all the corporations terminate their separate existences and become parties to a new one.

    Conglomerate merger An acquisition, which is not horizontal or vertical, by one company of another.

    Horizontal merger Merger between business competitors, such as manufacturers of the same type of products or distributors selling competing products in the same market area.

    Short-form merger Merger of a 90 percent subsidiary into its parent.

    Vertical merger Union with corporate customer or supplier.

midnight deadline Midnight of the next banking day after receiving an item.

mining partnership A specific type of partnership for the purpose of extracting raw minerals.

minor Under the age of legal majority (usually eighteen).

mirror image rule An acceptance cannot deviate from the terms of the offer.

misdemeanor Less serious crime.

mislaid property Property which an owner has put deliberately in a certain place that she is unable to remember, as distinguished from lost property, which the owner has left unwittingly in a location she has forgotten. See also **lost property**.

misrepresentation Any manifestation by words or other conduct by one person to another that, under the circumstances, amounts to an assertion not in accordance with the facts. A "misrepresentation" that justifies the rescission of a contract is a false statement of a substantive fact, or any conduct which leads to a belief of a substantive fact material to proper understanding of the matter in hand. See also **deceit**; **fraud**.

    Fraudulent misrepresentation False statement made with knowledge of its falsity and intent to mislead.

    Innocent misrepresentation Misrepresentation made without knowledge of its falsity but with due care.

Negligent misrepresentation Misrepresentation made without due care in ascertaining its falsity.

M'Naughten Rule Right/wrong test for criminal insanity.

modify Change the lower court's judgment.

money Medium of exchange issued by a government body.

monopoly Ability to control price or exclude others from the marketplace.

mortgage A mortgage is an interest in land created by a written instrument providing security for the performance of a duty or the payment of a debt.

mortgagor Debtor who uses real estate to secure an obligation.

multinational enterprise Business that engages in transactions involving the movement of goods, information, money, people, or services across national borders.

multiple product order Order requiring an advertiser to cease and desist from deceptive statements on all products it sells.

murder Unlawful and premeditated taking of another's life.

mutual mistake Where the common but erroneous belief of both parties forms the basis of a contract.

necessaries Items needed to maintain a person's station in life.

negligence The omission to do something which a reasonable person, guided by those ordinary considerations which ordinarily regulate human affairs, would do, or the doing of something which a reasonable and prudent person would not do.

> *Culpable negligence* Greater than ordinary negligence but less than gross negligence.

negligence *per se* Conclusive on the issue of negligence (duty of care and breach).

negotiable Legally capable of being transferred by indorsement or delivery. Usually said of checks and notes and sometimes of stocks and bearer bonds.

negotiable instrument Signed document (such as a check or promissory note) containing an unconditional promise to pay a "sum certain" of money at a definite time to order or bearer.

negotiation Transferee becomes a holder.

net assets Total assets minus total debts.

no arrival, no sale A destination contract, but if goods do not arrive, seller is excused from liability unless such is due to the seller's fault.

no-fault insurance Compensates victims of automobile accidents regardless of fault.

nonconforming use Preexisting use not in accordance with a zoning ordinance.

nonprofit corporation One whose profits must be used exclusively for the charitable, educational, or scientific purpose for which it was formed.

nonsuit Action in form of a judgment taken against a plaintiff who has failed to appear to prosecute his action or failed to prove his case.

note See **promissory note.**

novation A novation substitutes a new party and discharges one of the original parties to a contract by agreement of all three parties. A new contract is created with the same terms as the original one; only the parties have changed.

nuisance Nuisance is that activity which arises from the unreasonable, unwarranted, or unlawful use by a person of his own property, working obstruction or injury to the right of another or to the public, and producing such material annoyance, inconvenience, and discomfort that law will presume resulting damage.

obiter dictum See **dictum.**

objective fault Gross deviation from reasonable conduct.

objective manifestation What a reasonable person under the circumstances would believe.

objective satisfaction Approval based upon whether a reasonable person would be satisfied.

objective standard What a reasonable person under the circumstances would reasonably believe or do.

obligee Party to whom a duty of performance is owed (by delegator and delegatee).

obligor Party owing a duty (to the assignor).

offer A manifestation of willingness to enter into a bargain, so made as to justify another person in understanding that his assent to that bargain is invited and will conclude it. Restatement, Second, Contracts, § 24

offeree Recipient of the offer.

offeror Person making the offer.

open-ended credit Credit arrangement under which debtor has rights to enter into a series of credit transactions.

opinion Belief in the existence of a fact or a judgment as to value.

option Contract providing that an offer will stay open for a specified period of time.

order A final disposition made by an agency.

order paper Payable to a named person or to anyone designated by that person.

order to pay Direction or command to pay.

original promise Promise to become primarily liable.

output contract See **contracts.**

palpable unilateral mistake Erroneous belief by one party that is recognized by the other.

parent corporation Corporation which controls another corporation.

parol evidence Literally oral evidence, but now includes prior to and contemporaneous, oral, and written evidence.

parol evidence rule Under this rule, when parties put their agreement in writing, all previous oral agreements merge in the writing and the contract as written cannot be modified or changed by parol evidence, in the absence of a plea of mistake or fraud in the preparation of the writing. But the rule does not forbid a resort to parol evidence not inconsistent with the matters stated in the writing. Also, as regards sales of goods, such written agreement may be explained or supplemented by course of dealing, usage of trade, or course of conduct, and by evidence of consistent additional terms, unless the court finds the writing to have been intended also as a complete and exclusive statement of the terms of the agreement. UCC § 2–202.

part performance In order to establish part performance taking an oral contract for the sale of realty out of the statute of frauds, the acts relied upon as part performance must be of such a character that they reasonably can be naturally accounted for in no other way than that they were performed in pursuance of the contract, and they must be in conformity with its provisions. See UCC § 2–201(3).

partial assignment Transfer of a portion of contractual rights to one or more assignees.

partition The dividing of lands held by joint tenants, copartners, or tenants in common into distinct portions, so that the parties may hold those lands in severalty.

partnership An association of two or more persons to carry on, as co-owners, a business for profit.

> Partnerships are treated as a conduit and are, therefore, not subject to taxation. The various items of partnership income (gains and losses, etc.) flow through to the individual partners and are reported on their personal income tax returns.
>
> *Limited partnership* Type of partnership comprised of one or more general partners who manage business and who are personally liable for partnership debts, and one or more limited partners who contribute capital and share in profits but who take no part in running business and incur no liability with respect to partnership obligations beyond contribution.
>
> *Partnership at will* One with no definite term or specific undertaking.

partnership capital Total money and property contributed by partners for permanent use by the partnership.

partnership property Sum of all of the partnership's assets.

past consideration An act done before the contract is made.

patent Exclusive right to an invention.

payee The person in whose favor a bill of exchange, promissory note, or check is made or drawn.

payer or **payor** One who pays or who is to make a payment, particularly the person who is to make payment of a check, bill, or note. Correlative to "payee."

payor bank A bank by which an item is payable as drawn or accepted. UCC § 4–105(b). Correlative to "Drawee bank."

per capita This term, derived from the civil law and much used in the law of descent and distribution, denotes that method of dividing an intestate estate by which an equal share is given to each of a number of persons, all of whom stand in equal degree to the decedent, without reference to their stocks or the right of representation. The opposite of *per stirpes*.

per stirpes This term, derived from the civil law and much used in the law of descent and distribution, denotes that method of dividing an intestate estate where a class or group of distributees takes the share to which its deceased would have been entitled, taking thus by its right of representing such ancestor and not as so many individuals. The opposite of *per capita*.

perfect tender rule Seller's tender of delivery must conform exactly to the contract.

perfection of security interest Acts required of a secured party in the way of giving at least constructive notice so as to make his security interest effective at least against lien creditors of the debtor. See UCC §§ 9–302 through 9–306. In most cases, the secured party may obtain perfection either by filing with the secretary of state or by taking possession of the collateral.

performance Fulfillment of one's contractual obligations. See also **part performance**; **specific performance**.

periodic tenancy Lease with a definite term that is to be continued.

personal defenses Contractual defenses which are good against holders but not holders in due course.

personal property Any property other than an interest in land.

petty crime Misdemeanor punishable by imprisonment of six months or less.

plaintiff The party who initiates a civil suit.

pleadings The formal allegations by the parties of their respective claims and defenses.

> *Rules or codes of civil procedure* Unlike the rigid technical system of common law pleading, pleadings under federal and state rules or codes of civil procedure have a far more limited function, with determination and narrowing of facts and issues being left to discovery devices and pretrial conferences. In addition, the rules and codes permit liberal amendment and supplementation of pleadings.
>
> Under rules of civil procedure, the pleadings consist of a complaint, an answer, a reply to a counterclaim, an answer to a cross-claim, a third-party complaint, and a third-party answer.

pledge A bailment of goods to a creditor as security for some debt or engagement.

> Much of the law of pledges has been replaced by the provisions for secured transactions in Article 9 of the UCC.

possibility of reverter The interest which remains in a grantor or testator after the conveyance or devise of a fee simple determinable and which permits the grantor to be revested automatically of his estate on breach of the condition.

possibility test Under the statute of frauds, asks whether performance could possibly be completed within one year.

power of appointment A power of authority conferred by one person by deed or will upon another (called the "donee") to appoint, that is, to select and nominate, the person or persons who is or are to receive and enjoy an estate or an income therefrom or from a fund, after the testator's death, or the donee's death, or after the termination of an existing right or interest.

power of attorney An instrument authorizing a person to act as the agent or attorney of the person granting it.

power of termination The interest left in the grantor or testator after the conveyance or devise of a fee simple on condition subsequent or conditional fee.

precatory Expressing a wish.

precedent An adjudged case or decision of a court, considered as furnishing an example or authority for an identical or similar case afterwards arising or a similar question of law. See also **stare decisis**.

preemptive right The privilege of a stockholder to maintain a proportionate share of ownership by purchasing a proportionate share of any new stock issues.

preference The act of an insolvent debtor who, in distributing his property or in assigning it for the benefit of his creditors, pays or secures to one or more creditors the full amount of their claims or a larger amount than they would be entitled to receive on a *pro rata* distribution. The treatment of such preferential payments in bankruptcy is governed by the Bankruptcy Act, § 547.

preliminary hearing Determines whether there is probable cause.

premium The price for insurance protection for a specified period of exposure.

preponderance of the evidence Greater weight of the evidence; standard used in civil cases.

prescription Acquisition of a personal right to use a way, water, light, and air by reason of continuous usage. See also **easement**.

presenter's warranty Warranty given to any payor or acceptor of an instrument.

presentment The production of a negotiable instrument to the drawee for his acceptance, or to the drawer or acceptor for payment; or of a promissory note to the party liable, for payment of the same. UCC § 3–504(1).

presumption A presumption is a rule of law, statutory or judicial, by which a finding of a basic fact gives rise to the existence of presumed fact, until presumption is rebutted. A presumption imposes on the party against whom it is directed the burden of going forward with evidence to rebut or meet the presumption, but does not shift to such party the burden of proof in the sense of the risk of nonpersuasion, which remains throughout the trial upon the party on whom it was originally cast.

price discrimination Price differential.

price fixing Any agreement for the purpose and effect of raising, depressing, fixing, pegging, or stabilizing prices.

prima facie Latin. At first sight; on the first appearance; on the face of it; so far as can be judged from the first disclosure; presumably; a fact presumed to be true unless disproved by some evidence to the contrary.

primary liability Absolute obligation to pay a negotiable instrument.

principal *Law of agency* The term "principal" describes one who has permitted or directed another (*i.e.*, an agent or a servant) to act for his benefit and subject to his direction and control. Principal includes in its meaning the term "master" or employer, a species of principal who, in addition to other control, has a right to control the physical conduct of the species of agents known as servants or employees, as to whom special rules are applicable with reference to harm caused by their physical acts.

> *Disclosed principal* One whose existence and identity are known.
> *Partially disclosed principal* One whose existence is known but whose identity is not known.
> *Undisclosed principal* One whose existence and identity are not known.

principal debtor Person whose debt is being supported by a surety.

priority Precedence in order of right.

private carrier Carrier which limits its service and is not open to the general public.

private corporation One organized to conduct either a privately owned business enterprise for profit or a nonprofit corporation.

private law The law involving relationships among individuals and legal entities.

privilege Immunity from tort liability.

privity Contractual relationship.

privity of contract That connection or relationship which exists between two or more contracting parties. The absence of privity as a defense in actions for damages in contract and tort actions is generally no longer viable with the enactment of warranty statutes (*e.g.*, UCC § 2–318), acceptance by states of the doctrine of strict liability, and court decisions which have extended the right to sue to third-party beneficiaries and even innocent bystanders.

probable cause Reasonable belief of the offense charged.

probate Court procedure by which a will is proved to be valid or invalid, though in current usage this term has been expanded to include generally all matters and proceedings pertaining to administration of estates, guardianships, etc.

procedural due process Requirement that governmental action depriving a person of life, liberty, or property be done through a fair procedure.

procedural law Rules for enforcing substantive law.

procedural rules Rules issued by an administrative agency establishing its organization, method of operation, and rules of conduct for practice before it.

procedural unconscionability Unfair or irregular bargaining.

proceeds Consideration for the sale, exchange, or other disposition of collateral.

process *Judicial process* In a wide sense, this term may include all the acts of a court from the beginning to the end of its proceedings in a given cause; more specifically, it means the writ, summons, mandate, or other process which is used to inform the defendant of the institution of proceedings against him and to compel his appearance, in either civil or criminal cases.

    Legal process This term is sometimes used as equivalent to "lawful process." Thus, it is said that legal process means process not merely fair on its face but valid in fact. But properly it means a summons, writ, warrant, mandate, or other process issuing from a court.

profit corporation One founded for the purpose of operating a business for profit.

profit à prendre Right to make some use of the soil of another, such as a right to mine metals; carries with it the right of entry and the right to remove.

promise to pay Undertaking to pay an existing obligation.

promisee Person to whom a promise is made.

promisor Person making a promise.

promissory estoppel Arises where there is a promise which promisor should reasonably expect to induce action or forbearance on part of promisee and which does induce such action or forbearance, and where injustice can be avoided only by enforcement of the promise.

promissory note An unconditional written promise to pay a specified sum of money on demand or at a specified date. Such a note is negotiable if signed by the maker and containing an unconditional promise to pay a sum certain in money either on demand or at a definite time and payable to order or bearer. UCC § 3–104.

promoters In the law relating to corporations, those persons who first associate themselves for the purpose of organizing a company, issuing its prospectus, procuring subscriptions to the stock, securing a charter, etc.

property Interest that is legally protected.

    Abandoned property Intentionally disposed of by the owner.

    Lost property Unintentionally left by the owner.

    Mislaid property Intentionally placed by the owner but unintentionally left.

prosecute To bring a criminal proceeding.

protest A formal declaration made by a person interested or concerned in some act about to be done, or already performed, whereby he expresses his dissent or disapproval or affirms the act against his will. The object of such a declaration usually is to preserve some right which would be lost to the protester if his assent could be implied, or to exonerate him from some responsibility which would attach to him unless he expressly negatived his assent.

    Notice of protest A notice given by the holder of a bill or note to the drawer or indorser that the bill has been protested for refusal of payment or acceptance. UCC § 3–509.

provisional credit Tentative credit for the deposit of an instrument until final credit is given.

proximate cause Where the act or omission played a substantial part in bringing about or actually causing the injury or damage and where the injury or damage was either a direct result or a reasonably probable consequence of the act or omission.

proxy (Contracted from "procuracy.") Written authorization given by one person to another so that the second person can act for the first, such as that given by a shareholder to someone else to represent him and vote his shares at a shareholders' meeting.

public corporation One created to administer a unit of local civil government or one created by the United States to conduct public business.

public disclosure of private facts Offensive publicity given to private information about another person.

public law The law dealing with the relationship between government and individuals.

puffery Sales talk that is considered general bragging or overstatement.

punitive damages Damages awarded in excess of normal compensation to punish a defendant for a serious civil wrong.

purchase money security interest Security interest retained by a seller of goods in goods purchased with the loaned money.

qualified fee Ownership subject to its being taken away upon the happening of an event.

quantum meruit Expression "quantum meruit" means "as much as he deserves"; describes the extent of liability on a contract implied by law. Elements essential to recovery under quantum meruit are (1) valuable services rendered or materials furnished (2) for the person sought to be charged, (3) which services and materials such person accepted, used, and enjoyed, (4) under such circumstances as reasonably notified her that plaintiff, in performing such services, was expected to be paid by the person sought to be charged.

quasi Latin. As if; almost as it were; analogous to. Negatives the idea of identity but points out that the conceptions are sufficiently similar to be classed as equals of one another.

quasi contract Legal fiction invented by common law courts to permit recovery by contractual remedy in cases where, in fact, there is no contract, but where circumstances are such that justice warrants a recovery as though a promise had been made.

quasi in rem See **in rem**.

quasi in rem jurisdiction Jurisdiction over property not based on claims against it.

quiet enjoyment Right of a tenant not to have his physical possession of premises interfered with by the landlord.

quitclaim deed A deed of conveyance operating by way of release; that is, intended to pass any title, interest, or claim which the grantor may have in the premises but neither professing that such title is valid nor containing any warranty or covenants for title.

quorum When a committee, board of directors, meeting of shareholders, legislature, or other body of persons cannot act unless at least a certain number of them are present.

rape Unlawful, nonconsensual sexual intercourse.

ratification In a broad sense, the confirmation of a previous act done either by the party himself or by another; as, for example, confirmation of a voidable act.

    In the law of principal and agent, the adoption and confirmation by one person, with knowledge of all material facts, of an act or contract performed or entered into in his behalf by another who at the time assumed without authority to act as his agent.

rational relationship test Requirement that legislation bear a rational relationship to a legitimate governmental interest.

real defenses Defenses that are valid against all holders, including holders in due course.

real property Land, and generally whatever is erected or growing upon or affixed to land. Also, rights issuing out of, annexed to, and exercisable within or about land. See also **fixture**.

reasonable man standard Duty of care required to avoid being negligent; one who is careful, diligent, and prudent.

receiver A fiduciary of the court, whose appointment is incident to other proceedings wherein certain ultimate relief is prayed. He is a trustee or ministerial officer representing the court, all parties in interest in the litigation, and the property or funds entrusted to him.

recognizance Formal acknowledgment of indebtedness made in court.

redemption The realization of a right to have the title of property restored free and clear of a mortgage, performance of the mortgage obligation being essential for such purpose. (b) Repurchase by corporation of its own shares.

reformation Equitable remedy used to reframe written contracts to reflect accurately real agreement between contracting parties when, either through mutual mistake or unilateral mistake coupled with actual or equitable fraud by the other party, the writing does not embody the contract as actually made.

regulatory license Requirement to protect the public interest.

reimbursement Duty owed by principal to pay back authorized payments agent has made on principal's behalf. Duty owed by a principal debtor to repay surety who pays principal debtor's obligation.

rejection The refusal to accept an offer; manifestation of an unwillingness to accept the goods (sales).

release The relinquishment, concession, or giving up of a right, claim, or privilege, by the person in whom it exists or to whom it accrues, to the person against whom it might have been demanded or enforced.

remainder An estate limited to take effect and be enjoyed after another estate is determined.

remand To send back. The sending by the appellate court of a cause back to the same court out of which it came, for the purpose of having some further action taken on it there.

remedy The means by which the violation of a right is prevented, redressed, or compensated. Though a remedy may be by the act of the party injured, by operation of law, or by agreement between the injurer and the injured, we are chiefly concerned with one kind of remedy, the judicial remedy, which is by action or suit.

rent Consideration paid for use or occupation of property. In a broader sense, it is the compensation or fee paid, usually periodically, for the use of any property, land, buildings, equipment, etc.

replevin An action whereby the owner or person entitled to repossession of goods or chattels may recover those goods or chattels from one who has wrongfully distrained or taken such goods or chattels or who wrongfully detains them.

reply Plaintiff's pleading in response to the defendant's answer.

repudiation Repudiation of a contract means refusal to perform duty or obligation owed to other party.

requirements contract See **contracts.**

res ipsa loquitur "The thing speaks for itself"; permits the jury to infer both negligent conduct and causation.

rescission An equitable action in which a party seeks to be relieved of his obligations under a contract on the grounds of mutual mistake, fraud, impossibility, etc.

residuary Pertaining to the residue; constituting the residue; giving or bequeathing the residue; receiving or entitled to the residue. See also **legacy, residuary legacy.**

respondeat superior Latin. Let the master answer. This maxim means that a master or employer is liable in certain cases for the wrongful acts of his servant or employee, and a principal for those of his agent.

respondent In equity practice, the party who makes an answer to a bill or other proceeding. In appellate practice, the party who contends against an appeal; *i.e.,* the appellee. The party who appeals is called the "appellant."

restitution An equitable remedy under which a person who has rendered services to another seeks to be reimbursed for the costs of his acts (but not his profits) even though there was never a contract between the parties.

restraint on alienation A provision in an instrument of conveyance which prohibits the grantee from selling or transferring the property which is the subject of the conveyance. Many such restraints are unenforceable as against public policy and the law's policy of free alienability of land.

restraint of trade Agreement that eliminates or tends to eliminate competition.

restrictive covenant Private restriction on property contained in a conveyance.

revenue license Measure to raise money.

reverse An appellate court uses the term "reversed" to indicate that it annuls or avoids the judgment, or vacates the decree, of the trial court.

reverse discrimination Employment decisions taking into account race or gender in order to remedy past discrimination.

reversion The term reversion has two meanings. First, it designates the estate left in the grantor during the continuance of a particular estate; second, it denotes the residue left in grantor or his heirs after termination of a particular estate. It differs from a remainder in that it arises by an act of law, whereas a remainder arises by an act of the parties. A reversion, moreover, is the remnant left in the grantor, while a remainder is the remnant of the whole estate disposed of after a preceding part of the same has been given away.

revocation The recall of some power, authority, or thing granted, or a destroying or making void of some deed that had existence until the act of revocation made it void.

revocation of acceptance Rescission of one's acceptance of goods based upon a nonconformity of the goods which substantially impairs their value.

right Legal capacity to require another person to perform or refrain from performing an act.

right of entry The right to take or resume possession of land by entering on it in a peaceable manner.

right of redemption The right (granted by statute only) to free property from the encumbrance of a foreclosure or other judicial sale, or to recover the title passing thereby, by paying what is due, with interest, costs, etc. Not to be confounded with the "equity of redemption," which exists independently of statute but must be exercised before sale. See also **equity of redemption.**

right to work law State statute that prohibits union shop contracts.

rights in collateral Personal property the debtor owns, possesses, or is in the process of acquiring.

risk of loss Allocation of loss between seller and buyer where the goods have been damaged, destroyed, or lost.

robbery Larceny from a person by force or threat of force.

rule Agency statement of general or particular applicability designed to implement, interpret, or process law or policy.

rule against perpetuities Principle that no interest in property is good unless it must vest, if at all, not later than twenty-one years, plus period of gestation, after some life or lives in being at time of creation of interest.

rule of reason Balancing the anticompetitive effects of a restraint against its procompetitive effects.

sale Transfer of title to goods from seller to buyer for a price.

sale on approval Transfer of possession without title to buyer for trial period.

sale or return Sale where buyer has option to return goods to seller.

sanction Means of enforcing legal judgments.

satisfaction The discharge of an obligation by paying a party what is due to him (as on a mortgage, lien, or contract) or what is been awarded to him by the judgment of a court or otherwise. Thus, a judgment is satisfied by the payment of the amount due to the party who has recovered such judgment, or by his levying the amount. See also **accord and satisfaction.**

scienter Latin. Knowingly.

seal Symbol that authenticates a document.

secondary liability Obligation to pay is subject to the conditions of presentment, dishonor, notice of dishonor, and sometimes protest.

secret partner Partner whose membership in the partnership is not disclosed.

Section 402A Strict liability in tort.

secured bond A bond having a lien on specific property.

secured claim Claim with a lien on property of the debtor.

secured party Creditor who possesses a security interest in collateral.

secured transaction A transaction founded on a security agreement. Such agreement creates or provides for a security interest. UCC § 9–105(h).

securities Stocks, bonds, notes, convertible debentures, warrants, or other documents that represent a share in a company or a debt owed by a company.

Certificated security Security represented by a certificate.

Exempt security Security not subject to registration requirements of 1933 Act.

Exempt transaction Issuance of securities not subject to the registration requirements of 1933 Act.

Restricted securities Securities issued under an exempt transaction.

Uncertificated security Security not represented by a certificate.

security agreement Agreement that grants a security interest.

security interest Right in personal property securing payment or performance of an obligation.

seisin Possession with an intent on the part of him who holds it to claim a freehold interest.

self-defense Force to protect oneself against attack.

separation of powers Allocation of powers among the legislative, executive, and judicial branches of government.

service mark Distinctive symbol, word, or design that is used to identify the services of a provider.

servient Land subject to an easement.

setoff A counterclaim demand which defendant holds against plaintiff, arising out of a transaction extrinsic to plaintiff's cause of action.

settlor Creator of a trust.

severance The destruction of any one of the unities of a joint tenancy. It is so called because the estate is no longer a joint tenancy, but is severed. Term may also refer to the cutting of crops, such as corn, wheat, etc., or to the separation of anything from realty.

share A proportionate ownership interest in a corporation.

Shelley's case, rule in Where a person takes an estate of freehold, legally or equitably, under a deed, will, or other writing, and in the same instrument there is a limitation by way of remainder of any interest of the same legal or equitable quality to his heirs, or heirs of his body, as a class of persons to take in succession from generation to generation, the limitation to the heirs entitles the ancestor to the whole estate.

The rule was adopted as a part of the common law of this country, though it has long since been abolished by most states.

shelter rule Transferee gets rights of transferor.

shipment contract Seller is authorized or required only to bear the expense of placing goods with the common carrier and bears the risk of loss only up to such point.

short-swing profits Profits made by insider through sale or other disposition of corporate stock within six months after purchase.

sight draft An instrument payable on presentment.

signature Any symbol executed with intent to validate a writing.

silent partner Partner who takes no part in the partnership business.

slander Oral defamation.

small claims courts Inferior civil courts with jurisdiction limited by dollar amount.

social security Measures by which the government provides economic assistance to disabled or retired employees and their dependents.

sole proprietorship A form of business in which one person owns all the assets of the business, in contrast to a partnership or a corporation.

sovereign immunity Foreign country's freedom from a host country's laws.

special warranty deed Seller promises that he has not impaired title.

specific performance The doctrine of specific performance is that where damages would compensate inadequately for the breach of an agreement, the contractor or vendor will be compelled to perform specifically what he has agreed to do; e.g., ordered to execute a specific conveyance of land.

With respect to the sale of goods, specific performance may be decreed where the goods are unique or in other proper circumstances. The decree for specific performance may include such terms and conditions as to payment of the price, damages, or other relief as the court may deem just. UCC §§ 2-711(2)(b), 2-716.

standardized business form A preprinted contract.

stare decisis Doctrine that once a court has laid down a principle of law as applicable to a certain state of facts, it will adhere to that principle and apply it to all future cases having substantially the same facts, regardless of whether the parties and property are the same or not.

state action Actions by governments, as opposed to actions taken by private individuals.

state-of-the-art Made in accordance with the level of technology at the time the product is made.

stated capital Consideration other than that allocated to capital surplus, received for issued stock.

statute of frauds A celebrated English statute, passed in 1677, which has been adopted, in a more or less modified form, in nearly all of the United States. Its chief characteristic is the provision that no action shall be brought on certain contracts unless there be a note or memorandum thereof in writing, signed by the party to be charged or by his authorized agent.

statute of limitation A statute prescribing limitations to the right of action on certain described causes of action; that is, declaring that no suit shall be maintained on such causes of action unless brought within a specified period after the right accrued.

statutory lien Interest in property, arising solely by statute, to secure payment of a debt.

stock "Stock" is distinguished from "bonds" and, ordinarily, from "debentures" in that it gives a right of ownership in part of the assets of a corporation and a right to interest in any surplus after the payment of debt. "Stock" in a corporation is an equity, representing an ownership interest. It is to be distinguished from obligations such as notes or bonds, which are not equities and represent no ownership interest.

Capital stock See **capital**.

Common stock Securities which represent an ownership interest in a corporation. If the company has also issued preferred stock, both common and preferred have ownership rights. Claims of both common and preferred stockholders are junior to claims of bondholders or other creditors of the company. Common stockholders assume the greater risk, but generally exercise the greater control and may gain the greater reward in the form of dividends and capital appreciation.

Convertible stock Stock which may be changed or converted into common stock.

Cumulative preferred Stock having a provision that if one or more dividends are omitted, the omitted dividends must be paid before dividends may be paid on the company's common stock.

Preferred stock is a separate portion or class of the stock of a corporation that is accorded, by the charter or by-laws, a preference or priority in respect to dividends, over the remainder of the stock of the corporation, which in that case is called common stock.

Stock warrant A certificate entitling the owner to buy a specified amount of stock at a specified time(s) for a specified price. Differs from a stock option only in that options are granted to employees and warrants are sold to the public.

Treasury stock Shares reacquired by a corporation.

stock option Contractual right to purchase stock from a corporation.

stop payment Order for a drawee not to pay an instrument.

strict liability A concept applied by the courts in product liability cases in which a seller is liable for any and all defective or hazardous products which unduly threaten a consumer's personal safety. This concept applies to all members involved in the manufacture and sale of any facet of the product.

strict scrutiny test Requirement that legislation be necessary to promote a compelling governmental interest.

subagent Person appointed by agent to perform agent's duties.

subject matter jurisdiction Authority of a court to decide a particular kind of case.

subject to the mortgage Purchaser is not personally obligated to pay the debt, but the property remains subject to the mortgage.

subjective fault Desired or virtually certain consequences of one's conduct.

subjective satisfaction Approval based upon a party's honestly held opinion.

sublease Transfer of less than all of a tenant's interest in a leasehold.

subpoena A subpoena is a command to appear at a certain time and place to give testimony upon a certain matter. A subpoena duces tecum requires production of books, papers, and other things.

subrogation The substitution of one thing for another, or of one person into the place of another with respect to rights, claims, or securities. Subrogation denotes the putting of a third person who has paid a debt in the place of the creditor to whom he has paid it, so that he may exercise against the debtor all the rights which the creditor, if unpaid, might have exercised.

subscribe Literally, to write underneath, as one's name. To sign at the end of a document. Also, to agree in writing to furnish money or its equivalent, or to agree to purchase some initial stock in a corporation.

subscriber Person who agrees to purchase initial stock in a corporation.

subsidiary corporation Corporation controlled by another corporation.

substantial performance Equitable doctrine protects against forfeiture for technical inadvertence, trivial variations, or omissions in performance.

substantive due process Requirement that governmental action be compatible with individual liberties.

substantive law The basic law of rights and duties (contract law, criminal law, tort law, law of wills, etc.), as opposed to procedural law (law of pleading, law of evidence, law of jurisdiction, etc.).

substantive unconscionability Oppressive or grossly unfair contractual terms.

sue To begin a lawsuit in a court.

suit "Suit" is a generic term of comprehensive significance that applies to any proceeding in a court of justice in which the plaintiff pursues, in such court, the remedy which the law affords him for the redress of an injury or the recovery of a right.

Derivative suit Suit brought by a shareholder on behalf of a corporation to enforce a right belonging to the corporation.

Direct suit Suit brought by a shareholder against a corporation based upon his ownership of shares.

summary judgment Rule of Civil Procedure 56 permits any party to a civil action to move for a summary judgment on a claim, counterclaim, or cross-claim when he believes that there is no genuine issue of material fact and that he is entitled to prevail as a matter of law.

summons Writ or process directed to the sheriff or other proper officer, requiring him to notify the person named that an action has been commenced against him in the court from which the process has issued and that he is required to appear, on a day named, and answer the complaint in such action.

superseding cause Intervening event that occurs after the defendant's negligent conduct and relieves him of liability.

supreme law Law that takes precedence over all conflicting laws.

surety One who undertakes to pay money or to do any other act in event that his principal debtor fails therein.

suretyship A guarantee of debts of another.

surplus Excess of net assets over stated capital.

tangible property Physical objects.

tariff Duty or tax imposed on goods moving into or out of a country.

tenancy Possession or occupancy of land or premises under lease.

Joint tenancy Joint tenants have one and the same interest, accruing by one and the same conveyance, commencing at one and the same time, and held by one and the same undivided possession. The primary incident of joint tenancy is survivorship, by which the entire tenancy on the decease of any joint tenant remains to the survivors, and at length to the last survivor.

Tenancy at sufferance Only naked possession which continues after tenant's right of possession has terminated.

Tenancy at will Possession of premises by permission of owner or landlord, but without a fixed term.

Tenancy by the entirety A tenancy which is created between a husband and wife and by which together they hold title to the whole with right of survivorship so that, upon death of either, the other takes the whole to the exclusion of the deceased's heirs. It is essentially a "joint tenancy," modified by the common law theory that husband and wife are one person.

Tenancy for a period A tenancy for years or for some fixed period.

Tenancy in common A form of ownership whereby each tenant (i.e., owner) holds an undivided interest in property. Unlike the interest of a joint tenant or a tenant by the entirety, the interest of a tenant in common does not terminate upon his or her prior death (i.e., there is no right of survivorship).

tenancy in partnership Type of joint ownership that determines partners' rights in specific partnership property.

tenant Possessor of a leasehold interest.

tender An offer of money; the act by which one produces and offers to a person holding a claim or demand against him the amount of money which he considers to be due, in satisfaction of such claim or demand, without any stipulation or condition.

Also, there may be a tender of performance of a duty other than the payment of money.

tender of delivery Seller makes available to buyer goods conforming to the contract and so notifies the buyer.

tender offer General invitation to all shareholders to purchase their shares at a specified price.

testament Will.

testator One who makes or has made a testament or will; one who dies leaving a will.

third-party beneficiary One for whose benefit a promise is made in a contract but who is not a party to the contract.

Creditor beneficiary Where performance of a promise in a contract will benefit a person other than the promisee, that person is a creditor beneficiary if no purpose to make a gift appears from the terms of the promise, in view of the accompanying circumstances, and performance of the promise will satisfy an actual, supposed, or asserted duty of the promisee to the beneficiary.

Donee beneficiary The person who takes the benefit of the contract even though there is no privity between him and the contracting parties. A third-party beneficiary who is not a creditor beneficiary. See also **beneficiary.**

time paper Payable at definite time.

time-price doctrine Permits sellers to have different prices for cash sales and credit sales.

title The means whereby the owner of lands or of personalty has the just possession of his property.

title insurance Provides protection against defect in title to real property.

tort A private or civil wrong or injury, other than breach of contract, for which a court will provide a remedy in the form of an action for damages. Three elements of every tort action are the existence of a legal duty from defendant to plaintiff, breach of that duty, and damage as proximate result.

tortfeasor One who commits a tort.

trade acceptance A draft drawn by a seller which is presented for signature (acceptance) to the buyer at the time goods are purchased and which then becomes the equivalent of a note receivable of the seller and the note payable of the buyer.

trade name Name used in trade or business to identify a particular business or manufacturer.

trade secrets Private business information.

trademark Distinctive insignia, word, or design of a good that is used to identify the manufacturer.

transferor's warranty Warranty given by any person who transfers an instrument and receives consideration.

treaty An agreement between or among independent nations.

treble damages Three times actual loss.

trespass At common law, trespass was a form of action brought to recover damages for any injury to one's person or property or relationship with another.

Trespass to chattels or personal property An unlawful and serious interference with the possessory rights of another to personal property.

Trespass to land At common law, every unauthorized and direct breach of the boundaries of another's land was an actionable trespass. The present prevailing position of the courts finds liability for trespass only in the case of intentional intrusion, or negligence, or some "abnormally dangerous activity" on the part of the defendant. *Compare* **nuisance.**

trespasser Person who enters or remains on the land of another without permission or privilege to do so.

trust Any arrangement whereby property is transferred with the intention that it be administered by a trustee for another's benefit. A trust, as the term is used in the Restatement, when not qualified by the word "charitable," "resulting," or "constructive," is a fiduciary relationship with respect to property, subjecting the person by whom the title to the property is held to equitable duties to deal with the property for the benefit of another person, which arises through a manifestation of an intention to create such benefit. Restatement, Second, Trusts § 2.

Charitable trust To benefit humankind.

Constructive trust Wherever the circumstances of a transaction are such that the person who takes the legal estate in property cannot also enjoy the beneficial interest without necessarily violating some established principle of equity, the court will immediately raise a constructive trust upon the conscience of the legal owner, so as to convert him into a trustee for the parties who in equity are entitled to the beneficial enjoyment.

Inter vivos trust Established during the settlor's lifetime.

Resulting trust One that arises by implication of law, where the legal estate in property is disposed of, conveyed, or transferred, but the intent appears or is inferred from the terms of the disposition, or from the accompanying facts and circumstances, that the beneficial interest is not to go to or be enjoyed with the legal title.

Spendthrift trust Removal of the trust estate from the beneficiary's control.

Testamentary trust Established by a will.

Totten trust A tentative trust which is a joint bank account opened by the settlor.

Voting trust A trust which holds the voting rights to stock in a corporation. It is a useful device when a majority of the shareholders in a corporation cannot agree on corporate policy.

trustee In a strict sense, a "trustee" is one who holds the legal title to property of another, while, in a broad sense, the term is sometimes applied to anyone standing in a fiduciary or confidential relation to another, such as agent, attorney, bailee, etc.

trustee in bankruptcy Representative of the estate in bankruptcy who is responsible for collecting, liquidating, and distributing the debtor's assets.

tying arrangement Conditioning a sale of a desired product (tying product) on the buyer's purchasing a second product (tied product).

ultra vires Acts beyond the scope of the powers of a corporation, as defined by its charter or by the laws of its state of incorporation. By the doctrine of ultra vires, a contract made by a corporation beyond the scope of its corporate powers is unlawful.

unconscionable Unfair or unduly harsh.

unconscionable contract See contracts.

underwriter Any person, banker, or syndicate that guarantees to furnish a definite sum of money by a definite date to a business or government in return for an issue of bonds or stock. In insurance, the one assuming a risk in return for the payment of a premium.

undisputed debt Obligation whose existence and amount are not contested.

undue influence Term refers to conduct by which a person, through his power over the mind of a testator, makes the latter's desires conform to his own, thereby overmastering the volition of the testator.

unemployment compensation Compensation awarded to workers who have lost their jobs and cannot find other employment.

unenforceable Contract under which neither party can recover.

unfair employer practice Conduct in which an employer is prohibited from engaging.

unfair labor practice Conduct in which an employer or union is prohibited from engaging.

unfair union practice Conduct in which a union is prohibited from engaging.

Uniform Commercial Code One of the Uniform Laws, drafted by the National Conference of Commissioners on Uniform State Laws, governing commercial transactions (sales of goods, commercial paper, bank deposits and collections, letters of credit, bulk transfers, warehouse receipts, bills of lading, investment securities, and secured transactions).

unilateral mistake Erroneous belief on the part of only one of the parties to a contract.

union shop Employer can hire nonunion members, but such employees must then join the union.

universal life Ordinary life divided into two components, a renewable term insurance policy and an investment portfolio.

unliquidated debt Obligation that is uncertain or contested in amount.

unqualified indorsement (see **indorsement**) One that imposes liability upon the indorser.

unreasonably dangerous Danger beyond that which the ordinary consumer contemplates.

unrestrictive indorsement (see **indorsement**) One that does not attempt to restrict the rights of the indorsee.

usage of trade Any practice or method of dealing having such regularity of observance in a place, vocation, or trade as to justify an expectation that it will be observed with respect to the transaction in question.

usury Collectively, the laws of a jurisdiction regulating the charging of interest rates. A usurious loan is one whose interest rates are determined to be in excess of those permitted by the usury laws.

value The performance of legal consideration, the forgiveness of an antecedent debt, the giving of a negotiable instrument, or the giving of an irrevocable commitment to a third party. UCC § 1-201(44).

variance A use differing from that provided in a zoning ordinance in order to avoid undue hardship.

vendee A purchaser or buyer; one to whom anything is sold. See also **vendor.**

vendor The person who transfers property by sale, particularly real estate; "seller," being more commonly used for one who sells personally. See also **vendee.**

venue "Jurisdiction" of the court means the inherent power of the court to decide a case, whereas "venue" designates the particular county or city in which a court with jurisdiction may hear and determine the case.

verdict The formal and unanimous decision or finding of a jury, impaneled and sworn for the trial of a cause, upon the matters or questions duly submitted to it upon the trial.

vertical privity Who is liable to the plaintiff.

vertical restraints Agreements among parties at different levels in the distribution chain.

vested Fixed; accrued; settled; absolute. "To be "vested," a right must be more than a mere expectation based on an anticipation of the continuance of an existing law; it must have become a title, legal or equitable, to the present or future enforcement of a demand, or a legal exemption from the demand of another.

vested remainder Unconditional remainder that is a fixed present interest to be enjoyed in the future.

vicarious liability Indirect legal responsibility; for example, the liability of an employer for the acts of an employee or that of a principal for the torts and contracts of an agent.

void Null; ineffectual; nugatory; having no legal force or binding effect; unable, in law, to support the purpose for which it was intended.

This difference separates the words "void" and "voidable": *void* in the strict sense means that an instrument or transaction is nugatory and ineffectual, so that nothing can cure it; *voidable* exists when an imperfection or defect can be cured by the act or confirmation of the person who could take advantage of it.

Frequently, the word "void" is used and construed as having the more liberal meaning of "voidable."

voidable Capable of being made void. See also **void.**

voir dire Preliminary examination of potential jurors.

voluntary Resulting from free choice. The word, especially in statutes, often implies knowledge of essential facts.

voting trust Transfer of corporate shares' voting rights to a trustee.

wager (gambling) Agreement that one party will win or lose depending upon the outcome of an event in which the only interest is the gain or loss.

waiver Terms "estoppel" and "waiver" are not synonymous; "waiver" means the voluntary, intentional relinquishment of a known right, and "estoppel" rests upon principle that, where anyone has done an act or made a statement that would be a fraud on his part to controvert or impair, because the other party has acted upon it in belief that what was done or said was true, conscience and honest dealing require that he not be permitted to repudiate his act or gainsay his statement. See also **estoppel.**

ward An infant or insane person placed by authority of law under the care of a guardian.

warehouse receipt Receipt issued by a person storing goods.

warehouser Storer of goods for compensation.

warrant, v. In contracts, to engage or promise that a certain fact or state of facts, in relation to the subject matter, is, or shall be, as it is represented to be. In conveyancing, to assure the title to property sold, by an express covenant to that effect in the deed of conveyance.

warranty A warranty is a statement or representation made by a seller of goods, contemporaneously with and as a part of a contract of sale, though collateral to express the object of the sale, having reference to the character, quality, or title of goods, and by which the seller promises or undertakes to ensure that certain facts are or shall be as he then represents them.

The general statutory law governing warranties on sales of goods is provided in UCC § 2–312 et seq. The three main types of warranties are (1) express warranty; (2) implied warranty of fitness; (3) implied warranty of merchantability.

warranty deed Deed in which grantor warrants good clear title. The usual covenants of title are warranties of seisin, quiet enjoyment, right to convey, freedom from encumbrances, and defense of title as to all claims. *Special warranty deed* Seller warrants that he has not impaired title.

warranty liability Applies to persons who transfer an instrument or receive payment or acceptance.

warranty of title Obligation to convey the right to ownership without any lien.

waste Any act or omission that does permanent injury to the realty or unreasonably changes its value.

white-collar crime Corporate crime.

will A written instrument executed with the formalities required by statutes, whereby a person makes a disposition of his property to take effect after his death.

winding up To settle the accounts and liquidate the assets of a partnership or corporation, for the purpose of making distribution and terminating the concern.

without reserve Auctioneer may not withdraw the goods from the auction.

workers' compensation Compensation awarded to an employee who is injured, when the injury arose out of and in the course of his employment.

writ of certiorari. Discretionary review by a higher court. See also **certiorari.**

writ of execution Order served by sheriff upon debtor demanding payment of a court judgment against debtor.

zoning Public control over land use.